INTERNATIONAL LAW IN DOMESTIC LEGAL ORDERS

Series Editors

ANDRÉ NOLLKAEMPER

Professor of Public International Law at the University of Amsterdam

AUGUST REINISCH

Professor of International and European Law at the University of Vienna

Legal Monism

INTERNATIONAL LAW IN DOMESTIC LEGAL ORDERS

The topic of international law in domestic legal orders has risen in prominence since the end of the Cold War. The last decades have witnessed a tremendous increase in international agreements on various subjects, impacting on domestic law and proving to be relevant to domestic litigation. These changes mean that domestic courts have the potential to make a greater contribution to the application and development of international law. This series analyses and examines these trends, looking at questions of international law in domestic legal orders from a variety of perspectives.

OTHER BOOKS PUBLISHED IN THIS SERIES

The Interpretation of International Law by Domestic Courts
Uniformity, Diversity, Convergence
Edited by Helmut Philipp Aust and Georg Nolte

Domestic Application of the ECHR
Courts as Faithful Trustees
Eirik Bjorge

The Role of National Courts in Applying International Humanitarian Law
Sharon Weil

The Privileges and Immunities of International Organizations in Domestic Courts
August Reinisch

Legal Monism

Law, Philosophy, and Politics

PAUL GRAGL

OXFORD
UNIVERSITY PRESS

OXFORD
UNIVERSITY PRESS

Great Clarendon Street, Oxford, OX2 6DP,
United Kingdom

Oxford University Press is a department of the University of Oxford.
It furthers the University's objective of excellence in research, scholarship,
and education by publishing worldwide. Oxford is a registered trade mark of
Oxford University Press in the UK and in certain other countries

First Edition published in 2018

Impression: 1

Published in the United States of America by Oxford University Press
198 Madison Avenue, New York, NY 10016, United States of America

British Library Cataloguing in Publication Data
Data available

Library of Congress Control Number: 2018936197

ISBN 978–0–19–879626–8

Printed and bound by
CPI Group (UK) Ltd, Croydon, CR0 4YY

For Jennifer
—quo domum—

Preface

The principal thought which inspired this book is my refusal to accept contradictions in the traditional Aristotelian sense, namely that contradictory statements cannot both be true in the same sense and at the same time. To say that 'it is raining' and that 'it is not raining' violates the logical law of non-contradiction[1] and does not make sense unless one changes the meaning of the word 'raining' (e.g. to 'snowing'). But then one also has to accept that the subject of the conversation is no longer concerned with 'rain'. There are of course new and interesting trends in logic such as dialetheism, which holds that there can be true contradictions,[2] but I must admit that my traditional (and hopefully not close-minded) philosophical upbringing prevents me from warming to these new and nonetheless fascinating concepts. For the real crux of the matter is its extension to the law, and what consequences follow from contradictory commands both logically and practically in a legal context: logically, the non-resolution of conflicts between norms originating in different bodies of law (say, national and international law) subverts the meaning of 'legal validity', which constitutes, after all, the very existence of a legal norm; and practically, leaves legal addressees (i.e. individuals, including myself and you, the most esteemed reader of these lines) out in the cold world of contradicting obligations and unresolved disputes. Just imagine your own confusion back in the day when you asked your mother whether you could go out longer on a Saturday night and she referred you to your father, who then said: 'Ask your mother'.

It is my opinion that such a plurality of authorities leads nowhere and only causes legal uncertainty. As a philosopher, I am also a seeker of clarity and answers, and consequently, I am not a big fan of legal pluralism. As a committed international and EU lawyer, my vision is a global legal order which realizes peace through law, and thus I am not a big fan of legal dualism or monism under the primacy of national law, which both—ultimately—fall back to nineteenth-century conceptions of state sovereignty and the deification of the state. Therefore, it is the mission of this book to present, examine, and defend the concept of legal monism as a solution to these problems. Monism is not an overly popular theoretical choice to describe the relationship between different bodies of law these days, and dualism and particularly pluralism take centre stage in current legal theoretical studies. Yet this gave me all the more reason not to jump on the dualist/pluralist bandwagon and to join the apparently declining monist camp. This book represents my research of the last three years on how legal monism can be saved from obsoleteness and how it can be maintained as a viable legal theory to resolve normative conflicts and to explain the relationship

[1] See Aristotle, *Metaphysics* (ed and transl Jonathan Barnes, *The Complete Works of Aristotle, Vol 2*; Oxford University Press, 1984) 1011b13–14.

[2] See e.g. Graham Priest, *In Contradiction: A Study of the Transconsistent* (2nd edn; Clarendon Press, 2006).

between legal orders. In other words, it attempts to revive an old concept to deal with very contemporary problems.

These contemporary problems include, to name just a few, the toxic fallout of the political year 2016: the decision of the United Kingdom to leave the European Union (Brexit), the election of Donald Trump in the United States, the general rise of populism and irrational political choices, and—most of all—the dire consequences of these facts: a growing disrespect for human rights, representative democracy, and the rule of law. I consider these three cultural achievements the crucial heritage of the Age of the Enlightenment upon which the modern world was built. However, these achievements appear to be in severe danger. Legal monism, however, includes a healthy respect for all these principles, and with this book, I will do my part to uphold, protect, and promote these values.

This book was mostly written at Queen Mary University of London, where I was very fortunate to meet remarkable people and colleagues who directly or indirectly contributed to this project. For their constant support, advice, and encouragement I would like to thank Valsamis Mitsilegas, who continuously helped me with my career trajectory at Queen Mary; Malgosia Fitzmaurice, with whom I spent hundreds of morning coffees talking shop and from whom I received invaluable assistance concerning academic life; Roger Cotterrell, who acted as my academic mentor during my first three years at Queen Mary and who, more as a legal pluralist, provided me with excellent counterarguments to be taken into account; Maks Del Mar, who also showed me the other side of things in legal theory and offered me enormously constructive comments; and Violeta Moreno-Lax, Angelos Dimopoulos, and Nick Bernard, with whom I spent many hours discussing the intricacies of EU law.

This book was, however, also written in Graz, Austria, especially outside of term time. At the University of Graz, I am very grateful to Joseph Marko, who opened my eyes to law beyond positivism and the political sciences (in particular in terms of democracy theory and constructivism in international relations). I am also very much indebted to the anonymous reviewers who provided me with immensely helpful and constructive comments, thereby pushing my project in the right direction. I would also like to thank Kirsten Schmalenbach from the University of Salzburg for her unwavering and constant support throughout the years, as well as her invaluable advice and expertise. Lastly, my sincerest gratitude goes to Gerd Oberleitner for his organizational support in finishing this project and to Matthias Klatt for actively supporting this habilitation at the University of Graz—without them, the habilitation process would have never been possible.

Outside academia, but nonetheless in my hometown of Graz, my thanks also go to my parents, who have always supported me with all their hearts. My last and biggest thank you goes to my lovely wife Jennifer. As I wrote in my first book, I am immensely grateful for your constant moral support, your help with the delicacies of the English language, and your patience with my endless talk about too much philosophy and too much law. But I am also grateful for your patience with my chosen career path, the long times apart, the professional insecurities, and my very own personal Odyssey. Thank you so much! *Quo domum.*

Table of Contents

III. CONCLUSION

List of Figures

Table of Cases

INTERNATIONAL COURTS

International Court of Justice

Permanent Court of International Justice

International Criminal Tribunal For The Former Yugoslavia

Court of Justice of The European Union

Court of Justice of the European Union

General Court

Canada

Czech Republic

France

Germany

India

Ireland

Israel

Italy

List of Abbreviations

CJEU	Court of Justice of the European Union
ECHR	European Convention on Human Rights
ECtHR	European Court of Human Rights
EU	European Union
ICJ	International Court of Justice
ICJ Statute	Statute of the International Court of Justice
ICTY	International Criminal Tribunal for the Former Yugoslavia
PCIJ	Permanent Court of International Justice
TEU	Treaty on European Union
TFEU	Treaty on the Functioning of the European Union
UN	United Nations
UN Charter	Charter of the United Nations
VCLT	1969 Vienna Convention on the Law of Treaties

PART I

INTRODUCTION AND THEORY

1
Introduction

1. The Principal Question

Is there only one 'law', i.e. only one legal system, in this world? And if in the affirmative, how is this unitary legal system shaped and structured? How does such a monist conception fare against other competing theories, such as dualism and pluralism, which seem—given the fragmented status of the law—to describe and explain reality much better (at least *prima facie*)? Is there any moral dimension to monism, which could help bring about a cosmopolitan legal order under global democracy and peace? These are, concisely, the questions which the book at hand will attempt to answer. Although the question what it means 'to be one' sounds rather trivial, let alone quixotically metaphysical,[1] it is not, as will be shown comprehensively. The issue whether a certain thing or object indeed is one and not many particularly applies to the law as such and the relationship between allegedly different and distinct legal orders, most prominently national law, international law, and the law of the European Union (EU). Accordingly, the overarching aim of this book is to explore and analyse the theory known as *legal monism* and its claim that, from the perspective of international law, all laws form part of the law of the world community. Yet exploration and analysis alone are not sufficient at this point to make this book attractive to the reader. It is well known that monism has long gone out of fashion and, as an utterly 'moribund notion', it has been suggested that it 'be put to rest'.[2] Thus, this book will not only depict and scrutinize legal monism, but also fill a lacuna by advocating for its revival in thinking about the law.

The subsequent sections will present the central problem to be discussed, and the benefits of a theoretical analysis of legal monism as well as the scope of this book.

[1] Graham Priest, *One* (Oxford University Press, 2014) xv.

[2] Armin von Bogdandy, 'Pluralism, Direct Effect, and the Ultimate Say: On the Relationship between International and Domestic Constitutional Law' (2008) 6 *International Journal of Constitutional Law* 397, 397. For an overview see also the critique in Beatrice I. Bonafé, 'International Law in Domestic and Supranational Settings' in Jörg Kammerhofer and Jean d'Aspremont (eds), *International Legal Positivism in a Post-Modern World* (Cambridge University Press, 2014) 382–6.

2. Framing the Problem

A. How theories come about: normative conflicts and relationships between different bodies of law

It is an undisputable fact that legal norms occasionally conflict with each other. This possibility of a conflict arises especially whenever different legal norms have repercussions on one another and hence suggest different ways of dealing with a problem or point to different directions.[3] More concretely, norm conflicts usually occur if two substantially incompatible legal norms claim to be valid and applicable at the same time and in the same place;[4] for example if one norm commands a person to close an open door, whilst another norm prohibits the same person to do so.[5] This situation amounts to a so-called 'narrow' conflict that cannot be resolved through consistent interpretation of the two opposing norms, as the observance or application of one norm necessarily involves the violation of the other.[6] In the context of this book, it is important to note that different bodies of law (e.g. international law, national law, EU law) also often end up in conflict with one another. For example, in accordance with the definitions provided above, an international legal norm could obligate a state to prohibit torture in any event, whilst the domestic law of the same state commands the national authorities to torture terrorist suspects, making joint obedience impossible. Given the broad scale of normative conflicts,[7] suffice it to say at this point that the existence of such conflicts is the underlying cause for devising theories on how to resolve them. The crucial element nevertheless is the varying approaches these different theories take towards the (potential) resolution of such norm conflicts between national, supranational, and international law. This is exactly where the research question of this book comes into play.

The question of how to theorize the relationship between international and non-international law is far from being definitively answered. In fact, to this date this problem is still being discussed widely, and occasionally even controversially.[8] One might say that this legal fissure is as old as the concept of international law itself,[9] but the discussion became more intense in the period after the First World War and

[3] C. Wilfred Jenks, 'The Conflict of Law-Making Treaties' (1953) 30 *British Yearbook of International Law* 401, 404; Dirk Pulkowski, *The Law and Politics of International Regime Conflict* (Oxford University Press, 2014) 145.

[4] Heiko Sauer, 'Vorrang ohne Hierarchie' (2013) 44 *Rechtstheorie* 503, 503.

[5] Georg Henrik von Wright, *Norm und Handlung* (Scriptor, 1979) 53–4 and 81.

[6] Hans Kelsen, *General Theory of Norms* (reprint; Clarendon Press, 2011) 123; Erich Vranes, 'The Definition of "Norm Conflict" in International Law and Legal Theory' (2006) 17 *European Journal of International Law* 395.

[7] See e.g. Joost Pauwelyn, *Conflict of Norms in Public International Law* (Cambridge University Press, 2003).

[8] Christine Amrhein-Hofmann, *Monismus und Dualismus in den Völkerrechtslehren* (Duncker & Humblot, 2003) 16.

[9] Alfred Verdross, 'Vierhundert Jahre Völkerrechtswissenschaft' (1933) 63 *Stimmen der Zeit* 36, 36.

continued so after 1945.[10] It was particularly the inter-war period between 1918 and 1939 that gave rise to the development of the most influential theoretical underpinnings of the relationship between international and municipal law.[11] Today, the close-knit commercial and political interdependence among states, which has led to an increasing interpenetration of international and municipal law across a plethora of areas, such as human rights, environmental law, or international investment law (where the same field of law is subject to regulation at both the international and domestic planes), has exacerbated this issue. Thus, the relationship between international and non-international law is currently often presented as 'a clash at a level of high theory'.[12] Yet such a strictly theoretical treatment of the relationship between international and domestic law is today all the more important, since whilst international law is developing at an unprecedented pace, the risk arises that this growth could be seriously impaired by not giving sufficient weight to theoretical reflection.[13]

This is mainly because the definition of the relationship between international and domestic law is connected to various aspects: the concept of law in general, the structure of the international legal community, the foundations and sources of international law,[14] the degree of interdependence and interconnection between these two bodies of law,[15] and the question of how to resolve normative conflicts between them. This issue also necessarily touches upon questions such as whether international law is directly applicable by domestic organs; whether international law is directly binding on individuals and whether it can also be invoked by them; or whether it must be transformed prior to having any such effects; and if transformed, whether the rules thus incorporated can subsequently be changed or overridden by an act of the municipal legislature. This theoretical conundrum of the relationship between international law and domestic law has therefore led to two opposing doctrines: *monism* and *dualism*. And even though speaking about these two concepts has almost become a sinful act in international legal theory, it remains unable to disentangle itself from this traditional vocabulary.[16] Even former

[10] Luigi Ferrari-Bravo, 'International and Municipal Law: The Complementarity of Legal Systems' in Ronald St. John MacDonald and Douglas M. Johnston (eds), *The Structure and Process of International Law: Essays in Legal Philosophy, Doctrine, and Theory* (Martinus Nijhoff, 1983) 715.

[11] Janne Nijman and André Nollkaemper, 'Introduction' in Janne Nijman and André Nollkaemper (eds), *New Perspectives on the Divide between National and International Law* (Oxford University Press, 2007) 2.

[12] James Crawford, *Brownlie's Principles of Public International Law* (8th edn; Oxford University Press, 2012) 48.

[13] Joseph G. Starke, 'Monism and Dualism in the Theory of International Law' (1936) 17 *British Yearbook of International Law* 66, 66.

[14] Pierre-Marie Dupuy, 'International Law and Domestic (Municipal) Law' in Rüdiger Wolfrum (ed), *Max Planck Encyclopedia of Public International Law* (2nd edn; Oxford University Press, 2013) para 1.

[15] Aslan Abashidze, 'The Relationship between International and Municipal Law: Significance of Monism and Dualism Concepts' in Marko Novaković (ed), *Basic Concepts of Public International Law: Monism & Dualism* (University of Belgrade, 2013) 23.

[16] George Rodrigo Bandeira Galindo, 'Revisiting Monism's Ethical Dimension' in James Crawford and Sarah Nouwen (eds), *Select Proceedings of the European Society of International Law, Vol 3* (Hart Publishing, 2012) 141.

President of the International Court of Justice Rosalyn Higgins accurately pinpointed that '[a]t the heart of any chapter on international and national law is always an explanation of the two theories of monism and dualism'.[17] As a result, monism and dualism, as the classical and traditional approaches to theorize the relationship between international and domestic law, still are a practical first step to engage with this intriguing topic.

B. What the law is: one, two, or many?

The obvious existence of more than one body of law brings us back to the questions pondered at the very outset of this book. Seeing that there is an evident dichotomy in the law (namely between law that originates from domestic systems such as states, on the one hand, and law that originates from the international system through states and international organizations working together, on the other hand), how can the law still be considered to be a unitary system? The following sections will now provide a concise overview of the different theories to deal with the relationship between different bodies of law; an in-depth analysis will then follow in Chapter 2 of this book.

(1) Public international law as 'non-law'

The first thesis to regard the relationship between legal orders is that international law is not really law, but mere 'positive morality'.[18] Therefore, according to a realist worldview, states may freely disregard their international obligations, if these obligations run counter to their interests. Thus, in the end, speaking about normative conflicts comes down to brute power, not normativity, and the term 'international law' itself is to be regarded as an oxymoron.[19] Yet despite the scholarly analysis of the question of whether international law is law,[20] this assumption is hardly taken seriously any more these days, and the lack of enforcement and efficiency of international law appears not to be an outright objection to its legal nature, but a feature of its historical development.[21] Suffice it to say that this issue will be touched upon in this book, but not be discussed extensively or as a theory in its own right.

[17] Rosalyn Higgins, *Problems and Process—International Law and How We Use It* (Oxford University Press, 1994) 205.

[18] H.L.A. Hart, *The Concept of Law* (2nd edn; Clarendon Press, 1994) ch 10, especially 221–6.

[19] See e.g. Stephen D. Krasner, 'Realist Views of International Law' (2002) 96 *Proceedings of the Annual Meeting of the American Society of International Law* 265, 265–6.

[20] See, inter alia, Anthony D'Amato, 'Is International Law Really "Law"?' (1984/1985) 79 *Northwestern University Law Review* 1293; John R. Bolton, 'Is There Really "Law" in International Affairs?' (2000) 10 *Transnational Law and Contemporary Problems* 1; Jack L. Goldsmith and Eric A. Posner, *The Limits of International Law* (Oxford University Press, 2006).

[21] Starke, 'Monism and Dualism' (n 13) 69; Hersch Lauterpacht, *The Function of Law in the International Community* (reprint; Oxford University Press, 2011) 399–405.

(2) Distinct and separate legal orders: dualism

The second theory is dualism, which regards, as the name suggests, different legal orders as two entirely distinct and separate bodies of law. All of them differ in sources and grounds of validity, subjects and addressees, and substance.[22] Consequently, every legal order is to be regarded as self-contained, since within each system the only existing and valid rules are those which form part of that system. The gaps between legal orders can nonetheless be bridged and external norms thereby be made relevant for the system, in particular through rules of reference, which incorporate external norms or which obligate authorities to take these norms into account when interpreting their own law. But nevertheless, as 'foreign' norms, any international law provision per se remains a mere fact and lacks a legal character in national law[23] until duly incorporated, and thereby dualism would generally leave the resolution of normative conflicts to domestic law itself and its rules of reference. This could either result in international law substantially prevailing over ordinary domestic law if, for instance, the international legal norm in question is also, concurrently, a constitutional principle of the domestic legal system in question. Or, if this is not the case, this scenario can result in domestic law simply ignoring relevant international obligations.

In this light, dualism appears to be the most straightforward manner of conceptualizing the relationship between legal orders. It is intuitively plausible inasmuch as constitutional orders principally presuppose an independently existing international legal order, and if that were not the case, it would not make sense why constitutions usually contain rules of reference, stating the relevance of international norms within the domestic sphere.[24] Furthermore, especially long-standing conflicts between national and international courts concerning the supremacy of international and EU law seem to demonstrate that there is considerable resistance against a unifying perspective of the law.[25] Therefore, one should ask how the law can possibly be one, if there are conflicts between bodies of law. Is not the very distinctness of legal orders the ultimate underlying cause of norm conflicts in the first place? And since normative conflicts are an undisputable fact, it hence appears indisputable that legal orders are distinct from one another.[26]

[22] Heinrich Triepel, *Völkerrecht und Landesrecht* (C. L. Hirschfeld, 1899) 9 ff, 27 ff, and 228 ff.

[23] Dionisio Anzilotti, *Corso di diritto internazionale, Vol I* (3rd edn; Athenaeum, 1928) 41 ff; Dionisio Anzilotti, *Corso di diritto internazionale privato* (Athenaeum, 1925) 57.

[24] Alexander Somek, 'Kelsen Lives' (2007) 18 *European Journal of International Law* 409, 421.

[25] Neil MacCormick, *Questioning Sovereignty* (Oxford University Press, 1999) 131–3; Mattias Kumm, 'The Jurisprudence of Constitutional Conflict: Constitutional Supremacy in Europe Before and After the Constitutional Treaty' (2005) 11 *European Law Journal* 262, 262–307.

[26] Leaving aside at this point that this conclusion does not necessarily follow from the premise and could be considered an argument *cum hoc ergo propter hoc*. We do not know with absolute certainty whether normative conflicts are caused by the distinctness of legal orders.

(3) Law as a monolith: monism

The third theory is monism, which will take the centre stage of this book. Again, monism holds, as its name implies, that all bodies of law form part of one single legal system. Consequently, and in contrast to dualism, there is no difference in grounds of validity, substance, and subjects as well as addressees between international, supranational, and national law. This unity, however, can be explained in different terms, e.g. through *sociological* facts, wherein the cohabitation of human beings across borders and the beneficial results from compliance with cross-border relations constitute legal unity;[27] through *natural law*, which is common to all humans and which thereby functions as the source of normativity and the ultimate international limit to the validity of positive-legal norms, depriving them of their claim to authority if they contradict the postulates of justice;[28] or lastly, through the *epistemological* terms of the pure theory of law, arguing that if various bodies of law are considered to be simultaneously valid orders of binding norms, then it becomes inevitable to comprehend both as one system.[29] In this light, any construction other than monism will necessarily result in an equivocation or outright denial of the legal nature of international law.[30] Beyond these substantial differences, monism can also be viewed from entirely different angles when it comes to the resolution of norm conflicts. Either international law is based on national law, because states 'create' international law, which means that under the primacy of national law, all conflicts are resolved in favour of national law.[31] Or domestic law is subordinate to international law, which constrains the powers and jurisdictions of international legal subjects, entailing, under the primacy of international law, the resolution of all conflicts in favour of international law.[32]

In contrast to dualism, monism can provide for a clear and predicable resolution of such conflicts: either by arguing that monism necessarily entails logical consistency and that as a result, normative conflicts cannot logically exist within a unitary legal system, since hierarchically superior norms always invalidate inferior norms in contradiction to them;[33] or by relying on positive-legal mechanisms that are capable of telling us in a definite and conclusive manner which legal norm ought to prevail.[34] Thus, it is crucial to acknowledge that the existence of normative conflicts does not prevent a monist construction of the law and on the contrary, legal conflict itself is possible only if legal norms form part of the same system.[35] Monists have realized

[27] Georges Scelle, *Précis de droit des gens: Principes et systématique, Vol 1: Introduction, le milieu intersocial* (Sirey, 1932) 6 ff and 31.

[28] Alfred Verdross, *Die Einheit des rechtlichen Weltbildes auf Grundlage der Völkerrechtsverfassung* (Mohr, 1923); Alfred Verdross, *Die Verfassung der Völkerrechtsgemeinschaft* (Springer, 1926).

[29] Hans Kelsen, *Pure Theory of Law* (2nd edn; University of California Press, 1967) 332.

[30] Somek, 'Kelsen Lives' (n 24) 425; Starke, 'Monism and Dualism' (n 13) 74.

[31] Hans Kelsen, *Principles of International Law* (Rinehart & Company, 1952) 435–7.

[32] Ibid., 437–8.

[33] Hans Kelsen, *Introduction to the Problems of Legal Theory: A Translation of the First Edition of the Reine Rechtslehre or Pure Theory of Law* (transl Bonnie Litschewski Paulson and Stanley L. Paulson; Clarendon Press, 1997) 112.

[34] Kelsen, *General Theory of Norms* (n 6) 125.

[35] Michael Green, 'Hans Kelsen and the Logic of Legal Systems' (2003) 54 *Alabama Law Review* 365, 407–8.

that it is the very existence of conflicts that presupposes a unified normative perspective, because such a conflict between entirely incompatible norms only arises if the legal addressee of this norm feels to be bound by both. The addressee is consequently not only committed to both norms, but also has an interest in resolving this predicament in a meaningful way. These conditions represent the very foundations of a unified system.[36]

(4) 'The more the merrier': pluralism

Yet this long-standing dichotomy of monism and dualism did not go unchallenged, and subsequently the question was raised whether any of them was actually correct. Perhaps the law was neither one unitary system nor distinctly separated in two legal orders, but simply 'many', and the argument was made that a pluralist conception of the law was much more plausible. Legal pluralism is therefore the last theory to be presented at this point, and it emphasizes the fact that the current state of the law is better described and characterized by multiple uncoordinated, co-existing, and overlapping bodies of law, and that there inherently is diversity amongst them. Since these legal orders make competing claims of authority and impose conflicting norms on their respective addressees,[37] legal pluralism aims, in its most basic form, at explaining the apparent non-hierarchical co-existence of legal orders by referring to their heterarchical nature and the pluralism of legal systems—may they be national, supranational, or international—without any of them being supreme.[38] Hence, a pluralist approach to the interplay between various legal orders allows for compromises between international and domestic courts, and inconsistencies and normative conflicts between their decisions should be welcomed rather than regretted.[39] Instead of trying to find a definite legal answer to the question of which court has the last say, legal pluralism acknowledges their competing claims and contents itself with the state of suspense between them. Legal pluralism does not require any overarching legal conflict-resolution mechanism and states that any rules to this end are set by each legal order for itself. In this vein, normative conflicts among multiple overlapping legal orders are unavoidable and sometimes even desirable in order to engage in a mutual dialogue.[40] Norm conflicts may thus be resolved by political, and not necessarily legal means.

In conclusion, it is crucial to underline the differences between pluralism and dualism, and between pluralism and monism, especially to clarify again pluralism's

[36] Alexander Somek, *The Cosmopolitan Constitution* (Oxford University Press, 2014) 194 fn 93; Alexander Somek, 'Monism: A Tale of the Undead' in Matej Avbelj and Jan Komárek (eds), *Constitutional Pluralism in the European Union and Beyond* (Hart Publishing, 2012) 353.

[37] Brian Z. Tamanaha, 'Understanding Legal Pluralism: Past to Present, Local to Global' (2008) 30 *Sydney Law Review* 375, 375.

[38] Neil MacCormick, 'The *Maastricht*-Urteil: Sovereignty Now' (1995) 1 *European Law Journal* 259, 259.

[39] Nicholas W. Barber, 'Legal Pluralism and the European Union' (2006) 12 *European Law Journal* 306, 328.

[40] See e.g. Paul Schiff Berman, 'Global Legal Pluralism' (2006/2007) 80 *Southern California Law Review* 1155; Nico Krisch, *Beyond Constitutionalism* (Oxford University Press, 2010) 286.

distinguishing features: legal pluralism appears to share one quality with dualism, which is the original distinctness of various bodies of law, which can only be bridged by rules of reference. Yet whereas dualism considers different legal orders to be tangent[41] or, at most, intersecting circles,[42] pluralism envisages them as partially or even completely overlapping, thereby resulting in potentially unresolvable normative conflicts. The main difference to monism is much clearer: in contrast to a unitary conception of the law which is hierarchically structured, pluralism considers law to be heterarchical and akin to floating islands in a vast ocean, which may be connected via causeways or sometimes piled upon each other.

C. Why monism appears to be dead: an obituary?

Given this range of theories to explain and resolve (or to refrain from resolving) normative conflicts among different bodies of law, one must face the question again why one should be a monist and why this book should actually attempt to defend it. So why, among all these theories, should monism be the correct one and why is it worth discussing and defending? These are legitimate questions and since the criticism of dualism and pluralism will be presented and analysed throughout the book in order to defend monism, the principal arguments against monism will first be presented here to set the scene.

Monism appears to be dead these days, having silently passed away sometime during the second half of the twentieth century. As a dissenting position among legal theories, it has never had much support outside the circle of those who were somehow influenced by the Vienna School of Jurisprudence and the pure theory of law.[43] The somewhat limited or even obsolete relevance of monism boils down to the critique that it simply is 'unreal, artificial and strictly beside the point, because it assumes something that has to exist for there to be any controversy at all—and which in fact does not exist—namely a common field in which the two legal orders . . . both simultaneously have their spheres of activity'.[44] In contrast to dualism and pluralism, monism is not terribly appealing on the intuitive level[45] and seems to hold no explanatory power. Beyond that, it stands accused of being useless in providing solutions to the concrete problems regarding the relationship between different bodies of law, as domestic courts sometimes apply 'foreign' norms and sometimes refuse to do so, thus preventing any coherent theoretical picture to emerge.[46]

Dualism seems to be a more realistic and straightforward manner of conceptualizing the relationship between legal orders. The arguments against monism have therefore turned to empirically more accurate alternatives where the choice of one

[41] Triepel, *Völkerrecht und Landesrecht* (n 22) 111.

[42] Walter Rudolf, 'Incorporation of Customary International Law into Municipal Law' in Grigory I. Tunkin and Rüdiger Wolfrum (eds), *International Law and Municipal Law* (Duncker & Humblot 1988) 24–5.

[43] Somek, 'Monism' (n 36) 344.

[44] Gerald Fitzmaurice, 'The General Principles of International Law' (1957-II) 92 *Recueil des Cours* 1, 71.

[45] Somek, 'Monism' (n 36) 347.

[46] Crawford (n 12) 50; Bonafé (n 2) 383.

legal order over the other needs to be made with regard to the reality of the international legal system.[47] In this vein, the dualist Triepel criticized monism for failing to 'pay attention to the realities' of the law: Russian and English laws simply do not belong to the same legal system, and Dutch and Chinese laws are not dependent upon the same sole basic norm.[48] Similarly, H.L.A. Hart saw the unity of law as a fallacious assumption because of its blurring of what laws of validating purport say about other laws and their mutual mode of recognition[49]—a mistake that was seen as being out of touch with reality. Because of its persuasive power, this attack on monism's alleged neglect of the empirical reality of the law seems very convincing and hence continues to define one of the most recurrent counter-arguments throughout the years.[50] Consequently, dualism has been commended as a perfect portrait of the hard realities of the modern and contemporary condition of politics around the world, because of its confirmation by state practice throughout the last centuries up to the present time. Legal orders remain separate political communities, and any interaction between international and municipal norms is merely based on constitutional provisions giving effect to international law via transformation, not a unitary and common ground of validity.[51]

Beyond the realm of dualism, the argument that the reality which we can empirically observe is in contradiction to monism is also being used by dualism's most recent offspring,[52] legal pluralism, claiming to depict law beyond the simple duality of international and domestic law and to describe law as it is based on actual social reality.[53] Accordingly, the world of law is a 'disorder of orders', and—given the lack of any single meta-principle of authority such as the supremacy of international law—each of these legal orders must negotiate their boundary relations with one another themselves.[54] Under this premise, a unitary construction of the law becomes inconceivable.

The argument that reality undermines any possibility of monism being more than a thought experiment becomes even more powerful when being corroborated with actual judgments that support a profoundly dualist or pluralist conception of the relations between legal orders.[55] This judicial 'anti-monist' practice has even

[47] Somek, 'Kelsen Lives' (n 24) 421–2.

[48] Heinrich Triepel, 'Les rapports entre le droit interne et le droit international' (1923-I) 1 *Recueil des Cours* 77, 86.

[49] H.L.A. Hart, 'Kelsen's Doctrine of the Unity of Law' in Stanley L. Paulson and Bonnie Litschewski Paulson (eds), *Normativity and Norms: Critical Perspectives on Kelsenian Themes* (reprint; Clarendon Press, 2007) 563.

[50] Galindo (n 16) 142.

[51] Gaetano Arangio-Ruiz, 'International Law and Interindividual Law' in Janne Nijman and André Nollkaemper (eds), *New Perspectives on the Divide between National and International Law* (Oxford University Press, 2007) 20.

[52] Somek, 'Monism' (n 36) 344.

[53] Eugen Ehrlich, *Fundamental Principles of the Sociology of Law* (Harvard University Press, 1936) 501.

[54] Neil Walker, 'Beyond Boundary Disputes and Basic Grids: Mapping the Global Disorder of Normative Orders' (2008) 6 *International Journal of Constitutional Law* 373, 385–91.

[55] See e.g. Gráinne de Búrca, 'The European Court of Justice and the International Legal Order after *Kadi*' (2010) 51 *Harvard International Law Journal* 1, 31; Paul Schiff Berman, 'Federalism and International Law through the Lens of Legal Pluralism' (2008) 73 *Missouri Law Review* 1149, 1167 ff.

led international lawyers to show some resistance to accepting the supremacy of international law *in toto* over municipal law.[56] The rejection of the supremacy of international law over domestic constitutional law by several national supreme and constitutional courts entails that 'there is no legal rule to decide which norm should prevail' nor a 'legal rule to resolve the competing claims to authority raised by the international and the domestic constitutional actors'.[57] Therefore, less attention should be paid to the formal sources of the law and more to the substance of the rules in question, for example fundamental rights, which should trump less important norms.[58] Similarly, state practice demonstrates a certain reluctance of accepting the supremacy of international law as a formal principle. In fact, its acceptance is contingent on substantive conformity with fundamental values laid down in municipal law.[59] Lastly, there is a logical argument against monism: why do so-called monist legal orders find it necessary to proclaim the supremacy of international law within domestic law, if international law itself claims to prevail in cases of conflict?[60] The answer is that international law is not supreme per se and by itself; its supremacy is rather conditional upon the recognition of this supremacy in domestic law. This self-referential nature is, after all, paradoxical,[61] because the very act of asserting the supremacy of international law in a deferential monist manner necessarily undermines this very supremacy by confirming its own final authorship and authority in constitutional law.[62] A monist approach of national constitutions is therefore seen as a voluntary and sovereign decision of states, which can always be revised and changed.[63]

In conclusion, the problem is that monism is not without major flaws. From an academic and objective view, the idea of the unity of law needs to be subjected to the same close scrutiny as any other theory. Yet although monism seems to be the most criticized theory of all, this should not discourage any research on its merits and benefits. On the contrary, such criticism is to be seen as an enticement to rise to the challenge. Accordingly, it is the objective of this book to offer a seemingly untimely defence of legal monism and show that monism is not dead, but very much alive.[64] Monism's great legacy is to be highlighted and commended, namely its hitherto

[56] Galindo (n 16) 142.

[57] Anne Peters, 'Supremacy Lost: International Law Meets Domestic Constitutional Law' (2009) 3 *Vienna Online Journal on International Constitutional Law* 170, 196.

[58] Ibid., 197.

[59] André Nollkaemper, 'Rethinking the Supremacy of International Law' (2010) 65 *Zeitschrift für Öffentliches Recht* 65, 68 and 83.

[60] George Slyz, 'International Law in National Courts' (1995/1996) 28 *New York University Journal of International Law and Politics* 65, 71.

[61] Neil MacCormick, 'Risking Constitutional Collision in Europe?' (1998) 18 *Oxford Journal of Legal Studies* 517, 525.

[62] Neil Walker, 'Late Sovereignty in the European Union' in Neil Walker (ed), *Sovereignty in Transition* (Hart Publishing, 2003) 11, fn 23.

[63] Anne Peters, 'Rechtsordnungen und Konstitutionalisierung: Zur Neubestimmung der Verhältnisse' (2010) 65 *Zeitschrift für Öffentliches Recht* 1, 21.

[64] Somek, 'Monism' (n 36) 347.

unsurpassed analytical edge[65] and internal logic, its exclusive capability to resolve normative conflicts predictably and exclusively through legal means,[66] and its inherently moral conception about how to change the world for the better in times of fragmentation.[67]

3. An Analysis of Legal Monism: The Scope of This Book

The main argument of this book is that legal monism is logically and empirically better suited to describe, explain, and conceptualize the relationship between different bodies of law than other theories. Furthermore, it will also be argued that monism is morally superior to other concepts. Thereby the deficiencies of dualism and pluralism will be systematically revealed, and demonstrated that they do not really offer any useful alternatives to monism.[68] Admittedly, in contrast to monism, dualism and pluralism may display appealing features such as 'good, progressive, tolerant, non-domineering'—in contrast to the characteristics of monist and hierarchically ordered systems: 'bad, regressive, intolerant, domineering'.[69] But perhaps the time is ripe to be 'un-chic' and go back to the traditional roots of monism and commend its explanatory power and normative superiority against the intuitive appeal of dualism and pluralism. Francis Bacon correctly claimed that scientific progress only began when scientists started to look at experience.[70] Yet modern historians of science also keep emphasizing that if you start from experience alone without theoretical presuppositions, you are more likely to discover Aristotle's mechanics than Galileo's.[71] Similarly, Immanuel Kant attributed the revolutions in modern science to Copernicus's courage to contradict, and not to conform to the testimony of the senses.[72] This statement should by no means be understood as anti-empiricist. On the contrary, the positive law is the essential empirical datum with which every lawyer needs to work. The *caveat* in this respect is, however, that one should not always rely on intuition alone to explain the law and the relationships between different legal bodies. Monism seems to be counter-intuitive, but this argument in itself is insufficient to disprove it as a theory altogether. Physicists will agree, if one thinks of the highly counter-intuitive field of quantum mechanics.[73]

65 Markus Kotzur, 'Über Monismus und Dualismus hinaus: Ansätze zu einer Neukonzeptualisierung des Völkerrechts mit einer konstitutionellen Matrix' in Marko Novaković (ed), *Basic Concepts of Public International Law: Monism & Dualism* (University of Belgrade, 2013) 165.

66 Somek, 'Kelsen Lives' (n 24) 422–3.

67 Galindo (n 16) 144.

68 Somek, 'Monism' (n 36) 347.

69 J.H.H. Weiler, 'Prologue: Global and Pluralist Constitutionalism—Some Doubts' in Gráinne de Búrca and J.H.H. Weiler (eds), *The Worlds of European Constitutionalism* (Cambridge University Press, 2012) 14.

70 See Francis Bacon, *The New Organon* (John Bill, 1620).

71 Richard Westfall, *The Construction of Modern Science* (Cambridge University Press, 1977) 21 ff.

72 Immanuel Kant, *Kritik der reinen Vernunft* (Johann Friedrich Hartknoch, 1781/1787) B xxii.

73 This is nonetheless the point where the analogy ends, given the methodological split between natural sciences and the humanities.

Thus, in order to corroborate the main argument of this book, monism will be defended in three steps, which will in turn form the main three parts of this book: first, logical and epistemological arguments; secondly, practical and empirical arguments; and, thirdly, normative and moral arguments. The individual steps within this three-prong approach necessarily build upon each other and should be seen as a sequence of arguments: if monism does not make sense from a logical and epistemological perspective, a sceptic might certainly ask whether it is empirically and practically relevant. Should this, in turn, not be convincing either, then, the argument will conclude, why not at least make the best of monism's moral benefits?

A. Logical and epistemological arguments for legal monism

Legal monism can take many forms, but the main argument will be that even though legal monism per se may not necessarily be an epistemological problem,[74] its logical and epistemological manifestation in the form of the pure theory of law is the most persuasive one in contrast to the other proposed models. The reason for this is that monism becomes an epistemological problem once one encounters its predominant underlying questions. At the outset, there is the ontological question, namely: what is the law? And more concretely: what is valid law? Subsequently, the epistemological question arises, namely: how can valid law be cognized? How can valid law be distinguished from something that is not valid law and hence not law at all? Yet, although the principal distinction between ontology ('what is') and epistemology ('our apprehension of what is') is crucial, the two cannot always be strictly separated, as cognition is obviously inextricably bound to ontological commitments, which is—in the case of the law—the commitment of all lawyers and all legal theories to the existence of the law itself. The argument, therefore, is that it is not so much the existence of the law itself that is at stake here, but the way in which we ascertain whether something is law or not. Thus, the law undoubtedly presents itself as an epistemological problem, especially if we intend to cognize it as a meaningful object.[75] Without an answer to this question, it is impossible to defend legal monism, because if we do not know how to cognize valid law in the first place, how could we then possibly cognize it as a unity?

To find out what truly constitutes law, this book will defend legal positivism, but not positivism in a strict Hartian sense, according to which the law 'can be identified by reference to social facts alone'.[76] Legal positivism in this context should rather be seen in the tradition of the pure theory of law, which underscores law's dual position as both a posited act that is not dependent on facts, and as a normative command that is not dependent on morality.[77] The thrust of separability, in any direction, is

[74] Danilo Zolo, 'Hans Kelsen: International Peace through International Law' (1998) 9 *European Journal of International Law* 306, 323.

[75] Marek Zirk-Sadowski, 'Legal Epistemology and Transformation of Legal Cultures' in Mark Van Hoecke (ed), *Epistemology and Methodology of Comparative Law* (Hart Publishing, 2004) 23.

[76] Joseph Raz, *Ethics in the Public Domain* (Oxford University Press, 1994) 211.

[77] Stanley L. Paulson, 'The Neo-Kantian Dimension of Kelsen's Pure Theory of Law' (1992) 12 *Oxford Journal of Legal Studies* 311, 320.

epistemological, and that by eliminating moral and factual criteria from the cognition of legal validity, this theory intends to bring to the fore what truly constitutes law.[78] The central term is 'legal validity', which is conterminous with the law's very existence. Legal norms may be invalidated owing to various reasons, and it is even possible that certain norms are annulled *ex tunc*, i.e. as if they had never existed. But this only happens retrospectively. This means that the expression 'invalid law', i.e. law that is concurrently invalid and existent, is a contradiction in terms. Legal validity always comprises the very existence of a legal norm.

To cut a long introduction short, this is exactly where legal monism comes into play in an epistemological manner. The overall argument of this book is that both dualism and pluralism make the mistake of using the term 'legal validity' whilst changing its meaning unnoticeably within the argument, thus committing the logical fallacy of 'equivocation'. Both theories state that different legal orders are equally valid, either in entirely distinct (dualism) or overlapping spheres (pluralism). Let us now use the example of the prohibition of torture from above again, and we will see that a considerable problem arises. If the prohibition of torture, as laid down in several treaties as an absolute, unexceptionable, and non-derogable right,[79] is valid law, and the domestic command to torture terrorist suspects in state x is valid law, then there is a narrow normative conflict that cannot be resolved through consistent interpretation. The problem is, however, that one cannot understand both occurrences of 'valid law' as meaning exactly the same thing.[80] A dualist state might resolve the conflict in favour of national law, claiming 'national interests to have priority', thereby effectively denying the validity of the international norm in question.[81] And a pluralist-minded state would most likely refrain from resolving the conflict at all, which would subject the whole situation to a dilemma for the individuals involved. What both scenarios have in common is that legal validity must simply have a different meaning within the dualist and pluralist theories: in dualism, the validity of an international norm is denied in favour of national law on extra-legal grounds, and hence the international legal norm is somehow 'less' valid than national law; in pluralism, the logical rule of non-contradiction would also demand a different meaning, since eventually one of the two norms would be applied arbitrarily, either by action (the national norm) or by omission (the international norm), but without any legal specification. This entails that the two legal norms in conflict are valid in a different sense[82] without any legal grounding. Yet since 'legal validity' is equivalent with the very existence of a legal norm, the assumption of 'less' validity or simply a varying degree of validity is incommensurable with an objectively comprehensible analysis of the law.

[78] Alexander Somek, 'The Spirit of Legal Positivism' (2011) 12 *German Law Journal* 729, 738.

[79] See, inter alia, Article 7 of the International Covenant on Civil and Political Rights; Article 2(2) and (3) of the Convention against Torture and Other Cruel, Inhuman or Degrading Treatment or Punishment; Article 3 of the European Convention on Human Rights.

[80] Green (n 35) 366–7.

[81] Although one could argue that this approach effectively amounts to a monist stance under the primacy of national law, thus turning dualism in a version of monism.

[82] Green (n 35) 367.

Thus, whether or not one subscribes to monism depends on whether or not one takes the normativity and existence of the law—that is, its validity—seriously.[83] The choice for monism affects the question of whether it is law that one claims to be describing, because only legal monism allows for the concurrent and same meaning of legal validity of legal norms, originating in different bodies of law. Furthermore, only monism allows for conflict-resolution in a clear and predictable way, either by plainly giving preference to one specific body of law, say, national law, or international law.[84] Having said that, dualism and pluralism not only fail semantically and logically, but also because they entail legal uncertainty for all individuals and addressees involved. Logically and epistemologically speaking, legal monism hence remains the only viable option to describe the relationship and to resolve conflicts between different bodies of law. This hypothesis will be further depicted and scrutinized in Chapter 3 of this book.

B. Descriptive and practical arguments for legal monism

At this point, sceptics might certainly argue that legal monism may be 'correct in theory, but it is of no use in practice'.[85] They might continue that monists can devise any theory describing reality in a unitary way all they want, and this theory can certainly be logically, semantically, and epistemologically plausible. But this does not mean that this theory is empirically correct, i.e. that it has any real explanatory power concerning the positive law. The main argument, therefore, is that the choice for a monist conception of the law cannot be exclusively justified on the basis of logic and epistemology. Practitioners of the law will most likely not care for sophisticated philosophy, since they have to deal with the law as it is, and not as it is envisaged by those kept isolated in their ivory towers.

The central research questions of this chapter will consequently be how and to which extent legal monism applies in practice, and whether it is capable of describing legal reality as well as or even better than the competing theories of dualism and pluralism. As discussed above, law becomes uncertain when too much law 'exists' and norms of different bodies of law as a result conflict with each other. Normative conflicts are severe problems, not only for lawyers, but also for those subject to the law, because if such conflicts remain unresolved, legal subjects will find themselves in the legal desert of a dilemma,[86] uncertain what legal norm to follow. Conflicts pressure us to resolve them somehow, for instance, by giving preference to one legal norm over another.[87] The problem with dualism and pluralism is that they do not provide

[83] Somek, 'Kelsen Lives' (n 24) 422–3.

[84] For the sake of clarity, it should briefly be stated that this book will subsequently make the argument in favour of *monism under the primacy of international law*.

[85] See Immanuel Kant, 'Über den Gemeinspruch: Das mag in der Theorie richtig sein, taugt aber nicht für die Praxis' in Immanuel Kant (ed), *Gesammelte Schriften* (Deutsche Akademie der Wissenschaften, 1923) AA 8:273.

[86] Lando Kirchmair, 'The Theory of the Law Creators' Circle: Re-Conceptualizing the Monism-Dualism-Pluralism Debate' (2016) 17 *German Law Journal* 179, 193.

[87] Jörg Kammerhofer, *Uncertainty in International Law: A Kelsenian Perspective* (Routledge, 2011) 139.

any certain and definite rules on this very conflict resolution. Whenever dualists and pluralists perceive conflicts and the positive law itself does not provide them with a watertight and absolute conflict-resolution rule, they stop looking for answers in the law. They might look for answers in politics, sociology, or morality, but not in the law itself. This is highly troubling, as mingling the distinctively legal with non-legal elements further erodes legal certainty and the rule of law.[88]

Conversely, monism clearly does provide for such conflict-resolution rules, and it will be shown how this works in practice. The first assumption is that monism takes the concept of legal validity seriously. Subsequently, it is perfectly normal for any body of law to encounter conflicts in the form of objection to a validity claim that is external to its own rules of operation.[89] Usually, legal orders lay down the conditions necessary for the production of valid law in their constitution,[90] but dualism and pluralism assume that, owing to some factor which cannot be accounted for from the perspective of these conditions, a new law might fail to be valid because of the existence and operation of another body of law. And since neither dualism nor pluralism can incorporate into the system the very conditions under which such a failure may occur, the concept of legal validity disintegrates under such 'heterarchy as an organizing principle'[91] and becomes utterly meaningless. Monism, on the other hand, is interested in the dynamics of the law, and how the law is legally created and potentially annulled in the case of deficiencies or conflicts. In this respect, monism does not stop looking for answers to normative conflicts, but rather asks: what will happen next? What is the legal significance of the two norms in question? If the other norm in question were not a legal norm at all, but a moral norm or political courtesy, the separability thesis would certainly require that the *legal* norm be applied. The second question of monism is: what will *legally* happen next?[92]

To answer this question, Chapter 4 of this book will investigate what happens in the event of a conflict in the relationship between different bodies of law. Monism will be 'tested' on the basis of the positive law and it will then be determined whether it can be falsified or not, in particular on the basis of the relationship between public international law and national law, and between European Union law and Member State law. Chapter 4 will demonstrate that monism is capable of providing a resolution to normative conflicts and, whatever may happen, the law will seize the opportunity to create more law. Thus, the overall argument of this book will be that dualism and pluralism do not provide for a better explanation of the positive law. Descriptively and practically speaking, legal monism remains the only viable option to explain the relationship and to resolve conflicts between different bodies of law.

[88] Brian Z. Tamanaha, 'The Folly of the "Social Scientific" Concept of Legal Pluralism' (1993) 20 *Journal of Law and Society* 192, 193–4.

[89] Somek, 'Monism' (n 36) 354.

[90] Most often, in the relevant constitutional provisions on the legislative branch, its objectives, composition, and functioning. See e.g. Article I of the United States Constitution.

[91] Daniel Halberstam, 'Constitutional Heterarchy: The Centrality of Conflict in the European Union and the United States' in Jeffrey L. Dunoff and Joel P. Trachtman (eds), *Ruling the World? Constitutionalism, International Law, and Global Governance* (Cambridge University Press, 2009) 354.

[92] Somek, 'Monism' (n 36) 354–5.

C. Normative and moral arguments for legal monism

Yet for any remaining sceptics both the epistemological and empirical viability of legal monism might not be good enough. This, however, does not rule out the possibility that there might be convincing *normative* arguments for the adoption of a monist view of the law under the primacy of international law. Such arguments might even have the advantage of being able to defend monism if the strong, 'scientific' argument for monism turns out to be indefensible. The crucial point is that the works of the proponents of the Vienna School of Jurisprudence also offer the resources to come up with something more substantive in the way of a normative defence of monism, particularly if the writings on 'extra-legal' influences—ideological criticism, democracy, and pacifism as well as cosmopolitanism—are taken into due consideration.

In other words, once could ask what follows from legal monism in a normative sense. Is it capable of improving the world, and if yes, in what way? Is there any ethical dimension to it which would give it a moral edge over alternative theories? The central question of Chapter 5 of this book will therefore be how monism's moral superiority can be shown by way of three extra-legal influences in the works of Hans Kelsen and the other thinkers of the pure theory of law. And, indeed, as will be discussed in detail, the ideological criticism of natural law, the defence of representative democracy as well as constitutional review, and a pacifist, cosmopolitanist as well as constructivist view of international relations are highly conducive to a monist view of the law under the primacy of international law and mutually reinforcing concepts.

Therewith this introduction returns to the principal question of this book, namely whether there only is 'one law'. *Prima facie*, the answer appears to be in the affirmative, but the philosophical, legal, and political issues involved cannot be easily dismissed. They deserve a thorough, detailed, and systematic analysis to confirm this answer. This book will take up this task.

2

Theorizing the Relationship between Different Bodies of Law

1. Introduction and Overview

The aim of this book is to defend a monist view of the law. Yet before such a defence can be carried out in a comprehensive and scrutinizing fashion, it should first be clarified what the main theoretical competitors of monism are and by which distinctive features they are characterized. The introduction could, so far, only provide a very brief insight and overview of the principal theories on the relationship between legal orders, namely monism, dualism, and pluralism. This chapter will therefore describe these theories in more detail in order to set the scene for the subsequent defence of monism.

At this point, it should be noted that legal monism will only be described in rather broad strokes and brushes here, since the remainder of this book is dedicated to its further detailed depiction, analysis, and defence anyway. This rough overview in section 2 will only serve to give an outline of the different versions of monism, which will then help make the case for the epistemological-normative version of monism as envisaged by the pure theory of law. Section 3 will delve into dualism, its main characteristics, and a critical appraisal, whilst section 4 will depict and criticize legal pluralism and its most prominent varieties. Section 5 will then offer a conclusion on the theoretical approaches discussed here, thereby paving the way for the subsequent main parts of this book.

2. Legal Monism

As is well-known at this point, monism regards all legal orders and all bodies of law as one single legal system (hence: μόνος; *mónos*). All monist doctrines—and there are many varieties, as will be shown below—are therefore based on the theoretical postulate that the law has to be understood as a unity and that its validity can only logically be derived from one common source.[1] For this reason, monism in its purest

[1] Pierre-Marie Dupuy, 'International Law and Domestic (Municipal) Law' in Rüdiger Wolfrum (ed), *Max Planck Encyclopedia of Public International Law* (2nd edn; Oxford University Press, 2013) para 11.

form means that the rules of international law in particular and all 'foreign' rules in general form part of domestic law (or any other body of law, depending on the chosen legal viewpoint). However, apart from this common ground, these various manifestations of monism have different approaches, and even though they have all been labelled 'monist', not all of them fit the term 'monism'[2] in the way in which this book understands and will defend it.

Monism can roughly be divided along three axes: First, monism can differ concerning the methodological approach employed, i.e. it can be based on either non-positivist or positivist grounds. Secondly, with a more concrete focus on normative conflicts, monism can differ as to the question which body of law shall have the last say: under the primacy of national law, normative conflicts are resolved in favour of national law, whilst under the primacy of international law, international legal norms will prevail. Thirdly, and lastly, there may also be a difference concerning the outcome of this conflict-resolution: whereas radical monism considers the superseded norm to be null and void, moderate monism merely assumes its subsequent voidability. All of these variables or characteristics can be combined with each other, resulting in different schools of thinking along the lines set out in Figure 1 below:[3]

School of Thought / Approach Towards Normative Conflicts	*Non-positivist* (sociological or natural-legal)	*Positivist* (positivism *stricto sensu* or epistemological-normative positivism)
Primacy (of international or national law)	*National Law:* G.F.W. Hegel	*National Law:* Georg Jellinek, André Décencière-Ferrandière, Max Wenzel
	International Law: Hugo Krabbe, Léon Duguit, Georges Scelle, Alfred Verdross, Hersch Lauterpacht	*International Law:* Josef Laurenz Kunz, the younger Hans Kelsen
Consequence (radical invalidity or moderate voidability)	*Radical:* G.F.W. Hegel, Hugo Krabbe	*Radical:* the younger Hans Kelsen
	Moderate: Alfred Verdross, Léon Duguit, Georges Scelle	*Moderate:* the older Hans Kelsen, as influenced by Verdross, Merkl, and Kunz

Figure 1 Different monist approaches.

Given these various views, this section on monism will be divided into three subsections. The first will offer a short historical introduction, whereas the second will discuss non-positivist theories of legal monism in all its facets, and the third,

[2] Davíd Thór Björgvinsson, *The Intersection of International and Domestic Law* (Edward Elgar Publishing, 2015) 20.

[3] Note that this figure does not claim to be complete or exhaustive in terms of proponents; it simply aims at giving an overview of the colourful bouquet that is legal monism.

conversely, will illustrate positivist monist theories. Attentive readers will of course already be aware of the fact that this book will defend monism in the following combination: positivist as envisaged by the pure theory of law, under the primacy of international law, and moderate (the field on the bottom right of the figure above). Nonetheless, as briefly mentioned above, this defence will not be carried out here, but in Chapter 3 of this book, as the following subsections are only intended to give a short descriptive overview of all varieties of legal monism including their respective shortcomings.

A. Origins: philosophy, natural law, and the unity of human society

At the outset, a short historical introduction seems apposite. Monism is far older than dualism or pluralism and was, at least at the time of its inception, firmly rooted in philosophy. Philosophical monism was first discussed by the pre-Socratic philosopher Parmenides who held that only one single thing exists.[4] The concept of Parmenidean monism itself is, however, not self-explanatory, and therefore has to be broken down into three different versions: material, numerical, and predicational monism. *Material* monism—which asserts that the world is made of one single underlying substance—is of no concern here, nor will *numerical* monism be discussed, which claims that there is only one thing or item in the universe. These are issues better left to the natural sciences or metaphysics, respectively, to resolve. What will be important in the context of this book on legal monism is *predicational* monism. According to this specific notion, each thing that exists can be only one thing; it can thus only hold one predicate, and must hold it in a principally strong way. Consequently, in order to be a genuine entity, a thing must be a predicational unity, with a single account of what it is.[5] In terms of the law, this predicate is legal validity and thus its normative binding nature, as this book will explain.

Beyond pure philosophy, monism has also always been intricately related with natural law. Owing to the close bonds between the European approach to international law and Christian (later rationalist) natural law, a unitary conception of the law was the only conceivable and accepted view of the legal world. Yet not only did this early notion of monism regard natural law as the same source of international and domestic law,[6] it also considered individuals to be subjects and addressees of international law, at least until the second half of the nineteenth century.[7] Early Catholic scholars were careful to reconcile state sovereignty with a monist construction of the law, according to which sovereignty merely represented a delegation from international law as a superior legal order—a competence rather than an omnipotence.[8] Despite his emphasis on the consensual nature of the law of nations,

[4] Hermann Diels and Walther Kranz, *Die Fragmente der Vorsokratiker* (4th edn; Weidmannsche Buchhandlung, 1922) 28B 8.3–8.6.

[5] Patricia Kenig Curd, 'Parmenidean Monism' (1991) 36 *Phronesis* 241, 242–3.

[6] Walter Rudolf, *Völkerrecht und deutsches Recht* (Mohr Siebeck, 1967) 130.

[7] Johann Caspar Bluntschli, *Das moderne Völkerrecht der civilisirten Staten* (C.H. Beck, 1878) 68 ff; Robert von Mohl, *Staatsrecht, Völkerrecht und Politik, Bd 1* (Laupp, 1860) 586, 597, and 599 ff.

[8] Joseph G. Starke, 'Monism and Dualism in the Theory of International Law' (1936) 17 *British Yearbook of International Law* 66, 67–8.

Francisco Suárez hence stressed in the sixteenth century that every state is a member of a universal society which requires a system of law in order to function properly.[9] Even Jean Bodin, the founder of the modern notion of sovereignty, expressed that this very sovereignty was derived from a higher legal order.[10] Hugo Grotius, lastly, saw these different bodies of law in a maternal relationship, in which human nature, from which arise mutual relations of society, is the mother of the law of nature. The offspring of natural law are obligations imposed upon states that arise from mutual consent; and these obligations are, in the end, the mother of municipal law. Natural law, including mutual relations and obligations deriving from mutual consent, is therefore the ancestor of domestic law, and the latter is inconceivable without the former.[11] The nineteenth century, however, saw the rise of legal positivism and the idea of dualism, and monism, together with its predominantly theological and natural-legal pedigree, entered a state of decline. It would not rise to its old heights again until the early twentieth century.[12]

B. Non-positivist theories of legal monism

(1) The primacy of national law

First ideas of a non-positivist concept of monism under the primacy of national law can be traced back to G.F.W. Hegel. Hegel's view of the law is to be considered non-positivist as he regards the law not as derived from an autonomous normative source, but merely as a result of the will of the state, and 'the nation State is, [as] the spirit in its substantial rationality and immediate actuality ... the absolute power on earth ...'.[13] The welfare of the state should be its own supreme law, especially in its relations with others.[14] Highly sceptical of international law and its universalistic claim as understood by Kant,[15] Hegel reveals his conception that eventually, state law shall reign supreme in the relationship between domestic and international law as the latter is derived from the former: international rules can only be created through the particular sovereign will of individual states, and without the state and its consent, international law in itself cannot claim to be valid law. Thus, he regards international law as mere 'external state law', which is dependent on the will of the state and its choice whether or not it respects its obligations vis-à-vis other states.[16] Because of the sovereign will of the state, there cannot be one single universal legal order above national law; in fact, there are as many international

[9] Francisco Suárez, *De legibus, Vol II* (Johannes Keerberg, 1612) chapter 19, n 9.
[10] Jean Bodin, *De re publica libri sex* (Jacob Dupuys, 1576) book I, chapter viii.
[11] Hugo Grotius, *De iure belli ac pacis* (Nicolas Buon, 1646) Prolegomena, para 16.
[12] Anthony H. O'Brien-Thomond, 'Positivism and Monism in International Law' (1948) 8 *Franciscan Studies* 321, 339, and 344–5; Christine Amrhein-Hofmann, *Monismus und Dualismus in den Völkerrechtslehren* (Duncker & Humblot, 2003) 146–51.
[13] Georg Wilhelm Friedrich Hegel, *Elements of the Philosophy of Right* (transl H.B. Nisbet; Cambridge University Press, 1991) para 331.
[14] Ibid., para 336.
[15] Armin von Bogdandy and Sergio Dellavelle, 'Georg Wilhelm Friedrich Hegel (1770–1831)' in Bardo Fassbender and Anne Peters (eds), *The Oxford Handbook of the History of International Law* (Oxford University Press, 2012) 1127.
[16] Hegel (n 13) paras 330 and 333.

legal orders as there are states,[17] as every single national legal order, when entering into international relations with other states, spawns another set of international norms.[18] Lastly, it remains to be mentioned that Hegel's monism under the primacy of national law is unquestionably radical. Although Hegel concedes that treaties should be observed, any treaty ceases to be valid once it comes into conflict with the will and the welfare of the state.[19] Only by insisting on this strong stance towards sovereignty, the state—as a person in its own right—can be free to develop and maintain its own will.[20]

Hegel's deeply individualistic conception of international law as based on each sovereign state's 'external state law' exerted a strong influence on legal positivist thought in the nineteenth century,[21] both on state-centred monists and dualists alike. His thoughts on the law were nonetheless not widely and comprehensively acknowledged in their original form, because their inevitable consequences were simply unacceptable for lawyers. If one really agrees with Hegel's international law doctrine, then one must also accept that international norms cannot be valid in the light of contravening state will. But this result is entirely irreconcilable with the principle of *pacta sunt servanda*,[22] perhaps *the* cornerstone of the international legal order and, beyond that, an undoubtedly positive-legal provision of both customary and treaty law. A Hegelian monist conception under the primacy of national law is therefore to be rejected in its entirety if one takes legal validity seriously.

(2) The primacy of international law

After its decline in the nineteenth century (and disregarding its Hegelian state-centred interlude), monism began its new rise in the early twentieth century with jurists hailing from very different schools of thought. Despite their distinct methodological approaches, all of these scholars share the same conviction, namely that monism is only conceivable under the primacy of international law. Differences among them emerge again, however, when looking at the consequences this primacy entails for contravening national law.

Under the impressions left by the First World War, Hugo Krabbe developed a radically new conception of the state, which is, in his view, identical to its legal order.[23] This entails that the power of all governmental authorities is reducible to the intellectual and spiritual force of legal norms, which, in turn, are based on the

[17] Amrhein-Hofmann (n 12) 246–7; Steven V. Hicks, 'Hegel on Cosmopolitanism, International Relations, and the Challenges of Globalization' in Andrew Buchwalter (ed), *Hegel and Global Justice* (Springer, 2012) 24.

[18] It is therefore highly debatable whether this particular form of monism can really be considered monist. This argument will be discussed in Chapter 3, section 5.B.

[19] Hegel (n 13) para 336.

[20] Ibid., para 331.

[21] Bruno Simma, 'The Contribution of Alfred Verdross to the Theory of International Law' (1995) 6 *European Journal of International Law* 33, 40.

[22] Alfred Verdross, *Die Einheit des rechtlichen Weltbildes auf Grundlage der Völkerrechtsverfassung* (Mohr, 1923) 6–8.

[23] See Walter Schiffer, *Die Lehre vom Primat des Völkerrechts in der neueren Literatur* (Deuticke, 1937) 28.

further irreducible legal consciousness of humans.[24] Thus, the basis of the law is subjective and individual psychology becomes binding as law if the majority of the people have this particular legal consciousness.[25] A fortiori, he argues that international law cannot be dependent on the will of sovereign states, because states do not possess legal consciousness; only individuals do, and hence they are the subjects of international law, not states. Through this shared individual legal consciousness, international law becomes real and valid law endowed with the same qualities as domestic law. The crucial point is that since international law is conferring rights as well as imposing obligations on a larger number of addressees than national law, it must necessarily possess a legal value that is superior to that of domestic law. The radical twist in Krabbe's theory is, however, that in the case of conflict between the two bodies of law, international law necessarily prevails and even denies the validity of the domestic legal act in question automatically.[26] Criticism of his view focused mainly on his 'Messianic' tone, which visualizes an already evolving 'world State'[27] that enforces its law through supranational[28] means, thereby superseding national law. Such a radical view of international law automatically invalidating contravening national law is, however, out of touch with reality and cannot be seen as a correct explanation of the positive law.

A more moderate tone regarding the consequences of normative conflicts can be found in both the sociological French school of law and schools of thoughts more inclined towards and influenced by natural law doctrine. With regard to the former, especially Léon Duguit and his student Georges Scelle developed notable monist conceptions of the law. Similar to Krabbe, they disassociate the law from the state and trace it back to the psychological faculties of the individual.[29] Law is consequently rooted in the sociological and biological facts of any given community, and thus in human cohabitation and solidarity.[30] The validity of the law can, in sociological terms, therefore be best summarized in the formula *ubi societas ibi ius*.[31] As in Krabbe's theory, the law originates from the spirit and consciousness of individuals and, subsequently, through the behaviour of different groups and communities towards each other; these inter-social norms become international legal norms via the international legal consciousness.[32] However, in stark contrast to Krabbe, Duguit

[24] Hugo Krabbe, *Die moderne Staatsidee* (2nd edn; Martinus Nijhoff, 1919) 1–9, 44, 48, and 82; Hugo Krabbe, *Die Lehre von der Rechtssouveränität* (Wolters, 1906) 5, 155, 170, and 187.

[25] Hugo Krabbe, 'L'idée moderne de l'état' (1926-III) 13 *Recueil des cours* 513, 570; Krabbe, *Moderne Staatsidee* (n 24) 83–4.

[26] Krabbe, *Moderne Staatsidee* (n 24) 263, 268, and 280–1.

[27] O'Brien-Thomond (n 12) 346.

[28] Krabbe had in fact already used the term 'supranational' long before the creation of the European Union and its supranational legal order; Krabbe, *Moderne Staatsidee* (n 24) 279, denoting international law as 'supranational constitutional law'.

[29] See O'Brien-Thomond (n 12) 347; Björgvinsson (n 2) 22.

[30] Léon Duguit, *Traité de droit constitutionnel, Vol II* (2nd edn; Boccard, 1923) 2; Georges Scelle, *Précis de droit des gens: Principes et systématique, Vol 1: Introduction, le milieu intersocial* (Sirey, 1932) 3.

[31] Heinz Wagner, 'Monismus und Dualismus: eine methodenkritische Betrachtung zum Theorienstreit' (1964) 89 *Archiv des öffentlichen Rechts* 212, 231.

[32] Léon Duguit, *Traité de droit constitutionnel, Vol I* (2nd edn; Boccard, 1921) 99; Scelle, *Précis de droit des gens* (n 30) 2–5 and 14–15. See also Josef L. Kunz, 'Die Rechts- und Staatslehre Léon Duguits' (1926/1927) 1 *Revue internationale de la théorie du droit* 140, 149.

considers the evolution of an overarching 'world State' not a necessary result of this legal consciousness,[33] and Scelle even concludes that international law lacks the required organs to enforce its norms. Accordingly, international law uses domestic institutions such as the judiciary to be enforced, which 'splits the role' of municipal judges, thereby making them concurrently national and international judges (*dédoublement fonctionnel*).[34] The difference between Duguit and Scelle is, nonetheless, that Duguit resolves norm conflicts in favour of international law on the basis of a hierarchy, putting the 'world legal consciousness' on top, which constitutes the yardstick for all positive domestic law.[35] Scelle, conversely, regards monism as a fusion of legal consciousness that makes a definite hierarchy obsolete, as national law is inevitably absorbed—as the inferior legal order—into an organized international community.[36] A persisting norm conflict thus becomes impossible: either the contravening national legal norm gives way or, if the inter-social solidarity proves to be too weak to prevail, national law applies and the hitherto monist cohesion disintegrates again.[37] This view is much more moderate than Krabbe's, but ultimately takes the edge off the suggested primacy of international law. In fact, Scelle endorses both versions of primacy (national as well as international), although his main assumption rests on the notion of the primacy of international law. This contradiction remains unresolved throughout his works.

Natural law scholars follow a similarly moderate approach towards the primacy of international law and the ensuing resolution of normative conflicts. Hersch Lauterpacht, for instance, openly acknowledges the current imperfections of international law, but emphasizes that this state of transition will eventually lead to a world state.[38] He concedes that his version of monism is not always consistent, as it was deduced 'from the actual practice of States and judicial tribunals',[39] which is riddled with contradictions. Yet this dualist separation of systems in reality does not shake the primacy of international law, in Lauterpacht's view. On the contrary, since history has a *telos*, it is an ethical maxim that dualist interferences with the supremacy of international law are merely provisional and will eventually subside, hence giving way to the transition of international law into a true law subordinating domestic law.[40]

Another proponent of a more naturalist stance is Alfred Verdross. It is perhaps too simplistic a step to put Verdross in the category of natural lawyers, given his

[33] Léon Duguit, *Souveraineté et Liberté* (Alcan, 1922) 116.
[34] Scelle, *Précis de droit des gens* (n 30) 43.
[35] Duguit, *Traité de droit constitutionnel, Vol I* (n 32) 196.
[36] Georges Scelle, 'Règles générales du droit de la paix' (1933-IV) 46 *Recueil des cours* 331, 334, and 353.
[37] Scelle, *Précis de droit des gens* (n 30) 31.
[38] Hersch Lauterpacht, 'The Nature of International Law and General Jurisprudence' in Elihu Lauterpacht (ed), *International Law: Being the Collected Papers of Hersch Lauterpacht, Vol 2: The Law of Peace* (Cambridge University Press, 1975) 19–20.
[39] Hersch Lauterpacht, 'General Rules of the Law of Peace' in Elihu Lauterpacht (ed), *International Law: Being the Collected Papers of Hersch Lauterpacht, Vol 1: General Works* (Cambridge University Press, 1975) 214.
[40] Ibid., 229.

involvement with the pure theory of law, and his work containing many elements of the epistemological-normative positivism of the Vienna School (inter alia, the hierarchy of norms and the concept of the basic norm). Ultimately, however, his embrace of Christian natural law puts him in the natural law camp. In his conception, all law is derived from a basic norm rooted 'in the objective realm of values'.[41] This very realm culminates in the basic norm of *pacta sunt servanda*, which is of both positive-legal and ethical nature and creates the entire international legal community by subjecting all states to the positive international legal order.[42] His version of monism is nevertheless much more moderate and nuanced than his predecessors': according to his thinking, international law is also regarded as supreme, but it concurrently highlights that international law determines a margin of action for each state, effectively delimiting its liberty of action.[43] Nevertheless, a normative conflict between international and municipal law does not entail the latter's invalidity *ex tunc*, but rather its voidability *ex nunc*. This means that municipal norms in violation of international law remain valid law until their modification or annulment.[44] International courts therefore only apply international law and can order states to nullify domestic legislation that is contrary to international law,[45] but they can of course not invalidate such national norms themselves. There simply is no positive-legal basis for such a radical assumption, as originally proposed by Krabbe.

(3) *Critique of non-positivist theories*

The central argument of this book is that non-positivist theories of monism are flawed, and that, as a result, preference will be given to an epistemological-normative positivist theory of monism as understood by the pure theory of law. Despite this section's focus on *non*-positivist theories of the law, the same counterarguments also apply to theories of the law that are positivist *stricto sensu* (i.e. or positivist-empiricist) and which deem legal validity to be derived from social or other empirical facts or social convention (as H.L.A. Hart's rule of recognition does, for example[46]). Thus, positivism in the meaning used here should not be confused with this empiricist facts-based positivism, but be understood as the above-mentioned epistemological-normative positivist theory of the Vienna School of Jurisprudence. An extensive and detailed analysis of this issue will be provided in Chapter 3, which will also explain the legal scientific programme pursued by the proponents of this School.[47] Therefore, suffice it to say at this point that grounding the law in extra-legal concepts

[41] Alfred Verdross, *Die Verfassung der Völkerrechtsgemeinschaft* (Springer, 1926) 23.

[42] Alfred Verdross, 'Grundlagen und Grundlegungen des Völkerrechts—ein Beitrag zu den Hypothesen des Völkerrechtspositivismus' (1921) 29 *Niemeyers Zeitschrift für internationales Recht* 65–91; Alfred Verdross, 'Le fondement du droit international' (1927-I) 16 *Recueil des cours* 247, 286.

[43] Verdross, 'Le fondement' (n 42) 287; Dupuy (n 1) paras 17–18.

[44] Verdross, *Verfassung der Völkerrechtsgemeinschaft* (n 41) 37.

[45] Alfred Verdross, 'Droit international public et droit interne' (1954) 32 *Revue de Droit International, de Sciences Diplomatiques et Politiques* 219, 221–3.

[46] H.L.A. Hart, *The Concept of Law* (2nd edn; Clarendon Press, 1994) 92.

[47] See Chapter 3, section 2.

such as psychology, social facts, or natural law is doomed to failure, if one intends to be working with an objective concept of legal validity. In the words of Josef L. Kunz, such a course of action is tantamount to an outright renunciation of a 'true science of the law'.[48]

In addition to the vagueness that is inherent in concepts such as 'consciousness', 'sentiment of justice',[49] 'social convention', or 'morality', it has been sufficiently demonstrated by Gottlob Frege[50] and Edmund Husserl[51] that rigid psychologism, i.e. the reduction of the laws of logic to psychological states of the mind, is a dead concept.[52] However, Frege provided us with a non-empirical account of the meanings that logic investigates, resulting in the birth of modern symbolic logic,[53] which transcends individual psychological states. The same must be true of the law, because replacing an objective ground of validity of the law with explanations drawn from psychology, sociology, or even morality (which also widely differs among individuals and states) necessarily results in *subjective* validity. The law, however, such as logic, transcends and constrains everyone's will, social status, and ethical conviction,[54] and as such, in order to be truly objective, the concepts of legal validity and legal meaning need to be completely de-psychologized, desociologized, and demoralized.[55] The law—in Frege's modified words—does not have the task, as psychology does, 'of investigating minds and contents of consciousness owned by individual men'.[56] The task of the law is to objectively regulate behaviour, and this is only possible if one knows what valid law is. Frege's anti-psychologist stance was strongly influenced by Kant[57] who both, in turn, then immensely influenced Kelsen in particular and the pure theory of law in general. A detailed explanation of the Kantian and neo-Kantian sources of this epistemological-normative positivist theory will be provided in Chapter 3, particularly in order to deal with criticism of Kelsen's use of Kantian methodology and terminology, which has unquestionably hampered appreciation of this theory in the Anglo-American world.[58]

The second and third thrusts of criticism do not concern the non-positivist basis of the above-mentioned theses. They are, rather, directed against any radical form of monism, especially concerning Krabbe's approach. Any version of radical monism which claims that national law in breach of international law is automatically

[48] Kunz, 'Rechts- und Staatslehre' (n 32) 149.
[49] Ibid.
[50] Gottlob Frege, *The Foundations of Arithmetic* (2nd edn; Blackwell, 1959) v–vii and 33–8.
[51] Edmund Husserl, *Logical Investigations, Vol I* (transl J.N. Findlay; Routledge, 1970).
[52] See e.g. Francis J. Pelletier, Renée Elio, and Philip Hanson, 'Is Logic All in Our Heads? From Naturalism to Psychologism' (2008) 88 *Studia Logica: An International Journal for Symbolic Logic* 3, 3–66; Charles Sanders Peirce and Joseph Jastrow, 'On Small Differences in Sensation' (1885) 3 *Memoirs of the National Academy of Sciences* 73, 73–83.
[53] Michael Green, 'Hans Kelsen and the Logic of Legal Systems' (2003) 54 *Alabama Law Review* 365, 367–8.
[54] Ibid., 389 and 392.
[55] Hans Kelsen, *Hauptprobleme der Staatsrechtslehre* (2nd edn; Mohr-Siebeck, 1923) v–vi.
[56] Gottlob Frege, 'Thoughts' in Brian McGuinness (ed), *Gottlob Frege: Collected Papers on Mathematics, Logic, and Philosophy* (Blackwell, 1984) 369.
[57] Hans Sluga, *Gottlob Frege* (Routledge, 1980) 58–64; Gottfried Gabriel, 'Frege als Neukantianer' (1986) 77 *Kant-Studien* 84, 84–101.
[58] Green (n 53) 366 and 369.

invalidated *ex tunc*, is to be rejected. Such a theory is not supported by the positive law and does therefore lack any explanatory power. States would most likely need to adopt a constitutional provision providing for such automatic invalidation or, at least, for an obligation of domestic authorities to disregard the national legal act in question, before such a radical manifestation of monism could be considered realistic.[59] The other point of criticism relates to monism under the primacy of national law which is also to be rejected. Such an approach would reduce the existing principle of *pacta sunt servanda* and binding nature of international law in general to an absurdity. Yet it is a fact that states comply with international law (at least most of the time[60]), and that its validity and binding force are not dependent on the actions of states acting on their own. A single state may withdraw from a multilateral treaty, thus opting out from its respective obligations, but the validity of the treaty itself transcends this unilateral action and is therefore not dependent on it.

These last two arguments—the degree of radicalism in monism and the issue of primacy—will be discussed again in the subsequent section, because positivist theories contain these elements as well. The same points of criticism will of course apply accordingly.

C. Positivist theories of legal monism

(1) The primacy of national law

The Hegelian doctrine of state sovereignty proved to be very influential, especially on Georg Jellinek. Given the prevalence of natural law in international law textbooks in the mid-nineteenth century, his intent was to establish international law scientifically and as genuine law, and this endeavour could only succeed by applying a strict positivist methodology in this field and by dispensing entirely with international law's philosophical and natural-law basis.[61] To this end, he argues that under a positivist view, the foundation of international law cannot differ from that of state law,[62] and only the state, which establishes law as the 'sovereign will of all',[63] can be considered to be a law-creating entity. In this vein, Jellinek assumes that, if only the empirically verifiable will of the state can be regarded as the process of law-creation, then international law is necessarily grounded on the free will of the community of states.[64] To overcome the destructive Hegelian construct of 'external state law', Jellinek envisages a truly binding law of nations on the basis of a voluntarist

[59] Antonio Cassese, 'Towards a Moderate Monism: Could International Rules Eventually Acquire the Force to Invalidate Inconsistent National Laws?' in Antonio Cassese (ed), *Realizing Utopia: The Future of International Law* (Oxford University Press, 2012) 192.

[60] See the famous statement by Louis Henkin, *How Nations Behave* (Columbia University Press, 1979) 47: 'Almost all nations observe almost all principles of international law and almost all of their obligations almost all the time'. Beyond that, the argument of non-compliance is, in itself, not a sound argument against the validity and binding nature of international law, as will be discussed later on.

[61] Jochen von Bernstorff, *The Public International Law Theory of Hans Kelsen* (Cambridge University Press, 2010) 26–7.

[62] Georg Jellinek, *Die rechtliche Natur der Staatenverträge* (Hölder, 1880) 2.

[63] Ibid. [64] Ibid., 2–3.

premise,[65] which finds its basis in the so-called theory of 'self-limitation'. It holds that international law is placed on equal footing with state law, but only by virtue of state law itself. A fortiori, international law is only binding on the state because of its own choosing of limiting itself within the boundaries of international law. Should the interests of the state thereby be unduly curtailed, the state remains entitled to disengage itself at any time from its international legal obligations.[66]

Other proponents of this positivist version of monism under the primacy of national law include, inter alia, André Décencière-Ferrandière who regards international law—given the absence of a centralized legislature of the international legal order—as a mere projection of municipal law.[67] Similarly, for Max Wenzel, international law simply is national law, and the former's validity therefore rests on the latter's. This unitary view of the law makes irresolvable norm conflicts impossible, but it does not prevent states from acting lawfully under municipal law and concurrently acting in violation of international law.[68] Wenzel argues that the principle of *pacta sunt servanda* is not to be seen as constraining the freedom of states to act in any way they want, because this very principle forms part of national law and hence national law can determine the rules under which a state may withdraw from a treaty.[69] Thus, the validity of every single treaty is grounded in the domestic legal act that authorizes the states to conclude such treaties, and every treaty has as many grounds of validity as there are parties to it.[70]

Even though none of these monist versions under the primacy of national law can be considered eminently radical, there are certain elements to be criticized. Verdross, for example, draws attention to the self-defeating nature of the self-limitation theory if one acknowledges the legal nature of international law. For if states may unilaterally change their will in breach of their treaty obligations, then international law is not an objectively binding legal order, and it would not make sense to accept it as such; and if, conversely, states maintain the objectively binding nature of international law, then the concept of self-limitation becomes absurd.[71] Beyond that, monists such as Jellinek and Wenzel cannot evade the question as to whether their unitary construction of the law really is monist. In fact, the assumption that a multitude of national legal orders governs the entire legal universe and that international law only exists as within state law rather speaks in favour of a pluralist system. Therefore, state law co-exists in a disconnected and disjointed way, and norm conflicts become again—due to the lack of an overarching international legal order—utterly irresolvable.[72] Ultimately, under such a monism, international law disintegrates in as many national legal orders as there are states. Genuine *legal* relations within the strictest

[65] von Bernstorff (n 61) 30. [66] Jellinek (n 62) 7 and 40.

[67] André Décencière-Ferrandière, 'Considérations sur le droit international dans ses rapports avec le droit de l'État' (1933) 40 *Revue Générale de Droit International Public* 45, 64–6.

[68] Max Wenzel, *Juristische Grundprobleme* (Dümmler, 1920) 403 and 406–7.

[69] Ibid., 502–8 and 511.

[70] Max Wenzel, 'Der Begriff des Gesetzes in der Reichsverfassung' (1927) 4 *Veröffentlichungen der Vereinigung der Deutschen Staatsrechtslehrer* 136, 141 ff.

[71] Verdross, *Verfassung der Völkerrechtsgemeinschaft* (n 41) 14.

[72] Gustav Walz, *Völkerrecht und staatliches Recht* (Kohlhammer, 1933) 57–8.

meaning of the word cannot exist in such a conception.[73] It must therefore be highlighted again that monism under the primacy of national law eventually collapses into something else and ceases to be monism, thereby becoming an oxymoron.

(2) The primacy of international law

We will now turn to the epistemological-normative positivist school of thought, usually known as the Vienna School of Jurisprudence, and their respective versions of monism. The reader should be aware that the present subsection is not intended to provide an exhaustive illustration and examination of this specific monist approach. It rather aims at presenting its main features by way of a shortened and simplified introduction, whereas an in-depth analysis can be found in Chapter 3 of this book.

The principal aim of the proponents of this school is to excise from their scientific scrutiny of the law any moral, psychological, sociological, and political data, hence 'purifying' the law from any non-legal elements.[74] The central issue of the pure theory of law therefore is to ascertain what the ultimate ground of legal validity is. Thus, in order to establish the law as an objective normative science, the factual 'is' needs to be strictly distinguished from the normative 'ought' in the sense of David Hume's argument that prescriptive statements cannot be logically derived from descriptive statements.[75] The conclusion of Hans Kelsen, the most prominent thinker of the pure theory of law, is that the validity of the law is derived neither from a higher extra-legal normative order such as natural law or morality, nor from social or empirical facts.[76] The validity of a particular legal act can only be determined by examining the process of its creation through the hierarchy of norms, as originally envisaged by Kelsen's student Adolf Julius Merkl. According to Merkl, the existence and thus validity of every legal norm is determined by a superior norm, whose validity, in turn, is again determined by a superior norm.[77] This chain of validity can of course not go on indefinitely and will normally be concluded by the supreme positive norm of any given legal order, which is the constitution.[78] But what lies beyond the constitution and its historical predecessors, such as the historically first constitution? What is the source of validity of the constitution, if this source can be grounded in neither morality nor in a factual basis such as the effective and authorizing power of the state? The answer to this question can be found in the doctrine of the *Grundnorm* (or basic norm), which is the transcendental-logical precondition of the law. This norm is not

[73] Albert Bleckmann, *Allgemeine Staats- und Völkerrechtslehre: Vom Kompetenz- zum Kooperationsvölkerrecht* (Heymanns, 1995) 422.

[74] O'Brien-Thomond (n 12) 347–8.

[75] David Hume, *A Treatise of Human Nature* (John Noone, 1738) book III, part I, section I.

[76] Hans Kelsen, *Pure Theory of Law* (2nd edn; University of California Press, 1967) 1.

[77] Adolf Julius Merkl, 'Prolegomena einer Theorie des rechtlichen Stufenbaus' in Hans R. Klecatsky, René Marcic, and Herbert Schambeck (eds), *Die Wiener rechtstheoretische Schule: Schriften von Hans Kelsen, Adolf Merkl, Alfred Verdross, Band 2* (Verlag Österreich, 2010) 1098–9.

[78] Kelsen, *Pure Theory* (n 76) 194; Adolf Julius Merkl, *Die Lehre von der Rechtskraft entwickelt aus dem Rechtsbegriff* (Deuticke, 1923) 213 and 217.

posited but is necessarily presupposed a priori by anybody wishing to cognize valid law.[79] In one of its various manifestations[80] it states that one ought to behave as the individuals who created the first constitution have ordained.[81] The *Grundnorm* is therefore capable of explaining three issues: first, the validity of the law without any reference to extra-legal elements; secondly, the normativity of the law; and last, the hierarchical nature of legal orders.[82] In this vein, the pure theory of law considers the law to retain a certain hybrid status by combining legal-positivist elements, namely the posited nature of the law as it *is* (and not as it should be in terms of justice and fairness) with its normative and behaviour-regulating character (e.g. its command that somebody *ought* to do something or *ought* to refrain from doing something). The epistemological element of the pure theory of law, lastly, is its claim that the validity of the law can only be cognized and ascertained by the hierarchy of norms, which in turn presupposes the existence of the non-posited *Grundnorm*.

These claims, however, are not limited to domestic law alone, and were subsequently extrapolated to international law and its relationship to national law. For Kelsen, legal dualism hence is an untenable position for several reasons: First, it is simply not true that international law and national law govern different legal areas. On the contrary, both claim to regulate human behaviour in the same way, not only addressing individuals directly (e.g. by conferring individual rights on them),[83] but also those individuals acting as officials of the state. The 'State', in Kelsen's line of argumentation, does not exist as an entity separate from its legal order; in fact it is identical to its own legal order and can therefore only function through individuals acting on its behalf.[84] Otherwise 'international law would not obligate or authorize anybody to anything'.[85] Secondly, if inferior law can only be created validly by superior law, then only two options are possible to conceive of the relationship between national and international law: either one of them is subordinated to the other one in a monist manner, or they stand side-by-side in a somehow coordinated fashion. Yet such coordination would presuppose a third and even higher body of law, determining the creation of both national and international law. Since such a third and superior body does not exist, however, the dualist construction is not sustainable.[86] Finally, the assumption of two distinct legal orders in terms of validity is only conceivable within the meaning of alternatives: either one or the other normative system can be presupposed as valid, but not both at the same time. Valid law

[79] Kelsen, *Pure Theory* (n 76) 201–5.

[80] Stanley L. Paulson, 'Die unterschiedlichen Formulierungen der "Grundnorm"' in Aulis Aarnio and others (eds), *Rechtsnorm und Rechtswirklichkeit* (Duncker & Humblot, 1993) 53–74.

[81] Hans Kelsen, *General Theory of Law and State* (reissue edn; Transaction Publishers, 2007) 115.

[82] Hans Kelsen, 'On the Basic Norm' (1959) 47 *California Law Review* 107, 107.

[83] Hans Kelsen, *Das Problem der Souveränität und die Theorie des Völkerrechts* (Tübingen: Mohr-Siebeck, 1920) 124–31.

[84] Hans Kelsen, *Principles of International Law* (Rinehart, 1952) 438–44; Kelsen, *Problem der Souveränität* (n 83) 4–21.

[85] Kelsen, *General Theory* (n 81) 342.

[86] Kelsen, *Pure Theory* (n 76) 332. See also Paul Guggenheim, *Lehrbuch des Völkerrechts: Band 1* (Recht und Gesellschaft, 1948) 22–3 and 22 fn 7, equally rejecting such a 'third' construction.

is thus necessarily a unitary legal order, as otherwise the concept of validity would become meaningless.[87]

Based on these principal preliminary considerations, Kelsen develops his monist view of the law. At this point, attention needs to be drawn to the differences in thought of the younger and the older Kelsen, and to the other proponents of the Vienna School of Jurisprudence who considerably influenced him in this progress. The younger Kelsen develops his own version of radical monism under the primacy of international law. In this view, the *Grundnorm* of all law is to be found at the top of international law. This norm, as the source and foundation of all law, enables the creation of inferior norms, including those of national law. Thus, the legal order of municipal law and the authority of states to exercise jurisdiction in their territory is delegated and derived from international law. For the younger Kelsen, only monism under the primacy of international law is possible, as the primacy of national law would inevitably lead to a denial of international law as genuine law,[88] subjecting it to a subjectivist conception of validity under the imperialism of the most powerful states.[89] Furthermore, the superior norms of international law not only govern the creation of inferior norms, but also their abrogation. Very similar to Krabbe's approach,[90] the radical factor of Kelsen's theory thus is that due to their superior rank over domestic law, international norms have the power to invalidate any municipal rules in contravention to them. In fact, he even goes so far as to claim that each and every norm of the inferior system in breach of the norms of the superior system is null and void *ex tunc*, both under international and municipal law. The consequence of this is that there never existed a valid norm to begin with; normative conflicts between domestic and international law are therefore necessarily impossible.[91] However, as already discussed above, such a radical version of monism has been abandoned, since positive law cannot support it.

This evident deficiency in Kelsen's theory did nevertheless not remain unnoticed. Under the influence of Verdross' much more moderate and hence more realistic conception of monism,[92] the older Kelsen further develops his theories and mitigates his rather drastic theory by integrating these moderate components in his writings.[93] Upon this transition from radical to moderate monism,[94] Kelsen later acknowledges that a domestic legal norm in breach of international law remains valid until this very validity is repealed by another domestic norm. In this regard, he emphasizes that this situation does not endanger the unity of the law, as a useful analogy of national law shows: even in national law, statutes in contravention to the constitution are not automatically null and void, but need to be repealed by

87 Kelsen, *Problem der Souveränität* (n 83) 104–5; Kelsen, *Pure Theory* (n 76) 328–9 and 333–44.

88 Kelsen, *Problem der Souveränität* (n 83) 196–205.

89 Ibid., 317–19.

90 Krabbe, *Moderne Staatsidee* (n 24) 263, 268, and 280–1.

91 Kelsen, *Problem der Souveränität* (n 83) 111–14.

92 Verdross, 'Droit international public et droit interne' (n 45) 221; Alfred Verdross, *Völkerrecht* (5th edn; Springer, 1964) 113.

93 Hans Kelsen, 'Les rapports de système entre le droit interne et le droit de l'état (1926-IV) 14 *Recueil des cours* 231, 315–17.

94 Wagner (n 31) 212; Alfred Rub, *Hans Kelsens Völkerrechtslehre* (Schulthess, 1995) 426.

particular constitutional procedures. The same is true for the relationship between domestic and international law, and in case a state refuses to comply with its international obligations and to invalidate the national legal norm in question, this behaviour will be considered a delict under international law and may be sanctioned accordingly.[95]

The last aspect of the older Kelsen's conception of monism to be discussed here is his so-called 'choice hypothesis': in contrast to his earlier view that monism is only possible under the primacy of international law, he later states that both versions of monism—under the primacy of national law and the primacy of international law—are epistemologically and equally correct. The decisive choice for one of them is not grounded in logic or epistemology, but ideology ('pacifism versus State sovereignty'), and therefore an objective legal science needs to keep a healthy distance from this choice to retain its purity.[96] Kelsen's students Verdross and Kunz, however, disagreed with this result. To counter Kelsen's choice hypothesis, they argued that monism under the primacy of international law is not a mere choice between equal ideologies, but also a logical precondition for the postulated unity of the law, as only this manifestation of monism can explain the connection between international and national as one single system.[97] Otherwise, there would exist as many international legal orders as there are international legal subjects.

Accordingly, proponents of a monist conception under the primacy of international law consider, as the name aptly suggests, international law to prevail over domestic law in the case of conflict, as it sits at the apex in terms of legal validity. Presently, this notion, accepting the primacy of international law in one form or another, is the only one of interest.[98] Indeed, if one takes the example of state creation and the entry of new states into the international legal community, it is generally accepted that international law binds them without their consent. In the same way, if an old regime is overthrown by a revolution, or a constitution is peacefully modified or replaced by a new one, international law continues to confer rights and impose obligations on international legal subjects. Therefore, the sole scientific construction justified based on monism is that international law conditions state law and that it must somehow give way in the case of conflict.[99]

D. Interim conclusion

Before continuing with an examination of dualism and pluralism, the main points of the above discussion should be briefly summarized. As has been shown, the only

[95] Kelsen, *Pure Theory* (n 76) 330–1. [96] Ibid., 342–6.

[97] Josef L. Kunz, 'On the Theoretical Basis of the Law of Nations' (1925) 10 *Transactions of the Grotius Society* 115, 139; Josef L. Kunz, 'La primauté de droit des gens' (1925) 6 *Revue de droit international et de legislation comparée* 556, 572 ff; Josef L. Kunz, *Völkerrechtswissenschaft und Reine Rechtslehre* (Deuticke, 1923) 82; Alfred Verdross, 'Völkerrecht und staatliches Recht' in Hans Robert Engelmann (ed), *Die völkerrechtswidrige Kriegshandlung und der Strafanspruch der Staaten* (Engelmann, 1920) 33 ff; Verdross, 'Grundlagen und Grundlegungen' (n 42) 82–3.

[98] Dupuy (n 1) para 12. [99] Starke (n 8) 77.

monist choice still viable after this critique is its epistemological-normative positivist version as envisaged by the pure theory of law; moderate; and under the primacy of international law. To be more concrete, non-positivist theories of the law are to be rejected because of their diluting effect on the law and its validity. By taking recourse to non-objective grounds such as morality, social convention, or psychology, they make an exact determination of valid law impossible. And if the term 'validity' is bereft of its objective meaning, it does not make sense to talk about law any more. Thus, only an epistemological-normative positivist theory of the law as represented by the pure theory of law can objectively determine what the law is, primarily on the basis of the hierarchy of norms.

Furthermore, monism only has explanatory power in its moderate form. Any radical manifestations which deem contravening law to be automatically null and void do not correspond to the law as it is. Therefore, any law in breach of a superior norm is not invalid *ab initio*, but can merely be invalidated in accordance with existing procedural rules. Preference is hence given to *voidability* over *invalidity*. Should this invalidation not be executed accordingly, sanctions can subsequently be employed to ensure the unity of the law.

Lastly, the above discussion has also demonstrated that if one takes the validity of the law and thus international law as genuine law seriously, monism is only conceivable under the primacy of international law. Otherwise international law cannot be an objectively valid legal order that is binding on its legal subjects, and it merely remains a projection of external state law. To connect this assumption to the above-mentioned considerations on moderate monism, this also entails that normative conflicts between national and international law will be resolved in favour of the latter, but again not through automatic invalidation, but procedural voidability. Chapter 3 of this book will take up this issue again, further illustrate and scrutinize this version of monism and defend it against criticism.

3. Legal Dualism

A. Origins: philosophy and the will of the state

In the same way as monism, philosophical dualism dates back to ancient Greece. The dualism of material objects and immaterial ideas shapes Plato's entire metaphysics,[100] whilst Aristotle's much milder dualism distinguishes between material organs and immaterial intellect.[101] Modern philosophical dualism, however, was most prominently first discussed by René Descartes in his *Meditations* on the philosophy of mind. This Cartesian dualism basically states that there is a foundational distinction between the material body and the immaterial mind of a

[100] Plato, *Phaedo* (ed John M. Cooper, Hackett, 1997) 78b4–84b8.

[101] Aristotle, *De Anima* (ed and transl Jonathan Barnes, *The Complete Works of Aristotle, Vol 1* (Oxford University Press, 1984) 429a10–429b9.

human, even though he concedes to a certain degree of interaction between those two entities.[102]

Legal dualism, in turn, regards international and domestic law as two separate legal systems (hence: δύο; *dyo*). These legal systems are self-contained, since within each system the only rules that exist and can claim validity are those that are part of the system. Strictly speaking, given the fact that the systems under consideration are more than just two, it would be more appropriate to designate this conception as 'pluralism' rather than 'dualism'. Yet, since pluralism (as will be shown below) denotes a very different idea, it seems to be preferable to continue using the more traditional term 'dualism'.[103]

Dualism was mainly shaped by the beginning 'fall of natural law'[104] and the rise of legal positivism after the Treaty of Westphalia. As one of the first proponents of dualism in the eighteenth century, Emer de Vattel elevated states to the exclusive subjects of international law and stressed that it was their voluntary will to be bound by the law of nations, which enabled them to engage in international relations.[105] By construing international law on the basis of a positivist understanding of the law, the doctrine of state sovereignty became the central tenet in determining the relationship between national and international law.[106] The sovereign state remains the centre of gravity, and by viewing international and municipal law as quite distinct normative realities,[107] and by underlining the importance of the state in founding international law on the basis of consent, national self-determination and political processes can withstand external interference by international law.[108]

(1) Radical dualism: Heinrich Triepel

The dualist doctrine was and still is deeply rooted in the Hegelian notion of the state will.[109] This inspired Heinrich Triepel to a radical vision of dualism, postulating that the source of national law is the will of the state itself, whilst the source of international is the common will (*Gemeinwille*) of states.[110] Consequently, international and national law not only have two disparate sources of law, but also are disparate legal orders. By using a geometrical metaphor, Triepel regards these two systems as circles that may, at the most, touch one another, but which can never intersect.[111]

[102] René Descartes, 'Meditations on First Philosophy' in John Cottingham, Robert Stoothoff, and Dugald Murdoch (transl), *The Philosophical Writings of René Descartes, Vol II* (Cambridge University Press, 1984) 1–62.

[103] Giorgio Gaja, 'Dualism—A Review' in Janne Nijman and André Nollkaemper (eds), *New Perspectives on the Divide Between National and International Law* (Oxford University Press, 2007) 52–3.

[104] Mónica García-Salmones Rovira, *The Project of Positivism in International Law* (Oxford University Press, 2013) 33–4.

[105] Emer de Vattel, *Le droit des gens, ou principes de la loi naturelle, 2 vols* (Apud Liberos Tutior, 1758).

[106] Mary Ellen O'Connell, 'Peace and War' in Bardo Fassbender and Anne Peters (eds), *The Oxford Handbook of the History of International Law* (Oxford University Press, 2012) 278.

[107] Starke (n 8) 67–8.

[108] David Feldman, 'Monism, Dualism, and Constitutional Legitimacy' (1999) 20 *Australian Yearbook of International Law* 105, 107.

[109] Starke (n 8) 68.

[110] Heinrich Triepel, *Völkerrecht und Landesrecht* (C.L. Hirschfeld, 1899) 28–30.

[111] Ibid., 111.

Triepel explains this utter separation of the two systems on the basis of the public/private divide.[112] Accordingly, Triepel contrasts agreements (similar to contracts among individual persons), based on the union of identical wills, to further shared interests, with treaties that serve contrary interests and can hence only transcend state sovereignty by domestic implementation.[113] States can therefore not be bound by international norms against their will.[114] This entails that international and national law essentially differ from each other in three aspects:[115] first, with regard to their respective sources, international law is based on the collective will of the states, whereas municipal law is based on the state's constitution; and this difference in sources necessarily implies a difference in the grounds of validity.[116] Secondly, there is a considerable difference concerning the subjects and addressees whom these two legal systems govern: international law regulates inter-state law and thus the relations between states, whilst domestic law deals with legal relations between individuals inter se and between individuals and the state's organs.[117] Lastly, different sources and different addressees also necessitate a difference in substance and entail that international and national law are concerned with dissimilar areas of law by way of complementarity.[118]

The logical consequence of this normative separation is the impossibility of normative conflicts between international and domestic law, and, accordingly, the incapability of international law to derogate contravening national law and vice versa.[119] Another necessity of the dualist notion is that international law cannot be automatically or directly applied in municipal law; states can decide for themselves if and under which conditions they give effect to international norms in their own legal systems, and international law remains silent on this matter. Thus, to be applicable, international law must have been transformed or incorporated into domestic law, and it is consequently merely operative as part of that domestic legal order, and not as international law per se[120]—because international law, by itself, can only generate rights and obligations for states, but not for individuals.[121]

This approach avoids questions pertaining to the supremacy of one legal system over the other, as they share no common field of application.[122] In case of conflict between international and national law, radical dualists would consequently assume that a domestic court would apply domestic law, and that such court would decide which rule ought to prevail.[123] The effective performance and enforcement of

[112] García-Salmones Rovira (n 104) 34. [113] Triepel (n 110) 45–52.

[114] Robert Pfeffer, *Das Verhältnis von Völkerrecht und Landesrecht* (Mohr Siebeck, 2009) 83.

[115] Luzius Wildhaber and Stephan Breitenmoser, 'The Relationship between Customary International Law and Municipal Law in Western European Countries' (1988) 48 *Zeitschrift für ausländisches öffentliches Recht und Völkerrecht* 163, 170.

[116] Triepel (n 110) 27 ff. [117] Ibid., 11 ff.

[118] Ibid., 9, 11, and 228 ff. [119] Ibid., 257 ff.

[120] Wildhaber and Breitenmoser (n 115) 170–1.

[121] Triepel (n 110) 228–9; Walz (n 72) 238–9.

[122] Robert Jennings and Arthur Watts (eds), *Oppenheim's International Law* (9th edn; Longman, 1992) 53.

[123] James Crawford, *Brownlie's Principles of Public International Law* (8th edn; Oxford University Press, 2012) 48.

international law is therefore heavily dependent on the openness of the domestic legal order in question.

(2) *Moderate dualism: Dionisio Anzilotti*

Over time, this radical position gave way to a more moderate view of dualism, which can be found in the writings of Dionisio Anzilotti. Principally Anzilotti defends the sovereign powers of states[124] and agrees with Triepel that international and national law differ with regard to their respective addressees and grounds of validity.[125] He sees international law based on the principle of *pacta sunt servanda*, while municipal law is grounded on the duty to obey the legislator's commands.[126] Furthermore, he holds, in accordance with Triepel, that international law can only impose obligations on states, not individuals, and that it cannot impact on the validity of contravening domestic law.[127] Hence international law can only claim validity within the municipal legal sphere by virtue of the state's own legislation, implementing and transforming international law into national law. Thereby the substance of the original international norms thus transformed is being changed vis-à-vis the national legal addressees.[128] The consequence of this view is, as in Triepel's notion of dualism, the exclusion of normative conflicts between international and domestic law.[129]

Yet, the crucial and distinguishing factor in Anzilotti's dualist view is that he never carried his views to an extreme. On the contrary, his dualism is somewhat tempered by the observation that there exist, within various domestic systems,[130] rules that tend 'to ensure the compliance with some obligations under international law',[131] for example *renvoi*,[132] or the doctrine of consistent interpretation. Therefore, the former can be used to establish and perpetuate a more or less smooth continuity between international and national law,[133] while the latter enables national judges to construe a domestic, transformed norm in the light of the original international norm[134] in order to avoid incurring responsibility under international law.[135] But nevertheless, as 'foreign' norms, any international law provision remains a mere fact and lacks legal character in national law.[136] The moderating element is, nonetheless, that these international norms should be taken into account by the state.[137]

[124] Georg Nolte, 'From Dionisio Anzilotti to Roberto Ago: The Classical International Law of State Responsibility and the Traditional Primacy of a Bilateral Conception of Inter-State Relations' (2002) 13 *European Journal of International Law* 1083, 1084.

[125] Dionisio Anzilotti, *Corso di diritto internazionale, Vol I* (3rd edn; Athenaeum, 1928) 38 ff and 41 ff.

[126] Ibid., 38 ff. [127] Ibid., 41 ff. [128] Ibid., 45 ff. [129] Ibid., 42.

[130] Giorgio Gaja, 'Positivism and Dualism in Dionisio Anzilotti' (1992) 3 *European Journal of International Law* 123, 123, and 136.

[131] Anzilotti, *Corso di diritto internazionale* (n 125) 60.

[132] Ibid., 42 ff; Stefan Griller, 'Völkerrecht und Landesrecht—unter Berücksichtigung des Europarechts' in Robert Walter, Clemens Jabloner, and Klaus Zeleny (eds), *Hans Kelsen und das Völkerrecht* (Manz, 2004) 86.

[133] Rudolf (n 6) 141; Walz (n 72) 260.

[134] Anzilotti, *Corso di diritto internazionale* (n 125) 41; Walz (n 72) 239.

[135] Pfeffer (n 114) 85.

[136] Anzilotti, *Corso di diritto internazionale privato* (Athenaeum, 1925) 57.

[137] *Certain German Interests in Polish Upper Silesia (Merits)* [1926] PCIJ Series A, No 7, 19.

Of course, even in Anzilotti's moderate version of dualism, the fundamental element remains that international and municipal law are two disconnected and disparate bodies of law. After all, the determination whether a specific domestic act is indeed in breach of international law is only relevant from the aspect of international law itself, but not in terms of municipal law.[138] Nevertheless, the main achievement of Anzilotti's thinking is that he freely concedes to the existence of reciprocal influence of international law on the shaping of domestic law and vice versa[139]—despite the normative fissure between these two bodies of law.

(3) *Appraisal and critique*

Proponents of a realist outlook on international relations might argue that dualism, as a theoretical model to explain the dealings of states with the international community, represents a theory that is true to life and conforms better than any other explanation to the apparently chaotic relations between states. In a world driven by self-interest, the anarchical absence of a central law enforcer, and brute power politics, international law is left incapable of making constitutional and binding demands on states, and merely serves as a coordinating tool. Such a Machiavellian conception of the relationship between domestic and international law seems to conform easily to the interests of all states: utility, expedience, and power;[140] a judicial mistrust of extrinsic legal sources;[141] the protection of sovereignty, and an aversion to an imperfect international legal order.[142]

However, this is too pessimistic an observation and must not only be rejected because of its purely empirical nature (which does not allow for any inferences concerning the normative claims of international law[143]), but also because of other weighty objections to the traditional features of dualism. First, there are obvious difficulties in accepting the difference in sources of international and domestic law. Without resorting to artificial constructions such as 'tacit consent', it is problematic to trace all norms of international law back to *pacta sunt servanda*. This would not only disregard customary international law, but also general principles of law which form part of both international and domestic law with manifold reciprocal influences.[144]

[138] Griller (n 132) 86.

[139] *Consistency of Certain Danzig Legislative Decrees with the Constitution of the Free City* [1935] PICJ Series AB, No 65 (Individual Opinion by M. Anzilotti) 63; Rudolf (n 6) 142.

[140] A. Claire Cutler, 'The "Grotian Tradition" in International Relations' (1991) 17 *Review of International Studies* 41, 50, and 61.

[141] Jonathan Turley, 'Dualistic Values in the Age of International Legisprudence' (1992/1993) 44 *Hastings Law Journal* 158, 210–11.

[142] David M. Aaron, 'Reconsidering Dualism: The Caribbean Court of Justice and the Growing Influence of Unincorporated Treaties in Domestic Law' (2007) 6 *Law and Practice of International Courts and Tribunals* 233, 240–1.

[143] Again, 'ought' statements do not logically follow from 'is' statements; see Hume (n 75) book III, part I, section 1.

[144] Starke (n 8) 73; Dupuy (n 1) para 6.

Secondly, the hypothesis that international legal norms are exclusively addressed to states is no longer realistic, and even convinced traditionalists must admit that international organizations have joined the ranks of international legal subjects.[145] Moreover, it is also untrue that international law cannot reach out towards individuals and confer upon them rights and obligations.[146] The International Court of Justice (ICJ) confirmed this view in the *LaGrand* case when it held that Article 36(1) of the Vienna Convention on Consular Relations, governing the rights of arrested foreign nationals to consular protection, 'creates individual rights'.[147] After all, the individual is the addressee of 'international subjective rights'[148] and it is therefore beside the point that these rights must be transposed into domestic law in order to become effective.[149]

Lastly, concerning substance, it is simply not true that international and municipal law govern diverse areas: to begin with, if this were the case, the doctrine of consistent interpretation would be absurd, since if there were no overlap in substance, it would not make any sense to construe domestic norms in conformity with similar international norms. Moreover, it is common practice that domestic courts apply norms which have a counterpart in international law.[150]

Fully fledged dualism would allow for unrestrained state sovereignty[151] and hence become a threat to the status of public international law as genuine law.[152] But the law-making process on the international level has been diversified in many regards and it is no longer necessary to look at examples from supranational organizations in order to find sources that are not based on the express will and consent of states.[153] In fact, the great majority of observers today acknowledges that consent alone, as proposed in a dualist view, cannot satisfactorily explain the obligatory nature of international law.[154] It is today common for international legal norms to bind states without any form of express or implied consent,[155] which further undermines the Hegelian theory of self-limitation under which states only bind themselves to international law by virtue of their own national law.[156] *Ius cogens* norms, for example,

[145] See e.g. *Reparation for Injuries Suffered in the Service of the United Nations (Advisory Opinion)* [1949] ICJ Rep 174; and *Interpretation of the Agreement of 25 March 1951 between the WHO and Egypt (Advisory Opinion)* [1980] ICJ Rep 73, para 37.

[146] Gaja, 'Dualism' (n 103) 55.

[147] *LaGrand (Germany v United States of America)* [2001] ICJ Rep 466, para 77.

[148] Evelyne Lagrange, 'L'efficacité dans l'ordre juridique interne des normes internationales concernant la situation des personnes privées' (2012) 356 *Recueil des cours* 239, 275.

[149] Anne Peters, 'Rechtsordnungen und Konstitutionalisierung: Zur Neubestimmung der Verhältnisse' (2010) 65 *Zeitschrift für Öffentliches Recht* 1, 15.

[150] Christina Eckes and Stephan Hollenberg, 'Reconciling Different Legal Spheres in Theory and Practice: Pluralism and Constitutionalism in the Cases of *Al-Jedda, Ahmed,* and *Nada*' (2013) 20 *Maastricht Journal of European and Comparative Law* 220, 241.

[151] Wagner (n 31) 227.

[152] John Tasioulas, 'The Legitimacy of International Law' in Samantha Besson and John Tasioulas (eds), *The Philosophy of International Law* (Oxford University Press, 2010) 98.

[153] Dupuy (n 1) para 6.

[154] Jutta Brunnée, 'Consent' in Rüdiger Wolfrum (ed), *Max Planck Encyclopedia of Public International Law* (2nd edn; Oxford University Press, 2013) para 2.

[155] Starke (n 8) 73.

[156] Hersch Lauterpacht, *The Function of Law in the International Community* (reprint; Oxford University Press, 2011) 417.

are valid and binding on all international legal subjects without requiring them to consent to them *individually*, because the crucial component of their character is, in the words of Article 53 of the Vienna Convention on the Law of Treaties (VCLT), their acceptance and recognition by *the international community of states as a whole*. Furthermore, Article 53 of the VCLT explicitly disallows any derogations from *ius cogens* norms and restricts their modification to subsequent norms of the same character. This not only applies to all parties to the VCLT, but to the international community in its entirety due to the customary legal nature of Article 53 of the VCLT.[157]

In addition to peremptory norms, treaties also increasingly delegate powers from the ratifying subjects to treaty-based bodies with quasi-legislative or quasi-judicial character. These bodies, such as the United Nations Security Council acting under Chapter VII of the United Nations Charter,[158] are authorized under their respective founding treaty to develop and ascertain the specific content of the obligations imposed upon the treaty parties. This means, in other words, that although states have consented to a specific treaty, subsequent decisions can be taken without their consent by these treaty-based bodies.[159]

In the end, dualists must face a veritable dilemma from which they cannot successfully escape: either they admit, as 'true dualists', to the irresolvability of normative conflicts between international and municipal law and thereby sacrifice the legal validity of international law[160]—which would then expose them to the accusation of being 'deniers of international law'; an allegation which even a radical dualist such as Triepel would have vehemently dismissed.[161] Or, conversely, if dualism were to claim instead that domestic constitutional law comprehensively regulated the resolution of normative conflicts between municipal and international law, this would in turn reveal dualism to be monism in disguise, namely monism that accords primacy to domestic law.[162] This entails that if one accepts that international law contains valid and binding norms, dualism is untenable and eventually collapses into monism or denies international law its legal nature. In this vein, Alfred Verdross points out that even Triepel must be considered a monist,[163] when he considers international law to be a commander who can only emerge victorious from a battle if his generals (the states) obey his orders.[164] But this military metaphor is not thought from within

[157] Eric Suy, 'Article 53 Convention of 1969' in Olivier Corten and Pierre Klein (eds), *The Vienna Conventions on the Law of Treaties: A Commentary, Vol II* (Oxford University Press, 2011) para 5; *Accordance with International Law of the Unilateral Declaration of Independence in Respect of Kosovo (Advisory Opinion)* [2010] ICJ Rep 403, para 81.

[158] Other prominent examples include, inter alia, the North Atlantic Treaty; the International Criminal Tribunals for the Former Yugoslavia and Rwanda; the International Criminal Court; the World Trade Organization; the North American Free Trade Agreement; the United Nations Convention on the Recognition and Enforcement of Foreign Arbitral Awards; the Chemical Weapons Convention; the Vienna Convention for the Protection of the Ozone Layer; the Montreal Protocol on Substances that Deplete the Ozone Layer; and the Convention on Biological Diversity.

[159] Mattias Kumm, 'The Legitimacy of International Law: A Constitutionalist Framework of Analysis' (2004) 15 *European Journal of International Law* 907, 914.

[160] Assuming that a staunch dualist would most probably not deny the legal validity of domestic law; see also Alexander Somek, 'Kelsen Lives' (2007) 18 *European Journal of International Law* 409, 424–5.

[161] Triepel (n 110) 27–8. [162] Somek, 'Kelsen Lives' (n 160) 424–5.

[163] Alfred Verdross, *Einheit des rechtlichen Weltbildes* (n 22) 52 ff.

[164] Triepel (n 110) 271.

sovereignty, but from the vantage point of international law, from where the states, as generals, are seen as subordinate to the commands of international law.[165] This is nothing less than confused monism.[166] Owing to these significant shortcomings and its inability to describe and explain the reality of law, the concept of dualism in the relation between international and municipal law must be rejected.

B. Political ideologies and the divergence of doctrine and practice

As the previous two sections have shown, the dichotomist rift between dualism and monism has been discussed for a long time, often with strong ideological and political undertones,[167] and this argument sometimes even turned into a bitter dispute with reciprocal political accusations. After a cooling down, the topic was later revived in a different context:[168] when the CJEU ruled that the law of the EU possessed direct effect[169] in and supremacy[170] over the law of the Member States, it principally did so to enable EU norms to enter entirely different legal systems[171] in a uniform way and thus to bridge the significant differences between monist (Belgium, France, Luxembourg, and the Netherlands) and dualist countries (Germany and Italy).[172] In the aftermath of these ground-breaking rulings, however, the situations which had given new impetus to the ancient dispute of monism versus dualism were swiftly met by practical measures on the part of the CJEU to avoid a battle of principles, e.g. by setting boundaries to the spread of direct effect[173] or by reacting to criticism that the supremacy of EU law might endanger the protection of constitutionally guaranteed fundamental rights.[174]

Although the theoretical debate on monism and dualism is less significant today than it used to be during the inter-year wars, it is, nonetheless, not entirely settled.[175] The political ideologies which shaped the doctrines of monism and dualism are still extant and continue to permeate international law- and policy-making. In an admittedly over-simplified depiction, this doctrinal clash can therefore be seen as an argument between the partisans of national sovereignty (i.e. dualists and state-centric

[165] Amnon Lev, 'The Transformation of International Law in the 19th Century' in Alexander Orakhelashvili (ed), *Research Handbook on the Theory and History of International Law* (Edward Elgar Publishing, 2011) 138.

[166] Alexander Somek, 'Monism: A Tale of the Undead' in Matej Avbelj and Jan Komárek (eds), *Constitutional Pluralism in the European Union and Beyond* (Hart Publishing, 2012) 348–50.

[167] Dupuy (n 1) para 2.

[168] Luigi Ferrari-Bravo, 'International and Municipal Law: The Complementarity of Legal Systems' in Ronald St. John MacDonald and Douglas M. Johnston, *The Structure and Process of International Law: Essays in Legal Philosophy Doctrine and Theory* (Martinus Nijhoff, 1983) 715.

[169] Case 26/62 *van Gend en Loos* [1963] ECR 1.

[170] Case 6/64 *Costa v ENEL* [1964] ECR 585.

[171] Paul Craig, 'Once Upon a Time in the West: Direct Effect and the Federalization of EEC Law' (1992) 12 *Oxford Journal of Legal Studies* 453, 472.

[172] Bruno de Witte, 'Direct Effect, Primacy, and the Nature of the Legal Order' in Paul Craig and Gráinne de Búrca (eds), *The Evolution of EU Law* (2nd edn; Oxford University Press, 2011) 325.

[173] Case 152/84 *Marshall* [1986] ECR 723, para 48.

[174] Case 29/69 *Stauder* [1969] ECR 419, para 7; Case 11/70 *Internationale Handelsgesellschaft* [1970] ECR 1125.

[175] Wagner (n 31) 212.

monists) and the idealistic believers in internationalism and pacifism (i.e. international law-centric monists).[176] Another major issue is the fact that these rather clear-cut legal theories are not easily transferable to reality. Even though states under the influence of the Common Law usually tend to follow dualist traditions more than Civil Law countries, and in many of the latter a strong trend towards a form of moderate monism is increasing,[177] the actual legal systems of many states do not fit precisely in either of these two categories of monism and dualism. The results are new denotations such as hybrid monist countries, where domestic courts sometimes apply international law, in particular treaties, directly as law, and sometimes not, depending on certain criteria.[178] Moreover, the practice of both international and domestic courts has further blurred the lines between the two bodies of law and thus made the distinction between international and municipal law even less clear than in the times when the scope of application of international law could be regarded as solely regulating the relations of states amongst themselves.[179] The demise of the dichotomy of monism and dualism prepared the ground for other approaches of theorizing the relationship between different legal orders, most importantly legal pluralism.

4. Legal Pluralism

A. Growing criticism of the monism-dualism dichotomy

Strong criticism has been voiced that theorizing the relationship between international and municipal law merely based on either monism or dualism constitutes a false dichotomy, since this statement elegantly avoids the fact that there may be other 'in-between' options to describe this relationship.[180] Therefore, the concepts of monism and dualism have become subject to fervid criticism. Armin von Bogdandy notes that the theoretical dichotomy of monism and dualism should cease to exist for discussing the relationship between international and domestic law, and even likens these two concepts to creatures of the horror genre as 'intellectual zombies'.[181] The criticism expressed in this regard is predominantly fuelled by the argument that monism and dualism only have limited relevance and little explanatory value,[182] in particular with regard to the current and ongoing circumstances of

[176] Dupuy (n 1) para 23. [177] Ibid., para 26.

[178] David Sloss, 'Treaty Enforcement in Domestic Courts: A Comparative Analysis' in David Sloss (ed), *The Role of Domestic Courts in Treaty Enforcement: A Comparative Study* (Cambridge University Press, 2014) 6–7.

[179] Jennings and Watts (n 122) 54.

[180] Markus Kotzur, 'Overcoming Dichotomies: A Functional Approach to the Constitutional Paradigm in Public International Law' (2012) 4 *Goettingen Journal of International Law* 585, 590.

[181] Armin von Bogdandy, 'Pluralism, Direct Effect, and the Ultimate Say: On the Relationship between International and Domestic Constitutional Law' (2008) 6 *International Journal of Constitutional Law* 397, 400.

[182] Markus Kotzur, 'Über Monismus und Dualismus hinaus—Ansätze zu einer Neukonzeptualisierung des Völkerrechts mit einer konstitutionellen Matrix' in Marko Novaković (ed), *Basic Concepts of Public International Law: Monism & Dualism* (University of Belgrade, 2013) 160–3.

legal fragmentation in international law.[183] To begin with, international law itself is not only *horizontally* deeply fissured and fragmented, i.e. between its different legal areas.[184] Beyond that, it is also *vertically* fragmented. This form of fragmentation relates to the fragmentation of the international legal order in its relationship to non-international legal orders, such as national law. Therefore, the pluralist character of the relationship between international and domestic law is of a different kind than the relationship between different international regimes.[185]

The theoretical problem lawyers are facing these days is that the relationship between international and domestic law appears to be theoretically incomprehensible. The current global legal order seems to be 'a rugged, mountainous terrain: highly uneven, difficult to get a grasp of, and certainly not formed according to neat and clear principles'.[186] Interactions between municipal and international norms present themselves as 'strange loops and tangled hierarchies',[187] and constitutional hierarchies have become discontinuous and incomplete.[188] Particularly phenomena such as the emergence of new actors on the international plane alongside the range of 200-odd states, the proliferation of international courts and tribunals, and the extension of international rights and obligations to individuals and legal persons add a considerable element of multidimensionality,[189] which appears to be indescribable on the basis of existing international legal theories. It seems that the interplay between legal orders is shaped by dissent in a world of multiple overlapping normative communities, which further contribute to a 'world of legal conflict' and 'jurisdictional hybridity'.[190] In this light, the main thrust of criticism against the dichotomy of dualism and monism is directed against its shortcomings in describing and explaining the empirical legal world of interactions and interrelationships—which seems virtually impossible in the light of the existing complexities in law.

This criticism sowed the seeds which later bore fruit in the movement commonly known as *legal pluralism*, aiming at explaining the apparent non-hierarchical co-existence of legal orders with reference to their interacting and heterarchical nature and thus the pluralism of constitutional systems without any of them being supreme.[191]

[183] Samantha Besson, 'European Legal Pluralism after *Kadi*' (2009) 5 *European Constitutional Law Review* 237, 258.

[184] See International Law Commission, 'Fragmentation of International Law: Difficulties Arising from the Diversification and Expansion of International Law—Report of the Study Group of the International Law Commission, Finalized by Martti Koskenniemi' UN Doc A/CN.4/L.682, 13 April 2006, para 488.

[185] Geir Ulfstein, 'The Relationship between Constitutionalism and Pluralism' (2012) 4 *Goettingen Journal of International Law* 575, 581.

[186] Nico Krisch, *Beyond Constitutionalism* (Oxford University Press, 2012) 225.

[187] Douglas R. Hofstadter, *Gödel, Escher, Bach: An Eternal Golden Braid* (reprint; Penguin, 2000) 684.

[188] Mireille Delmas-Marty, *Towards a Truly Common Law: Europe as a Laboratory for Legal Pluralism* (Cambridge University Press, 2002) 59.

[189] Sionaidh Douglas-Scott, *Law after Modernity* (Hart Publishing, 2013) 81–4.

[190] Paul Schiff Berman, *Global Legal Pluralism: A Jurisprudence of Law Beyond Borders* (Cambridge University Press, 2013) 3 and 25, and chapter 2.

[191] Neil MacCormick, 'The *Maastricht*-Urteil: Sovereignty Now' (1995) 1 *European Law Journal* 259, 259.

The subsequent section will therefore briefly depict and explain the main arguments of the pluralist approach.

B. Origins and development of legal pluralism

As a philosophical concept dealing with the question of how many substances exist, pluralism was already comprehensively theorized by the pre-Socratic philosopher Empedocles, who argued that the diversity of nature could not be reduced to one single principle.[192] This concept was subsequently also present in law, for example in Roman law, where a *ius gentium* and a *ius civile* existed alongside one another,[193] or in medieval law, in which codified and customary law co-existed with canon law and *lex mercatoria*.[194] The origins of modern legal pluralism, however, lie in fields as diverse as anthropology,[195] sociology,[196] and colonialism,[197] especially when the introduction of European law in colonies around the world created a plurality of legal orders because of pre-existing indigenous legal systems, mostly based on tribal customs.[198]

Today, legal pluralism has long since moved beyond its original focus on legal anthropology and sociology.[199] In a more general fashion, it has been defined as 'that state of affairs, for any social field, in which behaviour pursuant to more than one legal order occurs'.[200] The fact that we distinguish between various sets of rules on different levels (local, regional, national, supranational, international), on different subject-areas (criminal law, contract law, administrative law) or sources (statutes, treaties, judicial decisions) reflects that law is highly pluralistic in a plethora of facets. Consequently, the reality of legal pluralism, i.e. the co-existence of multiple legal norms and rules in the same time-space context, also implies divergence and conflict rather than convergence and harmony. The same is true for the relationship between national, international, and EU law, which are informed by 'the multidirectional interaction of local, national, and international norms'.[201] At this level of transnational legal pluralism, we find a rich and often competing proliferation of rules and norms.[202] This also means that in most cases of normative competition and conflict, the absence of a clear-cut hierarchy between these different legal orders precludes the resolution of such conflicts on the basis of definite rules, especially if

[192] Diels and Kranz (n 4) B84.

[193] Barry Nicholas, *An Introduction to Roman Law* (revised edn; Oxford University Press, 1975) 19 and 54.

[194] Brian Z. Tamanaha, 'Understanding Legal Pluralism: Past to Present, Local to Global' (2008) 30 *Sydney Law Review* 375, 377.

[195] Leopold Pospisil, *Anthropology of Law: A Comparative Theory* (Harper and Row, 1971).

[196] Eugen Ehrlich, *Grundlegung der Soziologie des Rechts* (Duncker & Humblot, 1913).

[197] Kwamena Bentsi-Enchill, 'The Colonial Heritage of Legal Pluralism' (1969) 1 *Zambia Law Journal* 1.

[198] Sally Engle Merry, 'Legal Pluralism' (1988) 22 *Law and Society Review* 869, 869–70.

[199] Douglas-Scott (n 189) 109.

[200] John Griffiths, 'What is Legal Pluralism?' (1986) 24 *Journal of Legal Pluralism* 1, 2.

[201] Paul Schiff Berman, 'A Pluralist Approach to International Law' (2007) 32 *Yale Journal of International Law* 301, 311–12.

[202] Douglas-Scott (n 189) 109.

there are issues of prevalence with regard to the relationship between international and domestic law.

Having said that, it is important to note that pluralism is not dualism. Dualism would imply that all domestic legal systems have the same features, as opposed to international law,[203] whilst legal pluralism does not assume that they are all the same. Consequently, dualism is not capable of giving an accurate account of how the relationship between the international and non-international legal orders functions, as the mutual integration of these different legal orders largely works on the basis of domestic constitutional provisions, respective legislation, and the decisions of the judiciary.[204] It thus seems impossible to integrate all these different approaches into a dualist theoretical framework.

One may therefore sum up that legal pluralism underscores the value of diversity and difference among different normative systems, as well as the subsequent undesirability and implausibility of monism, which strives for coherence between different legal systems.[205] Pluralism acknowledges that normative overlaps and conflicts between these systems exist and will continue to exist, as long as there is no overarching and ordering institution or principle which would be able to harmonize any of these conflicts. Nevertheless, there are certain distinctive strands of legal pluralism which vary in their degree of how interconnected they regard the plurality of legal orders. The next sections will now examine these main pluralist strands, but also their shortcomings, in more depth.

C. Legal pluralist varieties

(1) Radical legal pluralism

According to Jonathan Griffiths, radical legal pluralism rejects all claims for any dominant institution or normative ordering framework.[206] Neil MacCormick further develops this view by theorizing the non-hierarchical relationship between Member State and EU law. In his opinion, the absence of hierarchical relations entails that the interpretative power of the highest decision-making authorities of the different systems must be ultimate, but only within each single system. Thus, it is for the CJEU to interpret and apply Union law in the last resort and in a finally authoritative way, whilst equally it must be for the highest constitutional or supreme court of each Member State to interpret and apply its national norms, and 'hence to interpret the interaction of the validity of [EU] law with higher level norms of validity in the given State system'.[207] Resulting normative conflicts would not be

[203] Crawford (n 123) 50 fn 17; Jean L. Cohen, 'Sovereignty in the Context of Globalization: A Constitutional Pluralist Perspective' in Samantha Besson and John Tasioulas (eds), *The Philosophy of International Law* (Oxford University Press, 2010) 272–8.

[204] Ulfstein, 'Constitutionalism and Pluralism' (n 185) 581.

[205] Gráinne de Búrca, 'The ECJ and the International Legal Order: A Re-Evaluation' in Gráinne de Búrca and J.H.H. Weiler, *The Worlds of European Constitutionalism* (Cambridge University Press, 2012) 128.

[206] Griffiths (n 200) 5–8.

[207] Neil MacCormick, *Questioning Sovereignty* (Oxford University Press, 1999) 118.

'logically embarrassing', since strictly speaking these decisions originate from the point of view of different systems. Furthermore, accepting a radically pluralist conception of legal systems also entails acknowledging that not every legal problem can be solved legally, because instead of an absence of legal answers, there is a superfluity of them.[208] As a result, there is no overarching principle that could tell us which legal answer should prevail over the other one.

Yet concurrently MacCormick admits that such a situation is 'practically embarrassing to the extent that the same human beings or corporations are said to have and not have a certain right'.[209] As a consequence, this 'radical' pluralism is highly problematic from the viewpoint of legal certainty, as any person involved in such a case would be lost in a 'shameful absence of the rule of law'.[210] The question remains, however, if this concept is in fact pluralist. If no choice between competing claims is made, this person is left with the decision of two courts, or *two monisms*. Within the domestic jurisdiction, the domestic monism is correct, whereas within the supranational or international jurisdiction, the supranational or international monism is correct. The result is a kind of 'double monism' where two hierarchies exist, but none of them is pluralist. If, conversely, MacCormick's concept is construed as 'disjunctive monism' in which both domestic and international courts endorse either a solution derived from domestic law or a solution derived from international law, a truly radical pluralism would exist: on some days, the courts may adhere to domestic monism, on other days they may choose international monism.[211]

Ronald Dworkin correctly identifies such 'checkerboard laws' as dismaying, because they would treat similar scenarios of, say, racial discrimination or abortion differently on completely arbitrary grounds, and would thus strongly encroach upon the overall integrity of a legal system.[212] Consequently, legal pluralism in its most radical form is highly unsatisfactory. In theoretical terms, it may either imply that no interaction exists between legal orders, which would reduce it to the above-mentioned notion of 'double monism', a form of pseudo-pluralism in monist disguise; or that sometimes communication in fact takes place, but merely on arbitrary grounds, which eventually imperils the legal order in its entirety. In practical terms, radical pluralism in both manifestations is irreconcilable with accountability and the rule of law,[213] which are being entirely undermined by arbitrariness and legal uncertainty. In the worst case, this could lead to a situation where pure power politics and ideologies take over a legal system and impose the interests of a few powerful over democratically legitimized legislation,[214] which ultimately means that radical pluralism is not a viable option to theorize the relationship between legal orders.

[208] Ibid., 119.

[209] Neil MacCormick, 'Risking Constitutional Collision in Europe?' (1998) 18 *Oxford Journal of Legal Studies* 517, 530.

[210] Douglas-Scott (n 189) 229.

[211] Pavlos Eleftheriadis, 'Pluralism and Integrity' (2010) 23 *Ratio Juris* 365, 373–4.

[212] Ronald Dworkin, *Law's Empire* (Hart Publishing, 1986) 179 and 184.

[213] Douglas-Scott (n 189) 126.

[214] García-Salmones Rovira (n 104) 142.

(2) *Pluralism under international law*

Mindful of the risk of normative conflicts inherent in an unregulated pluralism of legal orders, MacCormick subsequently softened his approach, when he recognized the greater potential for coordination in the overarching framework of international law.[215] Accordingly MacCormick proposes a 'pluralism under international law' wherein the validity of both Member State and EU law depend on international law, which imposes 'a framework on the interactive but not hierarchical relations between systems'.[216] Any remaining normative conflicts between the Member State and EU courts could then be resolved through their having recourse to international law without concurrently obliterating the pluralist core assumption of heterarchy.[217] Therefore, both national and EU law are hierarchically subordinate to the international legal order,[218] which also entails that both Member State and Union courts must take into account their mutual obligations under international law.[219]

But concurrently, MacCormick admits that this particular strand of pluralism is in fact just an instance of monism, with the notable exception that both the Member State and EU legal orders enjoy equal ranks juxtaposed with one another, only subordinated to international law.[220] This approach could help diminish the risk of normative collisions, since the Member State courts ought to have regard to 'the international obligations which still subsist notwithstanding, or indeed because of, the fact that [Union] law is a "new legal order *sui generis*" '.[221] Yet despite its appealing charm, there are certain shortcomings in this concept of 'pluralism under international law' which deserve closer scrutiny. First, although one might say that a 'fallback' to international law in disputes between Member States inter se and between Member States and the EU could be permissible (e.g. if intra-Union proceedings eventually fail[222]), the CJEU has already clarified that infringement proceedings under Articles 258 and 259 TFEU represent a departure from the traditional dispute settlement mechanisms of international law.[223] As a result, general international law, including the law of state responsibility, does not play a major role in Union-internal proceedings,[224] and the Member States are prohibited from unilaterally adopting corrective measures on their own authority to prevent any failure by other Member States to comply with EU law.[225] This approach conforms to the rule set out in Article 344 TFEU and thus the Member States' obligation not to submit disputes regarding the interpretation or application of EU law to any court

[215] Krisch (n 186) 73. [216] MacCormick, *Questioning Sovereignty* (n 207) 118.
[217] Klemen Jaklic, *Constitutional Pluralism in the EU* (Oxford University Press, 2014) 188.
[218] Eleftheriadis (n 211) 374. [219] MacCormick, *Questioning Sovereignty* (n 207) 120.
[220] MacCormick, 'Risking Constitutional Collision in Europe?' (n 209) 530.
[221] MacCormick, *Questioning Sovereignty* (n 207) 121.
[222] Bruno Simma, 'Self-Contained Regimes' (1985) 16 *Netherlands Yearbook of International Law* 111, 123–9.
[223] Anthony Arnull, *The European Union and Its Court of Justice* (2nd edn, Oxford University Press, 2006) 44.
[224] Joined Cases 90/63 and 91/63 *Commission v Luxembourg and Belgium* [1964] ECR 625, 631.
[225] Case 232/78 *Commission v France (Mutton and Lamb)* [1979] ECR 2729, para 9.

other than the CJEU.[226] This fact blatantly contradicts MacCormick's assumption that the EU and the Member States, as equal partners, may resolve any normative conflicts between them by hearkening back to the rules of international law. As the guardian of an autonomous legal order, the CJEU would never allow such a course of action.

Secondly, pluralists themselves criticize this approach for taking the edge out of pluralism, because it accepts pluralism not on the systemic level, but only on the grounds of an institutional structure. Different parts of one given legal order operate on a basis of coordination, and within the framework of common rules but without a clearly defined hierarchy.[227] Griffiths himself disapproves of such a soft legal pluralism as completely unrelated to the original idea of legal pluralism, as it would essentially remain dependent on centralized state law.[228]

Lastly, there is significant controversy on whether 'pluralism under international law' in the end collapses into monism, as MacCormick himself concedes somehow. Although it has been argued that this approach does not imply an ultimate subordination of EU and Member State law under international law (thereby maintaining a genuine 'pluralism' which merely utilizes international law as an additional practical device),[229] it is more convincing to assume that we are back to where we started. If the effect of EU law within national law is a question of international law, we are effectively back to monism and dualism.[230] This does not mean that MacCormick's interpretation is not sophisticated, but the point is that it is apparently not sufficiently controversial to be described as 'pluralist'. Whilst radical pluralism posits a plethora of distinct legal systems, each with its own *Grundnorm* or rule of recognition, pluralism under international law posits a single legal system, i.e. international law, with domestic legal orders, including the European Union, as subsets contained with it. This is a concept which both Hart and Kelsen could easily accommodate within their respective theories.[231] This means, in conclusion, that pluralism under international law is not a viable option to theorize the relationship between international and domestic law either, simply because it is not a theory of its own, but monism in disguise.

(3) Constitutional pluralism

A more recent and more prevalent strand of pluralism can be found in the idea of 'constitutional pluralism', which attempts to combine pluralism and constitutionalism. The latter notion refers to the basic objective of constituting and limiting government powers for the protection of equal rights of citizens by means of

[226] See in this respect the seminal Case C-459/03 *Commission v Ireland (Mox Plant)* [2006] ECR I-4635.

[227] Krisch (n 186) 73. [228] Griffiths (n 200) 8. [229] Jaklic (n 217) 210.

[230] Eleftheriadis (n 211) 375.

[231] Nicholas W. Barber, 'Legal Pluralism and the European Union' (2006) 12 *European Law Journal* 306, 326.

constitutional rules of a superior legal rank.[232] Constitutionalism in international law or the constitutionalization of international law pertains to the development of constitutional structures in international law, for instance rules establishing a certain normative hierarchy and core norms, from which no derogation is permitted.[233] Beyond that, the constitutionalization of international law also encompasses the development of both centralized and decentralized enforcement mechanisms (e.g. Security Council measures under Chapter VII of the United Nations Charter versus state responsibility and countermeasures); the rights and obligations of individuals (for instance human rights and international criminal law), and the differentiation and consolidation of international law in various legal fields, ranging from international trade law to environmental law.

By embracing both the existence of a plurality of legal orders and their constitutionalized nature, Neil Walker draws attention to the incommensurability of the authority claims emanating from these legal orders.[234] In other words, it is impossible to ascertain which validity claims are stronger and which are weaker in the case of normative conflict. Constitutional pluralism hence implies that legitimate authority can originate from a variety of sources, while there are no guidelines, principles, or rules to decide which one to follow in the case of conflict.[235] As a result, it is the purpose of constitutional pluralism to carve out a third way of conceiving the legal world in a meaningful way, namely on the middle ground between hierarchical integration on the one hand and radical pluralism on the other. Thereby this concept aims at describing how legal coherence in constitutional terms is possible even in the absence of a strict legal hierarchy.[236] But apart from this descriptive task, constitutional pluralism also pursues a normative goal, holding that the only practical and acceptable ethic of political responsibility is to be premised upon 'mutual recognition and interpenetration of constitutional sites located at different levels'.[237] Ultimately, the question of which court constitutes the ultimate arbiter in such a constitutionalized pluralist system can consequently only be answered through judicial dialogue, and not by simply labelling one court the supreme authority. In this sense, judicial dialogue emphasizes the value of respectful interaction between courts and thus offers a viable model for conflict-managing communication through accommodation.[238]

[232] Ernst-Ulrich Petersmann, 'Multilevel Trade Governance in the WTO Requires Multilevel Constitutionalism' in Christian Joerges and Ernst-Ulrich Petersmann (eds), *Constitutionalism, Multilevel Trade Governance and Social Regulation* (Hart Publishing, 2006) 6.

[233] Alexander Orakhelashvili, *Peremptory Norms in International Law* (Oxford University Press, 2008) 9.

[234] Neil Walker, 'The Idea of Constitutional Pluralism' (2002) 65 *Modern Law Review* 317, 338.

[235] Jan Klabbers, 'Setting the Scene' in Jan Klabbers, Anne Peters, and Geir Ulfstein (eds), *The Constitutionalization of International Law* (Oxford University Press, 2011) 29.

[236] Mattias Kumm, 'The Moral Point of Constitutional Pluralism' in Julie Dickson and Pavlos Eleftheriadis (eds), *Philosophical Foundations of European Union Law* (Oxford University Press, 2012) 217.

[237] Neil Walker, 'Late Sovereignty in the European Union' in Neil Walker (ed), *Sovereignty in Transition: Essays in European Law* (Hart Publishing, 2006) 4.

[238] Federico Fabbrini, *Fundamental Rights in Europe: Challenges and Transformations in Comparative Perspective* (Oxford University Press, 2014) 22; Aida Torres Pérez, 'The Challenges for Constitutional Courts as Guardians of Fundamental Rights in the European Union' in Patricia Popelier, Armen

This concept appears to apply first and foremost to the European Union and its Member States, in which no order or court can be identified as ultimately controlling this legal order made up of EU and Member State law.[239] The fundamental rights disputes between the CJEU and the German Constitutional Court, especially, show that the EU and Member State courts were often involved in boundary disputation—a fact that Walker considers a crucial symptom of the current authority predicament.[240] Hence when faced with boundary questions, the Member State courts were in fact willing to countenance the claims to authority stemming from the CJEU, but only on the basis of their respective constitutions, and not on the terms assumed by EU law itself.[241] But the eventual *constitutional* result is that every Member State court must, in case of conflict with domestic law, apply Union law in its entirety and set aside any national provision in conflict with it.

There is, however, also considerable criticism of the concept of constitutional pluralism and, particularly, its normative assessment,[242] which remains problematic for three reasons. The first issue inherent in constitutional pluralism is its lack of legal certainty, or in Dworkinian terms, its lack of respect for the values of integrity and coherence. It is evident that every legal order seeks to maintain the unity and consistency of its legal norms. Legal integrity requires national, European, and international judges and officials to speak with the same voice and to apply the law in the same manner. Accordingly, informal communication and dialogue between different legal orders is not sufficient to guarantee legal certainty. Every legal order needs to accommodate in its law a legal nexus to international law to provide a firm theory for its effective recognition, reception, and application as good and comprehensible legal decisions.[243] The simplest way to do so would be to create a constitutional provision which clarifies the respective domestic legal order's stance towards international law. Constitutional pluralism is not capable of doing this requirement justice, since it can only explain the interaction between different legal orders as sporadic, casuistic, and coincidental encounters, but not the eventual resolution of conflicts arising from these encounters. A judicial dialogue which could result in the annulment of pivotal policy measures agreed in common should always take place in a structured and formal way, and not through unilateral statements and informal dialogue.[244] The rationale of this incommensurability is therefore inferior to all other proposals which provide substantive reasons underpinning their positions and offer solutions to normative conflicts.[245]

Mazmanyan, and Werner Vandenbruwaene (eds), *The Role of Constitutional Courts in Multilevel Governance* (Intersentia, 2013) 49 and 75.

[239] Douglas-Scott (n 189) 111.

[240] Neil Walker, 'Beyond Boundary Disputes and Basic Grids: Mapping the Global Disorder of Normative Orders' (2008) 6 *International Journal of Constitutional Law* 373, 394.

[241] Neil Walker, 'Constitutionalism and Pluralism in Global Context' in Matej Avbelj and Jan Komárek (eds), *Constitutional Pluralism in the European Union and Beyond* (Hart Publishing, 2012) 21.

[242] Kumm, 'Moral Point' (n 236) 217–18.

[243] Eleftheriadis (n 211) 380–1 and 388.

[244] Julio Baquero Cruz, 'The Legacy of the Maastricht-Urteil and the Pluralist Movement' (2008) 14 *European Law Journal* 389, 414.

[245] Jaklic (n 217) 57.

Secondly, constitutional pluralism also fails on the applicative level by rejecting any sort of hierarchy and thus giving in to a messy network where the rule of law ceases to have any effect. Although it is correct that the validity of Member State law does not depend on and cannot be affected by European Union or international law, the existence of normative conflicts requires the existence of a normative hierarchy at the level of application as a prerequisite to solve these conflicts. If concrete conflicts cannot be resolved through consistent interpretation, they cannot be left unanswered; in fact, such questions must be determined by giving supremacy to one norm over another, either by disapplying the inferior norm or by invalidating it,[246] hence clearly stating what the law is. In EU law, direct conflicts with Member State constitutional law are not difficult to resolve. If any secondary Union act violates fundamental rights, it can be invalidated or amended without loss of face for any of the actors involved.[247] As a result, different forms of judicial resistance to the supremacy of Union law are best understood as exceptional instances of institutional disobedience rather than examples of constitutional pluralism.[248] In the end, it is crucial that clear and unambiguous decisions state what the law is and thus guarantee the continuing rule of law.

Lastly, constitutional pluralism must—as other forms of pluralism—accept the accusation that it merely is monism in disguise. Walker correctly claims that constitutional pluralism should not lead to a new unity or fixed hierarchy of constitutional authority[249] (otherwise, what innovative value would pluralism have?[250]), but eventually it settles into a new form of constitutional monism. Maybe the centripetal forces towards hierarchy and unity in constitutional logic and in the lawyers' constitutional mind-sets are too strong and incorrigible as to allow for anything else than the form of a state-centred model. It does not matter whether lawyers talk about the European Union, the United Nations, or international law in general, there always is a tendency towards a new manifestation of legal autonomization and a reduction to unity.[251] It is therefore reasonable and, *prima facie*, plausible that Mattias Kumm describes constitutional (or cosmopolitan[252]) pluralism as the concept 'that the refusal of a legal order to recognize itself as hierarchically integrated into a more comprehensive legal order is justified, if the more comprehensive legal order suffers from a structural legitimacy deficit that the less comprehensive legal order does not

[246] Baquero Cruz, 'Legacy' (n 244) 415.

[247] Gareth Davies, 'Constitutional Disagreement in Europe and the Search for Pluralism' in Matej Avbelj and Jan Komárek (eds), *Constitutional Pluralism in the European Union and Beyond* (Hart Publishing, 2012) 279.

[248] Julio Baquero Cruz, 'Legal Pluralism and Institutional Disobedience in the European Union' in Matej Avbelj and Jan Komárek (eds), *Constitutional Pluralism in the European Union and Beyond* (Hart Publishing, 2012) 249–67.

[249] Walker, 'Late Sovereignty' (n 237) 4.

[250] See Jaklic (n 217) chapter 7 (190–225) entitled 'A True Novelty'.

[251] Walker, 'Constitutionalism and Pluralism' (n 241) 18–19.

[252] Mattias Kumm, 'The Cosmopolitan Turn in Constitutionalism: On the Relationship between Constitutionalism in and beyond the State' in Jeffrey L. Dunoff and Joel P. Trachtman (eds), *Ruling the World? Constitutionalism, International Law, and Global Governance* (Cambridge University Press, 2009) 258–324.

suffer from'.[253] There appears to be no reason to disagree with such a concept of subsidiarity, especially if such a structural legitimacy deficit pertains to the protection of human rights, and said refusal is capable of protecting human rights vis-à-vis any interferences stemming from the more comprehensive legal order. But the theoretical problem with this approach is that it amounts to a monist construction, because the introduction of such 'rules of refusal' merely constitutes a further recourse to overarching meta-principles governing the legal system as a whole. This is the same as Mireille Delmas-Marty's 'pluralisme ordonné',[254] which attempts to identify and impose ordering structures so that legal pluralism is not required to be interpreted as inherently infinite, chaotic, and entropic.[255] Thus, constitutional pluralism seems to eventually collapse back into monism.

D. Interim conclusion: pluralist deficiencies

The foregoing sections do not claim to give a complete picture of all extant strands of legal pluralism, but merely try to offer a brief overview of the pluralist idea, its main approaches, and certain points of criticism. Such an endeavour to illustrate all forms of legal pluralism would certainly deserve a book in its own right, as Nico Krisch,[256] Paul Schiff Berman,[257] and other scholars[258] excellently demonstrated in their respective works. At this point, suffice it to say that it is not the task of the book at hand to exhaustively present all pluralist variants, such as Daniel Halberstam's 'interpretative pluralism',[259] Mattias Kumm's 'cosmopolitan constitutionalism',[260] or Miguel Poiares Maduro's 'contrapunctual pluralism'.[261] The main purpose of the preceding sections was to demonstrate that legal pluralism is a distinct and very illustrative concept to theorize and explain the increasing complexity of our current legal world. Legal pluralism is, beyond all these variations, an attempt to neutrally 'stand beyond the perspective of any particular system'[262] and to come to terms with the normative framework underlying the heterarchical co-existence of legal orders.[263]

However, the question remains whether the descriptive and empirical appeal of legal pluralism also represents a viable normative and analytical basis.[264] The overall answer of this book to this question will be in the negative, because legal pluralism

[253] Kumm, 'Moral Point' (n 236) 220.

[254] Mireille Delmas-Marty, *Les forces imaginantes du droit (II): Le pluralisme ordonné* (Seuil, 2006).

[255] Douglas-Scott (n 189) 121.

[256] Krisch (n 186).

[257] Berman, *Global Legal Pluralism* (n 190).

[258] See e.g. Jan Klabbers and Touko Piiparinen (eds), *Normative Pluralism and International Law: Exploring Global Governance* (Cambridge University Press, 2013); and Victor M. Muñiz-Fraticelli, *The Structure of Pluralism* (Oxford University Press, 2014).

[259] Daniel Halberstam, 'Constitutional Heterarchy: The Centrality of Conflict in the European Union and the United States' in Jeffrey L. Dunoff and Joel P. Trachtman (eds), *Ruling the World? Constitutionalism, International Law, and Global Governance* (Cambridge University Press, 2009) 326–55.

[260] Kumm, 'Cosmopolitan Turn' (n 252) 258–324.

[261] Miguel Poiares Maduro, 'Contrapunctual Law: Europe's Constitutional Pluralism in Action' in Neil Walker (ed), *Sovereignty in Transition: Essays in European Law* (Hart Publishing, 2006) 501–38.

[262] Walker, 'Late Sovereignty' (n 237) 18.

[263] Baquero Cruz, 'Legacy' (n 244) 413.

[264] Krisch (n 186) 78.

is both empirically and normatively deeply flawed and not a viable concept to theorize the relationship between domestic and international law. But a *caveat* seems appropriate at the outset: This critique is only directed at legal pluralism itself, not at pluralism in its synonymous meaning of diversity, which is an essential social element of discourse in the Habermasian sense,[265] and which needs to be maintained in any event.

5. Conclusion

This analysis has shown that all three concepts to theorize the relationship between international and non-international law—monism, dualism, and pluralism—may have their explanatory merits. Yet at the same time they all are, to a certain extent, defective and flawed. It is a fact that different bodies of law appear to be intricately intertwined with each other, and sometimes they seem to be even mutually dependent or at least constantly borrowing principles and norms from one another. One might consequently say that international law and domestic law, for example, are substantively interlaced, even though they remain institutionally separated. Especially regarding the question of conflicts and their resolution, they all differ extensively and do not provide one single solution or even any solution at all. Ultimately, it becomes obvious that there may be no comprehensive and correct theory to describe and analyse this very interrelationship.

Monism appears to disregard the realities of state sovereignty and power politics and hence the empirical fact that international law remains entirely distinct from domestic legal orders if the latter do not wish to give effect to the former. Consequently, international law as such cannot invalidate domestic legislation in contravention to international norms. Beyond that, critics of monism might also argue that although certain legal systems could be labelled as monist because their constitutions contain automatic adaption mechanisms for international norms, the existence of such constitutional provisions is a choice obviously made on the basis of a dualist or pluralist premise by each domestic legal system.[266] One could therefore conclude that dualism or pluralism is the 'default mode' of every municipal legal order, and that monism is merely a choice by switching the constitutional levers of said order from the option of 'closed' dualism or pluralism to 'open' monism.

Having said that, however, dualism equally has only limited power to describe, explain, and assess this continuing interaction and exchange, and may thus not be able to provide a realistic representation of the interplay between domestic and international norms and systems.[267] In the light of this continuing and thriving

[265] See Jürgen Habermas, *Faktizität und Geltung* (Suhrkamp, 1998).

[266] Gaetano Arangio-Ruiz, 'International Law and Interindividual Law' in Janne Nijman and André Nollkaemper (eds), *New Perspectives on the Divide between National and International Law* (University Press, 2007) 20.

[267] Janne Nijman and André Nollkaemper, 'Beyond the Divide' in Janne Nijman and André Nollkaemper (eds), *New Perspectives on the Divide between National and International Law* (Oxford University Press, 2007) 341.

interrelationship, one could also raise the question whether a principle such as dualism can realistically exist, as not only the number of international obligations increases across different areas traditionally considered domestic issues, but also because international law is gradually becoming part of municipal law, rendering the frontiers of these two bodies of law increasingly permeable.[268]

As a result, introducing a concept such as legal pluralism was intended to overcome this strict dichotomy of monism and dualism by acknowledging that there may be a third option of describing distinct legal orders. Yet it failed to achieve this end. The notion of a plurality of legal orders without any interactional rules is built upon a flawed analytical foundation which can be shown to disregard hierarchical structures that are essential to upholding legal certainty and the rule of law. Furthermore, legal pluralism was revealed to be either oxymoronic or monistic, which renders this concept completely defective for theorizing the relationship between different bodies of law. This ultimately means that legal pluralism must either be reconstructed from scratch or retired in its entirety.[269]

Since the present book does not intend to 'reinvent' pluralism, but rather to apply legal monism to the interplay between legal orders, it will follow the latter approach, namely retire legal pluralism. Beyond that, it must also be recalled at this point that dualism continues to be unacceptable to international lawyers because of its legal degradation of the international legal order. As a result, if one plans to take international law seriously and to conceive of it as a quasi-cosmopolitan legal order, having the normative force of guiding the behaviour of its subjects, it logically follows that law must be seen, along the lines of Immanuel Kant's idea of 'systematic unity',[270] as a monist entity. Otherwise, the law, in its international dimension and its reciprocal relationship between international and municipal law, can neither be imagined nor realized.[271] Monism is the only logical choice, and therefore the next chapter will present, analyse, and defend the concept of legal monism in further detail.

[268] Geir Ulfstein, 'The International Judiciary' in Jan Klabbers, Anne Peters, and Geir Ulfstein (eds), *The Constitutionalization of International Law* (Oxford University Press, 2011) 143.

[269] Brian Z. Tamanaha, 'The Folly of the "Social Scientific" Concept of Legal Pluralism' (1993) 20 *Journal of Law and Society* 192, 192–3.

[270] Immanuel Kant, *Kritik der reinen Vernunft* (Johann Friedrich Hartknoch, 1781/1787) A 693/ B 721.

[271] Mario Prost, *The Concept of Unity in Public International Law* (Hart Publishing, 2012) 167.

PART II

FROM PHILOSOPHY TO LAW AND POLITICS

3

The Epistemological Necessity of Legal Monism

1. Introduction

This chapter will now discuss monism in its positivist-epistemological manifestation as the most viable concept to theorize the relationship between different legal orders. Yet at the outset, some clarifications seem to be in order. To begin with, it should be emphasized that this chapter is not about Hans Kelsen alone. Most of the academic literature in Anglo-American legal theory seems to focus exclusively on him, which does not do justice to the other thinkers and writers of the Vienna School of Jurisprudence.[1] Kelsen may have been the most prominent proponent of this particular school of legal thinking, but the most notable influences on his work—particularly by Adolf Julius Merkl, Alfred Verdross, and Josef L. Kunz—will not be neglected here.

A. Analytic versus continental philosophy?

The subsequent analysis should not only be seen as a mere defence of monism as envisaged by the pure theory of law, but also as the theoretical groundworks for the central problem examined in this book, namely the resolution of normative conflicts between different bodies of law. It should, however, not remain unmentioned that this 'third way' between positivism in its empiricist version and natural law, remains highly controversial,[2] especially in Anglo-American scholarship—whereas it is held in more esteem in Austria (where the proponents of the Vienna School of Jurisprudence worked, lived, and continue to influence the law in both theory and practice to this day[3]);

[1] It is of course impossible to give a full account of this literature on Kelsen in English at this point. For some selected publications see e.g. the references in Michael Green, 'Hans Kelsen and the Logic of Legal Systems' (2003) 54 *Alabama Law Review* 365, 365 fn 3.

[2] See Deryck Beyleveld and Roger Brownsword, 'Normative Positivism: The Mirage of the Middle-Way' (1989) 9 *Oxford Journal of Legal Studies* 463, 464.

[3] Especially concerning Kelsen's contribution to the Austrian Constitution of 1920 and the establishment of the Austrian Constitutional Court; see e.g. Thomas Olechowski, 'Der Beitrag Hans Kelsens zur österreichischen Bundesverfassung' in Robert Walter and others (eds), *Hans Kelsen: Leben—Werk—Wirksamkeit* (Manz, 2009) 211–30.

Italy;[4] and, intriguingly, throughout Latin America.[5] This book is not concerned with the question of whether this local esteem is justified, or with 'preaching to the converted' there. This would not be an intellectual challenge at all. Since this book is written in English, it is mostly addressed to an Anglo-American audience that remains sceptical about the pure theory of law. This introduction will therefore provide the chance for a rapprochement between this theory, which was mostly shaped by Kantianism and neo-Kantianism, and English-speaking jurisprudence, which, conversely, traces its origins back to analytic philosophy. This divide in methodology and philosophical roots heavily hampers the appreciation of the pure theory of law[6]—even though one should be aware that such a harsh distinction between analytic versus continental philosophy along a geographical tilt (the Anglophone countries versus continental Europe) amounts to a grotesque oversimplification.[7] Some early influences on analytic philosophy can be found in Austria and Germany,[8] whilst continental philosophy has also found its way into English-speaking academia in various forms.[9] Thus, to soften this alleged divide and to offer a sympathetic account of the Kantianism of the pure theory of law to more 'analytically' minded readers, this introduction will briefly follow Michael Green's excellent illustration of the common ground shared between pure theorists and analytic philosophers. This common ground can be found in the logical analysis of language.[10]

B. The logical analysis of language and anti-psychologism

To this end, Green provides the example of Beatrice saying that 'John is happy, and he is not happy', and adds that if we wish to interpret her statement as possibly true, we cannot understand both occurrences of the word 'happy' as meaning the same thing. She could mean, for instance, that John is 'happy' *in one sense* (regarding his private life), and not 'happy' *in another sense* (in his job). This logical rule of non-contradiction is *necessary*, in the sense that it is impossible for this sentence to be true if both occurrences of the word 'happy' mean the same thing, as well as *formal*, in the sense that everybody can understand this rule without knowing the meaning of the word 'happy'.[11] Equally, as already touched upon in Chapters 1 and 2,[12] it

[4] Norberto Bobbio and Danilo Zolo, 'Hans Kelsen, the Theory of Law, and the International Legal System: A Talk' (1998) 9 *European Journal of International Law* 355, 355–6.

[5] See e.g. John Linarelli, 'Anglo-American Jurisprudence and Latin America' (1996/1997) 20 *Fordham International Law Journal* 50, 78; Josef L. Kunz, 'An Introduction to Latin-American Philosophy of Law' (1964) 15 *University of Toronto Law Journal* 259, 272.

[6] Green (n 1) 366.

[7] James Chase and Jack Reynolds, *Analytic versus Continental: Arguments on the Methods and Value of Philosophy* (Acumen, 2011) 1.

[8] In particular, logical positivism and proponents such as Gottlob Frege, Ludwig Wittgenstein, Moritz Schlick, Rudolf Carnap, and Ernst Mach.

[9] Simon Glendinning, *The Idea of Continental Philosophy* (Edinburgh University Press, 2006) 92, mentioning ideas and movements such as pragmatism, feminism, post-structuralism etc., which are all non-analytic in the strictest sense.

[10] Green (n 1) 366. [11] Ibid., 366–7.

[12] See Chapter 1, section 2A and Chapter 2, section 2B(3).

is logically impossible to say that 'norm ϕ is valid, and norm ϕ is not valid', if both occurrences of the word 'valid' are to be understood as meaning exactly the same thing. So if we think of such sentences in entirely empirical terms and replace them with psychological states,[13] logic loses its necessity and formality and it becomes psychologically possible to think that norm ϕ is concurrently valid and not valid. If this psychologism were true, then assuming a difference in the meaning of 'valid' and 'invalid' would be reasonable only if Beatrice was working with a mental system to which the logical law of non-contradiction applied. The two main problems with this approach are that on the one hand, it is impossible to reach this conclusion without an empirical enquiry into her psychological states, and that, on the other hand, whatever the conclusions of this enquiry are, they would be inapplicable to any other person. Thereby objective rules for the interpretation of meaning would simply vanish.[14]

To counter this psychologist stance, the neo-Kantian Hermann Cohen argues that, in order to avoid talking about the source of the necessary laws of logic, which could only be either metaphysical or empirical,[15] these laws must be justified immanently through themselves, and logical structure is hence based on an axiomatic root.[16] For if we challenge the necessity of the laws of logic, we cannot help but to either claim that these laws follow inevitably from the character of the representing subject (thus reducing them to mere psychological states and bereaving them of their necessity) or to appeal to a higher eternal law (thus resorting to metaphysical speculation). The solution to this problem is to manifest the necessity of the axiom by treating it as an axiom instead of trying to prove it as such.[17] Gottlob Frege subsequently followed up on this axiomatic method and argued that logical rules concern the necessary relations between meanings.[18] For Frege, it is crucial to regard the meanings with which logic is concerned as being independent from human beings and their psychological states and activities.[19] Otherwise, logic would not be a set of necessary, but contingent laws.[20] 'Meaning' thus constitutes a third way between empirical facts and metaphysical speculation.[21] Frege considers the method through which logical truths are justified as a case of logic justifying itself, and the question of why and how we can acknowledge a law of logic to be true can only be answered by reducing said law to another law of logic. And where this is not possible, logic can give no

[13] Richard R. Brockhaus, 'Realism and Psychologism in 19th Century Logic' (1991) 51 *Philosophy and Phenomological Research* 493, 495–6; John Stuart Mill, *A System of Logic, Vol I* (Parker, 1843) 1–2.

[14] Green (n 1) 396.

[15] Hermann Cohen, *Logik der Reinen Erkenntnis* (Cassirer, 1922) 12.

[16] Fritz-Joachim von Rintelen, 'Philosophical Idealism in Germany: The Way from Kant to Hegel and the Present' (1977) 38 *Philosophy and Phenomological Research* 1, 23–4.

[17] Green (n 1) 396–7.

[18] Gordon P. Baker and Peter Michael Stephen Hacker, *Frege: Logical Excavations* (Blackwell, 1984) 35–7; Harold W. Noonan, *Frege: A Critical Introduction* (Polity Press, 2001) 195.

[19] Gottlob Frege, 'Logic' in Hans Hermes and others (eds), *Gottlob Frege: Posthumous Writings* (University of Chicago Press, 1979) 126–7.

[20] Green (n 1) 397.

[21] Gottlob Frege, 'Thoughts' in Brian McGuinness (ed), Gottlob Frege: *Collected Papers on Mathematics, Logic, and Philosophy* (Blackwell, 1984) 363.

answer to that question.[22] Consequently, the laws of logic reveal themselves through the use of the axiomatic method.[23] By clearly distinguishing between the contingent empirical enquiry as to why we accept the laws of logic and the necessity of those laws themselves,[24] Frege exemplifies the approach of the neo-Kantians.[25] Yet at the same time, Frege is—as the founder of modern mathematical logic—usually regarded as the father of analytic philosophy as well, in particular because of his influence through Bertrand Russell on the Anglophone sphere of philosophy.[26]

To cut a long analysis short, it is pivotal to highlight that what Frege is to the interpretation of languages, the pure theory of law is to the interpretation of legal systems.[27] In response to strictly empiricist trends in legal theory that effectively undermine legal meanings, Kelsen especially intended to save the logical analysis of the law by adopting a (neo-)Kantian epistemology of legal meaning.[28] In this context, the Anglo-American reasons traditionally put forth for rejecting the pure theory of law appear to lose their purchase.

Conversely, criticism has also been voiced that Kelsen's account of the law is devoid of any social or political aspects that would give the law content and significance,[29] turning the pure theory of law into an 'exercise in logic and not in life'.[30] However, it is hardly a criticism of a logic of the law that it does not provide us with all the necessary information that we require to interpret a legal system, because this logic of the law only concerns the *necessary* and *formal* rules for interpretation, not its actual content. And the fact that this logical framework needs to be filled in with content drawn from morality, social facts, and politics does not mean this very framework does not exist or is unimportant. Such an argument would actually amount to rejecting the existence or significance of the law of non-contradiction simply because it does not and cannot tell us what particular words mean.[31]

C. Kantian transcendental philosophy for non-continentals

Green notes that another thrust of criticism directed against the pure theory of law found in Anglo-American jurisprudence pertains to the unfamiliar Kantian terminology Kelsen and his colleagues use to frame their arguments. Scholars trained

[22] Gottlob Frege, *The Basic Laws of Arithmetic* (transl Montgomery Furth; University of California Press, 1964) 15.

[23] Brockhaus (n 13) 115–19; Baker and Hacker (n 18) 122; Green (n 1) 397.

[24] Frege, *Basic Laws* (n 22) 15.

[25] Green (n 1) 398.

[26] Anthony Kenny, 'Frege, Gottlob' in Ted Honderich (ed), *The Oxford Companion to Philosophy* (2nd edn; Oxford University Press, 2005) 316; Chase and Reynolds (n 7) 17.

[27] Green (n 1) 368.

[28] Hans Kelsen, *Introduction to the Problems of Legal Theory: A Translation of the First Edition of the Reine Rechtslehre or Pure Theory of Law* (transl Bonnie Litschewski Paulson and Stanley L. Paulson; Clarendon Press, 1997) 7; Hans Kelsen, 'Natural Law Doctrine and Legal Positivism' (as an appendix) to Hans Kelsen, *General Theory of Law and State* (reissue edn; Transaction Publishers, 2007) 394.

[29] Jeremy Waldron, '"Transcendental Nonsense" and System in the Law' (2000) 100 *Columbia Law Review* 16, 48–9; Karl N. Llewellyn, *Jurisprudence: Realism in Theory and Practice* (Chicago University Press, 1962) 356 fn 5.

[30] Harold J. Laski, *A Grammar of Politics* (Allen & Unwin, 1938) vi.

[31] Green (n 1) 368.

in this tradition do not see how legal theory could possibly depend upon working through arcane issues as presented in Kantian transcendental idealism. Yet Kelsen's Kantianism is merely the response to empiricist objections that legal meanings are not proper objects of knowledge, and thus rejecting the logic of legal systems as envisaged by the pure theory of law because of its inherent Kantian ideas is like rejecting symbolic logic because the philosophical arguments that made it possible are too arcane.[32]

It must be admitted, however, that Kant's language, vocabulary, and writing style are indeed convoluted and difficult to understand, even for native German speakers. But once his original intention has been explained, it will become clear why there is no reason to shy away from his philosophy, which was not only crucial for Kelsen, but for Frege as well. If we remember the problem of how to cognize whether a given legal norm is objectively valid or not,[33] then we will see that the same problem troubled Kant, but regarding judgments about the world in general. He asks 'how subjective conditions of thinking should have objective validity',[34] given that every judgment appears to be fully describable in psychological terms, or by replacing those terms with those drawn in physics, biology, sociology, or other empirical sciences. Where can the *necessity* required for objectively valid judgments be found? To answer this question, traditional rationalists would usually resort to metaphysics and locate this necessity in an eternally existing and unitary soul. Kant, however, prefers a middle way between rationalism and empiricism[35] and points to the (admittedly) opaque concept of the transcendental thinking self.[36]

This transcendental self is best understood as always accompanying a subject's experiences and representations.[37] In other words, whatever a person is thinking, there always is a subject of thought which can never be made an object. Even when a person is observing his or her own thoughts, this subject will be the observer, and not the observed. Since this transcendental self can never be an object of empirical experience, the fact that everything about a person that he or she can experience is describable in psychological or other empirical terms, does not mean that these descriptions exhaust what it is to be *this person*.[38] The reason for this is that the self which thinks cannot be an object of experience.[39] In fact, it shows itself *through* experience and the fact that all experience is experience *for* a unified subject of thought. An analogy might be helpful to understand Kant's thoughts fully and, to this end, Green compares this relationship between the transcendental self and the world it experiences to the relationship between the eye and the visual field. Nobody can see their own eye, which is responsible for the visual field *within the visual field*. One could certainly hold up a mirror and then see something within the visual field that is rightly called 'this person's eye'. But the eye in the visual field is not the eye

[32] Ibid., 369. [33] See Chapter 2, section 2B(3).
[34] Immanuel Kant, *Kritik der reinen Vernunft* (Johann Friedrich Hartknoch, 1781/1787) A 89–90/ B 122.
[35] Green (n 1) 391–2.
[36] Kant, *Kritik der reinen Vernunft* (n 34) B 131–4. [37] Ibid., B 131–2.
[38] Green (n 1) 392.
[39] Henry E. Allison, *Kant's Transcendental Idealism* (revised edn; Yale University Press, 2004) 276–9.

responsible *for* the visual field.[40] Thus, to return to Kant's original thought, it becomes clear that since the unity of the transcendental self is not experienced, its unifications of ideas can be regarded as objectively valid. Owing to its nature of being a necessary (and hence not being experienced as a contingent) self, the transcendental self can unite all thoughts in a non-contingent manner, and by doing so, it can represent necessary connections in nature.[41]

Kant's 'Copernican' conclusion is that it is not our knowledge that must conform to objects, but that objects must conform to our knowledge.[42] But does he thereby not risk being accused of either solipsism[43] or rationalism in disguise? Kant's answer is in the negative, as the transcendental self is not an eternal soul in the rationalist sense, existing alongside the empirical self, which is known through psychology, biology, and physics. According to Kant, it is impossible to make such judgments about the thinking self.[44] The fact that this transcendental self is different from the empirical self known through experience is no more representable than the fact that the two are the same.[45] To make either of these claims is illegitimately to treat the transcendental self as a possible object of experience.[46] But the transcendental self is a *condition for*, not an *object of* knowledge,[47] in the same way as Frege treats the ultimate foundation of the laws of logic as an axiom instead of trying to prove it as such.

This short outline of Kant's transcendental idealism should be sufficient to explain his *via media* between rationalism and empiricism, which paved the way for Frege's logical groundwork between these two extremes, and which, eventually, influenced the pure theory of law, trying to find a way between metaphysical natural law and empiricist sociology or psychology. Having said that, the main intention of this section was to make Kant's transcendental philosophy and Kelsen's subsequent use of this vocabulary much more accessible and comprehensible to philosophers and lawyers who feel uncomfortable with the 'Continental' tradition. This will be particularly important when Kelsen's use of the *transcendental* a priori in a legal sense will be explained.

D. Overview

After this *tour de force* in the philosophical groundwork of the pure theory of law, it is now time to tackle this theory itself, but of course with the relevant references to Kantian and neo-Kantian philosophy. The subsequent sections will consequently

[40] Green (n 1) 392 and fn 119. See also Ludwig Wittgenstein, *Tractatus Logico-Philosophicus* (Kegan Paul, 1922) para 5.633: '[Y]ou do *not* see the eye. And nothing *in the visual field* allows you to infer that it is seen by an eye'.

[41] Kant, *Kritik der reinen Vernunft* (n 34) B 141–2.

[42] Ibid., B xvi and A 369–70/B 519–21.

[43] See e.g. Hilary Putnam, 'Why Reason Can't Be Naturalized' (1982) 52 *Synthese* 3, 10.

[44] Kant, *Kritik der reinen Vernunft* (n 34) B 399–432.

[45] Ibid., B 409.

[46] Green (n 1) 393–4.

[47] Robert C. Solomon, *From Rationalism to Existentialism: The Existentialists and Their Nineteenth-Century Backgrounds* (Rowman & Littlefield, 2001) 21; H.E. Matthews, 'Strawson on Transcendental Idealism' (1969) 19 *Philosophical Quarterly* 204, 216–17.

follow the claim that only a monist approach to the relationship between different bodies of law is logically and epistemologically conceivable, and thereby revive the allegedly 'undead'[48] concept of monism. Section 2 will examine the Kantian and neo-Kantian sources of the pure theory of law and how Kant's ideas of the transcendental a priori and mathematical antinomies shaped Kelsen's thoughts on an objective legal science. After that, section 3 will continue with an exposition of the obscure concept of the *Grundnorm* and why this concept is and remains the lynchpin of the pure theory of law. A doctrine intricately related with the *Grundnorm* is the hierarchy of norms, which will be critically analysed in section 4, both in its manifestation as the chain of validity and the chain of derogation. In section 5, legal monism will finally take the centre stage and be discussed comprehensively, particularly in its moderate version under the primacy of international law. Section 6 will engage with Kelsen's most prominent critics, namely H.L.A. Hart and Joseph Raz, who consider his monism highly implausible. A concluding section 7 will then summarize the findings of this chapter and set the scene for Chapter 4 of this book.

2. Legal Epistemology and the Synthetic A Priori of Law: Kantian and Neo-Kantian Sources

Given the long-term dominant status of natural law within the system of the 'law of nations', it is not surprising that public international law has not been a very popular subject among legal positivists. It is certainly correct to say that legal positivists such as Thomas Hobbes,[49] Jeremy Bentham,[50] John Austin,[51] and H.L.A. Hart[52] wrote about international law to a certain extent, but it is nevertheless also true that none of them expressed himself at length on the subject. Hans Kelsen, Adolf Julius Merkl, Alfred Verdross, and Josef L. Kunz, as the leading proponents of the Vienna School of Jurisprudence therefore remain the only major figures of modern analytic jurisprudence to have had a great deal to say about international law[53] and its relationship with national law. However, before the epistemological value of legal monism can be demonstrated in detail, the subsequent sections must first deal with the more abstract elements of this theory, especially its analysis of the law itself.

Kelsen begins his *Pure Theory of Law* in both editions with the statement that, as a theory of positive law in general, its purpose is to know and to cognize its subject

[48] Alexander Somek, 'Monism: A Tale of the Undead' in Matej Avbelj and Jan Komárek (eds), *Constitutional Pluralism in the European Union and Beyond* (Hart Publishing, 2012).

[49] Thomas Hobbes, *Leviathan* (Andrew Crooke, 1651) ch XX.

[50] Who is credited with coining the term 'international law'; Jeremy Bentham, *An Introduction to the Principles of Morals and Legislation* (reprint; Athlone Press, 1970) 296.

[51] John Austin, *The Province of Jurisprudence Determined* (reprint; Hackett Publishing, 1998) 127, denying international law its legal status as mere 'positive international morality'.

[52] H.L.A. Hart, *The Concept of Law* (2nd edn; Clarendon Press, 1994) ch X.

[53] Hedley Bull, 'Hans Kelsen and International Law' in Richard Tur and William Twining (eds), *Essays on Kelsen* (Clarendon Press, 1986) 321.

matter, i.e. the law, to be able to describe it.[54] Thus, this theory needs to be understood as a universal epistemological tool that can cognize *any* positive legal order. Although Kelsen concedes that he writes as a jurist, not a professional philosopher, he explicitly states that the source of his epistemological thoughts, elaborated in his theory, are based on Kant's transcendental philosophy and the philosophy of his neo-Kantian successors.[55] In the *Critique of Pure Reason*, Immanuel Kant undertook to search for the principles of our experience that are both genuinely informative and universally and necessarily true—the so-called *synthetic* a priori that provides us with knowledge independent of empirical experience (a priori), but nonetheless carries new information that goes beyond the mere clarification of what was already implicit in the given concepts (*synthetic*).[56] Similarly, as Kelsen intended his theory to be capable of cognizing and identifying any given legal order a priori,[57] it is therefore commonly accepted that Kelsen was following Kantian and neo-Kantian as well as Humean sources in his legal theory.[58]

This chapter (and this book in general) consequently builds upon the understanding that Kelsen's intellectual development from *c* 1921 to 1960 (his so-called 'classical phase') was shaped by a 'transcendental undergirding for legal science',[59] and it is this richest and most rewarding period in all of Kelsen's work that remains most interesting for legal theory.[60] It is nonetheless important to emphasize that Kelsen remained a jurist and did not become a Kantian legal moralist, and that Kelsen's legal scientific cosmopolitanism is certainly not based on Kant's ethical cosmopolitanism.[61] The philosophical foundation of the pure theory of law is, quite the contrary, as Kelsen himself pointed out, based on Kantian philosophy in the interpretation that it has undergone through the neo-Kantian Cohen and his interpretation of Kant's epistemological philosophy.[62] Since Kelsen placed essential reliance and importance on epistemological arguments in conceiving a sound theory of legal knowledge,[63] Kelsen's Kant was the Kant of epistemology in the *Critique of Pure*

[54] Kelsen, *Introduction* (n 28); Hans Kelsen, *Pure Theory of Law* (2nd edn; University of California Press, 1967) 1.

[55] Hans Kelsen, 'The Pure Theory of Law, "Labandism", and Neo-Kantianism: A Letter to Renato Treves' in Stanley L. Paulson and Bonnie Litschewski Paulson (eds), *Normativity and Norms: Critical Perspectives on Kelsenian Themes* (reprint; Clarendon Press, 2007) 173.

[56] Kant, *Kritik der reinen Vernunft* (n 34) A 10/B 14–19.

[57] Hans Kelsen, *Das Problem der Souveränität und die Theorie des Völkerrechts* (Mohr-Siebeck, 1920) vi.

[58] Hans Kelsen, 'Rechtswissenschaft und Recht' in Stanley L. Paulson (ed), *Die Rolle des Neukantianismus in der Reinen Rechtslehre: Eine Debatte zwischen Sander und Kelsen* (Scientia, 1988) 340–1; Hans Kelsen, *Society and Nature: A Sociological Enquiry* (Kegan Paul, 1946) 262.

[59] Carsten Heidemann, *Die Norm als Tatsache: Zur Normentheorie Hans Kelsens* (Nomos, 1997) 43.

[60] Stanley L. Paulson, 'Four Phases in Hans Kelsen's Legal Theory? Reflections on a Periodization' (1998) 18 *Oxford Journal of Legal Studies* 153, 155.

[61] Mónica García-Salmones Rovira, *The Project of Positivism in International Law* (Oxford University Press, 2013) 328–31.

[62] Kelsen, 'Letter to Renato Treves' (n 55) 171.

[63] Stefan Hammer, 'A Neo-Kantian Theory of Legal Knowledge in Kelsen's Pure Theory of Law?' in Stanley L. Paulson and Bonnie Litschewski Paulson (eds), *Normativity and Norms: Critical Perspectives on Kelsenian Themes* (reprint; Clarendon Press, 2007) 177.

Reason, and not the Kant of moral philosophy in the *Metaphysics of Morals* and the *Critique of Practical Reason*.[64]

A. The juridico-transcendental question

The standard account of Kelsen's early interrelationship with Kantian and neo-Kantian philosophy is provided by Kelsen himself in the 'Foreword' to the second edition of his habilitation.[65] Therein he draws the reader's attention to Oscar Ewald's book review of the first edition of 1911[66] describing the book as 'an attempt, carried out with logical rigour, to introduce the *transcendental method* into legal philosophy'.[67] Ewald continues to remark that not only the Kantian method proved crucial for Kelsen's theories, but also *neo*-Kantian thinking in the form of the above-mentioned Hermann Cohen's interpretation of Kant, in particular his anti-psychologist interpretation of the legal will that 'coincides in a most remarkable way with Kelsen's'.[68] Interestingly, Kelsen himself claims that he could not have based his theory on Cohen's neo-Kantian philosophy while writing his habilitation. In fact, these similarities must have been of an instinctive nature,[69] as he had not known Cohen's views at that time. Only after Ewald's review had brought his attention to the wide-ranging parallels between his concept of the legal will and Cohen's views, Kelsen repeatedly professed himself to neo-Kantianism.[70]

The pivotal point for neo-Kantianism and its reception of Kant was the central question of Kant's theoretical philosophy, 'What can I know?'[71] and its transcendental import. 'Transcendental' cognition, in Kant's words, is not concerned with the actual objects of cognition, 'but the manner how we cognize objects, in so far as this may be possible a priori'.[72] This is where Kelsen raises the juridical version of this transcendental question by asking 'how is positive law *qua* object of cognition, *qua* object of cognitive legal science, possible?'[73] By raising this question with respect to law, Kelsen follows Cohen[74] who 'tried to apply the transcendental method beyond the field of natural science' to normative questions.[75] In the second edition of the *Pure Theory of Law* (1960), Kelsen further refines this question and explicitly uses by analogy a concept of Kant's epistemology:

Kant asks: 'How is it possible to interpret without a metaphysical hypothesis, the facts perceived by our senses, in the laws of nature formulated by natural science?' In the same way,

[64] Stanley L. Paulson, 'On the Kelsen-Kant Problematic' in Ernesto Garzón Valdés and others (eds), *Normative Systems in Legal and Moral Theory* (Duncker & Humblot, 1997) 198.

[65] Ibid.

[66] Hans Kelsen, *Hauptprobleme der Staatsrechtslehre* (2nd edn; Scientia, 1923) xvii.

[67] Oscar Ewald, 'Die deutsche Philosophie im Jahre 1911' (1912) 17 *Kant-Studien* 382, 397 (emphasis added).

[68] Ibid., 397–8.

[69] Hans Kelsen, 'Autobiographie' in Matthias Jestaedt (ed), *Hans Kelsen im Selbstzeugnis* (Mohr-Siebeck, 2006) 37.

[70] Kelsen, *Hauptprobleme* (n 66) vi and xvii.

[71] Kant, *Kritik der reinen Vernunft* (n 34) A 805/B 833.

[72] Ibid., B 26.

[73] Kelsen, 'Rechtswissenschaft und Recht' (n 58) 128.

[74] Hermann Cohen, *Ethik des reinen Willens* (2nd edn; Cassirer, 1907) 29.

[75] Kelsen, 'Rechtswissenschaft und Recht' (n 58) 128.

the Pure Theory of Law asks: 'How is it possible to interpret without recourse to meta-legal authorities, like God or nature, the subjective meaning of certain facts as a system of objectively valid legal norms describable in rules of law?'[76]

This question visibly reflects Kelsen's principal methodological interest, which is to view law normatively as an 'ought' that is entirely distinct from the empirical facts of 'is', yet without thereby walking into the trap of a metaphysical (i.e. natural-legal) reading of moral principles into the positive law for the sake of normativity.[77] Kelsen's *legal* a priori therefore intends to be a Kantian *transcendental* a priori, and his construction of the concept of 'ought' hence represents the ambitious attempt to complement Kant's table of categories by one additional category.[78]

B. Kant's mathematical antinomies and Kelsen's jurisprudential antinomy

The first step in Kelsen's programme to answer the juridico-transcendental question is to adhere strictly to the separation of 'is' and 'ought' and thereby to eliminate from the object of legal cognition all alien elements and everything that is not strictly law, such as politics, psychology, sociology, and ethics.[79] More concretely, Kelsen emphasizes that the purity of a theory of legal cognition must be secured in two directions: firstly, it is to be secured against the 'is' and 'the claims of a so-called "sociological" point of view', and secondly it must also be 'secured against the claims of the natural law theory, which [...] takes legal theory out of the realm of positive legal norms and into the realm of ethico-political postulates'.[80] Thereby Kelsen follows Kant's and Frege's middle way between empiricism and metaphysics.

Stanley L. Paulson argues that three principal points can be drawn from the text quoted above to illustrate Kelsen's strategy in setting up his legal theory.[81] First, from a *historical* angle, Kelsen considers the Western tradition in legal philosophy and jurisprudence as informed by two fundamental types of theory that may be retraced to writings as early as Aristotle's *Nicomachean Ethics*:[82] natural law, according to which positive law is subject to morality; and legal positivism, which considers law as an empirical fact. Secondly, traditional jurisprudence has understood natural law theory and positivism not only as mutually exclusive, but also as entirely exhaustive of any other possibilities. Ergo any 'pretender theories' claiming to be distinct

[76] Kelsen, *Pure Theory* (n 54) 202.
[77] Hammer, 'Neo-Kantian Theory' (n 63) 181–2; Kelsen, *Pure Theory* (n 54) 67–9.
[78] Robert Alexy, 'Hans Kelsens Begriff des relativen Apriori' in Robert Alexy and others (eds), *Neukantianismus und Rechtsphilosophie* (Nomos, 2002) 194.
[79] Kelsen, *Pure Theory* (n 54) 1.
[80] Kelsen, *Hauptprobleme* (n 66) v.
[81] Stanley L. Paulson, 'The Neo-Kantian Dimension of Kelsen's Pure Theory of Law' (1992) 12 *Oxford Journal of Legal Studies* 311, 313–14.
[82] Aristotle, *Nicomachean Ethics* (ed and transl Jonathan Barnes, *The Complete Works of Aristotle, Vol 2* (Oxford University Press, 1984) 1134b 18–19, distinguishing between φύσις (phýsis; 'nature') and νόμος (nómos; 'convention').

from both traditional theories ultimately turn out to be disguised versions of the one or the other. Lastly, it can be concluded from Kelsen's juridico-transcendental question that he rejects both traditional theories. Neither of them is defensible, as their proponents confuse law with morality or law with fact, respectively, and fail to see that the law has a 'specific meaning'[83] of its own.[84]

Kelsen correctly remarks that these conceptions present us with a veritable dilemma: on the one hand, jurists usually acknowledge a particular connection between the realms of law and value or fact,[85] 'as the content of a legal obligation [. . .] can only be human behaviour'.[86] But on the other hand, jurists also accept that there is a logical dichotomy between 'is' and 'ought' and that one cannot logically conclude the latter from the former.[87] In other words, jurists must either side with the *morality thesis*—which considers law and morality inseparable—and therefore hold that the nature of law is ultimately explicable in moral terms;[88] or they must go with its antithesis, the separability thesis,[89] and argue—in Hart's words—that 'it is in no sense a necessary truth that laws reproduce or satisfy certain demands of morality, though in fact they have often done so'.[90] Once we equate the morality thesis with natural law theory and the separability thesis with legal positivism, a jurisprudential antinomy arises, as these traditional theories appear to be both mutually exclusive and jointly exhaustive of any other possibilities. Seeing that Kelsen rejects them both, we must face the antinomy that no answer to the juridico-transcendental questions can be given.[91]

The underlying philosophical source of Kelsen's jurisprudential antinomy can be found in Kant's mathematical antinomies. Therein Kant argues that both rationalists and empiricists present 'equally illuminating, clear and irrefutable evidence'[92] for a system of cosmological ideas, for example the idea that the universe is spatially and temporally finite (thesis) or infinite (antithesis).[93] As one can see quite obviously, these two ideas are necessarily incompatible with each other and cannot be solved based on pure reason alone.[94] Furthermore, logic dictates that if two propositions (such as the thesis and the antithesis in this case) are incompatible, then their conjunction results in a self-contradiction of the form '$p \wedge \neg p$'.[95] This means that

[83] Kelsen, *Introduction* (n 28) 33. [84] Paulson, 'Neo-Kantian Dimension' (n 81) 314.
[85] Hans Kelsen, *Allgemeine Staatslehre* (Springer, 1925) 19.
[86] Kelsen, *Introduction* (n 28) 109. [87] Kelsen, *Allgemeine Staatslehre* (n 85) 62.
[88] Paulson, 'Neo-Kantian Dimension' (n 81) 318.
[89] H.L.A. Hart, 'Positivism and the Separation of Law and Morals' (1957/1958) 71 *Harvard Law Review* 593–629. For the term 'separability thesis' itself see Jules L. Coleman, 'Beyond the Separability Thesis: Moral Semantics and the Methodology of Jurisprudence' (2007) 27 *Oxford Journal of Legal Studies* 581–608.
[90] Hart, *The Concept of Law* (n 52) 181–2.
[91] Paulson, 'Neo-Kantian Dimension' (n 81) 319.
[92] Immanuel Kant, 'Prolegomena zu einer jeden künftigen Metaphysik, die als Wissenschaft wird auftreten können' in Immanuel Kant (ed), *Gesammelte Schriften* (Deutsche Akademie der Wissenschaften, 1911) AA 4:340.
[93] Kant, *Kritik der reinen Vernunft* (n 34) A 424–29/B 452–27.
[94] Ibid., A 409/B 435 ff.
[95] Aristotle, *Posterior Analytics* (ed and transl Jonathan Barnes, *The Complete Works of Aristotle, Vol 1* (Oxford University Press, 1984) 77a 26–34; Aristotle, *Metaphysics* (ed and transl Jonathan Barnes, *The Complete Works of Aristotle, Vol 2* (Oxford University Press, 1984) 1011b 13–15.

thesis and antithesis not only exclude each other, but also, together, exhaust every other possibility too. Kant of course rejects thesis and antithesis alike and intends, by demonstrating the predicament in which epistemology finds itself, to show a way out.[96] Kant's solution to the mathematical antinomies is a middle way, which shows that such antinomies merely rest on a fallacy of ambiguity, as they draw on principles relating to appearances given to our intuition, but concurrently also try to reach conclusions which can only be true if they were considered as existing in themselves apart from their relation to the mind.[97]

The antinomy of the morality and separability theses presents Kelsen with a similar problem as the mathematical antinomies did in Kant's case. In fact, an answer to the juridico-transcendental question seems only possible if we regard the two propositions of the jurisprudential antinomy as a false dichotomy and acknowledge, as Paulson explains, that there are in sum *four* theses to reckon with, not merely two. He stresses that the relation between law and morality does not exhaust all possibilities, as it fails to consider the relation between law and fact. In this context, the *reductive thesis* claims that law is ultimately grounded on and explicable in factual terms. It hence purports the inseparability of law and fact and represents, *per definitionem*, an aspect of the legal positivist theory. Conversely, its antithesis is the *normativity thesis* that claims the separability of law and fact[98] and thus reflects—albeit tacitly, as Kelsen does—a part of natural law theory.[99]

When juxtaposing these four different theses, the following picture in Figure 2 emerges:[100]

law and fact / law and morality	*normativity thesis* (separability of law and fact)	*reductive thesis* (inseparability of law and fact)
morality thesis (inseparability of law and morality)	natural law theory	(legal reductionism)
separability thesis (separability of law and morality)	pure theory of law	(empirico-)positivist theory of law

Figure 2 The pure theory of law between legal positivism and natural law.

96 Paulson, 'Neo-Kantian Dimension' (n 81) 314.
97 Kant, *Kritik der reinen Vernunft* (n 34) A 517–19/B 545–7.
98 Paulson, 'Neo-Kantian Dimension' (n 81) 319.
99 Kelsen, *Hauptprobleme* (n 66) 7.
100 Paulson, 'Neo-Kantian Dimension' (n 81) 320. Note, however, that Paulson considers the juxtaposition of the morality and reductive theses resulting in legal reductionism a contradiction in terms, whereas Martin van Hees, *Legal Reductionism and Freedom* (Kluwer Law, 2000) 41–3, regards it as a possibility because of positive morality's belonging to the realm of facts.

Kelsen's solution is—as Kant's reply to the antinomies—a middle way and can be characterized as an attempt to combine the separability thesis and the normativity thesis. Law is, on the one hand, separate from morality as an act 'posited' by a human being, and therefore a positive 'is'; but at the same time it is, on the other hand, separate from fact by being obeyed, and if not obeyed, by being applied, which amounts to a normative 'ought'.[101] In other words, the 'ought' is irrevocably separated from the 'is', and yet the former is to be treated as a descriptive 'is', because of its posited nature. Through this combination, Kelsen succeeds in resolving the jurisprudential antinomy, yet omits to answer the question as to what constitutes the source of the law's normativity and hence validity. We will return to this issue below in section 3.

C. Legal purity and scientific rigour

On the basis of these considerations, Kelsen formulates a legally pure and scientifically rigorous theory.[102] He argues that since we are immediately aware of the fact that a *describing* statement is fundamentally different from a *prescribing* statement, the science of law can be clearly distinguished from the natural or causal sciences.[103] Whilst natural law theories conflate the empirical principle of causality ('metals expand when being heated') with the normative-legal concept of imputation ('an individual committing murder is punishable by ten to twenty years of imprisonment'[104]), the pure theory of law is very exact about the differences between the empirical and legal sciences. Although the latter operates analogously to the natural sciences—by linking premises and conclusions through a logical copula—this very copula itself is different. Causality describes empirical facts, whereas imputation relates to consequences that ought to happen under the applicable law.[105] Thus, the pure theory of law is a theory of that which ought to be in a positivist legal aspect, and not of that which empirically exists; and the object of investigation of the science of law is legal norms, not empirical reality. Yet, concurrently it is the science of law as it is, and not as it should be. Kelsen admits that this might appear to be a contradictory assertion, but this is not the case. The pure theory of law claims to describe and analyse positive law, i.e. legal reality, in contrast to ideas of justice, or how the law should ideally be.[106]

This claim is also of utmost importance in delineating law from non-legal normative systems, such as morality and politics. Kelsen postulates that natural law

[101] Hans Kelsen, 'On the Pure Theory of Law' (1966) 1 *Israel Law Review* 1, 2.

[102] Cf., however, the criticism voiced against the alleged impurity of the pure theory of law in e.g. Víctor Arévalo Menchaca, 'Die "Unreinheit" der Reinen Rechtslehre' [1984] *Rechtstheorie (Beiheft 5)* 131–58.

[103] Kelsen, *Pure Theory* (n 54) 5–6.

[104] Hans Kelsen, *General Theory of Law and State* (reissue edn; Transaction Publishers, 2007) 91–2.

[105] Hans Kelsen, 'Was ist die Reine Rechtslehre?' in Hans R. Klecatsky, René Marcic, and Herbert Schambeck (eds), *Die Wiener rechtstheoretische Schule: Schriften von Hans Kelsen, Adolf Merkl, Alfred Verdross, Band 1* (Verlag Österreich, 2010) 500.

[106] Ibid., 501–2.

theory is mistaken when assuming the existence of absolute norms that outrank all positive law, because 'absolute values' simply do not exist. Even moral codes such as the Golden Rule remain meaningless as long as they are not codified in positive law and explicitly state what it exactly is that one should not do unto others.[107] The pure theory of law aims to be mere cognition and to stay clear of moral obligations and legal politics.[108] Natural law may well be regarded as an 'ethical-political' standard[109] for positive law, but nonetheless legal norms may at the same time be immoral, according to ethical standards.[110] As a result, the validity of a given posited legal norm is not dependent on its substantive moral value, but—as we will see later on—rather on the formal procedures under which it has been created (and thus on the question of whether it forms part of a given legal system[111]). In Kelsen's words, the reason for the validity of one given legal norm can only be the validity of another norm,[112] and not its conformity with moral standards.

3. The *Grundnorm*

A. A logical terminus

Although the pure theory of law impressively combines the positivity of law with its normativity, it does not, *prima facie*, answer the question of where the actual reason for the validity of norms is to be found. Kelsen himself argues that if the law is conceived as a system of norms, we must also enquire what constitutes the unity of a multitude of norms, and why a given norm is valid.[113] Regarding the first question, one must at the outset search for the distinctive criterion which makes a legal order 'one' legal order. Usually a positivist criterion is used in this regard according to which a legal order can only be considered a unitary legal order if every single legal act can be derived from one legal source or authority.[114] Conversely, if there is more than one source, then there is more than one legal order. In a unitary legal order, the source can be decisionistic (as in John Austin's theory, where the legal act is based on the sovereign's decision);[115] factualist (as in Hart's theory where the so-called *rule*

[107] Hans Kelsen, 'Die Grundlagen der Naturrechtslehre' in Hans R. Klecatsky, René Marcic, and Herbert Schambeck (eds), *Die Wiener rechtstheoretische Schule: Schriften von Hans Kelsen, Adolf Merkl, Alfred Verdross, Band 1* (Verlag Österreich, 2010) 744.

[108] Lars Vinx, *Hans Kelsen's Pure Theory of Law: Legality and Legitimacy* (Oxford University Press, 2007) 10.

[109] Kelsen, *Pure Theory* (n 54) 204–5.

[110] Jörg Kammerhofer, 'Hans Kelsen's Place in International Legal Theory' in Alexander Orakhelashvili (ed), *Research Handbook on the Theory and History of International Law* (Edward Elgar, 2011) 146.

[111] Eugenio Bulygin, 'Das Problem der Geltung bei Kelsen' in Stanley L. Paulson and Michael Stolleis (eds), *Hans Kelsen: Staatsrechtslehrer und Rechtstheoretiker des 20. Jahrhunderts* (Mohr-Siebeck, 2005) 82–3.

[112] Kelsen, *Pure Theory* (n 54) 198.

[113] Ibid., 193.

[114] Carlos E. Alchourrón and Eugenio Bulygin, *Normative Systems* (Springer, 1971) 4; Joseph Raz, *The Concept of a Legal System: An Introduction to the Theory of Legal System* (2nd edn; Oxford University Press, 1980) 18.

[115] Austin (n 51) 208.

of recognition is based upon social practice);[116] or analytical (as in Kelsen's works). We now know that the validity of a given norm can be found neither in extra-legal norms such as morality (because the 'is' of the posited norm cannot be derived from the 'ought' of a moral rule) nor in empirical facts (because the 'ought' of the posited norm cannot be derived from the 'is' of a statement about reality).[117] Yet since a legal system is not a mere haphazard set of norms, but a system of normative interrelation,[118] the origin of legal validity must somehow be localized. The reason for the validity of a given norm lies in a 'higher', or hierarchically superior norm. Kelsen certainly admits that the search for the reason of a norm's validity cannot go on indefinitely, like the search for the cause of an effect.[119] Therefore, in order to avoid a *regressus ad infinitum*, this search is terminated by the highest norm, which represents the last reason of validity within a normative system.[120] Critics may, however, interject that the existence of such a supreme norm in positive law seems to be in contradiction with Kelsen's assumption that only natural law theories presuppose absolute values and norms. But he is nevertheless able to circumnavigate this issue by introducing the concept of the *Grundnorm* (or basic norm), which is the source and foundation of all law, and a necessary scientific hypothesis of the science of law.[121] In a way similar to Frege's axiomatic foundation of logic and Kant's transcendental self, this last and highest norm is presupposed and cannot be 'posited', i.e. it cannot be created by an authority whose competence to do so would have to derive from still a higher norm.

Prima facie, this seems to be a very obscure and metaphysical statement. In fact, however, when looking at the concept of the hierarchy of norms (*Stufenbaulehre*) in Kelsen's and Merkl's theory,[122] it will become evident that the notion of the basic norm forms a constitutive element in the pure theory of law. The central merit of this theory of perceiving legal norms in hierarchical structures, and a chain of validity, lies in its power to explain the structure and functioning of legal orders and their essential features. First, according to the 'chain of delegation' (*Delegationszusammen hang*),[123] the creation of each norm of a given legal system is determined by another, superior norm, whose creation is again determined by a superior norm;[124] whereas, second, according to the 'chain of derogation' (*Derogationszusammenhang*),[125] inferior norms conflicting with superior norms may be annulled and therefore invalidated.[126] Thus, the hierarchy of norms allows for a differentiated, continuously changing and shifting system of norms, which nonetheless remains a unified entity on the basis of the system's hierarchical chain of validity.[127] In epistemological terms,

[116] Hart, *The Concept of Law* (n 52) 92.
[117] Kelsen, *General Theory* (n 104) 110.
[118] Joseph Raz, *The Authority of Law* (2nd edn; Oxford University Press, 2009) 123.
[119] Kelsen, *Pure Theory* (n 54) 194.
[120] Kelsen, *General Theory* (n 104) 111.
[121] Joseph G. Starke, 'Monism and Dualism in the Theory of International Law' (1936) 17 *British Yearbook of International Law* 66, 74–5.
[122] This theory will be discussed in detail in section 4.
[123] Kelsen, *General Theory* (n 104) 113.
[124] Kelsen, *Pure Theory* (n 54) 233–6.
[125] Kelsen, *General Theory* (n 104) 153 ff.
[126] Kelsen, *Pure Theory* (n 54) 267–78.
[127] Peter Koller, 'Zur Theorie des rechtlichen Stufenbaus' in Stanley L. Paulson and Michael Stolleis (eds), *Hans Kelsen: Staatsrechtslehrer und Rechtstheoretiker des 20. Jahrhunderts* (Mohr-Siebeck, 2005) 106.

it is capable of resolving the questions of whether a certain norm is a valid legal norm and thus part of a given legal order, and whether a certain legal norm may have lost its validity and hence ceased to be part of a legal order, respectively.[128] Thereby the basic norm is the common source for the validity of all norms belonging to a given legal order,[129] and all norms whose validity can be traced back to one and the same basic norm form a normative system. It constitutes, as a common source and in a dynamic manner, the bond between all the various norms of which an order consists.[130]

In contrast to a strictly static legal order whose norms are valid on the strength of their content (e.g. 'do not lie' or 'do fulfil a promise'),[131] such a dynamic legal order has the clear advantage of containing valid norms regardless of their content.[132] Therefore, it is pivotal to emphasize that only the validity of norms, and not their contents, can be derived from the *Grundnorm*.[133] If the pure theory of law were to be a static system that assumed a basic norm of specific content (e.g. 'always be truthful'), only norms whose content was derived from the basic norm (e.g. 'do not lie'), and not any random legal norm, could be valid. In this case, Kelsen's theory would be downgraded to merely describing one particular legal order. What Kelsen, conversely, has in mind is to devise a theory of general jurisprudence,[134] which can describe *any* legal order, irrespective of its particular contents. As a result, any norm system presenting itself as a legal order essentially has a dynamic character, which means that a legal norm is not valid because it has a certain content, (i.e. because its content is logically deducible from a basic norm), but because it was created in a certain way, which is determined by the basic norm.[135]

Sceptics might nevertheless still wonder what the *Grundnorm* is. The most straightforward answer to the above question would be that the basic norm is Kelsen's reply to the juridico-transcendental question, which is only possible if law is to be considered as separated from both morality (as something posited) and from fact (as something normative). In a similar fashion to Kant's 'Copernican revolution' through which he realized that a priori (i.e. necessary) knowledge is not possible by conforming intuition to the nature of objects, but by conforming the object to our intuition,[136] Kelsen remarks that legal cognition is only possible if said '[c]ognition itself creates its objects, out of materials provided by the senses and in accordance with its immanent laws'.[137]

[128] Hans Tessar, *Der Stufenbau nach der rechtlichen Autorität und seine Bedeutung für die juristische Interpretation* (Verlag Österreich, 2010) 42.

[129] Kelsen, *Pure Theory* (n 54) 194–5.

[130] Kelsen, *General Theory* (n 104) 111.

[131] Kelsen, *Pure Theory* (n 54) 195.

[132] Which is, admittedly, a highly controversial argument, since this conception of law also allows—as Gustav Radbruch's famous critique of legal positivism demonstrates—for legal norms of arbitrary and criminal content, such as the laws of Nazi Germany, to be valid legal norms; Gustav Radbruch, 'Gesetzliches Unrecht und übergesetzliches Recht' (1946) 1 *Süddeutsche Juristen-Zeitung* 105, 107.

[133] Kelsen, 'Was ist die Reine Rechtslehre?' (n 105) 503.

[134] Dieter Kühne, 'Die Grundnorm als inhaltlicher Geltungsgrund der Rechtsordnung' [1984] *Rechtstheorie (Beiheft 5)* 193, 196.

[135] Kelsen, *Pure Theory* (n 54) 198.

[136] Kant, *Kritik der reinen Vernunft* (n 34) Preface to the 2nd edn, xvii.

[137] Kelsen, 'Natural Law Doctrine' (n 28) 434.

B. Localizing the *Grundnorm*

Having said that, it is fair to criticize that if the basic norm is presupposed and cannot be posited, it cannot form part of a legal order. In fact, the *Grundnorm*'s rather obscure nature has caused its fair share of criticism[138] where it was likened, among others, to a 'chimera'[139] or a 'mystery and mystique'.[140] It is therefore reasonable to say that this concept remains Kelsen's most notorious legal theoretical puzzle to date,[141] and that, as a philosophical stratagem, it appears to elude further explanation. Yet this construct is not the problem it is sometimes argued to be,[142] as Kelsen offers a response to this critique based on an illustrative example. When we ask why depriving individuals of their individual freedom by putting them in jail can be considered a valid legal act, the answer can be found in a judicial decision, ordering the imprisonment of these individuals. When asking why this specific decision is valid as part of a given legal order, the answer is because it has been created in conformity with a criminal statute. This statute, in turn, derives its validity from the constitution, as it has been created by a competent organ in the way the constitution prescribes. If we then ask why the constitution is valid, we might come across an older constitution, predating the one currently in force. Eventually we reach a constitution that is historically the first and which was laid down by a usurper, or by some assembly. The validity of this very first constitution is the last presupposition, or final postulate, on which the validity of all norms of a given legal order depends.[143]

But what lies beyond this historically first constitution? Where does its validity originate? The validity of the historically first constitution is also owed to a norm, since the individuals or the group of individuals who drafted and enacted it must have been in possession of the power to legislate. And it is this power of the first legislator that stems from the basic norm, that is, a norm 'included in the supposition'[144] that valid norms have been adopted by an organ bestowed with the competence to issue valid legal norms.[145] Thus, the basic norm of such a legal order is that one ought to behave as the individuals who created the first constitution have ordained.[146] For that reason the *Grundnorm* is not the product of free invention, or presupposed on arbitrary grounds in the sense that there is a choice between different basic norms.[147] Furthermore, it is important to note that the word 'historically' does not refer to the

[138] See most notably H.L.A. Hart, *Essays in Jurisprudence* and Philosophy (Clarendon Press, 1983) 338–9; Hart, *The Concept of Law* (n 52) 245–6; and Joseph Raz, 'Kelsen's Theory of the Basic Norm' (1974) 19 *American Journal of Jurisprudence* 94, 94–111.

[139] Jens-Michael Priester, 'Die Grundnorm—Eine Chimäre' [1984] *Rechtstheorie (Beiheft 5)* 211–44.

[140] Julius Stone, 'Mystery and Mystique in the Basic Norm' (1963) 26 *Modern Law Review* 34.

[141] Stanley L. Paulson, 'The Great Puzzle: Kelsen's Basic Norm' in Luís Duarte d'Almeida, John Gardner, and Leslie Green (eds), *Kelsen Revisited: New Essays on the Pure Theory of Law* (Hart Publishing, 2013) 43.

[142] Jörg Kammerhofer, 'Hans Kelsen in Today's International Legal Scholarship' in Jörg Kammerhofer and Jean d'Aspremont (eds), *International Legal Positivism in a Post-Modern World* (Cambridge University Press, 2014) 92.

[143] Kelsen, *General Theory* (n 104) 115.

[144] Kelsen, *Pure Theory* (n 54) 197.

[145] Uta Bindreiter, *Why* Grundnorm*? A Treatise on the Implications of Kelsen's Doctrine* (Kluwer Law, 2010) 23.

[146] Kelsen, *General Theory* (n 104) 115.

[147] Kelsen, *Pure Theory* (n 54) 201.

historical facts that brought about the constitution from any non-normative point of view, but to its normative pedigree. It denotes the genealogy of a constitution in the sense of a line of lawful constitutional 'heirs'.[148] The historically first constitution is consequently seen directly below the basic norm of a given legal order.[149] In Kelsen's words, the basic norm is—in contradistinction to the constitution in the positive legal sense—a constitution in a logical-juridical sense, which, however, eludes epistemic enquiries into the law.[150] On the contrary, only under this constitutive assumption or fiction it becomes possible to cognize the law as a specific object of knowledge.[151] In analogy to Kant's transcendental self, the *Grundnorm* is a *condition for* legal knowledge, and not an *object of* legal knowledge.

Eventually, through this conception of the *Grundnorm*, Kelsen can counter the argument mentioned at the beginning of this section, namely that a presupposed basic norm cannot form part of a given legal order.[152] For Kelsen, this does not constitute a problem, since this circumstance merely sheds light on the true status of the basic norm as a neo-Kantian transcendental notion and answer to the above-mentioned juridico-transcendental question[153] in the sense of Hermann Cohen's philosophy. The principal value of the basic norm accordingly is a means of explication[154] of utter pragmatic nature, since it facilitates the cognition of positive legal material and thus enables the lawyer to resolve problems of validity by appeal to derogation.[155]

C. Logical unity resolves normative conflicts

When taking this fundamental concept one step further, we see that the basic norm as the reason for the validity of all norms belonging to the same legal order also constitutes the unity of the multiplicity of these norms. A fortiori, this means that this very unity implies a description of this legal order in rules of law that do not contradict each other. Kelsen hastens, however, to add that it is certainly undeniable that legal organs may create conflicting norms, for example if one norm prescribes a certain behaviour and another norm prescribes another behaviour incompatible with the first;[156] for example, the obligation to fulfil a certain action and the concurrent prohibition to fulfil the same action.[157] In fact, it is quite common that a

[148] Bert van Roermund, 'Norm-Claims, Validity, and Self-Reference' in Luís Duarte d'Almeida, John Gardner, and Leslie Green (eds), *Kelsen Revisited: New Essays on the Pure Theory of Law* (Hart Publishing, 2013) 17.

[149] Rudolf A. Métall, 'Skizzen zu einer Systematik der völkerrechtlichen Quellenlehre' (1931) 11 *Zeitschrift für Öffentliches Recht* 416, 421; Jörg Kammerhofer, *Uncertainty in International Law: A Kelsenian Perspective* (Routledge, 2011) 232.

[150] Kelsen, *Pure Theory* (n 54) 199 and 204.

[151] van Roermund (n 148) 17.

[152] Bindreiter, *Why* Grundnorm*?* (n 145) 37.

[153] Kelsen, 'Letter to Renato Treves' (n 55) 174.

[154] Paulson, 'The Great Puzzle' (n 141) 60.

[155] Gerhard Luf, 'On the Transcendental Import of Kelsen's Basic Norm' in Stanley L. Paulson and Bonnie Litschewski-Paulson (eds), *Normativity and Norms: Critical Perspectives on Kelsenian Themes* (Oxford University Press, 2007) 233.

[156] Kelsen, *Pure Theory* (n 54) 205.

[157] Pablo E. Navarro and Jorge L. Rodríguez, *Deontic Logic and Legal Systems* (Cambridge University Press, 2014) 175.

legal subject may be the addressee of contradictory propositions. But the problem of such conflicting assertions is that they do not fit into a consistent and coherent legal order.[158]

Thus, since conflicts are regarded as anomalies, which imply shortcomings,[159] most of all legal uncertainty, they must somehow be satisfactorily resolved. The question remains, nonetheless, how this goal can be achieved. To begin with, Kelsen clarifies that such conflicts do not constitute logical contradictions *stricto sensu* of the word. Logical principles, most notably the principle of the exclusion of contradictions,[160] are applicable to assertions that are either true or false, which means that if a logical contradiction exists between the two assertions, only one or the other assertion can necessarily be true. Yet a norm cannot be true or false, but only either valid or invalid.[161] What can certainly be said is, however, that the assertion that a certain norm is valid according to a given legal order is either true or false. Consequently, logical principles including the principle of non-contradiction are applicable to rules of law describing legal norms and thus indirectly also to legal norms themselves. Hence if we say that two legal norms contradict each other, this means that only one of them can be regarded as objectively valid[162]—which, in turn, raises the question of how it is possible to cognize this very validity.

The answer can be found in the concept of the *Grundnorm*, which constitutes the source of the validity of a legal order and which functions as the terminus of the hierarchy of norms. Through this validity-relationship, the basic norm 'establishes the unity of the multiplicity of norms by being the basis for the validity of all norms belonging to this [normative] order'.[163] The *Grundnorm* thereby becomes an epistemologically essential element in the resolution of normative conflicts,[164] as it not only bestows validity on a given norm, but also enables the observer to identify whether a certain norm belongs to a given a legal order.[165] In other words, the basic norm is the apex of a closed and hierarchically ordered legal system[166] and hence enables us to interpret the material submitted to legal cognition as a meaningful whole, and to describe it in logically non-contradictory sentences.[167]

[158] Carlos E. Alchourrón and Eugenio Bulygin, 'The Expressive Conception of Norms' in Stanley L. Paulson and Bonnie Litschewski-Paulson (eds), *Normativity and Norms: Critical Perspectives on Kelsenian Themes* (Oxford University Press, 2007) 396.

[159] Joost Pauwelyn, *Conflict of Norms in Public International Law* (Cambridge University Press, 2003) 172.

[160] Aristotle, *On Interpretation* (ed and transl Jonathan Barnes, *The Complete Works of Aristotle, Vol 1* (Oxford University Press, 1984) 18a 28–19b 4, and Aristotle, *Metaphysics* (n 95) 1011b 26–7.

[161] Jørgen Jørgensen, 'Imperatives and Logic' (1937/1938) 7 *Erkenntnis* 288–96.

[162] Bindreiter, *Why* Grundnorm*?* (n 145) 142–7.

[163] Kelsen, *Pure Theory* (n 54) 197; Kelsen, *General Theory* (n 104) 111.

[164] Robert Walter, 'Entstehung und Entwicklung des Gedankens der Grundnorm' in Robert Walter (ed), *Schwerpunkte der Reinen Rechtslehre* (Manz, 1992) 47; Bindreiter, *Why* Grundnorm*?* (n 145) 31; Raz, *The Authority of Law* (n 118) 69.

[165] Stanley L. Paulson, 'Die unterschiedlichen Formulierungen der "Grundnorm"' in Aulis Aarnio and others (eds), *Rechtsnorm und Rechtswirklichkeit* (Duncker & Humblot, 1993) 64.

[166] Jürgen Behrend, *Untersuchungen zur Stufenbaulehre Adolf Merkls und Hans Kelsens* (Duncker & Humblot, 1977) 69.

[167] Kelsen, *Pure Theory* (n 54) 206–8.

Therefore, the derogation of one conflicting norm (for instance because it was not created in accordance with the hierarchy of norms) necessarily leads to the elimination of the conflict[168] whilst the concurrent cognition that one of these norms does not form part of the legal order in question through the *Grundnorm* safeguards its very consistency.[169] Later in life, Kelsen changed his view and claimed that such derogation can only occur positivistically, not a priori, which means through a posited norm decreed by a competent authority.[170] Yet this does not affect the overall concept of the basic norm, because even then, this posited norm would ultimately owe its validity to the *Grundnorm* through the positive-legal hierarchy of norms. Either way, the crucial point remains that the law must be understood as a meaningful whole and be describable in non-contradictory statements.[171]

D. Appraisal: the epistemological value of the *Grundnorm*

The nature of the basic norm may be summarized as a single, universal, organizing principle that governs a coherent and unified legal system.[172] This seems to be a simple and useful reference point if one intends to condense this theory into one single sentence. But to be more concrete, the ultimate epistemological value of the *Grundnorm* lies in the fact that despite its coinage by Kelsen, it is not dependent on his particular theoretical approach. In fact, all human beings must necessarily presuppose a basic norm when they perceive norms as norms, since this is the only way in which humans can conceive of them.[173] This necessity emerges from the *Grundnorm* as its expression of the is-ought dichotomy to deal with the problem of legal norms as posited and descriptive, yet also imperative and prescriptive entities.[174]

This is therefore the very first of the main three intertwining functions[175] of the basic norm, namely the termination of the infinite regress or the tautological circle of deriving an 'ought' from another 'ought' by presupposing the basic norm as a synthetic a priori in the Kantian sense. This self-reference avoids a logical circle by apriorizing the basic norm without bereaving it of its synthetic value.[176] As an epistemological tool and the concrete expression of the is-ought dichotomy,[177] it helps us perceive

[168] Alchourrón and Bulygin, 'Expressive Conception' (n 158) 393.

[169] Ewald Wiederin, 'Was ist und welche Konsequenzen hat ein Normenkonflikt?' (1990) 21 *Rechtstheorie* 311, 329.

[170] Hans Kelsen, *General Theory of Norms* (reprint; Clarendon Press, 2011) 125. See also section 4C.

[171] Kelsen, *Pure Theory* (n 54) 206.

[172] Isaiah Berlin, *The Hedgehog and the Fox* (2nd edn; Princeton University Press, 2013) 1–2.

[173] Kammerhofer, 'Kelsen in Today's Scholarship' (n 142) 94–5.

[174] Michael Potacs, 'Die Grundnormproblematik' in Stefan Griller and Heinz Peter Rill (eds), *Rechtstheorie: Rechtsbegriff—Dynamik—Auslegung* (Springer, 2011) 136–7.

[175] Kammerhofer, *Uncertainty* (n 149) 245–50 identifies four functions, the last of which (the identification and authorization of the norm-maker) is of little relevance at this point. See also Paulson, 'Die unterschiedlichen Formulierungen' (n 165) 58–63.

[176] Wolfgang Meyer-Hesemann, 'Zur rechtstheoretischen Rekonstruktion der Reinen Rechtslehre' [1984] *Rechtstheorie (Beiheft 5)* 63, 74–5.

[177] Robert Walter, 'Die Grundnorm im System der Reinen Rechtslehre' in Aulis Aarnio and others (eds), *Rechtsnorm und Rechtswirklichkeit* (Duncker & Humblot, 1993) 85.

the difference between empirical reality and the normative realm, which posits some status or behaviour as ideal. This idea of the 'ought' can be contained in a given norm only if the *Grundnorm* is being presupposed to be above each normative order.[178] It is therefore this normative interpretation that is the essential function of the basic norm and the precondition of the normativity of the object of cognizance,[179] i.e. the law.

The second main function of the basic norm is its role as the highest basis of validity of a legal normative order. The *Grundnorm* represents an answer to the questions: what constitutes the reason of the validity of a given legal norm and why is it valid? And why ought we to behave in conformity with this legal norm?[180] When following the is-ought dichotomy as a basis for Kelsen's normativism,[181] the ground of the validity for a given norm can only be another norm, which authorizes the creation of that norm in the first place.[182] Thus, the norms of a legal order form a hierarchy for which the conception of the *Grundnorm* helps to account. The hierarchy of norms requires some logic of norms, and the plausible basis for such a logic can be found in the basic norm.[183] As an axiomatic logical-normative terminus, it founds validity, but does not require any such foundation itself.[184] And it is self-referential and necessarily tautological,[185] as it answers by reference to itself by assuming validity.[186] In this vein, Kelsen concludes that we act under a legal hypothesis as if the normative order were valid, and from the assumption that it is valid, it follows that the whole legal order under it is valid.[187] Admittedly, this conception remains hypothetical, but if one accepts the dichotomy of 'is' and 'ought', it is necessarily the only possible one.[188]

Lastly, the *Grundnorm* constitutes the norm-creating and unifying force of the legal normative order[189] by establishing a validity-relationship between these norms and by being the basis for the validity of all norms belonging to this order.[190] Thereby Kelsen's notion of the basic norm helps to consolidate the vision of the law as a system. Legal norms are not autonomous entities,[191] 'standing coordinatedly side by side'; they can exist 'only as a part of such a system'.[192] Through the *Grundnorm*, the

[178] Kammerhofer, 'Kelsen in Today's Scholarship' (n 142) 95.
[179] Robert Walter, *Der Aufbau der Rechtsordnung* (2nd edn; Manz, 1974) 14–15.
[180] Kelsen, *Pure Theory* (n 54) 196.
[181] Jerzy Wróblewski, 'Kelsen, the Is-Ought Dichotomy, and Naturalistic Fallacy' (1981) 35 *Revue internationale de philosophie* 508, 509.
[182] Kelsen, *Pure Theory* (n 54) 196–7.
[183] Carsten Heidemann, 'Hans Kelsen and the Transcendental Method' (2004) 55 *Northern Ireland Legal Quarterly* 358, 362 and 365.
[184] Kammerhofer, 'Kelsen in Today's Scholarship' (n 142) 96.
[185] Stig Jørgensen, 'Grundnorm und Paradox' [1984] *Rechtstheorie (Beiheft 5)* 179, 188.
[186] Alfred Verdross, 'Zum Problem der völkerrechtlichen Grundnorm' in Hans R. Klecatsky, René Marcic, and Herbert Schambeck (eds), *Die Wiener rechtstheoretische Schule: Schriften von Hans Kelsen, Adolf Merkl, Alfred Verdross, Band 2* (Verlag Österreich, 2010) 1811.
[187] Kelsen, *Pure Theory* (n 54) 198–201; Kelsen, *General Theory* (n 104) 111.
[188] Kammerhofer, 'Kelsen in Today's Scholarship' (n 142) 96.
[189] Uta Bindreiter, 'Presupposing the Basic Norm' (2001) 14 *Ratio Juris* 143, 147; Behrend (n 166) 68–9.
[190] Kelsen, *Pure Theory* (n 54) 195.
[191] Mario Prost, *The Concept of Unity in Public International Law* (Hart Publishing, 2012) 73.
[192] Kelsen, *Pure Theory* (n 54) 47 and 201.

law becomes a closed system that regulates its own creation, application, and abrogation, and interrelates to the reality of society by creating and executing legal norms. Hence the basic norm represents the ultimate fount of the hierarchy of norms, which exists in every single legal order around the world; at least in the minimum shape of two hierarchical steps: norm-creating norms and those norms created accordingly.[193] Let us now discuss this concept of the hierarchy of norms in more detail.

4. The Hierarchy of Norms

A. Introduction and overview

The arguably most important elements of the pure theory of law are the dynamic concept of law and its theoretical basis, the hierarchy of norms.[194] The fundamental idea of this principle was first developed by Adolf Julius Merkl,[195] and only later incorporated by Kelsen into his pure theory of law. As will be shown in the subsequent sections, Merkl's doctrine of the hierarchy of norms remains, to date, a very rare innovation that legal theory was able to produce in the twentieth century:[196] from a theoretical viewpoint, it is still considered 'the most far-reaching and astute reply to the traditional doctrine of the sources of law'[197] and 'one of the most significant contributions to an exact cognition and objective description of positive law'.[198] It is remarkable that even scholars, who regard the pure theory of law to be built on sand, certify that the theory of the hierarchy norms stands on solid ground and that it will, more or less, endure.[199] In an almost paradoxical manner, even the most severe critics who excoriate Merkl's theory, attest its 'doctrinal usefulness'.[200] Empirically, this is all the more true, as this theory has influenced and fertilized legal doctrine to an extent that stands out in comparison to other legal-theoretical models.[201]

[193] Manfred Rotter, 'Die Reine Rechtslehre im Völkerrecht—eine eklektizistische Spurensuche in Theorie und Praxis' in Robert Walter, Clemens Jabloner, and Klaus Zeleny (eds), *Hans Kelsen und das Völkerrecht* (Manz, 2004) 57.

[194] Koller (n 127) 106.

[195] See e.g. Adolf Julius Merkl, 'Das doppelte Rechtsantlitz' in Hans R Klecatsky, René Marcic, and Herbert Schambeck (eds), *Die Wiener rechtstheoretische Schule: Schriften von Hans Kelsen, Adolf Merkl, Alfred Verdross, Band 1* (Verlag Österreich, 2010) 893–911; Adolf Julius Merkl, 'Prolegomena einer Theorie des rechtlichen Stufenbaus' in Hans R. Klecatsky, René Marcic, and Herbert Schambeck (eds), *Die Wiener rechtstheoretische Schule: Schriften von Hans Kelsen, Adolf Merkl, Alfred Verdross, Band 2* (Verlag Österreich, 2010) 1071–111.

[196] Ewald Wiederin, 'Die Stufenbaulehre Adolf Julius Merkls' in Stefan Griller and Heinz Peter Rill (eds), *Rechtstheorie: Rechtsbegriff—Dynamik—Auslegung* (Springer, 2011) 81.

[197] Stanley L. Paulson, 'Zur Stufenbaulehre Merkls in ihrer Bedeutung für die Allgemeine Rechtslehre' in Robert Walter (ed), *Adolf J. Merkl: Werk und Wirksamkeit* (Manz, 1990) 93.

[198] Hans Kelsen, 'Adolf Merkl zu seinem siebzigsten Geburtstag' (1959/1960) 10 *Österreichische Zeitschrift für Öffentliches Recht* 313, 313.

[199] Koller (n 127) 106.

[200] Werner Krawietz, 'Die Lehre vom Stufenbau des Rechts—eine säkularisierte politische Theologie?' [1984] *Rechtstheorie (Beiheft 5)* 255, 263.

[201] Wiederin, 'Stufenbaulehre' (n 196) 81–2, referring to its importance in, especially, constitutional legal practice in Austria, Germany, and Switzerland.

Before going into the details of this theory, a linguistic remark seems pertinent at this point: in German, both Merkl and Kelsen use the term *Stufenbau der Rechtsordnung*, which has been rendered as 'the hierarchical structure of the legal order' by the translator.[202] Unfortunately, however, it is impossible to reflect fully all three basic elements of the *Stufenbau* concept in English: namely, that the law is a dynamic process, always in *statu nascendi*, and not a static and permanently fixed structure; that this dynamic process from the general (constitution) to the particular (individual legal acts) is gradual and step-like; and that the various legal norms created in this process are held together in a hierarchical relationship, by both the chain of delegation and the chain of derogation.[203] Furthermore, Merkl emphasizes the necessary distinction between the content and the form of the law: although there is a sheer—indeed even infinite—number of conceivable contents the law might have, the number of the forms it can take is finite.[204] And it ultimately is the form of the law, not its substance, which allows for a structural analysis of a legal order.[205] This is where the central merit of this theory lies, namely in perceiving legal norms in hierarchical structures[206] and its power to explain the structure and functioning of legal orders as well as their essential features, which—until then—have not been fully understood. We will subsequently see that this idea that legal norms are related to one another in a hierarchical relationship changed the way of regarding the law, 'developing' it from a more or less homogeneous bundle of legal provisions to a differentiated, continuously changing, and shifting system of norms, which nonetheless remains a unified entity on the basis of the *Grundnorm*.[207]

The combination of the basic norm and the hierarchy of norms not only allows for maintaining the strong disparity of 'is' and 'ought',[208] but also enables the observer to resolve questions of whether a certain norm is a valid legal norm and thus part of a given legal order, and whether a certain legal norm may have lost its validity and hence ceased to be part of a legal order, respectively.[209] The subsequent sections will therefore depict and analyse the theory of the hierarchy of norms as first developed by Merkl and subsequently integrated by Kelsen into his *Pure Theory of Law*. Section B will focus on the development of the chain of delegation, while section C will critically examine the chain of derogation.

[202] Kelsen, *Pure Theory* (n 54) 221. Owing to the unfortunate neglect of Merkl's innovative ideas abroad and their immense overshadowing by Kelsen's theory, no translation of Merkl's writings into English exist to this day.

[203] William Ebenstein, 'The Pure Theory of Law: Demythologizing Legal Thought' (1971) 59 *California Law Review* 617, 642–3.

[204] Merkl, 'Prolegomena' (n 195) 1071–3.

[205] Walter, *Aufbau der Rechtsordnung* (n 179) 53–4; Heinz Mayer, 'Die Theorie des rechtlichen Stufenbaus' in Robert Walter (ed), *Schwerpunkte der Reinen Rechtslehre* (Manz, 1992) 38.

[206] Raz, *Concept of a Legal System* (n 114) 105; Catherine Richmond, 'Preserving the Identity Crisis: Autonomy, System and Sovereignty in European Law' (1997) 16 *Law and Philosophy* 377, 388.

[207] Koller (n 127) 106.

[208] András Jakab, 'Problems of the *Stufenbaulehre*: Kelsen's Failure to Derive the Validity of a Norm from Another Norm' (2007) 20 *Canadian Journal of Law and Jurisprudence* 35, 53.

[209] Tessar (n 128) 42.

B. The chain of delegation

(1) The necessary hierarchization of the law

Despite the complexities of highly developed legal systems and the usually large number of different shapes the law can take, Merkl asserts that any given legal order—even the most primitive one where a chieftain wields absolute power—necessarily consists of at least two normative levels. The reason for this is that even the very enthronization of said chieftain requires prior normative authorization.[210] Therefore, any legal order is necessarily ordered in a hierarchical manner and contains at least one level of 'absolute norm-creation' and one level of 'absolute norm-application'. A legal order may well possess more hierarchical levels than just these two, but a legal order consisting of only one legal form is inconceivable.[211] The assumption that the law is necessarily hierarchized has become subject to fervid criticism, most notably to the allegation that the hierarchy of norms is nothing less than a secularized and political theology, which conforms to the idea of a religiously and politically motivated hierarchization in the legal sphere.[212]

This accusation seems to be all the more fitting when considering that Merkl later changed his mind and also accepted that legal orders may only contain one single legal form,[213] which would, allegedly, only leave one superior metaphysical (or divine) norm, authorizing the single inferior norm. Yet this is exactly where Kelsen's and Merkl's theories meet, because when we presuppose, as Merkl did, something like a logical-transcendental 'source norm' (*Ursprungsnorm*) as an authorizing norm,[214] it becomes possible to imagine a legal order with only one single legal form below the source norm. The source norm itself is to be understood as the 'constitution in a legal-logical meaning'[215] that 'enthrones the law-creating authority'[216] and enables the observer to cognize the legal system as the product of a common source.[217]

Owing to these similarities with the key characteristics of Kelsen's *Grundnorm*[218] and, most importantly, the absence of any substantive content, any criticism of the hierarchy of norms because of their concealed theological and political nature must be dismissed. In fact, whether it is called source norm or basic norm is irrelevant, because as a transcendental a priori criterion, it allows for explaining the creation of different legal forms within any legal order[219] and without recourse to any metaphysical or divine sources.

210 Adolf Julius Merkl, *Die Lehre von der Rechtskraft entwickelt aus dem Rechtsbegriff* (Deuticke, 1923) 208–209, and fn 2; Adolf Julius Merkl, 'Gesetzesrecht und Richterrecht' in Hans R. Klecatsky, René Marcic, and Herbert Schambeck (eds), *Die Wiener rechtstheoretische Schule: Schriften von Hans Kelsen, Adolf Merkl, Alfred Verdross, Band 2* (Verlag Österreich, 2010) 1326.

211 Merkl, 'Das doppelte Rechtsantlitz' (n 195) 896; Merkl, 'Gesetzesrecht und Richterrecht' (n 210) 1325–6; Merkl, *Rechtskraft* (n 210) 210.

212 Krawietz (n 200) 260–1.

213 Merkl, 'Prolegomena' (n 195) 1073–6.

214 Ibid., 1091 and 1098; Merkl, *Rechtskraft* (n 210) 209 and 223.

215 Merkl, *Rechtskraft* (n 210) 209 fn 1.

216 Merkl, 'Gesetzesrecht und Richterrecht' (n 210) 1326.

217 Merkl, *Rechtskraft* (n 210) 210.

218 Martin Borowski, 'Concretized Norm and Sanction *qua* Fact in the Vienna School's *Stufenbaulehre*' (2014) 27 *Ratio Juris* 79, 82.

219 Wiederin, 'Stufenbaulehre' (n 196) 89–90.

(2) Conditions of norm-creation

More sophisticated legal orders usually possess more than two hierarchical levels of legal norms. It is typical of them to contain intermediate steps, which—in Merkl's parlance—are determining as well as determined norms. These norms, however, do not stand side by side in an unrelated fashion, but depend on one another in a genetic relationship.[220] And it is this connection, chain, or relation between *determining* norms (i.e. norms determining the creation and the validity of lower norms) and *determined* norms (i.e. norms whose creation and validity is determined by higher norms) to which Merkl refers as the chain of delegation or authorization.[221] This is where Merkl glimpses the specific dynamic element of law-creation: there is a necessary chain of delegation between determining and determined norms in the sense that the determined norm is not only created in accordance with the determining norm, but also by it.[222] This means that the higher norms usually contain the rules for creating lower norms by persons authorized to do so. The number of hierarchical levels is consequently determined by the sum of those norms that are subject to the same conditions of validity and which are hence of equal hierarchical rank.[223] Merkl enjoyed speaking in metaphors, and accordingly he likened the law to a river flowing down from the basic or source norm in step-like cascades or cataracts, where the legal science purifies its troubled waters in filter beds before it empties into the ocean of legal particularities.[224]

Beyond this dynamic character, the law also governs its own creation on the basis of its hierarchical nature. This means that one legal norm determines the method and way in which another norm is created, and—to some extent—the contents of that norm.[225] Furthermore, as a norm is valid because it has been created in a certain way determined by another norm, the latter is the immediate reason for the validity of the newly created norm and its 'belonging' to the same legal order. This relationship of hierarchical creation can be best presented as a relationship of super- and subordination, since the norm regulating the creation of another norm is the higher, the norm created in conformity with the former is the lower norm. The result is a legal order which does not consist of coordinated norms on equal levels, but of a hierarchy of different levels of legal norms. This chain of validity, pervading the lowest to the highest normative level brings about unity, since it eventually ends up in the presupposed basic norm. The *Grundnorm* therefore is the highest reason for the validity of norms, one created in conformity with another.[226]

220 Behrend (n 166) 16–17.
221 Merkl, 'Prolegomena' (n 195) 1098–9.
222 Merkl, *Rechtskraft* (n 210) 217; Merkl, 'Prolegomena' (n 195) 1098–9.
223 Koller (n 127) 109.
224 Merkl, 'Prolegomena' (n 195) 1101; Adolf Julius Merkl, 'Das Recht im Lichte seiner Anwendung' in Hans R. Klecatsky, René Marcic, and Herbert Schambeck (eds), *Die Wiener rechtstheoretische Schule: Schriften von Hans Kelsen, Adolf Merkl, Alfred Verdross, Band 1* (Verlag Österreich, 2010) 969; Theo Öhlinger, *Der Stufenbau der Rechtsordnung: Rechtstheoretische und ideologische Aspekte* (Manz, 1975) 9–10.
225 Kelsen, *General Theory* (n 104) 123–4; Merkl, 'Prolegomena' (n 195) 1099.
226 Kelsen, *Pure Theory* (n 54) 221–2.

In addition to Merkl's line of thought, Kelsen emphasizes another specific aspect of the *Stufenbau* doctrine: instead of the dichotomy of *determining* and *determined* norms, he uses the terms *general-abstract* and *individual-concrete* norms. The distinction between these two types of norms is inherent in the essence of the law and does not require any codification by positive legal norms to be effective. Moreover, these different steps are constituted by different legal forms, and the legal order, building upon these forms, hence appears as a sequence of a gradually increasing individualization and concretization of the law.[227] The result is that the further one moves downwards in the hierarchy of norms, the greater the concretization of the law,[228] since lower levels are bound by the decisions on content taken at higher levels.[229]

As an illustrative example of such a hierarchical legal order, Merkl and Kelsen cite the constitution as the highest level of positive law, which takes priority, both logically and genetically,[230] over all other legal norms, such as ordinary legislation and statutes, and hence governs their creation and thus their validity. Yet since the constitution is necessarily of general-abstract nature, it requires individualization and concretization through the law to be applicable in a meaningful way.[231] Legislation and statutes, in turn, determine ordinances, judicial decisions, and individual legal acts, such as contracts.[232] Therefore, it is important to note that the validity of the superior norm regulating the creation of the inferior norm always grounds the validity of that inferior norm, which means, *e contrario*, that lower-level legal norms are valid only if the constitution is valid. This *conditio sine qua non* formula, however, raises some issues that need to be addressed at this point.

(3) Consequences and problems

The usual depiction of the hierarchy of norms as a pyramid,[233] in which the creation and the validity of the law flows from the top to the bottom, has provoked its fair share of criticism. On the one hand, the proponents of the *Stufenbau* doctrine were criticized for failing to clarify whether this model only referred to an ideal legal order or whether it was to be understood as the description of a real legal order.[234] This criticism is, however, entirely unfounded, since the concept of the hierarchy of norms has to be distinguished from the concrete legal order to which it is being applied and from which it derives its content. In fact, all the *Stufenbau* doctrine does is to depict and identify the pre-existing hierarchical structure of a legal order, and it

[227] Kelsen, *Allgemeine Staatslehre* (n 85) 232–5.
[228] Borowski, 'Concretized Norm' (n 218) 84.
[229] Merkl, *Rechtskraft* (n 210) 221; Merkl, 'Prolegomena' (n 195) 1078–9; Kelsen, *Introduction* (n 28) 68; Kelsen, *Pure Theory* (n 54) 230.
[230] Wiederin, 'Stufenbaulehre' (n 196) 88.
[231] Kelsen, *Allgemeine Staatslehre* (n 85) 230–32; Kelsen, *Pure Theory* (n 54) 230.
[232] Merkl, *Rechtskraft* (n 210) 213 and 217; Merkl, 'Prolegomena' (n 195) 1078–83; Kelsen, *Pure Theory* (n 54) 221–67; Kelsen, *General Theory* (n 104) 123–36.
[233] Hans Kelsen, 'Die Selbstbestimmung des Rechts' in Hans R. Klecatsky, René Marcic, and Herbert Schambeck (eds), *Die Wiener rechtstheoretische Schule: Schriften von Hans Kelsen, Adolf Merkl, Alfred Verdross, Band 2* (Verlag Österreich, 2010) 1185.
[234] See Krawietz (n 200) 262, reproaching Merkl for freely switching between these two notions.

does not make any demands as to how the positive law be structured.[235] What Merkl describes as the 'ideal structure' of a legal order is the above-mentioned minimum of two hierarchical steps in contrast to the 'real structure' of many more legal forms.[236] Merkl's notion of the 'ideal structure' must therefore not be misunderstood as containing a normative dimension or as an *aliud* vis-à-vis existing legal orders. The ideal structure of the law rather denotes the fundamental structure that is a necessary and essential part of every single legal order, and ideal and real legal structures should be regarded as concentric circles.[237]

On the other hand, one could criticize the *Stufenbau* doctrine for failing to describe legal reality accurately. Several constitutions allow for irregular law-creation where specific hierarchical steps may be skipped (e.g. ordinances adopted directly on the basis of constitutional provisions, and not of a statute)[238] or where a legal act is partially based on the constitution and partially based on a statute,[239] thus leading to a situation where legislative and executive acts are to be considered coordinate and not subordinate acts.[240] Accordingly, Joseph Raz points out that the metaphor of a pyramid is oversimplified as it suggests that one norm can only determine or create norms on the subsequent and inferior level. He therefore proposes a 'tree diagram' that allows for norms that can authorize the creation of both general and individual norms, and authorities that can create both constitutional and individual norms.[241]

Merkl and Kelsen regarded this line of criticism as justified right from the outset and accepted that both the constitution and statutes may delegate certain types of ordinances, such as implementing ordinances.[242] They similarly concede that in a democratically and constitutionally governed state, certain steps may be omitted or even extended by introducing additional steps.[243] As a result, Merkl especially describes the relation between different legal forms in non-hierarchical metaphors, and likens the legal order to a widely branched system of legal forms, similar to the nerve system constituted by the brain or a system of blood vessels with the heart at its centre.[244] It appears that it was the label of a *hierarchy* of norms (which Merkl eventually chose) that significantly contributed to the success of this doctrine.[245] The problem with this very label is, nonetheless, that its memorable nature conceals the innovative and useful substance underneath it.[246] In the end, it is irrelevant which picture or metaphor one chooses to depict the hierarchical structure of the law,

[235] Walter, *Aufbau der Rechtsordnung* (n 179) 67.
[236] Merkl, 'Gesetzesrecht und Richterrecht' (n 210) 1326; Merkl, *Rechtskraft* (n 210) 215–16.
[237] Behrend (n 166) 19–20.
[238] See e.g. in Austria (Articles 18(3)-(5) B-VG) or Switzerland (Article 184 BV).
[239] See e.g. in Austria (Article 18(2) B-VG) or Germany (Article 80 GG).
[240] Erich Voegelin, 'Die Einheit des Rechtes und das soziale Sinngebilde Staat' (1930/1931) 5 *Zeitschrift für Theorie des Rechts* 58, 69.
[241] Raz, *Concept of a Legal System* (n 114) 99 fn 1.
[242] Merkl, 'Prolegomena' (n 195) 1095.
[243] Ibid., 1073–4; Adolf Julius Merkl, *Allgemeines Verwaltungsrecht* (Springer 1927) 174–5; Kelsen, *Pure Theory* (n 54) 224.
[244] Merkl, 'Recht im Lichte seiner Anwendung' (n 224) 969.
[245] Krawietz (n 200) 256.
[246] Wiederin, 'Stufenbaulehre' (n 196) 91 fn 57.

simply because it does not concern the underlying theoretical concept, but merely positive legal phenomena building upon this concept.[247]

Robert Walter expresses a similar, yet more fundamental critique. He draws attention to the fact that—in the case of constitutional or statutory amendment—superior norms are occasionally 'co-determined' by inferior norms.[248] In Austria, for example, the creation of superior constitutional norms is also determined by inferior ordinary legislation, such as the Act on the Rules of Parliamentary Procedure[249] or the Act on the Federal Law Gazette.[250] In the United Kingdom, comparably, statutes adopted by Parliament frequently empower government officials to fill gaps or further substantiate details of a policy laid down by primary legislation.[251]

Both examples appear rather to conform to a bottom-up approach, which would counteract the basic rationale of the hierarchy of norms. At this point, it needs to be recalled, however, that the *determining* relationship between norms of different hierarchical steps also comprises a *validating* relationship between them, and such temporal priority (or posteriority) must also be understood as logical priority (or posteriority). Insofar as one norm cannot exist without the relevant antecedent (i.e. superior and determining) norm, such a superior norm is necessary for the existence of the inferior norm.[252] In logical terms, such a conditional relationship is called replication, according to which the validity of a superior norm is a *necessary*, but not a *sufficient* condition for the validity of an inferior norm: (inferior) norm χ is valid only if (superior) norm ϕ is valid, and such a replication is false if the first premise is true and the second premise is false. Ergo it can be excluded that, in a legal order, norm ϕ is invalid whilst norm χ is valid.[253]

If applied to the examples above, it becomes obvious that the problem of an apparent bottom-up approach can be resolved satisfactorily: in the case of Austria, ordinary statutes may well influence how constitutional norms are being created, but it nonetheless remains possible to conceive of the ordinary statutes to be invalid without assuming the same for the statute amending the constitution. The reason for this is simple because if it were impossible to consider the constitution as a 'self-supporting structure' regarding ordinary statutes, then the constitution could necessarily never be effectuated if it addresses the legislature. In this case, it would be unfeasible to adopt an ordinary statute based on the constitution in the first place.[254] The same is true for the phenomenon of delegated legislation in the United Kingdom. Section 4(1) of the Legislative and Regulatory Reform Act 2006[255] explicitly lays down that no legislative power has been transferred to the executive

[247] Mayer, 'Theorie des rechtlichen Stufenbaus' (n 205) 41.
[248] Walter, *Aufbau der Rechtsordnung* (n 179) 62.
[249] Bundesgesetz über die Geschäftsordnung des Nationalrates (Geschäftsordnungsgesetz 1975), BGBl No 410/1975 as amended by BGBl I No 6/2014 and 99/2014.
[250] Bundesgesetz über das Bundesgesetzblatt (Bundesgesetzblatt 2004), BGBl I No 100/2003 as amended by BGBl I No 33/2013.
[251] Michael Asimow, 'Delegated Legislation: United States and United Kingdom' (1983) 3 *Oxford Journal of Legal Studies* 253, 253 fn 1.
[252] Merkl, 'Prolegomena' (n 195) 1094; Kelsen, *Pure Theory* (n 54) 221.
[253] Hubert Gerhard Fackeldey, *Handlungsnormen: Typologie und Logik* (Peter Lang, 2005) 232–3.
[254] Wiederin, 'Stufenbaulehre' (n 196) 95.
[255] 2006 c. 51.

decision-maker to be used as they see fit. A delegated legislator is, most importantly, only exercising power on behalf of the primary legislator, which means that it remains subject to Parliament's direction and control, and ultimately forms part of a hierarchical normative structure in Merkl and Kelsen's sense.

C. The chain of derogation

The picture of the normative hierarchy that Merkl and Kelsen painted so far remains incomplete without a second element, which is the *Derogationszusammenhang*, or the chain of derogation between norms. Whilst the chain of delegation concerns the *creation* of norms in a hierarchical system, the chain of derogation denotes the hierarchical structure of a legal order with respect to the *change* of norms, i.e. the derogating power of norms and their capability of abrogating or repealing the validity of other norms.[256] In this sense, derogation is the particular function of a norm whose content it is to repeal another norm. This usually happens if the legislator is authorized to adopt such a derogating norm and thereby repeals the validity of the prior norm.[257] Derogation may be complete (i.e. the norm ceases to exist entirely) or partial (i.e. the validity of a norm is being curtailed at the expense of another norm).[258] The subsequent sections will hence illustrate and analyse the crucial duplicity of the hierarchy of norms—delegation and derogation (which, as Walter warns, should not be mixed[259])—and elaborate on the differences between these two different chains.

(1) Merkl's concept of derogation

Merkl observes that norms are hierarchically ordered not only from a logical aspect (i.e. when assessing their interdependence under the chain of delegation), but also from a positive-legal viewpoint, concerning their legislating powers. This means, *in concreto*, that a norm having derogating power over another norm, which lacks such a power over the former, is of hierarchically superior rank in comparison to the latter. Conversely, if two norms are capable of derogating one another, they must inevitably have equal hierarchical rank.[260] Simply put, if norm φ can derogate norm χ, then the former is superior or posterior vis-à-vis the latter.[261] Although Merkl does not explicitly use these terms at this point, one can clearly see that these two results

[256] Bettina Stoitzner, 'Die Lehre vom Stufenbau der Rechtsordnung' in Stanley L. Paulson and Robert Walter (eds), *Untersuchungen zur Reinen Rechtslehre* (Manz, 1986) 63.
[257] Franz Bydlinski, *Juristische Methodenlehre und Rechtsbegriff* (2nd edn; Springer, 1991) 572.
[258] Jakab, 'Problems of the *Stufenbaulehre*' (n 208) 57; Öhlinger, *Stufenbau* (n 224) 22.
[259] Robert Walter, 'Die Lehre vom Stufenbau der Rechtsordnung' (1980) 13 *Archivum Iuridicum Cracoviense* 5, 9.
[260] Merkl, 'Prolegomena' (n 195) 1094.
[261] Jakab, 'Problems of the *Stufenbaulehre*' (n 208) 56.

follow the two traditional conflict-solving rules of superiority, *lex superior derogat legi inferiori*, and posteriority, *lex posterior derogat legi priori*.[262]

Subsequently, Merkl enumerates a sequence of legal forms, which stand to one another in a relationship of either superiority (constitutional provisions versus ordinary statutes; ordinary statutes versus ordinances; and ordinances versus judicial or administrative decision) or equality (federal and provincial statutes; and ordinary statutes and constitutional ordinances).[263] On the basis of these criteria, Merkl introduces another normative pyramid that is, as will be shown below, not identical to the chain of delegation, and thus raises interesting questions.

To begin with, Merkl highlights that every legal order is, at any time of its validity, self-contained, complete, and definite.[264] From this, he concludes that the law is, according to the normative-logical principle of *res iudicata*, immutable and unchangeable,[265] analogous to the total amount of energy that remains constant within an isolated system.[266] Thus, any changes in the law are not a necessary, but a mere contingent feature. It is only on the basis of positive legal provisions that existing norms can be modified, amended, or derogated; ergo any option for legal change must be enshrined in the legal order itself.[267] Hence, since the validity of norms is a normative-logical principle, a norm is necessarily valid until the conditions for derogation laid down in the determining norm are satisfied.[268] This means, vice versa, that if the positive law fails to govern how to amend and derogate the law, a legal norm remains unchangeable, even on the basis of the *lex posterior* principle.[269] Thereby Merkl provides evidence that *any* change or derogation of a legal norm requires an explicit authorization in the law itself, and that mere logical principles are insufficient. Accordingly, normative conflicts are merely contingent, and derogations simply possible, not necessary.[270] This finding not only had a considerable influence on Kelsen, who expressly agreed with Merkl in this regard,[271] but also on Hart, who considers the change or derogation of 'primary rules' (governing conduct

[262] Martin Borowski, 'Die Lehre vom Stufenbau des Rechts nach Adolf Julius Merkl' in Stanley L. Paulson and Michael Stolleis (eds), *Hans Kelsen: Staatsrechtslehrer und Rechtstheoretiker des 20. Jahrhunderts* (Mohr-Siebeck, 2005) 152; Wiederin, 'Stufenbaulehre' (n 196) 106.

[263] Merkl, 'Prolegomena' (n 195) 1094–5.

[264] Merkl, *Rechtskraft* (n 210) 234 and 238.

[265] Adolf Julius Merkl, 'Die Unveränderlichkeit von Gesetzen—ein normlogisches Prinzip' in Hans R. Klecatsky, René Marcic, and Herbert Schambeck (eds), *Die Wiener rechtstheoretische Schule: Schriften von Hans Kelsen, Adolf Merkl, Alfred Verdross, Band 1* (Verlag Österreich, 2010) 887; Adolf Julius Merkl, 'Die Rechtseinheit des österreichischen Staates' in Hans R. Klecatsky, René Marcic, and Herbert Schambeck (eds), *Die Wiener rechtstheoretische Schule: Schriften von Hans Kelsen, Adolf Merkl, Alfred Verdross, Band 1* (Verlag Österreich, 2010) 934; Merkl, *Rechtskraft* (n 210) 234.

[266] Wiederin, 'Stufenbaulehre' (n 197) 106. For the first law of thermodynamics see e.g. Martin Bailyn, *A Survey of Thermodynamics* (American Institute of Physics, 1994) 79.

[267] The potential for changing the law cannot be enshrined in the *Grundnorm* either, because this norm is necessarily unchangeable. If it were changeable, the identity and unity of a legal order could not be upheld; Merkl, *Rechtskraft* (n 210) 241 and 246.

[268] Behrend (n 166) 36–7; Merkl, *Rechtskraft* (n 210) 229–30.

[269] Adolf Julius Merkl, 'Zum Problem der Rechtskraft in Justiz und Verwaltung' in Hans R. Klecatsky, René Marcic, and Herbert Schambeck (eds), *Die Wiener rechtstheoretische Schule: Schriften von Hans Kelsen, Adolf Merkl, Alfred Verdross, Band 2* (Verlag Österreich, 2010) 990–1.

[270] Borowski, 'Lehre vom Stufenbau' (n 262) 135.

[271] Kelsen, *Problem der Souveränität* (n 57) 114 and 115 fn 1.

and behaviour) dependent on the existence of so-called 'secondary rules', which regulate the creation, change, and derogation of primary rules.[272]

Yet, even though Merkl stresses that the exact arrangement of the chain of derogation must be made by taking into account all positive legal requirements of a particular legal order,[273] the argument that such a chain of derogation within a parliamentary and democratic legal order is merely contingent remains unconvincing.[274] It is undoubtedly true that most positive legal orders are imperfect in providing for clear and obvious derogation rules. The reason for this lies in the incorrect assumption that derogation issues are resolvable on the basis of logical reasoning, and that, as a result, the positive law is not responsible for providing any solutions.[275] But this might ultimately lead to serious problems, as a democratic legal order with separated powers and a complex legal system cannot forego a hierarchical structure governed by a chain of derogation without concurrently giving up its democratic and constitutional nature. It may well be the case that ordinances derogate statutes,[276] but a legal order in which the constitution does not enjoy primacy over all other legal forms does not deserve to be called parliamentary, democratic, and—most importantly—constitutional. Similarly, the superiority of statutes and ordinances over individual legal acts is indispensable in such a legal order, and the hierarchization of the law under the chain of derogation in the constitution, general statutory norms, and individual legal acts becomes necessary.[277] Eventually, even Merkl concedes that derogation is necessary, simply to guarantee the identity of a given legal order through its own rules of change.[278]

This raises another problem, namely the relationship between the chain of delegation and the chain of derogation. Often it is simply assumed that every norm, which enjoys superiority in terms of delegation, also necessarily enjoys the same superiority with respect to derogation. Yet Merkl acknowledges a potential difference regarding delegation and derogation within a legal order. He concedes that the normative hierarchy in the context of delegation and derogation, respectively, does not necessarily correspond to each other. Even within one single legal order, there may be several normative hierarchies with different hierarchical steps,[279] and the chain of derogation cannot be deduced from the chain of delegation.[280]

[272] Hart, *The Concept of Law* (n 52) 93 ff. As Borowski, 'Concretized Norm' (n 218) 83 states that: '[I]t is remarkable that Merkl, already in 1931—thirty years before H.L.A. Hart published *The Concept of Law*—distinguished clearly between two different kinds of rule in the legal system' and that 'Hart's idea of secondary rules was already clearly present in Merkl's [theory of the hierarchy of norms]'.

[273] Merkl, 'Prolegomena' (n 195) 1096.

[274] Borowski, 'Lehre vom Stufenbau' (n 262) 153.

[275] Walter, 'Lehre vom Stufenbau' (n 259) 11.

[276] See Robert Walter, 'Können Verordnungen Gesetzen derogieren?' (1961) 16 *Österreichische Juristen-Zeitung* 2, 7, who nonetheless concludes in the end that ordinances may confine the effect of statutes in a legal order, but not completely annul them.

[277] Borowski, 'Lehre vom Stufenbau' (n 262) 153.

[278] Merkl, *Rechtskraft* (n 210) 239 and 259.

[279] Merkl, 'Prolegomena' (n 195) 1096 and 1103.

[280] Walter, *Aufbau der Rechtsordnung* (n 179) 67–8; Walter, 'Lehre vom Stufenbau' (n 259) 13.

Merkl demonstrates the duplicate or sometimes even antidromic[281] nature of these two hierarchical chains with the example of judicial decisions by courts of different jurisdictional levels and instances. For instance, the decision of a lower court determines the remedial decision of the higher court. Therefore, it appears that the chain of delegation is reversed in this case[282] and antidromic to the chain of derogation, according to which the higher court may certainly repeal the decision of the lower court.[283] This example of the duplicity and antidromicity of Merkl's two hierarchical chains is, however, somewhat dubious. The decision of the lower court may certainly *factually* determine the decision of the higher court, but not *normatively*. Consequently, there is no chain of delegation between these two decisions, which could be considered in a relationship of sub- and superordination. In fact, the relationship between the two decisions can be better characterized as a coordinated relation between norms of the same hierarchical rank; namely that of the relevant rules of procedure, usually contained in statutory law. And it is these rules that ultimately provide for the derogating power of a particular judicial decision. Hence there is no genuine antidromicity of the chains of delegation and derogation in the case of judicial decisions.[284]

It is nonetheless possible to find genuine examples of divergence in the positive law. There are, for instance, constitutional provisions that have been created in accordance with pre-existing other constitutional provisions (and which are therefore determining the former), but which may nevertheless have derogating power over the determining norm in question (in particular as to how subsequent norms may be created).[285] Having said that, however, there is nevertheless a close nexus between the chains of derogation and delegation: both demonstrate how law can be created, and it is therefore simply the authorization to create law that is depicted differently in these two hierarchical chains. The chain of delegation shows how certain provisions on the creation of legal norms *authorize to create* law and hence how the created law is deducible from this authorizing norm. The chain of derogation, conversely, reveals the extent to which certain legal norms are *authorized to derogate* other legal norms. Thus, the latter simply occupies a very specific area within the chain of delegation, and it would be practical to deduce the rules on derogation from the rules of delegation in a legal order[286] and to compare the conditions of norm-creation: norms that are more difficult to create (most notably constitutional provisions) are more significant than those that are easier to create (e.g. ordinary statutes). Therefore, provisions of higher sophistication in terms of their creation cannot be derogated by provisions of lower sophistication and thus have derogatory power over the latter.[287]

Opinions as to whether the chains of delegation and derogation are compatible tend to differ sharply, and Merkl himself seems to be lost in contradictions.[288] On

281 Behrend (n 166) 38. 282 Merkl, *Rechtskraft* (n 210) 215.

283 Merkl, 'Prolegomena' (n 195) 1097.

284 Behrend (n 166) 40; Borowski, 'Lehre vom Stufenbau' (n 262) 154–6.

285 Walter, *Aufbau der Rechtsordnung* (n 179) 66.

286 Ibid., 65, and Walter, 'Lehre vom Stufenbau' (n 259) 11 fn 17 and 13–14.

287 Mayer, 'Theorie des rechtlichen Stufenbaus' (n 205) 42–3.

288 Jörg Kammerhofer, 'Robert Walter, die Normkonflikte und der zweite Stufenbau des Rechts' in Clemens Jabloner and others (eds), *Gedenkschrift Robert Walter* (Manz, 2013) 254.

the one hand, he states that a norm derogating another norm can only be of superior rank vis-à-vis the latter; in other words, only the source of the latter's validity can be the reason for its invalidity.[289] On the other hand he also remarks that the positive-legal authorization to create specific norms does not comprise the authorization to change or derogate said norms.[290] In fact he doubts that the chain of derogation might be somehow deduced from the chain of delegation and claims, quite sceptically, that 'it would be fantastic to be able to glean from the form of a legal act the way it can be changed'.[291]

The ultimate reconciliation between the two hierarchical chains would, however, be in Merkl's interest, who considers this duplicity unsatisfactory and attempts to connect the two chains without organically combining them.[292] The most convincing argument in favour of a synchronous and unidirectional flow of the two chains is that their duplicity and antidromicity would lead to the peculiar result that every single legal order contained two different hierarchical systems, which would not only deviate, but also conflict with one another. Delegation and derogation cannot be two separate and independent criteria of normative hierarchy; in fact, they must be interrelated, because a clear-cut subordination of determined norms to determining norms is only possible if the superior norms concurrently have the power to derogate (i.e. repeal) their inferior counterparts.[293]

Yet, the problem with this view is that, ultimately, authorizing and derogating norms have, as Kelsen has shown, different normative functions.[294] While the former govern the creation of an 'ought', the latter regulate a 'non-ought'. Metaphorically speaking, the mother of a child is not necessarily its murderer, as the authorization to create differs from the authorization to annul.[295] Moreover, empirical reality also contradicts this view, since not all superior norms (with respect to the chain of delegation) also have the power to derogate inferior norms.[296] As a result, it may be an idealistic goal to attempt to reconcile the two chains with one another, but it also appears to be a dead end, as there is no connotatively necessary equality of the derogatory norms with the delegating norms on whose basis they have been created.[297] Such an assumption would, first, only defer the problem towards the norm-creating norms,[298] and, secondly, not be compatible with the generally accepted premise that the chain of derogation, as a contingent element, must not be superimposed on a given legal order, but be deduced from it itself.[299]

In conclusion, the chain of derogation should therefore be accepted as a useful tool, which must, nonetheless, be developed and conceptualized in the light of the observed positive legal order. To this date, a satisfactory solution to combine

[289] Merkl, *Rechtskraft* (n 210) 256. [290] Ibid., 260–1.
[291] Ibid., 299. [292] Merkl, 'Prolegomena' (n 195) 1094 ff.
[293] Koller (n 127) 110 and 112. [294] Kelsen (n 170) 96–101.
[295] Kammerhofer, 'Robert Walter' (n 288) 254–5.
[296] Walter, *Aufbau der Rechtsordnung* (n 179) 66.
[297] Wiederin, 'Stufenbaulehre' (n 196) 118.
[298] Rainer Lippold, *Recht und Ordnung* (Manz, 2000) 392.
[299] Walter, *Aufbau der Rechtsordnung* (n 179) 67–8; Walter, 'Lehre vom Stufenbau' (n 259) 6 and 14–15.

the chains of delegation and derogation has not been found and awaits further research.[300] But perhaps this duplicity and antidromicity issue is not as significant as is often presented, as it only concerns a positive legal area of the hierarchy of norms, and not its normative-logical foundations. Possibly, this also explains why Kelsen, who fully acknowledges the importance of Merkl's *Stufenbau* doctrine, only takes into consideration the chain of delegation.[301] Kelsen, as will be subsequently shown, therefore conceives of a different concept of derogation.

(2) Kelsen's early concept of derogation: logical resolvability of conflicts

In his early writings, Kelsen assumes that any conflicts between norms can be resolved on the basis of logical principles. This logical resolving of conflicts, however, only applies to cases of *material* derogation where a prior norm is implicitly annulled through a posterior norm that is substantially incompatible with the former.[302] *Formal* derogation, in contrast, denotes the procedure in which one specific norm is explicitly annulled without the promulgation of another norm, and does not involve a normative conflict.[303] In other words, Kelsen holds in his early views that normative conflicts brought about by substantial incompatibility can be resolved a priori, following the principle of non-contradiction.[304]

Norm conflicts necessarily entail that one of the norms in question is invalid. The principle of non-contradiction, however, is only applicable *per analogiam*, because, as already discussed above,[305] only assertions that are either true or false are subject to it. Norms, as 'ought' statements, cannot be true or false, but only valid or invalid. The principle of non-contradiction can therefore only be analogously or indirectly applied to the assertions describing the legal norms in question, thus basically equating the norm (*Rechtsnorm*) and the norm-describing assertion (*Rechtsnormsatz*).[306] This means that if such a norm-describing assertion is true, the described norm is valid; if the assertion is false, the norm is invalid.[307] Hence, it is impossible for norms to logically stand in contradiction with one another,[308] which also entails that the chain of derogation can be derived from the chain of delegation.[309]

A logical view of the hierarchy of norms means that (apparent) conflicts are possible between norms of the same level and between norms of different levels. The first conflict is, according to Kelsen, a conflict between norms created by the same organ (or even two different organs authorized to regulate the same subject matter)

[300] Borowski, 'Lehre vom Stufenbau' (n 262) 156; Wiederin, 'Stufenbaulehre' (n 196) 118.

[301] Kelsen, *Pure Theory* (n 54) 221; Kelsen, *General Theory* (n 104) 155.

[302] Robert Walter, 'Reine Rechtslehre und Gesetzgebungstechnik' in Harald Kindermann (ed), *Studien zu einer Theorie der Gesetzgebung 1982* (Springer, 1982) 148–9.

[303] Rudolf Thienel, 'Derogation: Eine Untersuchung auf Grundlage der Reinen Rechtslehre' in Robert Walter (ed), *Untersuchungen zur Reinen Rechtslehre II* (Manz, 1988) 23–4.

[304] Bindreiter, *Why* Grundnorm*?* (n 145) 142.

[305] See section 3C.

[306] Stanley L. Paulson, 'Zum Problem der Normenkonflikte' (1980) 66 *Archiv für Rechts- und Sozialphilosophie* 487, 494.

[307] Kelsen, *Pure Theory* (n 54) 74 and 205–6.

[308] Bindreiter, *Why* Grundnorm*?* (n 145) 144.

[309] Walter, *Aufbau der Rechtsordnung* (n 179) 59–60.

at different times. In this case, the validity of the later norm supersedes the validity of the earlier and contradictory norm under the *lex posterior* principle, because the authorization to prescribe changeable and thereby abolishable norms is presumed to be already included in that very authorization.[310] Legal science must necessarily proceed to this conclusion lest the relation between norms become meaningless. And meaningful normative relations include, as Kelsen puts it, a basic norm that comprises presupposed principles of interpretation such as the *lex posterior* rule[311]—a rule for which there is a fundamental preference in all systems.[312]

In contrast to conflicts of norms on the same level, Kelsen emphasizes that conflicts of norms between different levels are logically impossible.[313] The reason for this is that on each hierarchical level validity is made dependent on the conformity with norms of a superior level, and since inferior norms in contradiction to them cannot be valid, normative conflicts can be ruled out entirely in the sense of an automatic derogation.[314] The *lex superior* principle is therefore seen as authorizing the creation of only those inferior norms that correspond in content to the superior norm.[315] As such, it allows for the resolution of inconsistencies in any given legal order, and thus prevents *leges inferiores* from prevailing, which would topple a constitutional legal order into absurdity[316] and legal uncertainty. Hence any conflicts between norms of different hierarchical levels are self-contradictory, and occurrences such as 'unlawful' judicial decisions or 'unconstitutional' statutes would be null and void from the outset and not legal norms at all, as something that is null cannot be annulled.[317] This corresponds to an objective assessment of the correspondence between inferior and superior norms and is not dependent on an explicit act of will by an authorized organ.[318]

It should be noted that this is a very radical view, since any act that was not first authorized by a superior norm is to be considered automatically invalid. Moreover, because the authority or body that enacted the norm in question cannot have the concurrent authority to decide on its validity in the light of the constitution, this act of review rests by default with those to whom the act is addressed, namely the law-abiding citizen.[319] This assumption, i.e. that any single citizen may contest norms to the effect of automatic nullity, would, however, not only be extremely impractical, but also highly dangerous. In this vein, Kelsen cautiously backs away from

310 Kelsen, *Pure Theory* (n 54) 206; Kelsen, *General Theory* (n 104) 155–6.

311 Kelsen, *General Theory* (n 104) 402.

312 Ota Weinberger, 'The Expressive Conception of Norms: An Impasse for the Logic of Norms' in Stanley L. Paulson and Bonnie Litschewski Paulson (eds), *Normativity and Norms: Critical Perspectives on Kelsenian Themes* (reprint; Clarendon Press, 2007) 425.

313 Kelsen, *Pure Theory* (n 54) 208.

314 Inés Weyland, 'Idealism and Realism in Kelsen's Treatment of Norm Conflicts' in Richard Tur and William Twining (eds), *Essays on Kelsen* (Clarendon Press, 1986) 250.

315 Pierluigi Chiassoni, '*Wiener* Realism' in Luís Duarte d'Almeida, John Gardner, and Leslie Green (eds), *Kelsen Revisited: New Essays on the Pure Theory of Law* (Hart Publishing, 2013) 142.

316 Theodor Schilling, *Rang und Geltung von Normen in gestuften Rechtsordnungen* (Nomos, 1994) 400; Erich Vranes, '*Lex Superior, Lex Specialis, Lex Posterior*—Zur Rechtsnatur der "Konfliktlösungsregeln"' (2005) 65 *Zeitschrift für ausländisches öffentliches Recht und Völkerrecht* 391, 398.

317 Kelsen, *Pure Theory* (n 54) 267–8.

318 Weyland (n 314) 251; Thienel (n 303) 37.

319 Kelsen, *Allgemeine Staatslehre* (n 85) 289–90.

this exclusive logical view on derogation. By introducing the subjective criterion of annullability to test the validity of such contentious norms, he then appears to take a first tentative step towards a positive-legal and anti-logical understanding.[320]

In his objective and logical reasoning so far, he would say that the statement 'a valid statute is "unconstitutional" ' is self-contradictory, because a statute can only be valid on the basis of the constitution. And an invalid statute cannot be presumed to be unconstitutional, as it is no statute at all and thus legally non-existent.[321] Yet, under a more subjective reasoning, the term 'unconstitutional' denotes that the statute in question can be repealed not only on the basis of an ordinary constitutional procedure, through which the statute is annulled by another statute (under the *lex posterior* rule), but also in accordance with a special procedure provided for by the constitution, such as a review mechanism before a constitutional court.[322] In other words, an act of will to derogate the norm in question is required.[323] This means, a fortiori, that until the statute in question is not repealed, it must be presumed as valid and cannot be regarded as unconstitutional. Consequently, there is no such thing as a logical *ab initio* 'nullity' in law, and any errors in the law are mollified by the concept of voidability or annullability. Hence norms remain valid until their annulment,[324] which inevitably makes the decisions of a reviewing court always constitutive, not declaratory.[325]

Because of these considerations, Kelsen concludes that there can be no real contradictions between an inferior and a superior norm, because the higher norm determines the existence of its lower counterpart. This in fact means that any allegedly 'unconstitutional' or 'illegal' legal act must be presupposed as valid, but it nonetheless carries the possibility of being annulled if found in contravention to a superior norm. Accordingly, a contradiction between two norms of different levels cannot occur, and—most importantly—'the unity of the legal order can never be endangered by any contradiction between a higher and a lower norm in the hierarchy of law'.[326]

(3) Merkl's concept of the Fehlerkalkül

Merkl generally agrees with Kelsen that a legal act is only attributable to the state if it was actually determined by the respective superior norm, which entails that any minor defectiveness in this legal act would result in its absolute nullity.[327] Merkl,

[320] Stanley L. Paulson, 'On the Status of the *lex posterior* Derogating Rule' in Richard Tur and William Twining (eds), *Essays on Kelsen* (Clarendon Press, 1986) 243.

[321] Kelsen, *Pure Theory* (n 54) 271; Kelsen, *General Theory* (n 104) 155–6.

[322] Hans Kelsen, 'Wesen und Entwicklung der Staatsgerichtsbarkeit' in Hans R. Klecatsky, René Marcic, and Herbert Schambeck (eds), *Die Wiener rechtstheoretische Schule: Schriften von Hans Kelsen, Adolf Merkl, Alfred Verdross, Band 2* (Verlag Österreich, 2010) 1502 ff.

[323] Thienel (n 303) 37. [324] Kelsen, *Pure Theory* (n 54) 271 and 276–7.

[325] Kelsen, 'Wesen und Entwicklung' (n 322) 1520.

[326] Kelsen, *General Theory* (n 104) 161–2.

[327] Merkl, *Rechtskraft* (n 210) 287; Hans Kelsen, 'Über Staatsunrecht' in Hans R. Klecatsky, René Marcic, and Herbert Schambeck (eds), *Die Wiener rechtstheoretische Schule: Schriften von Hans Kelsen, Adolf Merkl, Alfred Verdross, Band 1* (Verlag Österreich, 2010) 823.

however, quickly adds that this assumption might well be justified from a theoretical perspective, but it nonetheless remains irreconcilable with legal reality, as even the slightest violation of a condition for the validity of a given legal act would automatically result in its immediate nullity. The expression 'unlawful' or 'invalid law' would for that reason be a *contradictio in adiecto*.[328] Accordingly, a faulty legal act would not even exist as such, and neither its repeal nor cassation or its amendment as a non-entity would be meaningful. As a result, only two types of legal acts could exist, and neither would allow for their derogation: (i) perfect legal acts whose repeal is *per definitionem* impossible; and (ii) non-legal acts that cannot have any legal effect and whose repeal is therefore meaningless.[329]

In order to resolve this antinomy, Merkl devises the theory of the *Fehlerkalkül* ('error-calculus'), which enables the law to accept a certain degree of deficiency in legal acts, whose actual gravity can then be determined on the basis of positive-legal provisions.[330] In other words, the concept of the *Fehlerkalkül* comprises those positive-legal provisions which permit taking into account such legal acts that have not been created in full accordance with the relevant determining norms.[331] It thereby allows to cognize deficient legal acts as valid law despite their deficiencies, and the expression 'invalid law' ceases to be a logical absurdity.[332]

The law accepts the inevitability of authorities making mistakes by lowering its own strict requirements, thereby permitting for a certain latitude between the ideal and the barely possible. This does not mean that law-positing authorities are entirely exempt from making mistakes; it only means that what the authority in question does within the margin of the existing *Fehlerkalkül* is to be regarded as valid law.[333] At the lower end, the law provides for the minimum or necessary conditions for a legal act to be valid, and if these conditions are not met, the legal act is indeed a legal nullity and can be ignored.[334] At the top, a legal act may qualify as satisfying the maximum or sufficient conditions, which means that it is perfectly valid and not subject to repeal on the grounds of illegality.[335] But the law may certainly content itself with less than this ideal maximum.[336] Therefore, any legal acts ranging between the minimum and the maximum conditions are to be regarded as *prima facie* valid, but nonetheless also open to being contested—which may result in declaring the act

[328] Adolf Julius Merkl, 'Justizirrtum und Rechtswahrheit' in Hans R. Klecatsky, René Marcic, and Herbert Schambeck (eds), *Die Wiener rechtstheoretische Schule: Schriften von Hans Kelsen, Adolf Merkl, Alfred Verdross, Band 1* (Verlag Österreich, 2010) 162.

[329] Christoph Kletzer, 'Kelsen's Development of the *Fehlerkalkül*-Theory' (2005) 18 *Ratio Juris* 46, 47.

[330] Merkl, 'Recht im Lichte seiner Anwendung' (n 224) 976; Merkl, *Rechtskraft* (n 210) 292–3.

[331] Concrete examples for the positive-legal grounding of the *Fehlerkalkül* are any provisions governing legal remedies or the right to appeal, and the constitutional review of statutes.

[332] Merkl, 'Prolegomena' (n 195) 1110; Merkl, *Allgemeines Verwaltungsrecht* (n 243) 196.

[333] Merkl, *Rechtskraft* (n 210) 296–7.

[334] Kletzer, 'Kelsen's Development' (n 329) 48; Tessar (n 128) 276; examples for this include an authority's obvious lack of jurisdiction; ultra vires acts; or evidently impermissible acts.

[335] Kletzer, 'Kelsen's Development' (n 329) 48; Borowski, 'Lehre vom Stufenbau' (n 262) 151. In other words, such a legal act has been created in perfect accordance with the respective determining norm.

[336] Schilling, *Rang und Geltung* (n 316) 581.

in question valid despite minor defects (at one end of the spectrum)[337] or in its utter invalidation (at the other end of the spectrum). So what the *Fehlerkalkül* does is not to correct the deficient legal act *ex post*, but merely to protect it from an inevitable logical slide into legal nullity.[338] Alternatively, it is not the deficiency of the legal act that is resolved, but only its consequences.[339]

Ultimately, however, there are three major problems with the theory of the *Fehlerkalkül*. First, it could be argued that the minimum conditions for a legal act to be above absolute and immediate nullity are nothing less than the conditions for the creation of the legal act in the first place. Secondly, the *Fehlerkalkül* depends upon positive regulation for its existence, which means that either all legal acts are immediately invalid if defective and if there is no provision regarding the *Fehlerkalkül* at all. Or, if there is such a provision, but no distinction between minimum and maximum conditions, even the least important conditions would be, by default, minimum conditions. In other words, all conditions for law-creation would need to be satisfied in every case.[340] The third and last problem is that the *Fehlerkalkül* may well succeed in explaining the existence of unlawful yet valid legal acts that can be repealed, but it fails to achieve the same result with respect to rulings of courts of last resort. In this case, the decision is final and its 'lawfulness' can no longer be contested. And since positive law itself accords this quality to such rulings (a point that will be shown to be untrue below), it is also evident that the legal order does not allow for any appeals against this decision.[341] Thereby deficient decisions can easily be perpetuated and never repealed. This problem inspired the older Kelsen to devise the theory of the *Alternativermächtigung* ('alternative authorization'), which will be discussed in the subsequent section.

(4) Kelsen's later concept of derogation: positive law and the Alternativermächtigung

After the second edition of the *Pure Theory of Law* in 1960, Kelsen takes a radical turn in his *General Theory of Norms* (published posthumously in 1979)[342] towards an anti-logical[343] and positivist approach to normative conflicts and derogation, without, however, explicitly building upon Merkl's writings.[344] This view is also in accordance with the predominant opinion on this matter, namely that logical inference among normative sentences is conceptually impossible.[345] Overall, the older Kelsen opines that derogation in general and the *lex posterior* rule in particular, are

337 Merkl, *Rechtskraft* (n 210) 301; Merkl, *Allgemeines Verwaltungsrecht* (n 243) 196.
338 Wiederin, 'Stufenbaulehre' (n 196) 122 and 127.
339 Günther Winkler, *Der Bescheid* (Manz, 1956) 40–1.
340 Kammerhofer, *Uncertainty* (n 149) 189.
341 Kelsen, *Pure Theory* (n 54) 269; Kletzer, 'Kelsen's Development' (n 329) 51.
342 Kelsen, *General Theory of Norms* (n 170).
343 In the sense of 'contingent' or 'a posteriori' and thus in contrast to 'necessary' and 'a priori'.
344 Paulson, 'On the Status' (n 320) 244; Thienel (n 303) 12.
345 Jørgensen (n 161) 288–96; Karel Engliš, 'Die Norm ist kein Urteil' (1964) 50 *Archiv für Rechts- und Sozialphilosophie* 305–16.

not logical principles, and that logical rules cannot be applied to normative conflicts.[346] Building upon these foundations, Kelsen also attempts to explain how inferior norms in obvious conflict with superior norms must be considered valid until formally repealed, thereby trading the logical principle of *lex superior* for the theory of 'alternative authorization'.

Kelsen explains that the term 'derogation' is a specific function of norms besides commanding, permitting, and authorizing, and it applies when the validity of an already valid norm is repealed by another norm.[347] This very function of derogation may occur in two different situations, namely: first, when there is *no* actual conflict and the norm-positing authority considers the validity of a valid norm to be undesirable and decides to repeal it (i.e. *formal* derogation); or second, when a conflict exists between norms (i.e. *material* derogation).[348] While the former case is relatively straightforward as the derogating norm is created and then loses its validity upon invalidation of the derogated norm,[349] the latter case is more interesting, but also more complex. Kelsen proceeds by stating that since the 'ought' of a legal norm is firmly tied to the act of will on the part of the norm-positing authority, this very 'ought' cannot be related to its own obedience, since obedience is a property not of the norm itself but of the behaviour that conforms to the norm—and therefore to an 'is'.[350] From this, he concludes that normative conflicts are completely different from logical contradictions.[351] Normative conflicts are rather situations where a legal subject must necessarily violate one norm by obeying another, because the content of the first norm is incompatible with the content of the second norm.[352] Consequently, Kelsen's normative irrationalism, i.e. the inexistence of logical relations between normative sentences, dictates that the principle of non-contradiction cannot be applied to them and must fail to resolve normative conflicts. Instead of using logical principles, such situations can only be resolved by one or the other norm losing its validity, for instance via derogation.[353]

The most remarkable feature of this view is that it presupposes the simultaneous validity of both conflicting norms, because if one the conflicting norms were invalid, there would be no conflict in the first place.[354] Ergo the validity of two conflicting norms is compatible with each other[355] and should hence not be seen as a contradiction,

[346] Alchourrón and Bulygin, 'Expressive Conception' (n 158) 383 ff.

[347] Hans Kelsen, 'Derogation' in Hans Kelsen and Ota Weinberger (eds), *Essays in Legal and Moral Philosophy* (Reidel, 1973) 261; Kelsen, *General Theory of Norms* (n 170) 106.

[348] Kelsen, *General Theory of Norms* (n 170) 107; Sven Ove Hansson, *The Structure of Values and Norms* (Cambridge University Press, 2001) 205–6.

[349] Thienel (n 303) 24; Kelsen, *General Theory of Norms* (n 170) 108 and 216.

[350] Hans Kelsen, 'Law and Logic' in Hans Kelsen and Ota Weinberger (eds), *Essays in Legal and Moral Philosophy* (Reidel, 1973) 231 and 239–40; Kelsen, *General Theory of Norms* (n 170) 219–20.

[351] Kelsen, 'Derogation' (n 347) 271; Kelsen, 'Law and Logic' (n 350) 235.

[352] Kelsen, *General Theory of Norms* (n 170) 123.

[353] Ota Weinberger, 'Kelsens These von der Unanwendbarkeit logischer Regeln auf Normen' in *Die Reine Rechtslehre in wissenschaftlicher Diskussion* [no editor] (Manz, 1982) 113; Kelsen, 'Law and Logic' (n 350) 211 ff and 235.

[354] Kelsen, *General Theory of Norms* (n 170) 213; Kelsen, 'Derogation' (n 347) 271–2; Kelsen, 'Grundlagen der Naturrechtslehre' (n 107) 712.

[355] Stanley L. Paulson, 'Stellt die "Allgemeine Theorie der Normen" einen Bruch in Kelsens Lehre dar?' in *Die Reine Rechtslehre in wissenschaftlicher Diskussion* [no editor] (Manz, 1982) 123 and 131–2.

but rather as a conflict of duties,[356] or a situation where two forces act in two diametrically opposed directions.[357] Yet the validity of the two conflicting norms is to be presumed only *prima facie*; which of the two will remain valid will be decided on the basis of positive legal norms and hence a contingent act of volition.[358]

If we now apply these considerations to normative conflicts between norms of the same level, the *lex posterior* principle evidently sheds its logical character. As Merkl already concluded, it is not the *lex posterior* rule that makes changes in the law possible, but it is rather the positivized authorization in the legal order to do so, which allows this rule to be conceived of in the first place.[359] Kelsen consequently regards the *lex posterior* principle as misleading as it gives the impression that derogation is an inherent function of the later (i.e. posterior) norm, whilst it is, in fact, the function of a *third* positive norm. This means that normative conflicts may, 'but need not be, solved by derogation, and derogation will take place only if it is stipulated by a norm-creating authority'.[360] In the same sense as a normative conflict is not a logical contradiction, derogation is not a logical principle, but the function of a positive norm, which may be applied even in situations where there is no normative conflict.[361] Thus, normative conflicts do not entail any consequences, unless a legal order contains explicit rules on how to resolve such conflicts.[362]

Let us now consider Kelsen's anti-logical thoughts for the problem of conflicts between norms of different levels and the *lex superior* principle. In a very similar way to his earlier work, Kelsen explains in the *General Theory of Norms* that so-called 'unconstitutional' statutes are of course valid, because the constitution empowers the legislator to enact statutory law in the first place.[363] What he does not mention any more, however, is that conflicts between norms of different hierarchical levels are logically impossible. One could therefore say that such a conflict between norms of different levels is a mere subsumption error, and the key to identifying such conflicts is to construe the superior norm as the 'material authorization norm' (*materielle Ermächtigungsnorm*)[364] vis-à-vis the conflicting inferior norm. This means, simply put, that the authorization of the inferior norm stems from the applicable superior norm,[365] which confers powers and concurrently limits the exercise of these powers. Hence normative conflicts occur if (i) the inferior norm does not fall within the area

[356] Kelsen, *General Theory of Norms* (n 170) 214; Kelsen, 'Derogation' (n 347) 271.

[357] Hans Kelsen, 'Recht und Logik' in Hans R. Klecatsky, René Marcic, and Herbert Schambeck (eds), *Die Wiener rechtstheoretische Schule: Schriften von Hans Kelsen, Adolf Merkl, Alfred Verdross, Band 2* (Verlag Österreich, 2010) 1208.

[358] Paulson, 'Bruch in Kelsens Lehre' (n 355) 131–2; Kazimierz Opałek, *Überlegungen zu Hans Kelsens "Allgemeiner Theorie der Normen"* (Manz, 1980) 32.

[359] Merkl, 'Rechtseinheit' (n 265) 930.

[360] Kelsen, *General Theory of Norms* (n 170) 125.

[361] Kelsen, 'Derogation' (n 347) 273.

[362] Wiederin, 'Normenkonflikt' (n 169) 328.

[363] Kelsen, *General Theory of Norms* (n 170) 125.

[364] Hans Kelsen, 'Les rapports de système entre le droit interne et le droit de l'état (1926-IV) 14 *Recueil des cours* 231, 271–4; Kelsen, *Pure Theory* (n 54) 148–9, 176–8, and 221 ff.

[365] Stanley L. Paulson, 'Material and Formal Authorization in Kelsen's Pure Theory of Law' (1980) 39 *Cambridge Law Journal* 172, 172. In contrast to material authorization, formal authorization denotes the process wherein authorization of an inferior norm flows from the power of the legal organ that creates, applies, or validates that norm.

of powers that have been conferred by the superior norm in the first place; or (ii) if the inferior norm is incompatible with the limits of exercising these powers. Yet the question remains, what happens if such conflicts remain unresolved?[366]

For Kelsen, both norms are certainly valid and remain valid, for the time being. By stating this, however, Kelsen must face the problem of justifying the validity of such conflicting inferior norms, because to say that they are both valid and yet in conflict with a superior norm is in contradiction with the basic tenet that norms are only valid if their creation has been authorized by higher norms.[367] It is interesting to note that a justification for this approach has already been envisaged in the first edition of the *Pure Theory of Law*, wherein Kelsen states that the constitution always aims for the validity of all statutes and their conformity with the constitution, even of those in violation of it—otherwise the latter could not be considered valid. The evidence for this is shown in the fact that the constitution prescribes not only that statutes should be created in a certain way and have a certain content, but also that if a statute was created other than in the prescribed way or has other than the prescribed content, it is not regarded as null and void *ex tunc*, but remains valid until it has been invalidated by the designated authority.[368] Thereby Kelsen resorts to the theory of *Alternativermächtigung* ('alternative authorization'), which states that the validity of such an 'unconstitutional' statute can be repealed by a special procedure provided for in the constitution, for instance before a constitutional court. Thus, there is no real conflict between norms, since if the norm in question is valid, it is also constitutional. In other words, the constitution both empowers the legislator to enact the statute in question, but concurrently also provides that the contested statute can be repealed by a special procedure.[369]

In this vein, what is usually termed the 'unconstitutionality' of a statute is not a logical contradiction between the statute and the constitution, but rather a condition laid down in the constitution for initiating a procedure that either invalidates or confirms the statute in question. From this point of view, the constitutional provisions governing the creation and the content of statutes can only be understood in connection with those provisions that govern 'violations' and the eventual invalidation of 'unconstitutional' statutes. Both categories nonetheless form a unity and have the character of alternative provisions, which are, nevertheless, distinguished by a disqualification of the second alternative in favour of the first.[370]

This is also where the evident merit of the 'alternative authorization' theory in comparison to the *Fehlerkalkül* theory comes into play. The latter holds that rulings by courts of last instance are, owing to their finality, not subject to the *Fehlerkalkül*, and that such rulings are not final in themselves, but only because of positive-legal provisions.[371] In contrast to that, 'alternative authorization' holds that this view is

[366] Paulson, 'Bruch in Kelsens Lehre' (n 355) 138.
[367] Weyland (n 314) 262; Kelsen, 'Derogation' (n 347) 272.
[368] Kelsen, *Introduction* (n 28) 72.
[369] Kelsen, *General Theory of Norms* (n 170) 125; Kelsen, 'Derogation' (n 347) 272.
[370] Kelsen, *Pure Theory* (n 54) 269; Kelsen, *General Theory of Norms* (n 170) 125; Paulson, 'Bruch in Kelsens Lehre' (n 355) 138–9.
[371] Kletzer, 'Kelsen's Development' (n 329) 51.

incorrect since appeals procedures are created by positive law, and hence all norm-creation must necessarily be, by default, final, unless an appeals procedure is expressly enacted.[372] However, as such an 'unlawful' final decision is valid and not subject to annullability or nullity *ab initio*, there must be a way to find legal rules on the basis of which the validity of such decisions can be explained.[373]

Kelsen claims that finality goes beyond non-annullability. Indeed, it means that the general norm predetermining the content of the judicial decision also authorizes the court itself to determine the content of the individual norm to be created. In a similar way to the problem of 'unconstitutional' statutes, the two norms form a unit, 'because the court of last instance is authorized to create either an individual legal norm whose content is predetermined by the general norm, *or* an individual norm whose content is not so predetermined, but is to be determined by the court of last instance for itself'.[374] Alternatively, the reason why decisions by lower courts are voidable is not only their 'unlawfulness', but also—and more importantly—the possibility, provided by the legal order itself, to bring about their definitive validity by the court of last instance.[375]

In conclusion, the resolution of any given normative conflict is something that necessarily turns on the existence of some positivized third meta-norm. Logic can only tell us whether there is a conflict, but it cannot tell us which of the conflicting norms is to be given preference. Derogation is thus not a logical function, but always the consequence of a positive legal norm.[376]

D. Appraisal: the epistemological value of the hierarchy of norms

The above analysis demonstrates that the theory of the hierarchy of norms, as devised and envisaged by the Vienna School of Jurisprudence, has a dual claim, namely to be both a tool for cognizing the law's essential structure *and* an empirically testable theory.[377] In the role of the former, it presents itself as an *ideal* legal order; in the role of the latter, it appears as a depiction of an actually existing *real* legal order.[378] Yet it should also be recalled at this point that the *Stufenbau*-theory must not be applied schematically: the cognition of hierarchical levels within any given legal order may only be derived from an existing positive legal order, which means, vice versa, that they must not be 'read' into the positive law.[379]

The *Stufenbau* theory remains a core element of the pure theory of law, and its significance within the latter's overall theoretical framework should not be

372 Kammerhofer, *Uncertainty* (n 149) 189.

373 Kletzer, 'Kelsen's Development' (n 329) 52; Kammerhofer, *Uncertainty* (n 149) 190.

374 Kelsen, *Pure Theory* (n 54) 269.

375 Ibid., 269–70.

376 Chiassoni (n 315) 150.

377 Bernd-Christian Funk, 'Die Leistungsfähigkeit der Stufenbaulehre: Zur Wissenssoziologie eines reduzierten Positivismus' in Stefan Griller and Heinz Peter Rill (eds), *Rechtstheorie: Rechtsbegriff—Dynamik—Auslegung* (Springer, 2011) 195.

378 Behrend (n 166) 19–30; Stoitzner (n 256) 75–6.

379 Mayer, 'Theorie des rechtlichen Stufenbaus' (n 205) 45; Walter, 'Lehre vom Stufenbau' (n 259) 14.

underestimated.[380] In a logically clear manner, it explains how it is possible to cognize both the creation and the change of the law on the basis of the chains of delegation and derogation in conformity with the duality of 'is' and 'ought'. With respect to the first aspect, it shows us that law is necessarily organized in hierarchical structures, as norm-application requires a superior level of norm-creation in any event. This means, a fortiori, that individual norms are always determined by more general norms, which are ultimately derived from the *Grundnorm*, and that thus the law logically determines its own creation. Eventually, it is this very structure that enables the observer to cognize and understand whether a specific legal act forms part of a given legal order or not, and what degree of individuation a specific norm possesses.[381] The second aspect of the *Stufenbau* is the mirror image of creation, namely the change and derogation of the law. Thereby the hierarchy of norms also provides for a way to cognize whether any given norm is deficient or not,[382] and, if in the affirmative, how the positive law may govern its ultimate repeal. Beyond that, the theory of the *Fehlerkalkül* and its further development in the concept of the *Alternativermächtigung* mitigate the radical logical consequence of such deficiencies and protect deficient norms from being automatically invalid *ab initio*.

Yet what is most important in the context of this book is another valuable merit of the hierarchy of norms. This merit is that the concept of the *Stufenbau* and its transcendental apex in shape of the *Grundnorm* laid the theoretical foundations for extending the hierarchical structure of the law beyond national law. Via this step, the pure theory of law also accomplishes the integration of the international legal order and offers a unitary view of the law in entirety. This aspect will be discussed in the subsequent chapter.

5. Legal Monism: The Necessary Unity of National and International Law

It is well known that the proponents of the pure theory of law did not only concern themselves exclusively with national law and its epistemological foundations, but also wrote extensively about international law and its theoretical underpinnings.[383] In the context of this book, the main focus will especially be on the works of Kelsen and his students Verdross and Kunz; and more concretely on the relationship between international law and national law. The international legal aspects of the pure theory of law form an integral part of the overall theoretical construct of the Vienna

[380] Wiederin, 'Stufenbaulehre' (n 196) 84.

[381] Walter, *Aufbau der Rechtsordnung* (n 179) 16–19.

[382] Borowski, 'Lehre vom Stufenbau' (n 262) 151.

[383] See e.g. Robert Walter, 'Die Rechtslehren von Kelsen und Verdross unter besonderer Berücksichtigung des Völkerrechts' in Robert Walter, Clemens Jabloner, and Klaus Zeleny (eds), *Hans Kelsen und das Völkerrecht* (Manz, 2004) 37–49; Alfred Rub, *Hans Kelsens Völkerrechslehre: Versuch einer Würdigung* (Schulthess Polygraphischer Verlag, 1995); García-Salmones Rovira (n 61) 120–56; Jochen von Bernstorff, *The Public International Law Theory of Hans Kelsen* (Cambridge University Press, 2010).

School[384] and should not be neglected by anyone wishing to go beyond an entirely empirical approach to the law in order to find a reliable guide through an increasingly complex interrelationship between multiple bodies of law.[385]

Although Kelsen constructed a legal theory that reflected the world of the early twentieth century, it remains—owing to its underlying epistemological considerations—also highly topical and immensely interesting to the world of the early twenty-first century. The main reason for this lies in Kelsen's project to develop a genuine and universally valid science of law in general and international law in particular—a science of positive law in general which is universally applicable.[386]

A. From the demise of sovereignty to the unity of the law

(1) Sovereignty: a chimera

It is commonly held that sovereign states are coeval with the birth of the international society through the Peace of Westphalia in 1648. This further substantiates Bodin's and Hobbes' claim of 'absolute State sovereignty' who consider this feature to be a necessary condition for the very existence of states.[387] Thus, states not only wield absolute power within their territory and over their population, but are also absolutely independent in their external dealings. Austin later argues that since law is the command of the sovereign and there is no common sovereign governing the relations of states with each other, international *law* is merely 'positive international morality'.[388] Yet given the increasing interrelationship and interdependence between states and other international legal subjects, this strict denial of international law as genuine law has been somewhat mitigated by the concept of 'relative sovereignty', which claims that even though states are subject to international law, they remain equal inter se.[389] Nonetheless, the notion of sovereignty remains the central concept in international law to describe and define the state in international legal terms,[390] as well as to ward off the subjection of the state to international law.[391] In this vein, proponents of state sovereignty argue that although states may comply with their international obligations, international law lacks effective enforcement mechanisms and therefore the key features of genuine legal norms. Ultimately, it

384 Jörg Kammerhofer, 'Kelsen—Which Kelsen? A Reapplication of the Pure Theory to International Law' (2009) 22 *Leiden Journal of International Law* 225, 225.

385 Charles Leben, 'Hans Kelsen and the Advancement of International Law' (1998) 9 *European Journal of International Law* 287, 287.

386 Kelsen, *Pure Theory* (n 54) 1.

387 Jean Bodin, *De re publica libri sex* (Jacob Dupuys, 1576) Book II, chapter I; Hobbes (n 49) Book II, chapters 17–21.

388 Austin (n 51) 127.

389 See e.g. Hans Aufricht, 'On Relative Sovereignty' (1944) 30 *Cornell Law Quarterly* 137, 137–59; Paul Guggenheim, 'Les principes de droit international public' (1952-I) 80 *Recueil des cours* 1, 84–5; Georg Schwarzenberger, 'The Forms of Sovereignty' (1957) 10 *Current Legal Problems* 264, 269–71.

390 Stefan Griller, *Die Übertragung von Hoheitsrechten auf zwischenstaatliche Einrichtungen* (Springer, 1989) 15–26.

391 Hans Kelsen, 'Souveränität' (1929) 40 *Die neue Rundschau* 433, 434.

seems quite evident that sovereignty puts the legal quality of the international legal order in doubt.[392]

Because of their 'pre-scientific'[393] character, Kelsen considers the concepts of both relative and absolute sovereignty untenable and intends to 'radically eliminate'[394] them from the vocabulary of international law—*nota bene*, however, as will be explained below, only in their non-legal dimension.[395] The idea of relative sovereignty can be easily refuted as it involves a *contradictio in adiecto*: the original sense of sovereignty is that of supreme power, but if power is limited by law, it cannot be supreme. Thus, to use the term 'relative' in this context is to distort 'sovereignty's' proper and original sense.[396] Absolute sovereignty, or sovereignty in its original sense, on the other hand, amounts to an undue methodological syncretism and thereby to a (re-) amalgamation of 'is' and 'ought': while the anthropomorphic view of the state as an absolutization in the form of a Hobbesian Leviathan is reminiscent of natural law and therefore to be rejected, the interpretation of the state as the most effective and most powerful force reduces the law to mere facts and is equally unacceptable in the light of the dichotomy of 'is' and 'ought'.[397]

As a result, Kelsen argues that the pre-existing notion of sovereignty cannot be derived jurisprudentially from the content of the positive law or from within it. Otherwise, sovereignty would merely represent a bundle of substantive competences, while a loss of sovereignty would simply amount to a curtailment of said competences. Yet any list of such core competences must always be arbitrary, non-exhaustive,[398] and hence theoretically unjustifiable, since describing sovereignty as the totality of state competences transforms this very notion from an attribute of the state into a symbol of the state itself.[399] In fact, Kelsen postulates that sovereignty is a property of the legal order, and not of the state in its power and effectivity, because the state itself is identical to its legal order that created it in the first place.[400]

The term 'sovereign State' simply denotes positive law, and 'sovereignty' thus merely represents a declaration of independence by the lawyers who assume that they are dealing with a system claiming validity in its own right and not as part of a wider system. As the quality of a normative legal order,[401] the concept of sovereignty in Kelsen's terms must therefore be regarded as a formal and norm-logical category and can only be absolute to the extent that it is a predicate of the subject

392 Vinx, *Kelsen's Pure Theory of Law* (n 108) 178.

393 Hans Kelsen, 'Der Wandel des Souveränitätsbegriffs' in Hanns Kurz (ed), *Volkssouveränität und Staatssouveränität* (reprint; Wissenschaftliche Buchgesellschaft, 1970) 164.

394 Kelsen, *Problem der Souveränität* (n 57) 320.

395 Vinx, *Kelsen's Pure Theory of Law* (n 108) 179.

396 Kelsen, 'Les rapports' (n 364) 311–13.

397 Kelsen, *Problem der Souveränität* (n 57) 2, 7–8, and 85–101.

398 Kelsen, 'Wandel' (n 393) 173; Kelsen, 'Souveränität' (n 391): especially the principle of territorial jurisdiction and its mirror-image, the prohibition to act extraterritorially, cannot be equated with sovereignty. See also Rub (n 383) 417.

399 Hans Kelsen, 'Souveränität' in Karl Strupp (ed), *Wörterbuch des Völkerrechts und der Diplomatie—Band 2* (de Gruyter 1925) 555.

400 Kelsen, *General Theory* (n 104) 181 ff; Kelsen, *Hauptprobleme* (n 66) 97 ff.

401 Hans Kelsen, *Principles of International Law* (Rinehart 1952) 438.

legal order.[402] Consequently, a sovereign legal order is an absolutely independent or highest order if and only if all of its legal norms can be derived from a norm that is not itself derived from any other norm. This gives us a good indication of the entity in which Kelsen sees the norm-logical and hierarchical attribute of sovereignty, namely the *Grundnorm* of a legal order.[403] In other words, sovereignty can be jurisprudentially derived from the basic norm and is thus conterminous with the core tenets of the pure theory of law, i.e. that the law is a unitary order, hierarchically ordered, not further derivable from either natural law or empirical facts, and governing its own creation and derogation. The theory of sovereignty is thereby transformed into the theory of the identity of legal systems[404] and becomes completely disconnected from the personified state or another factual entity.[405] In fact, by reducing sovereignty to its legal dimension, its manifestation as a factual and political notion becomes a scientifically useless chimera.[406]

(2) *The legal quality of international law*

The most important consequence of Kelsen's redefinition of the concept of sovereignty in an epistemologically and legally pure manner is that it undermines the outright denial of the legal character of international law and thereby provides the observer with the first step in considering international law as a body of law in its own right. In the next step, Kelsen accordingly tackles this issue again and, by convincingly arguing in favour of the legal quality of international law, defies the doubters and deniers of international law.[407]

The main criticism directed against the legal nature of international law is that it lacks, owing to its decentralized nature, certain characteristics that national law undoubtedly possesses: first and foremost, effective coercion and enforcement[408] through, for instance, obligatory jurisdiction by international courts.[409] Yet this is not a sufficient argument to deny international law its legal quality, as Kelsen explains, thus dismissing both purely positivist and realist arguments, which claim that there can be no international law until such time as the power to coerce states is concentrated in the hands of one single authority.[410] The reason for this is that

[402] Kelsen, *Problem der Souveränität* (n 57) 4–9 and 40–4; Wilhelm Jöckel, *Hans Kelsens rechtstheoretische Methode* (Mohr-Siebeck, 1930) 67.

[403] Kelsen, *Problem der Souveränität* (n 57) 97–101.

[404] Kelsen, *Principles of International Law* (n 401) 438–44; Kelsen, *Problem der Souveränität* (n 57) 4–21.

[405] Stanley L. Paulson, 'Methodological Dualism in Kelsen's *Das Problem der Souveränität*' in Agostino Carrino (ed), *Kelsen e il problema della sovranità* (Edizione scientifiche italiane, 1990) 89–94; von Bernstorff (n 383) 65.

[406] Walter, 'Rechtslehren von Kelsen und Verdross' (n 383) 39.

[407] In particular his contemporaries such as Felix Somló, *Juristische Grundlehre* (2nd edn; Meiner, 1927) 167 ff; Alexander von Hold-Ferneck, 'Anerkennung und Selbstbindung. Ein Beitrag zur Lehre vom Wesen des Völkerrechts' (1929) 4 *Zeitschrift für Rechtsphilosophie* 161 ff; Walther Burckhardt, *Über die Unvollkommenheit des Völkerrechts* (Haupt, 1923).

[408] Austin (n 51) 127.

[409] Somló (n 407) 163 ff, arguing that the denial of the legal quality of international law is only convincing because of the lack of efficiency of the international legal order.

[410] Raymond Aron, *Guerre et paix entre les nations* (3rd edn; Calmann-Lévy, 1962) 704–12.

international law may well be a 'primitive' legal order, as Kelsen himself puts it, because of its lack of a centralized special legislature, executive, and judiciary.[411] In fact, one might even consider it 'constitutionally deficient', as Hart did.[412] Nonetheless, international law is genuine law for the following reasons:

First, Kelsen states that it is the essential feature of positive legal orders that they—in contrast to other positive normative orders—try to bring about lawful and to prevent unlawful behaviour by coercive measures.[413] Coercive measures regularly amount to the infliction of an evil, such as the deprivation of life, health, liberty, or economic values, or the application of physical force.[414] Furthermore, it is an essential feature of the law as a coercive legal order that such measures are applied by particular organs that have a community monopoly of force.[415] Thus, coercion prescribed as reaction against a certain behaviour, through an organ that has been entrusted with the application of force and coercive measures is *the* distinguishing feature of law.[416]

Second, this premise now raises the decisive question[417] whether 'international law provide[s] for coercive acts (enforcement actions) as the consequence of a certain conduct of States determined by international law'[418] through specific organs. For Kelsen, the answer is in the affirmative since international law indeed provides for coercive measures, namely in the form of decentralized self-help. This leaves the function of coercing defaulting subjects to lawful behaviour to the legal subjects injured by the delict and the force monopoly of the international legal community.[419] At this point, it is, however, crucial to note that such monopolization does not equal centralization.[420] Regarding the shape that such decentralized self-help may take, Kelsen principally accepts reprisals and war as adequate coercive measures, and even takes into account the centralization of the use of force in form of the United Nations Security Council.[421]

These considerations may appear very odd to the contemporary international lawyer who has been brought up on a steady diet of the prohibition of the use of force,[422] but they are nevertheless without prejudice to the theoretical foundations

[411] Kelsen, *Problem der Souveränität* (n 57) 266–67; Kelsen, *Principles of International Law* (n 401) 22, 36, and 139.

[412] Hart, *The Concept of Law* (n 52) 90–3 and 224–31, stating that there are only primary rules on rights and obligations in international law, but no secondary rules to settle questions of what these rules are or what their exact scope is.

[413] Hans Kelsen, 'Collective Security under International Law' (1954) 49 *Naval War College International Law Studies* 1, 101.

[414] Kelsen, *Pure Theory* (n 54) 33–4; Kelsen, *General Theory* (n 104) 50–1.

[415] Hans Kelsen, *Peace through Law* (University of North Carolina Press 1944) 3; Kelsen, *Pure Theory* (n 54) 36–7; Kelsen, *General Theory* (n 104) 21.

[416] Kammerhofer, 'Kelsen—Which Kelsen?' (n 384) 227–8.

[417] Alexander Somek, 'Kelsen Lives' (2007) 18 *European Journal of International Law* 409, 435.

[418] Kelsen, *Principles of International Law* (n 401) 22.

[419] Kelsen, *Problem der Souveränität* (n 57) 258; Kelsen, *Principles of International Law* (n 401) 14–15.

[420] Hans Kelsen, *Law and Peace in International Relations: The Oliver Wendell Holmes Lectures, 1940-1941* (Harvard University Press, 1942) 50.

[421] Kelsen, *Principles of International Law* (n 401) 20–89.

[422] Kammerhofer, 'Kelsen—Which Kelsen?' (n 384) 229.

of the legal quality of international law. The prohibition of the use of force may be the rule,[423] but exceptions in the form of self-defence or collective security[424] are still permissible. Without the lawful and coercive use of force, 'there is no international law',[425] and this very doctrine has now been enshrined in Chapter VII of the UN Charter.[426] Equally, reprisals (or in more modern parlance: countermeasures[427]), as acts that are in themselves illegal, may be adopted by one state in retaliation for the commission of an earlier illegal act by another state, but must always remain short of the use of force. From a practical perspective, these restrictions on the use of force are certainly welcome and not to be underestimated for a peaceful international legal order; but from a theoretical viewpoint, however, it is irrelevant whether the use of force in these specific forms of coercive measures has been curtailed or not. It is equally irrelevant whether these coercive measures are fully effective or not; it is sufficient that international law foresees them in one way or another.[428]

It follows from the above two premises that international law constitutes genuine law, according to Kelsen's definition. As long as the international legal order speaks of unlawful acts (delicts) and coercive measures to redress them (sanctions), international law is a legal order, no matter how inefficiently this order may work in singular cases. Thus, if such sanctions are provided for, public international law exists.[429]

(3) The epistemological necessity of legal unity

a. The unity of the object of cognizance

After having demonstrated that international law exists as proper law, and not as mere positive morality, Kelsen proceeds to the actual lynchpin of legal monism, which is its epistemological necessity flowing from the law as a unitary object of cognizance. Before going into the details of Kelsen's line of reasoning, it should be recalled at this point that Kelsen's thinking is undoubtedly rooted in Kantian and neo-Kantian philosophy. Kant deduces in his *Critique of Pure Reason* that cognition cannot be purely a priori or a posteriori; in fact, we must already have rational concepts available to us when the empirical manifold of impressions impinges upon our senses. Otherwise we could not make sense of these impressions. For Kant, these

423 See Article 2(4) of the UN Charter and *Military and Paramilitary Activities in and against Nicaragua (Nicaragua v United States)* [1986] ICJ Reports 14, para 290.

424 See Article 51 of the United Nations Charter.

425 Hans Kelsen, 'Völkerrechtliche Verträge zu Lasten Dritter' (1934) 14 *Prager Juristische Zeitschrift* 419, 427.

426 Hans Kelsen, *The Law of the United Nations* (Praeger, 1951) 727–37.

427 See International Law Commission, Articles on Responsibility of States for Internationally Wrongful Acts 2001 (ARS 2001), Commentary, introduction to Part III, Chapter II 'Countermeasures', para 1, in International Law Commission, *Report of the International Law Commission on the Work of its Fifty-Third Session*, UN Doc A/56/10 (2001) 29, 296.

428 Kelsen, *Law and Peace* (n 420) 15; Kelsen, *Allgemeine Staatslehre* (n 85) 124–5.

429 Somek, 'Kelsen Lives' (n 417) 435–6.

concepts are therefore a priori fundamental categories such as unity and multiplicity; reality and negation; or existence and possibility.[430]

From this follows the so-called principle of the necessary unity of apperception,[431] stating that all of my representations must be grounded in pure apperception, that is, in the thoroughgoing identity of the self in all possible representations.[432] This is the transcendental self, as illustrated above.[433] In other words, it must be the case that each of my representations can be attributed to myself; a subject that is not only the same for all of my self-attributions, but also that is distinct from these representations, and which can be conscious of them.[434] And is this very transcendental unity of apperception 'through which all of the empirical manifold given in an intuition is united in a concept of the object'?[435] In a nutshell, it is therefore the unitary consciousness of the observer that constitutes the unity of the observed object.

In the light of Kantian epistemology, Kelsen develops his thoughts based on an epistemological position according to which it is the method that creates the object of legal science. And this method transforms everything it affects, just as Midas turns everything into gold,[436] into a unitary object of cognition. The cognition of an object and the cognition of its unity is therefore the same. And even though Kelsen refrains from providing a final definition of the law as the object of cognition, it is possible to construe the following definition from his scientific programme: positive law is a system of coercive norms that have been posited by human beings for the regulation of their behaviour; and in addition this system must be effective and govern its own creation.[437] In the same sense as there is only one chemistry,[438] this definition and delimitation of the law creates a unity of all law and it thereby becomes an epistemological unit.[439]

The task of the jurist is therefore to conceive of the law as a system of 'ought'-propositions that is (at least before Kelsen's norm-logical turn) free of contradictions. Hence, it is the application of the a priori legal 'ought'-categories, carried out in the mind of the jurist, to posited norms that creates the law as an 'ought'-order[440]

430 Kant, *Kritik der reinen Vernunft* (n 34) A 77/B 102–A 80/B 106. Note that merely being able to detect that there are two impressions requires the concepts of existence and multiplicity.

431 Apperception is the apprehension of a mental state as one's own, or the self-ascription of self-attribution of a mental state; see Peter Strawson, *Bounds of Sense: Essay on Kant's* Critique of Pure Reason (Routledge, 1966) 93–4.

432 Kant, *Kritik der reinen Vernunft* (n 34) B 131–2.

433 See section 1C.

434 Kant, *Kritik der reinen Vernunft* (n 34) A 116/B 131–2 and B 134–5.

435 Ibid., B 139.

436 H.L.A. Hart, 'Kelsen's Doctrine of the Unity of Law' in Stanley L. Paulson and Bonnie Litschewski Paulson (eds), *Normativity and Norms: Critical Perspectives on Kelsenian Themes* (reprint; Clarendon Press, 2007) 563.

437 Heinz Mayer, Gabriele Kucsko-Stadlmayer, and Karl Stöger, *Grundriss des Österreichischen Bundesverfassungsrechts* (11th edn; Manz, 2015) para 2; Clemens Jabloner, 'Der Rechtsbegriff bei Hans Kelsen' in Stefan Griller and Heinz Peter Rill (eds), *Rechtstheorie: Rechtsbegriff—Dynamik—Auslegung* (Springer, 2011) 23.

438 Immanuel Kant, 'Die Metaphysik der Sitten' in Immanuel Kant (ed), *Gesammelte Schriften* (Deutsche Akademie der Wissenschaften, 1907) AA 6:207.

439 Kammerhofer, 'Kelsen—Which Kelsen?' (n 384) 234.

440 von Bernstorff (n 383) 79.

on the basis of the unifying *Grundnorm* as a transcendental category.[441] As a result, it becomes impossible to deny that the law, as the object cognitively created in this manner, is of an epistemologically unitary nature. For Kelsen, the epistemological unity of all law is the *conditio sine qua non* for the establishment of legal science as an independent discipline,[442] and it can only become this by fulfilling the postulate of the unity of its knowledge, and by succeeding in cognizing the law as a unitary system.[443] The ultimate conclusion of the postulate that the same ought to be cognized as the same[444] is, as Kelsen himself puts it, that '[t]he unity of the epistemological standpoint demands imperiously a monistic view'.[445]

b. The legal nature of international law entails legal unity

At this point, the genuine legal nature of international law becomes crucial for the systemic unity of the law in two aspects. First, the unity of the law can only be denied if one excludes the entire international legal order from the system of law. Only then would the two orders—national and international law—be located on two completely different levels of cognition and the epistemological unity would disappear.[446] The 'validity' of national law would then have a meaning different from the 'validity' of international law. In other words, one could say that the pure theory does not intend to prove the legal quality of international law; the only thing it is explicitly stating is that if one conceives of international law as law, then it necessarily is part of a unitary system of law, together with national law.[447]

Yet—and this is the second aspect that follows from the legal quality of international law—Kelsen observes that less radical proponents of state sovereignty do not utterly deny the existence or legal nature of international law.[448] In fact, most of them wish to perceive both international and municipal law as simultaneously valid legal orders.[449] To this end, they adopt a dualist outlook and maintain that national and international law are disparate legal orders; that they govern, because of their different sources, dissimilar substantive areas; that they address different legal subjects; and that normative conflicts between them are irresolvable.[450] However, this intermediary view of accepting international law as law, but simultaneously regarding it as being distinct from national law is indefensible, as '[t]here is no halfway house between monism and the theory that international law is not law'.[451]

[441] Stefan Hammer, 'Kelsens Grundnormkonzeption als neukantianische Erkenntnistheorie des Rechts?' in Stanley L. Paulson and Robert Walter (eds), *Untersuchungen zur Reinen Rechtslehre* (Manz, 1986) 215.

[442] von Bernstorff (n 383) 79.

[443] Kelsen, *Problem der Souveränität* (n 57) 152.

[444] Kammerhofer, 'Kelsen—Which Kelsen?' (n 384) 234.

[445] Kelsen, *Problem der Souveränität* (n 57) 123.

[446] Ibid., 124; von Bernstorff (n 383) 79–80.

[447] Theo Öhlinger, 'Die Einheit des Rechts: Völkerrecht, Europarecht und staatliches Recht als einheitliches Rechtssystem?' in Stanley L. Paulson and Michael Stolleis (eds), *Hans Kelsen: Staatsrechtslehrer und Rechtstheoretiker des 20. Jahrhunderts* (Mohr-Siebeck, 2005) 167–8.

[448] Kelsen, *Pure Theory* (n 54) 329.

[449] Kelsen, *Problem der Souveränität* (n 57) 120–2; Kelsen, *Principles of International Law* (n 401) 424 ff, comparing this argument to the dichotomy of positive law and morality.

[450] See in general Heinrich Triepel, *Völkerrecht und Landesrecht* (C. L. Hirschfeld 1899) and Dionisio Anzilotti, *Corso di diritto internazionale, Vol I* (3rd edn; Athenaeum, 1928).

[451] Starke, 'Monism and Dualism' (n 121) 74.

Epistemologically, it is—from a positive aspect—impossible not to place all normative material into a logical interpretative context, or to derive two legal systems from different sources. Beyond that it is—from a negative aspect—equally impossible to conceive of two equally valid and yet conflicting norms, just as it is impossible to conceive of a conflict between a moral rule ('you shall not kill') and a legal provision ('murderers are to be executed') and their simultaneous and continuous validity within one normative system.[452] One way or another, the validity of one of these rules will be contested.

Thus, to accept international law as genuine law necessarily results in conceiving of international and national law as a monist legal order. Yet nonetheless, another piece of the puzzle is still missing, as Kelsen's student Verdross points out. Verdross himself also regards international and national law as a unitary legal system (albeit from a natural law viewpoint[453]), but also implies that unity can only be achieved through a theory of norm-creating delegation.[454] Otherwise, and without such a theory, all norms purporting to delegate a subordinate legal order would merely *claim* to create unity, such as a madman might claim to delegate all the world's laws.[455] In other words, legal unity also requires that superior norms delegate the creation of inferior norms and that all of these norms are derived from one single source.[456]

c. Two versions of primacy

As discussed above,[457] the term 'delegation' encompasses the authorization, through the hierarchy of norms, to create norms, which thereby become delegated norms.[458] Applied to a monist system of international and national law, this also means that there is a chain of delegation connecting these two bodies of law. A fortiori, one of them must be subordinated to the other one, since the latter contains a norm that determines the creation of the norms of the former; hence the former has the reason of its validity in the latter. Ultimately, this validity is derived from a common *Grundnorm*, which concludes the hierarchy of norms and unifies international and national law into one legal order.[459] For the sake of completeness, however, Kelsen also mentions a scenario in which national and international law form an (allegedly) monist legal order in a coordinated way, standing side by side, delimiting their spheres of validity against one another. Yet, when considering the hierarchy of norms, this scenario becomes logically impossible as it would require a *third* superimposed body of law that would govern the formers' creation—but there is no such superior body of law above both international and national law.[460] Ergo,

[452] Kelsen, *Problem der Souveränität* (n 57) 107–14; Kelsen, *Pure Theory* (n 54) 328–9.

[453] See e.g. Alfred Verdross, *Die Einheit des rechtlichen Weltbildes* (Mohr-Siebeck, 1923); Alfred Verdross, *Die Verfassung der Völkerrechtsgemeinschaft* (Springer, 1926).

[454] Verdross, *Einheit des rechtlichen Weltbildes* (n 453) 76.

[455] Kammerhofer, 'Kelsen—Which Kelsen?' (n 384) 235–6.

[456] Kelsen, *Problem der Souveränität* (n 57) 107.

[457] See section 4B.

[458] Kelsen, 'Les rapports' (n 364) 271; Kelsen, *Problem der Souveränität* (n 57) 51.

[459] Kelsen, *Pure Theory* (n 54) 332; Kelsen, *Principles of International Law* (n 401) 408 ff.

[460] Hans Kelsen, 'Die Einheit von Völkerrecht und staatlichem Recht' (1958) 19 *Zeitschrift für ausländisches öffentliches Recht und Völkerrecht* 234, 234; Kelsen, *Pure Theory* (n 54) 332.

subordination of one body of law to the other one remains the only logical possibility. In this monist legal order, the delegated body of law forms part of the superior delegating body, since the *Grundnorm* of that superior body constitutes the validity of all norms, including those of the inferior body.[461]

What this initial monist view of national and international law does not identify is, however, the *direction* of delegation between those two bodies of law,[462] as the epistemological necessity of legal monism does not per se answer the question of which body of law—national or international law—delegates the creation of the other and which one prevails in the case of conflict. Kelsen formulates two versions of monism, namely monism under the *primacy of national law* and monism under the *primacy of international law*,[463] whereby the term 'primacy' denotes the respective superior body of law.[464] While he first held the primacy of international law to be the correct view,[465] he later changed his mind and argued that both standpoints—monism under international law or monism under national law—were equally correct. The reason for this lies in Kelsen's logical conclusion[466] that these two versions of monism are only distinct from one another in terms of ideological criteria, namely international pacifism or state sovereignty, but not concerning epistemological requirements.[467] Consequently, the legal scientist may, under the so-called 'choice hypothesis', freely choose between these two versions of monism. Kelsen justifies this postulate with reference to Max Planck,[468] and paraphrases that, just as both the geocentric and the heliocentric view of the universe are equally correct, because there is no absolute astronomic point of reference, there is no such absolute Archimedean point of reference either in the interconnection between two or more bodies of law[469] (except, of course, for the *Grundnorm* which, nevertheless, may be found in either national or international law). Whatever version of monism is eventually chosen, however, is irrelevant; the crucial point is that dualism and pluralism become logically untenable.

If one assumes that national law has primacy, the basic norm is located in this particular body of law, and it is hence the national legal order that delegates the creation of international law.[470] In this scenario international law owes its legal character to national law and is merely 'external state law' in the Hegelian sense that it is dependent on the will of the state and its choice whether or not to respect international norms.[471] International law therefore becomes a projection of national law,[472]

[461] Kelsen, *Principles of International Law* (n 401) 408–9; Kelsen, 'Einheit' (n 460) 234–5.

[462] Michael Giudice, 'Hart and Kelsen on International Law' in Leslie Green and Brian Leiter (eds), *Oxford Studies in Philosophy of Law, Vol 2* (Oxford University Press, 2013) 153–4.

[463] Kelsen, *Pure Theory* (n 54) 339–44.

[464] Kelsen, 'Einheit' (n 460) 235.

[465] Kelsen, *Problem der Souveränität* (n 57) 314–20; Kelsen, *Introduction* (n 28) 116–18.

[466] Joseph G. Starke, 'The Primacy of International Law' in Salo Engel and Rudolf A. Métall (eds), *Law, State, and International Legal Order* (University of Tennessee Press, 1964) 311.

[467] Kelsen, *Pure Theory* (n 54) 342–3.

[468] Max Planck, *Vorträge und Erinnerungen* (Hirzel, 1949) 311.

[469] Kelsen, *Pure Theory* (n 54) 345–6.

[470] Kelsen, 'Einheit' (n 460) 235–8; Kelsen, *Allgemeine Staatslehre* (n 85) 121 ff.

[471] Georg Wilhelm Friedrich Hegel, *Elements of the Philosophy of Right* (transl H.B. Nisbet; Cambridge University Press, 1991) paras 330 ff.

[472] André Décencière-Ferrandière, 'Considérations sur le droit international dans ses rapports avec le droit de l'État' (1933) 40 *Revue Générale de Droit International Public* 8, 64–6.

and the validity of every single treaty is grounded in the domestic legal act that authorizes the relevant state to conclude such treaties. Consequently, every treaty has as many grounds of validity as there are parties to it.[473] Alternatively, this acknowledgement of international law is nothing other than the adoption of a norm that subsequently delegates international law and thereby makes it part of national law.[474] For Kelsen, the overall result of this view is that international law is not binding for a state that has not recognized it,[475] and that dualism, which also requires national law explicitly to acknowledge international norms to be valid within the domestic sphere, ultimately collapses into this particular version of monism.[476]

The primacy of international law, in contrast, entails that the basic norm is presupposed to sit at the apex of the international legal order. This means that international law delegates domestic law and also prevails over it in the case of conflict, and that it is—most importantly—valid without the latter's acknowledgement.[477] This is possible, as Kelsen remarks, because the principle of effectiveness,[478] as a positive norm of international law,[479] 'determines both the reason for the validity and the territorial, personal, and temporal sphere of validity of the national legal orders'.[480] Therefore, the primacy of international law is based on the fact that the coexistence of the national legal orders in space and their temporal succession is only made legally possible by international law; that international law determines what a state is; and that states retain competences only as far as international law does not regulate a specific subject matter.[481]

Kelsen's 'choice hypothesis' was, however, heavily criticized by other members of the Vienna School of Jurisprudence, among them, most notably, Kelsen's own students, Alfred Verdross and Josef L. Kunz. Both disagree with the claim that lawyers might freely choose their preferred version of monism. In this vein, they highlight that only monism under the primacy of international law is best equipped to describe and take into account the international legal order as it is; not only from a political view and the potential harm unrestricted state sovereignty can do to the international legal order, but also from a norm-logical perspective. Ultimately, only the primacy of international law is able to guarantee the connection of the material of all positive rules of international law into one

[473] Max Wenzel, 'Der Begriff des Gesetzes in der Reichsverfassung' (1927) 4 *Veröffentlichungen der Vereinigung der Deutschen Staatsrechtslehrer* 136, 141 ff.

[474] Kelsen, *Problem der Souveränität* (n 57) 153; Kelsen, 'Einheit' (n 460) 235.

[475] Kelsen, *Pure Theory* (n 54) 334.

[476] Kelsen, 'Einheit' (n 460) 238. See also Rub (n 383) 422; Vinx, *Kelsen's Pure Theory of Law* (n 108) 180.

[477] Kelsen, *Pure Theory* (n 54) 336.

[478] According to which a legal order has to be effective to the extent that 'the norms created in conformity with [the constitution or international law] are by and large applied and obeyed': Kelsen, *Pure Theory* (n 54) 210; Kelsen, *Problem der Souveränität* (n 57) 94–101.

[479] That is, the relevant principles of national jurisdiction under public international law, and the existence of 'effective State governments' as organs of international law; see Kammerhofer, 'Kelsen—Which Kelsen?' (n 384) 242.

[480] Kelsen, *Pure Theory* (n 54) 336. [481] Ibid., 336–8.

system, not the primacy of national law. Hence, if one assumes a monist point of view, only the primacy of international law can place both bodies of law into a logically coherent framework.[482]

It is nevertheless also possible to construe Kelsen's insistence on the 'choice hypothesis' as a purely strategic move within the theoretical discourse. Not only was this meant to demonstrate the scientific objectivity of the pure theory of law, but it also succeeded, by putting the matter in such analytical theoretical terms, to reduce the primacy of national law to an absurdity.[483] And even though he never explicitly said so, it is generally agreed that Kelsen definitely builds his theory upon the primacy of international law.[484] With that in mind, he published a short, but all the more conclusive article on his monist theory,[485] which could be considered the *summa* of his theory of international law.[486] The subsequent section will consequently demonstrate that the primacy of international law is the only reasonable choice of monism—not only for political or ideological reasons, but also because of its logical and epistemological merits.

B. The inevitable primacy of international law

Kelsen does not tire of demonstrating that sovereigntists erroneously reinterpret the *political* postulate of state sovereignty into an essential *legal* truth.[487] The following sections will hence show that there are two compelling reasons in favour of the primacy of international law—one being politico-ideological, the other one epistemological and norm-logical—and that the way the pure theory of law views international law is not only an extension of what this theory has to say about constitutional law, but *a constitutional theory of international law in itself*.[488] For these reasons, it is only consequent that the primacy of international law over national law is today accepted in virtually all theoretical doctrines, if one adheres to a monist perspective of the law in the first place.

[482] See especially Josef L. Kunz, 'On the Theoretical Basis of the Law of Nations' (1925) 10 *Transactions of the Grotius Society* 115, 139; Josef L. Kunz, 'La primauté de droit des gens' (1925) 6 *Revue de droit international et de legislation comparée* 556, 572 ff; Josef L. Kunz, *Völkerrechtswissenschaft und Reine Rechtslehre* (Deuticke, 1923) 82; Alfred Verdross, *Die völkerrechtswidrige Kriegshandlung und der Strafanspruch der Staaten* (Engelmann, 1920) 33 ff; Alfred Verdross, 'Grundlagen und Grundlegungen des Völkerrechts' (1921) 29 *Niemeyers Zeitschrift für Internationales Recht* 65, 82–3.

[483] von Bernstorff (n 383) 106.

[484] See e.g. Albert Bleckmann, 'Monismus mit Primat des Völkerrechts' [1984] *Rechtstheorie (Beiheft 5)* 337, 337; Rub (n 383) 435; Öhlinger, 'Einheit' (n 447) 164; Starke, 'Primacy of International Law' (n 466) 75.

[485] Hans Kelsen, 'Zur Lehre vom Primat des Völkerrechts' (1938) 12 *Internationale Zeitschrift für Theorie des Rechts* 211, 211–16.

[486] Mario G. Losano, 'Kelsen's Theory on International Law during His Exile in Geneva' (2015) 28 *Ratio Juris* 470, 481.

[487] Kelsen, 'Lehre vom Primat' (n 485) 214.

[488] Tomer Broude, 'The Constitutional Function of Contemporary International Tribunals, Or Kelsen's Visions Vindicated' (2012) 4 *Goettingen Journal of International Law* 519, 528.

(1) *The ideological absurdity of the primacy of national law*

It is interesting to note that even the adherently scientific Kelsen is willing to admit that the choice between the two versions of monism has a political import,[489] and that even for him a monist concept under the primacy of national law may be too grotesque a notion to be actually tenable.[490] Without any regard for epistemological considerations and solely in the light of ideological criteria, Kelsen seems to prefer the primacy of international law over national law.[491] At the outset, it needs to be mentioned that both versions of monism are prone to abuse: since the primacy of international law is dedicated to pacifism and the superiority of the international legal order, it could be abused to declare national norms in contravention of international law null and void. On closer inspection, this alleged possibility is, however, utterly absurd, because there is no such annulment procedure in international law, as Kelsen specifies. The primacy of national law, on the other hand, is much more susceptible to abuse, as it values state sovereignty and interests over international obligations. It hence corresponds to a kind of dangerous imperialistic ideology that is much more realistic to transpire and to undermine the international legal order than global pacifism and its potential abuse.[492] Therefore, those inclined to embrace the anti-cosmopolitan conception of the relationship between national and international law will have to bear a very heavy burden of moral justification for their choice.[493]

(2) *The primacy of international law as an epistemological consequence*

Yet the reason for choosing between the two versions of primacy is not only of an ideological nature. In fact, there are also norm-logical arguments in favour of monism under the primacy of international law.[494] Kelsen considers the primacy of national law as parallel to a subjectivist philosophy which, in order to understand and make sense of the world, proceeds from the observer's own *ego* and thus only interprets the external world as the will and idea of the subject. Such a philosophy is incapable of comprehending other subjects and results in utter solipsism.[495] Its result is the incapability of the sovereign state to recognize the sovereignty of other subjects. Thereby, the concept of sovereignty, which is constitutive of the Westphalian system, is ironically undermined by the concept of sovereignty that subtends it.[496]

[489] Kelsen, *Introduction* (n 28) 124. See also Vinx, *Kelsen's Pure Theory of Law* (n 108) 181.
[490] Robert Pfeffer, *Das Verhältnis von Völkerrecht und Landesrecht* (Mohr-Siebeck 2009) 86–7.
[491] Somek, 'Kelsen Lives' (n 417) 421 fn 60.
[492] Kelsen, *Pure Theory* (n 54) 342–3; Kelsen, *Problem der Souveränität* (n 57) 317–19.
[493] Vinx, *Kelsen's Pure Theory of Law* (n 108) 181–2.
[494] François Rigaux, 'Hans Kelsen on International Law' (1998) 9 *European Journal of International Law* 325, 341.
[495] Kelsen, *Principles of International Law* (n 401) 435–8; Kelsen, *Problem der Souveränität* (n 57) 317–19.
[496] Jean L. Cohen, 'Sovereignty in the Context of Globalization: A Constitutional Pluralist Perspective' in Samantha Besson and John Tasioulas (eds), *The Philosophy of International Law* (Oxford University Press, 2010) 266; Somek, 'Monism' (n 48) 348.

Beyond that, it is evident that international law cannot be seen as a legal order merely enjoying validity on the basis of national acknowledgement, as international law's claim to validity precludes that its source of validity is based in national law. However, if one accepts the primacy of national law, the principle of *pacta sunt servanda* is also derived from national law. This means that every single state can, at any time, repeal the chain of delegation and thus the validity of international law. In a manner very similar to dualism, international obligations of states can, under this monist premise, only be self-imposed obligations, which can be unmade at any time by abolishing the respective municipal legal act authorizing the state to commit to said obligation.[497] Strictly speaking, the term international 'obligations' thus becomes an oxymoron that can never be relied upon against the will of the state.[498] This view obviously leads to a scenario of global anarchy where each state may refuse to be bound by international law and the very treaties it has concluded whenever its interests so dictate,[499] and where 200-odd states would virtually construe 200-odd different international legal orders. The international legal order would only exist at the behest of the national legal orders and, most absurdly, there would be as many international legal orders as there are national legal orders. Such an utter denial of international law would not only be conceptually impossible, but also empirically false.[500] In fact, it is generally accepted that the doctrine of state primacy is 'a denial of international law as law',[501] and must therefore be rejected, if one takes the notion of legal validity seriously. Today, nobody seriously endorses this version of monism any more,[502] and only monism under the primacy of international law is being accepted as a reasonable choice to theorize the relationship between municipal and international law under a monist premise.[503]

Consequently, if one accepts the legal character of international law, it can only be seen as a legal order *not* delegated by national law, regardless of whether one adheres to a subjective or objective worldview. The primacy of international law is hence also ideologically neutral and legally pure.[504] Additional norm-logical arguments in favour of the primacy of international law will now be discussed in more detail.

[497] Georg Jellinek, *Die rechtliche Natur der Staatenverträge* (Hölder, 1880) 9 ff and 46 ff.

[498] Stefan Griller, 'Völkerrecht und Landesrecht—unter Berücksichtigung des Europarechts' in Robert Walter, Clemens Jabloner, and Klaus Zeleny (eds), *Hans Kelsen und das Völkerrecht* (Manz, 2004) 95.

[499] Edwin Borchard, 'The Relation between International Law and Municipal Law' (1940) 27 *Virginia Law Review* 137, 142.

[500] András Jakab, 'Kelsens Völkerrechtslehre zwischen Erkenntnistheorie und Politik' (2004) 64 *Zeitschrift für ausländisches öffentliches Recht und Völkerrecht* 1045, 1051 fn 30.

[501] Starke, 'Monism and Dualism' (n 121) 77.

[502] Lando Kirchmair, *Die Theorie des Rechtserzeugerkreises* (Duncker & Humblot 2013) 22–3.

[503] Pierre-Marie Dupuy, 'International Law and Domestic (Municipal) Law' in Rüdiger Wolfrum (ed), *Max Planck Encyclopedia of Public International Law* (2nd edn; Oxford University Press, 2013) para 12.

[504] Heinz Peter Rill, 'Internationales, supranationales und nationales Recht—eine Einheit' in Clemens Jabloner and others (eds), *Gedenkschrift Robert Walter* (Manz, 2013) 683 fn 24.

a. The *Grundnorm* of international law

To begin with, it is crucial to recall that the term 'monism under the primacy of international law' affirms, in a strictly scientific analysis, that each national legal order is not only restricted by international law (e.g. in questions of territorial jurisdiction), but also delegated by it.[505] The ultimate reason for this chain of delegation lies in and logically follows from the *Grundnorm* of international law, which thereby also constitutes the *Grundnorm* of the entire legal order (i.e. international law *plus* national legal orders).

Kelsen postulates that international treaties are not per se valid, but depend on the customary international principle of *pacta sunt servanda* (which is held to be the basic norm by Verdross and Anzilotti, respectively[506]). Customary international law in its entirety, in turn, is determined by the basic norm that might be formulated along the lines of 'States ought to behave as they have customarily behaved'[507]—or, in more succinct terms: *consuetudines sunt servandae*. This step, i.e. to consider one specific legal source as the 'substance' of the *Grundnorm*, is initially necessary, because the theory of the basic norm cannot explain the existence of more than one simultaneous norm-creating norm at the top of a positive legal order (as is the case in positive international law where custom, treaties, and general principles of law rank as equal sources of international law). Yet, given its formal and transcendental nature, it is highly problematic to bestow a particular content on the *Grundnorm* and to regard either of these principles—*pacta sunt servanda* or *consuetudines sunt servandae*—as the respective basic norm of international law. Consequently, resistance to choosing a content-laden basic norm quickly formed both inside and outside the Vienna School of Jurisprudence.[508]

With respect to the *pacta sunt servanda* principle as the potential *Grundnorm*, Verdross argues that it directly refers to international treaties that can be concluded either explicitly (the regular and problem-free option) or tacitly (a more intricate option). In the latter case, the result is a *pactum tacitum*, through which customary international law is created.[509] This means that customary international law is created through a tacit treaty between states,[510] and that the *Grundnorm* concurrently creates two sources, namely treaty and custom as tacit treaty law. The problem with this argument is, however, that although it would put the two sources of international law on a par with each other[511] by simply treating custom as a special case of treaty law, it merely focuses on the subjective aspect of customary law (i.e. the

[505] Starke, 'Primacy of International Law' (n 466) 308.

[506] Verdross, *Verfassung der Völkerrechtsgemeinschaft* (n 453) preface, 21–3, and 30–1; Dionisio Anzilotti, *Corso di diritto internazionale* (2nd edn: Athenaeum 1912) 49–50.

[507] Kelsen, *General Theory* (n 104) 369; Kelsen, *Principles of International Law* (n 401) 417–18.

[508] von Bernstorff (n 383) 163.

[509] Verdross, *Verfassung der Völkerrechtsgemeinschaft* (n 453) 32 and 43–4.

[510] Niels Petersen, 'Customary Law without Custom? Rules, Principles, and the Role of State Practice in International Norm Creation' (2007) 23 *American University International Law Review* 275, 295.

[511] An assumption that would be in accordance with positive international law where there is—notwithstanding *ius cogens norms*—no formal hierarchy among the sources of law; see Article 38 of the Statute of the International Court of Justice, and Hugo Thirlway, *The Sources of International Law* (Oxford University Press, 2014) 132–41.

opinio iuris) and neglects state practice. In this light, practice would cease to be a constituent element of customary international law and be degraded to be nothing more than an auxiliary in identifying it.[512] Furthermore, by reducing customary international law to treaty law, one would also need to accept that customary norms can, in the same way as treaties, be formally terminated, be invalid owing to an error in consent, or exclude newly emerging states from their validity[513]—a conclusion that is, as is well known, plain wrong. Therefore, the *pactum tacitum* theory has long been abandoned.

Lastly, there are two more objections in the light of the pure theory of law: first, the principle of *pacta sunt servanda* is a principle of positive international law, both as custom[514] and in its codified manifestation,[515] but the *Grundnorm*, as a transcendental category of legal cognition, does not have any substantive legal content.[516] And second, if one considers the norm-creating function of the *Grundnorm*, i.e. its authorizing the creation of positive law,[517] it is impossible to argue that it can be the simultaneous basis of more than one delegated source of law (i.e. both treaty and customary international law), since it is a construct of legal science, not a positive norm. As an epistemologically necessary category, it remains a transcendental entity, and cannot create a connection where there is none in positive law.[518] In sum, the principle of *pacta sunt servanda* cannot be the *Grundnorm* of international law, both for empirical and theoretical reasons.

The principle of *consuetudines sunt servandae* as the basic norm, as originally proposed by Kelsen, is equally flawed, because it puts customary international law at the top of the hierarchy of positive international law and thereby subordinates the entire international legal order to it. This approach is fraught with two major difficulties; one empirical, and one theoretical. To begin with, such an elevation of custom to the apex of all law would fly in the face of the legal reality of international law, where there is no formal hierarchy of sources, and hence all sources—treaties, custom, and general principles—rank as equals. No international lawyer can therefore accept that treaty law is somehow derived from custom. From a theoretical perspective, it remains controversial whether the principle of *consuetudines sunt servandae* is indeed a positive norm of international law or not.[519]

[512] Maarten Bos, 'Prolegomena to the Identification of Custom in International Law' in *Essays on International and Comparative Law* [no editor] (Springer, 1983) 2 fn 6; Hugh Thirlway, *International Customary Law and Codification* (Sijthoff, 1972) 59; Petersen (n 510) 295.

[513] Bleckmann, 'Monismus mit Primat des Völkerrechts' (n 484) 345.

[514] Kirsten Schmalenbach, 'Article 26' in Oliver Dörr and Kirsten Schmalenbach (eds), *Vienna Convention on the Law of Treaties: A Commentary* (Springer, 2012) para 20.

[515] Article 26 VCLT.

[516] Josef L. Kunz, 'The "Vienna School" and International Law' in Josef L Kunz (ed), *The Changing Law of Nations: Essays on International Law* (Ohio State University Press, 1934) 403–4; Métall, 'Skizzen' (n 149) 420.

[517] Paulson, 'Die unterschiedlichen Formulierungen' (n 165) 59 and 65–7.

[518] Kammerhofer, 'Kelsen—Which Kelsen?' (n 384) 247.

[519] Against this view, cf. e.g. Michael Schweitzer, '*Ius cogens* im Völkerrecht' (1971) 15 *Archiv des Völkerrechts* 197, 218–19. In favour of it, see e.g. Antonio Cassese, *International Law in a Divided World* (Clarendon, 1994) 152; Mark E. Villiger, *Commentary on the 1969 Vienna Convention on the Law of Treaties* (Martinus Nijhoff, 2009) 10 and 366.

If it is in fact a positive norm, then this would again conflict with the presupposition of the basic norm as a transcendental category of cognition. But even if it is not a positive legal norm, theoretical problems persist. On the one hand, if one regards the *consuetudines*-principle as the basic norm, it would ultimately amount to a *petitio principii*, because it would place customary international law at the top of the positive international legal order (merely below the *Grundnorm*) and the legal validity of all other customary international norms could then only be explained on the basis of customary law itself.[520] The pertinent problem is that customary international law—as the highest ranking positive law—is, in itself, incapable of creating further hierarchical steps of the normative pyramid, as all other thereby determined customary norms would be located on the same normative level.[521] Yet even Kelsen accurately acknowledges this problem by arguing that if a constitution is created by custom and if the law-applying organs are considered duly authorized to apply customary law, then this does not mean that custom is instituted as a law-creating act by the custom-created and hence positive-legal constitution. This would in fact result in a *petitio principii* because if the positive-legal constitution (i.e. a norm that regulates the creation of general norms) can be created by custom, then it must already be presupposed that custom is a law-creating fact. And this presupposition can only be the basic norm.[522]

In this sense, neither the principle of *pacta sunt servanda* nor the principle of *consuetudines sunt servandae* can serve as the basic norm of international law. The empirical problem remains that all sources of international law are equal, which cannot be explained by the theory of a basic norm that has been 'substantially charged'.[523] By doing this, it may explain that there only is one supreme norm of norm-creation, yet at the same time it thereby becomes subject to the criticism that it is in contradiction to the positive law. One last option would therefore be to return to a *Grundnorm* without any content, which merely sets out the transcendental conditions for a unified legal order: a terminus for the hierarchy of norms; the fount of the validity of all legal norms; and the unifying force of the legal order. Norm-creation, as Jörg Kammerhofer suggests, could then be explained by an explicit 'constitution of international law' or a 'historically first constitution' as a meta-meta-*stratum* above *pacta sunt servanda* and *consuetudines sunt servandae* as the meta-norms on law-creation. Although treaties, custom, and general principles would form separate branches of international law,[524] they would be connected by this superstructure, which regulates their interrelationship. This meta-meta-*stratum* would need to consist of positive norms, yet it remains doubtful whether such positive norms exist.[525]

[520] Kunz, '"Vienna School" and International Law' (n 516) 403–4; Métall, 'Skizzen' (n 149) 420; von Bernstorff (n 383) 164.

[521] Jörg Kammerhofer, 'Uncertainty in the Formal Sources of International Law: Customary International Law and Some of Its Problems' (2004) 15 *European Journal of International Law* 523, 538–40 and 549; Godefridus J.H. van Hoof, *Rethinking the Sources of International Law* (Kluwer Law, 1983) 107.

[522] Kelsen, *Pure Theory* (n 54) 226.

[523] Bleckmann 'Monismus mit Primat des Völkerrechts' (n 484) 345.

[524] Grigory Tunkin, 'Is General International Law Customary Law Only?' (1993) 4 *European Journal of International Law* 534, 536.

[525] Kammerhofer, 'Hans Kelsen's Place' (n 110) 152.

A viable candidate for such a meta-meta-*stratum* could be, in Alfred Verdross and Bruno Simma's sense, 'inter-State consensus [as] the original source of international law'.[526] Hence, consensus would form the content of the highest positive norm of international law. However, there is a considerable doctrinal hurdle to this view, as one would then need to verify that there is such a positive norm of inter-state consensus. This will most likely prove impossible, since the emerging community of states did probably not agree on a catalogue of the sources of international law, neither explicitly nor tacitly. Another contender for the meta-meta-law of international law could be Article 38 of the Statute of the International Court of Justice as a manifestation of what is accepted as law-creating in international law.[527] It remains doubtful, however, whether this provision is of real epistemological value because there might be other sources of international law omitted in Article 38.[528]

Yet even though there might be supplemental and additional sources, Article 38 as the basis of all international legal sources has never been seriously disputed in practice.[529] But mere pragmatism and practical use alone are not sufficient at this point: if Article 38 were not to reflect the meta-meta-law of the international legal order, then its universal and undisputed use would not make this a correct statement. The validity of legal norms depends on other legal norms, and not practice. Thus, the enumeration of sources in this provision and its position as a meta-meta-law of international law is only correct if it corresponds to the number of meta-norms that exist, which means, a fortiori, that it is merely declaratory in nature. The reasoning behind Article 38 being declaratory is that it is generally accepted as such, and that the meta-norms on international law-creation (i.e. the sources of international law) are created by general acceptance. Consequently, the real claim here is that the epistemological position of Article 38 arises from its correspondence with the meta-meta-law's condition for meta-law creation. It nonetheless remains doubtful whether Article 38 really constitutes such a meta-meta-law for international law, and international lawyers remain rather sceptical about this claim, in particular because of this provision's non-exhaustive character.[530]

The problem is that the assumed 'constitution' of international law either lacks positivity (i.e. it only exists in the minds of international lawyers) or perceptibility (i.e. it is positive, but simply very difficult to perceive owing to its unwritten nature).[531] It is, however, indisputable that there are certain constitutionalizing

[526] Alfred Verdross and Bruno Simma, *Universelles Völkerrecht* (3rd edn; Duncker & Humblot, 1984) 59–60 and 324–7.

[527] Gerald Fitzmaurice, 'Some Problems Regarding the Formal Sources of International Law' in F. M. van Asbeck and others (eds), *Symbolae Verzijl. Présentées au Prof. J.H.W. Verzijl à l'occasion de son LXX-ième anniversaire* (Martinus Nijhoff, 1958) 173; Thirlway, *International Customary Law* (n 512) 36; Kammerhofer, *Uncertainty* (n 149) 209.

[528] Prakash Menon, 'An Enquiry into the Sources of Modern International Law' (1986) 64 *Revue de droit international, de sciences diplomatiques et politiques* 181, 182, arguing that Article 38 might not be exhaustive. See also Pauwelyn (n 159) 90; Kammerhofer, *Uncertainty* (n 149) 209–10.

[529] Maarten Bos, 'The Hierarchy among the Recognized Manifestations ("Sources") of International Law' (1978) 25 *Netherlands International Law Review* 334, 334.

[530] Kammerhofer, *Uncertainty* (n 149) 208–10.

[531] Kammerhofer, 'Uncertainty in the Formal Sources' (n 521) 550.

trends in international law, and that therefore the latter view is much more plausible. There is a positive-legal constitution of international law that regulates international law-making, but owing to its highly fragmented status, it is just very difficult to perceive. Yet fragmentation and difficulties in perceiving the elements of this constitution do not speak against its positive character—in the same way as the fragmented and mostly uncodified status of the United Kingdom's constitution does not speak against its constitutional nature.[532] In addition to Article 38 of the ICJ Statute, thus merely enumerating various sources of international law in a non-exhaustive manner, the meta-meta-norms of international law are complemented by various other sources on international law-creation, such as those rules of the 1969 Vienna Convention of the Law of Treaties on treaty-making, which are universally accepted;[533] the relevant rules on the creation of customary international law, as explained by the ICJ in the *North Sea Continental Shelf* case;[534] the gap-filling role of general principles to avoid the problem of *non liquet*;[535] certain types of unilateral declarations;[536] and decisions of international organizations.[537] Soft law, however, must be excluded from this list of international legal sources. The reason for this is that it lacks formally binding force, and given the strict binary character of the law as being either valid and existent or invalid and non-existent, there is no room for a grey area of being 'a little valid' in between.[538]

Thus, ultimately, if one can accept Article 38 of the ICJ Statute and an unwritten and yet positive 'constitution' of international law as the meta-meta-law of the international legal order, there would be no need to bestow any content upon the *Grundnorm* and it could remain the transcendental entity that it was originally envisaged to be. This *Grundnorm* would then constitute the reason for the validity of the quasi-constitution of international law, i.e. its meta-meta-law in the shape of Article 38 plus other sources of international law-making, which sets out the conditions for law-creation, i.e. the meta-law as constituted by the principles of *pacta sunt servanda, consuetudines sunt servandae*, etc.

[532] See Joint Committee on Draft Civil Contingencies Bill, First Report; 28 November 2003, H. L. 184 HC 1074, para 183, enumerating various sources and acts which could be taken to constitute the fundamental parts of British constitutional law.

[533] See International Law Commission, 'Fragmentation of International Law: Difficulties Arising from the Diversification and Expansion of International Law—Report of the Study Group of the International Law Commission, Finalized by Martti Koskenniemi', UN Doc A/CN.4/L.682, 13 April 2006, para 493.

[534] *North Sea Continental Shelf Cases (Germany v Denmark; Germany v Netherlands)* [1969] ICJ Rep 3, para 77.

[535] Hersch Lauterpacht, 'Some Observations on the Prohibition of *Non Liquet* and the Completeness of the Law' in F.M. van Asbeck and others (eds), *Symbolae Verzijl. Présentées au Prof. J.H.W. Verzijl à l'occasion de son LXX-ième anniversaire* (Martinus Nijhoff 1958) 196–221. Cf. also, however, *Legality of the Threat or Use of Nuclear Weapons (Advisory Opinion)* [1996] ICJ Rep 226, para 97, where the Court could not reach a definitive conclusion as to the legality or illegality of the use of nuclear weapons in extreme circumstances of self-defence.

[536] *Nuclear Tests (Australia v France)* [1974] ICJ Rep 253, paras 48–56.

[537] *Legal Consequences for States of the Continued Presence of South Africa in Namibia (South West Africa) Notwithstanding Security Council Resolution 276 (1970) (Advisory Opinion)* [1971] ICJ Rep 16.

[538] Jan Klabbers, 'The Redundancy of Soft Law' (1996) 65 *Nordic Journal of International Law* 167, 167–82.

b. The principle of effectiveness as the delegating norm of international law

The question nonetheless remains how international law delegates national law. The *Grundnorm* may be a necessary condition for the unity of the law, but it remains insufficient unless there are positive-legal norms that delegate the creation of inferior norms.[539] Kelsen argues that such a delegating norm can be found in the so-called 'principle of effectiveness' according to which a legal order has to be effective to the extent that 'the norms created in conformity with [the national constitution or international law] are by and large applied and obeyed'.[540] In this sense, 'effectiveness' denotes a positive norm of international law that 'determines both the reason for the validity and the territorial, personal, and temporal sphere of validity of the national legal orders'.[541] This positive norm[542] is contained in the relevant principles governing national jurisdiction under public international law, and the existence of effective State governments as organs of international law, asserting their authority vis-à-vis the population within a particular circumscribed territory.[543] This rule of 'effective government' thereby defines the organs of the state for international law just as a national statute would define the managing directors of a corporation as a legal person.[544]

Alternatively, effectiveness acts as a delegating nexus between international and national law and delimits the competences and the scope of application of national legal orders with respect to the international legal order.[545] Thus, the following picture as seen in Figure 3 emerges:[546]

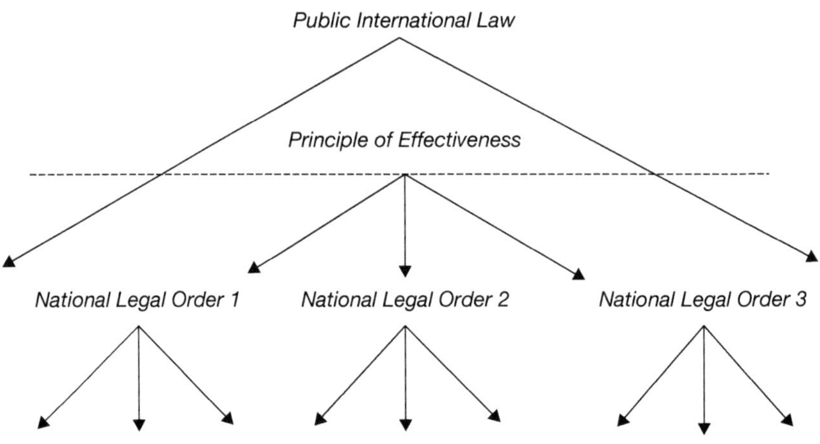

Figure 3 The primacy of international law and the principle of effectiveness.

[539] Kelsen, *Problem der Souveränität* (n 57) 107. [540] Kelsen, *Pure Theory* (n 54) 210.

[541] Kelsen, *Principles of International Law* (n 401) 214–15; Kelsen, 'Einheit' (n 460) 242.

[542] The existence of this positive norm of international law is also evidenced by Verdross, *Verfassung der Völkerrechtsgemeinschaft* (n 453) 133.

[543] Kelsen, *Problem der Souveränität* (n 57) 240–1. See also Kammerhofer, 'Kelsen—Which Kelsen?' (n 384) 242; von Bernstorff (n 383) 92.

[544] Kammerhofer, 'Kelsen—Which Kelsen?' (n 384) 242; Rub (n 383) 459–61.

[545] Kelsen, *Problem der Souveränität* (n 57) 101; Kelsen, 'Zur Lehre vom Primat' (n 485); Kelsen, 'Einheit' (n 460) 238–9.

[546] See Marcelo Neves, 'Grenzen der Autonomie des Rechts in einer asymmetrischen Weltgesellschaft: Von Luhmann zu Kelsen' in Hauke Brunkhorst and Rüdiger Voigt (eds), *Rechts-Staat: Staat, internationale Gemeinschaft und Völkerrecht bei Hans Kelsen* (Nomos, 2008) 309.

In terms of substance, and when solely regarding national legal orders, the effectiveness principle is hence nothing less than the *Grundnorm* of national law which, by taking into account the international legal order, becomes a positive norm.[547] Yet, it has been argued that the existence of several basic norms, even in the light of their relativity to international law, would not only be meaningless,[548] but also inconsistent with Kelsen's own unitary theory of the law. If international law and all the national legal orders had a *Grundnorm* of their own, this would not amount to a monist, but a pluralist system, since the unity of the legal order can only be safeguarded by tracing all norms back to one and only one basic norm. To counter this argument, one may certainly assume that the various basic norms of national law merely represent a working hypothesis, which is only maintained as long as international law is disregarded.[549]

This reply is partly correct, but the overall solution to this problem is more complex. It is incorrect that Kelsen assumes—allegedly inconsistently—a transcendental (and thus non-positive) *Grundnorm* for an isolated view of national law, and concurrently a positive-legal *Grundnorm* for national law when considering international law. Kelsen only postulates a transcendental basic norm of national law in his early writings and before international law comes into play.[550] Therefore, Kelsen does not claim a cumulative,[551] but an alternative co-existence of the various basic norms of international and national law. This co-existence simply depends on the viewpoint of the legal scientist (hence the wording *alternative* co-existence).[552] Yet it is evident that monism under the primacy of international law only allows for one perspective, and this is a single *Grundnorm* at the apex of the international legal order, thereby delegating the national legal orders.

Kelsen admits that the delegation of national law by international law via the principle of effectiveness may strike the reader as absurd, because from a historical perspective, the national legal orders unquestionably preceded the creation of international law.[553] This point, however, mistakes a logical relation of norms with historical facts. In the same manner as the family as a legal community is older than the state, family law is now delegated by the respective national constitution;[554] and just as historical settlements and cities such as Vienna or London predate the states of Austria or the United Kingdom, their municipal laws and ordinances are now delegated by the respective national legal orders.[555] Similarly, it is wrong to assume that the various legal orders within a federal system were merely curtailed, but not delegated by the federal constitutional order. In fact, it is this very curtailment that implies the authorization of the federation to legislate outside these legal limitations.

[547] Jöckel (n 402) 32; Rub (n 383) 423; Kelsen, *Pure Theory* (n 54) 214–15.

[548] Cohen, 'Context of Globalization' (n 496) 267.

[549] Bleckmann 'Monismus mit Primat des Völkerrechts' (n 484) 344–5.

[550] Rub (n 383) 423 fn 71. See Kelsen, *Allgemeine Staatslehre* (n 85) 250–1.

[551] As erroneously criticized by Bleckmann 'Monismus mit Primat des Völkerrechts' (n 484) 344–5.

[552] Öhlinger, 'Einheit' (n 447) 163 fn 16, referring to the criticism of Bleckmann 'Monismus mit Primat des Völkerrechts' (n 484) 344–5.

[553] From a historical perspective, it is irrelevant whether one pinpoints the birth of international law to 1648 or before; states or state-like entities undoubtedly existed before that.

[554] Kelsen, *Pure Theory* (n 54) 338–9; Kelsen, 'Einheit' (n 460) 241.

[555] Dupuy (n 503) para 14; Bleckmann 'Monismus mit Primat des Völkerrechts' (n 484) 339.

Admittedly, the chain of delegation and norm-creation between international and national law might not be as perceptible as in federations, but it nonetheless exists.[556]

This analogy to federal legal orders also brings to mind Kelsen's 'three circles theory' (*Drei-Kreise-Theorie*) to describe the interplay of laws within a federal system, where the overall constitution (*Gesamtverfassung*) delegates both the law of the federation and the federated states.[557] In such a system, the laws of the latter two circles are of equal rank and stand coordinatedly side by side, which means that normative conflicts between them are resolved on the basis of the coordinating and overarching first 'circle'.[558] Applied to the relationship between national and international law, a picture emerges of sovereign and equal states that—in a decentralized way—enforce international law but nonetheless remain subject to it, such as the federation and the federated states are subject to the overall constitution.

To give another example, not only is the extent of every state's sovereignty and jurisdiction defined by international legal norms,[559] but it is also the duty of every international legal subject to bring its domestic law into conformity with international law.[560] If in default of its obligations under international law (which also includes the failure to transform international legal norms into national law), the state exposes itself to the legal consequences prescribed by international law.[561] Indeed, if one takes the example of state creation and the entry of new states into the international legal community, the existence of a chain of delegation between international and national law on the basis of the effectiveness principle becomes even more obvious, as it is generally accepted that international law can—in certain situations—automatically bind states without their consent.[562]

The same hypothesis applies to existing states: in the same way as if an old regime is overthrown by a revolution, or a constitution is peacefully modified or replaced by a new one, international law continues to confer rights and impose obligations on international legal subjects.[563] Aristotle may have been right in the context of the Greek *polis* to state 'that when the constitution changes its character and becomes different,

[556] Starke, 'Primacy of International Law' (n 466) 315.

[557] Kelsen, *Allgemeine Staatslehre* (n 85) 199.

[558] Hans Kelsen, 'Die Bundesexekution' in Zaccaria Giacometti and Dietrich Schindler (eds), *Festgabe für Fritz Fleiner zum 60. Geburtstag* (Mohr-Siebeck, 1927) 166.

[559] See the different theories on Statehood and recognition, which are all determined by international law itself, in e.g. James Crawford, *The Creation of States in International Law* (2nd edn; Oxford University Press, 2006) 3–173.

[560] *Treatment of Polish Nationals and other Persons of Polish Origin or Speech in the Danzig Territory (Advisory Opinion)* [1932] PCIJ Series A/B, No 44, 24.

[561] Kelsen, *Pure Theory* (n 54) 337.

[562] Kelsen, *General Theory* (n 104) 381. This view is rather uncontroversial regarding customary international law and also speaks against the aforementioned *pactum tacitum* theory: see e.g. Jules Basdevant, 'Règles générales du droit de la paix' (1936) 58 *Recueil des cours* 471, 515; Grigory Tunkin, 'Remarks on the Juridical Nature of Customary Norms of International Law' (1961) 49 *California Law Review* 419, 426. Concerning treaties, however, the problem of 'universal succession versus *tabula rasa*' comes into play at this point: see e.g. Matthew Craven, 'The Problem of State Succession and the Identity of States under International Law' (1998) 9 *European Journal of International Law* 142, 142–62; Gerhard Hafner and Gregor Novak, 'State Succession in Respect of Treaties' in Duncan B. Hollis (ed), *The Oxford Guide to Treaties* (Oxford University Press, 2012) 396–427.

[563] Kelsen, *Problem der Souveränität* (n 57) 224–9.

the State too remains no longer the same'.[564] Yet if one takes into account international law, the principle of effectiveness inevitably determines the existence of the state and its legal order, and its continuity and legal identity remain, despite violent changes of its constitution.[565] This 'identity thesis' in cases of changes—may they be of territorial,[566] governmental,[567] or populational nature[568]—has all the more been confirmed by certain rules of positive international law.[569] Therefore, the sole scientifically sound construction justified on the basis of monism is that state law is conditioned and delegated by international law.

c. The chain of derogation and the turn from radical to moderate monism

So far, the discussion of the primacy of international law has only examined the chain of delegation between international and national law, and it is now clear that norm-logically speaking, international law delegates national law. What has been missing in this debate, however, is what ought to happen in the case of a conflict between national and international norms. In this respect, the concept of primacy of international law also requires that preference be given to the respective norm of international law, and that a contravening norm of national law must give way.[570] This is where Merkl's chain of derogation (albeit in a slightly modified form) comes into play.

As we have seen above,[571] Kelsen claims, in his early writings, that monism under the primacy of international law entails a radical consequence, namely that any national norm in contravention of international law is null and void *ex tunc*. The reason for the nullity of the national legal norm lies in the logical contradiction arising from its unlawfulness under international law.[572] Yet since this theory of radical monism stands in obvious contrast to reality where national norms in violation of international norms are certainly *not* automatically null and void *ex tunc*[573] (simply because international law does not envisage a process by which the illegal national norm in question could be declared invalid), this radical view has long gone out of fashion and is not seriously supported any more. There is no positive-legal principle that international law prevails over national law through the invalidation of the latter—in a similar way to national constitutional provisions that decree the invalidating supremacy of federal law over sub-federal law.[574]

564 Aristotle, *Politics* (ed and transl Jonathan Barnes, *The Complete Works of Aristotle, Vol 2* (Oxford University Press, 1984) 1276b; Kelsen, *General Theory* (n 104) 368–9.

565 Kelsen, *General Theory* (n 104) 369. See also Konrad G. Bühler, *State Succession and Membership in International Organizations* (Kluwer, 2001) 9.

566 Article 15 of the Vienna Convention on Succession of States in Respect of Treaties and Article 29 VCLT.

567 Krystyna Marek, *Identity and Continuity of States in Public International Law* (Librairie Droz, 1968) 24–73.

568 Crawford (n 559) 678.

569 Marek (n 567) 12.

570 Starke, 'Primacy of International Law' (n 466) 308.

571 See ch 2, section 2C(2).

572 Kelsen, *Allgemeine Staatslehre* (n 85) 125; Kelsen, *Problem der Souveränität* (n 57) 113.

573 Antonio Cassese, 'Towards a Moderate Monism: Could International Rules Eventually Acquire the Force to Invalidate Inconsistent National Laws?' in Antonio Cassese (ed), *Realizing Utopia: The Future of International Law* (Oxford University Press, 2012) 187–99.

574 See e.g. Article 31 GG ('Bundesrecht bricht Landesrecht'); Article VI, clause 2 of the United States Constitution ('Supremacy Clause').

In this context, Verdross develops his idea of moderate monism[575] that, occasionally, national courts apply national law in violation of international law only provisionally. International law certainly retains its supreme position in Verdross' view, but by providing states with a particular margin of action (i.e. their delimited competences), it forgoes its automatic invalidating power[576] and restricts itself to the voidability *ex nunc* of unlawful national law. Verdross therefore compares this situation of conflicting norms to a federal state where laws allegedly in violation of superior laws remain valid until abrogated by the respective authority (either the legislature or the constitutional court). The same applies to national laws in violation of international law: they remain valid until formally abrogated by the competent authority.[577] National law thus only has provisional quality, since international law, despite its normative priority, possesses neither the power nor the procedures to invalidate contravening national law. This provisional quality of national law is the result of the decentralized and often ineffective nature of international law, which is nevertheless strengthened by international courts that, by applying international law, can order states to nullify domestic legislation in contrast to international law.[578] In this vein, Verdross regards his monism as a systematic concept of an international constitution at the top of the unitary legal order, whereby international constitutional law fulfils the external constitutional function by defining the outer limits of the national legal orders' jurisdictional spheres.[579]

One could therefore say that whereas radical monism focuses on primacy in terms of *validity* only, moderate monism conforms better to reality by restricting itself to declaring the national norm in question to be simply inapplicable. Moderate monism consequently underlines the primacy of international law in terms of *applicability*. From this follows the requirement that the defaulting state bring its law into compliance with international law.

Verdross' mediating considerations had a lasting influence on Kelsen,[580] and in his 'moderate turn',[581] he mitigates his radical monist conception to a more moderate version in the spirit of his student Verdross. This is where Kelsen's later concept of derogation, also partly influenced by Merkl's *Fehlerkalkül*, comes into play to deal with normative conflicts between national and international law. By turning away from logic and towards the positive law, Kelsen accepts that normative conflicts between international and national law are exactly analogous to conflicts between the constitution and ordinary statutes. In the same manner as a so-called

[575] Alfred Verdross, 'Droit international public et droit interne' (1954) 32 *Revue de Droit International, de Sciences Diplomatiques et Politiques* 219, 221; Alfred Verdross, *Völkerrecht* (5th edn; Springer, 1964) 113.

[576] Dupuy (n 503) paras 17–18.

[577] Verdross, *Verfassung der Völkerrechtsgemeinschaft* (n 453) 37; Verdross, *Völkerrecht* (n 575) 113 ff.

[578] Verdross, 'Droit international public' (n 575) 221–3.

[579] Thomas Kleinlein, 'Alfred Verdross as a Founding Father of International Constitutionalism' (2012) 4 *Goettingen Journal of International Law* 385, 408.

[580] See e.g. Rotter (n 193) 61; Öhlinger, 'Einheit' (n 447) 165–6; García-Salmones Rovira (n 61) 343. For an explicit acknowledgement of Verdross' influence on Kelsen's works, see Kelsen, *Hauptprobleme* (n 66) xv.

[581] Heinz Wagner, 'Monismus und Dualismus: eine methodenkritische Betrachtung zum Theorienstreit' (1964) 89 *Archiv des öffentlichen Rechts* 212, 212: 'Kehre'; Rub (n 383) 426.

unconstitutional statute remains valid law until formally abrogated, national law in violation of international law remains in force until formally voided by the competent authority.[582] Alternatively, one could argue that the unitary legal order of national and international law anticipates the malfunctioning of the legal system and attributes a different legal effect than automatic nullity in order to allow for the provisional validity of otherwise faulty legal norms between their creation and their annulment.[583] This aspect is to be seen under the above-mentioned doctrine of the *Alternativermächtigung* ('alternative authorization'), which, to a certain extent, accepts and receives Merkl's *Fehlerkalkül* in a modified shape into the analysis of the relationship between international and national law.[584]

Given the decentralized nature of international law, the decision on how to handle norms in contrast with international law usually rests with the national courts.[585] This means that the national norms which create the norm in question and provide for a procedure to derogate it, can be construed to the effect that they already provide for either the derogation or the confirmation of the domestic norm allegedly in violation of international law. If, for one, the norm in violation of international law is effectively annulled, the conflict is resolved; and if, alternatively, this norm remains valid and confirmed as such, one can argue that there is no material contradiction between the domestic and the international norm.[586]

Nonetheless, one must also consider that a given national legal order might not provide for such a resolution via alternative authorization. Yet even in this case, the assumed unity between national and international law is not punctured, as the enactment of national law that is contrary to international law can be sanctioned as a violation of international law by other states or international subjects through reprisals short of the use of force. This should, eventually, prompt the defaulting state to redress the illegal situation accordingly.[587] It must therefore be emphasized that a violation of international law is not disproving monism under the primacy of international law, as no delict is in contradiction to the law; it is in fact a condition determined by law.[588] In other words, a norm cannot be violated. On the contrary, it is indispensable to the validity of norms that it is possible to commit or omit the act triggering the sanction. As has been pointed out, 'as long as the international system speaks of unlawful acts and sanctions, it is a legal system, no matter how inefficiently the system may work in singular cases'.[589] But the mere existence of a threat of sanctions is the minimum requirement to speak of a legal system.

Thus, the reaction to a delict and its redress constitute a derogating act that further confirms the unity of the law. Even after his norm-logical turn, Kelsen affirmed that a legal norm can 'be repealed only in a certain manner prescribed by itself or by a norm of the same order'.[590] In other words, derogation is only possible between

[582] Kelsen, *Pure Theory* (n 54) 330–1.
[583] Kletzer, 'Kelsen's Development' (n 329) 48–9.
[584] Wagner (n 581) 229; Rub (n 383) 466.
[585] Kelsen, *Pure Theory* (n 54) 331.
[586] Rub (n 383) 468.
[587] Rill, 'Internationales, supranationales und nationales Recht' (n 504) 681–2.
[588] Kelsen, *Principles of International Law* (n 401) 422–3.
[589] Somek, 'Kelsen Lives' (n 417) 435–6.
[590] Kelsen, 'Derogation' (n 347) 265.

norms of the same legal order, and the identity of said legal order is determined by the legal reference point all of its norms share—i.e. the *Grundnorm*, which caps the norm-creating chain of delegation.[591] Norms that do not belong to a given legal order can never trump or invalidate norms of this legal order because they simply exist outside of its remit, unrelated and unconnected to it. Therefore, derogation is only possible within the same legal order, and the legal consequences applicable to any violations of international law are further proof of legal monism.

(3) Consequences: no differences in the law

a. No difference in sources

One of the most important consequences of a monist conception of the relationship between international and national law is that it allowed Kelsen to pioneer recognition of the role of the individual in international law by rejecting the core tenets of dualism.[592] Hence it becomes difficult to maintain the dualist doctrine that international and national law are based on different grounds of validity (the common will of the states versus the historically first constitution)[593] and that they consequently have different sources (the sources enumerated in Article 38(1) of the ICJ Statute versus the respective sources of national law).[594] For dualists, it is the will of individual states that is, by way of a law-creating 'agreement', transformed into the common will of the states (*Gemeinwille*). And only this common will can then, in turn, function as a source for international law that is separate from that of national law.[595]

For Kelsen, this line of reasoning is of course flawed. He criticizes that neither the concept of the will (as a psychological term[596]) nor the factual creation of norms (as an empirical *factum brutum*) can be the constitutive element of legal validity, since this validity—because of the dichotomy of the 'is' and 'ought'—can only be derived from the *Grundnorm*.[597] The admittedly different forms of norm-creation in national and international law must therefore be traced back to one single basic norm. Even if dualists and pluralists accepted the hypothesis of the *Grundnorm*, but concurrently maintained their argument by referring to the existence of various and distinct basic norms, the argument of the necessary unity of cognition of the law would apply and underscore that there can only be one *Grundnorm* and, a fortiori, only one valid legal order. Otherwise, if they continue to uphold their argument of a variety of basic norms, they must also accept a conceptual difference in the term 'legal validity' and therefore the consequence that the law will be bereft of any objective meaning.

[591] Kammerhofer, 'Kelsen—Which Kelsen?' (n 384) 241.

[592] Somek, 'Kelsen Lives' (n 417) 418, also emphasizing that Kelsen's argument in favour of individuals is solely based on his theory, and not a normative consequence of it.

[593] Triepel (n 450) 111 ff; Griller, 'Völkerrecht und Landesrecht' (n 498) 96–7.

[594] John R. Bolton, 'Is There Really "Law" in International Affairs?' (2000) 10 *Transnational Law and Contemporary Problems* 1, 3–8.

[595] Triepel (n 450) 63 ff; Anzilotti, *Corso di diritto internazionale* (n 506) 26.

[596] von Bernstorff (n 383) 71.

[597] Kelsen, *Problem der Souveränität* (n 57) 105–6 and 135; Rub (n 383) 423–4.

This is certainly possible, but only at the price of giving up discussing 'the law' and changing the subject to something different.

b. No difference in substance and subjects

The second argument against a unitary conception of the law follows directly from the alleged difference in sources, namely that international and national law govern two substantially different bodies of law (norms regulating inter-state relations versus norms regulating individual behaviour) and hence perform different legal functions in different systems.[598] For dualists, this also means that international and national law necessarily relate to different addressees (states versus individuals).[599] These arguments are equally unacceptable for Kelsen. For him, it is wrong to claim that national law regulates the relations that are rooted within one state, whilst international law regulates the relations that transcend the sphere of these purely domestic affairs. The reason for this is that every so-called domestic affair of a state can be made the subject of a treaty and thereby be transformed into a foreign affair. Ultimately, Kelsen considers this attempted distinction between the subject matter of international and national law to be a simple tautology, since the assertion that national law governs domestic affairs and that international law governs foreign affairs boils down to the truism that national law regulates what is regulated by national law, and international law regulates what is regulated by international law.[600]

Thereby the pure theory of law clarifies that the law does not regulate pre-existing relations; in fact, it is the law that creates these relations by governing the rights of obligations of legal subjects.[601] In this sense, the subject matter of the law is derived from the subjects of the law, and the relationship of international law vis-à-vis national law is principally the same as the relationship between national law (i.e. the state) and the individual. Therefore, legal subjects—may they be states or individuals—are personified sub-orders of the legal order in its entirety and derived from it. According to the identity thesis, which holds that the state is identical to its legal order,[602] the relationship between both the individual and the state and between the state and the international legal order are hence mere normative links between different legal subjects that are themselves the personified entity of a derived bundle of rights and obligations.[603] As a consequence, Kelsen rejects the formal distinction between subordinating and coordinating legal relations in this matter since all legal subjects, including the state, are equally subordinated to the law. Accordingly, it is incorrect to contrast international law as a *coordinating* legal order with national law as a *subordinating* legal order.[604] International law does not

[598] Triepel (n 450) 11 ff; David Feldman, 'Monism, Dualism, and Constitutional Legitimacy' (1999) 20 *Australian Yearbook of International Law* 105, 106.

[599] Anzilotti, *Corso di diritto internazionale* (n 450) 281 and 320; Triepel (n 450) 11 ff.

[600] Kelsen, *General Theory* (n 104) 364–5.

[601] Kelsen, *Problem der Souveränität* (n 57) 125–8; Kelsen, 'Les rapports' (n 364) 281.

[602] See section 5A(1) on sovereignty.

[603] Kelsen, *Problem der Souveränität* (n 57) 126–7; von Bernstorff (n 383) 72.

[604] Hans Kelsen, 'Zur Grundlegung der Völkerrechtslehre. Eine Auseinandersetzung mit Heinrich Drost' (1946) 1 *Österreichische Zeitschrift für öffentliches Recht* 20, 31–32; Hans Kelsen, 'Théorie générale du droit international public. Problèmes choisis' (1932-IV) 42 *Recueil des cours* 116, 131.

simply coordinate between national legal orders, it delegates them. Thus, it becomes evident that every subject matter that can be regulated by national law is open to regulation by international law as well.[605]

Furthermore, this line of reasoning entails for Kelsen that a difference in subjects is equally inconceivable, because the legal subject is not an entity that predates the legal order, but something that is created by the latter.[606] Dualists may be right that *some* rules of international law only address states and hence exclusively govern inter-state relations,[607] but for Kelsen it is logically incorrect to regard *all* rules of international law as being directed at states and not to regard individuals as addressees of international norms alongside states. And even if international law did not regulate the conduct of individuals, there was nothing to prevent the international legal order from expanding its reach in this respect.[608] Moreover, Kelsen argues that the object of legal norms is always the conduct of individuals. *Prima facie*, it might seem that international law only governs the conduct of states, but eventually, this simply means that individual human behaviour regulated by international law can be attributed to the state as the personified unity of a bundle of norms.[609] In conclusion, both international and national law regulate the behaviour of individual humans, and the fact that this behaviour can be attributed through legal norms to different personified legal sub-orders of the overall unified legal order is without detriment to their shared regulatory object.[610] In other words, international law determines what ought to be done directly to individuals, yet it may also delegate the further determination of the individual (as, for instance, an organ or representative of the state) who ought to do this, to be established by national law.[611]

c. No validity through transformation

This notion of delegating the further determination of the individual responsible under or entitled by international law is closely connected to the concept of transformation. The doctrine of transformation is based upon a more modest version of dualism in the spirit of Anzilotti, which accepts that the generally separated spheres of national and international law may intersect at times. Yet before this intersection can take place and international norms can have any effect within national law, they need to be expressly and specifically transformed into domestic law using constitutional mechanisms. In other words, international law is 'recast' by the creation of parallel norms of domestic law, and compliance with changes on the international plane is dependent on internal legislative modifications. The validity of the national

[605] Kelsen, *General Theory* (n 104) 365.
[606] Kelsen, *Problem der Souveränität* (n 57) 108–9; Kelsen, 'Les rapports' (n 364) 266.
[607] Giorgio Gaja, 'Dualism—A Review' in Janne Nijman and André Nollkaemper (eds), *New Perspectives on the Divide between National and International Law* (Oxford University Press, 2007) 54–5.
[608] Giorgio Balladore Pallieri, 'Le dottrine di Hans Kelsen e il problema dei rapporti fra diritto interno e diritto internazionale' (1935) 27 *Rivista di diritto internazionale* 24, 74.
[609] Kelsen, *Problem der Souveränität* (n 57) 128; Kelsen, *Pure Theory* (n 54) 327.
[610] von Bernstorff (n 383) 72; Somek, 'Kelsen Lives' (n 417) 418; Leben, 'Kelsen and the Advancement' (n 385) 301.
[611] Kelsen, 'Théorie générale' (n 604) 121.

legal norm is thereby decoupled from its international pendant, and only the former will be domestically applied.[612]

Kelsen clearly rejects the idea that the validity of international legal norms within national law is dependent on a prior national provision providing for this very validity.[613] Although it is true that the international legal order lacks enforcement bodies and must therefore rely on enforcement through national authorities,[614] Anzilotti is mistaken in his views on transformation as a necessary element in bestowing domestic validity on international law. Again, the international legal order does not obligate states as such and as real collectives, but only addresses individuals, which means that the state can only manifest itself through its organs. And if individuals act as organs or representatives of their state, the obligation to act is then imputed to the national legal order of the state.[615] Otherwise, we would need to deal with the self-contradictory hypothesis that the state has a double legal personality (national and international) yet while being one and the same state. This would lead to the absurd conclusion that there is a substance of the state that is independent of its legal personality,[616] and hence to a juristic duplication of every single state.[617]

The correct view is that international law leaves it to the state to ascertain the personal element on how to give effect to international norms, which remain incomplete since they only govern a substantial element and thereby the behaviour which, if complied with, will prevent any future penalizing sanctions. Transformation may be necessary from the viewpoint of national law, but not international law. All a state is doing by enacting the statute concerned is merely fulfilling its international obligations or exercising its international rights.[618] If, however, transformation is considered necessary in order to bind the organs of the state, then this would concurrently mean that international law does not even govern its own substance.[619] And by asserting that international law does not bind individuals, proponents of the transformation doctrine deny that international law is binding at all, because none but individuals can ever be bound.[620]

[612] Ignaz Seidl-Hohenveldern, 'Transformation or Adoption of International Law into Municipal Law' (1963) 12 *International and Comparative Law Quarterly* 88, 88.

[613] Hans Kelsen, 'La transformation du droit international public en droit interne' (1936) 43 *Revue générale de droit international public* 5, 5.

[614] Kelsen, *Principles of International Law* (n 401) 193–4, where he provides examples such as extradition treaties.

[615] Kelsen, 'La transformation' (n 613) 9 fn 1 and 14.

[616] Kelsen, 'Les rapports' (n 364) 23; Kelsen, 'La transformation' (n 613) 22.

[617] Kelsen, *General Theory* (n 104) 376–7; Charles Leben, *The Advancement of International Law* (Hart Publishing, 2010) 116–17: in this sense, one could also ask why such a duplicated State, say the two Frances of national and international law, would not be able to conclude treaties with each other—a clearly absurd conclusion.

[618] Kelsen, *Principles of International Law* (n 401) 194; Kelsen, *General Theory* (n 104) 378.

[619] Kelsen, 'La transformation' (n 613) 6–11.

[620] J. Walter Jones, 'The "Pure" Theory of International Law' (1935) 16 *British Yearbook of International Law* 5, 8.

C. Appraisal and conclusion

The merit of legal monism undoubtedly lies in its unambiguous distinctness and unsurpassed analytical edge.[621] These qualities result from the scientific-objective programme of the Vienna School of Law, which draws on (neo-)Kantian epistemology, and not politics, psychology, sociology, brute facts (i.e. positivism), or metaphysics (i.e. natural law) to construct a theory of law in general.[622] The foregoing sections not only demonstrated that the sovereignty of the state is a chimera, as it is ultimately identical to the legal order of that very state, but also that the unity of international and national law (*scilicet* legal monism) is a logical and epistemological consequence of the strictly scientific demands of the pure theory of law. One must realize what Kelsen, Merkl, Verdross, and Kunz took from Kant and his philosophy, namely that the observer's epistemological position influences and affects the world one perceives. In other words, it is predicated on the assumption by the observer cognizing the law and whether this observer wants to see it as one or not.[623]

In this light, this unitary view is nothing less than establishing the normativity of the law via a hypothetical identification of legal validity which, ultimately, is achieved by means of the *Grundnorm*. Despite its enduring puzzling nature, it is crucial to underscore that it is the hypothesis of the basic norm that provides the positive law with an epistemological basis and thereby enables the observer (i.e. the jurist) to cognize an effective and coercive normative system as valid. And if the jurist accepts this legal system as valid, monism becomes logically necessary, as legal validity remains indivisible and not subject to gradation. National law is not valid in a different sense than international law, and hence only a monist construction of the law is possible.[624]

Admittedly, the jurist nevertheless remains free to embrace a dualist or pluralist construction of the law which then becomes epistemologically and logically possible[625]—but only at the dear price of contaminating the purity of law by reducing legal validity to factual-empirical criteria[626] or of giving up the concept of legal validity and the legal nature of the international legal order altogether. By producing an equivocation in the term 'legal validity', both dualists and pluralists should understand that what they are actually talking about may no longer be law.[627] Thus, the concept of legal monism protects the law from methodological arbitrariness[628] and acts, through the *Grundnorm*, as a functional precondition of the legal science and thereby as an epistemological tool to outline its object of cognizance.[629]

621 Markus Kotzur, 'Über Monismus und Dualismus hinaus: Ansätze zu einer Neukonzeptualisierung des Völkerrechts mit einer konstitutionellen Matrix' in Marko Novaković (ed), *Basic Concepts of Public International Law: Monism & Dualism* (Faculty of Law, University of Belgrade, 2013) 165.

622 Jakab, 'Kelsens Völkerrechtslehre' (n 500) 1055–6.

623 Kant, *Kritik der reinen Vernunft* (n 34) A 42/B 59.

624 See also Öhlinger, 'Einheit' (n 447) 167–8, arguing that the pure theory of law does not intend to prove the legal quality of international law; its purpose merely is to state that if one accepts international law as law, then it must form a unitary legal body with international law.

625 Theodor Schilling, 'Das Verhältnis zwischen Völkerrecht, Gemeinschaftsrecht und staatlichem Recht' in Stefan Griller and Heinz Peter Rill (eds), *Rechtstheorie: Rechtsbegriff—Dynamik—Auslegung* (Springer 2011) 153–6.

626 Rub (n 383) 454.

627 Somek, 'Kelsen Lives' (n 417) 425.

628 Hammer, 'Kelsens Grundnormkonzeption' (n 441) 226.

629 Walter, *Aufbau der Rechtsordnung* (n 179) 13; Rotter (n 193) 56.

The next consequence of a unitary view of the law is that national and international law are connected by a hierarchy of norms, which enables the observer to comprehend the composition of any given legal order, including its delegating and derogating relations. And although Kelsen highlights that strictly scientifically seen, the question of primacy within this hierarchy of norms is indeterminate (i.e. either national or international law may sit at the top of the chain of delegation), a closer scrutiny reveals that one needs to go beyond Kelsen to see that the primacy of national law is epistemologically (and practically) untenable. This version of primacy would result in macerating the concept of legal validity since international law—as law—would then only exist at the behest of national legal orders and, on top of that, in as many manifestations as there are national legal orders—a clearly absurd outcome, if one claims that international law is genuine law.[630]

Lastly, legal monism has the benefit of being able to overcome the decentralized nature of international law by showing, again with reference to the *Grundnorm*, that the law is a unitary object of cognition, and that this unitary view also informs and influences the substance of international law.[631] If one assumes that national and international law are derived from one single basic norm and that international law delegates national law, then by necessity, there can be no difference in sources, substance, and subjects of these two bodies of law. This also entails that normative conflicts between national and international law are not principally irresolvable, as dualism and pluralism claim. Because of its clear structure and one single concept of legal validity, legal monism can provide for a clear resolution of such conflicts—either by disapplying the relevant national norm in conflict with international law or by resorting to sanctions—in clear conformity with the law.

However, the epistemological claims for legal monism by the Vienna School of Jurisprudence did not remain unchallenged. To give a balanced and complete picture of legal monism, the subsequent section will explore the main arguments against the views of the pure theory of law, but also try to rebut them in a satisfactory and convincing manner.

6. Legal Monism: Critique and Rebuttal

In addition to the direct and intuitive appeal of both dualism and pluralism, the main reason why legal monism is out fashion these days among legal theorists is that prevailing opinion holds that it has, as envisaged by the pure theory of law, been decisively refuted by two of the most eminent current legal theorists, namely H.L.A. Hart in his essay 'Kelsen's Doctrine of the Unity of Law'[632] and Joseph Raz in his book *The Concept of a Legal System*.[633] In general, Hart and Raz also argue

630 Rill, 'Internationales, supranationales und nationales Recht' (n 504) 683 fn 24.
631 Bleckmann 'Monismus mit Primat des Völkerrechts' (n 484) 347.
632 Hart, 'Kelsen's Doctrine' (n 436).
633 Raz, *Concept of a Legal System* (n 114).

that laws exist as part of legal systems[634] or that there is a system-constituting social rule, i.e. the rule of recognition, which specifies the membership conditions of legal norms.[635] Yet neither of them ever went as far as Kelsen, Verdross, or Kunz and declared that all legal norms in the world necessarily formed part of a unitary legal order.[636] According to their criticism, legal monism fails to offer a satisfactory theory of the identity of legal systems and therefore is simply not a viable legal theory, because it leads to obviously absurd consequences. The membership of norms in a given legal system can only be ascertained with reference to the social practices of identification that characterize the activity of the primary law-applying institutions of that legal system.[637]

Given the impact of this criticism on the substantial value of the pure theory of law as a theory to conceive of the law in general and on legal monism in particular, a scrutinizing analysis of Hart's and Raz's arguments deserves a section in its own right to conclude this part on the epistemological merits of legal monism. These arguments, which, in principle, take the form of an attack on the most basic tenets of legal monism, must be duly addressed and credibly rebutted to maintain monism in the sense of the pure theory of law as a viable theory.[638]

This section intends to counter the overall claims by Hart and Raz that legal monism as presented by Kelsen is either trivially true and therefore not interesting, or interesting, but false. In fact, it will be argued that monism is both logically true and interesting, since it can provide the lawyer with new information that goes beyond mere tautological truths. Through its central conceptions (such as the strict dichotomy of 'is' and 'ought', the basic norm, and the hierarchy of norms), the pure theory of law succeeds in explaining the objective meaning of norms,[639] which is 'legal validity', and in satisfactorily resolving conflicts between norms of different bodies of law. Only monism takes the concept of legal validity seriously, and therefore it cannot be uninteresting to lawyers.

A. H.L.A. Hart and Kelsen's unity doctrine

According to Hart, it is Kelsen's most serious mistake to claim that all valid laws necessarily form a single system. The monist theory of national and international law, Hart continues, is simply unsuccessful because of the major fallacies Kelsen overlooked when envisaging this doctrine.[640] Despite certain similarities between Hart and Kelsen and the latter's (albeit limited) influence on the former, Hart is rather anxious to clarify that his theory differs from the pure theory of law in important

[634] Joseph Raz, 'The Identity of Legal Systems' (1971) 59 *California Law Review* 795, 795–815.
[635] Hart, *The Concept of Law* (n 52) 92. [636] Giudice (n 462) 148.
[637] Vinx, *Kelsen's Pure Theory of Law* (n 108) 182.
[638] *Nota bene* that Hart and Raz only concentrate on legal monism as presented by Kelsen and neglect other scholars of this school of thought. This lack of engagement with these other thinkers is a regrettable restriction, but needs to be accepted as a fact at this point.
[639] Brian H. Bix, 'Rules and Normativity in Law' in Michał Araszkiewicz and others (eds), *Problems of Normativity, Rules, and Rules-Following* (Springer 2015) 135.
[640] H.L.A. Hart, 'Answers to Eight Questions' in Luís Duarte d'Almeida, James Edwards, and Andrea Dolcetti (eds), *Reading HLA Hart's* The Concept of Law (Hart Publishing, 2013) 290.

ways.[641] Hart is a force to be reckoned with, and there is no way around his arguments. These very arguments will now be discussed in three separate steps:[642] (i) the strong version of monism; (ii) the problem of the basic norm; and (iii) the principle of validating purport and the weak version of monism.[643] All of these arguments will subsequently be subjected to close scrutiny in order to save legal monism from theoretical obsolescence and absurdity.

(1) The strong version of monism: logical and epistemological necessity

At the outset, Hart distinguishes two versions of legal monism in Kelsen's writings:[644] a strong version, according to which international and national law form one single legal order by logical and epistemological necessity;[645] and a weaker version, which states that although it is not necessarily true that all valid laws form one single legal order, it is, however, just the case, as an empirical contingency, that they do form such a single legal order.[646] Yet the first problem in Hart's argument is that this distinction between these two different versions of monism cannot be sustained. Kelsen nowhere expounds a weak version of monism by *exclusively* pointing to the existence of the effectiveness principle as *the* positive legal provision that anchors the recognition of states in the existence of efficacious territorial legal orders of coercive rule.[647]

Let us nonetheless engage with Hart's objections against Kelsen's strong version of monism. Because of his artificial distinction into a weak and strong version of monism, Hart erroneously postulates that very little is to be found in support of the stronger thesis in Kelsen's works—even though Kelsen's entire work rests on this alleged strong version and his epistemological claims as derived from Kant and the neo-Kantians. For Kelsen, monism is an epistemological postulate of legal theory, as it is logically impossible to conceive of simultaneously valid norms belonging to different and mutually independent systems.[648] Thus, quite the contrary is the case, and if there is any support for legal monism, it is to be found in these epistemological claims. Hart correctly summarizes that these claims can be reduced to the contention that all law forms a single system since there is a form of knowledge in the shape of legal cognition that studies both national and international law as subsumable under the single description 'valid laws' and hence constitutes 'its object'

[641] See A.W. Brian Simpson, *Reflections on* The Concept of Law (Oxford University Press, 2011) 114; Nicola Lacey, *A Life of HLA Hart: The Nightmare and the Noble Dream* (Oxford University Press, 2004) 249–53.

[642] See Giudice (n 462) 157.

[643] As a fourth argument, one could add Hart's criticism that Kelsen cannot accept conflicts between valid laws in analogy to the logical principle of non-contradiction; see Hart, 'Kelsen's Doctrine' (n 436) 565–74. However, since the older Kelsen has given up this claim and accepted the existence of normative conflicts (see section 4C(4)), this problem need not concern us at this point. See also the respective admittance in Hart, 'Eight Questions' (n 640) 290.

[644] Hart, 'Kelsen's Doctrine' (n 436) 554.

[645] Kelsen, *Pure Theory* (n 54) 329.

[646] See Kelsen, *General Theory* (n 104) 371–2; Kelsen, *Pure Theory* (n 54) 330–1.

[647] Somek, 'Kelsen Lives' (n 417) 426.

[648] Kelsen, *General Theory* (n 104) 363 and 373.

as a unity.[649] Hart, however, does not engage properly with Kelsen's use of Kant's unitary object of cognizance, and is to be criticized for brushing off this argument in one single sentence, stating: 'Surely we might as well attempt to deduce from the existence of the history of warfare or the science of strategy that all wars are one or all armies are one'.[650]

This objection fails for three reasons. First, Hart appears to misunderstand this particular element of Kantian philosophy. To conceive of specific objects as a transcendental unity does not mean that these objects are all the same—this would be too simple a solution. What this unity entails is, in Kant's words, a 'productive synthesis' of empirical data into one single concept.[651] Kant's transcendental unity of apperception is the a priori ground of all concepts through which all of the manifold given in an empirical sensation is a united concept of the object.[652] In other words, all wars or all armies are not one in the same way as all laws are not one. But what is the same is the conceptual cognition of these objects, and their belonging to their respective unitary concept of 'war', 'army', or 'law'. The Second World War is not the same as the American Civil War, but they form a unitary object of cognizance 'war' by being observed as an armed conflict between different parties. Equally, the crime of murder is not the same as the crime of theft, but they both form part of the unitary object of cognizance 'law' by being cognized as part of an effective, self-creating, and coercive normative system that has been posited by human beings for the regulation of their behaviour.[653] The *essentiale* of law ultimately is its validity, which is coterminous with its very existence[654] and not subject to gradation. Either a specific legal norm is valid and therefore exists, or it is invalid and therefore does not exist.[655] This means that all law forms a unitary object of cognizance *qua* validity, which derives from the *Grundnorm* as the very fount of this validity.

Secondly, Hart's argument does not work because his analogy of warfare does not work. Not only is it common sense that law and war are not relevantly similar, but it is also crucial to recall that Kelsen's legal monism flows from the logic of norms and the nature of normativity. Consequently, there is no reason why Kelsen would be committed to a similar account where, as in warfare as an empirical fact, logic and normativity have no application.[656] They would certainly apply to the *law* of warfare, but that is not what Hart means.

[649] Hart, 'Kelsen's Doctrine' (n 436) 564. [650] Ibid., 565.

[651] Kant, *Kritik der reinen Vernunft* (n 34) A 118–19, A 250–51 and B 139.

[652] Ibid., B 139–40.

[653] See Rill, 'Internationales, supranationales und nationales Recht' (n 504) 688; Jabloner, 'Rechtsbegriff' (n 437) 23.

[654] Kelsen thus follows the philosophical tradition which denies that existence is an additional property or predicate of entities; see Aristotle, *Metaphysics* (n 95) 1028a 13–15; David Hume, *A Treatise of Human Nature* (John Noone, 1738) book I, part II, section VI; Kant, *Kritik der reinen Vernunft* (n 34) A 600/B 628; Bertrand Russell, 'On Denoting' (1905) 14 *Mind* 479; Gottlob Frege, *The Foundations of Arithmetic* (2nd edn; Blackwell, 1959) para 53.

[655] Kelsen, *Pure Theory* (n 54) 10; Kelsen, 'Law and Logic' (n 350) 229.

[656] Giudice (n 462) 157.

Thirdly, Hart's implicit criticism that either Kelsen is right, but what he claims is trivially true and thus not interesting, or that Kelsen's claim is interesting but false, is also to be rejected. It might be correct to say that the way of how Kelsen reaches his epistemological conclusion based on Kantian and neo-Kantian philosophy is terrifyingly trivial, because to claim that all law is law *qua* being law and thus forms 'one law' is necessarily true, but this would of course not be an interesting claim. Analytic a priori claims ('all bachelors are unmarried') are certainly always and trivially true and hence uninteresting. The decisive argument is, however, that Kelsen's claims are not analytic a priori, but synthetic a priori claims in the Kantian sense[657] and therefore not necessarily uninteresting owing to their necessary nature. This means that his claims entail propositions whose predicate concepts are not already contained in the respective subjects,[658] or that certain interesting consequences follow from them that were not immediately perceptible.

The most important consequence of these synthetic a priori claims is that only the presupposition of one single *Grundnorm* allows for the cognition of valid law, whilst the assumption of two (as in dualism) or more basic norms (as in pluralism) prevents such cognition. The reason for that is that assuming the existence of more than one basic norm will necessarily result in an equivocation of the meaning of 'legal validity', which would thereby destroy the very essence of the law. Furthermore, in contrast to dualism or pluralism, monism does not surrender when it comes to normative conflicts. Instead, monism rather asks: what will happen next? What is the legal significance of the two norms in question? If the other norm in question is not a legal norm at all, but a moral norm or political courtesy, the dichotomy of 'is' and 'ought' would certainly require that the *legal* norm be applied. And in contrast to dualism and pluralism, which may attempt to resolve normative conflicts by taking recourse to extra-legal solutions, monism's subsequent question will always be: what will *legally* happen next?[659]

And this is exactly what is at stake in the question of whether the law forms one system or not, namely how the law is to be cognized and applied, and how lawyers can be enabled to resolve conflicts between legal norms. In sum, Hart's objection to the epistemological necessity of legal monism is mistaken and fails to convince on all grounds.

(2) The conundrum of the basic norm

Hart also takes considerable issue with the very basis of normativity in Kelsen's theory: the *Grundnorm*. In Hart's own theory, the foundation of a legal system lies in the 'rule of recognition' which, as an accepted and practised social rule, provides the criteria for identifying all types of rules as rules and hence members of a given

[657] See also William E. Conklin, *The Invisible Origins of Legal Positivism: A Re-Reading of a Tradition* (Kluwer Law, 2001) 221.

[658] Kant, *Kritik der reinen Vernunft* (n 34) A 6–7/B 10–11.

[659] Somek, 'Monism' (n 48) 354–5.

system.[660] Thus, in contrast to the transcendental nature of the basic norm, the rule of recognition is simply a sociological and present matter of fact that can be expressed by utterances such as 'it is the law that…' in the practice of courts, officials, and private persons.[661] By establishing this extra-systemic foundation of law on the basis of social practice, however, Hart unduly interfuses empirical facts and the normativity of the law and thereby transgresses the dichotomy of 'is' and 'ought'. In Humean and Kelsenian terms, such derivation of legal norms from social practice is unacceptable, but—in the context of this section—need not bother us any further at this point.

What is more important is Hart's critique of the *Grundnorm*, which he regards, when accepting the constitution as a living reality, as a needless reduplication 'to suggest that there is a further rule to the effect that the constitution (or those who "laid it down") are to be obeyed'.[662] This allegation of reduplication is based on the fact that the basic norm and the historically first constitution share two distinctive features, namely that both are effective and, as their validity is merely presupposed, non-valid.[663] The constitution cannot be valid unless the *Grundnorm* is presupposed, since the constitution's validity depends on authorization by a superior norm; and the *Grundnorm* itself is also non-valid because if it were valid, there would be no need of presupposing its validity.[664] In this light, Hart therefore does not see any added value in presupposing a transcendental basic norm if all it does is reduplicate the constitution on a higher and impalpable level.[665]

Equally, Hart considers a basic norm for international law to be a comic effort and an empty repetition of the rule that the society of states ought to observe certain standards of conduct as obligatory rules.[666] According to Hart, Kelsen's suggested basic norm of international law, *consuetudines sunt servandae*, that is, states should behave as they have customarily behaved, says nothing more than that those who accept particular rules also ought to observe a rule that the rules ought to be observed. This is, again, a useless reduplication of the fact that a set of rules is accepted as binding by states as binding rules.[667] Hence, Hart claims that Kelsen's *Grundnorm* of international law has no content and goes no distance in that a distinct and system-constituting rule exists above what Hart would call primary rules of obligation at the international level. Yet the problem is that Hart merely focuses on the abstractness of Kelsen's formulation of the basic norm, which makes him overlook its actual content.[668]

660 Hart, *The Concept of Law* (n 52) 100.

661 Ibid., 89 and 107.

662 Ibid., 246.

663 See Georg Henrik von Wright, *Norm and Action. A Logical Enquiry* (Routledge 1963) 196 and 199. The term 'non-valid' (instead of 'invalid') is used here because it can be argued that both 'validity' and 'invalidity' are norm-relative concepts, i.e. norms are invalid or valid only *in relation* to another norm permitting its issuing; thus, the basic norm of any given legal order is neither valid nor invalid, but non-valid.

664 Kelsen, *Pure Theory* (n 54) 201 ff.

665 Although the same objection holds, *mutatis mutandis*, against Hart's own rule of recognition; see Stephen Munzer, *Legal Validity* (Martinus Nijhoff 1972) 54.

666 *Nota bene* at this point that international law only takes up 'a relatively small and unimportant part' in Hart's theory; Hart, *The Concept of Law* (n 52) 4 and ch X in general.

667 Hart, *The Concept of Law* (n 52) 230.

668 Giudice (n 462) 159.

If we recall Kelsen's statement in this respect, he provides an account of a hierarchy of norms by stating that the basic norm of *consuetudines sunt servandae* allows for the development of customary international law as the first (and supreme) positive-legal stage within the international legal order. The customary rule of *pacta sunt servanda* then allows for the creation of treaties, which in turn, provides for the creation of treaty-based organizations and institutions.[669] But this is exactly the same system-constituting normative hierarchy Hart is establishing on the basis of his rule of recognition, albeit in a more elusive manner:[670] even though this hierarchy of validity-criteria is characterized by an order of relative subordination and primacy,[671] it remains rudimentary in comparison with Merkl's and Kelsen's *Stufenbau* doctrine and fails to grasp all the rules that are considered as applicable and binding in a given legal order.[672]

Hart's allegation of emptiness and reduplication becomes even more erroneous when one notices that it is also easy to accuse his rule of recognition of the same charge, e.g. by formulating it as 'unless they are required to do otherwise by valid positive law, officials must apply as valid the norms of their own customary behavior (and not, for example, norms of other people's customary behavior, or moral norms, etc.)'.[673] As already discussed above,[674] Kelsen may have formulated the basic norm of international law in a wrong way, because the norm of *consuetudines sunt servandae* does not live up to the actual non-existing hierarchy of sources in positive international law. However, it is no more accurate to claim that Kelsen's attempt amounts to a meaningless reduplication than it would be to say that Hart's concept of the rule of recognition amounts to an empty reduplication.[675]

Beyond that, as concluded above,[676] it is also possible to reinterpret the concept of the basic norm of international law to the effect that it remains contentless. By regarding it as a pure transcendental hypothesis (and therefore in contrast to Kelsen), the *Grundnorm* can prevent any allegations of reduplication. Furthermore, by allowing for the existence of Article 38 of the ICJ Statute and the other sources of international norms as the meta-meta-law on international law-creation,[677] this assumption also remains compatible with positive international law.

669 Kelsen, *Pure Theory* (n 54) 214–17; Kelsen, *Principles of International Law* (n 401) 417–18.

670 Bindreiter, *Why* Grundnorm*?* (n 145) 69 fn 3.

671 Hart, *The Concept of Law* (n 52) 105–7; this basically means that if certain rules have been identified as valid on the basis of a criterion and they then conflict with other rules, identified as being valid on the basis of another criterion, then the first validity criterion would prevail as superior.

672 Michael Pawlik, *Die Reine Rechtslehre und die Rechtstheorie H.L.A. Harts: Ein kritischer Vergleich* (Duncker & Humblot, 1993) 155–6; Bindreiter, *Why* Grundnorm*?* (n 145) 69 fn 3.

673 Giudice (n 462) 159–60.

674 See section 5B(2)a.

675 Giudice (n 462) 160. See also Jeremy Waldron, 'Who Needs Rules of Recognition?' in Matthew D. Adler and Kenneth E. Himma (eds), *The Rule of Recognition and the U.S. Constitution* (Oxford University Press, 2009) 327–49.

676 See section 5B(2)a.

677 Kammerhofer, *Uncertainty* (n 149) 210.

(3) *The weak version of monism: the principle of validating purport*

At the outset, it must be clearly emphasized again that Kelsen never distinguishes between a strong (i.e. necessary) and weak (i.e. contingent) version of monism. Let us nonetheless engage with Hart's criticism of Kelsen's 'principle of effectiveness' which, in Kelsen's words, legitimizes a coercive national legal order 'for the territory of its actual effectiveness as a valid legal order and the community constituted by this coercive order as a "State" in the sense of international law'.[678] Hart calls this chain of delegation between international and national law the relationship of *validating purport*, and argues that legal monism fails because it conflates this very relationship with the relationship of *validation proper*. Hart likens this to a situation where he writes a paper on Kelsen and concurrently receives a request from the Vice-Chancellor of Oxford University to write a paper on Kelsen. Hart concludes that without establishing the exact circumstances surrounding these events, it remains impossible to ascertain whether he indeed obeyed the request or not.[679]

The central problem at stake is that of two different intentional states of mind: *validation proper* denotes a situation where a norm is adopted with the intent of creating it on the basis of another one, for instance when a judge identifies a particular norm as valid law on the basis of an accepted rule of recognition or if a national parliament adopts a legal act in accordance with the relevant constitutional procedures. *Validating purport*, conversely, means that legal norms which fit a certain description, are deemed valid regardless of whether they were created to become members of the legal order containing that description.[680]

To emphasize his criticism, Hart provides the hypothetical example of the British Parliament passing the Soviet Laws Validity Act, which purports to declare all laws currently effective in the Soviet Union to be valid within the United Kingdom.[681] This does not, however, mean that British and Soviet law form one legal system, because it would be absurd to say that Soviet Law derives its validity from the relevant act of Parliament. Alternatively, it is evident that the law of the Soviet Union is valid in the Soviet Union regardless of the validating purport of the British statute, since its validity is derived from an accepted rule of recognition in the Soviet Union. Hart continues that the same holds true for the relationship between international and national law. He states that questions regarding the formation of one single system and the derivation of validity of national law from international law (*validation proper*) are not the same as questions of whether international law treats national law as forming part of a single system with itself and whether national law is valid according to international law on the basis of the principle of effectiveness.[682] Since the principle of effectiveness is hence a mere expression of validating purport built into positive international law, unity between two bodies of law cannot be established if one of them recognizes as valid for itself what is valid in the other. It

[678] Kelsen, *Pure Theory* (n 54) 210 and 336; Kelsen, *General Theory* (n 104) 350–1.
[679] Hart, 'Kelsen's Doctrine' (n 436) 556.
[680] Somek, 'Kelsen Lives' (n 417) 426–7; Hart, 'Kelsen's Doctrine' (n 436) 561–2.
[681] *Nota bene* that Hart first published this essay in 1968 when the Soviet Union still existed.
[682] Hart, 'Kelsen's Doctrine' (n 436) 562–3.

simply treats foreign rules in the same manner as its own rules, but it does not ingest these foreign rules.[683]

However, Hart's criticism cannot be sustained for three reasons. The first argument against Hart is his obvious misinterpretation of Kelsen. It is very unlikely that Kelsen would have failed to appreciate and to acknowledge the distinction between validation proper and validating purport. In his works, Kelsen heavily emphasizes the distinction between objective and subjective legal meaning. The 'ought' as the meaning of the norm may have a subjective dimension, i.e. it is treated as what someone wishes to be or not to be, for instance when somebody states in writing what ought to happen to their belongings after their passing. Hence the subjective meaning of this act is a testament. This, however, may not be sufficient, because from an objective viewpoint, it may not be a testament in the legal sense as some formalities were not observed. Thus, the objective meaning denotes what ought to happen independently of what anyone wishes to be or not to be.[684] After all, it is obvious that usurping and abusing the authority of public offices, as the famous Hauptmann von Köpenick did,[685] only satisfies the subjective, but not the objective meaning of the law, and that the lack of real legal authority results in the nullity of the alleged legal act.[686]

In the same vein, Kelsen would certainly also have rejected Hart's idea that the Vice-Chancellor of Oxford University can put himself in a genuine position of normative authority over Hart by merely purporting to give orders to him. Consequently, it is highly implausible to attribute to Kelsen a principle such as validating purport that involves an obvious confusion of objective and subjective legal meaning.[687] Furthermore, there is another aspect to this issue. Hart's distinction between validation proper and validating purport is of a substantive nature, which, however, is entirely beside the point to Kelsen's theory. Kelsen, as is well known, does not explore substance ('any kind of content might be law'[688]), but the form in which the legal substance is to be accounted for by legal science. *Prima facie*, it is true that subjective purport may or may not play a role in law-creation. Individual parties, for example, can agree to enter contractual relations through mere conduct that is not intended to create a norm.[689] In constitutional legal terms, some processes of norm-creation might require some intentional use of a particular rule,[690] but nevertheless, no law can be validly created by the authorized norm-creating body unless the relevant procedural rules are thoroughly complied with. Yet, what really matters in legal

683 Somek, 'Monism' (n 48) 348; Somek, 'Kelsen Lives' (n 417) 427.

684 See Kelsen, *Pure Theory* (n 54) 2–3.

685 Wilhelm Voigt (1849–1922), an impostor who masqueraded as a military officer and, with the help of unsuspecting soldiers, occupied the local city hall of Berlin-Köpenick, where he 'confiscated' a considerable amount of money from the treasury.

686 Kelsen, 'Über Staatsunrecht' (n 327) 848; Vinx, *Kelsen's Pure Theory of Law* (n 108) 78–100.

687 Lars Vinx, 'The Kelsen-Hart Debate: Hart's Critique of Kelsen's Legal Monism Reconsidered' in Jeremy Telman (ed), *Hans Kelsen in America – Selective Affinities and the Mysteries of Academic Influence* (Springer, 2016) 63–4.

688 Kelsen, *Pure Theory* (n 54) 198.

689 Through an 'implied-in-fact contract' or acquiescence, for example.

690 See e.g. rules on required majorities to either pass constitutional or 'ordinary' statutes.

theoretical terms is that whether or not a relation of validation is based on validation proper or sheer validating purport, it focuses on the particular *substance* of the legal norm in question[691]—clearly an issue with which Kelsen does not concern himself.

The second argument against Hart's criticism immediately follows from Kelsen's tacit rejection of the distinction between validating purport and validation proper. Hart's premise of 'weak monism' is only tenable under such a distinction, which he deems crucial in order to explain the phenomenon of 'system-relative validity', that is, the existence of several and different rules of recognition for different legal systems.[692] At best, Hart's critique is very weak, as it rests on a premise that Kelsen does not share:[693] first, because Kelsen cannot accept a social practice, such as Hart's rule of recognition, as a criterion for validity owing to its transgression of the is-ought dichotomy;[694] and, secondly, because even if one substitutes 'rule of recognition' with *Grundnorm*, the idea of various different basic norms for different legal systems flies in the face of Kelsen's legal-epistemological foundations.[695] Moreover, the fact that Kelsen does not and cannot support the principle of validating purport also helps defend the viability of monism under the primacy of international law. This monist version claims that one must, under epistemological considerations, necessarily view national and international as a unitary legal body in which international law is superior, and not, as Hart claims, because the principle of effectiveness purports to validate national law.[696]

Hart fails to acknowledge Kelsen's argument that the existence of a legal system—and thereby the defensibility of a certain construction of that legal system—depends on constraints of effectiveness. For Kelsen, it would not be scientific to postulate the existence of a particular legal order unless the behaviour it claims to govern also exhibits sufficient conformity with the norms of the system.[697] The consequence is that monism under the primacy of international law has to be compatible with these constraints of effectiveness in order to amount to a viable description of the law. This is in fact the case and can easily be demonstrated by pointing out the existing system of states and other international legal subjects that interact with one another on a regular basis. Moreover, they do so in recognition of international law, such as that no state—despite the occasionally serious scepticism—seriously denies the legal quality of international law, and that international obligations are complied with[698] lest states incur international responsibility and risk subsequent sanctions. Hart is therefore wrong in assuming that monism under the primacy of international law depends on nothing but a relation of validating purport between the principle of

691 Somek, 'Kelsen Lives' (n 417) 428.

692 Hart, 'Kelsen's Doctrine' (n 436) 575–6.

693 Somek, 'Kelsen Lives' (n 417) 427.

694 Bindreiter, 'Presupposing the Basic Norm' (n 189) 166–8; Pawlik (n 672) 189–91.

695 Öhlinger, 'Einheit' (n 447) 162–3.

696 Hart, 'Kelsen's Doctrine' (n 436) 563.

697 Vinx, 'Kelsen-Hart Debate' (n 687) 66; Kelsen, *Problem der Souveränität* (n 57) 94–101.

698 James L. Brierly, 'The Basis of Obligation in International Law' in Hersch Lauterpacht and Humphrey Waldock (eds), *The Basis of Obligation in International Law and Other Papers by the Late James Leslie Brierly* (Clarendon Press, 1958) 1–67; Rosalyn Higgins, *Problems and Process* (Clarendon Press, 1994) 13–16.

effectiveness and national law, and he fails to make the case that monism cannot account for state behaviour in a descriptively plausible way.[699]

The last argument against Hart's criticism is that monism is in fact able to accommodate the example of the Soviet Laws Validity Act quite well, since Hart fails to consider one of the most crucial elements of the pure theory of law: the *Stufenbau* doctrine. Hart is absolutely right in saying that the purported validation of Soviet law by the Soviet Laws Validity Act is not really what validates Soviet law (except for its use in British courts, but this is a question of the conflict of laws).[700] Yet Hart commits to an obvious *non sequitur* when assuming that it follows from the fact that the Soviet Laws Validity Act does not validate Soviet Law, that British and Soviet Law cannot possibly form part of one and the same legal order. If jurists take the viewpoint of monism under the primacy of international law, they can certainly argue that both British and Soviet Law form part of one legal order as they are both delegated by the principle of effectiveness under international law, and not by a validating relationship between British and Soviet Law.[701]

This makes perfect sense, if we remember the hierarchy of norms as originally devised by Merkl, according to which only superior norms can validate inferior norms, but legal norms of the same hierarchical level cannot validate one another.[702] Therefore, in a monist construction under the primacy of international law, where British and Soviet Law are located on an equal level of legal hierarchy, the Soviet Laws Validity Act, as a British legal act, can never be an authentic validation of Soviet law.[703] Monism does not claim that one national legal order validates another national legal order, and Hart fails in comparing the *horizontal* relationship between equal bodies of law (i.e. national law) with the *vertical* relationship between hierarchically different bodies of law (i.e. international law as the delegating and national law as the delegated body of law, respectively).

In sum, Hart's critique must therefore be rejected.

B. Joseph Raz and the identity of legal systems

Joseph Raz is the other legal theorist besides Hart who has critically engaged with Kelsen's theory and his monist claim. Thereby Raz formed very strong opinions and explicit views on Kelsen, which he follows through and defends with an impressive philosophic will. And although he somewhat rehabilitates Kelsen's reputation by defending him against Hart[704] on the basis of the strength and robustness he sees in Kelsen's writings, Raz is nonetheless of the opinion that Kelsen errs in stipulating the *Grundnorm* as an epistemological requirement at the apex of the legal order to

699 Vinx, 'Kelsen-Hart Debate' (n 687) 66.

700 Hart, 'Kelsen's Doctrine' (n 436) 562.

701 Vinx, 'Kelsen-Hart Debate' (n 687) 64.

702 Merkl, *Rechtskraft* (n 210) 217; Merkl, 'Prolegomena' (n 195) 1098–9.

703 Vinx, 'Kelsen-Hart Debate' (n 687) 65.

704 See e.g. Joseph Raz, 'Two Views of the Nature of the Theory of Law: A Partial Comparison' (1998) 4 *Legal Theory* 249–82; Raz, 'Kelsen's Theory' (n 138) 94–111; Raz, *Concept of a Legal System* (n 114) 147–67.

give unity to this very order.[705] *In concreto*, Raz argues that the reason why a basic norm is not necessary for the unity of the legal system can be easily understood by examining the following two cases: (i) there are non-identical legal orders that share a *Grundnorm*; and (ii) even without the *Grundnorm*, a unified legal order is possible.[706] As will become clear in the analysis below, the first argument refers to the hierarchy of norms and the chain of delegation, whilst the second argument deals with the basic norm itself. It will also become evident that Raz further develops the arguments by Hart, and that they are, for this reason, fairly similar.[707] And yet for the same reason Raz's criticism must fail, as it ends up misunderstanding and misconstruing Kelsen's theory.[708]

(1) Chains of validity and the identity of legal orders

At the outset, Raz offers a reconstruction of the most basic tenets of Kelsen's theory in the form of two (in his opinion: flawed) axioms from which two further theorems can be derived. For the purposes of the present section, only the first axiom is relevant, which reads as follows: 'Two laws, one of which directly or indirectly authorizes the creation of the other, belong to the same legal system'. From this, Raz derives the theorem that 'if one law authorizes the creation of another or if both are authorized by a third law, then both belong to the same legal system'.[709] Thereby this axiom and theorem introduce the concept of a chain of validity. Raz, however, emphasizes that they also demonstrate the flaws in Kelsen's theory: the derived theorem is false as the fact that two norms are linked by a chain of validity is in itself insufficient to guarantee that they in fact belong to the same legal order. And if the derived theorem is false, so must be the axiom from which it has been derived by way of *modus tollens*.[710]

Raz presents a simple example to illustrate his claim that the *Grundnorm* cannot be the decisive criterion for the unity of a given legal order, as it is possible to conceive of non-identical legal orders sharing a basic norm. If the first axiom—asserting that all the laws belonging to one chain of validity are part of one and the same legal order—were indeed true, the peaceful granting of independence to new states would be impossible.[711] Raz asks the reader to imagine that country A has a colony B, and that both territories are governed by the same legal order. Now imagine that the 'motherland' A grants independence to B on the basis of a law that confers exclusive and unlimited legislative powers over B to an assembly or parliament elected

[705] Christoph Kletzer, 'The Role and Reception of the Work of Hans Kelsen in the United Kingdom' in Robert Walter, Clemens Jabloner, and Klaus Zeleny (eds), *Hans Kelsen anderswo—Hans Kelsen abroad* (Manz, 2010) 158.

[706] Raz, *Concept of a Legal System* (n 114) 100–6; Raz, 'Kelsen's Theory' (n 138) 95.

[707] Vinx, 'Kelsen-Hart Debate' (n 687) 59 fn 1.

[708] Sylvie Delacroix, 'Hart's and Kelsen's Concepts of Normativity Contrasted' (2004) 17 *Ratio Juris* 501, 519; Kletzer, 'Hans Kelsen in the United Kingdom' (n 705) 158.

[709] Raz, 'Kelsen's Theory' (n 138) 95.

[710] Vinx, *Kelsen's Pure Theory of Law* (n 108) 185.

[711] Raz, *Concept of a Legal System* (n 114) 102–3; Raz, 'Kelsen's Theory' (n 138) 98.

by the residents of B.[712] Eventually, suppose that this assembly or parliament adopts a constitution that is generally recognized by the residents of B. Subsequently, elections are held and further laws are adopted according to this constitution, and quite naturally, the government, courts, and the population of B regard themselves as an independent state with an independent legal order.[713] And not only has this new state been recognized by all other states including A, the courts of A also regard the constitution and laws of B as a separate legal order distinct from their own.[714] And yet, despite all these facts, Raz highlights, it follows from Kelsen's first axiom that the constitution and laws of B are part of the legal order of A, since all laws of B were authorized by the independence-granting law of A in the first place and therefore belong to the same chain of validity and to the same legal order.[715] This proves that the 'basic norm cannot play the role assigned to it by Kelsen's criteria of membership and identity, and that these criteria fail to fulfil their function'.[716]

Nevertheless, Raz's argument is not as stringent as it seems *prima facie*. To begin with, Raz fails to see that what Kelsen has in mind when he talks about the unity of a legal order is not a sociological, historical, or political conception of unity, but a legal-normative conception. Kelsen postulates that only norms belonging to one and the same legal order can be valid, and hence the claim that the law of both A and B are valid is the same as claiming that both belong to one and the same legal order.[717] However, Kelsen is not committed to the claim that it is merely a law enacted in A, purporting to authorize the constitutional system of B, that establishes a chain of validity between A and B. Purported chains of validity are only legally significant if jurists in country B do not opt for their state's normative independence. But as already explained above with respect to Hart's critique, Kelsen never assumes that there is a chain of delegation between different states, and therefore jurists in B need not adopt the perspective of absolute normative independence to avoid a chain of validity between A and B. The second option to rebut Raz's argument and to show that there is no chain of validity, is to regard both the laws of A and B as parts of the overarching international legal order *qua* monism.[718]

Even if one adopts a monist view under the primacy of national law, the conclusion that there is only one legal order is inevitable. In this scenario, the basic norm would be located at the apex of A's legal order. Then the validity of B's constitution would be grounded in a norm of A's constitution, either directly granting validity to the laws of B (which would confirm Raz's critique, however),

[712] For the more complex question of a revolutionary and unpeaceful transfer of powers, see Raz, *Concept of a Legal System* (n 114) 103. See also the practical impact of this question on the Rhodesian Unilateral Declaration of Independence of 1965 in case *Madzimbamuto v Lardner-Burke* [1969] AC 645 (PC).

[713] Raz, *Concept of a Legal System* (n 114) 102–3; Raz, 'Kelsen's Theory' (n 138) 98.

[714] As the United Kingdom did concerning its Commonwealth Realms in the Statute of Westminster 1931, 22–3 Geo. 5 c. 4. See also Benjamin Spagnolo, *The Continuity of Legal Systems in Theory and Practice* (Hart Publishing, 2015) 35–6.

[715] Raz, 'Kelsen's Theory' (n 138) 98.

[716] Raz, *Concept of a Legal System* (n 114) 104.

[717] Kletzer, 'Hans Kelsen in the United Kingdom' (n 705) 159. See also Kelsen, *Pure Theory* (n 54) 221 ff.

[718] Vinx, *Kelsen's Pure Theory of Law* (n 108) 187.

or granting validity to international law, which in turn delegates the laws of B. Yet seeing that monism under the primacy of national law is not only practically, but also epistemologically absurd, it is much more plausible to start off from the perspective of monism under the primacy of international law. In this case, the chain of validity would arise from the basic norm of international law authorizing the positive rules of international law, which in turn authorize, under the principle of effectiveness, the constitutions of both A and B.[719] Reliance on the principle of effectiveness therefore has the advantage of explaining why the relationship of validating purport between the two states is entirely irrelevant regarding the validity of the laws of B. Once B became independent, it achieved effective control of its territory and hence, under the principle of effectiveness, only remains delegated by the international legal order, not A. And since B is neither connected to A via a chain of delegation nor normatively independent from international law, Raz's claim that Kelsen's alleged axiom and theorem are false is to be rejected. Kelsen's theory of the chain of delegation simply does not lead to the counter-intuitive example Raz imputes to it.[720]

(2) *Again: the* Grundnorm

Raz's second element of criticism introduces the second axiom of Kelsen's theory, which states that 'all the laws of a legal system are authorized directly or indirectly by one law' from which Raz derives the theorem that 'two laws, neither of which authorizes the creation of the other, do not belong to the same system unless there is a law authorizing the creation of both'.[721] This axiom and theorem give rise to the notion of the *Grundnorm*, which Raz considers equally flawed. Even without Kelsen's hypothesized basic norm, Raz says, a legal order can be unified, and therefore the theorem is false. And if the theorem is false, so is its respective axiom.[722]

To demonstrate his claim, Raz uses the example of a 'legally minded observer' coming to a country where laws can derive their validity either from a written constitution or a customary constitution.[723] This observer will subsequently wonder whether the codified and the customary constitutions belong to the same legal order. To answer this question, Kelsen would refer the observer to the *Grundnorm*, and reply that since neither of the constitutions depends on the other, and since there is no superior positive law that could delegate them, the two constitutions can only be authorized by the same basic norm. Ergo they belong to the same legal order. For Raz, however, this method represents a *petitio principii*, as he regards the basic norm

[719] Kletzer, 'Hans Kelsen in the United Kingdom' (n 705) 159.
[720] Alida Wilson, 'Joseph Raz on Kelsen's Basic Norm' (1982) 27 *American Journal of Jurisprudence* 46, 62; Vinx, *Kelsen's Pure Theory of Law* (n 108) 187–8.
[721] Raz, 'Kelsen's Theory' (n 138) 95.
[722] Raz, *Concept of a Legal System* (n 114) 100–6; Raz, 'Kelsen's Theory' (n 138) 95.
[723] See Kelsen, *General Theory* (n 104) 125 where Kelsen explicitly mentions the United Kingdom as having 'no "written" and hence no formal constitution'. Nonetheless 'the (material) constitution has the character of customary law . . .'.

mainly as a power-conferring norm, i.e. as authorizing norm-creation.[724] And to identify the relevant authorizing content of the basic norm, according to Kelsen, one must identify 'the facts through which an order is created and applied'.[725] Yet this will drive the observer to despair, because then he or she would only be able to identify the legal order with the help of the basic norm, whilst the basic norm can only be identified after the identity of the legal has been established. Therefore, the *Grundnorm* represents a vicious cycle and cannot solve the problem of identity and unity of legal orders.[726]

As a first step, one could counter this argument with reference to the pure theory's synthetic a priori truth that the customary constitution and the codified constitution cannot fail to belong to the same legal order if they are both valid law.[727] Thus, the question of whether the codified or the customary constitution belong to the same legal order or whether there are actually two distinct legal orders in force is not problematic for the Kelsenian legally minded observer once it is generally admitted that both are valid law. Hence it does not make sense to criticize Kelsen for not providing a criterion to answer this question.[728]

The problem is that a sceptic will not be convinced by the epistemological force of the pure theory of law. As a second step, one could therefore take recourse, as suggested by Lars Vinx, to our fictional protagonist, the Kelsenian law-abiding person.[729] The interest of such a person would be to determine what the law requires, and to do so, this person must presuppose the *Grundnorm* to cognize the normative nature of the law. Even an anarchist, according to Kelsen, could describe the law as a system of valid and behaviour-regulating norms without having to approve of this law.[730] Although Raz criticizes this element in Kelsen's theory as a moral statement and hence as an impurity, he eventually accepts the role of the basic norm as a means for the jurist to pretend that law is a valid system of norms.[731]

Persisting differences in this respect aside,[732] in the context of the present analysis, we can consequently agree that both Kelsen and Raz would accept such a fictitious law-abiding person. From an empirical point of view, this person could find that both the customary and the codified constitution are considered to be valid by large groups of members of society, and that he or she must therefore comply with both. Potential conflicts between the two constitutions, however, must somehow be resolved, which is only possible by presuming a *Grundnorm* that makes joint compliance possible. Thereby both custom and codified law become normatively coordinated parts of the same hierarchy of norms, and the question of whether there

[724] Raz, *Concept of a Legal System* (n 114) 66 and 147 ff, contrasting power-conferring with duty-imposing norms. See also Paulson, 'Die unterschiedlichen Formulierungen' (n 165) 59 and 64–7, discussing the *Grundnorm* in its function as a 'norm-creating authorization rule'.

[725] Kelsen, *General Theory* (n 104) 120.

[726] Raz, 'Kelsen's Theory' (n 138) 99.

[727] Kelsen, *Pure Theory* (n 54) 328–9.

[728] Vinx, *Kelsen's Pure Theory of Law* (n 108) 189.

[729] Ibid., 189–90.

[730] Kelsen, *Pure Theory* (n 54) 218 fn 82.

[731] See generally Joseph Raz, 'The Purity of the Pure Theory' (1981) 35 *Revue internationale de philosophie* 441, 441–59.

[732] For an in-depth critical discussion of Raz's view of normativity in Kelsen's theory see e.g. Wilson (n 720) 46–63; Bindreiter, *Why* Grundnorm*?* (n 145) 90–5; Delacroix (n 708) 512–18.

is one or whether there are two legal orders can never become a serious issue for the law-abiding person.[733] Nonetheless, a Razian sceptic could, at this point, simply reiterate their critique that this assumption is begging the question, since to claim that there must be a possibility to comply with both custom and statute because of their being valid is only possible if we already know that they both form part of the same legal order. What is required here is an independent criterion to resolve the issue of identity before the appeal to joint compliance is made.[734]

If we examine the relationship between international and national law, it becomes clear that a practice-based criterion, according to which the observer would simply opt for the validity of that body of law that enjoys a higher degree of effectiveness, would not work to establish the unity of the law. Kelsen himself acknowledges that there are no international law-applying institutions whose practice of recognition could provide for such a criterion.[735] The same applies by analogy to the example of the two constitutions. Vinx argues that if we assume instances of disagreement among the members of society and its legal practitioners as to whether there is a normative relation between the customary and the codified constitution, it is possible to imagine that some members of society or the jurists believe, while others deny that both constitutions are valid. Equally, one can imagine that both society and jurists agree that both are valid, while they disagree with respect to the nature of the normative relationship between them. It is exactly this example where practice-based or institutional criteria fail to provide a conclusive answer to the question of identity and unity of the law.

A solution can be found in the behaviour of the law-abiding person: if we presuppose the effectiveness of both constitutions, this law-abiding person will necessarily be biased towards construing the broadest possible set of effective rules as parts of one legal order. Thus, to deny a norm membership in the legal order would be tantamount to denying its legal validity. Yet since this person is interested in upholding the effects of the law, he or she will avoid this validity-annulling conclusion whenever possible[736]—in the same way as authorities interpret customary norms in accordance with the set of positive norms and vice versa in order to make them applicable without any normative conflicts.[737] As a result, Vinx concludes that the law-abiding person will base their judgments regarding the structure of the legal order in question on hypotheses that cannot be fully explained in terms of sociological or empirical observation. Once one adopts the perspective of law-abidingness, Raz's allegation of circularity does not apply any more, as this allegation presupposes agreement on the point that a satisfactory account of the identity of legal orders must be

[733] Vinx, *Kelsen's Pure Theory of Law* (n 108) 190; Kelsen, *Problem der Souveränität* (n 57) 94 fn 1.

[734] Vinx, *Kelsen's Pure Theory of Law* (n 108) 190.

[735] Kelsen, *Principles of International Law* (n 401) 269–70; Kelsen, *General Theory* (n 104) 339. Although Kelsen sees the then-emerging international judiciary as a first step towards such an international institution; see Kelsen, *Peace through Law* (n 415) 16.

[736] Vinx, *Kelsen's Pure Theory of Law* (n 108) 192–3.

[737] Valentin Petev, 'Rechtsquellenlehre und Reine Rechtslehre' [1984] *Rechtstheorie (Beiheft 5)* 273, 285.

one that appeals to purely descriptive criteria—an assumption the pure theory of law rejects altogether.[738]

In sum, Raz's critique must therefore be rejected.

7. Conclusion: An Overall Appraisal

After this extensive analysis, the present conclusion can certainly give only a very brief overall appraisal of the pure theory of law. To begin with, one should not underestimate the philosophical foundations of this theory in the spirit of Kant, his neo-Kantian successors and Gottlob Frege, looking for a middle way between the two extremes of metaphysical rationalism and brute empiricism. This middle way presents itself by way of a transcendental epistemology in the sense that cognition is not concerned with the actual objects of cognition, but the *manner how* we cognize objects, and, more importantly, in so far as this manner of cognition is possible a priori.[739]

Equally, one should not forget that Kelsen considers the pure theory of law to be a theory of *positive* law in general,[740] not an a priori theory. This means that it builds upon the empirically extant legal material and that it develops therefrom, in an abstracting fashion, a description of the characteristics that all legal structures share throughout space and time.[741] Yet what is of an a priori nature is the notion of the *Grundnorm* which, as a logico-transcendental presupposition for cognizing legal reality, is comparable to the Kantian categories,[742] making possible the constituting of experience in the first place. Like these categories, the *Grundnorm* shapes the sensory material, thereby condensing it into the unity of the object of cognition and making it accessible to the observing subject. By providing for the 'ought' of legal norms and hence their validity, the basic norm allows the jurist to interpret acts of will as legal acts, whilst the basic norm itself must be presupposed.[743] The reason for this is Hume's law, i.e. that norms can logically only be derived from other norms, not from facts.

Accordingly, by strictly distinguishing between the 'is' of the empirical and the 'ought' of the normative world, the pure theory of law accomplishes three goals: first, the stringent and consistent differentiation from extra-juridical elements, i.e. metaphysics in the shape of morality, and empirical facts in the form of sociology, politics, and psychology—a feat for which even Hart lauded Kelsen.[744] Secondly, it aims at the 'scientification' of the law through a descriptive methodology, thus describing what the law is, and not what it should be. Lastly, the pure theory of law can therefore describe the law as a self-creating system through the hierarchy of norms,

738 Vinx, *Kelsen's Pure Theory of Law* (n 108) 193.

739 Kant, *Kritik der reinen Vernunft* (n 34) B 26.

740 Kelsen, *Pure Theory* (n 54) 1.

741 Hammer, 'Kelsens Grundnormkonzeption' (n 441) 215 ff.

742 Kant, *Kritik der reinen Vernunft* (n 34) A 77/B 102–A 80/B 106.

743 Norbert Leser, 'Die Reine Rechtslehre im Widerstreit der philosophischen Ideen' in *Die Reine Rechtslehre in wissenschaftlicher Diskussion* [no editor] (Manz, 1982) 100–2.

744 Hart, 'Eight Questions' (n 640) 289.

culminating in the *Grundnorm* to avoid an infinite regress, according to which one can ascertain whether a certain legal norm is a member of a given legal order or not, entailing that non-members are to be presumed invalid. In a logically clear manner, it explains how it is possible to cognize both the creation and the change of the law on the basis of the chains of delegation and derogation in conformity with Hume's law.

The last substantial merit to be mentioned here is the pure theory's potential to be extrapolated beyond the boundaries of national law.[745] If we assume that a legal norm can only be valid if it has been created in full compliance with superior norms within the *Stufenbau*, and also accept international law as proper law, then it necessarily follows that all law, both national and international law, form part of one unitary legal order.[746] Furthermore, it is also evident that legal monism, as an epistemological necessity, is only conceivable under the primacy of international law, i.e. with a common *Grundnorm* and international law sitting at the top of the chain of delegation. Otherwise, if we assume the national legal orders to give validity to international norms, the notion of international law would be reduced to a mere absurdity, as there would be as many international legal orders as there are states and other international legal subjects. Thus, international law necessarily delegates national law logically, not historically, through the principle of effectiveness, both enabling states to be effective legal orders and constraining them in their powers on the international plane. Hence, in such a monist legal order, there can be no difference in source, substance, and subjects of these two bodies of law, which also entails that normative conflicts between national and international law are not principally irresolvable, as dualism and pluralism claim.

Despite considerable criticism by other eminent legal scholars such as Hart and Raz, legal monism has the unquestionable merit of being able to examine the structure of the law in a way that enables jurists to comprehend the legal material and eventually to put it into practice.[747] Particularly the pure theory of law has been described as being able to foster analytical thinking and problem-solving and to thereby support lawyers in solving concrete legal problems on the basis of a certain underlying academic standard.[748]

The question nevertheless remains whether these epistemological claims are also verifiable in the light of reality and whether monism really is better equipped to describe the law as it is. To this end, the next chapter of this book will hence examine whether this is indeed the case and closely scrutinize whether and the extent to which the premises of legal monism are applicable to the relationship between international law and national law on the one hand, and European Union law and Member State law on the other hand.

[745] Starke, 'Primacy of International Law' (n 466) 308–10.

[746] Somek, 'Kelsen Lives' (n 417) 451.

[747] Michael Thaler, 'Rechtsphilosophie und das Verhältnis zwischen Gemeinschaftsrecht und nationalem Recht' (2000) 8 *Journal für Rechtspolitik* 75, 76; Heinz Mayer, 'Rechtstheorie und Rechtspraxis' in Clemens Jabloner and Friedrich Stadler (eds), *Logischer Empirismus und Reine Rechtslehre: Beziehungen zwischen dem Wiener Kreis und der Hans Kelsen-Schule* (Springer, 2001) 319.

[748] Rill, 'Internationales, supranationales und nationales Recht' (n 504) 700.

4

The Descriptive Value of Legal Monism

1. Introduction: On Verifiability

The previous part of this book depicted and defended the strong epistemological value of the pure theory of law and its merits in construing the law, in a logical manner, as a unitary body. However, this is not sufficient to counter all criticism. Owing to the obvious *prima facie* discrepancy between legal monism and the reality of the law, the pure theory of law has often been accused of having an 'aura of unreality'[1] and therefore of being out of touch with the real world itself.[2] Furthermore, Hans Kelsen was reproached for jumping from 'reality into his own world of fancy, where reality is ignored or receives a surrealistic aspect',[3] and for ignoring history, state practice, and jurisprudence itself.[4] Given these allegations, it stands to reason that the choice for a monist conception of the law cannot be justified exclusively on the basis of epistemology and logic, and consequently a precise analysis is required as to whether two or more distinct bodies of law in fact blend into a unitary legal order or whether they evade such integration. Legal epistemology may be philosophically intriguing, but ultimately it stands accused of being quixotic,[5] let alone of being incapable of describing the real legal world. It appears that dualism or pluralism represent more straightforward manners of conceptualizing the relationship between different bodies of law. The issue therefore remains as to whether the pure theory of law in general and legal monism in particular, as theories of the law, can be verified or falsified on the basis of the law as it empirically and positively exists.

However, before delving into an empirical assessment of this theory, a few words on verifiability are in order. To begin with, it remains philosophically and scientifically unclear whether the truth of theories or statements can indeed be conclusively verified, as proponents of logical positivism might claim.[6] If we take into

[1] William Charles Starr, *Kelsen and Hart on International Law* (University of Wisconsin, 1977) 82.
[2] Alfred Rub, *Hans Kelsens Völkerrechslehre: Versuch einer Würdigung* (Schulthess Polygraphischer Verlag, 1995) 544.
[3] Jean Polydore Haesaert, 'Book Review: Hans Kelsen, *Principles of International Law*' (1953) 2 *American Journal of Comparative Law* 576, 579.
[4] Krystyna Marek, 'Paul Guggenheim, 1899–1977' (1987) 44 *Schweizerisches Jahrbuch für internationales Recht* 9, 11.
[5] Rub (n 2) 556–91.
[6] See e.g. Rudolf Carnap, 'Überwindung der Metaphysik durch logische Analyse der Sprache' (1931/1932) 2 *Erkenntnis* 219, 221–2; Moritz Schlick, 'Meaning and Verification' (1936) 45 *The Philosophical Review* 339, 339–69.

consideration the problem of induction,[7] it will never be possible to verify the statements of a theory conclusively, as tomorrow a new fact in contradiction to one of the statements might arise, which would then prove this theory wrong. As a result, it seems more apposite to think of the subsequent empirical assessment as a falsification test as envisaged Karl Popper: first, the question is whether the pure theory of law can actually be falsified. If this is not the case, it should be considered pseudoscience. This means that insofar as scientific statements relate to reality, they must be falsifiable, and insofar as they are not falsifiable, they do not relate to reality.[8] Only after that, as a second step, can the theory or statement in question be subjected to scrutiny in the light of empirical facts.

The term 'empirical' in itself, however, may be problematic in the context of the pure theory of law. If one starts off with its transcendental roots, one must also ask whether Kant's transcendental philosophy itself is falsifiable. Specific claims, such as the ominous 'thing-in-itself' denoting a given object as it exists independently of its cognitive relation to the human mind,[9] describe entities beyond human experience and thereby evade falsification, as they cannot be meaningfully assessed on the basis of a direct criterion. But then, conversely, certain other aspects of Kant's transcendental philosophy were in fact falsified over the last centuries. For instance, Kant's claim that space and time form a priori building blocks of our sensory experience,[10] was ultimately disproved by Einstein's theory of relativity and the unity of space-time.[11] This means that at least parts of transcendental theory or theories based on Kantian thought can be subjected to a falsification test.

A. The *Grundnorm* as an unfalsifiable axiom

Having said that, the question arises whether the same is true for the pure theory of law as a juridico-transcendental theory. The first aspect to be discussed is of a rather controversial nature and pertains to the concept of the *Grundnorm*. Alfred Verdross argues that the *Grundnorm* cannot be verified (and accordingly not be falsified) on the basis of the law's claim to validity, as law can only be considered valid under the premise that the *Grundnorm* delegates its creation and normative character.[12] Kelsen readily accepts that the basic norm is indeed beyond verification or falsification. In fact, it is its presupposed and hypothetical character which expresses its transcendental-epistemological, not transcendent-metaphysical quality. Since it is,

[7] That is, the problem that inductive reasoning on the basis of generalizations and inference of future events from past facts can never lead to justified knowledge. See David Hume, *An Enquiry Concerning Human Understanding* (A. Millar, 1748) section IV.

[8] Karl Popper, *Logik der Forschung* (8th edn; Mohr-Siebeck, 1984) 256.

[9] Immanuel Kant, *Kritik der reinen Vernunft* (Johann Friedrich Hartknoch, 1781/1787) A 249–60/B 306–16.

[10] Ibid., A 19–48/B 33–73.

[11] See Friedel Weinert, 'Einstein and Kant' (2005) 80 *Philosophy* 585–93.

[12] Alfred Verdross, 'Die Rechtstheorie Hans Kelsens' (1930) 59 *Juristische Blätter* 421, 423.

by definition, a non-posited norm, it is impossible to verify or falsify the existence or presupposition of the *Grundnorm*.[13]

A general defence of the pure theory of law as a falsifiable theory therefore has two options to handle this specific kind of criticism. As a first approach, one could accept the allegation of the basic norm's quasi-metaphysical nature[14] and argue that even Kant failed in his fight against metaphysics when he conceded that positive law cannot be based on itself, but requires a basis beyond positivity.[15] Similarly, Aristotle claims that the preconditions of sensual experience can hardly be of empirical nature and hence concludes that at least some metaphysics cannot be excluded a priori from any philosophical discussion about the foundations of knowledge and cognition.[16] One should accordingly accept that, when dealing with basic philosophical questions, it is virtually impossible to renounce metaphysics altogether. Furthermore, one should also avoid modern philosophy's disdain for metaphysics and approach it in an unprejudiced manner to do justice to the central task of philosophy, namely the investigation of the possibly invariant fundamental structures of our system of concepts and its implicit ontology.[17]

Nonetheless, it should be said in all honesty that such a pledge for metaphysics might not convince the sceptic and that an alternative approach is required. Therefore, it is perhaps best to consider the *Grundnorm* resembling a mathematical or logical axiom, as explained by Frege.[18] Even mathematics contains improvable axioms, which may possibly remain improvable forever.[19] This may sound disheartening, but in fact this is the inherent nature of axioms in any given theory: axioms themselves constitute unverifiable (and hence unfalsifiable) foundational assumptions upon which entire theories are built. But what can be deduced from axioms subsequently is, under the very assumption of these axioms, verifiable, falsifiable, and—ideally—exact. In this vein, the concept of the *Grundnorm* would also be in line with Kurt Gödel's first incompleteness theorem, which states that consistent theoretical systems always contain statements that are true, but ultimately unprovable within the boundaries of that theory.[20] Thus, the basic norm can also function as the unfalsifiable axiom of the pure theory of law,[21] and accordingly, a thorough

[13] Hans Kelsen, 'Recht, Rechtswissenschaft und Logik' (1966) 52 *Archiv für Rechts- und Sozialphilosophie* 545, 547.

[14] See Kelsen's own admission of this potential interpretation in Hans Kelsen, 'Die philosophischen Grundlagen der Naturrechtslehre und des Rechtspositivismus' in Hans R. Klecatsky, René Marcic, and Herbert Schambeck (eds), *Die Wiener rechtstheoretische Schule: Schriften von Hans Kelsen, Adolf Merkl, Alfred Verdross, Band 1* (Verlag Österreich, 2010) 278.

[15] Immanuel Kant, 'Die Metaphysik der Sitten' in Immanuel Kant (ed), *Gesammelte Schriften* (Deutsche Akademie der Wissenschaften, 1907) AA 6:229–30.

[16] Aristotle, *Metaphysics* (ed and transl J. Barnes, *The Complete Works of Aristotle, Vol 2* (Oxford University Press, 1984) especially book Λ.

[17] Otfried Höffe, *Kants Kritik der praktischen Vernunft* (C.H. Beck, 2012) 204.

[18] See Chapter 3, section 1B.

[19] See Tony Crilly, *The Big Questions: Mathematics* (Quercus, 2011) 6; Willard van Orman Quine, *Methods of Logic* (4th edn; Harvard University Press, 1982) 85–6.

[20] Kurt Gödel, 'Über formal unentscheidbare Sätze der Principia Mathematica und verwandter Systeme I' (1931) 38 *Monatshefte für Mathematik und Physik* 173, 175–6.

[21] See Rudolf Thienel, *Kritischer Rationalismus und Jurisprudenz* (Manz, 1991) 100–14.

assessment of a theory may exclude its axioms, because if its theorems are eventually proven wrong, there is no further need to engage with its axiom. Furthermore, the need for the *Grundnorm* as an axiom has already been discussed in detail in Chapter 3 of this book.

B. Law as a normative science between two extremes

The second aspect to be considered in this respect is Kelsen's vehement assertion that norms are norms, nothing else,[22] and hence expressions of the 'ought'.[23] In this light, legal norms, as 'ought' statements, cannot be true or false, but only valid or invalid.[24] Legal science, as envisaged by the pure theory of law, thus is a normativist science which deals with valid law, and wherein 'validity' is to be understood as the specific existence of legal norms. Accordingly, legal norms, belonging to the realm of 'ought' are not to be found by empirical means. 'Ought' statements are consequently not part of the empirical world, and Kelsen does not tire of explicitly denying any reference to reality or to the practice of social realities in any given legal order. Law, as a normative science, is to be an autonomous intellectual field and, as a result, in order to cognize what the 'ought' is, one has to restrict one's analytical work to an 'ought' on the level of logical necessity.[25] And even though Kelsen seems to take an incursion into reality and a realist aspect of the law by stating that legal norms are valid if they belong to a positive, coercive, and effective legal order,[26] he also underscores that the pure theory of law is not a theory about what happens in natural reality, but what ought to happen according to positive law.[27] In other words, the kind of cognition we use depends on the object of investigation: when cognizing facts, we use empirical cognition; when cognizing legal norms, we use normative cognition.[28]

Nonetheless, it is possible to assess and test the claims of the pure theory of law in reality. At the outset, Kelsen himself argues that there is no need for the behaviour of legal subjects to conform perfectly to what the legal norms prescribe. In fact, it is the antagonism between factual human behaviour and the normative order which gives meaning to this very order, because ultimately, it is the law's purpose to regulate social conduct. Neither a legal order that perfectly conforms to reality nor a legal order which is contradicted in every single aspect by human behaviour would

[22] See H.L.A. Hart, 'Kelsen Visited' (1962/1963) 10 *UCLA Law Review* 709, 710.

[23] Hans Kelsen, 'Die soziologische und die juristische Staatsidee' in Matthias Jestaedt (ed), *Hans Kelsen: Werke, Band 3; Veröffentlichte Schriften 1911–1917* (Mohr-Siebeck, 2010) 203.

[24] Hans Kelsen, *Pure Theory of Law* (2nd edn; University of California Press, 1967) 74 and 205–6.

[25] Hans Kelsen, *Das Problem der Souveränität und die Theorie des Völkerrechts* (Mohr-Siebeck, 1920) iv and 84; Hans Kelsen, *Hauptprobleme der Staatsrechtslehre* (2nd edn; Scientia, 1923) v–vi.

[26] Kelsen, *Pure Theory* (n 24) 30–58 and 208–14; Hans Kelsen, *General Theory of Law and State* (reissue edn; Transaction Publishers, 2007) 18–20 and 122.

[27] Hans Kelsen, 'Was ist die Reine Rechtslehre?' in Hans R. Klecatsky, René Marcic, and Herbert Schambeck (eds), *Die Wiener rechtstheoretische Schule: Schriften von Hans Kelsen, Adolf Merkl, Alfred Verdross, Band 1* (Verlag Österreich, 2010) 501.

[28] Hans Kelsen, 'Eine "Realistische" und die Reine Rechtslehre. Bemerkungen zu Alf Ross: On Law and Justice' (1959/1960) 10 *Österreichische Zeitschrift für öffentliches Recht* 1, 2.

be meaningful.[29] The existence of a legal order as determined by its conformity to empirical reality is therefore best seen as a matter of degree. Kelsen explains that the relationship between the validity and the effectiveness of a legal order principally constitutes the tension between the 'is' and the 'ought' and can be ascertained only by means of an upper and a lower borderline, as the agreement between reality and normativity must neither exceed a certain maximum nor fall below a particular minimum.[30] By putting normative 'validity' and empirical 'effectiveness' into an interrelationship, Kelsen equally avoids idealism where there is no relation whatsoever between these two principles, and realism where these two terms are regarded as identical.[31]

If we now look at the minimum threshold, one must acknowledge that the validity of a legal norm presupposes the possibility to behave in a way contrary to it, but if it remains permanently ineffective (i.e. falls below the minimum), it ceases to be valid.[32] If, on the other hand, law transgresses beyond the maximum threshold, this would amount to an identification of law with power, right with might, and validity with effectiveness, and law, being reduced to a mere 'is', would lose its normative import.[33] However, as long as the law remains between these two extremes and continues to oscillate between ineffectiveness and brute-fact positivism, it can be described and depicted within the confines of a testable and hence also falsifiable theory, as the observer can cognize whether a specific legal order has become obsolete by either being rendering completely ineffective through non-compliance (a more realistic option) or by being strictly adhered to in all instances (a less realistic option).

C. The correspondence theory of truth: the pure theory of law as a falsifiable theory

Critics of the pure theory of law consider it one of its main weaknesses that monism under the primacy of international law is only conceivable on the basis of a minimum effectiveness and minimum substance of international legal norms.[34] Kelsen subsequently acknowledges that the conception of a unitary legal order merely on a logical-epistemological basis is a necessary, but perhaps not a sufficient step. This means that the positive law—i.e. the law as it empirically exists—must also be taken into account to ascertain whether the pure theory of law is apt to describe legal reality.[35] Thus, and despite the above-mentioned possible existence of metaphysical

[29] Kelsen, *General Theory* (n 26) 120.
[30] Kelsen, *Pure Theory* (n 24) 211: 'A positivistic legal theory is faced by the task to find the correct middle road between two extremes which are both untenable'.
[31] Kelsen, *Pure Theory* (n 24) 211; Mario G. Losano, 'Das Verhältnis von Geltung und Wirksamkeit in der Reinen Rechtslehre' in *Die Reine Rechtslehre in wissenschaftlicher Diskussion* [no editor] (Manz, 1982) 95–6.
[32] Kelsen, *Pure Theory* (n 24) 11.
[33] Kelsen, *General Theory* (n 26) 121.
[34] See e.g. Walter Schiffer, *Die Lehre vom Primat des Völkerrechts in der neueren Literatur* (Deuticke, 1937).
[35] Kelsen, 'Eine "Realistische" und die Reine Rechtslehre' (n 28) 5.

axioms within an objective legal science, such a science, geared towards objective cognizance, has to be based on the so-called 'correspondence theory of truth' according to which the truth or falsity of a given statement is determined by how it relates to the factual world and whether it is able accurately to describe (i.e. corresponds to) this world.[36] When we use Kant's *Critique of Pure Reason* as the intellectual and epistemological basis for the pure theory of law, it becomes clear that although his transcendental approach discusses other truth theories,[37] the correspondence theory takes precedence therein.[38] In Kant's view, a statement about reality is true, if the statement is coherent with other statements and, more importantly, if the empirical matter corresponds to our sensations about it.[39] In other words, epistemological truth consists of consensual and coherent correspondence to reality, with the crucial addendum, however, that correspondence constitutes the apex and decisive criterion.[40]

An objective, merely descriptive, and yet similarly transcendental legal science such as the pure theory of law should consequently equally be based on the correspondence theory of truth.[41] The basic and therefore necessary assumptions of such an objective legal theory should thus include, first and foremost, the assumption of an objective meaning of legal norms as linguistic expressions; of the possibility to cognize such legal norms; and of the ability to describe them.[42] Kelsen aptly reacts and states that the pure theory of law can be an 'empirical' theory, i.e. a theory that is capable of describing the reality in terms of the correspondence theory. Yet to this end, it must nonetheless conform to the dichotomy of 'is' and 'ought' and not describe 'ought'-norms by way of 'is'-propositions. Furthermore, an 'empirical' science—in contrast to a 'metaphysical' theory—describes facts occurring in time and space as well as the meaning of certain human acts. Thus, the pure theory of law remains empirically testable and falsifiable, if it confines itself to the description of legal norms which are the meaning of empirical human acts occurring in space and time, and if it does not concern itself with norms arising from metaphysics, such as divine or natural law. The pure theory of law meets all of these conditions[43] and can accordingly be assessed as to whether it corresponds to reality within the spectrum

[36] For the philosophical foundations of the correspondence theory see e.g. Aristotle, *Metaphysics* (n 16) 1011b 26; David Hume, *A Treatise of Human Nature* (John Noone, 1738) book III, part I, section I; Alfred Tarski, 'The Concept of Truth in Formalized Languages' in John Corcoran (ed), *Logic, Semantics, Metamathematics: Papers from 1923 to 1938* (2nd edn; Hackett, 1983) 152–278; Ludwig Wittgenstein, *Tractatus Logico-Philosophicus* (Kegan Paul, 1922) propositions 2.21 and 2.222–2.224; Karl Popper, *Objective Knowledge: An Evolutionary Approach* (revised edn; Oxford University Press, 1979) 319–40.

[37] Such as the 'coherence theory', claiming that a statement is true if it fits coherently within a set of statements, or the 'consensus theory', holding that a statement is true as a matter of social agreement, for instance by the academic community.

[38] Dieter Lohmar, *Erfahrung und kategoriales Denken* (Springer, 1998) 46.

[39] Kant, *Kritik der reinen Vernunft* (n 9) A 20/B 34 and A 723/B 751.

[40] Ibid., B 114 ff.

[41] See e.g. Christoph von Mettenheim, *Recht und Rationalität* (Mohr-Siebeck, 1984) 94; Ota Weinberger, *Rechtslogik* (Duncker & Humblot, 1989) 84; Thienel, *Kritischer Rationalismus* (n 21) 134.

[42] Michael Potacs, 'Die Grundnormproblematik' in Stefan Griller and Heinz Peter Rill (eds), *Rechtstheorie: Rechtsbegriff—Dynamik—Auslegung* (Springer, 2011) 149.

[43] Kelsen, 'Eine "Realistische" und die Reine Rechtslehre' (n 28) 5.

of effectiveness at the minimum and full compliance at the maximum level—or in other words: whether two or more bodies of law conform to a monist view or not.

To this end, this chapter will subsequently assess the assumptions of the pure theory of law and, in particular, those of legal monism, namely between national law and public international law and between national law and European Union law. The objective of this assessment is to show whether monism is in fact capable of describing the legal reality as well as or even better than dualism or pluralism.

2. National Law and International Law

To find out whether legal monism really is superior in describing the relationship between international and national law, the following sections will now assess the current attitude of national law vis-à-vis the international legal order, in particular on the basis of the main points of criticism voiced by dualists and pluralists. This descriptive or empirical account will thereby scrutinize whether the epistemological claims of the pure theory of law live up to the day-to-day reality of the law. To this end, it will employ an approach that is traditionally used when examining the encounter of national and international law, namely to distinguish between the validity, the rank, and the applicability of international law within the domestic legal sphere.[44]

A. The validity of international law within national law

(1) The question of different grounds of validity

In this context, the term 'validity' does not refer to the question as to whether international law is genuine law and therefore valid. 'Validity' in this respect refers to the acceptance of international law as valid within the domestic sphere, which is a logical prerequisite for its subsequent application within the latter.[45] The pertinent problem is that dualists and pluralists claim that international and national law are based on different grounds of validity: whereas the validity of international law is argued to be derived from the common will of the states, a collective that is superior to that of individual states,[46] the validity of national law is based on the will of the state itself, and consequently its constitutional legal order.[47] This duality in grounds of validity logically entails a duality in sources according to which the sources of international law are those enumerated in Article 38(1) of the Statute of the International Court of Justice (ICJ), and the sources of national law those found in the respective

44 Helen Keller, *Rezeption des Völkerrechts* (Springer, 2003) 11–12.

45 Alfred Verdross and Bruno Simma, *Universelles Völkerrecht* (3rd edn; Duncker & Humblot, 1984) para 552, fn 34.

46 See e.g. Heinrich Triepel, *Völkerrecht und Landesrecht* (C.L. Hirschfeld, 1899) 111 ff.

47 David Feldman, 'Monism, Dualism, and Constitutional Legitimacy' (1999) 20 *Australian Yearbook of International Law* 105, 107; Joseph G. Starke, 'Monism and Dualism in the Theory of International Law' (1936) 17 *British Yearbook of International Law* 66, 70.

constitutions. Conceptions other than monism therefore consider different bodies of law as *prima facie* separated and self-contained legal systems, since within each system, the only existing rules are those that form part of the system. Nevertheless, in a subsequent step, rules which were not created within the system can become relevant for it if these rules are somehow referred to by a rule included in this system.[48] In a monist view, this rule would be the *Grundnorm*, which unifies law into one single legal order. Dualism, however, holds that there are no interferences between separate and different legal orders unless a given system allows for that by a specific rule; and pluralism similarly argues that legal orders are separate from each other with separate reference rules, but mutual validity. These differences between dualism and pluralism will be neglected at this point, since the crucial element that is common to both notions is that a rule of reference is required to consider external sources of law, such as international legal norms, as valid within another legal system.

International law itself does not provide any such reference rules, as it neither governs the status it occupies within domestic legal orders after reception[49] nor regulates the method by which states fulfil their international obligations.[50] The reason for this is the fact that general international law does not determine or prescribe its validity within domestic law,[51] but leaves the arrangements of its relationship with domestic law by way of a *renvoi* to the latter, thereby recognizing the relative legal autonomy of states and other subjects under international law.[52] Dualists and pluralists therefore consider international law as external and foreign to domestic law, which entails that international legal norms are in constant need of domestication, e.g. by transforming international norms into domestic norms, in order to regard them as valid law.[53] Hence both dualism and pluralism sharply distinguish between the validity of international law per se (as external law), and the validity of international law in its manifestation *as domestic law* (as internal law).

This can lead to situations where a state may regard an international rule as valid and consider itself bound by it without accepting it as valid in its national law. Accordingly, if a legal norm is not considered valid in the internal legal sphere, it cannot have any effect *within* a domestic legal order. In other words, if national authorities deny particular international legal norms domestic validity, these norms may not be domestically applicable. This entails that, only an international norm which has successfully crossed the validity threshold of domestic law can be a source of rights and obligations in that legal order.[54] The question thus remains as to how international legal norms can cross this threshold and become domestically valid.

[48] Giorgio Gaja, 'Dualism—A Review' in Janne Nijman and André Nollkaemper (eds), *New Perspectives on the Divide Between National and International Law* (Oxford University Press, 2007) 52–3.

[49] Luzius Wildhaber and Stephan Breitenmoser, 'The Relationship between Customary International Law and Municipal Law in Western European Countries' (1988) 48 *Zeitschrift für ausländisches öffentliches Recht und Völkerrecht* 163, 164.

[50] Ignaz Seidl-Hohenveldern, 'Transformation or Adoption of International Law into Municipal Law' (1963) 12 *International and Comparative Law Quarterly* 88, 90.

[51] André Nollkaemper, *National Courts and the International Rule of Law* (Oxford University Press, 2012) 68–9.

[52] Wildhaber and Breitenmoser (n 49) 164.

[53] Başak Çalı, *The Authority of International Law* (Oxford University Press, 2015) 138.

[54] Nollkaemper, *National Courts* (n 51) 130.

(2) The role of national legal provisions on international law

The answer to the above question is that states generally use their national legal provisions as the principal instrument to 'validate' international legal norms domestically. Thereby states may declare themselves to be either monist or non-monist in nature, which opens up a couple of possibilities to deal with international norms within domestic law. First, at the extreme ends of the spectrum, a state can be fully monist and regard international law as domestically valid *ab initio*; or it can be totally non-monist and make the domestic validity of all international legal norms dependent on pre-existing national rules of reference. Between these two options, both monists and non-monists can, secondly, accept the notion that some particular international legal norms of peremptory character are automatically binding, irrespective of the state's consent or constitutional legal order—which results in the creation of a sub-category of monist norms even for non-monist systems. *Ius cogens* norms would then exist alongside international legal norms, which require transformation to be considered domestically valid by the state in question. And lastly, it is possible that some domestic legal orders might consider themselves monist for one source of international law (for instance customary law), but non-monist for another (for instance treaties)[55] in a hybrid fashion.[56]

To arrange their individual relationship with the international legal order, states have, in principle, two instruments at their disposal: adoption and transformation,[57] which will be examined in detail in the subsequent section.

What these instruments have in common, however, is the claim that the ultimate power to consider and treat international legal norms as valid within the domestic sphere rests with the states themselves and is hence contingent on domestic law.[58] This statement illustrates that there is a difference of formal sources between national and international law, and it thus raises the crucial question whether the states' ultimate power to give domestic validity to international norms—may it be through adoption or transformation, or the increasingly blurred lines between these instruments—proves monism wrong. Dualists and pluralists might therefore argue that although certain legal systems could be labelled as monist because their constitutions contain automatic adoption mechanisms for international norms, the existence of such constitutional provisions is a choice obviously made on the basis of a dualist or pluralist premise, by each domestic legal system.[59] One could accordingly conclude that dualism or pluralism are the 'default modes' of every municipal legal

[55] Dinah Shelton, 'Introduction' in Dinah Shelton (ed), *International Law and Domestic Legal Systems* (Oxford University Press, 2011) 2–3.

[56] David Sloss, 'Domestic Application of Treaties' in Duncan B. Hollis (ed), *The Oxford Guide to Treaties* (Oxford University Press, 2012) 369.

[57] The theory of '*ad hoc* execution' (*Vollzugstheorie*), predominant in Germany, will be disregarded at this point owing to it being an amalgam of the adoption and transformation theories.

[58] Nollkaemper, *National Courts* (n 51) 69.

[59] Gaetano Arangio-Ruiz, 'International and Interindividual Law' in Janne Nijman and André Nollkaemper (eds), *New Perspectives on the Divide Between National and International Law* (Oxford University Press, 2007) 20.

order, and that monism is merely a choice by switching the constitutional levers of said order from non-monism to monism.

If we now assume, in following the claims of the pure theory of law on legal monism, that international law is valid independently from domestic validation, does this mean that monism can be falsified on the basis of the dualist and pluralist arguments that make the domestic validity of international law dependent on such national rules of reference? In other words, is the claim that only domestic validation *qua* national legal provisions makes international law valid, a good and falsifying argument against monism?

a. Adoption

The principle of 'adoption' denotes the legal instrument through which international legal norms are declared automatically valid within the domestic sphere without the need to modify their contents or character as international legal norms or to create parallel domestic norms.[60] This goal is typically achieved if a national legal provision (the 'receptor') incorporates the international norm into the domestic legal order. Adoption is therefore usually associated with a monist stance, as the automatic validation and incorporation of international norms into national law does not change their legal nature and thereby perpetuates their connection with other norms of international law.[61] However, a clear distinction should be made between the adoption of customary international law and international treaties.

With respect to customary international law, prominent examples of such receptors can be found in uncodified form in common law jurisdictions, such as the *Paquete Habana* judgment in which the United States Supreme Court held that '[i]nternational law is part of our law …'.[62] In a similar manner, customary international law is adopted in English Law by the courts, regarding it as valid law without any Act of Parliament, from which 'it follows … inexorably that the rules of international law, as existing from time to time, do form part of English law'.[63] In civil law jurisdictions, such general receptors are regularly found in codified constitutional provisions, such as Article 25 of the German Basic Law (GG) and Article 9(1) of the Austrian Federal Constitution (B-VG), which state that the generally recognized rules of international law are regarded as integral parts of federal law. Other examples of adopting receptors with respect to customary international law include, just to name a few, Article 94 of the Dutch Constitution;[64] Article 10(1) of the Italian Constitution; and Articles 15(4) and 17 of the Russian Constitution.

What can be deduced from the adoption method regarding customary international law is that these receptors within national legal orders create a stronger

[60] Wildhaber and Breitenmoser (n 49) 171.

[61] Pierre-Marie Dupuy, 'International Law and Domestic (Municipal) Law' in Rüdiger Wolfrum (ed), *The Max Planck Encyclopedia of Public International Law* (2nd edn; Oxford University Press, 2013) para 57.

[62] *The Paquete Habana* 175 US 677 (1900).

[63] *Trendtex Trading Corp v Central Bank of Nigeria* [1977] QB 529, 554 (Lord Denning MR).

[64] *Nota bene*, however, only *per analogiam*; see J.F.H. van Panhuys, 'The Netherlands Constitution and International Law' (1953) 47 *American Journal of International Law* 537, 557.

harmony between domestic and international law than any other method of giving municipal validity to international norms.[65] Moreover, there is a practical aspect to it. Since the formation and development of international custom is by no means a static concept and therefore a rather dynamic and assiduous process,[66] it is much more effective to also incorporate these norms in a continuous manner. In other words, if a given constitution expressly refers to these rules, it does not aim at 'petrifying' them at the moment of their reception, but constantly to adopt them as they develop further. This allows the national judiciary and legislature to interpret these rules in a dynamic fashion and to accommodate the ever-changing character of customary international law. If, on the other hand, the pertinent customary rules had been transformed and thus codified in written form in domestic law at the time of enactment of the constitution in question,[67] these domestic manifestations of customary international law would always lag behind their international counterparts, as the latter would be subject to constant modification by changing practice and *opinio iuris*.

Similarly, there exist general receptors for international treaties, which, in the words of William Blackstone[68] and Article VI clause 2 of the United States constitution, declare treaties concluded by the respective state to be part of the law of the land.[69] Thus, a municipal provision (often of constitutional nature) makes all or particular treaties automatically part of domestic law and thereby validates them internally without the need for prior implementing legislation.[70] Other examples for this approach include, inter alia, Article 9(1) in conjunction with Articles 49(2) and 50 of the Austrian Constitution; Article 10 of the Constitution of the Czech Republic; Article 98 of the Japanese Constitution; Article 55 of the French Constitution; Article 93 of the Dutch Constitution;[71] and Articles 93 and 151 of the Constitution of Egypt.

In contrast to the rather vague notion of customary international law, these explicit provisions on the adoption of international agreements are highly significant, since treaties, as codified norms, thereby enter into a more direct and precise competition with the main body of domestic law. Furthermore, laws are usually only binding and valid within a given domestic legal order if they have obtained prior

[65] Dupuy (n 61) para 59.

[66] Roozbeh (Rudy) B. Baker, 'Customary International Law in the 21st Century: Old Challenges and New Debates' (2010) 21 *European Journal of International Law* 173, 181.

[67] Seidl-Hohenveldern (n 50) 93–4.

[68] William Blackstone, *Commentaries on the Laws of England, Vol IV* (Clarendon Press, 1765–1769) ch 5.

[69] This apparently monist stance should, however, be taken *cum grano salis*, as treaty provisions in conflict with the Constitution or superseded by domestic *leges posteriores* are not considered valid within US law; see e.g. David Sloss, 'United States' in David Sloss (ed), *The Role of Domestic Courts in Treaty Enforcement: A Comparative Study* (Cambridge University Press, 2009) 510.

[70] André Nollkaemper, 'The Effects of Treaties in Domestic Law' in Christian J. Tams, Antonios Tzanakopoulos, and Andreas Zimmermann (eds), *Research Handbook on the Law of Treaties* (Edward Elgar Publishing, 2014) 138.

[71] To be interpreted, however, in conjunction with unwritten constitutional law; see André Nollkaemper, 'The Netherlands' in David Sloss (ed), *The Role of Domestic Courts in Treaty Enforcement: A Comparative Study* (Cambridge University Press, 2009) 331.

approval, for instance by an act of the legislative branch. Treaties as adopted by the domestic receptor, conversely, also become valid and binding if they were only concluded as simplified agreements by the executive branch and without any legislative act.[72] Thus, their legal nexus with other international norms is maintained, and treaties can be made applicable in their entirety and without rescinding their synallagmatic relationship. It follows logically that no parallel domestic norms need to be enacted and that norms with the same content are valid in all municipal legal systems bound by them, accordingly reaching a complete unification of the respective international norms.[73] The principle of adoption is therefore regarded as a domestic requirement to apply international law 'as is', which classifies it as part of the monist doctrine.[74]

b. Transformation

In contrast to the underlying monist tone of adoption, the doctrine of 'transformation' rests upon a staunch dualist basis and thus the perception that any international legal norm must be expressly and specifically 'transformed' into municipal law using constitutional mechanisms before it can be considered domestically valid. Alternatively, international law is 'recast' by the creation of parallel norms of domestic law, which results in a duplicate existence of international norms: on the one hand the international legal norm itself, governed by international law, and on the other hand its mirror image whose ground of validity is derived from the domestic legal order alone.[75]

Scholarly literature and practice usually distinguish between *special* and *general* transformation. Special transformation is extremely reminiscent of its dualist pedigree to the extent that each international norm must be transformed into a domestic norm to be valid law within the internal legal order in question. Owing to this coexistence of an international and a non-international norm, the latter's validity is decoupled from the former's, and only the latter will be regarded as valid law. General transformation, conversely, appears to be more evocative of the concept of monism and refers to a situation where transformed international law is considered to be valid within a domestic legal order either on the basis of a particular domestic legal act, or on the grounds of a constitutional provision requiring international law to be transformed in lock, stock, and barrel.[76]

General transformation may appear similar to adoption, but theoretically it is not the same. For what both examples of transformation—in contrast to adoption—have

[72] Seidl-Hohenveldern (n 50) 101–2; Sloss, 'Domestic Application' (n 56) 373.

[73] Dupuy (n 61) para 57.

[74] Walter Rudolf, *Völkerrecht und deutsches Recht* (Mohr Siebeck, 1967) 154; Stefan Griller, *Die Übertragung von Hoheitsrechten auf zwischenstaatliche Einrichtungen* (Springer, 1989) 352–3.

[75] Kirsten Schmalenbach, 'Article 27' in Oliver Dörr and Kirsten Schmalenbach (eds), *Vienna Convention on the Law of Treaties: A Commentary* (Springer, 2012) para 31.

[76] Annemie Schaus, 'Article 27 Convention of 1969' in Olivier Corten and Pierre Klein (eds), *The Vienna Conventions on the Law of Treaties: A Commentary, Vol I* (Oxford University Press, 2011) 698; Wildhaber and Breitenmoser (n 49) 171.

in common is that it is the particular piece of domestic legislation which is internally valid, and not the international legal norm in question. Hence, all legal effects flow from the domestic legal source, never the international one.[77] In this vein, one should again sharply distinguish between the transformation of customary international law and international treaties.

Given that national legal orders—if they refer to the domestic role of customary international law at all—regularly consider customary norms as automatically incorporated into municipal law,[78] it has sometimes been denied that transformation of customary international law into municipal law is even theoretically possible, especially since such a procedure would not make any practical sense. Beyond that, such a provision prescribing the transformation of international custom would be a highly artificial legal construction, since future and thus unforeseeable developments on the international level should ideally be transformed as well.[79] Yet this idea principally amounts to an application of the adoption doctrine which intends to adjust itself to the great variability of customary rules.[80] It can therefore be argued that the constant transformation of customary international law would in the end overstrain every legal order. If any given domestic legal system were to require customary international law to be transformed to be municipally applicable, the legislative branch would then be under the obligation explicitly to confirm all changes and creation of general international norms. Otherwise, domesticated customary law would be petrified in the moment of transformation, incapable of dynamically accommodating any changes on the international level, which probably occur on a quotidian basis.[81] Taking into account the plethora of international norms emerging in a vastness of legal fields, national legislatures would at least once a year need to inspect all legal questions in these fields, and take respective action by, for instance, enacting according national legislation or by modifying pertaining treaty law. It is beyond any reasonable doubt that no legal order in the world would ever be able to fulfil such a monumental and Sisyphean task.[82] Adoption of customary law therefore remains the more practical solution.

The transformation of treaties, conversely, is an entirely different matter. In strictly non-monist states, no treaties can have the formal status of law (and thus be considered valid), unless the respective legislature formally adopts a domestic legal act to incorporate the treaty as domestic law.[83] The most prominent examples of

[77] Schmalenbach, 'Article 27' (n 75) para 31.
[78] Seidl-Hohenveldern (n 50) 93.
[79] Dupuy (n 61) para 101.
[80] Karl Josef Partsch, *Die Anwendung des Völkerrechts im innerstaatlichen Recht* (C.F. Müller, 1964) 167.
[81] Kristen Walker and Andrew D. Mitchell, 'A Stronger Role for Customary International Law in Domestic Law?' in Hilary Charlesworth and others (eds), *The Fluid State: International Law and National Legal Systems* (Federation Press, 2005) 126, considering the US Alien Tort Claims Act of 1789 (28 USC § 1350) to be an example of transformed customary international law.
[82] Wildhaber and Breitenmoser (n 49) 176–7; Verdross and Simma (n 45) para 541.
[83] Sloss, 'Domestic Application' (n 56) 370.

this approach include, inter alia, Austria,[84] the United Kingdom (UK)[85] and all the Commonwealth states,[86] India,[87] Italy,[88] and Germany.[89]

There are several arguments that speak in favour of transformation and its advantageous effects on the national legal order: the protection of state sovereignty and the autonomy of the national legal order; the separation of powers within a state (i.e. the difference between the executive concluding the treaty and the legislative domestically validating it);[90] and the imperfection of treaty provisions, which can be overcome by more precise incorporating national legal acts.[91] Conversely, there are nevertheless also considerable disadvantages to the transformation method. Its most significant disadvantage is its 'uncoupling' effect, which principally disconnects the substance of the treaty from the substance of the respective transformed domestic law. Eventually, it is the domestic law that is applied and interpreted by the municipal authorities, which may adversely affect compliance with the treaty.[92]

Similarly, the 'lifespan' of the domestic legal act is not be governed by the life of the treaty itself, but by the validity of the relevant transforming act.[93] This might lead to the absurd result that the transformed legal act would continue to exist even if the parallel treaty was terminated. This not only locks the domestic legal order in a static way where compliance with changes on the international plane remains dependent on internal legislative modifications, but also supports a situation in which the treaty and the corresponding domestic act drift further apart, for instance owing to sovereignty-centric interpretation, untransformed international judicial decisions, and the leeway of the municipal legislature.[94] This disparity can certainly be softened by consistent interpretation which allows for a certain degree of continuity between the international treaty and the domestic legal act when it comes to its application and effects within a municipal legal order.[95] However, it cannot belie the fact that the respective grounds of validity of the two legal acts are different and separate from each other which, ultimately, may entail legal consequences that are entirely different from the adoption method.

[84] Article 50(2) Z 4 B-VG.

[85] *Re McFarland* [2004] UKHL 17; ILDC 102 (UK 2004).

[86] Brian Opeskin, 'Constitutional Modelling: The Domestic Effect of International Law in Commonwealth Countries: Part I' [2000] *Public Law* 607, 622–6.

[87] Supreme Court, *Daya Singh Lahoria v India*, AIR 2001 SC 1716; ILDC 170 (IN 2001) [A1].

[88] Corte costituzionale, *EP v Municipality of Avellino*, Case no 349/2007; (2008) 91 *Riv Dir Intern* 230; ILDC 301 (IT 2007) [6.1].

[89] Article 59(2) GG.

[90] See David Haljan, *International Law and the Separation of Powers* (TMC Asser, 2013) especially 13–86.

[91] David M. Aaron, 'Reconsidering Dualism: The Caribbean Court of Justice and the Growing Influence of Unincorporated Treaties in Domestic Law' (2007) 6 *The Law and Practice of International Courts and Tribunals* 233, 240–1; Schmalenbach, 'Article 27' (n 75) para 32.

[92] Robert Pfeffer, *Das Verhältnis von Völkerrecht und Landesrecht* (Mohr-Siebeck, 2009) 133.

[93] Ibid.; Partsch (n 80) 43 and 111.

[94] Heinhard Steiger, 'The Relationship of German National Law with Public International Law and with European Community Law' in A.J.A. Vandamme and Jan-Herman Reestman (eds), *Ambiguity in the Rule of Law* (Europa Law Publishing, 2001) 67; Schmalenbach, 'Article 27' (n 75) para 32.

[95] Dionisio Anzilotti, *Corso di diritto internazionale, Vol. I* (3rd edn; Athenaeum, 1928) 41; Rudolf (n 74) 162–3 and 170–1; Pfeffer (n 92) 134.

(3) *Consequential arguments against monism*

After this depiction of these two different approaches of domestic law towards the international legal order, the question now remains what this means for a monist view of the law as envisaged by the pure theory of law. As briefly mentioned above, the above doctrines share the principally non-monist assumption that international law can only claim to be valid within domestic law if domestic law itself allows for this very validity of international legal norms. To use a metaphor, international law may freely flow into domestic law, but the latter remains in control of the water tap and can, if it so wishes, turn it completely off to stop the flow. Monists may correctly interject at this point, however, that this assumption does not affect the validity of the international legal order itself. In other words, the absence of *internal* validity is without prejudice to the *external* validity of international law, and international law continues to exist even when not adopted, transformed, or implemented otherwise into municipal law. Thus, both a non-monist and a monist interpretation of municipal provisions, bestowing validity within the domestic sphere on international law, becomes possible.[96]

The problem nevertheless remains that dualism or pluralism appear to be more convincing at this point. Monists may be right in claiming that the internal and external validity of international law are two very different kinds of phenomena, but it is this very assumption that eventually undermines monism and its core tenet. Legal monism claims that there is only one ground of validity, namely the *Grundnorm* at the apex of the international legal order, and this postulate is hence incompatible with the argument that there are two manifestations of validity, i.e. internal and external validity. Thus, by claiming that only domestic validation *qua* national legal provisions can render international law internally valid, both dualism and pluralism start from the basic principle that there is more than one ground of validity and thereby make a very convincing and falsifying argument against monism.

In concreto, the argument against monism claims that if there are two or more grounds of validity, there can be no hierarchy of norms or chain of delegation connecting these distinct bodies of law. Domestic law cannot be delegated by international law, as postulated by monism under the primacy of international law on the basis of the principle of effectiveness.[97] If domestic law is not delegated by international law, then it is not derived from the same *Grundnorm*; and if it is not derived from the same *Grundnorm*, then there is no unitary body law. *Ergo*, dualists and pluralists conclude that monism is wrong and thereby falsified.

The transformation method clearly speaks in favour of such an anti-monist reading. Anzilotti observes that compliance with international obligations can only be ensured by such specific rules within the various domestic systems,[98] and that

[96] Stefan Griller, 'Völkerrecht und Landesrecht—unter Berücksichtigung des Europarechts' in Robert Walter, Clemens Jabloner, and Klaus Zeleny (eds), *Hans Kelsen und das Völkerrecht* (Manz, 2004) 101.

[97] See Kelsen, *Pure Theory* (n 24) 336; Hans Kelsen, *Principles of International Law* (Rinehart, 1952) 214–15; Kelsen, *Problem der Souveränität* (n 25) 94–101.

[98] Anzilotti, *Corso di diritto internazionale* (n 95) 60.

international law therefore remains heavily dependent on these transformation provisions.[99] Thus, states can decide for themselves if and under which conditions they give effect to international norms in their own legal systems. And in order to be internally valid, international law must have been transformed into domestic law, and it is consequently merely operative as part of that domestic legal order, and not as international law per se[100]—because international law, by itself, can only generate rights and obligations for states, but not for individuals.[101] Therefore, simply because international law remains distinct and clearly separated from national law, it is highly implausible to see these two legal orders as one body of law.

However, the same argument also holds true for the adoption doctrine. Although this approach is usually associated with monism, dualism and pluralism opine that it cannot prove a unitary conception of the law. The assumption that international law delegates national law, as asserted by monism, is an artificial brainchild, and therefore it is wrong to consider constitutional provisions purporting to adopt international norms as a tendency towards or even as conclusive proof of monism.[102] The underlying problem with such provisions is that they can be read, on the one hand, as merely declaratory of effects that international law would in any event produce within domestic law. In this case, they can be understood as a clear monist recognition of the superiority of international law. On the other hand, however, such adoption rules can also be construed as evidence of the need for a constitutional device to assure the smooth validation of international norms within municipal law. Thereby these provisions are an indicator of international law only becoming relevant because of this reference,[103] not as a legal force in itself. The argument concludes that monism could hence only be verified as a valid theory once constitutional provisions of this kind (i.e. adoption rules) have become mere declaratory statements of domestic constitutions.[104]

In sum, dualism and pluralism therefore maintain that the state constitutes the disjunctive factor between national and international law,[105] simply because it is not international law that delegates national law, but the domestic legal orders representing the very prerequisite for the existence of international law as a coordinating legal order.[106]

[99] Griller, 'Völkerrecht und Landesrecht' (n 96) 86.

[100] Wildhaber and Breitenmoser (n 49) 170–1.

[101] Triepel, *Völkerrecht und Landesrecht* (n 46) 228–9; Gustav Walz, *Völkerrecht und staatliches Recht* (Kohlhammer, 1933) 238–9.

[102] Rudolf (n 74) 146–7. See also Heinz Peter Rill, 'Internationales, supranationales und nationales Recht—eine Einheit' in Clemens Jabloner and others (eds), *Gedenkschrift Robert Walter* (Manz, 2013) 692–3.

[103] Luigi Ferrari-Bravo, 'International and Municipal Law: The Complementarity of Legal Systems' in Ronald St. John MacDonald and Douglas M. Johnston, *The Structure and Process of International Law: Essays in Legal Philosophy Doctrine and Theory* (Martinus Nijhoff, 1983) 737; Gaja (n 48) 60.

[104] Michael Potacs, 'Das Verhältnis zwischen der EU und ihren Mitgliedstaaten im Lichte traditioneller Modelle' (2010) 65 *Zeitschrift für öffentliches Recht* 117, 121; Rudolf (n 74) 146–7.

[105] Alexander Hold-Ferneck, *Lehrbuch des Völkerrechts I* (Meiner, 1930) 111.

[106] Rudolf (n 74) 146.

(4) *Monist arguments in the context of validity*

Following up on the theories of the Vienna School of Jurisprudence, it is unquestionable that a common ground of validity of all legal norms constitutes *the* necessary feature of a unitary legal order.[107] In accordance with Merkl's theory of the hierarchy of norms, the ground of validity of all norms can be found in those provisions of a legal order which govern the conditions for the valid creation and existence of other norms,[108] and which, in turn, are conditioned by the basic norm. Dualism, however, claims that international and national law are based on different legal sources and hence also on different grounds of validity.[109] In the light of the hierarchy of norms, one could therefore say that international law and national law differ from one another regarding their respective chains of delegation, because they regulate the conditions of valid creation of legal norms independently from each other.[110]

a. Transformation does not falsify monism

Having said that, however, anti-monist theories nonetheless fail to substantiate convincingly why national law and the law of other international legal subjects should not be delegated and constrained by international legal norms—although it should also be frankly admitted that such delegation and constraint are rather weakly grounded in customary international law[111] *qua* the principle of effectiveness. Nevertheless, under general international law, all states are obliged to recognize the sovereignty of other states, and the rules delimiting the areas of such sovereignty must necessarily be laid down by some higher legal order and not by national law alone.[112] Neither can dualism or pluralism be justified by arguing that states historically preceded the international legal order and that thus national law delegates international law.[113] As has already been discussed above,[114] historical facts are not to be confused with norm-logical conditions. States may predate international law such as cities may predate the states in which they are located, but this is without prejudice to the fact that international law delegates national law in the same way as national law delegates the relevant rules of city administration.

It follows that, in the context of transformation and adoption, it should also be clearly emphasized that the international legal order is not concerned with the method by which international legal subjects discharge their international

[107] Rill, 'Internationales, supranationales und nationales Recht' (n 102) 695.

[108] Adolf Julius Merkl, *Die Lehre von der Rechtskraft entwickelt aus dem Rechtsbegriff* (Deuticke, 1923) 217; Adolf Merkl, 'Prolegomena einer Theorie des rechtlichen Stufenbaus' in Hans R. Klecatsky, René Marcic, and Herbert Schambeck (eds), *Die Wiener rechtstheoretische Schule: Schriften von Hans Kelsen, Adolf Merkl, Alfred Verdross, Band 2* (Verlag Österreich, 2010) 1098–9.

[109] Potacs, 'Verhältnis' (n 104) 126.

[110] Rill, 'Internationales, supranationales und nationales Recht' (n 102) 696.

[111] Ibid.

[112] Joseph G. Starke, 'The Primacy of International Law' in Salo Engel and Rudolf A. Métall (eds), *Law, State, and International Legal Order* (University of Tennessee Press, 1964) 314. Even though some of these rules might be reflected in national norms, for instance rules that statutes are not to have extra-territorial application.

[113] Rill, 'Internationales, supranationales und nationales Recht' (n 102) 693.

[114] See Chapter 3, section 5B(2)b.

obligations. Any method would appear to be equally acceptable as long as it is an appropriate means to realize this objective. Accordingly, a state or any other international legal subject may even decide not to enact any general validation procedure at all to ensure that its internal law conforms to international law and its obligations under it.[115] But the existence or non-existence of an international legal duty to transform international law into domestic law is of little importance to the problem concerning direct relations between these two bodies of law. In fact, the very existence of the transformation method in itself does not falsify monism, as the freedom of states to pursue the performance of their obligations in the fashion they find most suitable evidently finds its limits in the responsibility that the subject in question may incur for failure to comply with said obligations. Positive international law itself, namely Article 27 of the Vienna Convention on the Law of Treaties (VCLT),[116] bars states from invoking any of their domestic laws to derogate from their international obligations, and consequentially obligates them to adjust their internal law so as to allow them to comply with their duties.[117] Transformation is thus—from the perspective of international law—*stricto sensu* not necessary. It may be necessary from the point of view of municipal law, because the respective constitution requires the legislative to do so; but by enacting the law concerned, the domestic actor in question simply fulfils its international obligations or exercises its international rights—but it does not transform, recast, metamorphose, or convert in any way international into non-international law[118] and thereby create an additional ground of validity. International law, as valid law, is binding in itself and not in need of legal duplication. Lastly, owing observance of its norms is not optional, particularly when taking into account the principle of *pacta sunt servanda* as a quasi-constitutional norm of international law.[119]

Verdross rightly points out that international law acknowledges the relative autonomy of domestic legal systems, as the international legal system is neither capable nor authorized to annul any municipal legal acts in contravention to international norms.[120] But this does not mean that the transformation of international law creates an additional ground of validity; transformation solely remains a vehicle to ensure compliance. In fact, when assuming that national law is delegated by international law, transformation merely extends the hierarchy of norms within the domestic sphere, starting at the *Grundnorm* of the overall legal order, running down international law via the principle of effectiveness into municipal law, and provisionally terminating in the transformed domestic legal act. Therefore, the unity of the legal order and monism are not falsified on the basis of the transformation approach.

[115] Seidl-Hohenveldern (n 50) 90.

[116] See also *Certain Questions of Mutual Assistance in Criminal Matters (Djibouti v France)* [2008] ICJ Rep 177, para 124, regarding the customary legal character of Article 27 VCLT.

[117] Schaus (n 76) 698.

[118] Kelsen, *Principles of International Law* (n 97) 194–5.

[119] Josef L. Kunz, 'The Meaning and the Range of the Norm *Pacta Sunt Servanda*' (1945) 39 *American Journal of International Law* 180, 181. See also *Exchange of Greek and Turkish Populations (Advisory Opinion)* [1925] PCIJ Series B No 10, 20.

[120] See Alfred Verdross, *Die Einheit des rechtlichen Weltbildes auf Grundlage der Völkerrechtsverfassung* (Mohr, 1923).

b. Adoption does not falsify monism

Equally, dualism or pluralism cannot be proven on the basis of so-called 'international law-friendly' constitutional provisions. If it were true that monism could not be confirmed as a valid theory until such provisions became mere declaratory statements,[121] then dualism and pluralism, as theories about reality, would probably remain unchallenged and also unfalsifiable.[122] The reason for this is that it is very unlikely that general state practice plus relevant *opinio iuris* will ever result in the creation of a rule obligating domestic authorities to apply international norms under their duty to put into effect genuine national law. And even if such a customary international rule developed, national law would remain valid besides the relevant international norms, erroneously suggesting a 'double ground of validity' and that there are two different basic norms at work. Yet the real reason is that individual obligations of state officials and authorities could only be enforced on the basis of national law, not international law.[123]

This manner of creating obligations and respective sanctions for national authorities and officials does not disprove monism, because even if international law were only binding on states, this would not undermine the unity of the law. States are enjoined from breaching international norms,[124] and even if they do violate international law, the relevant contravening national legal acts are illegal and hence voidable.[125] Ultimately, should the defaulting state not annul the illegal national norm in question, the law of state responsibility would apply and the unity of national and international law would be upheld in any event. As explained above,[126] the enactment of national law in contravention to international law does not puncture the theoretical connection and the unity between the two legal orders, as such instances can be sanctioned as violations of the defaulting state's international obligations.[127]

It is of course also possible to enact national legislation that would directly bind national officials under international law. But such a course of action would not save dualism or pluralism either because, in this case, international law would lose its legal character and validity (as the said officials would in fact only be bound by the national legal act). Non-monist theories, however, claim that both national and international law are valid legal orders,[128] and consequently neither dualists nor pluralists deny the legal character of international law.

[121] Rudolf (n 74) 146–7.

[122] Which would mean that dualism or pluralism would not be scientific theories at all, but mere metaphysics; see e.g. Popper, *Logik der Forschung* (n 8) 13–14 and 41.

[123] Rill, 'Internationales, supranationales und nationales Recht' (n 102) 694.

[124] Kirsten Schmalenbach, 'Article 26' in Oliver Dörr and Kirsten Schmalenbach (eds), *Vienna Convention on the Law of Treaties: A Commentary* (Springer, 2012) para 1, pointing out that international law is binding on international legal subjects and that Article 26 of the Vienna Convention and the quasi-restatement of the principle of *pacta sunt servanda* can only be of proclamatory and symbolic nature.

[125] Rill, 'Internationales, supranationales und nationales Recht' (n 102) 694.

[126] See Chapter 3, section 5B(2)c.

[127] Hans Kelsen, *Introduction to the Problems of Legal Theory: A Translation of the First Edition of the Reine Rechtslehre or Pure Theory of Law* (transl Bonnie Litschewski Paulson and Stanley L. Paulson; Clarendon Press, 1997) 110; Kelsen, *General Theory* (n 26) 372; Kelsen, *Pure Theory* (n 24) 331.

[128] Rill, 'Internationales, supranationales und nationales Recht' (n 102) 694.

c. Conclusion: what non-monist theories fail to explain

Subsequently it becomes evident that neither dualism nor pluralism can convincingly explain why international and national law should not have a common and unitary ground of validity.[129] Monism under the primacy of international law, conversely, is capable of illustratively showing that the *Grundnorm* of all legal norms is that very norm which allows for the existence of customary international law according to which other law can be validly created.[130] With reference to Article 38(1) of the ICJ Statute and the fact that there is no hierarchy of norms within international law, as custom and treaties might supersede one another,[131] lawyers might, however, disagree with the notion that every legal norm is delegated by customary international law. One could nonetheless, on the one hand, follow Kelsen's suggestion to assume a *Grundnorm* with the content of *consuetudines sunt servandae*,[132] which places the hierarchical superiority of customary international law in the logical assumption that the conclusion of international treaties would be impossible without the pre-existing customary rule of *pacta sunt servanda*.[133] However, it has already been pointed out[134] that this claim is, given the reality of the law, highly problematic and controversial, since it is indeed true that custom and treaty law enjoy equal rank among the sources of international law. On the other hand, one could also apply Kelsen's assumption in a slightly modified form and presuppose the *Grundnorm* without any content and with Article 38 of the ICJ Statute as the meta-meta-stratum above the norm-creating meta-rules of *pacta sunt servanda* and *consuetudines sunt servandae*. This would not only better conform to reality, but could also explain how international law is being created without placing any of its sources above the others. In this picture, the *Grundnorm* gives validity to the 'constitution of international law', i.e. Article 38 of the ICJ Statute, according to which customary and treaty norms are subsequently created.[135] And among these sources, it is customary law that delegates national law via the principle of effectiveness.

Thus, dualism and pluralism fail in explaining the relationship between different bodies of law if they simply duplicate or even multiply the respective grounds of validity.[136] If we remember, the core claim of dualism is that owing to the different

[129] Potacs, 'Verhältnis' (n 104) 126–7.

[130] Rill, 'Internationales, supranationales und nationales Recht' (n 102) 696; François Rigaux, 'Hans Kelsen on International Law' (1998) 9 *European Journal of International Law* 325, 327; Rosalyn Higgins, 'Equality of States and Immunity from Suit: A Complex Relationship' (2012) 43 *Netherlands Yearbook of International Law* 129, 130, arguing that the equality of States functions as the *Grundnorm* from which other essential rules flow—such as the prohibition of the use of force, non-intervention, and sovereign immunity.

[131] Posterior treaties may always override prior customary international law (except for *ius cogens* norms), whereas subsequent practice is to be taken into account in the application of a treaty under Article 31(3)(b) of the VCLT.

[132] Kelsen, *General Theory* (n 26) 369; Kelsen, *Principles of International Law* (n 97) 417–18.

[133] Jörg Kammerhofer, 'Hans Kelsen's Place in International Legal Theory' in Alexander Orakhelashvili (ed), *Research Handbook on the Theory and History of International Law* (Edward Elgar Publishing, 2011) 152.

[134] See the discussion in Chapter 3, section 5B(2)a.

[135] Jörg Kammerhofer, *Uncertainty in International Law* (Routledge, 2011) 209.

[136] Davíd Thór Björgvinsson, *The Intersection of International Law and Domestic Law* (Edward Elgar Publishing, 2015) 3.

grounds of validity of international and national law, international law is only valid and applicable within national law if the latter explicitly provides for this, e.g. by transforming or adopting international law into national legal norms. In this vein, it has, however, been argued that dualists could generally accept monism as soon as international law becomes an effective and enforceable legal order. If this were to happen, a dualist explanation of the interplay between national and international law would become artificial, as the respective grounds of validity would be falsely duplicated,[137] in the same manner as pluralism fails to succeed by introducing several basic norms.[138] From a monist perspective, this is a desirable result, but it does not explain why two or more grounds of validity would exclude a chain of delegation between international and national law. Indeed, monism can—albeit to a very limited extent—accept two or more grounds of validity. For instance, the historically first constitution may well continue to exist as the fount of validity for national law besides the *Grundnorm* of international law, but only under the premise of alternative co-existence, in which the respective ground of validity depends on the viewpoint of the legal scientist.[139] Thus, if the legal scientist limits her or his focus to national law, thereby entirely excluding the international legal order, the historically first constitution can easily be accepted as a basic norm. Yet once international law enters the cognition of the legal scientist, the *Grundnorm* must necessarily shift to the apex of the international legal order. The *immediate* fount of validity of national law remains the constitution, but international law logically delegates the constitution, and consequently, the *overall* fount of legal validity is the basic norm of international law. Accordingly, the unity of national and international law remains intact. Equally, the above-mentioned decentralized character and weak enforcement mechanisms of international law can neither justify dualism nor pluralism: monism certainly acknowledges that one may deny the unity of international and national law on the basis of the former's lack of effectivity, but only at the price of forfeiting its legal nature. Yet a definition of the law that excludes international law verifies neither dualism nor pluralism.[140]

Ultimately, however, it becomes evident that the apparent openness of national constitutions vis-à-vis international law only ensures smooth compliance,[141] but does not indicate a potential plurality of grounds of validity. It is therefore absolutely mistaken to view the adoption method as a commitment to monism and transformation as an expression of non-monism. Whatever the attitude of a national constitution towards international law may be, i.e. openly embracing or entirely

[137] Griller, 'Völkerrecht und Landesrecht' (n 96) 100.

[138] See Wolf-Dietrich Grussmann, 'Grundnorm und Supranationalität—Rechtsstrukturelle Sichtweisen der Europäischen Integration' in Thomas von Danwitz and others (eds), *Auf dem Wege zu einer Europäischen Staatlichkeit* (Boorberg, 1993) 56 ff.

[139] Theo Öhlinger, 'Die Einheit des Rechts: Völkerrecht, Europarecht und staatliches Recht als einheitliches Rechtssystem?' in Stanley L. Paulson and Michael Stolleis (eds), *Hans Kelsen: Staatsrechtslehrer und Rechtstheoretiker des 20. Jahrhunderts* (Mohr-Siebeck, 2005) 163 fn 16.

[140] Rill, 'Internationales, supranationales und nationales Recht' (n 102) 695.

[141] Gaja (n 48) 60.

inimical, this cannot change or adversely affect the principal unity of international and national law.[142]

B. The hierarchy of international law vis-à-vis national law

(1) The supremacy of international law: claims and doubts

The second aspect to be considered is the hierarchical rank of international law and national law. This necessarily involves the concept of 'supremacy', relating to the problem of normative conflicts between international and national law and thus the question of which body of law ultimately prevails.[143] This certainly also raises the question of whether this supreme status is held by national law or international law. In the context of monism as understood by the pure theory of law, the straightforward answer to this question is certainly that supremacy must follow primacy; i.e. since each and every domestic legal order is conditioned and delegated by international law as a higher legal order, preference must logically be given to the international norm in question in the event of conflict, which means that the repugnant municipal norm must give way ('supremacy').[144] As a result, especially to avoid semantic confusion, the term 'primacy' is to be understood in the context of the chain of delegation, whereas the concept of 'supremacy' should be seen against the background of the chain of derogation.[145]

The supremacy of international law is therefore regarded as a monist conception, which not only implies coordination between international and domestic law, but also continuously guarantees the binding character of the former.[146] In this light, the principle of supremacy has been described as 'one of the great principles of international law, informing the whole system and applying to every branch of it'.[147] Thereby it requires that states exercise their powers in accordance with international law, not domestic law alone,[148] which highlights the fact that there cannot be any legal rule without the existence of some principles taking precedence over others deemed to be of lesser importance.[149] In other words, allowing states to prioritize their municipal law over international law would effectively corrode the efficacy of the latter.[150]

[142] Rill, 'Internationales, supranationales und nationales Recht' (n 102) 692 fn 80.

[143] Riccardo Pisillo-Mazzeschi, 'Die reine Lehre Kelsens und die Realität des heutigen Völkerrechts' in Agostino Carrino and Günther Winkler (eds), *Rechtserfahrung und Reine Rechtslehre* (Springer, 1995) 140.

[144] Starke, 'Primacy of International Law' (n 112) 308.

[145] See especially Matej Avbelj, 'Supremacy or Primacy of EU Law—(Why) Does it Matter?' (2011) 17 *European Law Journal* 744, which examines the discrepancy between these two notions in EU law.

[146] Gaja (n 48) 61.

[147] Gerald Fitzmaurice, 'The General Principles of International Law Considered from the Standpoint of the Rule of Law' (1957-II) 92 *Recueil des cours* 5, 85.

[148] Gerald Fitzmaurice, *The Law and Procedure of the International Court of Justice, Vol II* (Grotius, 1986) 587.

[149] Fitzmaurice, 'General Principles of International Law' (n 147) 69.

[150] Nollkaemper, *National Courts* (n 51) 281.

This stance appears to be confirmed by the general agreement that failure to observe international law in the domestic legal sphere entails the responsibility of the state (or any other relevant actor), and that the latter cannot rely upon its constitution (or legal basis in general) as an excuse for non-compliance.[151] Furthermore, rulings of international courts and tribunals of the past reinforce this view, stating, inter alia, that 'a treaty is superior to the constitution, which latter must give way. The legislation of the republic must be adapted to the treaty, not the treaty to [international law]'.[152] In line with this decision, the Permanent Court of International Justice (PCIJ) held that 'a State cannot adduce as against another State its own Constitution with a view to evading obligations incumbent upon it under international law or treaties in force'.[153]

The same principle has been endorsed by positive international law itself which establishes in Article 27 of the VCLT[154] that 'a party may not invoke the provisions of its internal law as justification for its failure to perform a treaty'. Similarly, Articles 3 and 32 of the Draft Articles on State Responsibility bar states from relying on their internal law to escape international responsibility. The question of the supremacy of international legal norms *qua ius cogens* norms is, *prima facie*, not relevant at this point, since *ius cogens* norms are primarily concerned with the relationship of international rules inter se. Therefore, their superior status over incompatible international acts does not by itself translate to the relationship between international and national law.[155]

What supremacy does not involve, however, is automatic invalidation of the contravening domestic legal norm, as correctly pointed out by Verdross.[156] International law does not provide any procedures or mechanisms effectively to bring about the necessary changes of domestic legislation in violation of international rules.[157] Accordingly, owing to this procedural deficiency, doubts have been raised whether the supremacy of international law is absolute in the sense that any attempt

[151] Felice Morgenstern, 'Judicial Practice and the Supremacy of International Law' (1950) 27 *British Yearbook of International Law* 42, 43; Fulvio Maria Palombino, 'Compliance with International Judgments: Between Supremacy of International Law and National Fundamental Principles' (2015) 75 *Zeitschrift für ausländisches öffentliches Recht und Völkerrecht* 503, 504.

[152] *Case of the Montijo (United States of America v Colombia); Agreement between the United States and Colombia of August 17, 1874, Award of 26 July 1875* in John Bassett Moore (ed), *History and Digest of International Arbitrations to which the United States Has Been A Party, Vol 2* (Government Printing Office, 1898) 1440.

[153] *Treatment of Polish Nationals and Other Persons of Polish Origin and Speech in the Danzig Territory (Advisory Opinion)* [1932] PCIJ Series A/B No 44, 24.

[154] It is interesting to note that with the exception of Costa Rica and Guatemala, claiming that Article 27 only refers to secondary, not constitutional law, no other state made a reservation to this provision. What is more, the reservations made by Costa Rica and Guatemala were objected to (concerning their compatibility with the object and purpose of the Vienna Convention) by Finland, Germany, Sweden, and the UK. See 1155 UNTS 331.

[155] Alexander Orakhelashvili, *Peremptory Norms in International Law* (Oxford University Press, 2006) 541.

[156] Verdross, *Einheit des rechtlichen Weltbildes* (n 120).

[157] Antonio Cassese, 'Towards a Moderate Monism: Could International Rules Eventually Acquire the Force to Invalidate Inconsistent National Laws?' in Antonio Cassese (ed), *Realizing Utopia. The Future of International Law* (Oxford University Press, 2012) 191.

to give precedence to municipal law is unlawful.[158] Supremacy as a merely formal principle remains highly controversial, and in practice the movement towards a fully supremacy-based international legal order remains limited in its scope. Since supremacy turns a blind eye to substance and effect, states may consider this principle, by itself, insufficient to indicate what the law is, and refrain from giving effect to an international obligation in certain situations.[159] Consequently, international law may reign supreme on the international level, but on the domestic level, states may resist international law's claim to supremacy[160] and thereby counteract this core tenet of monism under the primacy of international law.

(2) Domestic law's attitude towards the supremacy of international law

In a similar fashion to the question of validity of international norms vis-à-vis municipal law, states may or may not include a provision in their legal order which regulates the hierarchical rank of international legal norms within domestic law. But traditionally, constitutions do contain such a clause which sometimes explicitly or implicitly accepts the supremacy of international law over all domestic law or over secondary (i.e. statutory law) only; or which puts received international legal norms on a par with or below secondary law,[161] thus fully subjecting them to the *lex posterior* principle and potential supersession by posterior domestic legislation.[162] However, although this latter scenario does not release states from their international obligations and can easily be remedied through consistent interpretation (unless there is explicit legislative intent to breach these international obligations),[163] the existence of such constitutions, either 'open' or 'closed' towards the supremacy of international law mirrors, again, a monist or dualist/pluralist stance towards the international legal order. Resistance to the supremacy of international law is probably as old as international law itself, and as an empirical fact, most states declared their constitutions to be supreme in this respect.[164] In other words, the ultimate power to provide international legal norms with supremacy over domestic law and within domestic law rests with the national legal orders.[165] But if this power arises from domestic law,

[158] Nollkaemper, *National Courts* (n 51) 281.

[159] Sir Arthur Watts, 'The International Rule of Law' (1993) 36 *German Yearbook of International Law* 15, 22.

[160] Arangio-Ruiz (n 59) 35.

[161] Anne Peters, 'Supremacy Lost: International Law Meets Domestic Constitutional Law' (2009) 3 *Vienna Journal on International Constitutional Law* 170, 171–2.

[162] See e.g. Thomas H. Lee and David L. Sloss, 'International Law as an Interpretive Tool in the Supreme Court, 1861–1900' in David L. Sloss, Michael D. Ramsay, and William S. Dodge (eds), *International Law in the U.S. Supreme Court: Continuity and Change* (Cambridge University Press, 2011) 141.

[163] Benedetto Conforti, *International Law and the Role of Domestic Legal Systems* (Martinus Nijhoff, 1993) 44 and 47.

[164] Anne Peters, 'The Globalization of State Constitutions' in Janne Nijman and André Nollkaemper (eds), *New Perspectives on the Divide Between National and International Law* (Oxford University Press, 2007) 260.

[165] Daniel Thürer, 'Internationales "Rule of Law"—innerstaatliche Demokratie' (1995) 5 *Schweizerische Zeitschrift für internationales und europäisches Recht* 454, 472.

international law cannot, by itself, claim supremacy, which would eventually render a monist view under the primacy of international law highly implausible.

Thus, if we again assume, in accordance with the claims of the pure theory of law and legal monism, that international law is supreme independently from domestic law, does this mean that monism can be falsified on the basis of the dualist and pluralist arguments that make the domestic supremacy of international law dependent on such national constitutional provisions? In other words, is the claim that only the explicit domestic bestowal of supremacy *qua* national legal provisions makes international law supreme, a good and falsifying argument against monism, because states may give or take away this granting of supremacy any time and at their own discretion?

a. Constitutions accepting the supremacy of (parts of) international law

In a similar way to the adoption method discussed above, domestic legal orders that accept the supremacy of international law—be it entirely or only partially—are usually considered to be representative of a monist attitude towards international law.[166] Accepting international law's claim to supremacy over municipal law, however, appears rather to be the exception than the rule. The vanguard in this respect are the Constitution of Belgium[167] and the Constitution of the Netherlands,[168] which both grant international law—to a certain extent—precedence over national constitutional law. A special case of this particular version of supremacy is that of international human rights treaties, especially the European Convention on Human Rights (ECHR), which means that a constitution explicitly grants these treaties precedence over domestic law, but not international law in general.[169] Another interesting case can be found in the Swiss Constitution, which expressly accepts *ius cogens* norms as superior norms.[170] Hence, these constitutions have been described as the 'most monist'[171] legal systems in existence.

Below this extremely international law-friendly approach, there are certain constitutions that reject the supremacy of international law vis-à-vis constitutional law, but accept it to rank on a par with it and thereby to prevail over ordinary legislation. Until 2008, the Austrian Constitution, for instance, allowed for treaties to enjoy constitutional rank and thus to effect revisions of or supplements to the constitution itself. As these treaties of constitutional nature were not incorporated into the main

[166] Morgenstern (n 151) 57.

[167] *Nota bene*, however, that there is no explicit constitutional provision to this effect, and that this matter was decided by the Belgian Supreme Court in *État Belge v SA 'Fromagerie Franco-Suisse Le Ski'*, Cour de Cassation, 1ère chambre, 27 May 1971; and *Vlaamse Concentratie*, Cour de Cassation, 2ème chambre, 9 November 2004, para 14.1.

[168] Article 91(3). Even though this provision only explicitly mentions the supremacy of treaties over statutory law, this also applies to the constitution itself: see e.g. Nollkaemper, 'The Netherlands' (n 71) 334.

[169] Article 20 of the Constitution of Romania; Article 11 of the Constitution of Slovakia; Article 10 of the Constitution of the Czech Republic; Article 90(5) of the Constitution of Turkey.

[170] Articles 139(3) and 194(2) of the Constitution of Switzerland.

[171] John H. Jackson, 'Status of Treaties in Domestic Legal Systems: A Policy Analysis' (1992) 86 *American Journal of International Law* 310, 334.

text of the constitution itself, this led to an extremely confusing fragmentation of the law. Since 2008, the reformed Article 50 B-VG now states that treaties—with the exception of the European Union treaties—can no longer revise or supplement the Austrian constitution outside the procedural framework for constitutional amendment.[172] This means that even though existing treaties will not be bereft of their constitutional status, newly concluded treaties will be equal to ordinary legislation and accordingly not have the power to derogate constitutional law.[173]

With respect to customary international law, Article 9(1) B-VG does indeed declare the 'generally accepted rules of international law' to be an integral part of federal law, but remains silent concerning their hierarchical rank within the Austrian legal order. The prevailing view is, however, that the level of a customary international norm within Austrian law depends on the content of the rule, which means that a particular customary rule will have the rank of federal constitutional law, if the federal legislator was required to adopt a constitutional provision to create a domestic legal act with the same content; and that it will have the rank of federal statutory law, if the federal legislator would need to adopt a federal statute to regulate the subject matter in question.[174] Similarly, the Italian Constitution may grant international treaties constitutional rank which, however, depends on the formal status of the concrete national legal act (*ordine di esecuzione*), implementing the treaty in question.[175] Customary international law and EU law, conversely, constitute yardsticks that constrain the Italian legal system and thus its constitution.[176]

b. Constitutions rejecting the supremacy of international law

As briefly mentioned at the beginning of the previous section, the majority of states does not accept the supremacy of international law over their constitutions, but usually makes the acceptance of international obligations within the domestic legal sphere dependent on substantive conformity with fundamental values enshrined in municipal law.[177] Hence the overall effect of the principle of supremacy—most notably in the case of normative conflicts—is contingent on its ability to conform to such fundamental values. Yet since such conformity cannot be presumed in the first place, national legislatures retain the power to deny the supremacy of international law on the basis of constitutional provisions.[178] Viewing domestic law as independent from the supreme status of international law and thus not subject to any automatic changes on the international level naturally corresponds to a non-monist outlook.[179]

[172] Peters, 'Supremacy Lost' (n 161) 185–6.

[173] Heinz Mayer, Gabriele Kucsko-Stadlmayer, and Karl Stöger, *Grundriss des Österreichischen Bundesverfassungsrechts* (11th edn; Manz, 2015) para 228.

[174] Elisabeth Handl-Petz, 'Austria' in Dinah Shelton (ed), *International Law and Domestic Legal Systems* (Oxford University Press, 2011) 89; Mayer, Kucsko-Stadlmayer, and Stöger (n 173) para 220.

[175] Augusto Sinagra and Paolo Bargiacchi, *Lezioni di diritto internazionale pubblico* (Giuffrè, 2009) 234–5.

[176] Articles 10 and 117 of the Italian Constitution.

[177] Nollkaemper, *National Courts* (n 51) 282; Peters, 'Supremacy Lost' (n 161) 187.

[178] Thürer (n 165) 472.

[179] Björgvinsson (n 136) 34.

At the most extreme end of the non-monist spectrum, there are examples of constitutions that explicitly claim the supremacy of national constitutional law over (parts of) international law, such as the Constitution of Belarus;[180] the Constitution of Georgia;[181] and the Constitution of South Africa.[182] A special case is the UK, where treaties are in no way supreme under the (unwritten) British Constitution; in fact, they are not even equal to domestic law and can be superseded by it, although this is rare.[183] Of a lesser non-monist degree are constitutions that clearly grant international law supremacy over statutory legislation, but not over the constitution itself, for instance Article 28(1) of the Constitution of Greece; Article 123 the Constitution of Estonia; Article 91(3) of the Constitution of Poland; and Article 79 of the Constitution of Russia.

Another prominent non-monist example can be found in Germany which, however, follows a certain mixed approach regarding the rank of the different sources of international law. According to Article 59(2) GG, treaties enjoy the rank of federal statutory law, thus following the 'life' of the respective domestic act that transformed the treaty into national law (*Zustimmungsgesetz*).[184] The 'general rules of international law', as Article 25 GG denotes all non-treaty-based international law, conversely, prevail over statutory law. Despite the clear wording of this provision, it has been debated whether incorporated general international law might nonetheless be superior[185] to the constitution in the case of conflict. This argument is not convincing, because the framers of the constitution explicitly mention the supremacy of general international law over statutory law, but not over constitutional law, nor did they declare it to be an integral part of German law (as Article 140 GG does, for example).[186] Beyond that, it is—in particular from a monist aspect—interesting to note that logical objections have been raised against the potential 'ultra-constitutional' rank of incorporated general international law in German law: since it is undisputed that the rank of a legal norm is determined by the rank of the creator of this norm, it follows that the norm cannot be of a rank superior to that of its creator. In fact, if one accepts the existence of legal norms that are superior to those of the constitution,[187] then their very existence and therefore their supreme status cannot depend on the national constitution.[188] Consequently, the mezzanine

[180] Article 116 stating that international agreements found to be unconstitutional by the Constitutional Court shall be deemed invalid.

[181] Article 6(2) declaring the precedence of the Constitution over international treaties in the case of normative conflicts.

[182] Section 232 incorporating customary international law only to the extent that it is not inconsistent with the Constitution or an Act of Parliament.

[183] Anthony Aust, 'United Kingdom' in David Sloss (ed), *The Role of Domestic Courts in Treaty Enforcement: A Comparative Study* (Cambridge University Press, 2009) 479.

[184] Albert Bleckmann, *Grundgesetz und Völkerrecht* (Duncker & Humblot, 1975) 277; Pfeffer (n 92) 169–70.

[185] See e.g., Ingolf Pernice, 'Art. 25' in Horst Dreier (ed), *Grundgesetz-Kommentar: Band II* (2nd edn; Mohr-Siebeck, 2006) paras 25–6, arguing that *ius cogens* norms prevail over constitutional law.

[186] Pfeffer (n 92) 169.

[187] As the German Federal Constitutional Court generally does: BVerfGE 1, 18—*Südweststaat*, 23 October 1951, para 151.

[188] Rudolf (n 74) 265.

status of incorporated general international law, i.e. between constitutional and statutory law, has been confirmed by the Bundesverfassungsgericht.[189]

In older constitutions, express provisions on the hierarchical status of domestic vis-à-vis international law are rare. Article VI clause 2 of the United States Constitution, for example, declares that '[t]his Constitution, and the laws of the United States which shall be made in pursuance thereof; *and all treaties made, or which shall be made, under the authority of the US., shall be the supreme law of the land* ...',[190] yet remains silent on how to resolve normative conflicts. This question was therefore mostly answered in constitutional case law through which the Supreme Court established the supremacy of the Constitution over international treaties. This entails that any conflicts between the Constitution and treaties are resolved in favour of the former[191]—a stance which the Supreme Court justifies with the language of Article VI clause 2, the history of its adoption, the objections of the framers, and constitutional history.[192] As a consequence, when the United States enter into treaty obligations, they are routinely subjected to conflicting constitutional provisions.[193] Treaties, however, rank higher than state laws and take precedence in the case of conflict,[194] whereas treaties and federal statutes enjoy equal rank. In this regard, courts attempt to resolve normative conflicts through interpretation.[195] Only should this approach fail, will they resort to the *lex posterior principle*, according to which later-in-time treaties prevail over prior inconsistent federal law, and later-in-time federal law prevails over prior inconsistent treaties.[196] Thus, the courts ensure that all treaty norms only have effects in domestic law within constitutional limits.[197]

c. Domestic courts rejecting the supremacy of international law

Definitive codified provisions on accepting or rejecting the supremacy of international law are regularly complemented by the decisions of domestic courts that may claim to have the last word on the question of supremacy, thereby challenging the performance of international obligations in contravention to particular municipal legal norms.[198] Hence national legal systems, while generally being open to international law, might insist on guarding certain policy areas from external influences, which usually results in retaining full sovereignty and hindering

[189] BVerfGE 6, 309—*Reichskonkordat*, 26 March 1957, 363; BVerfGE 37, 271—*Solange I*, 29 May 1974, 278–279; BVerfGE 111, 307—*Görgülü*, 14 October 2004, 318.

[190] Emphasis added.

[191] See also Restatement (Third) of Foreign Relations Law, § 115(2) (1987).

[192] *Reid v Covert*, 354 US 1, 16–17 (1957).

[193] See e.g. the US reservation to the Genocide Convention of 1948, 1021 UNTS 277: '[N]othing in this Convention requires or authorizes legislation or other action by the United States of America prohibited by the Constitution of the United States as interpreted by the United States'. See also the declaration by Germany stating that this can only be interpreted 'as not in any way affecting the obligations of the United States of America as a State Party to the Convention'.

[194] *Ware v Hylton*, 3 US (3 Dall) 199 (1796).

[195] *Trans World Airlines, Inc. v Franklin Mint Corp.*, 466 US 243, 252 (1984).

[196] *Chae Chan Ping v United States*, 130 US 581, 602 (1889); *Whitney v Robertson*, 124 US 190, 194 (1888); *Edye v Robertson*, 112 US 580, 597–8 (1884).

[197] Sloss, 'United States' (n 69) 509.

[198] Nollkaemper, *National Courts* (n 51) 282; Peters, 'Supremacy Lost' (n 161) 193.

the implementation of the international norm in question.[199] The reason for this domestic judicial resistance is twofold: first, international law has become much more regulatory in fields that were traditionally governed by national law alone, most prominently concerning the rights and obligations of individuals in general and human rights in particular;[200] and, secondly, international law lacks the same standard and quality in terms of the rule of law,[201] which makes domestic courts more reluctant to accept international norms not conforming to municipal standards of protection.[202] The result of this is a widening gap between international law (which continues to claim supremacy over national legal orders) and domestic law (where courts may resist this claim with reference to fundamental rights protection). Interestingly, the scope of this problem differs widely between the various sources of international law: while it is marginal or even non-existent regarding customary international law, there are abundant issues with respect to treaty performance and decisions of international organizations,[203] particularly when courts argue that decisions go beyond the original powers granted to such organizations by their respective founding treaty.[204]

Examples of such judicial resistance include the Constitutional Chamber of the Supreme Tribunal of Justice of Venezuela, which declared that 'above the Supreme Court of Venezuelan Justice, and to the effects of domestic law, there is no supranational, transnational or international court', and that decisions of such organs 'will not be executed in Venezuela if they contradict the Venezuelan Constitution'.[205] Similarly, the Supreme Court of Sri Lanka stated that it could not give effect to views of the Human Rights Committee that were in conflict with the constitution.[206] In France, Article 55 of the constitution, expressly providing treaties supremacy over statutory law, was accordingly interpreted by the Conseil d'État to the effect that 'the supremacy thus granted to international agreements does not apply, within domestic law, to constitutional provisions'.[207] This position was subsequently confirmed by the Conseil Constitutionnel, holding that 'when international agreements . . . contain a clause contrary to the Constitution, challenging constitutionally guaranteed rights and freedoms or undermining the conditions essential for the exercise of national sovereignty, the authorization to ratify such agreements calls for

199 Palombino (n 151) 506–7.

200 Antônio Cançado Trindade, *The Construction of a Humanized International Law* (Brill, 2015) 871; Antonios Tzanakopoulos, 'Domestic Courts in International Law: The International Judicial Function of National Courts' (2011) 43 *Loyola of Los Angeles International and Comparative Law Review* 133, 143.

201 James Crawford, 'International Law and the Rule of Law' (2004) 24 *Adelaide Law Review* 3, 6–12.

202 Nollkaemper, *National Courts* (n 51)283 and 285.

203 Ibid., 284.

204 Thomas Gehring, 'Treaty-Making and Treaty Evolution' in Daniel Bodansky, Jutta Brunnée, and Ellen Hey (eds), *The Oxford Handbook of International Environmental Law* (Oxford University Press, 2007) 466.

205 *Rafael Chavero Gazdik*, Constitutional Chamber Award No 1.942, 15 July 2003, Case No 01-0415; ILDC 1286 (VE 2003).

206 *Singarasa v Attorney General*, SC Spl (LA) No 182/99; ILDC 518 (LK 2006).

207 *Sarran et Levacher*, 30 October 1998, Revue Française de Droit Administratif 1998, n 141081–1090.

a constitutional revision'.[208] This is also in line with Article 54 of the constitution, explicitly stating the same requirement for a constitutional amendment in the case of a treaty in violation of the constitution. National sovereignty is therefore given the final word.[209]

To date, one of the most extreme examples of rejecting the supremacy of international law can be found in a judgment of the Italian Constitutional Court, following the *Jurisdictional Immunities* case decided earlier by the ICJ. In this case, the ICJ had found that Italy had breached its international obligations by denying Germany jurisdictional immunity from civil suits before Italian courts for crimes committed in Italy during the Second World War.[210] Subsequently, the Italian Parliament approved legislation according to which the judgments issued by Italian courts in violation of the relevant international legal norms on state immunity could be annulled. This implementing act, however, was found to be unconstitutional by the Italian Constitutional Court for various reasons, most notably because, by virtue of Article 134 of the constitution, the Constitutional Court is the only court entrusted with constitutional review, and because fundamental rights (in particular access to justice) constitute a limit to the reception of international law under Article 10(1) of the constitution. The Court therefore concluded that the international rule on state immunity could not prevail over domestic law and annulled the legal act in question.[211] In this light, when rejecting the supremacy of the international legal order and favouring constitutional law principles, the Constitutional Court was certainly guided by a domestic view of the claimed supremacy of international law. This approach can consequently and without doubt be qualified as non-monist.[212] Similarly, the German Federal Court held in an extremely dualist fashion that a treaty that has been transformed into national law on the basis of a statutory 'command to apply international law' (*Rechtsanwendungsbefehl*), only has the same hierarchical rank and status of said statute. This means that subsequent non-compliance with the original treaty can be justified (at least in terms of national law) by a superseding *lex posterior*, effectively 'overriding the treaty'.[213]

Yet there are also instances where national courts send somewhat mixed signals regarding the supremacy of international law. In the *Görgülü* case, for example, the German Federal Constitutional Court highlighted, on the one hand, that the constitution does not forego the sovereignty contained in the German Constitution and interpreted the relationship between international law and the German legal order in a strictly non-monist manner.[214] *In concreto*, it declined to give effect to a judgment of the European Court of Human Rights (ECtHR) because of its restrictive

[208] *Traité établissant une Constitution pour l'Europe*, decision no 505 DC, 19 November 2004, (2004) JORF 19885, para 7.

[209] Emmanuel Decaux, 'France' in Dinah Shelton (ed), *International Law and Domestic Legal Systems* (Oxford University Press, 2011) 217.

[210] *Jurisdictional Immunities of the State (Germany v Italy; Greece Intervening)* [2012] ICJ Rep 99.

[211] Decision No 238, 22 October 2014.

[212] Massimo Lando, 'Intimations of Unconstitutionality: The Supremacy of International Law and Judgment 238/2014 of the Italian Constitutional Court' (2015) 78 *Modern Law Review* 1028, 1037.

[213] BVerfG, 2 BvL 1/12—*Treaty Override*, 15 December 2015, paras 49–51, 74, 77, and 88.

[214] BVerfGE 111, 307—*Görgülü* (n 189) paras 34–5.

effect on national fundamental rights.[215] Thereby it regarded the binding force of the ECHR in a reductionist way and argued that it would not constitute a strict prescript for the German authorities, but merely a text to be 'taken into account' within the limits of constitutional law.[216] On the other hand, however, the Constitutional Court also recognized the existence of a 'gradually developing international community of democratic states under the rule of law'[217] and paved the way for constitutional complaints against instances of alleged disregard of ECtHR judgments by domestic authorities.[218]

Ultimately, the overall result is an emerging picture of domestic courts resisting the supremacy of international law, picking and choosing when to accept and when to reject it. The question remains, nonetheless, what this 'supremacy à la carte', i.e. a supreme status that is, after all, contingent on the will of the states, means for a monist view of the law.

(3) Consequential arguments against monism

In a similar fashion to the question of validity discussed above, the foregoing analysis shows that the supremacy of international is not generally accepted among states. Quite the contrary, a blanket acceptance of this supreme status over constitutional law seems to be the exception, and the rule is that international legal norms may be on a par with the constitution; or rank below it, but prevail over secondary legislation; or enjoy the same hierarchical status as statutory law. Should any doubts remain, it has been shown that domestic courts are also usually very eager to rein in the claimed superior position of international law. In the context of this book, it becomes inevitable to ask what this means for a monist view of the law as envisaged by the pure theory of law. As briefly mentioned above, the problem with a monist understanding under the primacy (and thus supremacy) of international law in this context is the following: in practice, it does not matter whether a constitution or a court accepts or rejects the supremacy of international law, since both approaches are based on the principally non-monist assumption that international law can only claim supremacy within domestic law if domestic law itself allows for this very supremacy of international legal norms.[219] Accordingly, non-monists do not deny that, in order to avoid the breach of obligations under international law, international law should prevail over municipal law. Yet nonetheless it remains a fact that an ensuing non-application of domestic law owing to the supreme status of international law is based on domestic law itself, for example on a constitutional provision or a constitutional court decision which requires compliance with international law.[220] In this light, the claimed supremacy of international law is only

[215] Ibid., para 32. [216] Ibid., paras 47–50. [217] Ibid., para 36.
[218] Ibid., para 63.
[219] Antonios Tzanakopoulos, 'Judicial Dialogue as a Means of Interpretation' in Helmut Philipp Aust and Georg Nolte (eds), *The Interpretation of International Law by Domestic Courts* (Oxford University Press, 2016) 86 fn 80.
[220] Rudolf (n 74) 146–7.

apparent, since it is dependent on the status it is given in municipal law—a status which can always be reversed by a change in the relevant law[221] through a *lex posterior* or, assuming that the hierarchical rank of a transformed international norm is equivalent to the transformative act itself, through a derogating higher norm in the domestic system in question. At this point, monists may of course object and argue that denying international law its supreme status within domestic law does not automatically affect the supremacy of the international legal order itself. Again, the absence of *internal* supremacy would be without prejudice to the *external* supremacy of international law, and ultimately, international law continues to be supreme in the case of conflict even when not given this status in domestic law. Thus, the question of supremacy cannot be answered in an unequivocal manner and a stalemate between monism and dualism as well as pluralism appears to be inevitable, as all interpretations are equally plausible.[222]

The problem for monism is, however, that the dualist and pluralist views seem to be more convincing when it comes to the question of supremacy. Monism is arguably correct in emphasizing the difference between the internal and external supremacy of international law, and yet again, this very assumption—the distinction between two legal orders—undercuts the core tenet of monism, namely the necessary existence of one single legal order. If there only is one ground of validity, found in the *Grundnorm* of international law, then there can also be only one hierarchy of norms, one chain of delegation, and one chain of derogation, which is not compatible with the argument that the supremacy of international law stops at the intersection of domestic and international law. Accordingly, the dualist and pluralist claims that municipal law might have the last word on the supremacy of international norms within domestic law, makes a very convincing and falsifying argument against monism.

The practice of states rejecting the supremacy of international law certainly speaks against monism. Even though it is correct to say that international law does not allow states and other international legal subjects to rely on their internal law to derogate from their international obligations, it never claimed the same supremacy within the municipal sphere. Especially this scenario, i.e. the existence of domestic law in violation of international law, is compensated on the international level by the law of state responsibility,[223] according to which injured parties may resort to countermeasures short of the use of force or demand reparation or compensation, and the law of treaties itself, most notably Article 60 of the VCLT.[224] In the light of these legal instruments, it is highly questionable whether states can be required on the international plane to change their domestic law in contravention to international law. International law does not require such municipal law to be invalidated *qua* international law itself, which means that only domestic law itself can effectively

[221] Gaja (n 48) 61. [222] Schaus (n 76) 700.

[223] *Gabčíkovo-Nagymaros Project (Hungary v Slovakia)* [1996] ICJ Rep 7, para 47.

[224] For the relevance in distinguishing between the two responses see Bruno Simma and Christian J. Tams, 'Reacting against Treaty Breaches' in Duncan B. Hollis (ed), *The Oxford Guide to Treaties* (Oxford University Press, 2012) 580–2.

change, amend, or annul the legal act in question.[225] Hence, it is merely a truism that when international law imposes on a state the duty to change its laws in order to comply with its international obligation, this state is duty-bound to repeal or amend the problematic legal act[226]—a view that was also confirmed by the PCIJ in the *Exchange of Greek and Turkish Populations* case.[227] The question of how states fulfil this obligation is nonetheless entirely left to them themselves.[228] Therefore, the task of resolving potential normative conflicts between international and domestic legal norms rests with the respective national actors.[229]

The same arguments apply to constitutional systems which, more or less, accept the supremacy of international law. In the same manner as the adoption of international law—usually regarded as a sign of openness towards international law—has been shown to be utterly dependent on positive provisions of national law, the acceptance of the supremacy of international law also hinges on the same conditions. This means that even after declaring that international law is to prevail over domestic law in normative conflicts, national law is still capable of imposing extensive constraints on the enforcement of international law in the internal sphere. Thus, (allegedly) monist systems operate on the same basis as non-monist systems.[230] As a result, the overall monist appearance of these constitutional orders should not obscure the fact that better compliance with international law is not necessarily achieved through supremacy-accepting constitutional provisions.[231] Hence, ultimately, the supremacy of international law can only be realized if domestic courts are in a position to review the domestic act in question for its compatibility with international law, which is partly dependent on direct effect. If, however, no judicial review is available, any constitutional provisions granting supremacy to international law remain a dead letter.[232]

These arguments seem plausible and convincing, yet the question remains whether they conclusively falsify monism or not.

(4) Monist arguments in the context of supremacy

The attack on the supremacy of international law is not only of theoretical concern, as it may prove the pure theory of law wrong. Beyond that, this approach will, in the long run, also turn out to be extremely detrimental to the concept of law itself, since it is difficult to see how the general principle of supremacy can be qualified by domestic law without necessarily undermining the international legal order itself. Recognition of the potential power of states to prioritize their own law over binding international obligations will ultimately undermine the effectiveness

[225] Albert Bleckmann, 'Vorrang des Völkerrechts im Landesrechtsraum? Zum Urteil der belgischen Cour de cassation vom 27. Mai 1971' (1972) 32 *Zeitschrift für ausländisches öffentliches Recht und Völkerrecht* 516, 526.

[226] Cassese, 'Towards a Moderate Monism' (n 157) 188.

[227] *Exchange of Greek and Turkish Populations (Advisory Opinion)* (n 119) 20.

[228] Bleckmann, 'Vorrang des Völkerrechts' (n 225) 526.

[229] Peters, 'Supremacy Lost' (n 161) 186.

[230] Morgenstern (n 151) 66.

[231] Conforti (n 163) 26.

[232] Peters, 'Supremacy Lost' (n 161) 186.

of international norms by obliterating the boundaries of legality,[233] and thereby reinforce already existing perceptions of international law as non-law or mere positive morality, which remains unenforceable against state sovereignty.[234] Furthermore, basing resistance to the supremacy of international law on substantive values such as fundamental rights, democracy, the rule of law, or legitimacy in general, leads to further fragmentation of the law owing to the difficulties in identifying such values, which may perhaps exclusively be attributed to 'liberal democracies',[235] but which are not shared by all states. These grounds for justifying non-performance are too open-ended to work effectively and with certainty. If international law allowed such challenges, its end would indeed be near.[236]

Therefore, the rationale for constitutions to pay tribute to international law cannot derive from the national legal orders themselves, and accordingly it does not make sense to label these constitutions or national legal orders—depending on their degree of openness towards the supremacy of international law—as monist, dualist, or pluralist. Instead, the rationale for the binding nature, effectiveness, and influence of international law on domestic must necessarily arise from its supremacy and the impermissibility for municipal legal systems to affect the performance and application of international legal norms.[237] In other words, only a monist understanding of the law under the primacy of international law is a reasonable choice to follow. The following sections will now examine possible arguments to bolster this rationale and to defend monism against falsification in the context of supremacy.

a. The sensitivity of international law

At the outset, it is crucial to note that international law is not completely insensitive to the concerns of domestic law, especially when it comes to the protection of fundamental rights. International law in fact provides a variety of instruments through which states can guarantee the immunity of constitutional principles to the effect of international obligations.[238] Derogating from international supremacy is, for instance, allowed under Article 46 of the VCLT, which resolves tensions between constitutional orders and the principle of democracy on the one hand, and the efficiency of international law on the other hand in favour of the latter.[239] Whereas the first part of this provision confirms that states may not invoke their internal law to escape international obligations, the second part states that this rule does not apply if the international obligation is invalid because of a manifest violation of an internal law of fundamental importance. This may include reasons such as

[233] André Nollkaemper, 'Rethinking the Supremacy of International Law' (2010) 65 *Zeitschrift für öffentliches Recht* 65, 73–4; Nollkaemper, *National Courts* (n 51) 287.

[234] Yuval Shany, 'Toward a General Margin of Appreciation Doctrine in International Law?' (2006) 15 *European Journal of International Law* 908, 912.

[235] Giulio Bartolini, 'A Universal Approach to International Law in Contemporary Constitutions: Does It Exist?' (2014) 4 *Cambridge Journal of International and Comparative Law* 1287, 1319.

[236] Nollkaemper, *National Courts* (n 51) 287–8.

[237] Bartolini (n 235) 1289.

[238] Nollkaemper, 'Rethinking Supremacy' (n 233) 71.

[239] Michael Bothe, 'Article 46 Convention of 1969' in Olivier Corten and Pierre Klein (eds), *The Vienna Conventions on the Law of Treaties: A Commentary, Vol II* (Oxford University Press, 2011) 1097.

the expression of consent of the state to be bound by an organ not entitled to do so[240] or the violation of competence rules in federally-structured states. This provision nonetheless emphasizes the exceptional character of the ground for invalidating consent[241] and thus gives precedence to the security of treaties, the good faith of the other contracting parties over countervailing considerations, and thereby also to the supremacy of international law over the complexities and uncertainties of pertinent domestic provisions.[242]

Alternatively, international law also permits explicit references to domestic law in international obligations to derogate from its supremacy.[243] An example for this can be found in Article 36(2) of the Vienna Convention on Consular Relations stating that '[t]he rights referred to in paragraph 1 of this article [i.e. communication, information, and visits between consular officers and the nationals of the sending state, especially in the case of arrest] shall be exercised in conformity with the laws and regulations of the receiving State . . .'. This entails that a state which applies domestic law when performing Article 36(1) will principally not be in conflict with its international obligations and hence no issue of supremacy will arise.[244] In the *Avena* case, the ICJ accordingly endeavoured to accommodate the relevant domestic act of the United States (which effectively prevented Mexico from retaining private counsel for arrested nationals) with the Convention and concluded that it would be premature to conclude that there was indeed a violation of international law.[245]

Other interesting examples of such sensitivity towards domestic law can be found in the ECHR system which, although lacking supremacy in the strong sense as found in European Union law, remains unrivalled in its effectiveness and achievements, mainly because of the ECtHR and its sophisticated and detailed jurisprudence.[246] In controversial cases, such as the protection of morals,[247] where the ECtHR is unable to determine a consensus among states, they are allowed a certain (albeit limited) margin of appreciation to assess whether a human rights violation has actually taken place. Upon entry into force of Protocol No 15 to the ECHR, this principle will subsequently also be expressly incorporated into the preamble to the Convention.[248]

[240] See e.g. *Land and Maritime Boundary between Cameroon and Nigeria (Cameroon v Nigeria; Equatorial Guinea Intervening)* [2002] ICJ Rep 303, paras 262–8.

[241] See Final Draft, Commentary to Art 43, para 12; statements by the representatives of Australia, Senegal, Sweden, and the Ukrainian SSR; Official Records of the United Nations Conference on the Law of Treaties, First Session (Vienna, 26 March–24 May 1968), Summary Records of the Plenary Meetings and of the Meetings of the Committee of the Whole, UN Doc A/CONF.39/11, 239, 241–2.

[242] Thilo Rensmann, 'Article 46' in Oliver Dörr and Kirsten Schmalenbach (eds), *Vienna Convention on the Law of Treaties: A Commentary* (Springer, 2012) paras 21–5.

[243] Fitzmaurice, *Law and Procedure* (n 148) 591.

[244] Nollkaemper, 'Rethinking Supremacy' (n 233) 72.

[245] *Avena and Other Mexican Nationals (Mexico v United States of America)* [2004] ICJ Rep 12, para 113. See also the judgment of the US Supreme Court in *Sanchez-Llamas v Oregon & Bustillo v Johnson*, 126 S Ct 2669.

[246] Alastair Mowbray, 'The Creativity of the European Court of Human Rights' (2005) 5 *Human Rights Law Review* 57–79.

[247] See in particular ECtHR, *Handyside v United Kingdom*, App no 5493/72, 7 December 1976, paras 47–9.

[248] Article 1 of Protocol No 15 to the Convention, adopted on 24 June 2013; CETS 213.

Secondly, it has also been established that local remedies are key to the settlement of international disputes. Thus, the requirement that these local or domestic remedies be exhausted before an international court can be involved in a dispute is today generally accepted as a customary international norm.[249] A specific example of this rule is enshrined in Article 35(1) ECHR, which has been interpreted by the ECtHR as having three crucial purposes: first, to afford states the opportunity of preventing or redressing alleged human rights violations before those allegations are submitted to the Court;[250] secondly, to codify the presumption that states provide individuals with effective remedies, thus underlining the subsidiarity of the ECHR system vis-à-vis domestic law;[251] and, thirdly, eventually to give the Court—should the case nonetheless be brought before it—the benefit of taking into consideration the views of the national courts before ruling on the matter itself.[252] In other words, this rule and the jurisprudence of the Court can be seen as a sign of respect towards national courts, which are primarily responsible for interpreting and applying domestic law and hence better positioned to resolve legal disputes.[253]

The last examples of sensitivity and deference towards municipal law are Articles 41 and 53 ECHR. Article 41 ECHR provides the ECtHR with the power to afford just satisfaction to the party injured by a human rights violation, if the internal law of the respondent in question does not allow or allows only for partial reparation to be made. This means, *a contrario*, that this provision gives states considerable discretion as to the manner of execution of a judgment and the effecting of restitution or compensation.[254] Similarly, Article 53 ECHR allows states discretion in affording individuals with a standard of protection that is higher than that of the Convention, thereby establishing the ECHR as a minimum threshold for human rights protection.[255]

Dualists and pluralists might argue at this point that this very sensitivity of international law vis-à-vis national law is proof for the latter's ultimate power to dictate the terms. This, however, is not the case, and quite the opposite is true. Exceptions are certainly important, as not all individual situations are equitably decidable on the ground of general norms. But without these general norms and rules, international law would become unable to perform its functions and thereby

[249] Chittharanjan Felix Amerasinghe, Local Remedies in International Law (2nd edn; Cambridge University Press, 2004) 3.

[250] ECtHR, *Selmouni v France*, App no 25803/94, 28 July 1999, para 74; ECtHR, *Hentrich v France*, App no 13616/88, 22 September 1994, para 33; ECtHR, *Remli v France*, App no 16839/90, 23 April 1996, para 33.

[251] ECtHR, *Akdivar v Turkey*, App no 21893/93, 16 September 1996, para 65; ECtHR, *Eberhard and M. v Slovenia*, App nos 8673/05 and 9733/05, 1 December 2009, para 103.

[252] ECtHR, *A and Others v United Kingdom*, App no 3455/05, 19 February 2009, para 154; ECtHR, *Burden v United Kingdom*, App no 13378/05, 29 April 2008, para 42.

[253] ECtHR, *Huvig v France*, App no 11105/84, 24 April 1990, para 28. See also ECtHR, *Kemmache v France (No 3)*, App no 17621/91, 24 November 1994, para 37.

[254] ECtHR, *Papamichalopoulos and Others v Greece (Article 50)*, App no 14556/89, 31 October 1995, para 34.

[255] Helen Keller and Alec Stone Sweet, 'Assessing the Impact of the ECHR on National Legal Systems' in Helen Keller and Alec Stone Sweet (eds), *A Europe of Rights: The Impact of the ECHR on National Legal Systems* (Oxford University Press, 2008) 702–3.

ineffective.[256] Therefore, these exceptions do not disprove the supremacy of international law and thereby a monist view; on the contrary, they do nothing but prove the existence of a rule,[257] as otherwise exceptions would be meaningless. This is also confirmed by the original meaning of the phrase '*exceptio probat regulam in casibus exceptis*' found in Roman law, which denotes that a stated exception implies the existence of a rule to which it is the exception.[258] These instruments and devices do not exclude the application of the principle of supremacy; they merely aim at reducing potential conflicts. Whereas Article 41 ECHR, for example, simply moderates the effects of the principle of supremacy, the performance of the obligation itself remains entirely subject to this principle.[259] Even if we assume a situation in which domestic law does not allow for a full reparation to be made, the ECtHR can—in the last resort—give full effect to the obligation to provide reparation,[260] and subsequently, the respondent state in question would not be permitted to rely on its internal law to justify its non-performance.[261] Similarly, Article 36(2) of the Vienna Convention on Consular Relations states that the deference to municipal law is 'subject to the proviso, however, that the said laws and regulations must enable full effect to be given to the purposes for which the rights accorded under this Article are intended'.[262] In a nutshell, the general point is that, ultimately, it is international law which determines what matters are regulated by domestic law and the extent to which they are regulated by domestic law.[263]

Thus, the sensitivity of international law to domestic law and its most fundamental rules, as depicted and examined above, is not proof against monism, as these mechanisms do not result in a general exception to the principle of supremacy in international law, as exemplified by Article 27 of the VCLT as well as Articles 3 and 32 of the Draft Articles on State Responsibility. Beyond these explicit limits and exceptions, the principle of supremacy fulfils its regular functions[264] and should rather be seen as confirmation of monism under the primacy of international law.

b. Reservations

Another option to reconcile international law's claim to supremacy and domestic resistance to it can be found in the formulation of reservations, aimed at safeguarding municipal law by stating that the application of the treaty in question must be compatible with national law.[265] Thereby, potential normative conflicts can be prevented in the first place.[266]

256 See Luís Duarte d'Almeida, *Allowing for Exceptions: A Theory of Defences and Defeasibility in Law* (Oxford University Press, 2015) 3.

257 Palombino (n 151) 505.

258 Marcus Tullius Cicero, *Pro Balbo* (revised edn; transl R. Gardner, Loeb, 1989) XIV, 32.

259 Nollkaemper, 'Rethinking Supremacy' (n 233) 72.

260 See e.g. ECtHR, *Ruslan Umarov v Russia,* App no 12712/02, 3 July 2008, para 168.

261 See Article 32 of the Draft Articles on State Responsibility.

262 *LaGrand (Germany v United States of America)* [2001] ICJ Rep 466, paras 90–1, concluding that on this very legal basis, the US was clearly in breach of its international obligations.

263 Fitzmaurice, *Law and Procedure* (n 148) 592.

264 Nollkaemper, 'Rethinking Supremacy' (n 233) 73.

265 Palombino (n 151) 523; Peters, 'Supremacy Lost' (n 161) 191.

266 Nollkaemper, *National Courts* (n 51) 285.

The power of states is nevertheless not unrestricted in this regard. Not only are other states rather reluctant to accept broadly and vaguely formulated reservations through which the legal effects of specific treaty provisions on domestic law are purported to be excluded,[267] but international law itself also provides instruments to counter the watering down of its supremacy and prevailing effects. In principle, reservations to exclude or modify the legal effect of treaty provisions 'in order to preserve the integrity of *specific* norms of the internal law'[268] are certainly permissible, but only as long as they are not of an undefined nature and therefore fall foul of the object and purpose of the treaty in question, as set forth in Article 19(c) of the VCLT. Despite the inherently enigmatic nature of the 'object and purpose' test, it is now commonly accepted that reservations worded in vague and general language, which does not allow for its scope to be ascertained, are to be considered incompatible with the object and purpose of a treaty.[269]

It has been argued that in the context of reservations, Article 27 of the VCLT and therewith the supremacy of international law would be entirely irrelevant, as they in fact only apply 'once the extent of the State's obligations has been determined, that is, once the issue of reservations has been addressed and resolved'.[270] This contention, however, is neither persuasive[271] nor entirely correct, especially when considering the case law of international courts. The root of the problem is that the expression of consent to be bound by a certain treaty, to which an impermissible reservation has been made, is contradictory in itself, and such an inherent paradox cannot be resolved by interpretation. This may entail, on the one hand, that a state which formulated a reservation that is incompatible with the object and purpose of the treaty did not become a party to it all, as held by the ICJ in its *Advisory Opinion in Reservations to the Genocide Convention*.[272] On the other hand, impermissible reservations can also result in the severance of the reservation from the ratification, according to which the former is declared invalid whilst the latter is kept intact, as concluded by the ECtHR in the *Belilos* case.[273]

The question of which legal consequence follows a reservation impermissible under Article 19(c) VCLT remains highly controversial to this day, but it is eventually not relevant to the question of monism. Ultimately, the existence of reservations does not falsify the unity of the law, since it is the international legal order which decides on their ultimate permissibility and thus validity in the light of the law of treaties. Accordingly, should a reservation be declared impermissible and invalid, the treaty in question remains intact and international law in general supreme.

[267] Edward T. Swaine, 'Reserving' (2006) 31 *Yale Journal of International Law* 307, 348–9.

[268] Rule 3.1.11 of the Guide to Practice on Reservations to Treaties, as adopted by the International Law Commission (ILC) Drafting Committee; International Law Commission, 'Reservations to Treaties', UN Doc A/CN.4/L.705 (2007) (emphasis added).

[269] Rule 3.1.7 of the Guide to Practice on Reservations to Treaties (n 268).

[270] William Schabas, 'Reservations to the Convention on the Rights of the Child' (1996) 18 *Human Rights Quarterly* 472, 480.

[271] Palombino (n 151) 524.

[272] *Reservations to the Convention on Genocide (Advisory Opinion)* [1951] ICJ Rep 15, 21.

[273] ECtHR, *Belilos v Switzerland*, App no 10328/83, 29 April 1988, para 60. See also Human Rights Committee, General Comment No 24, UN Doc CCPR/C/21/Rev.1/Add.6, para 18.

c. Turning inter-order conflicts into intra-order conflicts

The last option to reconcile international legal supremacy and contravening domestic law is the so-called 'internationalization of national values' technique, whereby the rule of law at both the municipal and international level can possibly be preserved.[274] In this vein, it has been argued that declaring tensions between domestic fundamental rights in conformity with international law, on the one hand, and international obligations as normative conflicts in terms of supremacy, on the other hand, is a category mistake, as such tensions could be resolved at the international level. Hence there really is no conflict between international and national law, but a conflict between different international legal norms which can be entirely dealt with at the international level. Three scenarios should consequently be distinguished from one another in this regard.[275]

First, one could think of a situation in which a fundamental right is invoked by a state as justification for non-compliance with an international obligation, and this very fundamental right corresponds to a rule of *ius cogens*. In such a scenario, the *ius cogens* norm would prevail over the 'ordinary' international obligation in question by invalidating it,[276] and the state could thus freely prioritize the fundamental right in question. As a result, no issue of supremacy would arise,[277] because under a monist view, peremptory norms undoubtedly sit at the apex of positive law, which in turn encompasses both domestic and international law.[278]

Secondly, there are scenarios in which tensions might arise between an internationally protected human right not, however, rising to the level of a *ius cogens* norm, and an obligation under a United Nations Security Council resolution, which is superior over conflicting obligations, according to Article 103 of the United Nations Charter. Such a tension could be resolved either through interpretation or the invalidation of the Security Council resolution in question. Should either of these approaches fail, the result would be that within the international legal order, obligations arising under the resolution would have to prevail. An international court would then find that it could not give precedence to international human rights law in the light of Article 103 of the UN Charter.[279] An example of this *modus operandi* can be found in the *Behrami and Saramati* decision by the ECtHR, in which the Court ultimately attributed the alleged human rights violations to the United Nations over which, however, it does not have jurisdiction *ratione personae*.[280] For a domestic court, this issue remains irrelevant unless it follows the international conflict rule, as did the British House of Lords in the *Al-Jedda* case, giving priority to Article 103 of the UN

[274] Palombino (n 151) 525; Bleckmann, 'Vorrang des Völkerrechts' (n 225) 527.

[275] Nollkaemper, 'Rethinking Supremacy' (n 233) 79–81.

[276] See Article 53 VCLT.

[277] Nollkaemper, 'Rethinking Supremacy' (n 233) 80.

[278] See also the judgment of the International Criminal Tribunal for the Former Yugoslavia (ICTY) in *Prosecutor v Furundžija*, IT-95-17/1-T (1998), paras 153–5; Orakhelashvili, *Peremptory Norms* (n 155) 542–3 and 545.

[279] Nollkaemper, 'Rethinking Supremacy' (n 233) 80.

[280] ECtHR, *Behrami and Behrami v France and Saramati v France, Germany, and Norway*, App nos 71412/01 and 78166/01, 2 May 2007, paras 144–52.

Charter, but nonetheless emphasizing the importance of human rights under the ECHR.[281]

Lastly, there are situations in which the fundamental right in question is neither of *ius cogens* character nor in conflict with an obligation under the UN Charter. *Ergo* there is a conflict between two international legal norms of equal hierarchical status. In this scenario, the relevant rules governing the resolution of conflicts between international norms apply,[282] which may well result in the one international legal norm corresponding to the fundamental right in question to prevail. Thus, no question of supremacy arises.[283]

Despite these straightforward options to prevent normative conflicts and to uphold the supremacy of international law concurrently, they may not offer conclusive solutions in all cases.[284] For instance, in the case of conflict, an international court will usually try to establish the supremacy of one norm over the other,[285] but might ultimately fail, since one of the parties is not a party to the treaty in question. A domestic court, conversely, will attempt to balance the two obligations binding on the state.[286] Examples of this approach can be found in cases such as *Short v Netherlands*, wherein the Dutch Supreme Court resolved a conflict between an obligation under a bilateral extradition treaty and the ECHR in favour of the latter, based on the conclusion that a balance of interests clearly privileged the refusal to extradite persons to countries where they might face capital punishment.[287] Given the restricted jurisdictional powers of international courts, the outcome of this case could have been entirely different had it taken place before an international court. However, the question remains whether these potential discrepancies, resulting in an *aporia* incapable of resolving conflicts between national sovereignty and international law's claim to supremacy, are sufficient to disprove a monist outlook on the relationship between national and international law.[288] As the subsequent conclusion will show, the answer to this question is clearly in the negative.

d. Conclusion: what non-monist theories fail to explain

In sum, the existence of states and national courts resisting the supremacy of international law is not an argument against this very supremacy in particular and

[281] *R (Al-Jedda) v Secretary of State for Defence* [2007] UKHL 58, [2008] 1 AC 332 at para 39 (Lord Bingham). Cf. also, however, ECtHR, *Al-Jedda v United Kingdom*, App no 27021/08, 7 July 2011, para 109, in which the Strasbourg Court concluded that the UN Security Council resolution neither explicitly nor implicitly required the UK to place an individual considered to constitute a security risk in indefinite detention without charge.

[282] See International Law Commission, 'Fragmentation of International Law: Difficulties Arising from the Diversification and Expansion of International Law', Report of the Study Group of the International Law Commission; finalized by Martti Koskenniemi, UN Document A/CN.4/L.682, 13 April 2006.

[283] Nollkaemper, 'Rethinking Supremacy' (n 233) 80.

[284] Palombino (n 151) 525–6.

[285] Ulf Linderfalk, 'The Principle of Rational Decision-making—As Applied to the Identification of Normative Conflicts in International Law' (2013) 73 *Zeitschrift für ausländisches öffentliches Recht und Völkerrecht* 591, 612.

[286] Nollkaemper, 'Rethinking Supremacy' (n 233) 80.

[287] *Short v Netherlands*, Nos 13.949 and 13.950, 30 March 1990.

[288] Palombino (n 151) 527.

monism under the primacy of international law in general. States do not participate in the international legal order with the purpose of disregarding international law or enter international legal commitments with the intention of violating them.[289] From a pragmatic viewpoint, states may certainly respect international law in certain situations only because it furthers their own interests, e.g. if inter-state co-operation is absolutely necessary or an issue is of common concern. However, at the very minimum, international law is generally respected in good faith. This is also confirmed in the sense that there is no empirical evidence to demonstrate that there is a clear intention *not* to respect international law among states.[290] Thus, it is interesting to note that states do—in the case of non-compliance—provide excuses and exceptions in order to justify their specific behaviour, rather than rejecting the supremacy of international law in an outright fashion.[291] Even the German Bundesverfassungsgericht, despite effectively accepting that a national *lex posterior* can override a statute which gives domestic effect to a bilateral tax treaty, expressly mentions that its decision is restricted to German law. It hence acknowledges that international law is and remains supreme and that Germany cannot rely on this decision to justify a breach of its obligations vis-à-vis the other contracting party who may react to this situation by denunciating,[292] or terminating or suspending the treaty in the case of a material breach,[293] or by demanding restitution, compensation or satisfaction.[294] The decision is consequently without prejudice to Article 27 of the VCLT and the principle of *pacta sunt servanda*,[295] and accordingly not detrimental to the supremacy of international law in general.

Therefore, non-monist theories simply fail to explain the reality of the relationship between international and municipal law. International law itself not only determines its own binding character,[296] but also its supreme status, as evidenced by the law of treaties, since the determination of whether a treaty is voidable because of contravening domestic law is to be made in accordance with the law of treaties, not domestic law.[297] And similarly, such contravening municipal law is not automatically invalidated by superior international law (as claimed by radical monism, which is of course irreconcilable with reality), but merely indicated as voidable by international law as the respective *lex superior*. In other words, international law allows for a certain

[289] Çalı (n 53) 70–1. Cf. also, however, Surabhi Ranganathan, 'Responding to Deliberately Created Treaty Conflicts' in Christian J. Tams, Antonios Tzanakopoulos, and Andreas Zimmermann (eds), *Research Handbook on the Law of Treaties* (Edward Elgar Publishing, 2014) 447–75, discussing the practice of states to create new treaties in order to challenge or change existing treaties. This practice may be a fact, but in this case, states attempt to change the law ex post, and not in the first place when they enter the original international legal obligations.

[290] Harold Hongju Koh, 'Why Do Nations Obey International Law?' (1996/1997) 106 *Yale Law Journal* 2599, 2599, especially fn 2; Çalı (n 53) 71.

[291] Rosalyn Higgins, *Problems and Processes: International Law and How We Use It* (Oxford University Press, 1994) 7.

[292] If the treaty contains a provision regarding termination, denunciation, or withdrawal; see Article 56 VCLT.

[293] See Article 60 VLCT.

[294] See Articles 34–38 of the Draft Articles on State Responsibility.

[295] BVerfG, 2 BvL 1/12—*Treaty Override* (n 213) paras 47 and 60–3.

[296] Schaus (n 76) 700.

[297] Schmalenbach, 'Article 27' (n 75) para 24.

degree of deficiency in domestic legal acts in the sense of Merkl's *Fehlerkalkül*, which states that legal acts in violation of superior law are valid, but subject to contestation and eventual annulment.[298] One could also resort to Kelsen's theory of the *Alternativermächtigung* ('alternative authorization'), which holds that the validity of a municipal legal act in violation of international law can be repealed,[299] and since such a repeal procedure does not exist in international law, the law of state responsibility must be applied accordingly. Thereby, the unity between national and international is not endangered by national laws and courts, challenging the supremacy of international law, because such challenges can be sanctioned as violations of international obligations by other states or international organizations. This should, ultimately, force the defaulting state to remedy the situation in contravention to international law accordingly.[300] Hence a violation of international law by denying it its supreme status within domestic law is not disproving monism under the primacy of international law. In fact, dualism or pluralism do not falsify monism by distinguishing between two or more legal orders wherein the violation of international law within the domestic sphere is sanctioned by measures on the international level. Quite the contrary, it is the very existence of the law of state responsibility and legal consequences that speaks in favour of a unitary and monist view of the law in its entirety.

The choice for monism becomes even more obvious when one thinks of the relationship between national and international law in federal terms, such as the abovementioned[301] 'three circles theory', which Kelsen uses to describe the interplay of laws within a federal system, where the overall federal constitution delegates both the law of the federation and the federated states.[302] In such a unitary legal order, federal laws and the laws of the federated states may well have the same hierarchical rank, but they both remain subject to the overarching federal constitution. Analogously, some international norms ('federal law') and domestic norms ('state law') may be on a par with one another (e.g. within domestic law on the basis of a constitutional provision), but they are all inferior to functional or quasi-constitutional norms of international law (the 'federal constitution'), such as *ius cogens* norms, Article 27 of the VCLT, and Article 103 of the UN Charter. In other words, these norms can be deduced as functional norms from the structure of the international legal order and from the shrinking legal competences of the states which are part of this legal order.[303]

The theory of a moderate monism under the primacy of international law, as first proposed by Verdross[304] and then taken up by Kelsen,[305] is thus definitely

[298] Merkl, *Lehre von der Rechtskraft* (n 108) 293; Merkl, 'Prolegomena' (n 108) 1110.

[299] Hans Kelsen, *General Theory of Norms* (reprint; Clarendon Press, 2011) 125; Hans Kelsen, 'Derogation' in Hans Kelsen and Ota Weinberger, *Essays in Legal and Moral Philosophy* (Dordrecht: Reidel, 1973) 272; Kelsen, *Pure Theory* (n 24) 271 ff.

[300] Rill, 'Internationales, supranationales und nationales Recht' (n 102) 681–2.

[301] See Chapter 3, section 5B(2)b.

[302] Hans Kelsen, *Allgemeine Staatslehre* (Springer, 1925) 199.

[303] Starke, 'Primacy of International Law' (n 112) 311 and 314–15.

[304] Alfred Verdross, 'Droit international public et droit interne' (1954) 32 *Revue de Droit International, de Sciences Diplomatiques et Politiques* 219, 221; Alfred Verdross, *Völkerrecht* (5th edn; Springer, 1964) 113. See also in general Anke Brodherr, *Alfred Verdross' Theorie des gemäßigten Monismus* (Utz, 2005).

[305] Kelsen, *Pure Theory* (n 24) 330–1.

compatible with the way positive law presents itself—in fact, it is better suited to explain how the supremacy of international law works *in praxi*. Again, non-compliance with international obligations—may it be through national legal acts in violation of the supremacy of international law or domestic courts contesting this supremacy—does not endanger the unity of the law or disprove monism: national legal orders may freely give preference to domestic norms over international norms binding on them as they like, but this does not release them from the legal consequences of their default. In no way does this prove a potential plurality of grounds of validity or the supremacy of national law. It is therefore entirely incorrect to view particular constitutions as monist, dualist, or pluralist, depending on which rank they allow international norms within municipal law. Whatever the attitude of a national constitution towards international law may be, i.e. openly embracing its supremacy or classifying it as inferior to domestic law, this cannot change or adversely affect the principal unity of international and national law.[306]

C. The applicability of international law within national law

(1) The question of differences in substance and addressees

The last argument to be discussed in the context of the relationship between international and domestic law is the question of the former's applicability within the latter. 'Applicability' is therefore to be understood to consist of two distinctive and yet closely related questions: first, whether international and national law govern essentially different subject areas and thus distinct legal substances; and, secondly, given the question of different subject matters, whether international law is also addressing and conferring rights upon individuals.[307]

Non-monist theories claim that a difference in sources between international and national law also necessitates a difference in substance, which means that these distinct legal orders regulate dissimilar areas of law by way of complementarity.[308] These substantially different bodies of law can be classified into norms governing inter-state relations (i.e. international legal norms) versus norms governing individual behaviour (i.e. national legal norms), thus performing different functions and excluding each other from their respective legislative processes.[309] Alternatively, international law is regarded as the law applying to the international legal community per se, that is states, of which individuals do not partake.[310] The immediate consequence of this difference in substance is the non-monist claim of difference in addressees and legal subjects, namely states versus individuals: international law regulates inter-state law and thus the relations between states, whilst domestic law

[306] Rill, 'Internationales, supranationales und nationales Recht' (n 102) 692 fn 80.
[307] Pisillo-Mazzeschi (n 143) 135–6.
[308] Triepel, *Völkerrecht und Landesrecht* (n 46) 9, 11, and 228 ff.
[309] Arangio-Ruiz (n 59) 17.
[310] Gaja (n 48) 54; Starke 'Monism and Dualism' (n 47) 70.

deals with legal relations between individuals inter se and between individuals and the state's organs.[311] This argument eventually entails that individuals cannot be directly affected by international law, and are to be mediated through municipal legal provisions in order to have rights and obligations.[312]

According to monism under the primacy of international law as envisaged by the pure theory of law, conversely, there is no distinction in substance and subjects between international and national law. Not only can any allegedly domestic legal affair be equally governed by a treaty and hence be made an international legal affair,[313] but individuals can also be subjects of international law in a direct manner without the mediating effect of states, as the relationship between both the individual and the state and between the state and the international legal order are mere normative links between different legal subjects that are themselves the personified entity of a derived bundle of rights and obligations.[314]

With respect to substance and subject matter, international law remains generally silent on its own reach and therefore largely constitutes a body of neutral rules,[315] which is why there are no explicit references to the question of substance to be found in national law. Yet, although the involvement of international law has spread out beyond its primary concern, i.e. the protection and preservation of peace, and now encompasses and regulates areas as diverse as the environment, space, human rights, and trade, there obviously is no catalogue of enumerated 'competences' as in federal legal orders, which would clearly assign international law and national law their respective subject matters. The only exceptions to this rule are exemplified by the most basic and therefore cogent norms of international law restricting the reach of national law, namely the general principles on the (un)lawfulness of extraterritorial acts,[316] the prohibition of the use of force,[317] and other *ius cogens* norms in general.[318]

Similarly, international law does not provide an exhaustive list of the addressees to whom it applies. It is of course trite to say that states remain the principal subjects of international law, and that, according to Article 1 of the Montevideo Convention, states as the primary 'persons' of international law, should possess certain qualities, such as a permanent population, a defined territory, and a

[311] Triepel, *Völkerrecht und Landesrecht* (n 46) 11 ff.

[312] Regarding the concept of mediation, see *Mavrommatis Palestine Concessions* [1924] PCIJ Series A No 2, 12; Anne Peters, *Jenseits der Menschenrechte: Die Rechtsstellung des Individuums im Völkerrecht* (Mohr-Siebeck, 2014) 49.

[313] Kelsen, *General Theory* (n 26) 364–5.

[314] Kelsen, *Problem der Souveränität* (n 25) 126–7.

[315] Higgins, *Problems and Processes* (n 291) 39.

[316] See especially *The 'Lotus' (France v Turkey)* [1927] PCIJ Series A No 10.

[317] Article 2(4) of the UN Charter and the corresponding customary rule as confirmed in *Military and Paramilitary Activities in and against Nicaragua (Nicaragua v United States of America), Jurisdiction and Admissibility* [1984] ICJ Rep 392, para 73. See also the exceptions to this rule in the right to self-defence under Article 51 of the UN Charter and collective measures under Chapter VII of the UN Charter.

[318] Of which there is, however, no exhaustive catalogue: Orakhelashvili, *Peremptory Norms* (n 155) 36–66.

government. Furthermore, it is nowadays also accepted that international organizations represent addressees of international legal norms.[319] The question of whether individuals are addressees and subjects of international law, however, is more controversial and opinions in this regard are strongly divided, both over the status and the legal position of the individual in international law as well as what constitutes the background and boundaries of this legal position.[320] It is undisputable that individuals now have rights under international law, in particular those rights enshrined in human rights treaties, as well as international legal obligations, especially international criminal responsibility.[321]

The problem remains, however, that these international rules are not attended by a specific means of enforcement belonging to individuals. In other words, individuals currently have a plethora of international rights and obligations, but principally only a few remedies under international law to enforce them.[322] It is of course true that a wide range of treaties now provide individuals with access to international courts and tribunals,[323] but individuals nonetheless remain in principle dependent on national law as their first port of call. This raises the question of how national law deals with the issue of enforceable rights at the domestic level. Nominally, monist states may declare all international legal norms as applicable and thus enforceable for individuals, whilst nominally non-monist states might argue that the substance between the two bodies of law is entirely different and subsequently deny individuals their internationally granted rights—especially if the international norm in question has not been transformed into national law and the individual is therefore equally unable to rely on the domestic manifestation of this right. In this light, it is crucial to examine which role instruments such as direct effect and consistent interpretation play, and what this means for a monist view of the relationship between international and national law.

(2) National courts as the ultimate arbiters of applicability

Courts may give effect to international law and thereby ensure its domestic applicability and enforcement in two ways, either direct or indirect.[324] To begin with, the concept of *direct* effect denotes a situation in which domestic courts enforce international obligations as such, and without relying on the substance of an additional

[319] *Reparation for Injuries Suffered in the Service of the United Nations (Advisory Opinion)* [1949] ICJ Rep 174.

[320] Alexander Orakhelashvili, 'The Position of the Individual in International Law' (2000) 31 *California Western International Law Journal* 241, 241.

[321] *Prosecutor v Tadić*, IT-94-1-AR72, ICTY, Appeals Chamber, Decision on the Defence Motion for Interlocutory Appeal on Jurisdiction, paras 128–37.

[322] Andrew Clapham, 'The Role of the Individual in International Law' (2010) 21 *European Journal of International Law* 25, 27.

[323] See e.g. Article 34 of the European Convention on Human Rights; Article 44 of the Inter-American Convention on Human Rights; Articles 1–5 of the Optional Protocol to the International Covenant on Civil and Political Rights; and Articles 8–16 of the International Convention for the Elimination of All Forms of Racial Discrimination.

[324] Nollkaemper, *National Courts* (n 51) 117.

intervening municipal legal act, for instance the transformed international legal norm.[325] Thus, the critical question is whether domestic judges may or must apply international law in a direct manner; a feature that is best described by the term 'self-executing'.[326] This can lead to a situation where this principle of direct effect, broadly understood as direct applicability, can be relied on by individuals against the forum state, and accordingly be used in a narrower and rights-conferring as well as rights-enforcing meaning.[327]

There are, however, certain conditions that need to be satisfied in order to allow for the direct effect of international norms:[328] first, the norm in question must be domestically valid to be a source of enforceable rights in a given municipal legal order.[329] This means that in monist states, where international law automatically forms part of national law, direct effect can be granted more easily than in non-monist states, in which international law only becomes domestically valid upon transformation or incorporation in general.[330] Yet, validity is merely a necessary, but not a sufficient criterion in this respect: secondly, one must also enquire the intent of the treaty parties and whether they actually intended the international legal norms in question to be individually applicable and enforceable within the domestic sphere.[331] Lastly, an international legal norm requires to be deemed complete by a national court in order to have direct effect. This means that this norm must be sufficiently clear and precise (i.e. not worded generally and vaguely)[332] and unconditional (i.e. not requiring subsequent national legislation).[333] If these criteria are fulfilled, individuals can find themselves in a position to rely directly on international rules before national courts.

Beyond that, international law might also be applied and enforced in an indirect manner, since direct effect might not be possible if the conditions for its application are not fulfilled—which then leaves consistent interpretation (or its synonymous term: indirect effect) as another viable option to give effect to international law within national law. Consistent interpretation can principally be distinguished from direct effect in that international norms are not enforced in the absence of a provision of domestic law but, conversely, through a provision of domestic law.[334] Hence,

[325] See e.g. Verdross and Simma (n 45) 550; Griller, *Übertragung von Hoheitsrechten* (n 74) 355.

[326] See Jordan J. Paust, 'Self-Executing Treaties' (1988) 82 *American Journal of International Law* 760, 766 ff.

[327] André Nollkaemper, 'The Duality of Direct Effect in International Law' (2014) 25 *European Journal of International Law* 105, 109. For the distinction between direct effect in a broader sense (i.e. direct applicability) and direct effect *stricto sensu* see also J. A. Winter, 'Direct Applicability and Direct Effect: Two Distinct and Different Concepts in Community Law' (1972) 9 *Common Market Law Review* 425, 425–38.

[328] See generally Nollkaemper, *National Courts* (n 51) 130–8.

[329] See e.g. Australian High Court, *Minister for Immigration and Ethnic Affairs v Teoh* [1995] HCA 20; 128 ALR 358.

[330] Morgenstern (n 151) 68.

[331] Stefan Riesenfeld, 'The Doctrine of Self-Executing Treaties and *US v. Postal*: Win at Any Price?' (1980) 74 *American Journal of International Law* 892, 895–6.

[332] Nollkaemper, *National Courts* (n 51) 136–8.

[333] Carlos Manuel Vázquez, 'Treaties as Law of the Land: The Supremacy Clause and the Judicial Enforcement of Treaties' (2008/2009) 122 *Harvard Law Review* 599, 606.

[334] Nollkaemper, *National Courts* (n 51) 140–1.

the defining difference is that when a court bestows *direct* effect to a rule of international law, it uses this rule as an autonomous and independent basis for its decision, whilst in the case of *indirect* effect, the court uses the international legal rule to interpret a rule of domestic law in conformity with international law. Following the landmark decision of the United States Supreme Court in the *Charming Betsy* case, holding that domestic law '[o]ught never to be construed to violate the law of nations, if any other possible construction remains . . .',[335] consistent interpretation is now regarded as a judicial instrument to ensure coherence between national and international law and to prevent any normative conflicts in the first place.

As a consequence, the doctrine of consistent interpretation allows domestic courts to give effect to international obligations which—albeit binding on the state—have not been duly or fully transformed into municipal law and as such do not form part of the law actually applicable by the courts. Such scenarios mostly arise in dualist states where the courts may bridge the gaps in effectiveness of treaties between their entry into force and their domestic implementation.[336] Basically, the courts engage in the interpretation of not directly applicable international norms when construing 'consubstantial' domestic norms, i.e. formally unrelated, but substantially similar or identical municipal norms,[337] thus practically clarifying ambiguous domestic provisions.[338] Thereby national judges can—in the parlance of Georges Scelle's hypothesis of *dédoublement fonctionnel*[339]—act as quasi-agents of international law and enforce the rights and obligations of individuals enshrined in international legal norms.

What direct effect and consistent interpretation have in common, however, is the fact that they are both contingent on domestic law, which means that the international and municipal legal orders remain self-contained in a non-monist sense.[340] Both instruments necessarily presume a general or specific rule of reference in international law to apply international law and to enforce individual rights.[341] Therefore, any effects of international law within national law—may they be direct or indirect—are subject to national law and the will of the national legislator, which may or may not allow for such effects. Since the concrete implementation and discharge of international legal obligations is entirely within the discretion of states and hence part of their *domaine reservé*, the direct and indirect effect of international law can therewith be also fully excluded.[342] Accordingly, states pronounce themselves as

[335] *Alexander Murray v the Schooner Charming Betsy*, 6 US (2 Cranch) 64 (1804) 118.

[336] Nollkaemper, *National Courts* (n 51) 143.

[337] Tzanakopoulos, 'Domestic Courts' (n 200) 178.

[338] *Suresh v Canada (Minister of Citizenship and Immigration) and Attorney-General of Canada* [2002] 1 SCR 3; 37 Admin LR (3d) 159; ILDC 186 (CA 2002) paras 93–8, where the Canadian Supreme Court used Article 2(1)(b) of the International Convention for the Suppression of the Financing of Terrorism to clarify what is meant by 'terrorism' in s 19 of the Immigration Act.

[339] Georges Scelle, *Précis de droit des gens: principles et systématique* (Sirey, 1932 and 1934) vol I: 43 and 56; vol II: 10–11; Georges Scelle, 'Règles générales du droit de la paix' (1933-IV) 46 *Recueil des cours* 327, 358–9.

[340] Gaja (n 48) 52.

[341] Nollkaemper, *National Courts* (n 51) 120.

[342] Peters, *Jenseits der Menschenrechte* (n 312) 443; Bleckmann, *Grundgesetz und Völkerrecht* (n 184) 282.

either nominally monist or non-monist in nature. However, whatever their ultimate stance is—open or inimical towards international law—the ultimate power to regulate the effects of international law within domestic law rests with them,[343] and thus individuals can be said to be merely mediated through municipal law—an argument which clearly speaks against monism.

Thus, if we again assume, in accordance with the claims of the pure theory of law and legal monism, that international law is addressing individuals and conferring rights and obligations on them independently from domestic law, does this mean that monism can be falsified on the basis of non-monist arguments that make the domestic application and enforcement of international law dependent on national provisions and the domestic judiciary? In other words, is the claim that only the explicit domestic bestowal of rights and obligation on individuals *qua* national legal provisions and judicial decisions makes international law domestically enforceable, a good and falsifying argument against monism, because states may give or take away this granting of applicability any time and at their own discretion?

a. Quasi-monist legal orders and applicability

If national law recognizes direct effect, it can function as a very powerful sword to ensure the application and enforcement of international law on the municipal level. In this context, the metaphorical expression 'sword' therefore denotes a process through which international rights and obligations can pierce the shield of the domestic legal order in question and possibly protect individual rights where national law falls short of this. Consequently, this sword function becomes especially strong if it is combined with the supremacy of international law, thus also prevailing over conflicting national legal provisions.[344] Nonetheless, from a theoretical point of view, the two different concepts of supremacy and direct effect should in principle be regarded as entirely distinct, and a conflation of them should be avoided.[345]

Direct applicability and effect are mostly associated with monist countries, even though—as the following analysis will show—the situation is much more nuanced in reality.[346] Constitutions rarely refer to the issue of applicability, but there are certain exceptions to this rule.[347] In Germany, for example, references to the effects of international law can be found in the constitution itself. The second sentence of Article 25 GG states that the general rules of international law 'shall take precedence over the [federal] laws and directly create rights and duties for the inhabitants of the federal territory'. This wording is, however, rather misleading. This provision does not establish the direct effect of international law per se within German law, i.e. in its narrow and rights-conferring sense, but merely declares international law to be directly applicable by national courts and authorities, if all conditions

[343] Keller, *Rezeption des Völkerrechts* (n 44) 15.

[344] Nollkaemper, 'Duality of Direct Effect' (n 327) 112; Peters, 'Supremacy Lost' (n 161) 186.

[345] Ramses A. Wessel, 'Reconsidering the Relationship between International and EU Law: Towards a Content-Based Approach?' in Enzo Cannizzaro, Paolo Palchetti, and Ramses A. Wessel (eds), *International Law as Law of the European Union* (Brill, 2012) 20–1.

[346] Björgvinsson (n 136) 90.

[347] Shelton, 'Introduction' (n 55) 11.

for this are met.[348] Therefore, this provision has to be read as a presumption of direct applicability, which can always be rebutted.[349] And even though the German courts are largely open towards granting international direct applicability and effect[350] (a practice that is also supervised by the Bundesverfassungsgericht itself),[351] these consequences cannot be taken for granted. The reason for this is that, as discussed above,[352] Article 59(2) GG is construed as placing treaties on the same hierarchical rank as federal statutory law, by virtue of the domestic transforming act. Nevertheless, the legislature can also decide that the rank and effect of a given treaty vary in relation to other legal acts, which means that the potential direct effect of a treaty may effectively be thwarted by its domestically inferior status vis-à-vis other municipal legal acts.[353]

Similarly, Article 93 of the Dutch Constitution provides that '[p]rovisions of treaties and of resolutions by international institutions that are binding on all persons by virtue of their contents shall become binding after they have been published'. Thus, when determining whether a specific international legal norm has direct effect, the Dutch Supreme Court usually tests meticulously what the intention of the treaty parties in question was and whether a particular norm is sufficiently clear from its content.[354] Yet, even in the obviously monist Netherlands, the case law is far from consistent, and the question of whether a specific international legal norm is directly applicable or effective depends on which branch of the law is concerned—civil or administrative—and the political significance of the pending case.[355] In particular in the latter scenario, the Dutch courts have occasionally ruled that even if the international legal provision in question is to be considered directly effective, it would, in certain situations, lie outside their competence to apply this provision, if doing so would interfere with the duties of the political branches.[356]

In Austria, Article 9(1) B-VG sets out a monist approach by declaring customary international law to form part of the federal law, which means that all state organs, including the courts, have to apply customary rules of international law.[357] The Constitutional Court nonetheless found in several cases that customary international rules were insufficiently determined and would therefore not give rise to individual rights.[358] However, although it seems correct to conclude that whether

[348] BVerfGE 15, 25—*Jugoslawische Militärmission*, 30 October 1962, 33.

[349] Bleckmann, *Grundgesetz und Völkerrecht* (n 184) 295.

[350] See e.g. BVerwGE 134, 1—*Studienbeitragserhebung NWR*, 29 April 2009; BVerfGE 112, 1—*Bodenreform III*, 26 October 2004, 22.

[351] See BVerfGE 111, 307—*Görgülü* (n 189) para 61, and Article 100(2) GG, obliging courts to refer cases to the Constitutional Court if they are in doubt whether a particular international legal norm directly creates rights and obligations for individuals.

[352] See section 2B(2)b above.

[353] Björgvinsson (n 136) 90.

[354] See Supreme Court of the Netherlands, *E.O. v Public Prosecutor*, 18 April 1995, NJ (1995) No 619; Supreme Court of the Netherlands, *Railway Strike*, 30 May 1986, NJ (1986) No 688.

[355] Nollkaemper, 'The Netherlands' (n 71) 348.

[356] Evert A. Alkema, 'Netherlands' in Dinah Shelton (ed), *International Law and Domestic Legal Systems* (Oxford University Press, 2011) 417–18.

[357] Theo Öhlinger, 'Artikel 9, Absatz 1' in Karl Korinek and Michael Holoubek (eds), *Österreichisches Bundesverfassungsrecht—Textsammlung und Kommentar* (Springer, 2002) para 30.

[358] Constitutional Court (VfGH), VfSlg 1375/1931; VfSlg 3950/1961; VfSlg 7448/1974; VfSlg 11.508/1987; see also Administrative Court (VwGH), VwSlg 14.941 A.

or not a customary international norm actually provides for individual rights or obligations is a matter of the content of that rule and should hence be ascertained on a case-by-case basis,[359] the Constitutional Court appears to exclude direct effect in this context altogether and without exceptions—a position that is at odds with the wording of Article 9(1) B-VG itself.

The last example to be discussed at this point is the United States. Following the wording of Article VI of the constitution, declaring all treaties to be part of the law of the land as well as judges to be bound by them, Justice Marshall emphasized in *Foster v Neilson* that usually, international agreements require implementing legislation in order to have effect within municipal law. But this is not always necessary, for example if the political branches involved in creating the treaty make clear by means other than implementing legislation that they intended the treaty in question to be 'self-executing'.[360] The distinction between treaties that are self-executing and those which are not, is not absolutely precise and therefore still a matter of controversy. What is more important in this context, however, is the fact that recent case law has thrown into doubt this traditional monist understanding of the self-executing nature of international law within US law. In particular in *Medellín v Texas*, the Supreme Court held that it could not give effect to an obligation under the Vienna Convention on Consular Relations to which it had been ordered by the ICJ in the foregoing *Avena* case.[361] The reason for this was, in the view of the Supreme Court, that Article 94(1) of the UN Charter, obliging states to comply with ICJ judgments, was considered not to be of self-executing nature because it would be for the legislature to take appropriate action, not the judiciary.[362] Thereby the Supreme Court interpreted the overall monist provision of Article VI of the constitution to a very dualist effect.[363]

These examples demonstrate that the most basic difference between monist and non-monist approaches by national legal orders has become immensely blurred and that a clear classification in this regard seems not only very difficult, but maybe also obsolete.[364]

b. Quasi-dualist legal orders and applicability

In contrast to its function as a sword, direct effect can also be used as a shield by national authorities and courts, and thereby justify the non-application of international law within the domestic sphere. In this sense, direct effect does not describe a process, but constitutes a concept that contains a threshold requirement before international law can be applied. This means, *in concreto*, that if not all of

[359] Handl-Petz (n 174) 86–7; Öhlinger, 'Artikel 9, Absatz 1' (n 357) para 33.

[360] Supreme Court, *Foster v Neilson*, 27 US 2 Pet 253, 314 (1829).

[361] *Avena and Other Mexican Nationals* (n 245) 64. The obligation in question was to provide Mexican nationals, who had been denied consular access and consultation upon arrest by the American authorities, with review and reconsideration of the convictions and sentences.

[362] *Medellín v Texas*, 552 US 491 (2008).

[363] See Jeremy Telman, 'A Monist Supremacy Clause and a Dualistic Supreme Court: The Status of Treaty Law as U.S. Law' in Marko Novaković (ed), *Basic Concepts of Public International Law: Monism & Dualism* (University of Belgrade, 2013) 571–90.

[364] Björgvinsson (n 136) 89–90; Sloss, 'Domestic Application' (n 56) 376.

the above-mentioned criteria—validity, original intent, and completeness—are fulfilled, international norms cannot be applied and enforced before municipal bodies.[365] The criterion of validity is highly relevant especially in nominally dualist states, which usually require international law to be implemented and transformed into national law before it can have effect. Yet again, an analysis of the positive law will show that there are many nuances concerning non-monist states as well.[366]

The most prominent example in this respect is the UK, where there is no codified provision on the country's relationship towards international law, but nevertheless a crucial distinction between unimplemented and implemented treaties.[367] This means that if Parliament has enacted a statute to transform particular international rules into national law, the courts will basically apply the statute, not the international norm itself, and only consult the international norms in question to help ascertain the meaning of the statute.[368] In other words, the rule is that the courts apply international law indirectly, not directly. Accordingly, there are no special rules regarding the standing of individuals for the invocation of treaty rights,[369] which gives a clear and sound dualist picture of the law in the UK. Nonetheless, there are exceptions to the dualist rule that only incorporated treaties can be applied and relied on by individuals, for instance, if the piece of legislation in question refers expressly to a relevant but as yet unincorporated treaty,[370] or if the ratification of a treaty, where no incorporation has taken place, could give rise to legitimate expectations that the executive and the judiciary act in conformity with the treaty.[371] Hence it can be argued that the direct applicability and direct effect of international law in the dualist system of the UK is possible, if no parliamentary legislation is required to modify the existing law or add something to it, or if the division powers are not affected.

Similarly, Denmark is also usually regarded as a dualist legal order in which treaty provisions can only become part of domestic law upon legislative incorporation, which means that unincorporated treaties can neither be applied nor individually be relied on.[372] Nonetheless it has been noted that the Danish courts—to a certain extent—incorporate international legal norms by referring to them in their decisions. And although these norms do thereby not become binding law within the domestic sphere,[373] they are subsequently applied and enforced by the national courts. In this sense the traditional dualist view on the relationship between Danish law and

[365] Nollkaemper, 'Duality of Direct Effect' (n 327) 115.

[366] Björgvinsson (n 136) 91.

[367] See *Re McFarland* (n 85).

[368] Stephen C. Neff, 'United Kingdom' in Dinah Shelton (ed), *International Law and Domestic Legal Systems* (Oxford University Press, 2011) 622–3.

[369] *R v Lyons* [2002] UKHL 44, [2003] 1 AC 976, [2002] 3 WLR 1562, [2002] 4 All ER 1028, speech of Lord Hoffmann [27].

[370] See e.g. *R (Channel Tunnel Group Ltd) v Secretary of State* [2001] 119 ILR, 398 and 407–408.

[371] See e.g. *R v Secretary of State for the Home Department, Ex Parte Ahmed and Patel* [1998] INLR 570, 584 (Lord Woolf MR).

[372] See e.g. Jonas Christoffersen and Mikael Rask Madsen, 'The End of Virtue? Denmark and the Internationalisation of Human Rights' (2011) 80 *Nordic Journal of International Law* 257, 264–9.

[373] Björgvinsson (n 136) 93.

international law, which includes the argument that only incorporated international law can have domestic effect, is not suitable to describe this relationship between two allegedly distinct legal orders.[374]

What is even more surprising is that courts in dualist states in general developed various strategies to apply and enforce unincorporated treaties. The Australian High Court, for example, held that administrative decision-makers had to act in conformity with the Convention on the Rights of the Child, as individuals had, upon ratification of this convention, a legitimate expectation that the government would act in accordance with it.[375] The Canadian Supreme Court refused to follow this 'legitimate expectations' doctrine, but nonetheless emphasized that administrative decision-makers must exercise their discretion in compliance with the Convention, an incorporated treaty.[376] Another example includes the Supreme Court of Israel, which now applies the Fourth Geneva Convention in cases involving the Occupied Territories by way of standard practice, even though this treaty has not been made part of the domestic law.[377] Lastly, the Supreme Court of India also routinely applies unincorporated treaties, in particular to corroborate its interpretation of national law and to develop common law principles further.[378]

Again, as with the monist examples above, the increasing judicial application and enforcement of unincorporated international law in dualist states further blurs the line between monism and non-monism[379] and leaves an uneasy tension between the formal non-monist approach under the respective constitutional parameters and the judicial reality to overcome them.[380]

c. Consistent interpretation

In contrast to the principles of direct applicability and direct effect, reference to the concept of consistent interpretation is even more rarely found in national legal provisions. Examples of such scarce provisions include, inter alia, Article 39 of the South African Constitution, Article 11(2)(c) of the Constitution of Malawi, and Article 10(2) of the Spanish Constitution, which all, to varying degrees, require that international law be taken into account in the interpretation of national law. However, since such explicit provisions are extremely rare, the widespread practice of consistent interpretation can only be grounded on the activity of the national judiciaries which apply and follow this doctrine when dealing with cases at the interface of national and international law. This very practice includes both civil law and common law systems, and both monist states which automatically adopt

[374] Ole Spiermann, 'Højesterets anvendelse af folkeret i det 20 århundrede' [2001] *Juristen* 1, 2–3.

[375] *Minister of State v Teoh* (n 329).

[376] *Baker v Canada* [1992] 2 SCR 817.

[377] *Hamoked Center for the Defence of the Individual v IDF Commander* [2002] HCJ 3278/02, 57 PD (1) 385.

[378] See e.g. *Jolly George Verhese v Bank of Cochin* [1980] 2 SCR 913; *Transmission Corporation of Andhra Pradesh v Ch Prabhakar* [2004] Civil Appeal 6131 of 2002; *MV Elisabeth v Harwan Investment and Trading Pvt Ltd.* [1992] 1 SCR 1003.

[379] Melissa A. Waters, 'Creeping Monism: The Judicial Trend Toward Interpretive Incorporation of Human Rights Treaties' (2007) 107 *Columbia Law Review* 628, 650–2.

[380] Sloss, 'Domestic Application' (n 56) 373.

international law, and non-monist states which require transformation and incorporation via domestic legislation.[381]

In general, consistent interpretation is regularly applied in three scenarios:[382] first, if a provision of national law is ambiguous and may be clarified by reference to the underlying international norm;[383] secondly, whenever national law allows for it,[384] especially to prevent violations of international obligations in the case of varying meaning;[385] and, thirdly, in order to review the exercise of discretion by the executive branch in the light of international obligations and thus possibly to provide for grounds of review.[386] Accordingly, consistent interpretation is especially important in non-monist states, where there may be considerable delays between the entry into force of a treaty and its domestic implementation, because it enables courts to ensure compliance with international law if the political branches have not taken any steps towards this goal yet.[387] Yet consistent interpretation is equally crucial in monist states, where it may circumvent the shield of direct effect (i.e. situations in which not all conditions for direct effect are met), since it is—in contrast to direct effect—not contingent on any inherent qualities of a given international legal norm.[388]

Consistent interpretation is, however, no panacea for the resolution of all normative conflicts between domestic and international law. To begin with, there are major differences in how this principle is applied across the world. Although the practice itself is more or less uniformly applied, the conditions under which it can be triggered remain dependent on domestic law.[389] Clearly and unambiguously worded domestic legislation, for example, would definitely bar the use of consistent interpretation. If a legislative act makes the intent of the legislator perfectly plain, the courts are required to enforce the intent of the legislative irrespective of whether the domestic rule conforms to international law.[390] This also means that municipal courts are not required to comply with an interpretation which would actually result in a *contra legem* reading of the rule in question[391] or in international law

[381] Nollkaemper, *National Courts* (n 51) 147–9, and the numerous references to the individual States there, especially in fn 50–66.

[382] Nollkaemper, 'Effects of Treaties' (n 70) 147–8.

[383] See e.g. *Suresh v Canada* (n 338) paras 93–8.

[384] John F. Coyle, 'Incorporative Statutes and the Borrowed Treaty Rule' (2009/2010) 50 *Virginia Journal of International Law* 655, 676.

[385] See e.g. Australian High Court, *Povey v Qantas Airways Ltd and British Airways Plc* [2005] HCA 33; (2005) 216 ALR 427 (Separate Opinion of Kirby J).

[386] Margaret Allars, 'International Law and Administrative Discretion' in Brian R. Opeskin and Donald R. Rothwell (eds), *International Law and Australian Federalism* (Melbourne University Press, 1997) 256.

[387] Nollkaemper, 'Effects of Treaties' (n 70) 148. See also Supreme Court of Bangladesh, *State v Metropolitan Police Commissioner*, 60 DLR (2008) 660; ILDC 1410 (BD 2008) 28.

[388] Nollkaemper, 'Effects of Treaties' (n 70) 148. See also Council of the State of the Netherlands, *Ziers v Gedeputeerde Staten Gelderland*, Case No AB 1995/24 (1993).

[389] Coyle (n 384) 702; Nollkaemper, *National Courts* (n 51) 150.

[390] See e.g. US Court of Appeals, Second Circuit, in *Guaylupo-Moya v Gonzales and McElroy*, 423 F. 3d 121 (2d Cir 2005) para 35.

[391] Ward N. Ferdinandusse, *Direct Application of International Criminal Law in National Courts* (TMC Asser Press, 2006) 152.

taking precedence over domestic constitutional law.[392] This is where the doctrine of consistent interpretation reaches its limits: whereas direct effect, coupled with supremacy, allows for the enforcement of international law even against conflicting rules of domestic law, consistent interpretation cannot prevail over contravening domestic law and thus has to operate within the latter's boundaries.[393]

(3) Consequential arguments against monism

The discussion above shows that the question of applicability of international law within municipal law remains a controversial issue and that it remains, ultimately, apparently dependent on the will of the national legislature and judiciary. And even though the potential difference in substance between international and national law is not as relevant any more as it traditionally used to be, it is intrinsically linked to the issue of applicability. It has been suggested—in very dualist terms—that there is simply no common field in which both international and national law would simultaneously have their spheres of activity.[394] If there indeed is an overlap in substance and subjects between these two bodies of law, it is solely partial, which can be explained with reference to the essentially localized nature of particular international legal areas. International human rights law, in particular, is sometimes regarded as the paradigmatic driving force of monism, as this area of the law obviously succeeds in securing a modest degree of incorporation of international law into domestic law across the world.[395] The content of this law, however, will necessarily be intrinsically localized and hence, in a deeply pluralist sense, differ immensely among states.[396] In this vein, there are no parallels in substance between domestic and international law, and even if there are any, they are imperfect and unable to belie the existing underlying dualist and pluralist structures.[397] This presents a veritable problem for a monist view under the primacy of international law, as proposed by the pure theory of law.

The question of applicability of international law within national law and hence the difference in subjects between these two legal orders is also highly problematic in the light of monism. International law is neutral when it comes to the question of *how* it is applied and enforced on the national level. As the ICJ clarified in the second

[392] Malawi High Court, sitting as a Constitutional Court, *Evance Moyo v The Attorney General*, Constitutional Case No 12 of 2007, para 12; BVerfGE 111, 307—*Görgülü* (n 189) para 32; Irish High Court, *Kavanagh v Governor of Mountjoy Prison* [2002] IESC 13.

[393] Nollkaemper, *National Courts* (n 51) 162–3.

[394] Fitzmaurice, 'General Principles' (n 147) 71.

[395] André Nollkaemper, 'Inside or Out: Two Types of International Legal Pluralism' in Jan Klabbers and Touko Piiparinen (eds), *Normative* Pluralism and International Law: Exploring Global Governance (Cambridge University Press, 2013) 103.

[396] David Kinley, 'Bendable Rules: The Development Implications of Human Rights Pluralism' in Brian Z. Tamanaha, Caroline Sage, and Michael Woolcock (eds), *Legal Pluralism and Development: Scholars and Practitioners in Dialogue* (Cambridge University Press, 2012) 62.

[397] Nollkaemper, 'Inside or Out' (n 395) 103.

Avena case, international obligations are obligations of result,[398] which stop 'short at the outer boundaries of the State machinery',[399] and therefore the exact means of implementing international law is left to the respective national legal orders.[400] The neutrality of international law in this context is merely a reflection of its accepting the continuing differences in the methods through which states give effect to their international obligations.[401] As a result, the concepts of direct applicability and direct effect have a very weak international legal status, as it is the national legal systems which determine the conditions and consequences of international legal effects in the municipal sphere.[402] The same is true for the principle of consistent interpretation, which is regulated by national law, not international law, and can therefore not be considered a duty rooted in the international legal order.[403] Consequently, the congruence in subjects, as claimed by monism, is only apparent, since states may always deny to give effect to international law and therefore cut off individuals from their international rights and obligations.

The practice of national legal orders principally rejecting direct applicability and effect of international law obviously speaks in favour of a dualist or pluralist view and against monism. For such non-monist legal orders, the domestic validity of the international legal norm in question remains a crucial factor for its subsequent domestic application, which means that if no prior incorporation has taken place, application is very unlikely. However, even if such application occurs and the lines between non-monism and monism become blurred, this is not attributable to any underlying monist conviction or particular friendliness vis-à-vis international law. On the contrary, the 'coupling' of international and national law via the principles of direct applicability, direct effect, and consistent interpretation is dependent on the degree of how 'loose' or 'tight' national law wants to be with its international counterpart,[404] and these considerations are mostly based on practical *ad hoc* decisions. Indeed, it has been argued that the readiness to accept the effects of international

[398] *Request for Interpretation of the Judgment of 31 March 2004 in the Case Concerning Avena and Other Mexican Nationals (Mexico v United States of America) (Mexico v United States of America)* [2009] ICJ Rep 3, para 44.

[399] International Law Commission, 'Report of the Commission to the General Assembly on the Work of Its Twenty-Ninth Session, 9 May–29 July 1977', Commentary to Article 21 of the Draft Articles on State Responsibility: 'Breach of an International Obligation Requiring the Achievement of a Special Result Adopted on First Reading' (1977) *Yearbook of the International Law Commission, Volume II, Part Two*,19, para 1.

[400] *Request for Interpretation of the Judgment of 31 March 2004* (n 398) para 44.

[401] Max Sørensen, 'Die Verpflichtungen eines Staates im Bereich seiner nationalen Rechtsordnung aufgrund eines Staatsvertrages' in Rechts- und staatswissenschaftliche Fakultät an der Universität Wien (ed), *Menschenrechte im Staatsrecht und im Völkerrecht* (C.F. Müller, 1967) 21.

[402] Nollkaemper, *National Courts* (n 51) 124–5.

[403] Jean D'Aspremont, 'The Systemic Integration of International Law by Domestic Courts: Domestic Judges as Architects of the Consistency of the International Legal Order' in Ole Kristian Fauchald and André Nollkaemper (eds), *The Practice of International and National Courts and the (De-)Fragmentation of International Law* (Hart Publishing, 2012) 153.

[404] Ferrari-Bravo (n 103) 737.

law depends heavily on the perceived legitimacy of the norm in question, which is in turn dependent on its substantive quality.[405]

The same *caveat* applies to nominally monist legal systems that (albeit only *prima facie*) accept the direct applicability and direct effect of international law and also strive to interpret national law in consistency with their international obligations. While the states exemplarily depicted above display an overtly friendly approach towards the domestic effects of international rules in their constitutions and the criterion of validity should accordingly not be an issue for them (as they usually follow the adoption technique), they do not pursue a uniform line either. In a fashion similar to that of dualist or pluralist states, monist legal orders can and will probably refuse to give effect to international legal norms if doing so would interfere with the constitutional separation of powers between the apolitical judiciary on the one hand and the political executive and legislative branches on the other hand, which usually hold the relevant competences in foreign affairs.[406] In this sense, the application of international law and its effects on individuals are often curtailed to protect basic constitutional principles.

Thus, the distinction between monism, dualism, and pluralism seems to have reached a point where it does not hold any theoretical value any more, as national legal orders alternate between these approaches on an *ad hoc* basis. What can be concluded, however, is that the key to the domestic application of international law lies in domestic law itself,[407] and if this very body of law does not wish to enforce the international rights and obligations of individuals, then the divergence of subjects between national and international law cannot be overcome. Again, these arguments seem convincing, yet the question remains whether they conclusively falsify monism or not.

(4) Monist arguments in the context of applicability

If we now remember the core tenets of the pure theory of law in general and of monism under the primacy of international law in particular, it becomes clear that the above arguments cannot be accepted. Since this theory argues that all law can be traced back to its epistemologically necessary fount, i.e. the *Grundnorm*, then there can only be one law, which entails that there is only one substance of the law. Hence every subject matter that can be regulated by national law is open to regulation by international law as well.[408] Subsequently, since the relationship between international law and national law is principally the same as the relationship between national law (i.e. the state) and the individual, all legal subjects—states, international organizations, individuals, etc.—are personified sub-entities of the legal order in its

[405] Niels Petersen, 'Determining the Domestic Effect of International Law through the Prism of Legitimacy' (2012) 72 *Zeitschrift für ausländisches öffentliches Recht und Völkerrecht* 223, 226, and 231.

[406] Peters, *Jenseits der Menschenrechte* (n 312) 458–9.

[407] Anne Peters, 'Rechtsordnungen und Konstitutionalisierung: Zur Neubestimmung der Verhältnisse' (2010) 65 *Zeitschrift für Öffentliches Recht* 3, 21; Arangio-Ruiz (n 59) 31–2.

[408] Kelsen, *Problem der Souveränität* (n 25) 107; Kelsen, *General Theory* (n 26) 364–5.

entirety and derived from it. This means, in conclusion, that states as well as individuals constitute bundles of rights and obligations,[409] and that there is no normative difference between them. The following sections will now examine possible arguments to bolster the rationale that law, as one substance, addresses all legal subjects equally, and to defend monism against falsification in the context of applicability.

a. Law as a homogeneous substance

To begin with, both dualism and pluralism are mistaken in claiming that international and national law are distinct from each other because of their difference in substance. This argument can be easily rebutted in two steps and has therefore already been abandoned. The first counterargument is that an exchange and flow of legal norms between domestic and international law is an observable fact. For example, the 'general principles of law', mentioned as a source of international law in Article 38 of the ICJ Statute, undoubtedly embody ideas which were first developed on the domestic plane and then transplanted into the international legal order.[410] International courts or tribunals commonly use general principles of law to avoid *non liquet* situations.[411] To this end, they may find that there are principles which are, *in substance*, recognized by domestic law, and subsequently, these principles are deduced, extracted, and applied to international legal problems.[412] Such a *modus operandi* would be conceptually and factually impossible if there were no common substantial ground shared between international and national law, as dualism or pluralism claim.

Moreover, it is also a fact that this normative exchange flows the other way, i.e. from international law into domestic law, as many international norms address domestic issues that are concurrently also addressed by domestic norms. Thus, today it is common practice that domestic courts apply norms which have a counterpart in international law.[413] Such 'consubstantial' or 'multi-sourced equivalent norms'[414] may exist in their original form in international law as well as in municipal law, either as transformed international law or even as pre-existing domestic law.[415] Accordingly, such norms are conferring rights or obligations upon the same legal subject, are similar or identical in their normative content, and have been created through different law-creating avenues.[416] The most prominent examples of such substantially coinciding norms include municipal rules which are substantially

[409] Jochen von Bernstorff, *The Public International Law Theory of Hans Kelsen* (Cambridge University Press, 2010) 72; Kelsen, *Problem der Souveränität* (n 25) 126–7.

[410] Ferrari-Bravo (n 103) 718.

[411] See e.g. Robert Kolb, *The International Court of Justice* (Hart Publishing, 2013) 745–6.

[412] See Hugo Thirlway, *The Sources of International Law* (Oxford University Press, 2014) 95.

[413] Christina Eckes and Stephan Hollenberg, 'Reconciling Different Legal Spheres in Theory and Practice: Pluralism and Constitutionalism in the Cases of *Al-Jedda, Ahmed*, and *Nada*' (2013) 20 *Maastricht Journal of European and Comparative Law* 220, 241.

[414] Tomer Broude and Yuval Shany, 'The International Law and Policy of Multi-Sourced Equivalent Norms' in Tomer Broude and Yuval Shany (eds), *Multi-Sourced Equivalent Norms in International Law* (Hart Publishing, 2011) 1–15.

[415] Tzanakopoulos, 'Domestic Courts' (n 200) 143.

[416] Broude and Shany, 'Multi-Sourced Equivalent Norms' (n 414) 5.

reflective of existing international rules, for instance rules of interpretation,[417] and constitutional rights reflecting internationally protected rights, most importantly substantially similar or identical human rights.[418] The most obvious examples in this respect include the International Covenant on Civil and Political Rights (ICCPR) and the ECHR, but also other fundamental rights protected under customary international law, and even some rights of *ius cogens* nature, for instance the prohibition of torture.[419]

Beyond that, another argument in this context needs to be considered. If it really were the case that international and domestic law governed entirely distinct areas and that there were no substantial overlaps, the doctrine of consistent interpretation would be meaningless, because then it would be absurd to construe domestic norms in conformity with obviously similar or identical international norms. It therefore becomes trivial to say that the subject matter of international law is reflected in rules that are in the interest of all states.[420] Accordingly, such a distinction between domestic law and international law in substance becomes obsolete once we talk about cross-boundary issues such as environmental protection, human rights, and other areas of law which are clearly regulated by both domestic and international law.

The second counterargument against non-monist claims is the question of why such difference in substance between national and international law (if such a difference in fact exists) would necessarily disprove monism. Again, an analogy with federalism will help make the case for monism, especially if one remembers that in federal systems, federal states are usually given certain powers by the federation proper which did not previously belong to them.[421] As in a dualist view, where national and international law would co-exist side by side, without any substantial overlap and clear-cut boundaries as to what area of law is governed by which body of law, the same constellation can be envisaged in a federal system. This would consequently more or less amount to 'dual federalism'—a concept which was prevalent in the United States until 1937[422] and basically stated that governmental powers are divided into mutually exclusive spheres between the federal government and the governments of the federal states. They were each considered sovereign regarding the competences committed to them and were prohibited from interfering with the competences committed to the other,[423] which meant that there was no concurrent jurisdiction and hence no substantial overlap between the federal and the state

[417] Thomas Bingham, 'International Law in National Courts' in James Crawford and Margaret Young (eds), *The Function of Law in the International Community: An Anniversary Symposium* (Lauterpacht Centre for International Law, 2008) 3.

[418] Pisillo-Mazzeschi (n 143) 146–7.

[419] Tzanakopoulos, 'Judicial Dialogue' (n 219) 86.

[420] Godefridus J.H. van Hoof, *Rethinking the Sources of International Law* (Kluwer, 1983) 68; Christos Rozakis, *The Concept of Jus Cogens in the Law of Treaties* (North-Holland, 1976) 61.

[421] Starke, 'Primacy of International Law' (n 112) 314–15.

[422] See Supreme Court, *United States v Morrison*, 529 US 598 (2000) and Ernest A. Young, 'Dual Federalism, Concurrent Jurisdiction, and the Foreign Affairs Exception' (2000/2001) 69 *George Washington Law Review* 139, 139.

[423] Supreme Court, *McCulloch v Maryland*, 17 US 316 (1819) 410.

governments.[424] However, even if such a dual federal concept were to be the case in the relationship between international and national law, it would be compatible with monism. In the same manner as American dual federalism described the rules of a unitary constitutional system under the supremacy of the constitution itself,[425] which was in turn subordinated to the unifying meta-constitutional philosophy of dual federalism[426] (i.e. its quasi-*Grundnorm*), the substance of national law and the substance of international law can be imagined to be subject to the formal constitution of international law, delegating them both. In fact, the emerging picture would conform to Kelsen's above-mentioned theory of the three circles, and would be plausible within the remits of the positive law.

What is even more plausible, however, is the idea of cooperative federalism.[427] As in the United States after 1937, it has also become impossible to define and police the boundaries of (only apparently) clear-cut substance areas[428] between national and international law. As the United States Supreme Court held in the landmark decision which paved the way for cooperative federalism,[429] one can analogously argue with regard to the substance of international and national law that they are not alien to each other. Quite the contrary, they coexist within the same territory, and they share the same concerns, especially in the case of cross-boundary and cross-cutting problems, such as environmental and fundamental rights protection. Substantial overlap is inevitable, and in the same way as federal states and the federal government, international and national law are mutually complementary parts of a single legal order whose parts will be applied in accordance with the powers of the respective law-applier.[430] Lastly, it should also be emphasized that a certain difference in substance is quite normal and should not be interpreted as evidence against monism: complete congruence between different substantial bodies of law would not only be unrealistic, but also extremely absurd, as every single subject area of the law would then be regulated at least twice, which would result in meaningless over-regulation without any added value.

Thus, in conclusion, one can effortlessly see that international law not only governs inter-state relations, but also inter-individual questions of economic, commercial, and social nature, both in treaties and custom.[431] In a Kelsenian sense, law is certainly to be seen in its formal dimension, but formal does not mean vacuous.[432] Hence it would be completely erroneous to suppose that international law, encompassing the entire world, was purely formal,[433] merely addressing states

[424] Charles W. Needham, 'The Exclusive Power of Congress over Interstate Commerce' (1911) 11 *Columbia Law Review* 251, 255.

[425] See the Supremacy Clause in Article VI, section 2 of the US Constitution.

[426] Robert Schütze, *From Dual to Cooperative Federalism: The Changing Structure of European Law* (Oxford University Press, 2009) 79.

[427] Ibid., 101. [428] Young, 'Dual Federalism' (n 422) 139.

[429] *Carmichael v Southern Coal & Coke Co.*, 301 US 495 (1937) 526.

[430] Edward S. Corwin, 'The Passing of Dual Federalism' (1950) 36 *Virginia Law Review* 1, 19.

[431] Pisillo-Mazzeschi (n 143) 135.

[432] Paul Ricoeur, *Oneself as Another* (transl Kathleen Blamey; University of Chicago Press, 1990) 263.

[433] Emmanuelle Jouannet, 'Universalism and Imperialism: The True-False Paradox of International Law?' (2007) 18 *European Journal of International Law* 379, 386–7.

and restricting their jurisdictional reach, and without any substantial content relating to individuals. Hence the argument that monism can be disproved by referring to a possible difference in substance between national and international law is unfounded and can be dismissed.

b. International law addresses all legal subjects, including individuals

Similarly, the argument that international and national law have different subjects and addressees is not tenable any more. Even convinced traditionalists must admit that states ceased to be the exclusive addressees of international law and that international organizations have joined the ranks of international legal subjects.[434] Kelsen argues that if individuals are legal subjects under national law, and national and international law form part of a unitary legal order, then they must necessarily be legal subjects under international law as well.[435] Similarly, Verdross considers it a 'faulty attitude'[436] to ignore individuals as international legal subjects and argues, as early as 1920, that international treaties, such as the Hague Convention on the Creation of an International Prize Court,[437] may bestow international legal subjectivity on individuals as well.[438]

In 2001, the ICJ confirmed this view in the *LaGrand* case when it held that Article 36(1) of the Vienna Convention on Consular Relations, governing the rights of arrested foreign nationals to consular protection, 'creates individual rights'.[439] More recently in the *Diallo* case from 2012, the ICJ examined in detail the individual rights of Mr Diallo, a Guinean national, who had been expelled from the Democratic Republic of Congo, where he had been running various business enterprises.[440] In the end, the ICJ decided in favour of Guinea (and hence Mr Diallo) and held that the sum awarded to Guinea in the exercise of diplomatic protection of Mr Diallo was intended to provide reparation for the latter's injury.[441] It thus substantially transformed a case involving the diplomatic protection of a national mediated through his home country into a case about individual rights protection.[442] This means that the ICJ effectively managed to detach the case from the dogmatic straitjacket of international law as pure inter-state law and did not even attempt to translate Mr Diallo's individual rights back into the rights of his home state as

[434] See e.g. *Reparation for Injuries* (n 319); and *Interpretation of the Agreement of 25 March 1951 between the WHO and Egypt (Advisory Opinion)* [1980] ICJ Rep 73, para 37.

[435] Kelsen, *Principles of International Law* (n 97) 96 ff and 140 ff.

[436] Verdross, *Einheit des rechtlichen Weltbildes* (n 120) 46.

[437] See Articles 3–5 of the Convention (XII) Relative to the Creation of an International Prize Court; The Hague, 18 October 1907; this agreement, however, was never ratified and never entered into force.

[438] Alfred Verdross, *Die völkerrechtswidrige Kriegshandlung und der Strafanspruch der Staaten* (Engelmann, 1920) 34.

[439] *LaGrand* (n 262) para 77.

[440] *Ahmadou Sadio Diallo (Republic of Guinea v Democratic Republic of the Congo) Preliminary Objections* [2007] ICJ Rep 582, paras 34 ff.

[441] *Ahmadou Sadio Diallo (Republic of Guinea v Democratic Republic of the Congo) Compensation Owed by the Democratic Republic of the Congo to the Republic of Guinea* [2012] ICJ Rep 324, para 57.

[442] Sandy Ghandhi, 'Human Rights and the International Court of Justice: The *Ahmadou Sadio Diallo* Case' (2011) 11 *Human Rights Law Review* 527, 528.

mediated rights,[443] as the PCIJ did in *Mavrommatis*.[444] Similarly, Article 33(2) of the International Law Commission's Draft Articles on State Responsibility clearly states that the provisions on the actual content of international state responsibility 'is without prejudice to any right, arising from the international responsibility of a State, which may accrue directly to any person or entity other than a State'. After all, the individual is the addressee of 'international subjective rights'[445] and it is therefore beside the point that these rights must be transposed into domestic law to become effective.[446]

Anti-monists might argue at this point that the arguments above may be true, but only on the international legal plane. After all, international and domestic law are separate and distinct and the ICJ can therefore enforce individual rights in international law in any way it deems correct, but this remains without consequences for national law. Whether the national legal orders apply and enforce international individual rights domestically, for instance via the principles of direct effect or consistent interpretation, is up to them, and states therefore have the last say in this. This sounds convincing, but is ultimately incorrect. To begin with, it must be emphasized that the neutrality of international law towards the question of whether states are required or not to allow direct applicability or direct effect in their domestic legal order is highly deceptive.[447] In other words, the traditional opinion that these instruments are entirely dependent on national law and the will of the legislator as well as the judiciary is wrong.[448] The reason for this is simple: the fact that international law does not obligate states to allow for direct effect does not negate the influence the international legal order exerts over this instrument. Indeed, as long as the conditions for direct effect are fulfilled, the influence of international law will be considerable,[449] since the instruments of direct applicability and direct effect primarily amount to questions of treaty interpretation.[450] For example, every treaty party is obliged to achieve the full exercise of the individual rights enshrined in a given treaty to the maximum of its available resources, which will usually include the adoption of legislative measures (i.e. an obligation of the legislature) or at least a corresponding interpretation by the municipal courts (i.e. an obligation of the judiciary),[451] which will probably give direct effect to the respective treaty provisions. Even the United States Supreme Court mentioned in the dualist-inspired *Medellín* case 'our obligation to

[443] Bruno Simma, 'Human Rights Before the International Court of Justice: Community Interests Coming to Life?' in Christian J. Tams and James Sloan (eds), *The Development of International Law by the International Court of Justice* (Oxford University Press, 2013) 311.

[444] *Mavrommatis Palestine Concessions* (n 312).

[445] Evelyne Lagrange, 'L'efficacité dans l'ordre juridique interne des normes internationales concernant la situation des personnes privées' (2012) 356 *Recueil des Cours* 239, 275.

[446] Peters, 'Rechtsordnungen und Konstitutionalisierung' (n 407) 15.

[447] Nollkaemper, *National Courts* (n 51) 127.

[448] Peters, *Jenseits der Menschenrechte* (n 312) 443.

[449] Thomas Buergenthal, 'Self-Executing and Non-Self-Executing Treaties in National and International Law' (1992-IV) 235 *Recueil des cours* 303, 319.

[450] Peters, *Jenseits der Menschenrechte* (n 312) 443.

[451] See e.g. the Swiss Federal Supreme Court, BGE 136 I 290–295, *X v Z*, 4 May 2010, paras 2.3.1–2.3.2.

interpret treaty provisions to determine whether they are self-executing'.[452] As a result, the issue whether an international norm is directly effective boils down to the test whether it is of 'such kind that the provision can function as an objective rule in the national legal order'.[453] Thus, in determining whether a treaty should be directly applied and have direct effect, courts generally place much weight on interpretation and the intention of the parties,[454] and by doing so, they follow international legal provisions,[455] such as Articles 31 and 32 VCLT on treaty interpretation.

This means that the questions of direct applicability and direct effect are not exclusively within the jurisdiction of national law. On the contrary, they are of a mixed international and municipal nature[456] and therefore—and this is the crucial element in the context of monism—also necessarily form part of the international legal order.[457] In other words, giving effect to these instruments is not entirely within the will of the national legal orders, which speaks against dualism and pluralism. By asking the question of what was originally promised, international law takes into account that states can conclude treaties which require its parties to guarantee that its relevant provisions enjoy the status as directly applicable and effective law.[458] This means, a fortiori, that the questions of direct applicability and direct effect can also be conclusively decided by international courts, as the PCIJ did in its *Jurisdiction of the Courts of Danzig* opinion,[459] whose decisions should then—according to the supreme status of international law—prevail over contravening national law or the decisions of the municipal courts. This approach may of course not always prevent domestic courts from disallowing for the direct applicability or the direct effect of international norms,[460] but such a behaviour can, in turn, certainly be sanctioned under international law itself, either through the law of state responsibility or the respective treaty provisions on its enforcement. This argument clearly speaks in favour of a unitary view of the law where violations of the superior body of law through legal acts on the inferior plane can and will be sanctioned through the rules of the former.

The same holds true for the concept of consistent interpretation which is also of mixed international and domestic pedigree. As such, it constitutes both an inherent element of the international legal requirement to perform international obligations and of the national mandate to construe domestic law in accordance and consistency with international law. Of course it is true that disregarding this principle per se

[452] *Medellín v Texas* (n 362) 37.

[453] Supreme Court of the Netherlands, *Railway Strike* (n 354).

[454] See e.g. Belgium, Court of Cassation, *Art Research & Contact Naamloze Vennootschap v BS*, Case No C 00 0391 N; ILDC 44 (BE 2001).

[455] Peters, *Jenseits der Menschenrechte* (n 312) 444.

[456] Albert Bleckmann, 'Self-Executing Treaty Provisions' in Rudolf Bernhardt (ed), *Encyclopedia of Public International Law, Vol VII* (North-Holland, 1984) 414.

[457] Karen Kaiser, 'Treaties, Direct Applicability' in Rüdiger Wolfrum (ed), *The Max Planck Encyclopedia of Public International Law* (2nd edn; Oxford University Press, 2013) paras 6 and 8.

[458] Nollkaemper, *National Courts* (n 51) 127; Buergenthal (n 449) 319; Sørensen (n 401) 26.

[459] *Jurisdiction of the Courts of Danzig (Pecuniary Claims of Danzig Railway Officials Who Have Passed into the Polish Service against the Polish Railways Administration) (Advisory Opinion)* [1928] PCIJ Series B No 15, 17–18.

[460] Peters, *Jenseits der Menschenrechte* (n 312) 444.

would not amount to a violation of international law, because it is simply an instrument to give effect to international law,[461] very similar to the rules of treaty interpretation laid down in Articles 31 and 32 of the VCLT from which national courts may deviate in their interpretative enterprises without automatically violating international law.[462] Yet states are nonetheless obliged under the general law of state responsibility effectively to resolve and eliminate any violations of international law rooted in domestic law,[463] which may or may not occur on the basis of consistent interpretation. Accordingly, consistent interpretation is merely one of many ways for states to avoid violations of their international obligations. But coincidentally, in most cases, a refusal to interpret national law in harmony with the corresponding international rule will result in such a violation of international obligations, thus entailing legal consequences under international law. This proves again that acts on the national level have effects on the international plane, which only further bolsters the idea of a monist system of both national and international law.

Hence the argument that monism can be disproved by referring to a possible difference in subjects and addressees between national and international law is unfounded and can be dismissed.

c. Conclusion: what non-monist theories fail to explain

The analysis above has shown that neither dualism nor pluralism can convincingly explain why international and national law should not share the same substance or the same addressees. In contrast to the issues of validity and supremacy in the relationship between international and domestic law, there now is broad consensus between proponents of different theories that the differences in substance and subjects are too marginal and negligible to justify a concept which would clearly distinguish between entirely different legal orders. Even outspoken critics of Kelsen who usually do not hold back in their disapproval of the pure theory of law in other points, readily concede to the superiority or partial correctness of the monist theory with respect to the questions of substance and subjects.[464] Surprisingly, even H.L.A. Hart pays Kelsen enormous respect in this regard when he writes that his attack on 'the crude and confusing theory that international and municipal law are independent or different systems because international law applies to states and municipal law to individuals' is illuminating and not be quarrelled with.[465]

[461] Nollkaemper, *National Courts* (n 51) 150.

[462] Richard Gardiner, *Treaty Interpretation* (2nd edn; Oxford University Press, 2015) 126, provided, however, that Articles 26 and 27 of the VCLT are complied with.

[463] See e.g. *Avena and Other Mexican Nationals* (n 245) para 138; Kirsten Schmalenbach, 'Article 53' in Oliver Dörr and Kirsten Schmalenbach (eds), *Vienna Convention on the Law of Treaties: A Commentary* (Springer, 2012) para 55; Peters, *Jenseits der Menschenrechte* (n 312) 329.

[464] Rub (n 2) 461 and fn 337 on the same page. Fernando Téson, 'The Relations between International Law and Municipal Law: The Monism/Dualism Controversy' in Michael Bothe and Raul E. Vinuesa (eds), *International Law and Municipal Law* (Duncker & Humblot, 1982) 109.

[465] H.L.A. Hart, 'Kelsen's Doctrine of the Unity of Law' in Stanley L. Paulson and Bonnie Litschewski Paulson (eds), *Normativity and Norms: Critical Perspectives on Kelsenian Themes* (reprint; Clarendon Press, 2007) 558–9.

In the context of substance, it is indisputable that modern international law has crossed the traditional boundary of inter-state law areas, merely regulating the co-existence of states, and has attracted new competences[466] that were previously entirely within the domain of national law. Indeed, the most persuasive fact in favour of monism and against dualism and pluralism is that if there were no congruence or overlap in substance between international and domestic law, then there could not be any normative conflicts between those two bodies of law. However, the fact that such normative conflicts exist, proves that it is possible that both national and international law can regulate the same legal substance. Dualists and pluralist must hence accept that there is no subject which, by its own nature, can exclusively be governed by domestic law, but not international law.[467]

Similarly, anti-monists also admit that although many rules of international law only address states, the absolute view that international law cannot address individuals is somewhat dated.[468] For the pure theory of law, the status of individuals as addressees of international legal norms is just a logical consequence of the unity of the law and the identity of the state with its legal order. Although it is correct that there are crucial differences between individual persons and the legal person of the 'State', there is principally no conceptual difference between them, because ultimately, the law always governs the conduct of physical human beings.[469] The state is nothing other than a section of the overall monist legal order, restrained by international law, which entails that individuals are not only addressees of this section of the law, but also of international law itself.[470] Non-monists may of course criticize the theoretical foundations of this conclusion,[471] but they cannot deny the fact that monism is capable of aptly describing the position of individuals as addressees and subjects of the international legal order. One may of course interject that individuals lack the capacity to create international legal norms, as they do not themselves as private persons participate in the formation of customary international or in concluding treaties.[472] This argument, however, fails for two reasons: first, even in undemocratic states, where individuals are barred from participating in the law-making process, one must admit that they remain subject to this very law; and, secondly, one could also argue that individuals are indirectly involved in the international law-making process through the representation of their state—a situation that is comparable to representative democracies. Thus, the fact that individuals are not directly partaking in the creation of international law is not an argument against their legal personality under international law.

466 Rub (n 2) 462; Pisillo-Mazzeschi (n 143) 135.

467 Téson (n 464) 109.

468 Gaja (n 48) 55. See also G Balladore Pallieri, 'Le dottrine di Hans Kelsen e il problema dei rapporti fra diritto interno e diritto internazionale' (1935) 27 *Rivista di diritto internazionale* 24, 74, who—as early as 1935—had already noted that even if international law did not address individuals, nothing prevented it from expanding its reach in this regard.

469 Pisillo-Mazzeschi (n 143) 145; Téson (n 464) 109.

470 Hans Kelsen, 'Théorie générale du droit international public. Problèmes choisis' (1932-IV) 42 *Recueil des cours* 116, 141–72; Hans Kelsen, 'Théorie du droit international public' (1953-III) 84 *Recueil des cours* 1, 66–107.

471 Pisillo-Mazzeschi (n 143) 146.

472 An argument that even Kelsen acknowledged: Kelsen, 'Théorie générale' (n 470) 268.

Accordingly, the greatest success of monism under the primacy of international law lies in the fact that it not only describes the *lex lata* better than dualism or pluralism, but that it was also able to anticipate this development, i.e. the continuing individualization and humanization of international law. The unmediated effect of international legal norms on individuals in combination with direct access to international courts represents an enormous breakthrough towards a more effective universal and unitary law.[473] Consequently, even if national authorities refuse to apply international law directly, to give it direct effect, or to interpret national law in consistency with it, this is not verifying dualism or pluralism, nor falsifying monism. On the contrary, the fact that international law bestows certain rights and obligations on individuals and eventually controls whether states comply with these obligations, clearly speaks in favour of monism under the primacy of international law.

D. Conclusion

The foregoing sections discussed and examined the relationship between national law and international law along the main attack points against monism under the primacy of international law, namely the validity, supremacy, and applicability of international norms within domestic law. In other words, it investigated whether these two bodies of law have different sources or share the same ultimate fount of validity; whether they are disconnected from each other or linked by the same chain of delegation and derogation and how normative conflicts between them are to be resolved; and whether they are distinct in substance and addressees or whether they share the same substance-matter and legal subjects.

By comparing the main claims of the pure theory of law concerning monism under the primacy of international law with the law as it is, it has been shown that this theory has not been conclusively disproven and falsified. It is of course undoubtedly true that dualism and pluralism possess an enormous explanatory value in our legally fragmented world, driven by the brute *realpolitik* of the powerful and the lack of centralized enforcement authorities. At first glance, monism appears to be a cold logical device, out of touch with reality, and therefore deeply counter-intuitive. Yet this does not mean that it is wrong.[474] On the contrary, one must look deeper to realize that the positive law does not necessarily falsify this theory. In this sense, the foregoing analysis demonstrated that monism can describe the reality of the law as well as or even better than dualism or pluralism.

International and municipal law form part of the same unitary legal order via a common *Grundnorm*, located at the apex of the international legal order, and one must accept this statement unless she or he is prepared to forfeit the legal nature of international law. Accordingly, a definition of the law that excludes international law neither verifies dualism nor pluralism.[475] The same is true for the supremacy of

[473] von Bernstorff (n 409) 148.

[474] See Yvan I. Russell and Fernand Gobet, 'What Is Counterintuitive? Religious Cognition and Natural Expectation' (2013) 4 *Review of Philosophy and Psychology* 715–49. *Nota bene* also the counter-intuitive nature of undisputable facts such as heliocentrism and a spherical Earth.

[475] Rill, 'Internationales, supranationales und nationales Recht' (n 102) 695.

international law and the interconnection of international and national law through the same chain of delegation and derogation,[476] which is perfectly capable of explaining not only the fact that international law itself determines its own binding character, but also its supreme status vis-à-vis national law. This means that violations of international obligations entail legal consequences in the form of sanctions, for example. Lastly, it has also been convincingly shown that even staunch non-monists must accept that international and national law share the same substance and the same addressees, especially individuals. Overall, monism appears to be the better theory to describe and explain the positive law and emerges unfalsified from this test.

Finally, a clear distinction needs to be made concerning monism's weakest and strongest point: admittedly it is true that monism cannot ensure the substantive unity of the law by unifying its primary rules, i.e. by guaranteeing that there are no normative conflicts between two bodies of law. The younger Kelsen was wrong in assuming that such conflicts are logically impossible, because normative conflicts do exist and must be acknowledged as such. But what monism can guarantee is the formal unity of the law,[477] which is a unity of secondary rules. Kelsen correctly elaborated that this unity is not about logical consistency and the absence of conflicts, but about the processes by which national and international law are assembled together,[478] namely a chain of delegation and a chain of derogation. And especially regarding the latter, it cannot be emphasized enough that international law provides for legal consequences, in case states violate their international obligations. Admittedly, these consequences may sometimes be ineffective or not entirely enforceable, but the fact that they exist proves that international and national law form part of one unitary legal order.

3. National Law and European Union Law

In the same fashion as in the previous sections on the relationship between international law and domestic law, the subsequent ones will now assess whether legal monism is also superior in describing the relationship between the law of the European Union (EU) and the law of its Member States, in particular on the basis of the main positions and constellations conceivable between those two bodies of law. This descriptive account will thereby study whether the epistemological claims of the pure theory of law live up to the daily reality of positive law.

[476] Manfred Rotter, 'Die Reine Rechtslehre im Völkerrecht—eine eklektizistische Spurensuche in Theorie und Praxis' in Robert Walter, Clemens Jabloner, and Klaus Zeleny (eds), *Hans Kelsen und das Völkerrecht* (Manz, 2004) 80.

[477] See also Joseph Raz, 'The Identity of Legal Systems' (1971) 59 *California Law Review* 795, 796, and his basic distinction between the substantive/material and the formal unity of the law.

[478] Mario Prost, *The Concept of Unity in Public International Law* (Hart Publishing, 2012) 47 and 73–4.

A. Introduction: the pure theory of law and EU law

To begin with, one should note the fact that the members of the Vienna School of Jurisprudence wrote extensively about national law and international law. In contrast to that, it is more noteworthy that there certainly is no mention of the EU or its historical predecessors in the writings of Kelsen, Merkl, Verdross, or any other member of the Vienna School of Jurisprudence. They never dealt with questions of European integration in general or the European Union in particular[479] for three obvious reasons: first, the project of European integration was neither foreseeable at the beginning of the twentieth century nor well-developed as late as 1960 when the second edition of the *Pure Theory of Law* was published.[480] Secondly, the European project and its institutions were not a priority for lawyers in the early days of its existence,[481] and particularly not in the United States, where Kelsen spent his last years[482] and where his work was generally ignored. Lastly, in the 1960s, the European Economic Community was still commonly perceived as nothing more than an ordinary international organization, and not as inherently different from others.[483] The only statement by Kelsen that could be construed as anticipatory of the ultimate development of the European Union is that

> [t]he creation of a real, that is to say, technically perfect, judicature, even though it be only within a specific collectivity of States, must precede any strivings after the establishment of international legislative organisms as also any attempt to codify international law.[484]

Despite or because of this lack of an analysis of EU law in the light of the pure theory of law, there were some attempts to examine its legal structure in terms of monism, the *Grundnorm*, and the hierarchy of norms, especially after the Union had further developed and consolidated into its current form. Yet, because of the EU's idiosyncratic and *sui generis*[485] nature, which defies any categorizing in 'nation Statehood' terms, doubts have emerged whether the pure theory of law is in fact capable of describing and explaining the interplay between the law of the Union and its Member States. And since the theory was regarded as unable to account for the contemporary European legal order,[486] it was subsequently dismissed as an unsuitable model.[487]

[479] See Jürgen Busch and Tamara Ehs, 'The EU as "Rechtsgemeinschaft": A Kelsenian Approach to European Legal Philosophy' (2008) 85 *Rivista internazionale di filosofia del diritto* 195, 198.

[480] Heinz Mayer, 'Reine Rechtslehre und Gemeinschaftsrecht' in Robert Walter, Clemens Jabloner, and Klaus Zeleny (eds), *Hans Kelsen und das Völkerrecht* (Manz, 2004) 121–2.

[481] Busch and Ehs (n 479) 198 and 198 fn 9, specifically mentioning that Kelsen had stopped working one to two years before his death in 1973.

[482] See e.g. Jeremy Telman, 'A Path Not Taken: Hans Kelsen's Pure Theory of Law in the Land of the Legal Realists' in Robert Walter, Clemens Jabloner, and Klaus Zeleny (eds), *Hans Kelsen anderswo—Hans Kelsen Abroad* (Manz, 2010) 353–76.

[483] Busch and Ehs (n 479) 199.

[484] Hans Kelsen, *The Legal Process and International Order* (Constable, 1935) 19.

[485] Case 6/64 *Costa v ENEL* [1964] ECR 585.

[486] See inter alia, Neil MacCormick, 'Beyond the Sovereign State' (1993) 56 *Modern Law Review* 1, 13; Neil MacCormick, 'The *Maastricht*-Urteil: Sovereignty Now' (1995) 1 *European Law Journal* 259, 263–4; Werner Schroeder, *Das Gemeinschaftsrechtssystem* (Mohr-Siebeck, 2002) 206–55.

[487] See e.g. F.E. Dowrick, 'A Model of the European Communities' Legal System' (1983) 3 *Yearbook of European Law* 169–237.

One should nevertheless not content oneself with this conclusion. On the contrary, as the pure theory of law is 'a theory of positive law in general, not a specific legal order',[488] it should be very much capable of describing the relationship between EU law and its Member States. In fact, if one is inclined to take this theory seriously, every effort should be made to extrapolate it from the existing theorems to the relationship between the EU and the national legal orders—in the same way as it was first extrapolated from national law to the international legal sphere.

Indeed, the question has been raised whether and the extent to which the law of the EU—which claims to be legally autonomous from both Member State and international law—and the project of European integration in general can be considered 'a late confirmation of the Pure Theory of Law'.[489] This claim will be discussed in the subsequent sections and on the basis of principal four models to describe the relationship between national and European Union law:[490] (1) a pluralist model between EU law and the Member States, devoid of primacy and clear hierarchical structures; (2) a constitutional dualist model in which the Member States are clearly contrasted with a distinct EU legal order; (3) a monist model under the primacy of Member State law; and (4) a monist model under the primacy of EU law.

B. The relationship between EU and national law in the light of different models

We should now enquire whether the relationship between Union law and Member State law is describable in terms of the pure theory of law. At the outset, however, one must also admit to the question of whether it makes any sense to force the jurisprudence of the CJEU, which is chiefly shaped by pragmatism and functionality, into a rigid theoretical corset.[491] And even though issues such as the legal autonomy, supremacy, direct effect, and the potential *Kompetenz-Kompetenz* of EU law were sometimes seen as an excellent opportunity to revisit various legal theoretical approaches to explain the complex relationship between EU and national law,[492] it has been suggested that 'in the case of the EU, recently revived interest in the theory of legal systems is best strangled at birth . . .'.[493] Cynics even opine that in interpreting a badly drafted regulation 'concerning the fat content of skimmed-milk powder, there is no place for competing national theories of legal philosophy'.[494] *Au contraire*,

[488] Kelsen, *Pure Theory* (n 24) 1.

[489] Öhlinger, 'Einheit' (n 139) 168.

[490] Tobias Kruis, *Der Anwendungsvorrang des EU-Rechts in Theorie und Praxis* (Mohr-Siebeck, 2013) 7–8.

[491] Schroeder (n 486) 197.

[492] See e.g. Mark L. Jones, 'The Legal Nature of the European Community: A Jurisprudential Analysis Using H.L.A. Hart's Model of Law and a Legal System' (1984) 7 *Cornell International Law Journal* 1; Ines Weyland, 'The Application of Kelsen's Theory of the Legal System to European Community Law—The Supremacy Puzzle Resolved' (2002) 21 *Law and Philosophy* 1.

[493] Julie Dickson, 'Towards a Theory of European Union Legal Systems' in Julie Dickson and Pavlos Eleftheriadis (eds), *Philosophical Foundations of European Union Law* (Oxford University Press, 2012) 29.

[494] Jack Mackenzie Stuart, *The Acceptance of Community Law in the English Legal Order* (Zentrum für Europäisches Wirtschaftsrecht, 1991) 6.

this book argues, because the CJEU emulates—just as any other court—the ideal of law as a system. Thereby it attempts to resolve normative conflicts by way of decisions that can be coherently placed into one single system under the overarching principles of the rule of law and legal certainty.[495] Whether these aspirations to establishing one single system, consisting of EU law itself and the national legal orders of the Member States, can correctly be described in terms of legal monism and the pure theory of law is a different question. Let us now investigate whether such a description makes sense.

(1) The Stufenbau *doctrine and European Union law*

If one tries to apply the elements of the pure theory of law to European Union law, it is certainly best to start with the least controversial part of this theory, namely the hierarchy of norms. The most practical aspect of this particular component is that it can be applied regardless of any other theoretical preconditions, and accordingly, it can also be used as a model to explain and describe the normative hierarchies within EU law itself[496] (while disregarding the relationship with Member State law at this point, which is of course much more contentious). The necessity of such a hierarchical model of norms to establish and safeguard the unity of Union law was already recognized in Declaration No 16 of the Final Act to the Treaty of Maastricht, in which it was agreed 'to review the classification of [Union] acts with a view to establishing an appropriate hierarchy between the different categories of acts'.[497] However, no formal hierarchy of norms was introduced in the subsequent Treaties, and the only underlying rule was that legislative acts would be superior to executive acts.[498] In order to guarantee a higher degree of democratic legitimacy and a better separation of powers,[499] the Lisbon Treaty retained the existing hierarchy of norms, but made it more visible and formal than previous Treaties.

There is no express mention in the Treaties of the position of primary EU law within the hierarchy of norms, but it has always been accepted in a logical way and long before the Lisbon Treaty that primary law undoubtedly sits at the apex of the normative hierarchy of EU law and prevails over secondary law.[500] Primary law consists of the Treaties themselves, amending and accession treaties, the Charter of Fundamental Rights[501] as well as general principles,[502] Protocols, and Annexes

[495] Henry G. Schermers, 'The Role of the Member States in Filling Lacunae in EC-Law' in Roland Bieber and Georg Ress (eds), *Die Dynamik des Europäischen Gemeinschaftsrechts* (Nomos, 1987) 311–12.

[496] Catherine Richmond, 'Preserving the Identity Crisis: Autonomy, System, and Sovereignty in European Law' (1997) 16 *Law and Philosophy* 377, 388–9.

[497] OJ C 191/101, 29 July 1992.

[498] Koen Lenaerts and Marlies Desomer, 'Towards a Hierarchy of Legal Acts in the European Union? Simplification of Legal Instruments and Procedures' (2005) 11 *European Law Journal* 744, 745.

[499] See European Convention, 'Final Report of Working Group IX on Simplification', CONV 424/02, 29 November 2002, 2.

[500] Jacques Ziller, 'Hierarchy of Norms, Hierarchy of Sources, and General Principles in European Union Law' in Ulrich Becker and others (eds), *Verfassung und Verwaltung in Europa: Festschrift für Jürgen Schwarze zum 70. Geburtstag* (Nomos, 2014) 343–4.

[501] See the reference in Article 6(1) TEU.

[502] Takis Tridimas, *The General Principles of EU Law* (2nd edn; Oxford University Press, 2007) 50–1.

to the Treaties, and it thus forms the constitutional backbone of the European Union. International agreements concluded by the Union institutions rank below primary law, but above secondary law, on a mezzanine rank, which is not only reflected in the wording of Articles 267(1)(b), 216(2), and 218(11) TFEU, but also in the case law of the Court of Justice.[503] Secondary law in the form of legislative acts, as defined by Articles 288 and 289 TFEU, ranks below this tier, and includes regulations, directives, and decisions.[504] Furthermore, Articles 290 and 291 TFEU contain details regarding delegating and implementing acts which, as tertiary law, can be considered executive acts and therefore below the legislative acts mentioned above.

a. The chain of delegation in European Union law

This EU hierarchy of norms was, however, not only criticized for being incomplete,[505] but also for not fitting the *Stufenbau* doctrine.[506] The first point might be correct, but does not form part of the analysis at hand. Regarding the second point, it should be noted that this criticism both predates the entry into force of the Lisbon Treaty (which introduced a much more sophisticated hierarchy of norms) and is, as will be shown, unjustified. The EU hierarchy of norms, as presented in its current post-Lisbon form, undoubtedly constitutes a *Stufenbau* in the sense of a dynamic legal order and a chain of validity. The constitution, in a manner of speaking, from which one starts to arrange the positive law, is primary law. The validity of secondary law is, thus, entirely dependent on the rules of law-creation laid down in primary law (i.e. Articles 288 and 289 TFEU). The validity of tertiary law, in turn, is dependent on both the conditioning secondary legal act and the relevant primary legal rules (i.e. Articles 290 and 291 TFEU). This view is also mirrored in the Court's understanding of Union law as organized as a 'system of sources'[507] and, *expressis verbis*, in a 'hierarchy of norms',[508] according to which 'a measure of secondary legislation cannot derogate from a provision of the Treaty'.[509] One can therefore clearly see a chain of delegation or validity running down from the 'constitution' of primary law to legislative acts in the form of secondary law and to executive acts in the shape of tertiary law, wherein the validity of the inferior act is dependent on the rules of law-creation enshrined in the respective superior layer of the law.

[503] Case 181/73 *Haegeman* [1974] ECR 449, para 5; Case C-61/94 *Commission v Germany (International Dairy Arrangement)* [1996] ECR I-3989, para 52; Case 104/81 *Kupferberg & Cie KG (Kupferberg I)* [1982] ECR 3641, para 14.

[504] Deidre Curtin and Tatevik Manucharyan, 'Legal Acts and Hierarchy of Norms in EU Law' in Anthony Arnull and Damian Chalmers (eds), *The Oxford Handbook of European Union Law* (Oxford University Press, 2015) 106–10.

[505] Ibid., 123–4.

[506] Schroeder (n 486) 203 and 307 ff; Dowrick (n 487) 181.

[507] Case 34/73 *Variola* [1973] ECR 981, para 8.

[508] Case C-103/96 *Eridania Beghin-Say* [1997] ECR I-1453, para 15; Joined Cases C-246/94 to C-249/94 *Agricola Zootecnica and Others* [1996] ECR I-4373, para 31.

[509] Joined Cases T-24/93 to T-26/03 and T-28/93 *Compagnie maritime belge* [1996] ECR II-1201, para 152; Joined Cases C-90/90 and C-91/90 *Jean Neu and Others* [1991] ECR I-3617, para 12.

b. The chain of derogation in European Union law

The reverse (and yet intricately related) side to the chain of validity is the chain of derogation, or the question of how legal acts can be derogated in the case of their alleged illegality. The concept that the validity of a particular Union norm is determined and delimited by a superior norm is enshrined in the Treaties themselves, especially the action for annulment under Article 263 TFEU and the preliminary ruling procedure with regard to the validity of secondary law under Article 267(1)(b) TFEU. Both procedures are concerned with the legal basis of such acts and since every legislative measure must have a legal foundation in a Treaty provision or in a previous legislative measure itself based upon a Treaty provision, challenges to the validity of Union acts all regress back to the Treaties and to compatibility with them.

At the lowest end of the spectrum of validity, one may find so-called non-existent acts, which do not even satisfy the minimum or necessary conditions to be valid. In this case, the legal act would be a legal nullity and can be ignored.[510] In the case of EU law, however, only the CJEU is authorized to declare Union acts to be invalid,[511] and no legal act can be simply ignored, as validity must always be presumed until definitely disproven, even in the case of alleged absolute invalidity.[512] If a contested act has serious and manifest defects,[513] it can be regarded as non-existent and declared void by the Court, which would principally amount to a legal nullity in the light of the pure theory of law. Should this be the case, the non-existent act cannot produce any legal effects at all, as it never existed and was therefore void *ex tunc*. The Court is, nevertheless, quite reluctant to declare any acts as legally inexistent, as such declarations should be 'reserved for quite extreme situations',[514] and does not provide any clear guidelines as to what constitutes such a serious and manifest defect.[515] Between such non-existent acts and acts which were perfectly created in accordance with their respective delegating norms, Merkl's concept of the *Fehlerkalkül* could apply, but only if the positive law provides for this.[516] And this is indeed the case, as mentioned above, since both Article 263 TFEU and Article 267(1)(b) TFEU authorize the Court to invalidate any secondary law that has not been created in accordance with primary law,[517] because of the lack of competence, the infringement of an essential procedural requirement, the infringement of the Treaty or any rule of law relating to its application or the misuse of powers (in the case of Article 263 TFEU) and because of other grounds in violation of the relevant Treaty provisions raised before national courts (in the case of Article 267(1)(b) TFEU). Accordingly,

[510] Christoph Kletzer, 'Kelsen's Development of the *Fehlerkalkül* Theory' (2005) 18 *Ratio Juris* 46, 48.

[511] Case 314/85 *Foto-Frost* [1987] ECR 4199, para 15.

[512] Case C-137/92 P *Commission v BASF and Others* [1994] ECR I-2555, para 48; Case C-475/01 *Commission v Greece (Failure to Fulfil Obligations)* [2004] ECR I-8923, para 19.

[513] Joined Cases 15–33, 52, 53, 57–109, 116, 117, 123, 132 and 135–137/73 *Kortner and Others v Council, Commission, and Parliament* [1974] ECR 177, para 10; Case C-137/92 *Commission v BASF* (n 512) para 49; Case C-135/93 *Spain v Commission* [1995] ECR I-1651, para 18.

[514] Case C-137/92 *Commission v BASF* (n 512) para 50.

[515] Alexander H. Türk, *Judicial Review in EU Law* (Edward Elgar Publishing, 2009) 36.

[516] Merkl, *Lehre von der Rechtskraft* (n 108) 287 and 293.

[517] Mayer, 'Reine Rechtslehre und Gemeinschaftsrecht' (n 480) 136.

the CJEU views the validity of EU norms in a manner that is consistent with the pure theory of law, ascribing validity only if the norm has been created in perfect conformity with the respective determining superior norm.[518]

c. Extending the hierarchy of norms to the relationship with national law

At this point, the reader will have noticed that one crucial element of the pure theory of law has been omitted, namely the concept of the *Grundnorm*. The analysis of the *Stufenbau* of EU law above only discussed the positive law and started out with primary Union law, which constitutes the hierarchically highest legal layer. However, the chain of validity of EU law becomes much more difficult to trace once the validity of the EU Treaties themselves is questioned,[519] as there is, at least not within the Union system, another positive legal norm which could serve as the source of the Treaties' validity. But where is the *Grundnorm* of the Union legal order to be found? Where is this norm-creating and unifying force of this legal order located?

The search for the *Grundnorm* of the EU legal order requires us to go beyond the positive law of the Union,[520] where one finds several possible locations for it. The European Union Treaties may be valid: (i) because of a legal norm of public international law, which would make EU law part of the international legal order and determined by it; (ii) because of a *Grundnorm* in EU law itself which, however, exists independently alongside the basic norms of the Member States, and none of them can be traced back to one another; (iii) because of a legal norm of Member State law, in which case EU law would derived and determined by national law; or (iv) because of a presupposed *Grundnorm* in European Union law itself, which would provide it with an internal claim to validity and legal autonomy.[521]

Given the previous findings of this book,[522] the first reaction of a legal monist would be to point to option (i) as the correct answer, since the overall *Grundnorm* of the law would logically and epistemologically be located at the apex of international law. But let us disregard this option in the context of the present analysis and focus on the relationship between national and EU law alone. Under option (ii), the relationship between the Union and the Member States is seen in a pluralist light (where the Member States and the EU co-exist without any formal hierarchies based on the same basic norm, but where links and interdependencies may develop) or a dualist view (in which legal orders co-exist, but strictly separated from each other). In other words, in the pluralist or dualist perception, there are no pre-existing links between the different legal orders and the respective hierarchies of norms end in their respective basic norms without extending over the boundaries of these orders themselves. Links can only be established based on explicit provisions found in these legal orders, and a hierarchical order cannot simply be presupposed. Therefore, it should

[518] Richmond (n 496) 390. [519] Ibid., 391.

[520] Uta Bindreiter, *Why* Grundnorm*? A Treatise on the Implications of Kelsen's Doctrine* (Kluwer Law, 2010) 215–18.

[521] Richmond (n 496) 393; Miguel Poiares Maduro, 'Contrapunctual Law: Europe's Constitutional Pluralism in Action' in Neil Walker (ed), *Sovereignty in Transition* (Hart Publishing, 2003) 512; MacCormick, 'Beyond the Sovereign State' (n 486) 3.

[522] See Chapter 3, section 5B, and Chapter 4, section 2.

be mentioned that the wide-ranging acceptance of the *Stufenbau*-doctrine remains restricted to structuring and ordering the legal norms *within one body of law*. It has consequently been heavily contested whether its theoretical capacities and explanatory power can reach beyond positive Union law itself and construct, on the basis of a shared *Grundnorm*, a formal normative hierarchy between Member State and EU law.[523] In opposition to this understanding, however, options (iii) and (iv) assume that there is a common and shared *Grundnorm* and that a hierarchy of norms exists, formally connecting national and EU law. The only difference between those two perspectives is that option (iii) locates this basic norm in Member State law, whilst option (iv) pinpoints it within Union law itself.

In a nutshell, it hence becomes evident that the overall relationship between the Member States and European Union law boils down to the question of where the *Grundnorm* of the entire system is ultimately located (again deliberately disregarding international law at this point, even though fully aware that this is in contradiction to monism under the primacy of international law). In fact, if one takes into account the case law of the CJEU on the autonomy of EU law, then it can only be considered truly autonomous if it has its own *Grundnorm* and is not delegated or determined by Member State law. The following sections will now investigate this claim in the light of legal pluralism, dualism, monism under the primacy of national law, and monism under the primacy of EU law, respectively.

(2) Pluralism in the context of EU and Member State law

a. Neil MacCormick and legal pluralism in EU law

After the *Maastricht* decision of the Bundesverfassungsgericht in 1993,[524] it became apparent that there was an incommensurable clash between the Luxembourg Court and the German Constitutional Court: while the CJEU claims the autonomous validity and supremacy of EU law[525] as well as its own exclusive jurisdiction within the scope of application of Union law,[526] these claims were considered meaningless by the Bundesverfassungsgericht from its internal constitutional point of view. On a strong note, which resembles dualism, the court claims final authority for the German Constitution, but on a softer stance, which gives rise to the interconnecting elements of pluralism, EU law may enjoy relative validity and supremacy, yet only because of national law and not in itself.[527]

[523] Schroeder (n 486) 203, 225 ff, and 307 ff; Neil MacCormick, *Questioning Sovereignty* (Oxford University Press, 1999) 117–18; Neil Walker, 'The Idea of Constitutional Pluralism' (2002) 65 *Modern Law Review* 317, 317; Claudia Annacker, *Der fehlerhafte Rechtsakt im Gemeinschafts- und Unionsrecht* (Springer, 1998) 162 ff and 173; Potacs, 'Verhältnis' (n 104) 132–3.

[524] BVerfGE 89, 155—*Maastricht*, 12 October 1993.

[525] Case 6/64 *Costa v ENEL* (n 485) 593–4.

[526] Case 106/77 *Simmenthal II* [1978] ECR 629, para 14; Case 44/79 *Hauer* [1979] ECR 3727, para 14; Joined Cases C-6/90 and C-9/90 *Francovich* [1991] ECR I-5357, paras 38 ff.

[527] Julio Baquero Cruz, 'The Legacy of the Maastricht-Urteil and the Pluralist Movement' (2008) 14 *European Law Journal* 389, 412; George Letsas, 'Harmonic Law: The Case against Pluralism' in Julie Dickson and Pavlos Eleftheriadis (eds), *Philosophical Foundations of European Union Law* (Oxford University Press, 2012) 82.

In MacCormick's understanding, the developments and interactions between EU and Member State law are entirely incompatible with a monist view in the spirit of the pure theory of law. Even more, only a pluralist outlook could explain the existence of such overlapping and yet non-hierarchical legal systems, wherein no system could hence demand overall superiority over the other.[528] EU-centred monism does not make sense[529] if each of these interacting systems demands for their respective highest courts the exclusive right and authority to interpret the norms of their legal systems in a definitive and ultimate manner.[530] The essence of pluralism in the present context is that the national validity of EU law in the sense of the CJEU's claimed supremacy only results from the Member States' constitutional amendments allowing for validity and supremacy, whilst the Union legal order depends neither on the validity of any particular Member State's constitution nor on the sum of conditions which the Member States might impose. Thus, the relations between Union and states becomes interactive and heterarchical.[531] Conflicts between EU and national law are then decided based on what MacCormick calls *radical pluralism*: the absence of hierarchical relations entails that the interpretative power of the highest decision-making authorities of the different systems must be ultimate, but only within each single system. Consequently, it is for the CJEU to interpret and apply Union law in the last resort and in a finally authoritative way, whilst equally it must be for the highest constitutional or supreme court of each Member State to interpret and apply its national norms, and 'hence to interpret the interaction of the validity of [EU] law with higher level norms of validity in the given State system'.[532] As a result, MacCormick concludes that under such a radically pluralist outlook, 'not all legal problems can be solved legally', which is nevertheless 'not logically embarrassing, because strictly the answers are from the point of view of different systems'.[533]

As mentioned above,[534] MacCormick later recognizes the limitations inherent in such an unregulated and radical view,[535] particularly the slipping of legal judgments into political statements to resolve these conflicts,[536] and moderated his position on pluralism, looking to public international law as a source of conflict resolution. According to this *pluralism under international law*, the international legal order imposes 'a framework on the interactive but not hierarchical relations between systems', which conditions the validity of both national and Union law by coordinating them, yet not subordinating them to each other. International law would, in this

[528] MacCormick, '*Maastricht*-Urteil' (n 486) 264; MacCormick, *Questioning Sovereignty* (n 523) 117.

[529] Pavlos Eleftheriadis, 'Pluralism and Integrity' (2010) 23 *Ratio Juris* 365, 370.

[530] Neil MacCormick, 'Risking Constitutional Collision in Europe?' (1998) 18 *Oxford Journal of Legal Studies* 517, 529; MacCormick, *Questioning Sovereignty* (n 523) 117.

[531] MacCormick, *Questioning Sovereignty* (n 523) 117–18.

[532] Ibid., 118.

[533] Ibid., 119; MacCormick, 'Maastricht Urteil' (n 486) 264–5.

[534] See Chapter 2, section 4C(2).

[535] See e.g. Jan Komárek, 'Institutional Dimension of Constitutional Pluralism' in Matej Avbelj and Jan Komárek (eds), *Constitutional Pluralism in the European Union and Beyond* (Hart Publishing, 2012) 232.

[536] MacCormick, *Questioning Sovereignty* (n 523) 119.

scenario fill the apparent legal vacuum between the two legal orders by providing for the relevant legal obligations of both the EU and the Member States in order to resolve normative conflicts between them.[537] MacCormick, however, also acknowledges that this coordinating view under the auspices of international law could be criticized for being an instance of Kelsenian monism.[538]

b. Consequences: constitutional pluralism and the difference in validity

The element of distinctness between different legal orders is therefore not a sufficient condition for the existence of legal pluralism in the European Union,[539] since chains of validity can easily be constructed under international law. The decisive element of a pluralist view is that these distinct legal orders concurrently claim to be based on their own autonomous ground of validity, which means that their validity is not derived from each other.[540] The Member States claim legal autonomy *and* the EU claims legal autonomy, and this claim becomes necessarily incompatible and mutually exclusive regarding the validity, applicability, and supremacy of Union law within domestic law. One could also argue that there is a plurality of institutional normative orders and each has a functioning constitution in the sense of establishing and conditioning relevant government powers. The crucial aspect is, however, that each order acknowledges the legitimacy of the other one within its own sphere, but none asserts or acknowledges constitutional supremacy over another.[541] Neil Walker accordingly describes this concept as *constitutional pluralism*, which recognizes that the EU legal order has developed beyond the traditional boundaries of international law and now makes its own independent constitutional claims for autonomy, and these claims exist alongside the same claims of the Member States in a horizontal and heterarchical instead of a vertical and hierarchical way. States are thus no longer the sole constitutional authorities, but neither is the EU.[542]

Constitutional pluralism thereby accepts the possibility of legal inconsistency, i.e. the existence of normative conflicts between two or more legal orders.[543] But the pivotal point is that this normative conflict is not a conflict in terms of validity (which would only be possible on the basis of the same ground of validity), but in terms of applicability.[544]

In general, constitutional pluralism does not answer the question of what the exact ground of validity of the different legal orders is.[545] Constitutional pluralism

[537] Ibid., 118.

[538] MacCormick, 'Risking Constitutional Collision' (n 530) 530 and 532.

[539] Mattias Wendel, *Permeabilität im Europäischen Verfassungsrecht* (Mohr-Siebeck, 2011) 17.

[540] Anne Peters, *Elemente einer Theorie der Verfassung Europas* (Duncker & Humblot, 2001) 268 ff.

[541] MacCormick, *Questioning Sovereignty* (n 523) 104.

[542] Walker, 'Idea of Constitutional Pluralism' (n 523) 337; Neil Walker, 'Late Sovereignty in the European Union' in Neil Walker (ed), *Sovereignty in Transition* (Hart Publishing, 2003) 4.

[543] Nick W. Barber, 'Legal Pluralism and the European Union' (2006) 12 *European Law Journal* 306, 308–16.

[544] Stefan Kadelbach, *Allgemeines Verwaltungsrecht unter europäischem Einfluss* (Mohr-Siebeck, 1999) 24–5; Peters, *Elemente* (n 540) 273.

[545] Walker, 'Idea of Constitutional Pluralism' (n 523) 345, only mentioning that laws are 'valid in accordance with the system's ultimate criteria of validity'.

could, for instance, use Hart's rule of recognition to test which rules form part of a given legal order,[546] and as a result, each legal system would therefore possess and use its own unique rule of recognition to determine the validity of its legal norms. In the context of this book, it is nonetheless more relevant to discuss versions of constitutional pluralism with a certain Kelsenian spin. In this vein, Wolf-Dietrich Grussmann argues that the validity of EU law is not grounded in one national legal order alone. In fact, the Union legal order requires a *Grundnorm* of its own, which in no way impinges upon the claim to validity of the national legal orders that, in turn, is derived from their own respective basic norms. By assuming the existence of several basic norms, there can be no normative conflicts in terms of validity, only in terms of obligation.[547] In contrast to this conception, Theodor Schilling postulates that epistemologically speaking, such a plurality of basic norms would contradict the unity of legal orders as a principle of the rule of law, which would provide individuals with the legal certainty of what behaviour is expected of them.[548] Nonetheless, he proposes that every lawyer is free to examine either their own or a foreign legal order, a currently existing or a historical legal order, or a real or fictitious legal order (the so-called 'free choice thesis'). Therefore, they may also include a plurality of legal orders in their examination to the extent that every legal order has its own *Grundnorm*, and that they stand side by side and in an uncoordinated manner. If, however, this observer presumes that two given legal orders (say, international and national law) are somehow connected and that one is bound to incorporate the other one, they must also choose which legal order is valid, or which legal order incorporates which one, and to which legal order the *Grundnorm* relates.[549]

c. Arguments against the explanatory power of legal pluralism

This section will now test whether legal pluralism lives up to its expectations, i.e. whether it is capable of aptly describing and explaining the (allegedly) heterarchical relationship between the Member States and the European Union, regardless of whether one calls this conception 'constitutional pluralism', 'European legal pluralism', or even 'multilevel constitutionalism' in the sense of a *Verfassungsverbund* ('compound constitution').[550] It will be shown and argued that despite its overall intellectual appeal, legal pluralism in all its manifestations is highly problematic and ultimately fails accurately to describe legal reality. However, having said that, the following arguments should not be construed as an attack on *discursive* pluralism. This means that *pluralism in general* remains an essential element of legal discourse, argumentation, and interpretation, and the position of all actors and bodies of law

[546] H.L.A. Hart, *The Concept of Law* (2nd edn; Clarendon Press, 1994) 112–13.

[547] Grussmann (n 138) 59–64. See also Richmond (n 496) 408–409 for a similar approach.

[548] Theodor Schilling, 'Zum Verhältnis von Gemeinschafts- und nationalem Recht' (1998) 39 *Zeitschrift für Rechtsvergleichung, Internationales Privatrecht und Europarecht* 149, 150–1.

[549] Theodor Schilling, 'Das Verhältnis zwischen Völkerrecht, Gemeinschaftsrecht und staatlichem Recht' in Stefan Griller and Heinz Peter Rill (eds), *Rechtstheorie: Rechtsbegriff—Dynamik—Auslegung* (Springer, 2011) 154–6.

[550] See Ingolf Pernice, 'Multilevel Constitutionalism in the European Union' (2002) 8 *European Law Review* 511, 511.

involved need to be taken seriously. Yet it is also crucial that such discursive pluralism takes place within a coherent institutional and normative framework, but it is this very framework that *legal* pluralism threatens fatally to undermine.[551]

i. Pluralism's rejection of hierarchy

One of the most fundamental tenets of legal pluralism in all its forms is its rejection of any sort of hierarchy. Monists, dualists, and pluralists may agree that the validity of Member State law is not based on Union law, since the case law of the Court itself confirms that in the case of conflict, contravening national law is not invalidated by the CJEU, but must merely be disapplied.[552] But disagreement certainly ensues once it is claimed that a hierarchy of norms must necessarily exist at the level of application in order to deal with normative conflicts that cannot be prevented or resolved through consistent interpretation.[553] One pluralist answer could be that such conflicts should be left open and that it is exactly one of the purposes of a pluralist conception of the law 'to legitimate leaving that question open and that, at an empirical level, the fact that the question remains open is a simple description of the constitutional status quo in Europe and only serves to reinforce the value of constitutional pluralism'.[554] Other pluralist answers include the recourse to 'cosmopolitan values' in the form of overarching constitutional principles such as fundamental rights protection, democracy, and subsidiarity to deal with such conflicts.[555]

These answers, however, fail on two accounts: on the one hand, from a theoretical perspective, the introduction of such overarching principles would again amount to a version of monism under said principles, which could then provide for the relevant rules on conflict resolution.[556] On the other hand, it is important to emphasize that pluralism is also wrong from an empirical perspective. No pluralist author has been able to devise and formulate a convincing alternative conflict rule that could help decide which legal norm should enjoy supremacy in the case of a normative conflict.[557] Legal pluralism surrenders exactly to the question to which an answer is most needed, namely what happens when the constitutional conflict cannot be

[551] Baquero-Cruz (n 527) 414.

[552] Case 106/77 *Simmenthal II* (n 526) para 17; Joined Cases C-10/97 to C-22/97 *IN.CO.GE'90 and others* [1998] ECR I-63077 ff, para 21; Case C-290/94 *Commission v Greece (Free Movement of Workers)* [1996] ECR I-3285, para 29.

[553] Case 14/83 *Von Colson* [1984] ECR 1891, para 28, and Case C-106/89 *Marleasing* [1990] ECR I-4135, para 8, stating that national courts cannot be forced to adopt a *contra legem* interpretation of Member State law in order to achieve the results prescribed by EU law.

[554] Miguel Poiares Maduro, 'Three Claims of Constitutional Pluralism' in Matej Avbelj and Jan Komárek (eds), *Constitutional Pluralism in the European Union and Beyond* (Hart Publishing, 2012) 73.

[555] Mattias Kumm, 'The Moral Point of Constitutional Pluralism' in Julie Dickson and Pavlos Eleftheriadis (eds), *Philosophical Foundations of European Union Law* (Oxford University Press, 2012) 216.

[556] Martin Loughlin, 'Constitutional Pluralism: An Oxymoron?' (2014) 3 *Global Constitutionalism* 9, 29.

[557] Monica Claes, 'The Primacy of EU Law in European and National Law' in Anthony Arnull and Damian Chalmers (eds), *The Oxford Handbook of European Union Law* (Oxford University Press, 2015) 202.

prevented or resolved?[558] Pluralism's answer that such conflicts can and should remain unresolved is nevertheless not an empirical claim about constitutions,[559] as one constitutional order will always claim the last say on a given conflict. This claim and the subsequent exercise of competence necessarily results in a hierarchical order. On the one hand, it could be the national courts factually taking this role at the top of the hierarchy, for example by protecting their national fundamental rights. And even though this course of action would once and for all disprove the supremacy of EU law, it would nonetheless prove the existence of a normative hierarchy of one sort or another by resolving the conflict from within the law in contradiction to the claims of legal pluralism.[560] On the other hand, it could be the CJEU claiming the last word and hence confirming the supremacy of EU law, which is also better corroborated by empirical facts. Indeed, the Court's answer to the challenge of European integration as well as a uniform interpretation and application of Union law has been the establishment of a 'new legal order', according to which Union law takes precedence over national law. As will be shown, both the treaties and any norms derived from them are at a higher position in the hierarchy of norms than national law, and the principle of supremacy does therefore not simply function as a mere conflict rule. This does not mean that the Bundesverfassungsgericht does not influence the jurisprudence of the CJEU, but it means that this mutual relationship is undoubtedly shaped by certain hierarchical structures.[561]

Supremacy in application (*nota bene*: not in validity) necessarily implies a normative hierarchy, and in guaranteeing a core nucleus of shared values vital to the integrity of the Union legal order,[562] the CJEU has no choice but to follow a thoroughly hierarchical approach.[563] And even if one assumes that EU law and national law are derived from two different legal sources, this does not impinge on the concept of a hierarchical relationship between them—at least not on a hierarchical concept that differs from the Stufenbau doctrine and the chain of validity in terms of the pure theory of law. Thus, it is only consequential that the national courts accepted the supremacy of EU law and the ultimate judicial authority of the CJEU in the long run.[564] Even eventual and occasional resistance on part of the national courts does not disprove hierarchy; in fact, this only demonstrates that the CJEU and the Member State judiciaries are in disagreement on how exactly to determine this hierarchy.[565]

Supremacy is not a new concept, and if one compares the supremacy of Union law to the supremacy of international law, one will see that an implied supremacy clause

558 Alexander Somek, 'Monism: A Tale of the Undead' in Matej Avbelj and Jan Komárek (eds), *Constitutional Pluralism in the European Union and Beyond* (Hart Publishing, 2012) 343–79.

559 Loughlin (n 556) 25.

560 Piet Eeckhout, 'Human Rights and the Autonomy of EU Law: Pluralism or Integration?' (2013) 66 *Current Legal Problems* 169, 186.

561 Martin Nettesheim, 'EU-Recht und nationales Verfassungsrecht' [2002] *XX FIDE Report* 1, 74.

562 *In concreto*, the uniform interpretation and application of EU law.

563 Koen Lenaerts and José A. Gutiérez-Fons, 'The Constitutional Allocation of Powers and General Principles of EU Law' (2010) 47 *Common Market Law Review* 1629, 1664.

564 Peters, *Elemente* (n 540) 767.

565 Nettesheim, 'EU-Recht und nationales Verfassungsrecht' (n 561) 77.

can be found in every international agreement,[566] and in the context of EU law, in Declaration No 17 to the Treaties. The six founding Member States may or may not have agreed to the development of the supremacy principle in the case law of the Court, but they and all other Member States certainly agreed to it and accepted it when negotiating and ratifying the Lisbon Treaty *plus* Declaration No 17. The main difference between international law *stricto sensu* and Union law is, however, that the former has never claimed for its directly effective norms to become part of national law and to prevail over inconsistent norms of national law within national law.[567]

The *Melloni* case[568] is, in this regard, the best example for the existence of a hierarchical relationship between national and EU law as well as the anti-pluralist claim that conflicts can be resolved from within the law.[569] When asked whether a conviction *in absentia* in Italy and the request to Spain to surrender the convicted violated fair trial rights under the Spanish Constitution, the CJEU interpreted the Charter in the light of the relevant case law of the ECtHR[570] and ruled that the respective provisions of the European Arrest Warrant did not violate the fundamental right to a fair and public trial. Furthermore, and more crucially, it also held that Spanish constitutional law could not provide for a higher standard of protection if this interfered with the supremacy of Union law and thereby compromised its unity and effectiveness.[571] Subsequently—and this is the really remarkable point of this case—when being handed back the case from Luxembourg, the Spanish Constitutional Court unanimously changed its previously held doctrine on fair trial rights in order to reconcile Spanish law with the supremacy of EU law.[572]

The *Melloni* case consequently and quite visibly demonstrates that there are unquestionable limits to the capacities of national courts when dealing with Union law, and the fact that the Spanish Constitutional Court relented to the CJEU's ruling is proof against the pluralist claim of a heterarchical system of systems within the relationship between the Union and the Member States. And even if the Spanish Constitutional Court or the Bundesverfassungsgericht ignored a preliminary ruling or found that a certain EU legal act was indeed ultra vires, such a revolt would not contradict a hierarchical relationship—on the contrary, a revolt is necessarily directed against something already existing, which those revolting against it intend to overcome.[573]

566 Roman Kwiecień, 'The Primacy of European Union Law over National Law under the Constitutional Treaty' in Philipp Dann and Michał Rynkowski (eds), *The Unity of the European Constitution* (Springer, 2010) 74–5.

567 Eeckhout (n 560) 183.

568 Case C-399/11 *Melloni* [2013] ECLI:EU:C:2013:107.

569 Eeckhout (n 560)185.

570 See especially ECtHR, *Medenica v Switzerland*, App no 20491/92, 12 December 2001, paras 56-9; ECtHR, *Sejdovic v Italy*, App no 56581/00 (GC), 1 March 2006, paras 84, 86, and 98; ECtHR, *Haralampiev v Bulgaria*, App no 29648/03, 24 April 2012, paras 32–3.

571 Case C-399/11 *Melloni* (n 568) paras 55–64.

572 Tribunal constitucional, *Melloni*, Sentencia 26/2014, 13 February 2014.

573 Jochen Frowein, 'Die Europäisierung des Verfassungsrechts' in Peter Badura and Horst Dreier (eds), *Festschrift 50 Jahre Bundesverfassungsgericht—Band 1: Verfassungsgerichtsbarkeit—Verfassungsprozess* (Mohr-Siebeck, 2001) 214.

This fact, however, does not exclude the possibility that the CJEU enters into a dialogue with the national courts and works in cooperation with them. Again, conflicts between the EU and the Member States can be resolved from within the existing law, since Article 4(2) and (3) TEU can be regarded as EU law-inherent exceptions to the principle of absolute supremacy.[574] Article 4(2) TEU ensures that the 'Union shall respect [the Member States'] ... national legal identities, inherent in their fundamental structures, political and constitutional, inclusive of regional and local self-government'. This provision can certainly be interpreted as endorsing a pluralist vision of EU law, but it is much more plausible to see it as an exception to the rule of supremacy. In *Sayn-Wittgenstein*, for instance, the Court declared that the Austrian law on the abolition of nobility, effectively refusing to recognize all noble elements of a surname that were lawful in another Member State, was a legitimate and justified restriction on the free movement of persons. The reason for this was the respect for Austria's national identity as a Republic[575] and its historically contentious relationship with monarchy. Similarly, the CJEU did not shy away in the *Omega* case from giving precedence to the value of human dignity, as enshrined in Article 1 GG, over the free movement of goods. The simulated killing of other persons with laser guns can lawfully be prohibited, as the product in question is considered to be an affront to human dignity[576]—a right whose protection plays a pivotal role in Germany, given the atrocious crimes committed during the Second World War.

Beyond the protection of national identity, Article 4(3) TEU lays down the principle of sincere cooperation which obligates both the Union and the Member States, 'in full mutual respect, [to] assist each other in carrying out tasks which flow from the Treaties'. This provision thus complements Article 4(2) TEU and indicates the EU's duty to show consideration for the Member States' most fundamental constitutional norms and not to go beyond the competences which were conferred upon the Union. To conclude, these provisions permitting the Court a certain degree of judicial deference perfectly fit within the Union's claimed supremacy, as they do not question these conceptions, but presuppose them as a rule and accordingly formulate exceptions to them.[577]

Similar legal provisions regarding exceptions also exist in national law, especially in federally organized states such as Germany or Austria. Although Article 31 GG principally provides that federal law prevails over conflicting state law, it is now an established constitutional principle that the federation must show due consideration to the *Länder*,[578] particularly in cases where federal actions might otherwise encroach upon their competences.[579] The same principle applies in Austria where the federal government is also bound to respect the 'relative constitutional

[574] Peters, *Elemente* (n 540) 289–91.
[575] Case C-208/09 *Sayn-Wittgenstein* [2010] ECR I-13693, para 92.
[576] Case C-36/02 *Omega-Spielhallen* [2004] ECR I-9609, paras 39–41.
[577] Claes (n 557) 203.
[578] See e.g. BVerfGE 106, 310—*Zuwanderungsgesetz*, 18 December 2002, para 128.
[579] See e.g. BVerfGE 111, 226—*Juniorprofessur*, 27 July 2004.

autonomy' of the states[580] and to show due consideration to other regional authorities.[581] In conclusion, it needs to be mentioned that not only has the German Bundesverfassungsgericht already used the German constitutional principle of co-operation to relate to its manifestation in Union law,[582] but that it is also a very strong argument against pluralism that such exceptions also exist in nation states whose normative hierarchical structure and legal unity is beyond any doubt.

ii. Pluralism's incompatibility with pacta sunt servanda *and legal validity*

The second major argument against legal pluralism is that this concept, thought through to the end, claims that all legal systems, partly overlapping and conflicting with one another concerning the same acts and actors, are, at any point of time, equally valid. But thereby pluralism denies the legal consequences resulting from violations of the law, as the act in question might be unlawful within one legal system, but perfectly lawful within another one. Consequently, pluralism becomes incompatible with the principle of *pacta sunt servanda* which, besides its fundamental role in public international law, is as old and ubiquitous as the law itself.[583] One could even say, in more controversial terms, that this principle may be regarded as the positive legal foundation of the validity of all norms, historically predating all constitutions. For a contract or treaty (and thus legal rights and obligations) can necessarily only exist if parties are validly bound by it and if they cannot unilaterally withdraw from it on a whim, but only in accordance with the law in general or with the specific provisions of the contract or treaty in question.[584]

Thus, a pluralist view of the relationship between EU and Member State law would practically undermine the foundations of the law itself and fail, from a theoretical perspective, to provide a meaningful explanation of legal reality. From a practical perspective, pluralism equally fails, as positive law demonstrates. For the CJEU itself, the public international law principle of *pacta sunt servanda* is intrinsically connected with the ratification of the Treaties as a ground for the supremacy of Union law over national law.[585] Even MacCormick admits that the principle of *pacta sunt servanda*, 'as a more natural interpretation' and an overarching validating norm, needs to be taken into account to resolve normative conflicts.[586] However, it has also been argued that the principle itself might prove inapplicable as well as insufficient to justify the supreme status of EU law.[587]

In fact, if one follows this approach through to its conclusion, it becomes obvious that the principle of *pacta sunt servanda* is fundamentally incompatible

580 VfGH, VfSlg 11.669/1988; VfGH, VfSlg 16.241/2001. This autonomy is relative, as it remains limited by the fundamental principles of the Federal Constitution.

581 See e.g. VfGH, No G 5/80, VfSlg 8831/1980.

582 BVerfGE 89, 155—*Maastricht* (n 524) para 94; BVerfGE 75, 223—*Kloppenburg*, 8 April 1987, paras 25 and 48; BVerfGE 123, 267—*Lissabon*, 30 June 2009, paras 240 and 304.

583 See e.g. C. Wilfred Jenks, *The Common Law of Mankind* (Stevens & Sons, 1958) 143–5.

584 Peters, 'Rechtsordnungen und Konstitutionalisierung' (n 407) 53.

585 Case 6/60 *Humblet* [1960] ECR 559, 569; Case 9/65 *San Michele SpA* [1967] ECR 27, 30.

586 MacCormick, 'Risking Constitutional Collision' (n 530) 520, 527, and 531; MacCormick, *Questioning Sovereignty* (n 523) 117–21.

587 Marcus Klamert, *The Principle of Loyalty in EU Law* (Oxford University Press, 2014) 42.

with the *ex hypothesi* autonomy of EU law. Applying this principle to the relationship between national and EU law would entail that the individual ratifying acts of the Union Treaties by the Member States would constitute the ultimate legal basis for the full effect of EU law within the national legal orders. Accordingly, Union law would be partitioned into as many territorial acts as there are Member States, each having an independent legal basis, which would also be subject to review by the national (constitutional) courts. Such fragmentation would necessarily entail a denial of the indivisible and autonomous character of the EU legal order.[588]

Instead it has been suggested that it was their becoming a member through which the Member States have voluntarily accepted a 'workable supremacy'.[589] Consequently, to accept this supremacy voluntarily also means that compliance with it is not optional, but mandatory. In this light, it appears to be more apposite to discuss again the principle of sincere cooperation in Article 4(3) TEU as the bedrock of the requirement that Member States must not act contrary to their obligations under Union law. The case law of the CJEU on the development of the supremacy principle indeed demonstrates that the principle of sincere cooperation or loyalty is inspired and yet distinct from and far more enhanced than the more general concept of *pacta sunt servanda*:[590] on the one hand, the observance of legal obligations in good faith is at the heart of both *pacta sunt servanda* and the EU principle of loyalty,[591] as 'only together and in unison can the Member States act as treaty architects to change the direction of the integration project and create a revised common baseline'.[592] On the other hand, however, loyalty also encompasses other doctrines, such as state liability, which entails the duty of the Member States to adapt and rectify their national law in accordance with their obligations under EU law.[593] It is well known that Member States that fail to implement EU directives can, under certain conditions, be held liable by individuals before the CJEU,[594] even for breaches of EU law committed by national courts.[595] Given the constitutional principle of the separation of powers in the Member States, national resistance against this wide concept of state liability, potentially interfering with the independence of the judiciary, was expected. In fact, however, there is so far no proof that the Member State

588 René Barents, *The Autonomy of Community Law* (Kluwer, 2004) 16.

589 Case C-5/94 *Hedley Lomas* [1996] ECR I-2553, Opinion of Advocate General Léger, paras 106–7.

590 Case C-203/07 P *Greece v Commission (Abuja Project)* [2008] ECR I-8161, Opinion of Advocate General Mázak, para 83.

591 Klamert (n 587) 42–3.

592 Markus Puder, 'Supremacy of the Law and Judicial Review in the European Union: Celebrating *Marbury v. Madison* with *Costa v. ENEL*' (2004) 36 *George Washington International Law Review* 567, 579.

593 Klamert (n 587) 131–3.

594 See especially Joined Cases C-6/90 and C-9/90 *Francovich* (n 526) paras 33–6; Joined Cases C-46/93 and C-48/93 *Brasserie du Pêcheur and Factortame* [1996] ECR I-1029, paras 38–40 and 51; Joined Cases C-178/94, C-179/94 and C-188/94 to C-190/94 *Dillenkofer* [1996] ECR I-4845, paras 23 and 26–7.

595 Case C-224/01 *Köbler* [2003] ECR I-10239, paras 33–6.

courts would generally defy the respective requirements as stated by CJEU.[596] And even if national courts do so, as the Italian Corte Suprema di Cassazione did in *Traghetti*—first, when it declined to request an obligatory preliminary ruling, thus incurring state liability for the violation of Union law;[597] and, secondly, when it refused to comply with the CJEU's subsequent judgment[598]—there is no doubt that the relationship between the Member States and the EU is shaped by hierarchy and compulsion.[599] In the case of non-compliance, the binding nature of EU law will be enforced by the Commission through infringements proceedings under Article 258 TFEU, as in *Traghetti*, against the defaulting state.[600] As an interim conclusion, it should therefore be emphasized that legal pluralism—by reference to the existence of heterarchical legal structures, the resolvability of normative conflicts not through law but politics, and the synchronous equal validity of legal norms—is consequently not capable of providing a very convincing explanation for the interplay between the Member States and the EU at this point.

The explanatory flaws of legal pluralism become even more obvious when we look further into the preliminary ruling procedure under Article 267 TFEU. Given the dialogic format of this procedure, through which national courts can communicate with the CJEU, it has been characterized and described as a pluralist tool and hence a prime example of the management of overlapping or conflicting jurisdictional claims.[601] This pluralist outlook is, however, incorrect. Preliminary references are indeed essentially cooperative, but the agenda of this cooperation and the rules of engagement are exclusively set by the CJEU,[602] in particular when it comes to the obligation to request a preliminary ruling under Article 267(3) TFEU. This is now all the more the case, as national constitutional courts, which for a long time avoided such a formal cooperation with the CJEU on the basis of Article 267 TFEU, have now begun to request preliminary rulings for the first time.[603]

As has been shown above in the *Traghetti* case, the Member States and their courts may certainly refuse to give effect to Union law on grounds of violation of national constitutional law, but it is evident that such a breach of EU law will go neither unnoticed nor unpunished. A flouting of the binding effect of Union law and its supremacy in a pluralist sense is therefore not very persuasive, especially when considering the opinion of Advocate General Villalón in the *OMT* case, which was

[596] Björn Beutler, 'State Liability for Breaches of Community Law by National Courts: Is the Requirement of a Manifest Infringement of the Applicable Law an Insurmountable Obstacle?' (2009) 46 *Common Market Law Review* 773, 790.

[597] Case C-173/03 *Traghetti del Mediterraneo (TDM)* [2006] ECR I-5177, para 32.

[598] Corte Suprema di Cassazione, *Traghetti*, Decision of 10 June 2010.

[599] Takis Tridimas, 'The ECJ and the National Courts: Dialogue, Cooperation, and Instability' in Anthony Arnull and Damian Chalmers (eds), *The Oxford Handbook of European Union Law* (Oxford University Press, 2015) 407.

[600] Case C-379/10 *Commission v Italy (Failure to Fulfil Obligations)* [2011] ECR I-180.

[601] Walker, 'Idea of Constitutional Pluralism' (n 523) 347.

[602] Klamert (n 587) 213.

[603] See the very first request by the Bundesverfassungsgericht in BVerfGE 134, 366—*OMT*, 14 January 2014; the first request by the Spanish Tribunal Constitucional in the *Melloni* case, Pleno. Auto 86/2011, 9 June 2011, and the first request by the French Conseil Constitutionnel, *Jeremy F.*, Decision no 2013-314P QPC, 4 April 2013.

referred to the CJEU by the Bundesverfassungsgericht. He clarified once again that a reference for a preliminary ruling is not a procedural mechanism which is intended to facilitate the national courts' own validity review of EU acts. The overall purpose of the procedure under Article 267 TFEU is to safeguard that the review of validity is carried out uniformly, and this is only possible before the judicial body having exclusive jurisdiction to do so: the Court of Justice. This means that a national court is not permitted to include in a request for such a ruling the possibility that it will in fact later depart from the answer received. If it were possible for national courts to reserve for themselves the last word on the validity of EU legal acts, the preliminary ruling procedure would become merely advisory in nature and its functioning within the framework of the Treaties would be severely undermined.[604]

A pluralist reading of this procedure that would allow national courts to disregard the decisions of the CJEU because they claim the last say within national law, is hence not compatible with the fundamental principle of *pacta sunt servanda* and, a fortiori, the principle of sincere cooperation and loyalty as enshrined in Article 4(3) TEU. Accordingly, the Bundesverfassungsgericht eventually accepted the CJEU's preliminary ruling in *OMT*,[605] which therefore speaks against a pluralist interpretation of the relationship between EU and national law.

In conclusion, it is consequently evident that a pluralist outlook on the relationship between the European Union and the Member States is untenable. This relationship is undoubtedly shaped by (i) hierarchically structured enforcement mechanisms, not heterarchical co-existence without any formal links. These enforcement mechanisms can (ii) be found in EU law itself, and do not require informal political resolution. And (iii) these enforcement mechanisms allow to guarantee the supremacy of EU law over contravening Member State law, as they have accepted this very supremacy when becoming an EU Member State and cannot unilaterally disregard it. In this light, a pluralist view of the relationship between EU and Member State law fails at explaining this very relationship. If one follows the notion that the boundaries of the constitutional competence for the transfer of sovereign rights are not reliably established and that the cooperation of national and European organs is not sufficiently clarified, then this makes *tabula rasa* of EU law and totally ignores the preliminary reference procedure. This procedure, however, undoubtedly connects Member State law with the EU legal order and introduces a quasi-hierarchical principle, obligating the Member State courts in specific situations to refer a case to the CJEU.[606] Furthermore, conflicts between EU and national law are indeed resolvable, and within the scope of application of Union law, conflicts are resolved in favour of the supremacy of Union law and the disapplication of the contravening national norm.[607] Ultimately, legal pluralism fails to see that the law of the Member States and the EU are interlocked in certain hierarchical ways (even

[604] Case C-62/14 *OMT* [2015] ECLI:EU:C:2015:7, Opinion of Advocate General Villalón, paras 35 and 36.

[605] BVerfG, 2 BvR 2728/13, 2 BvR 2729/13, 2 BvR 2730/13, 2 BvR 2731/13, 2 BvE 13/13—*OMT II*, 21 June 2016.

[606] Baquero Cruz (n 527) 407 and 414.

[607] Case 106/77 *Simmenthal II* (n 526) para 17.

though it remains to be seen where the overall *Grundnorm* is to be localized). An anarchic plurality of legal orders without any means of integration and coordination is no *legal* order, and the term 'legal pluralism' is reduced to an oxymoron[608] that is not only entirely incompatible with the principle of *pacta sunt servanda*, but also leaves the resolution of normative conflicts to politics instead of the law, and surrenders individuals to the mercy of a legal *aporia*.[609]

iii. Arguments against the multiplication and free choice theses

The last major argument against legal pluralism in this context pertains to issues concerning the pluralist multiplication of the *Grundnorm* and the so-called 'free choice thesis'. These versions of legal pluralism envisage a pluralism of legal systems and basic norms which aim at construing the pure theory of law as compatible with legal pluralism.[610] With respect to the first view—let us call it for convenience the 'simple multiplication thesis'—it must be clearly underlined right at the beginning that a pluralist interpretation is utterly irreconcilable with the monist identity thesis that only one single legal order can be valid at the same spatial and temporal point.[611]

In order to set up his multiplication thesis, Grussmann correctly presumes at the outset that the ground of validity of the EU legal order is not derived from one single national legal order. Consequently, since the CJEU claims that Union law is autonomous, one must necessarily presuppose a *Grundnorm* of EU law, which may have developed through a legal revolution besides the pre-existing basic norms of the respective Member States. This contention is, in his view, also sufficiently supported by the relevant case law of the CJEU and the Bundesverfassungsgericht. Hence, by presupposing several different *Grundnormen*, the relationship between national and EU law no longer hinges on the concept and ground of validity. This step, according to Grussmann, leads to an understanding of this relationship in which there can be no normative conflicts in terms of validity, but only conflicts in terms of differing obligations, which, admittedly, may result in considerable dilemmas on the part of the norm addressee.[612] The norm addressee, i.e. the natural or legal person in question, must then concretely decide on a case-by-case basis what legal norm on the basis of what *Grundnorm* they accept as binding on themselves.[613]

[608] Loughlin (n 556) 23–4.

[609] Peters, 'Rechtsordnungen und Konstitutionalisierung' (n 407) 53; Matthias Jestaedt, 'Der Europäische Verfassungsverbund' in Christian Calliess (ed), *Verfassungswandel im europäischen Staaten- und Verfassungsverbund* (Mohr-Siebeck, 2007) 123.

[610] As suggested by, inter alia, Grussmann (n 138) 47–64; Richmond (n 496) 409–10 and 417–18; Udo di Fabio, 'Richtlinienkonformität als ranghöchstes Auslegungsprinzip? Überlegungen zum Einfluss des indirekten Gemeinschaftsrechts auf die nationale Rechtsordnung' (1990) 43 *Neue Juristische Wochenschrift* 947, 950–1.

[611] See Hans Kelsen, 'Die philosophischen Grundlagen der Naturrechtslehre und des Rechtspositivismus' in Hans R. Klecatsky, René Marcic, and Herbert Schambeck (eds), *Die Wiener rechtstheoretische Schule: Schriften von Hans Kelsen, Adolf Merkl, Alfred Verdross, Band 1* (Verlag Österreich, 2010) 247–52; Kelsen, *Allgemeine Staatslehre* (n 302) 130–2.

[612] Grussmann (n 138) 59–64; Bindreiter, *Why* Grundnorm*?* (n 520) 202.

[613] Jestaedt, 'Der Europäische Verfassungsverbund' (n 609) 124; Josef Isensee, 'Vorrang des Europarechts und deutsche Verfassungsvorbehalte—offener Dissens' in Joachim Burmeister (ed), *Verfassungsstaatlichkeit: Festschrift für Klaus Stern zum 65. Geburtstag* (C.H. Beck, 1997) 1239.

The pivotal problem with this argument is, however, that the source of bindingness of a given legal norm is none other than the subjective acceptance of this legal norm by the norm addressee, and thus, the conflict in terms of obligations necessarily presupposes the subjective acceptance of both legal norms in conflict with each other as *valid* norms. This argument therefore merely begs the question,[614] because if we think, for example, of public officials and their daily work, then they cannot simply regard a foreign legal order as entirely disconnected from domestic law. If they take notice of this foreign legal order and consider it to be domestically valid, then they will necessarily consider it as either inferior or superior to their own legal order.[615] Otherwise, they would never be able to resolve any legal issues resulting from the interplay between EU and national law, which would in turn contradict the positive legal principle of *Rechtstaatlichkeit* in the sense that any person must always be capable of recognizing what is legally required of them.[616] Examples of such positive legal norms include Article 20(3) GG in Germany or Article 18 B-VG in Austria, which state that the law binds all branches of the state and that all of their acts must be in accordance with the law.

Whatever normative conflicts between national and EU law are called, it is evident that legal pluralism does not only willingly accept them, but must also necessarily result in them. If we really regard EU and national law as entirely distinct in terms of validity, then this view also entails that every body of law claims the exclusive power and authorization to enforce the law and sanction any violations of it within itself. But this would also mean that if one body of law, say the EU, imposes a certain sanction for a breach of its law, for which there is no legal basis or authorization in national law, then the Member State would, in turn, also need to sanction this measure. The consequence of this would be a 'struggle for the law' and a deeply unpeaceful co-existence, which has, however, no empirical grounding. Certain Member State courts may grudgingly protest against the CJEU and its case law, but such a veritable legal war between the courts has definitely not transpired in reality.[617]

Even if we assume that Union law is only effective because the Member States allow for this, this does not undermine the argument against pluralism: in this case, officials and private individuals alike would localize the *Grundnorm* at the national level. If these officials and individuals, however, feel more inspired by the European project, then they may even presuppose the basic norm within EU law.[618] But they would never localize it simultaneously at the national level and the EU law, as this would subject them to a normative dilemma in the case of conflict. In fact, the multiple forms of interweaving between the law of the EU and the Member States speak against a pluralist multiplication of the *Grundnorm*. Both legal bodies refer to each

[614] Bindreiter, *Why* Grundnorm*?* (n 520) 202.
[615] Schilling, 'Zum Verhältnis' (n 548) 150. See also Kelsen, *Problem der Souveränität* (n 25) 102 ff.
[616] Theodor Schilling, *Rang und Geltung von Normen in gestuften Rechtsordnungen* (Nomos, 1994) 377.
[617] Jan Vollmeyer, *Der Staat als Rechtsordnung: Hans Kelsens Identitätsthese und ihre Bedeutung für den europäischen Konstitutionalisierungsprozess* (Nomos, 2011) 291–2.
[618] Schilling, 'Zum Verhältnis' (n 548) 151–2.

other and can therefore not be considered as several autonomous orders, but only as different levels of one single and common legal order.[619]

If we take again the preliminary ruling procedure, it becomes even more evident that the EU system of legal protection is proof for the supremacy of Union law and thus the unity of the legal order of EU and Member States. This kind of procedure implies and presupposes that EU legal acts are valid, applicable, and supreme within domestic law, and that individuals can rely on them and effectively enforce them before national courts. Lastly, it also relieves them, national judges, and other officials from the above-mentioned conflict in terms of obligation.[620] Thus, it appears to be more consistent not to take recourse to any form of a *Grundnorm* in a pluralist setting, as it is not only its very duplication or multiplication that betrays its crucial axiom, namely its norm-logical unity,[621] but also its inaccuracy in terms of the positive law.

A similar pluralist view that attempts to make fruitful use of the *Grundnorm* is the so-called 'free choice thesis', which allows for a free choice of the observer's viewpoint.[622] Under this hypothesis, the ever-changing point of view of the observer can be duly taken into account, and allows the observer to consider the national *Grundnorm* to be the correct one from the national perspective, and to regard the *Grundnorm* of EU law to be the correct one from a supranational perspective.[623] Legal orders can freely govern their mutual relationships, which means that answers to questions of autonomy, primacy, and the resolution of normative conflicts entirely depend on the observer's premises. Logical notions such as 'true' or 'false' cease to exist,[624] and the respective observers find themselves outside the perceived legal orders and see them as regulating their mutual relationship differently, yet equally plausibly.[625]

The opinion that every scholar and scientist is entirely free to choose his or her object of observation is of course correct and not to be criticized. At the same time, it is, however, equally correct that such a choice has a binding effect on the further course of action. This means that the observing scholar is not as free as thought in the first place. The pure theory of law, for example, avails itself of this freedom of choice by considering itself as 'a theory of positive law in general, not of a specific legal order' and by cognizing law as an effective and coercive legal order.[626] Moreover, this choice also includes the critical element of cognizing law as 'valid', which means that certain norms form part of a given legal order and that they are to be complied with[627] until formally invalidated by the competent authority.[628] As a consequence,

[619] Jestaedt, 'Der Europäische Verfassungsverbund' (n 609) 121.

[620] Olivier Gänswein, *Der Grundsatz unionsrechtskonformer Auslegung nationalen Rechts* (Peter Lang, 2009) 298.

[621] Wendel (n 539) 24; Schroeder (n 486) 249–50 and 254.

[622] Schilling, 'Verhältnis' (n 549) 153 ff.

[623] Richmond (n 496) 409–10 and 417–18; Schroeder (n 486) 250.

[624] Isensee, 'Vorrang des Europarechts' (n 613) 1265.

[625] Maduro, 'Contrapunctual Law' (n 521) 501.

[626] Kelsen, *Pure Theory* (n 24) 1 and 33 ff.

[627] Kelsen, *General Theory* (n 26) 35.

[628] Kelsen, *General Theory of Norms* (n 299) 108.

pluralism under the free choice by the observer becomes meaningless because it regards, just as traditional dualism does, legal validity in terms of degree. However, despite its critical stance towards the case law of the CJEU, not even the German Bundesverfassungsgericht disputes the legal validity of European Union law; it has warned that it might, *in extremis*, refuse to apply and give effect to Union law within the domestic legal order, but this is not the same as disputing and rejecting the validity of EU legal acts. Therefore, the thesis that any observer (above all a legal scientist) may cognize several unrelated legal orders, which all possess their own *Grundnorm*,[629] but are nonetheless equally valid, is a *petitio principii*.[630] The pluralist construction of the basic norm can therefore not be salvaged by a mere change in perspective of the observer, e.g. from the CJEU to the Bundesverfassungsgericht or vice versa, on the basis of a 'normative shuffling'.[631] Beyond that, this is a contradiction in itself, as only those norms can be considered valid within a given legal order whose origin can be traced back to the *Grundnorm* of this legal order.[632]

Pluralism hence appears to fall victim to an unresolvable paradox. This paradox can be found in the pluralist assumption that the European Union itself is, on an equal footing with the Member States, treated as an original and autonomous source of legal power. However, from a historical and international law perspective, it is entirely unquestionable that the Union is a creation of the Member States on the basis of international treaties and hence derives all powers from them through these very treaties.[633] Regardless of the question of whether these treaties evolved into a quasi-constitution later on, one must accept as a fact that all predecessor organizations of the EU were conceived as international organizations and that its birth certificate is an international treaty or sequence of treaties.[634]

Once concluded, these treaties may certainly take on a life of their own, and they may well be called autonomous in the sense that they are not continuously dependent on the national legal orders from which they are derived. But this autonomy nonetheless remains historically derivative from the individual ratifying acts of the Member States.[635] Even the principle of conferral in Article 5(2) TEU and the CJEU itself in *Costa v ENEL* concede that a transfer of powers from the Member States to the Union must have taken place in the beginning,[636] and this derivative nature cannot be adequately described and understood by a pluralist conception which regards the EU and the Member States as equally holding non-delegated

[629] Schilling, 'Verhältnis' (n 549) 155.

[630] Rill, 'Internationales, supranationales und nationales Recht' (n 102) 699.

[631] As suggested by Richmond (n 496) 409–10 and 417–18. Cf. the criticism by Schroeder (n 486) 250.

[632] Heiko Sauer, 'Vorrang ohne Hierarchie' (2013) 44 *Rechtstheorie* 503, 516; Öhlinger, 'Einheit' (n 139) 162–3.

[633] Martin Borowski, 'Legal Pluralism in the European Union' in Agustín José Menéndez and John Erik Fossum (eds), *Law and Democracy in Neil MacCormick's Legal and Political Theory* (Springer, 2011) 201.

[634] Robert Schütze, 'On "Federal" Ground: The European Union as an (Inter)National Phenomenon' (2009) 46 *Common Market Law Review* 1069, 1079.

[635] Theodor Schilling, 'The Autonomy of the Community Legal Order: An Analysis of Possible Foundations' (1996) 37 *Harvard International Law Journal* 389, 404.

[636] Case 6/64 *Costa v ENEL* (n 485) 593 and 594.

powers. To put it even more drastically by way of a thought experiment proposed by Martin Borowski, legal pluralism would principally not distinguish in the relation between the EU and the Member States if the Union had not been established via treaties ratified by the Member States, but had been created by means of coercion through a non-European force. Hence sovereign rights would not have been voluntarily transferred, but forcefully usurped by the European institutions.

This conception demonstrates that legal pluralism would, however, not see any decisive difference between the two scenarios: the legal system of the EU would be existent, socially effective, and lay claim to original and autonomous powers, and since this system would also be capable of restraining Member State law, one would have to concede to a plurality of legal systems. As a result, it must be emphasized that legal pluralism ignores the difference between voluntarily transferred and usurped powers, and such a conception is incapable of grasping the specific nature of EU law as historically derived from national law.[637]

Legal pluralism in general and the conception of various *Grundnormen* within a pluralist setting are therefore equally implausible and should be abandoned, because it amounts to nothing other than a *contradictio in adiecto*.[638] As discussed above, if one indeed assumes that there is a norm-genetical connection between EU and national law, then it seems to be based, *prima facie*, on the Member States' historical use of public international law, namely the very international treaties through which the EU was established. However, even though this model effectively discards legal pluralism as a viable theory to explain the relationship between Union and national law, it does not conform to the principle supremacy of EU law within a unitary legal order, as claimed by the CJEU. In fact, this 'international law' or 'derivative' thesis essentially amounts to a monist view under the primacy of national law, which would nevertheless undermine the supremacy, effectiveness, and unity of the European Union legal order. Such a fragmented legal order would certainly be unacceptable for the EU institutions and especially the CJEU. Yet, to date, the emphasis has exclusively been on terms such as 'historical' or 'historically derived', and the subsequent sections on monism will therefore discuss the extent to which this assumption is different from the question of whether one system is norm-logically derived from another.[639]

d. Conclusion: the shortcomings of legal pluralism

The previous sections have shown that the concept of legal pluralism in all its manifestations is utterly unable to sustain the claims made on its behalf. They all fail to offer a coherent description of and empirical evidence for their claims about the nature of existing relations between the Member States.[640] The legal observer must

[637] Borowski (n 633) 201–2.

[638] Schroeder (n 486) 262; Pavlos Eleftheriadis, 'Begging the Constitutional Question' (1998) 36 *Journal of Common Market Studies* 255, 259; Peter Badura, 'Supranationalität und Bundesstaatlichkeit durch Rangordnung des Rechts' in Jürgen Schwarze (ed), *Verfassungsrecht und Verfassungsgerichtsbarkeit im Zeichen Europas* (Nomos, 1998) 64 ff.

[639] See especially sections 3B(4) and 3B(5) below.

[640] Loughlin (n 556) 29.

certainly concede that the potential for a veritable conflict between national and EU law is deeply embedded in the system, but to this date prudence and pragmatism on both sides have successfully managed to prevent such conflicts from transpiring and escalating. The CJEU and the national courts may reach their decisions through different avenues, arguments, and normative starting points, but usually they arrive at convergent and compatible results.[641]

A scrutinizing look at the law as it is reveals that a pluralist rejection of hierarchy in this relationship is unsustainable, because EU law provides for hierarchically structured enforcement mechanisms to secure the application of Union legal acts over conflicting national legal norms. If the Member States refuse to comply, sanctions on part of the Union institutions can and will follow to safeguard the functioning of the EU legal order, which speaks against the pluralist assumption of heterarchical co-existence. There certainly are exceptions to this hierarchy and supremacy to allow for constitutional autonomy in sensitive areas, but EU law itself, not national law, regulates these exceptions. Equally, legal pluralism is entirely incompatible with the principle of *pacta sunt servanda* and legal validity, as the Member States freely and voluntarily entered into their obligations under EU law, which means that they must also comply with them. If they could choose and pick between different obligations and whether to follow them at times or not, the law itself would ultimately be undermined, and that is something no Member State has in mind. What would otherwise be the added explanatory value of a *legal* theory that tries to describe a plurality of legal systems, helplessly circling in autonomy, but that, on the same account, fails to explain that conflicts between these systems can be resolved on the basis of the *law*?[642]

In this respect, legal pluralism remains dangerously distant from legal reality and ignores that EU law forms, from both the national and supranational perspective,[643] an integral part of all national legal orders and takes effect within them. In applying the law, one legal norm will always prevail over another, regardless of whether the prevailing norm is national or supranational in nature. Thus, at this point, the question of which body of law sits at the top of this hierarchy is irrelevant (even though EU law seems to be the more plausible candidate in terms of applicability), since the very existence of a hierarchical structure speaks against a pluralist heterarchy of systems. Therefore, the pluralist equivocation in the concept of legal validity is entirely at odds with the *lex lata* and pluralists should honestly acknowledge that what they are talking about is no longer law.[644] In fact, the pluralist construction of the relationship between national and EU law appears simply to shift the predominant problems (above all, legal autonomy in all its facets: supremacy, legislative and judicial *Kompetenz-Kompetenz*, etc.) from the *legal* to the *extra-legal* sphere, which is of no use to the law itself and its problems at all.

[641] Baquero Cruz (n 527) 418; Maduro, 'Contrapunctual Law' (n 521) 524.

[642] Marcel Kaufmann, 'Permanente Verfassungsgebung und verfassungsrechtliche Selbstbindung im europäischen Staatenverbund' (1997) 36 *Der Staat* 521, 542; Schroeder (n 486) 253.

[643] Case 106/77 *Simmenthal II* (n 526) paras 17–18, and BVerfGE 73, 339—*Solange II*, 22 October 1986, 367.

[644] Alexander Somek, 'Kelsen Lives' (2007) 18 *European Journal of International Law* 409, 425.

Having said that, it is now also clear that the pluralist use of certain elements of the pure theory of law, most eminently the *Grundnorm*, cannot be grounded in empirical facts. A duplication or multiplication of the basic norm is not only theoretically and epistemologically meaningless, but also not verifiable on the basis of the positive law. If there is indeed a norm-genetical connection between national and EU law then, historically speaking, Union law is derived from Member State law (leaving aside subsequent developments at this point). And although this view disproves legal pluralism, it is not unproblematic either, as it undermines the position of a unitary EU legal order across all Member States. This issue will therefore be discussed later on, since it now seems that EU law may be superior in applicability, but not validity, and this divergence needs to be resolved or at least meaningfully explained in order to save monism.

In conclusion, it must be underscored again that legal pluralism should be abandoned as a theory to explain the relationship between EU and national law. In addition to highly contentious theoretical problems (above all the ultimate collapse of pluralism into either dualism or monism[645]), issues concerning its empirical explanatory power abound as well. This in itself does of course not verify a monist conception of this relationship, but it first of all shows that alternative models are not successful and should be challenged. The following sections will therefore focus on the traditional theories of dualism and monism.

(3) Dualism of European Union and national law

a. The paradoxes of direct effect and supremacy

In contrast to legal pluralism, a dualist view of the relationship between EU and Member State law does not accept an overlap and thus a temporal and spatial coexistence of these two bodies of law, but a tangency of them at the most. Even moderate dualism, which allows for an interpenetration of distinct legal orders, resolves the question of domestic legal effects of 'foreign' law on the basis of national legal sources. In other words, dualism requires national law to provide for an internal receptor in order to be able to receive Union law, whilst legal pluralism in all its manifestations, acknowledging the parallelism of incommensurable claims of constitutional autonomy, does not. In pluralist terms, EU law is not only valid, but also applicable in its own terms within national law, which may or may not resist these claims.[646]

Constitutional dualism in terms of European Union law has especially been discussed in terms of the relationship between the supremacy and the direct effect of EU law.[647] Whereas the former notion implies an integrated model wherein Union

645 Loughlin (n 556) 29; Eleftheriadis, 'Pluralism and Integrity' (n 529) 375.

646 Franz C. Mayer and Mattias Wendel, 'Multilevel Constitutionalism and Constitutional Pluralism' in Matej Avbelj and Jan Komárek (eds), *Constitutional Pluralism in the European Union and Beyond* (Hart Publishing, 2012) 137.

647 For the constitutional dualist model prevalent in Austria see e.g. Ludwig Adamovich (sen), Bernd-Christian Funk, Gerhart Holzinger, and Stefan Leo Frank, *Österreichisches Staatsrecht I: Grundlagen* (2nd edn; Springer, 2011) paras 01.045 and 17.060; Stefan Griller, 'Der Stufenbau der österreichischen Rechtsordnung nach dem EU-Beitritt' (2000) 8 *Journal für Rechtspolitik* 273, 282.

law implants itself on top of the hierarchy of Member State law, direct effect necessarily presupposes two distinct and separate legal orders of which EU law imposes specific effects on national law.[648] If one accepts the integrated model, direct effect appears as entirely superfluous and as a mere 'infant disease' of Union law.[649] If, conversely, one favours the dualist model of two distinct legal orders, then direct effect as defined in *Van Gen den Loos*[650] is and remains necessary in order to give domestic effect to particular EU legal norms. In this case, only directly effective legal norms enjoy supremacy over conflicting national law, and supremacy is downgraded to a mere remedy to be administered by the national courts in resolving conflicts between Union and national law.[651] One problem with these two models is that the CJEU provides support for both the monist integration and the dualist trigger model. The other problem is that the dualist model might effectively undermine the Union legal order, because if dualism necessarily militates against the idea of integration and causes national courts to regard EU law as a simple component or subspecies of national law,[652] then the Member State courts may always refuse to give direct effect and thus supremacy to Union law[653] (even though the CJEU has already put certain limits to the national judiciaries' procedural autonomy in this regard[654]).

b. Arguments against the explanatory power of dualism

The subsequent sections will now investigate whether the claims of dualism are empirically justified, and whether dualism is therefore better suited to explain and describe the relationship between Union and Member State law. It will be demonstrated that despite its obvious appeal in describing EU and national law as entirely distinct bodies of law, wherein the Member States (allegedly) have the last say as to whether Union acts are valid, applicable, effective, and supreme within domestic law, dualism remains highly problematic. Ultimately, a dualist approach to the relationship between national and Union law fails to describe the law as it is.

i. Not separated, but integrated legal orders

If one takes a closer look at a potential dualist relationship between EU and national law, the limits inherent in this approach become visible. To begin with, it is indisputable that there is a legal connection between national and Union law—regardless of the question of which body of law conditions and delegates the other. Contrary to dualism, these two bodies of law are not independent from each other and indeed

648 Kaarlo Tuori, *European Constitutionalism* (Cambridge University Press, 2015) 67–8.

649 See Pierre Pescatore, 'The Doctrine of Direct Effect: An Infant Disease of Community Law' (1983) 8 *European Law Review* 155–77.

650 Case 26/62 *Van Gend en Loos* [1963] ECR 1, 12.

651 Michael Dougan, 'When Worlds Collide! Competing Visions of the Relationship between Direct Effect and Supremacy' (2007) 44 *Common Market Law Review* 931, 934.

652 Ian Ward, 'Dualism and the Limits of European Integration' (1995) 17 *Liverpool Law Review* 29, 36.

653 Bruno de Witte, 'Direct Effect, Primacy, and the Nature of the Legal Order' in Paul Craig and Gráinne de Búrca (eds), *The Evolution of EU Law* (2nd edn; Oxford University Press, 2011) 339–40 and 346–8.

654 Case C-312/93 *Peterbroeck, Van Campenhout & Cie SCS* [1995] ECR I-4599, para 12.

have normative relevance for one another.[655] In this light, it will be argued that dualism is not defensible, because Union and Member State law form somehow integrated, and not separated, legal orders on the basis of the EU Treaties. Indeed, the negotiations on the European Coal and Steel Community (ECSC) show that it was rather a monist, and not a dualist view, that shaped the design of European integration. The term 'supranationality', especially, appeared spontaneously and was consequently accepted as a matter of fact during these negotiations.[656] It was exactly this term that was previously used by monists to describe the supremacy and direct applicability of international law within municipal legal orders. Especially the work of Hugo Krabbe, who postulated the ordering force of the law beyond the state,[657] was said to have influenced the burgeoning discussion on the relationship between legal orders during this time.[658] Accordingly, the ECSC was already described in the initial stages of the negotiations on the Treaty of Rome as a breaking point with dualism and beyond the traditional categories of the strict dichotomy of national and international law.[659]

Having said that, however, it is indisputably true that the Union Treaties contain some international law elements, first and foremost the instrument of infringement proceedings (Articles 258 and 259 TFEU) as a classical international legal enforcement mechanism between states inter se and between states and the EU institutions, practically excluding individuals. Yet at the same time, the Treaties also include strong signals against this 'ordinary' international reading. As the first anti-dichotomic signal, one must take into consideration a particularly constitutional mechanism, which envisages the direct application of European law by the national courts, namely the preliminary ruling procedure. First, the CJEU made it very clear that the national courts are obliged to apply EU law as valid law, and that they are free to reject the grounds put forward before them in support of the alleged invalidity of a Union legal act, if these grounds are unfounded. However, what they are not permitted to do is to declare such an act invalid on their own volition. Thus, if they have doubts regarding the validity of an EU legal act, they must always refer this case to the CJEU.[660]

Secondly, even if no preliminary ruling is requested, the national courts act as quasi-decentralized Union courts and are under the duty to apply, *ex officio*, EU law in a plethora of policy areas,[661] in particular in competition law. Especially Article 6 of Regulation 1/2003[662] lays down that '[n]ational courts shall have the power to

[655] Barents, *Autonomy* (n 588) 178.

[656] Paul Reuter, 'Le plan Schuman' (1952-II) 81 *Recueil des cours* 519, 545.

[657] Hugo Krabbe, *Die moderne Staatsidee* (2nd edn; Martinus Nijhoff, 1919) 278.

[658] Hauke Delfs, *Komplementäre Integration: Grundlegung und Konstitutionalisierung des Europarechts im Kontext* (Mohr-Siebeck, 2015) 168.

[659] Carl Friedrich Ophüls, 'Vom Internationalen zum Übernationalen' (1952) 2 *Das Parlament* 1, 2; Delfs (n 658) 168–9.

[660] Case 314/85 *Foto-Frost* (n 511) paras 14–15.

[661] Joined Cases C-430/93 and C-431/93 *van Schijndel and van Veen* [1995] ECR I-4705, para 15.

[662] Council Regulation (EC) No 1/2003 of 16 December 2002 on the implementation of the rules on competition laid down in Articles 81 and 82 of the Treaty (text with EEA relevance), OJ L 1–25, 4 January 2003.

apply Articles [101] and [102 TFEU]', i.e. the relevant rules on anti-competitive agreements and the abuse of market power. Last, after a preliminary ruling has been requested and the CJEU has handed down its decision, the referring court is bound by it in its application and interpretation of EU law.[663]

Although the wording of Article 267 TFEU gives the CJEU only the power to interpret the Treaties, and not to apply them to the facts of the particular case, the dividing line between interpretation and application is blurred. The CJEU may of course answer the referred question in such general terms that it effectively defers to the national judiciary on the point in issue or simply provide the national court with guidelines as to how to resolve the dispute. However, since some of the questions submitted to the CJEU are very detailed and intricate, they can only be answered by a very specific response; and the more detailed this interpretation of the CJEU is, the more it approximates application, thereby leaving the referring court no margin for manoeuvre.[664] Hence the first concluding argument against dualism is that Article 267 TFEU undoubtedly establishes a procedural mechanism that connects the Member State courts with the CJEU, and even though this system is not a fully developed federal appellate judiciary, a strictly dualist separation of European and national courts becomes unsustainable in the light of these facts.

The second of these Treaty-inherent anti-dualist indicators is Article 288(2) TFEU. This provision states that regulations are directly applicable within all Member States, which matches an integrated and monist model[665] better than a separated and dualist conception of this relationship. Dualist Member States may claim that the validity, supremacy, and applicability of Union law are all based on the relevant accession statute[666] or the specific constitutional authorization in conjunction with the accession statute,[667] but Article 288(2) TFEU makes it quite clear that it is not up to the Member States any more to decide how or whether an EU regulation becomes law of the land. Regulations do so in their original form and confer rights and duties within the domestic sphere without further legislative participation or transformation. In fact, the CJEU has already held that regulations 'come into force solely by their publication in the Official Journal' and that consequently, transformation not only is unrequired but also impermissible owing to its distorting effects on the effectivity and uniformity of Union law.[668] The principle of transformation, as a core element of and a crucial argument for dualism, however, thereby becomes entirely irrelevant. Thus, through Article 288(2) TFEU itself,

[663] See e.g. Case 69/85 *Wünsche* [1986] ECR 947, para 13; and Case C-173/09 *Elchinov* [2010] ECR I-8889, paras 29–30.

[664] Paul Craig and Gráinne de Búrca, *EU Law: Text, Cases, and Materials* (6th edn; Oxford University Press, 2015) 496–7.

[665] Tuori (n 648) 68.

[666] Thus in e.g. the UK see House of Lords, *R v Secretary of State for Transport (Factortame II)* [1991] 1 AC 603.

[667] Thus in e.g. Germany; see Article 23(1) GG in conjunction with Article 79(3) GG, and BVerfGE 89, 155—*Maastricht* (n 524).

[668] Case 39/72 *Commission v Italy (Slaughtering Premiums for Cows)* [1973] ECR 101, paras 15–17.

dualism becomes irrelevant, and the question of how EU law penetrates national law is no longer for the Member States to answer.[669]

As a counterargument, dualists will certainly point to Article 288(3) TFEU and argue that in contrast to regulations, directives generally require transformation into domestic law in order to be applicable and effective.[670] Directives hence lie closer to the idea of two distinct legal orders and a dualist view of EU and national law.[671] Yet there are a couple of arguments against this view as well: first, forms of cooperative federalism, wherein the federal parliament legislates and the federated legislatures subsequently implement and administer the legal act in question, are not a new thing and quite common across federal systems throughout the world. Examples include Article 12 B-VG in Austria, which authorizes the federal legislature to enact framework statutes (*Grundsatzgesetzgebung*) on certain public services. These statutes are subsequently implemented by the federal states by way of state law. Similarly, Article 75 GG provided for such framework legislation (*Rahmengesetzgebung*) in Germany, which was, however, abolished in the course of the 2006 Federalism Reform.[672] Even centralized, i.e. not federally organized states, such as Italy, rely on legislative instruments, which authorize the regions to implement more detailed legislation based on more generally drafted framework statutes.[673]

Interestingly, in comparison with the EU and the way in which directives are implemented by the Member States, there are certain limits on the United States federal government to implement federal legislation through the individual states. The US Supreme Court only rarely declares laws unconstitutional for violating the Tenth Amendment,[674] which states that the federal government only possesses those powers explicitly delegated to it by the constitution, whilst all other powers remain with the states. It nonetheless clarified that the federal government was not allowed to make use of state officials to enforce its law;[675] that federal law may provide for monetary incentives for states to comply with and implement national statutory law, but that Congress may nevertheless not compel states to enforce federal law;[676] and that federal legislation must not force states effectively to join the federal bureaucracy.[677] Owing to the similarities shared between directives and framework states in national federal systems, it has been remarked that especially the now defunct *Rahmengesetzgebung* in Germany astoundingly resembled the mechanism applied by Article 288(3) TFEU.[678]

[669] Case 94/77 *Zerbone* [1978] ECR 99, para 23.

[670] The potential direct effect of directives is an exception to this rule and will therefore be discussed separately below.

[671] Tuori (n 648) 68.

[672] See German Federal Gazette, BGBl I, Nr 41/2006, 31 August 2006.

[673] See Article 117(3) Costituzione Italiana. Note, however, that the term 'legislazione concorrente' (concurring legislation) appears to be a misnomer in this context.

[674] Erwin Chemerinsky, 'The Rehnquist Court and Justice: An Oxymoron?' (1999) 37 *Washington University Journal of Law and Policy* 1, 39.

[675] *Printz v United States*, 521 US 898 (1997).

[676] *New York v United States*, 505 US 144 (1992).

[677] *National Federation of Independent Business v Sebelius*, 132 S Ct 2566 (2012).

[678] Thomas Vandamme, 'EU Directives and Multilevel Governance—Can Lessons Be Drawn from Cooperative Federalism?' (2014) 21 *Maastricht Journal of European and Comparative Law* 341, 350–2.

The concluding argument against dualism therefore is that there are numerous national legal orders employing the same mechanism as the EU, and nobody disputes their legal unity. In the United States, as discussed above, the principle of cooperative federalism appears to be even weaker than in the European Union and, again, nobody contests the legal unity of the US legal order. The need for subsequent transposition of directives simply arises from the fact that directives are much better suited than directly applicable regulations to respect national legal traditions and to therefore leave as much scope for national decision as possible.[679]

In addition to this comparative analysis, other arguments against directives as evidence for a dualist conception of EU and national law include the wording of Article 288(3) TFEU itself and the subsequent case law of the CJEU. Regarding the former point, it is true that Article 288(3) TFEU leaves the choice of form and methods of implementation to the Member States. But this freedom does not entail that it is up to the Member States to decide whether or not to implement directives. In fact, it does not release them from the obligation to give effect to the provisions of a directive through national provisions of a legally binding nature.[680] The necessity of transposing directives is a requirement of EU law and not of domestic law, and of course not optional. The non-transposition of directives amounts, in the wording of the Court, to a sufficiently serious breach of Union law[681] and may give rise to state liability, if the directive confers identifiable rights on individuals and there is a causal link between the Member State's breach and the damage to the individual.[682] Regarding the latter point, the Court also clarified that the Member States must—even before the expiry of the transposition period—'refrain from taking any measures liable seriously to compromise the result prescribed'[683] by the directive in question. This means that, whilst directives may not be directly applicable in the same way as regulations, they form part of EU law and thereby also of national law from the time they enter into force, and not only as of their effective transposition into domestic law.[684] These findings clearly speak against dualism in the relationship between Union and Member State law.

The third and last argument against dualism is directed against its claim that the borders of non-overlapping separate legal orders must be clearly determined. This entails, in other words, that EU and Member State law each deal with a different legal substance and subject matter. If one thinks in particular of the general principles of Union law, as developed by the Court of Justice, then the dualist model leads to great practical difficulties and absurd results. For a dualist, the exact location of these principles is crucial, because if they are principles of national law, they

[679] Treaty of Amsterdam, Protocol No 30 on the Application of the Principles of Subsidiarity and Proportionality, paras 6 and 7, OJ C 340/173, 10 November 1997.

[680] Case 96/81 *Commission v Netherlands (Bathing Water)* [1982] ECR 1791, para 12.

[681] Joined Cases C-178 to 179 and 188 to 190/94 *Dillenkofer* (n 594) paras 21–3; Case C-5/94 *Hedley Lomas* [1996] ECR I-2553, paras 28–9.

[682] See the landmark cases in terms of state liability, Joined Cases C-6/90 and C-9/90 *Francovich* (n 526), and Joined Cases C-46/93 and C-48/93 *Brasserie du Pêcheur and Factortame* (n 594) paras 19–29.

[683] Case C-129/96 *Inter-Environnement Wallonie* [1997] ECR 7411, para 45.

[684] Klamert (n 587) 91–2.

cannot concurrently be principles of Union law, and vice versa. Hence, if the CJEU is referring to the general principles of EU law, then these principles are entirely different from the principles existing at the national level, operating under the same name. The consequence is that there would be a plethora of national principles in each Member State plus one Union principle with its own autonomous meaning, and each of these principles would have its own field of application.[685]

This view is utterly implausible in the face of legal reality. As is well known, the Court gradually read these general principles into EU law to fill gaps inherent in the EU legal order, and used, most importantly in this context, the national constitutional traditions common to the Member States to do so.[686] Beyond the protection of fundamental rights, the CJEU thereby developed the general principles of, inter alia, equal treatment and non-discrimination, proportionality, legal certainty, and legitimate expectations. The crucial point is that it was the administrative law of the Member States that has been immensely influential in shaping the law of the EU in this regard,[687] which, in turn, is then transplanted and reapplied to national law via Union legal acts. The influence of national law and its traditional principles on the development of Union law is therefore not to be underestimated. Accordingly, these reciprocal effects speak against a dualist and non-overlapping view of national and Union law.

Especially when it comes to substance, dualism is unable to account for its inability to draw exact borders between allegedly separated legal orders, and to sustain the argument of the substantive complementarity of Member State and Union law.[688] In reality, dualism solves nothing and remains incapable of providing satisfactory answers to the question of what should happen in the case of overlaps and conflicts. Under dualism, there would not be any substantial overlaps to begin with, but as the positive law demonstrates, these overlaps and conflicts exist:[689] otherwise, the duty of the Member States to disapply contravening national law[690] would not make much sense.

ii. The doctrine of direct effect as an argument against dualism

Another argument against dualism can be found in the principle of direct effect that EU law claims to have within Member State law, thus allowing individuals (who, as traditional dualism holds, are not legal subjects of any legal order other than national law) to rely directly on Union law under certain circumstances without prior transformation into domestic law. However, it should not be omitted at this point that, from a general international law perspective, the existence of a doctrine such as direct effect speaks rather in favour of dualism than against it. To give direct effect to a particular rule of international law does not mean that a domestic court applies

[685] Martijn W. Hesselink, 'How Many Systems of Private Law Are There in Europe?' Leone Niglia (ed), *Pluralism and European Private Law* (Hart Publishing, 2013) 227.

[686] Case 4/73 *Nold* [1974] ECR 491, para 13.

[687] Paul Craig, *EU Administrative Law* (2nd edn; Oxford University Press, 2012) 264 and 272.

[688] See Eleftheriadis, 'Pluralism and Integrity' (n 529) 388.

[689] Hesselink '(n 685) 225–9.

[690] Case 106/77 *Simmenthal II* (n 526) para 17.

this rule independently from domestic law. On the contrary, it is assumed that direct effect is contingent on domestic law and presumes a rule of reference within the latter.[691] In this regard, it becomes evident that non-national and national law remain self-contained.[692] Otherwise, if there were no separation between legal orders that needed to be bridged somehow, the existence of the doctrine of direct effect would not make sense.[693]

If we look closer, however, and consider the relevant case law of the Court of Justice and the goals it pursued therewith, sceptics will realize that the traditional international law arguments are not correct and that the direct effect of EU law constitutes a very strong argument against dualism, and not for it. In its early years, the Court had to deal with six very different founding Member States, and whilst Belgium, France, Luxembourg, and the Netherlands were more inclined towards a monist understanding, Italy and Germany followed a dualist stance. However, regardless as to which approach the founding Member States pursued vis-à-vis international law and treaties (thus including the original EU Treaties), the CJEU effectively discarded any dualist leanings among the Member States and levelled all differences[694] in one of the most important cases of European Union law: *Van Gend en Loos*. In this judgment, the Court made it very clear for the first time that the Treaties are more than ordinary agreements, merely creating mutual obligations between the contracting states. Having established institutions, whose exercise of powers affects both Member States and individuals, and having created the preliminary ruling procedure, which allows individuals to invoke Union law before national courts, these very individuals constitute legal subjects of EU law and enjoy rights conferred upon them by this new legal order.[695]

Even if one questions the usefulness of direct effect and goes as far as Pierre Pescatore, who describes it as 'nothing but the ordinary state of the law',[696] thus without raising the question of whether the Union legal act in question is directly effective or not, *Van Gend en Loos* was merely the initial spark for the further development of direct effect within Union law. Especially when we draw a particular contrast between the Union legal order and international law, the significance and strength of direct effect become obvious: the weakness of international law, i.e. that a treaty may not be enforceable before domestic courts prior to transformation, even if the treaty provisions themselves are apt to be applied by them, has not been reproduced in Union law. If we think of directives, it is correct to say that the wording of Article 288(3) TFEU, the 'choice of form and methods' left to the Member States in transposing directives, has become illusory, as this very discretion is now severely limited by the detailed and exhaustive nature of directives. Therefore, many of the provisions laid down in directives have direct effect and are not dependent on prior

[691] Nollkaemper, *National Courts* (n 51) 120; Nollkaemper, 'Duality of Direct Effect' (n 327) 105, 110.

[692] Gaja (n 48) 52.

[693] See Tuori (n 648) 67–8.

[694] Paul Craig, 'Constitutions, Constitutionalism, and the European Union' (2001) 7 *European Law Journal* 125, 131.

[695] Case 26/62 *Van Gend en Loos* (n 650) 12.

[696] Pescatore, 'Infant Disease' (n 649) 177.

transposition in order to be enforceable by individuals before domestic courts.[697] One could hence say that the CJEU claimed in *Van Gend en Loos* more than what international law requires, namely a rule of reference enshrined in domestic law. Effectively, the Court proclaimed a fully Union law-based version of direct effect, and thereby it stands out as a successful step to disconnect direct effect from Member State law: direct effect is a matter of EU law, not of domestic law.[698]

Moreover, it is crucial to highlight how the Member States reacted to this development. While it is rather easy to devise a principle such as direct effect to ensure the effectiveness of EU law within domestic law, even without prior transposition, it is much more difficult to assess the climate on the receiving end: will such a principle be accepted loyally in practice? Will it just be accepted grudgingly? Or will it be flatly rejected? Outright rejection would leave the CJEU worse off than before, whereas grudging acceptance could result in conflicts later on. Therefore, only loyal acceptance will ensure that direct effect can achieve its intended objective.[699] The fundamental importance of *Van Gend en Loos* and all other subsequent cases on direct effect is that the Member States indeed accepted that the direct effect of future EU legal acts of unknown content was no longer under their exclusive control, and that this control was now exercised by the CJEU. Direct effect is nowadays taken for granted, and this fact remains unrivalled elsewhere in the world.[700] Simply put, by ignoring the Member States' constitutional choice for dualism, direct effect furthers a monist understanding of the interplay between national and Union law.[701] Admittedly, a dualist conception of national and EU law may have been adequate in the very beginning, but once the Member States and the Union legal order as formally distinct entities had been merged into a unity in substance, they solidified as a monist legal order.[702]

In its absolute form, i.e. by maintaining a rigid separation of legal orders, dualism is not capable of describing the direct effect of Union law, which may even horizontally regulate legal relations between individuals.[703] In fact, in the interpretation of the CJEU, direct effect means that EU law forms an integral part of Member State law and is part of the 'law of the land'. Such an effect would be utterly inconceivable, should Union law be considered a legal order that is fully separate and independent from national law.[704] *Prima facie*, dualism appears to provide a loose description of the relationship between EU and Member State law, but ultimately, it does not fit with what the CJEU is saying, because that is resolutely monist.[705] And yet,

[697] Case C-316/93 *Vaneetveld* [1994] ECR I-763, Opinion of Advocate General Jacobs, 773–4.

[698] Nollkaemper, 'Duality of Direct Effect' (n 327) 106 and 110.

[699] Anthony Arnull, *The European Union and Its Court of Justice* (2nd edn; Oxford University Press, 2006) 168.

[700] Nollkaemper, 'Duality of Direct Effect' (n 327) 106.

[701] Tuori (n 648) 61.

[702] Ingolf Pernice, 'Theorie und Praxis des Europäischen Verfassungsverbundes' in Christian Calliess (ed), *Verfassungswandel im europäischen Staaten- und Verfassungsverbund* (Mohr-Siebeck, 2006) 68.

[703] Case 36/74 *Walrave and Koch* [1974] ECR 1405, paras 18 and 21–2. Cf. also, however, Case 152/84 *Marshall* [1986] ECR 723, para 48, in which the Court confirmed that directives do not have horizontal direct effect and that they therefore do not impose obligations on individuals.

[704] Massimo La Torre, 'Legal Pluralism as Evolutionary Achievement of Community Law' (1999) 12 *Ratio Juris* 182, 192–3.

[705] Eleftheriadis, 'Pluralism and Integrity' (n 529) 387; Maduro, 'Contrapunctual Law' (n 521) 533.

ultimately, scepticism regarding this 'monist condensation' on part of the CJEU remains. Dualists (or even pluralists) will probably argue at this point that a monist view of this relationship is only possible to the extent that national law allows for this very monism by way of effective incorporation or reference rules—similar to the way in which states allow for the direct effect of general international law. Member States may resist this monism and simply refuse to give direct effect to certain EU legal norms before domestic courts for whatever reason. Consequently, the only way for EU law to assert itself in such a case of conflict is to resort to its own enforcement mechanisms.[706] This brings us to the question of whether the Union legal order is an effective coercive system and, if in the affirmative, whether this is another piece of evidence against dualism.

iii. EU law as an effective coercive legal order

One of the most plausible and most often used arguments of dualism against the unity of the law is the lack of enforcement mechanisms under international law.[707] However, as already briefly discussed above in the context of legal pluralism,[708] the law of the European Union does indeed have coercive and hierarchically structured enforcement mechanisms at its disposal, especially in the shape of Article 258 TFEU. It has therefore been argued that if the lack of enforcement mechanisms in fact were to be good evidence for dualism, this would be even less plausible for EU law because of the existence of rather effective enforcement mechanisms.[709] Thus, the dualist attack in this regard loses its purchase, since any violations of EU law by a Member State entail—in the same way as violations of national law—judicial proceedings which obligate the defaulting party to redress the violation or, in the event of non-compliance, to face legal sanctions. What is more, a decision finding national law in breach of Union law automatically results in the former's disapplication, and the dualist argument of two separate and distinct legal orders becomes untenable. This interaction of national and supranational law proves that violations of Union law do have immediate consequences on the domestic level.[710]

Dualists may of course counter this argument with reference to national legislation and the respective rules of reference which allow for the validity and applicability of EU law in national law in the first place. This legislation may always be revoked through a *lex posterior*, thus 'blocking out' the effects of Union law within the domestic legal order. This may be true, but the state in question nonetheless remains a Member State (unless it concurrently withdraws from the EU under Article 50 TEU) and hence also remains under the duty to fulfil its obligations under the Treaties. If, however, the relevant legislation were annulled or changed to the detriment of the effectivity of Union law, the respective Member State would be in breach of its obligations and infringement proceedings could be instigated. Should

[706] Potacs, 'Verhältnis' (n 104) 138.

[707] See e.g. Louis Henkin, 'International Law: Politics, Values, and Functions' (1989-IV) 216 *Recueil des cours* 19, 93.

[708] See section 3B(2)c.i above.

[709] Griller, 'Stufenbau' (n 647) 283 fn 79.

[710] Griller, 'Völkerrecht und Landesrecht' (n 96) 109–10.

the CJEU in the end decide that a Member State is in fact responsible for a violation of Union law, it goes without saying that the state in question is 'required to take the necessary measures to comply with the judgment of the Court'—as Article 260(1) TFEU sets forth. Dualists might, however, argue that any judgment of the CJEU, finding that a Member State is in breach of its obligations, is a mere declaratory judgment, and that the Court is not authorized to annul the unlawful domestic act at issue or explicitly to pronounce the Member State's obligation to redress the violation.[711]

This is true, but also without prejudice to the Member States' general duty to put an end to the infringement of Union law, which also means that incompatible domestic norms need to be annulled or modified accordingly.[712] This procedural interlacing undoubtedly speaks against a dualist view.

Dualists will nonetheless not be entirely convinced by this argument. What if the defaulting Member State proves to be extremely recalcitrant and refuses to comply with its duty to abide by the Court's judgment? This may certainly be a major issue, but in contrast to general international law, EU law possesses a very sophisticated follow-up procedure in the form of Article 260(2) and (3) TFEU. Under Article 260(2) TFEU, the Commission can, if it considers that the Member State in question has not taken the necessary measures to comply with the judgment of the CJEU, bring the case—again—before the Court. If the Court then finds that the Member State has not complied with its prior judgment, it may then request the Member State to pay a lump sum or penalty payment. Beyond that, Article 260(3) TFEU entitles the Commission to bring a case before the CJEU on the grounds that the Member State in question has failed to fulfil its obligations to notify measures transposing a directive. Similarly, if the Court then finds that there is an infringement, it may impose a lump sum or penalty payment on the Member State concerned.

Dualists must accept that both types of proceedings under Article 260 TFEU are viewed as coercive measures which place Member States under financial pressure to comply quickly and accordingly with CJEU judgments.[713] They undoubtedly represent the sharp end of the overall enforcement procedure, and with a distinctly less diplomatic and more formal legal flavour than the Article 258 TFEU stage.[714] So far, the threat of penalty or lump sum payments has been very successful in bringing the vast majority of Member States in line with outstanding judgments before being referred back to the CJEU. Equally, after these penalties have been imposed, they have principally been successful in securing compliance by the defaulting Member States. Certain problems persist of course, as some Member States may use these

[711] Diane de Bellescize, 'L'article 169 du Traité de Rome et l'efficacité du contrôle communautaire sur les manquements des États membres' (1977) 13 *Revue trimestrielle de droit européen* 173, 200.

[712] Joined Cases 314–316/81 and 83/82 *Procureur de la République v Waterkeyn* [1982] ECR 4337, para 14.

[713] Commission Communication, Memorandum on Applying Art 171 of the EC Treaty [now Art 260 TFEU], OJ C 242/6, 21 August 1996, para 4 and Case C-387/97 *Commission v Greece (Failure to Fulfil Obligations)* [2000] ECR I-5047, para 90.

[714] Craig and de Búrca (n 664) 460–1.

penalty payments to 'purchase' continued non-compliance,[715] or because occasionally, repeated referrals under Article 260 TFEU are necessary until the Member State eventually complies.[716] Some might even say that—given the absence of a 'European bailiff'—the most problematic aspect of this procedure remains the lack of a formal coercive mechanism for collection of the payment, if a Member State should refuse to comply.[717]

But this fact does not make dualism true. On the contrary, whilst dualism either contents itself with conflicts remaining unresolved or resolves such a conflict according to national law and the hierarchical rank national law gives EU law in the domestic sphere,[718] Article 260 TFEU undoubtedly contradicts this view: all conflicts between EU and Member State law are indeed resolved, and when being resolved, this occurs on the basis of Union law, not national law. Thus, if national law provides EU law with a rank inferior to domestic law or refuses to give it any effect at all (thereby rendering it ineffective in both cases), this approach certainly conflicts with the respective Member State's obligations under Union law and the latter's claim to direct effect and supremacy. Consequently, sanctions by the CJEU will ensure to guarantee compliance with these very obligations. And if a Member State persistently refuses to abide by the Court's judgments in a dualist fashion, thereby treating its obligations under EU law as nothing more than 'moral', not legal obligations, then we do not talk about law any more and dualism undermines itself.[719]

But even beyond this rather flimsy dualist approach, it seems possible to apply the pure theory's notion of the law as a coercive order to the law of the European Union. As already mentioned above,[720] Kelsen considers it an essential feature of the law that it—in contrast to other normative orders such as morality—attempts to foster lawful behaviour and to prevent unlawful behaviour through coercive measures. At first glance, coercive measures—in the form of an evil such as the deprivation of life, health, liberty, or economic values, or the application of physical forces[721]—can of course be imposed by both the law and bands of robbers, which begs the question of the way in which the law can be distinguished from brute force at gun-point. The distinguishing feature is that whilst the threat of a gang of robbers can be reduced to the statement that an evil *will be* inflicted, the command of a legal organ is interpreted as a statement that an evil *ought to be* inflicted. This means that in the latter case, an evil is inflicted by applying an objectively valid norm, stipulating a coercive act as a sanction to guarantee compliance with the law or penalize prior non-compliance.[722] Hence, it is an essential feature of the law as a coercive legal order that

[715] Brian Jack, 'Article 260(2) TFEU: An Effective Judicial Procedure for the Enforcement of Judgments?' (2013) 19 *European Law Journal* 404, 421.

[716] European Commission, '32nd Annual Report on Monitoring the Application of Union Law (2014)', COM(2015) 329, 15–16; European Commission, '31st Annual Report on Monitoring the Application of EU Law (2013)', COM(2014) 612 final, 5–6 and 13.

[717] Maria A. Theodossiou, 'An Analysis of the Recent Response of the Community to Non-Compliance with Court of Justice Judgments: Article 228(2) EC' (2003) 27 *European Law Review* 25, 39–40.

[718] Somek, 'Kelsen Lives' (n 644) 422–3.

[719] Ibid., 426.

[720] See Chapter 3, section 5A(2).

[721] Kelsen, *Pure Theory* (n 24) 33–4.

[722] Ibid., 44–50.

such measures are applied by particular organs which have a monopoly of force.[723] Thus, coercion prescribed as reaction against a certain behaviour, or the 'coercive order paradigm' (*Zwangsnormpostulat*), through an organ that has been entrusted with the application of force and coercive measures, is *the* distinguishing feature of the law.[724] Law within the meaning of the pure theory of law consequently constitutes a coercive order.[725]

Sceptics will argue at this point that the nature of a coercive legal order lies, *ultima ratio*, in the imposition of physical measures, for example carried out by the police or the military. And since EU law cannot physically force the Member States to implement judgments or to pay fines imposed under Article 260 proceedings, it cannot be regarded as a coercive legal order in Kelsen's sense.[726] One has to agree with the sceptics that what they consider to be a 'coercive theory' is in fact not defensible in the light of the law as it is. However, there are some considerable concerns with this sceptical position. To begin with, it needs to be emphasized that the element of 'coercion' within the pure theory of law is not a theory, but a mere conceptual characteristic of the law. Furthermore, it is crucial to add that what the sceptics understand as coercion or coercion theory is only loosely related to the pure theory of law which, at no point, considers physical or military measures as *the* exclusive enforcement measures. It is correct that Kelsen mentions physical force as a *possible* way to enforce the law against non-compliant behaviour coercively (and this needs to be seen against the original background of his writings, which is *national* legal theory)—but the use of physical force (in whatever way) remains only *one* way to enforce law amongst many other methods.[727] Another evil that can be inflicted is the deprivation of economic values—and this is the specific element of coercion—*against* the perpetrator's will.[728] Moreover, persistent non-compliance on the part of the defaulting Member State is not an argument against the coercive and effective nature of the European Union legal order, as long as Article 260 TFEU is regularly applied and as long as non-compliance is perceived as unlawful.[729]

Thus, EU law is certainly a coercive legal order in the sense of the pure theory of law.[730] In conclusion, the Member States certainly continue to be sovereign as they may always withdraw from the EU, but as long as they remain Member States, they are also part of the Union legal order, and any breaches of this law will be penalized. Therefore, the unity of the law is not endangered and dualism becomes implausible.

[723] Hans Kelsen, *Peace through Law* (University of North Carolina Press, 1944) 3; Kelsen, *Pure Theory* (n 24) 36–7; Kelsen, *General Theory* (n 26) 21.

[724] Jörg Kammerhofer, 'Kelsen—Which Kelsen? A Reapplication of the Pure Theory to International Law' (2009) 22 *Leiden Journal of International Law* 225, 227–8.

[725] Mayer, 'Reine Rechtslehre und Gemeinschaftsrecht' (n 480) 129.

[726] Schroeder (n 486) 211–15.

[727] Mayer, 'Reine Rechtslehre und Gemeinschaftsrecht' (n 480) 129 and fn 38.

[728] Kelsen, *Pure Theory* (n 24) 33.

[729] Rudolf Thienel, 'Geltung und Wirksamkeit' in Stanley L. Paulson and Robert Walter (eds), *Untersuchungen zur Reinen Rechtslehre* (Manz, 1986) 39; Somek, 'Kelsen Lives' (n 644) 430.

[730] Mayer, 'Reine Rechtslehre und Gemeinschaftsrecht' (n 480) 129–30.

c. Conclusion: the shortcomings of dualism

It may be controversial whether the Court of Justice of the EU, in its dealings with Member State law, follows a strictly monist approach.[731] Yet it is all the more certain that a dualist interpretation of this relationship is untenable. This would not only pose insurmountable problems in the face of contravening practice, but also prove dangerous to the unity and effectivity of the Union legal order, because by reducing EU law to mere inter-state law, it would be rendered ineffective until duly transformed into national law.[732] Hence, it is irrelevant whether the Member States intended for this monism or not: it is a fact that, particularly in *Van Gen den Loos* and *Costa v ENEL*, the CJEU cut the hitherto existing umbilical cord with general international law and discarded any dualist leanings on the part of the Member States.[733]

Ultimately, there is no added value to regarding EU law and Member State law as two separate legal orders or as a 'dualist constitution',[734] because thereby normative conflicts can neither be prevented nor satisfactorily be resolved. One can therefore summarize that, although so far a clear *chain of delegation* between national and EU law has not yet been proven, there is undoubtedly a positive-legal *chain of derogation* in place and at work between them. The only restriction to be taken into consideration at this point is that EU law indeed ranks higher than national law on the chain of derogation, yet not in terms of validity, but applicability. This difference in terms, however, does not speak in favour of dualism or against monism, as the effect is practically the same: even though contravening Member State law does not give way to superior EU law automatically, it must do so eventually. And even if Member States refuse to give effect to supreme Union norms, they must face the respective consequences in the shape of infringement proceedings and, potentially, further penalty payments. The two bodies of law are thus intricately intertwined and not separate legal orders.

It is consequently unquestionable that under the primacy of Union law as established by the Court, the conditions for the applicability of EU law are being governed by EU law itself, and not by the Member States' legal orders—which corresponds to a more or less moderate version of monism.[735] Within the scope of application of EU law,[736] normative conflicts between Union and national law are indeed resolvable on the basis of the primacy of EU law.[737] The same is all the more true for direct effect, which allows individuals to rely on Union law without prior transposition into domestic law.[738] Thus, direct effect ignores the Member States' constitutional choice for dualism and furthers a monist understanding of the interplay between national and Union law.[739] In the end, monism allows for a much more relaxed

[731] Peters, *Elemente* (n 540) 276. [732] Barents, *Autonomy* (n 588) 179–80.
[733] Robert Schütze, *An Introduction to European Law* (2nd edn; Cambridge University Press, 2012) 117.
[734] Peter Pernthaler, 'Die neue Doppelverfassung Österreichs' in Herbert Haller and others (eds), *Staat und Recht: Festschrift für Günter Winkler* (Springer, 1997) 773 ff; Schroeder (n 486) 188.
[735] de Witte, 'Direct Effect, Primacy' (n 653) 348–50; Peters, 'Rechtsordnungen und Konstitutionalisierung' (n 407) 21.
[736] See Article 51(1) of the Charter of Fundamental Rights, and Case C-617/10 *Åkerberg Fransson* [2013] ECLI:EU:C:2013:105.
[737] Griller, 'Stufenbau' (n 647) 283 fn 79. [738] Öhlinger, 'Einheit' (n 139) 168–9.
[739] Tuori (n 648) 61.

description of the relationship between national and Union law,[740] while dualism appears to be less plausible in the light of this complex legal interweaving.

In conclusion, a dualist view of the relationship between Member State and Union law appears to be of little practical use,[741] as it is unsuitable to resolve any legal issues. This raises the question of whether national and Union law are in fact derived from the same source of validity and whether there exists a chain of delegation between those two bodies of law; in other words: can monism better explain and describe this relationship than the pluralist and dualist models?[742]

(4) Monism under the primacy of national law

a. The unquestionable interlocking of EU and national law: monist choices

Seeing how close the links between Union and Member State law have become over the last decades, it is definitely not far-fetched to argue that they have evolved into one single system: 'Because the Court's [case law] to be applied at the national level effectively has been fully accepted in most Member States, the [Union] legal system does exist in fact at the national level and the national officials do act as [Union] officials'.[743] However, after having established that, upon their fusion into one legal order, Union law as well as national law now constitute the law of the land for every individual citizen,[744] two intricately related and immensely crucial elements of monism are still absent in this model, namely the *Grundnorm* and the chain of validity. The above analyses on pluralism and dualism have shown that it is more convincing to view the EU legal order as a monist system, but they did not answer the question as to where the source of validity of this unitary legal order is located. Does the *Grundnorm* of the overall Union system sit at the apex of national law, thus making the validity of Union law dependent on superior domestic norms? Or is the reverse assumption more plausible, namely that the *Grundnorm* of the overall system is located at the top of Union law, thus making the validity of Member State law dependent on superior EU norms?[745] The section at hand will now explore the former scenario, whilst the latter thesis will be examined in the subsequent section.

If one chooses a monist perspective, the relationship between European Union law and Member State law may well be considered from the aspect of monism under *the primacy of national law*. In this scenario, European Union law would, as 'external Member State law', norm-logically be delegated by the national legal orders where the *Grundnorm* of the entire system would be located. The chain of delegation would thus run from this national basic norm down, via the Union Treaties and secondary law, to the most individual legal acts adopted under EU law.

In more doctrinal terms, monism under the primacy of national law simply boils down to a specific version of the so-called 'international law theory'. It holds, in

[740] Griller, 'Stufenbau' (n 647) 284.
[741] Schroeder (n 486) 249.
[742] Barents, *Autonomy* (n 588) 183.
[743] Jones (n 492) 52.
[744] Ingolf Pernice, 'Multilevel Constitutionalism and the Treaty of Amsterdam: European Constitution-Making Revisited?' (1999) 36 *Common Market Law Review* 703, 712.
[745] See Jestaedt, 'Der Europäische Verfassungsverbund' (n 609) 121–2.

contrast to the '*sui generis* theory'[746] of EU law, that the Union legal order and its interactions with national law can be properly understood in terms of international law principles, notwithstanding its developed institutional structures and extensive jurisdictional scope. Although EU law is much more intrusive and enforceable than general international law, an explanation of its nature and features does not require any departure from established international legal principles.[747] In a nutshell, the Union is not an independent legal order at all, but simply a highly specialized area of international law; and principles such as direct effect and supremacy are not exotica of EU law, but merely indicators that a national court is obliged to reach decisions which are in accordance with the international obligations of the state in question.[748] The law of the European Union is nothing more than particular international law,[749] but there is a specific twist and crucial component to this theory which distinguishes it from monism under the primacy of international law (or a *genuine* 'international law theory' of EU law, as one might call it): international law-centred monism would locate the *Grundnorm* at the apex of the international legal order and hence assume that Union law may have originally been part of international law. In other words, it was international law which bestowed validity upon Union law in the first place.[750] In contrast to that, the state-centred 'international law theory' discussed below holds that the validity of international law (in this case: in the shape of the EU Treaties) depends on the Member States and it is the validity of their legal acts which gives validity to their international legal acts in turn. Under this monism under the primacy of national law, the *Grundnorm* is located within national law, and the Member States simply utilized international instruments such as treaties to create the European Union. International law thus acts as a mere conduit for the acts of the Member States and for bestowing validity on EU norms.

In this vein, the following section will now further engage with arguments in favour of such a monist view under the primacy of national law, whereas the section after that will subsequently critique and rebut it, thereby setting the scene for monism under the primacy of EU law.

b. EU law is derived from national law via international law

Overall, a monist approach under the primacy of Member State law is characterized by four main points of argumentation which consecutively rest upon one another.[751] First, as a kind of preliminary argument, it needs to be stressed that the underlying purpose of the EU still is, as the preamble to the Treaty on European Union lays down, 'to continue the process of creating an *ever closer union among the*

[746] For an excellent overview of these two theories see e.g. Robert Schütze, *European Constitutional Law* (Cambridge University Press, 2012) 67–71.
[747] Timothy Moorhead, *The Legal Order of the European Union* (Routledge, 2014) 112.
[748] Julie Dickson and Pavlos Eleftheriadis, 'Introduction: The Puzzles of European Union Law' in Julie Dickson and Pavlos Eleftheriadis (eds), *Philosophical Foundations of European Union Law* (Oxford University Press, 2012) 9.
[749] Pernice, 'Multilevel Constitutionalism and the Treaty of Amsterdam' (n 744) 711.
[750] Schroeder (n 486) 232–43.
[751] Schütze, *European Constitutional Law* (n 746) 70–1.

peoples of Europe'.[752] This expression suggests an inherently strong dynamic element in the European integration process[753] which seeks to unite the peoples of Europe in one single polity. The Bundesverfassungsgericht, however, took issue with this rather open-ended statement and clarified in its *Maastricht* decision that the Treaty on European Union only 'establishes an association of States [*Staatenverbund*] to realize an ever closer union of the peoples of Europe', and this association needs to be understood as organized as States, and not as 'a State based on the people of one European nation'.[754] Thus, the German Constitutional Court presented its 'no *demos* thesis' and offered a simple connection: as there is no European *demos*, the integration process must necessarily rely on domestic institutions such as democratically legitimized national parliaments.[755] The European Union simply does not have any *pouvoir constituant* in a democratically demanding sense, and consequently the primary source of democratic legitimacy for all legal acts adopted by the EU remains with the national peoples.[756]

This takes us to the second and perhaps most crucial point in this line of argumentation, which is that all legal authority of the Union is derived from the Member States and national law. When the six founding Member States created the ECSC and the European Communities in the 1950s by a series of international treaties, there was no shred of doubt that these entities were created as international organizations and that Community law practically was a particular subsystem within general international law. The choice for international law as the instrument for setting up this organization was not obvious, as some European federalists had hoped to create a United Europe on the basis of a federal constitution.[757] Yet, despite these federal and national legal efforts, the European governments involved chose instead to follow the traditional route of using international agreements to foster enhanced cooperation between them.[758]

The profoundly international legal nature of all Union Treaties is also evident in the use of the international law-inspired wording throughout them, such as: the High Contracting Parties that establish the European Union (Article 1 TEU);

[752] Preamble to the Treaty on European Union, as amended by the Treaty of Lisbon, OJ C326/1, 26 October 2012, indent 13 (emphasis added).

[753] Roland Bieber, Jean-Paul Jacqué, and J.H.H. Weiler, 'Introduction' in Roland Bieber, Jean-Paul Jacqué, and J.H.H. Weiler (eds), *An Ever Closer Union: A Critical Analysis of the Draft Treaty Establishing the European Union* (Office for Official Publications of the European Communities, 1985) 8.

[754] BVerfGE 89, 155—*Maastricht* (n 524) 89.

[755] Kalypso Nicolaïdis, 'European Demoicracy and Its Crisis' (2013) 51 *Journal of Common Market Studies* 351, 352.

[756] Christoph Möllers, 'Pouvoir constituant—Constitution—Constitutionalisation' in Armin von Bogdandy and Jürgen Bast (eds), *Principles of European Constitutional Law* (2nd edn; Hart Publishing, 2009) 186; Schütze, *European Constitutional Law* (n 746) 70.

[757] See e.g. Bernard Vayssière, *Vers une Europe fédérale? Les espoirs et les actions fédéralistes au sortir de la Seconde Guerre mondiale* (Peter Lang, 2006) 33 ff; and Christophe Réveillard, *Les premières tentatives de construction d'une Europe fédérale, des projets de la Résistance au Traité de la CED* (1940–1954) (Oeil, 2001).

[758] Jan Klabbers, 'Straddling the Fence: The EU and International Law' in Anthony Arnull and Damian Chalmers (eds), *The Oxford Handbook of European Union Law* (Oxford University Press, 2015) 55–62.

potential limitations to the territorial application of EU and the exclusion of particular parts of Member State territory from its reach (Article 354 TFEU);[759] and the fact that the Treaties *enter into force* upon *ratification* by the Member States (Article 357 TFEU).[760] No powers or competences on part of the EU are therefore original, but merely derivative of national law.[761]

In the words of the pure theory of law, the *Grundnorm* is hence located in national law, and the historically first constitution of all Member States consequently conditions their currently valid constitutions. And since the Union Treaties were ratified in accordance with the Member States' respective constitutional provisions on treaty ratification, the validity of the EU legal order continues to depend on national law, for instance, in the shape of the individual act of ratification or the very inner constitutional core (*integrationsfester Verfassungskern*) which remains entirely unaffected by EU law.[762] Accordingly, by establishing the Union on the basis of international agreements concluded and ratified by the Member States, the legal autonomy claimed by the CJEU is only apparent and remains derivative from national law. This, in turn, excludes so-called interpretative autonomy, and means that the ultimate powers and competences remain with the Member States.[763]

In the parlance of the Bundesverfassungsgericht, the Member States, as the contracting parties to the EU Treaties, are and remain the 'Masters of the Treaties' (*Herren der Verträge*),[764] having the last say over the validity and features of Union law. Eventually, this power also includes the inherent right of the Member States to amend and revise the Treaties at will. And since the Member States sit at the top of the chain of derogation, they may dispose of these Treaties as they wish. They could, for instance, amend the Treaties without regard to the procedural conditions for this laid down in the Treaties[765] or adopt an *actus contrarius* or *actus modificiens* to the Treaties,[766] and thus disintegrate the Union at their discretion. Ultimately, the EU has—under this version of monism—no original powers. This means that the powers conferred upon the Union by the Member States, may under no condition be extended or modified by the institutions or the CJEU.[767]

Thirdly, the consequence of this chain of validity, running from national law to EU law, is that a potential reversal of this very chain—i.e. giving Union law supremacy over national law—is only possible on the basis of national law itself, and not through EU law. Thus, Union law can never be considered autonomous, as its validity and supremacy within superior Member State law is based on a mediating or

[759] See also Article 29 VCLT, and Bruno de Witte, 'European Union Law: How Autonomous Is Its Legal Order?' (2010) 65 *Zeitschrift für Öffentliches Recht* 141, 144.

[760] Emphasis added.

[761] Kadelbach (n 544) 206; Schilling, 'Autonomy' (n 635) 404.

[762] Michael Thaler, 'Rechtsphilosophie und das Verhältnis zwischen Gemeinschaftsrecht und nationalem Recht' (2000) 8 *Journal für Rechtspolitik* 75, 77; Schilling, 'Zum Verhältnis' (n 548) 150.

[763] Schilling, 'Autonomy' (n 635) 403–409.

[764] BVerfGE 89, 155—*Maastricht* (n 524) para 190.

[765] Barents, *Autonomy* (n 588) 134–6.

[766] Rupert Scholz, 'Europäische Union und deutscher Bundesstaat' (1993) 12 *Neue Zeitschrift für Verwaltungsrecht* 817, 818.

[767] Barents, *Autonomy* (n 588) 135.

bridging domestic provision,[768] such as Article 23 GG for Germany or the European Communities Act 1972 for the UK. The validity and exact arrangement of this provision consequently depends on national constitutional law. Moreover, it is crucial to note that this is equally true for both so-called monist and non-monist constitutions, because even a complete monist opening-up of national law towards any form of external law presupposes the existence of a national legal act acknowledging and accepting this very openness.[769]

Monist constitutions may therefore take full account of the supreme status claimed by EU norms by granting them supremacy over all domestic law, whilst non-monist constitutions would resolve normative conflicts in accordance with the hierarchical rank which Union norms possess under the constitution. The existence of any constitutional integration barriers (*Integrationsschranken*) in the shape of principles such as democracy, the rule of law, fundamental rights protection, and subsidiarity[770] would then, in such non-monist systems, bar Union law from having unconditional supremacy over and effect within Member State law.[771] In other words, in the case of doubt, national law would then reclaim its original superior hierarchical position on the chain of validity and thereby rein in the claims of EU law to autonomous validity and supremacy over Member State law.

Last, monism under the primacy of national law also entails that EU legal acts which go beyond this national scope and transgress these constitutional integration barriers, may be considered ultra vires. Furthermore, since they sit at a higher echelon of the hierarchy of norms, the right to decide whether such an act is indeed ultra vires or not rests, ultimately, with the national courts.[772] Under this specific version of monism, the Union legal order is derived from national law via international law by way of a power transfer, which also becomes evident when taking into account Article 5(2) TEU and the principle of conferral. As the 'Masters of the Treaties', the Member States conferred and pooled only certain of their powers in the Union and its institutions, and therefore the legislative *Kompetenz-Kompetenz* continues to rest with them. This means, *e contrario*, that the EU only possesses those powers which have been conferred upon it through the Treaties in the first place.[773]

Let us now assume the following scenario to further elucidate what monism under the primacy of Member State law involves in this context: the CJEU upholds a contested piece of EU law on the basis that the Union legislature has validly exercised the competences which have been conferred upon it by the Treaties. Concurrently, however, a national constitutional court comes to the conclusion that the Union legislature acted in excess of its conferred powers, i.e. ultra vires. This national court

[768] Christoph U. Schmid, 'From Pont d'Avignon to Ponte Vecchio: The Resolution of Constitutional Conflicts between the European Union and the Member States through Principles of Public International Law' (1998) *18 Yearbook of European Law* 415, 419.

[769] Kadelbach (n 544) 206 fn 140.

[770] See in particular Article 23(1) GG in this respect.

[771] Potacs, 'Verhältnis' (n 104) 133 and 138–9.

[772] Schütze, *European Constitutional Law* (n 746) 71.

[773] Michael Dougan, 'The Convention's Draft Constitutional Treaty: Bringing Europe Closer to Its Lawyers?' (2003) 28 *European Law Review* 763, 765.

would then probably declare the EU act at issue to be inapplicable or to have no effect whatsoever within domestic law.[774]

The most plausible ground for reaching this conclusion will be that the national government as well as the national parliament themselves, when acceding to the EU Treaties, were bound by their constitution. Alternatively, under the principle of *nemo plus iuris transfere potest quam ipse habet*,[775] the Member States could have never transferred more competences upon the European Union than they themselves possessed in the first place. Therefore, and although the authority of treaty interpretation by the CJEU is unassailable in terms of EU law itself, this authority certainly comes to an end when the Court endorses an arrogation of competences which either never have or never could have been transferred to the Union.[776]

This conclusion has two crucial ramifications, one concerning the CJEU itself, the other one concerning the national courts and the ultimate consequence of such ultra vires acts under Member State-centred monism: first, one may have to accept that the EU Treaties have created institutions such as the CJEU which 'ensure that in the interpretation and application of the Treaties the law is observed'.[777] This is in contrast to general international law where, in the absence of treaty institutions, the contracting states usually resort to the instrument of auto-interpretation,[778] thus underlining their right to definitive interpretation of the treaty in question. Hence the CJEU may have extensive powers in comparison to other treaty regimes, but these powers do not include the right to go beyond what was originally given. The Court's claim to interpretative autonomy therefore fails, because the Member States have retained their power to auto-interpret the Treaties when it comes to the thorny issues of *Kompetenz-Kompetenz* and integrational barriers.[779]

In this light, the EU Treaties are nothing more than ordinary international agreements among the Member States, the compliance of which is simply policed by the CJEU.[780] Secondly, this right to auto-interpretation by the Member States entails that the national courts would consider any EU acts in contravention of their integrational barriers to be unlawful. The exact legal consequence of this unlawfulness would probably depend on the respective national constitution. Sitting higher atop the chain of derogation, national constitutions could, for instance, authorize their respective constitutional courts to declare Union law in breach of national law to be ineffective on the domestic level. And should national law not provide for

[774] Somek, 'Monism' (n 558) 356; Daniel Halberstam, 'Constitutional Heterarchy: The Centrality of Conflict in the European Union and the United States' in State' in Jeffrey L. Dunoff and Joel P. Trachtman (eds), *Ruling the World: International Law, Global Governance, Constitutionalism* (Cambridge University Press, 2009) 335–6.

[775] See the corresponding principle in the *Corpus Iuris Civilis, Digesta Book L*, Title XVII, 54, literally meaning that no one can confer on another person more rights than they themselves possess in the first place.

[776] Somek, 'Monism' (n 558) 356.

[777] Article 19(1) TEU.

[778] Leo Gross, 'States as Organs of International Law and the Problem of Autointerpretation' in Leo Gross (ed), *Essays on International Law and Organization* (reprint; Springer, 1984) 367–97; Schilling, 'Autonomy' (n 635) 404.

[779] Schilling, 'Autonomy' (n 635) 407.

[780] Alexander Somek, *Individualism: An Essay on the Authority of the European Union* (Oxford University Press, 2008) 214–16.

such an authorization in terms of Merkl's *Fehlerkalkül*, then the logical consequence would be to presume the absolute nullity of the legal act in question.[781]

c. Arguments against the explanatory power of monism under the primacy of national law

The following subsections will now look more closely into the claims of monism under the primacy of Member State law and test these claims. Thereby it will be examined whether they can be supported by the law as it is, and whether they are well suited to describe and explain the relationship between the Member States and the EU. Equally, it will then be demonstrated and argued that despite its *prima facie* appeal under the so-called 'international law theory', this version of monism remains highly problematic and ultimately fails accurately to describe the legal reality.

i. Demo(i)cracy and the chain of delegation

The first argument to be discussed is the claimed state-anchored chain of validity, which is alleged to be ultimately based on national democracy. Admittedly, it is true that there is no European state,[782] nor is there one single European *demos* which would constitute the first and necessary building block of a genuine European democracy. Since an in-depth analysis of the EU's alleged democratic deficit would go beyond the scope of this section and is not necessary at this point (as will be shown shortly), suffice it to say that democracy within the Union institutions is not perfect. And even though the EU is committed to democracy as a value,[783] it is not a democracy in the national sense, but more of a European *demoi*cracy, i.e. a polity of multiple *demoi*.[784]

However, this 'democracy argument' does not support monism under the primacy of Member State law, for two reasons. First, as has already been discussed above,[785] an analogy with general international law can be drawn: historically speaking, it is of course true—as even Kelsen admits—that national law preceded the creation of the international legal order, but it is nonetheless important to distinguish these historical facts from norm-logical conditions of delegation and validity, i.e. the logical delegation of national law by international law under the latter's primacy.[786]

In the same way, Member State law and their democracies preceded the creation of the European Union, but this does not tell us anything about the question as to which entity—EU or Member States—has primacy over the other. Secondly, despite its stressing of the various 'peoples of Europe',[787] thus implicitly denying the existence of a European *demos*, the Bundesverfassungsgericht does not support the idea in its *Maastricht* decision that the EU legal order may be norm-genetically derived from national constitutional law.[788] It is correct that this decision was mainly

781 Thaler (n 762) 77.

782 See Opinion 2/13 *EU Accession to the ECHR* [2014] ECLI:EU:C:2014:2454, para 156.

783 See Articles 2, and 9–12 TEU.

784 See particularly Kalypso Nicolaïdis, 'The New Constitution as European Demoi-cracy? (2004) 7 *Critical Review of International Social and Political Philosophy* 76–93.

785 See Chapter 3, section 5B(2)b.

786 Kelsen, *Pure Theory* (n 24) 338–9.

787 BVerfGE 89, 155—*Maastricht* (n 524) 89.

788 Schroeder (n 486) 229.

shaped by a view in which the Member States remain the centre point of the human community, living together in order,[789] but this underlying concept in itself does not make the German Constitutional Court regard the law of the European Union as a kind of external state law in the Hegelian sense. On the contrary, the Constitutional Court rather emphasizes the origins of EU law in public international law itself,[790] but not in the sense of it being instrumentalized and thus being delegated by national law. A more accurate description of its approach is a dualist position according to which EU and German law represent two separate legal orders wherein normative conflicts are resolved on the basis of the German Basic Law (that may or may not allow for the supremacy of Union law).[791]

Consequently, it is not the validity of the EU legal order itself which is dependent on German law, but simply its *domestic* validity and applicability within Germany.[792] Thus, from a purely domestic perspective, both dualism and monism under the primacy of Member State law lead to the same result, but this should not blind us to the underlying differences between these two positions. If dualism were true, a violation of EU law, allegedly justified by constitutional law,[793] would, after all, represent a failure to perform obligations under the Union Treaties vis-à-vis the other Member States under general international law.[794] This could then prompt legal consequences by way of infringement proceedings, for example. In contrast to that, a monist view under the primacy of Member State law would always exclude such a violation of EU law and its respective consequences, as it is inconceivable that superior (i.e. delegating) national law could ever be in breach of inferior (i.e. delegated) European Union law.[795]

It is, however, a fact that national law can indeed be incompatible with EU norms which is why enforcement mechanisms such as infringement proceedings as well as the preliminary ruling procedure exist, or principles such as supremacy and direct effect were developed. State-centred monists may argue at this point that the Member States only subject themselves to any procedures before the CJEU and the above-mentioned principles because of their respective constitutional provisions, giving effect to Union norms within domestic law. Accordingly, they might always revoke these provisions and therefore invalidate EU law. This view is, however, incorrect. As just mentioned above, the Bundesverfassungsgericht explained in *Maastricht* that not the validity of Union law per se was delegated by national law, but only its effects within it.[796] This means that the Member States may of course revoke these provisions any time they wish to do so. But this course of action does not make the validity

[789] Paul Kirchhof, 'Die Gewaltenbalance zwischen staatlichen und europäischen Organen' (1998) 53 *Juristen-Zeitung* 965, 966.

[790] BVerfGE 89, 155—*Maastricht* (n 524) 183, 187, 190, and 200; BVerfGE 75, 223—*Kloppenburg* (n 582) 242; and BVerfGE 73, 339—*Solange II* (n 643) 375 and 383–4.

[791] Schroeder (n 486) 230; Werner Meng, *Das Recht der Internationalen Organisationen—eine Entwicklungsstufe des Völkerrechts* (Nomos, 1979) 136.

[792] BVerfGE 89, 155—*Maastricht* (n 524) 190.

[793] See Article 27 of the VCLT.

[794] Assuming that no exception under Article 46 VCLT is applicable; see J.H.H. Weiler and Ulrich R. Haltern, 'The Autonomy of the Community Legal Order—Through the Looking Glass' (1996) 37 *Harvard International Law Journal* 411, 441.

[795] Schroeder (n 486) 230.

[796] BVerfGE 89, 155—*Maastricht* (n 524) 190.

of EU law dependent on national law, seeing that cancelling out the domestic effects of Union norms is tantamount to a Treaty infringement. In other words, as long as the Member States wish to be a part of the Union, they cannot simply revoke their respective legislation giving effect to EU law within their national law without the prospective of being sanctioned for this step. Thus, the validity of the Union legal order cannot be regarded to be delegated by national law.[797]

Furthermore, concerning the argument that the Union has no original powers and that all of its competences are derived from Member State law which can be withdrawn at any time, it has also been argued that the foundation and the nature of the EU's powers cannot be adequately explained in terms of primacy of national law. Accordingly, the Union's powers are best characterized by their original and independent character, and not their alleged delegation by national law. Hans Peter Ipsen, for example, opines that the European Union was created through a 'collective act' (*Gesamtakt*[798]) of the Member States' integrational powers. This, in turn, led to the establishment of an autonomous legal order which exists independently of the Member States.[799] But these powers were not merely delegated or transferred by the Member States, and the Union does not simply act as the Union's agent within these specific policy areas.[800]

In fact, the Treaties allocated the EU powers which are original in the sense that, owing to their scope and content, they cannot exist at the national level. Consequently, they cannot be considered to be transferred by national acts of ratification.[801] This is all the more confirmed by the Court's case law, according to which 'a [Union] provision must be interpreted in relation to and in the context of its own sources',[802] as well as by the Treaties themselves which mention, in Articles 4(1) and 13(2) TEU, a conferral of powers by the Treaties, not by the Member States. The law of the EU would then be better characterized by being delegated by general international law itself, and not by the detour of national law, merely utilizing international law in the form of international treaties. Regarding the content of these original powers, it suffices to mention Articles 2 to 4 TEU which are intended to protect and promote the general interest of the Union; the conferral of specific rights and obligations on citizens;[803] and the mandatory nature of EU law which is, in the words of the Court, 'definitive', 'unconditional', and 'irreversible'.[804]

By way of conclusion, it is of course correct to cite the above-mentioned principle *nemo plus iuris transfere potest quam ipse habet* in the context of the creation-process of the European Union to underline that nobody—not even states—can confer more rights and powers than they actually possess to somebody else. But this

[797] Bleckmann, *Grundgesetz und Völkerrecht* (n 184) 273.
[798] For more details, see section 3B(5)b.ii below.
[799] Hans Peter Ipsen, *Europäisches Gemeinschaftsrecht* (Mohr-Siebeck, 1972) 58 and 62–3.
[800] Martin Nettesheim, 'Kompetenzen' in Armin von Bogdandy and Jürgen Bast (eds), *Europäisches Verfassungrecht: Theoretische und dogmatische Grundzüge* (2nd edn; Springer, 2009) 397–8.
[801] Barents, *Autonomy* (n 588) 232–3. [802] Case 12/73 *Muras* [1973] ECR 963, para 7.
[803] Case 26/62 *Van Gend en Loos* (n 650) 1; Case 51/76 *VNO* [1977] ECR 113, para 23.
[804] Case 7/71 *Commission v France (Euratom Supply Agency)* [1971] ECR 1003; Case 106/77 *Simmenthal II* (n 526).

principle neglects the fact that transferring one's powers to another entity jointly with other partners creates something different and larger than the original powers of the sharers. By pooling the original sovereignty of the Member States at the European level, powers are now shared between them and their common European institutions.[805] And these institutions, together with the EU legal order, are more than just the sum of their cumulatively ceded and then reassembled parts in the shape of the Member States' original competences. The assumption that the law of the Union is norm-genetically derived from national law is therefore incorrect.[806]

ii. The chain of derogation, ultra vires acts, and Kompetenz-Kompetenz

State-centred monists might also argue that the fact that there is no chain of delegation running from national law (at the top of the hierarchy of norms) towards Union law, thereby bestowing validity on the latter, does not automatically mean that national law does not hold a superior position vis-à-vis EU law on the chain of derogation. Ultimately, the legislative *Kompetenz-Kompetenz* rests with the Member States, and this entails that the Union cannot unilaterally change the Treaties. Equally, the right to ultra vires review also remains with the national courts. Therefore, it is the Member States, not the Union, which have the power to derogate (i.e. repeal) EU norms.

The derogation of legal norms may, however, occur in different settings, and we should thus distinguish between various constellations. At the outset, derogation and ultra vires control not in relation to the Treaties, i.e. secondary law, will be discussed. In this vein, it should be emphasized right from the start that in the same manner as the CJEU can never invalidate contravening Member State law, so the national courts cannot invalidate EU law. Both courts remain the exclusive guardians of their respective bodies of law[807] and have declared that the validity of legal norms derived from the respective other legal order cannot be affected by the criteria of validity of their own legal order.[808] Therefore, it appears that there is no chain of derogation connecting Member State and Union law. However, to counter this argument, the CJEU will certainly point to the principle of supremacy in conjunction with the Member States' duty to disapply contravening national law.[809] This means that the contravening domestic act remains valid and may be fully operable in purely internal situations or once the Union act is repealed.[810] Thus, even though any national legal acts in violation of EU law do not need to be invalidated in the case of conflict, they must at least be disapplied, and this supremacy in—at least applicability—speaks in favour of a chain of derogation connecting EU and national law with the Union legal order on top. This resembles Alfred Verdross' model

805 Pernice, 'Multilevel Constitutionalism in the European Union' (n 550) 511.

806 Wendel (n 539) 23.

807 Case 11/70 *Internationale Handelsgesellschaft* [1970] ECR 1125; and Case 314/85 *Foto-Frost* (n 511).

808 BVerfGE 37, 271—*Solange I*, 29 May 1974, para 41; Case 6/64 *Costa v ENEL* (n 485) 592–3.

809 Case 106/77 *Simmenthal II* (n 526).

810 de Witte, 'Direct Effect, Primacy' (n 653) 190. See also Case C-314/08 *Filipiak v Dyrektor Izby Skarbowej w Poznaniu* [2009] ECR I-11049, para 82.

of moderate monism under the primacy of international law which also claims that domestic law in breach of international law is not automatically invalid, but simply needs to be disapplied or amended accordingly.[811]

In contrast to this view, the Member States will nonetheless insist on their constitutional or supreme courts' right to ultra vires review of EU legal acts as a last resort, should they be of the opinion that the Union legislature might have strayed beyond the competences expressly conferred upon it by the Treaties.[812] Hence if, say, the German Constitutional Court considers a specific piece of EU legislation to be ultra vires, it will—although it cannot invalidate it—declare it domestically inapplicable. And if we consider the *Simmenthal* doctrine of disapplication on part of the CJEU to be a manifestation of the chain of derogation, then the same applies to national law, which would then regard EU law as simply inapplicable by way of '*Simmenthal* reversed'. Does that mean that there is a chain of derogation with EU law at the end on one side and with national law at the end on the other side?

The answer to this question is in the negative. The above assumption of 'reversed *Simmenthal*' *qua* judicial ultra vires review does definitely not put the Member States on top of the hierarchy of norms in terms of derogation or disapplication of EU law. One only needs to work from within the existing Union system to see that a solution to this problem can be reached from Union law itself. If we assume that a normative conflict between the CJEU and a national court effectively results in the latter refusing to give effect to a particular EU norm (e.g. because it is allegedly ultra vires), there is general agreement that such a refusal will be sanctioned by infringement proceedings[813]—which would give the CJEU the last word in this matter in any case.[814] Furthermore, it is also settled case law—clearly mirroring Article 27 of the VCLT—that Member States cannot plead that the existence of constitutional barriers would justify failure to comply with their obligations under EU law.[815] Accordingly, it has been argued that any references to a Union act allegedly being ultra vires or not in accordance with a Member State's constitutional identity would ultimately fail before the CJEU as convincing arguments.[816] In particular in the *OMT* case, dissenting judge Lübbe-Wolff surmised that it was not the European Central Bank that had acted ultra vires, but the Bundesverfassungsgericht itself, which had attempted to apply a legal regime to a purely political or legislative, and thus ultimately non-justiciable, question.[817]

[811] Alfred Verdross, 'Droit international public et droit interne' (1954) 32 *Revue de Droit International, de Sciences Diplomatiques et Politiques* 219, 221; Alfred Verdross, *Völkerrecht* (5th edn; Springer, 1964) 113.

[812] Mattias Kumm, 'Who Is the Final Arbiter of Constitutionality in Europe: Three Conceptions of the Relationship between the German Federal Constitutional Court and the European Court of Justice?' (1999) 36 *Common Market Law Review* 351, 364.

[813] Rüdiger Stotz and Petra Škvařilová-Pelzl, 'Europarechtliche Gesetzeskontrolle' in Winfried Kluth and Günter Krings (eds), *Gesetzgebung: Rechtsetzung durch Parlamente und Verwaltungen sowie ihre gerichtliche Kontrolle* (C.F. Müller, 2014) 998–9, para 83.

[814] See Case C-62/14 *OMT* [2014] ECLI:EU:C:2015:400.

[815] Case C-358/03 *Commission v Austria (Workers' Protection)* [2004] ECR I-12055, para 13; Case C-111/00 *Commission v Austria (Biological Agents)* [2001] ECR I-7555, para 12.

[816] Walter Frenz, *Europarecht* (2nd edn; Springer, 2015) 416–17, para 1290.

[817] BVerfGE 134, 366—*OMT*, 14 January 2014; Sondervotum Lübbe-Wolff, paras 4, 7, and 9.

State-centred monists might in this context cite for further evidence the *Landtóva* judgment by the CJEU.[818] After several cases had been brought before the Czech Constitutional Court asking it to revisit the case in accordance with the preliminary ruling by the CJEU, the national court refused on the grounds that the Union had acted ultra vires in this regard, basically interfering with foundational constitutional principles.[819] This reaction was not only heavily criticized for being overtly blunt, entirely disproportionate, and highly undiplomatic,[820] but also because of its petty roots in a domestic dispute between the Czech Constitutional Court and the Supreme Administrative Court, as well as the signs of poor knowledge of EU law and of serious logical flaws in argumentation.[821] Yet, despite this obvious confrontational approach, this situation has not turned out to be as disruptive as it seemed. So far, this decision remains the only openly endorsed and thus completely isolated ultra vires review of Union law. Beyond that, even before the CJEU could have reacted upon another request for a preliminary ruling by the Supreme Administrative Court, this request was withdrawn[822] and the situation was resolved by the Czech Parliament, which repealed the national legal act at issue.[823]

Furthermore, even the very court that had initiated this scepticism vis-à-vis the CJEU—the Bundesverfassungsgericht—justified the outcome of a recent decision on the European Arrest Warrant by stating that the CJEU would have decided this case in the same way.[824] This, in itself, does not prove that the decision was correct and in accordance with EU law, but it nevertheless shows a certain degree of deference towards the Luxembourg Court and accepts, in principle, its last say. Furthermore, the CJEU has already reacted receptively to this practice and confirmed that national authorities are not obligated to execute the arrest warrant, if there is objective evidence for a substantial and systemic risk of inhuman or degrading treatment in the issuing Member State.[825] This is also in line with the *Honeywell* case, in which the Bundesverfassungsgericht demonstrated reticence about how to deal with alleged ultra vires acts. It highlighted that, before it will actually intervene, the breach must be manifest and significant, and—more importantly—the CJEU must always be given prior opportunity to review the measure in question.[826] This means that the Bundesverfassungsgericht intends to avoid any conflicts with the CJEU. Otherwise, should doubts persist, the Member States may also bring an action for annulment

[818] Case C-399/09 *Landtóva* [2011] ECR I-5573.

[819] Constitutional Court, *Slovak Pensions XVII*, 31 January 2012, Pl ÚS 5/12.

[820] Michal Bobek, 'Of Feasibility and Silent Elephants: The Legitimacy of the Court of Justice through the Eyes of National Courts' in Maurice Adams and others (eds), *Judging Europe's Judges* (Hart Publishing, 2013) 226.

[821] Robert Zbíral, 'A Legal Revolution of Negligible Episode? Court of Justice Decision Proclaimed *Ultra Vires*' (2012) 49 *Common Market Law Review* 1475, 1484 and 1487–8.

[822] Case C-253/12 *JS v Česká správa sociálního zabezpečení* [2013] ECLI:EU:C:2013:212.

[823] Jiří Zemánek, 'An "Entirely-Specific" Situation or a Routine Limitation of the National Autonomy? *Slovak Pensions XVII* of the Czech Constitutional Court' in Rainer Arnold (ed), *Limitations of National Sovereignty through European Integration* (Springer, 2016) 137.

[824] BVerfG, 2 BvR 2735/14—*Europäischer Haftbefehl*, 15 December 2015.

[825] Joined Cases C-404/15 and C-659/15 PPU *Aranyosi and Căldăraru* [2016] ECLI:EU:C:2016:198, para 104.

[826] BVerfGE 126, 286—*Honeywell*, 6 July 2010, paras 58–60.

on the grounds of lack of competence under Article 263(2) TFEU against the respective EU institution. Thereby the Court's jurisdiction can somewhat mitigate any remaining lack of clarity in ultra vires cases.[827]

This means that, factually, the Member States certainly retain the power to have their judges adopt false decisions—'false' not in the sense of a national court incorrectly interpreting Union law, but in the meaning of falsely believing in the supremacy of national law over EU law. But if they do so, they must also be willing to pay for it:[828] either by being 'sanctioned' under Articles 258 and 260 TFEU by the CJEU itself, or by having to pay damages to individuals in state liability cases by way of 'privatized' enforcement.[829] Thus, according to the law as it stands, all disputes are eventually decided by the CJEU itself, which entails that there is no evidence for a superior position of the Member States on the chain of derogation vis-à-vis Union law.

In addition to the question of potential derogation of EU law *qua* judicial review by national courts, we also need to consider the derogation of primary law, or the issue of which entity is in control of Treaty amendment. Even if one can accept that the CJEU might sit at the top of the chain of derogation by way of judicial *Kompetenz-Kompetenz*, it has been argued that this does not automatically include legislative *Kompetenz-Kompetenz* on the part of the European Union as a whole.[830] From a public international law perspective, the Member States will of course insist on their crucial role in being the ultimate 'Masters of the Treaties', as even after the entry into force of the Lisbon Treaty, amendments to the Treaties will still generally require the conclusion and ratification of an amending Treaty by all Member States under Article 48(2) TEU. Accordingly, the EU itself is unable to revise the Treaties and to change the division of competences between itself and the Member States unilaterally. However, when we look more closely into the issue of derogation *qua* Treaty amendment or revision, one will see that the Member States do not sit at the top of the chain of derogation either, or that, at least, they need to share this position with others. An important argument against the primacy of national law in this respect is that even though Treaty amendments must ultimately be ratified by all Member States, both the European Parliament and the Commission can now, under Article 48(2) or (6) TEU, also be the catalysts for Treaty reform.

The general pattern of the integration process does not support the theory that the Member States, as the ultimate 'Masters of the Treaties', take the position of a *pouvoir*

[827] Gretchen M. MacMillan, 'The European Union: Is It a Supranational State in the Making?' in Andreas Heineman-Grüder (ed), *Federalism Doomed? European Federalism between Integration and Separation* (Berghahn, 2002) 76.

[828] Somek, 'Monism' (n 558) 358.

[829] Alexander Somek, 'Inexplicable Law: Legality's Adventure in Europe' (2006) 15 *Transnational Law and Contemporary Problems* 627, 630–3.

[830] See also the debate between, on the one hand, Schilling, 'Autonomy' (n 635) 406–7, who regards the Union's lack of legislative *Kompetenz-Kompetenz* being 'at odds' with the Court's judicial *Kompetenz-Kompetenz*, thereby concluding that a legal order without the former cannot contain a court endowed with the latter; and, on the other hand, Weiler and Haltern, 'Autonomy' (n 794) 437, who consider these two types of competence to be distinct from each other and argue that one does not necessarily follow from the other.

constituant of the European Union. The process of European integration is—and despite its most recent difficulties—characterized by a continuous development of the *acquis communautaire*. Each of the new amendments of the existing Treaties, from Rome to Lisbon, constitutes a stage in the integration process which did not follow a classical international legal approach, but rather a constitutional amendment procedure, as set forth in Article 48 TEU.[831] This was explicitly confirmed by the CJEU when it held that the Treaties 'can only be modified by means of the amendment procedure carried out in accordance with [Article 48 TEU]',[832] thereby precluding the Member States from revising or amending the Treaties under general international law. Consequently, Treaty changes are now only possible within a constitutional framework which curtails the original powers of the Member States.

Moreover, the Member States apparently prefer the explicit rules of EU law on Treaty revision over those of international law. In particular the 'Euro crisis' has shown that the Member States are careful to follow EU law when amending the Treaties (in this case, Article 136(3) TFEU, which allows for the establishment of a financial stability mechanism).[833] In this context, one might however argue that the European Stability Mechanism[834] and the Fiscal Compact[835] were—owing to the resistance of the UK—established on the basis of 'ordinary' international agreements and thus outside the framework of primary Union law. This is true, but the core principles of Union law must nevertheless be respected, since these mechanisms function on the basis of one particular EU provision, namely Article 136(3) TFEU.[836] That is why the Court not only held in the *Pringle* case that the conclusion of these agreements was in accordance with Union law, but it also—for the first time—reviewed the validity of a Treaty amendment.[837] Prior to the introduction of the simplified revision procedure via the Lisbon Treaty, it was settled case law that the Court did not have the power to review revision Treaties.[838] The past reasoning was based upon the CJEU's lack of competence to review the Treaties under Article 267 TFEU, which, however, is not sound any more, since any post-Lisbon amendments also result from an act of a Union institution (which the Court has the competence to review under Article 267 TFEU). This should ultimately ensure that the Member States do not evade their obligations under Article 48 TEU to use the amendment procedure laid down therein.

[831] Barents, *Autonomy* (n 588) 159–60; Möllers (n 756) 185 ff.

[832] Case 43/75 *Defrenne v Sabena* [1976] ECR 455, para 58.

[833] European Council, Decision of 25 March 2011 Amending Article 136 of the Treaty of the Functioning of the European Union with regard to a Stability Mechanism for Member States Whose Currency is the Euro (2011/199/EU), OJ 2011 L91, 1.

[834] Treaty establishing the European Stability Mechanism; entered into force on 27 September 2012.

[835] Treaty on Stability, Coordination and Governance in the Economic and Monetary Union; entered into force on 21 December 2012, ratified by all EU Member States except for the UK, the Czech Republic, and Croatia.

[836] Matthias Ruffert, 'The European Debt Crisis and European Union Law' (2011) 48 *Common Market Law Review* 1777, 1790.

[837] Case C-370/12 *Pringle* [2012] ECLI:EU:C:2012:756, paras 47–67.

[838] Case C-253/94 *Roujansky v Council* [1995] ECR I-7, para 11.

It is of course true that no Treaty revision is possible without the Member States, because any amendments need to be ratified by all Member States in accordance with their respective constitutional requirements.[839] Hence national law still plays an important role, but this should not be overestimated. For given the constitutional restrictions imposed on them in the shape of Article 48 TEU, it is equally true that the Member States' derogating powers are somewhat delegated by this norm of European Union law. This is not a genuine legislative *Kompetenz-Kompetenz* in a domestic legal meaning, but it nevertheless supersedes the Member States' originally exclusive *Kompetenz-Kompetenz* on Treaty revision by involving primary EU provisions on how to derogate Union law. In other words, national law cannot claim to be hierarchically superior on the chain of derogation, as this very derogation procedure is governed by Union law itself. Therefore, if one wishes to identify the apex of the chain of derogation exactly in this context, then it is the entirety of the Member States acting jointly with the EU institutions under Article 48 TEU,[840] and only under this provision alone, in a similar way as three-fourths of all states in the United States must ratify constitutional amendments exclusively under Article V of the constitution.

State-centred monists might argue at this point that the three-fourths requirement under Article V of the US Constitution cannot be compared to the unanimity requirement under Article 48 TEU. Since the latter is much stricter, the Member States remain *the* decisive power in terms of Treaty revision. This argument, however, goes entirely amiss, as the key factor in derogation is not this difference in degree, but a difference in kind and the answer to the question of which body of law contains the rule on derogation: in both cases, it is not the single states or Member States, but the overarching EU or American federal law that exclusively regulates constitutional change.

In contrast to Article 48 TEU, the question remains how we should best characterize another candidate provision for a potential legislative *Kompetenz-Kompetenz* of the European Union: Article 352 TFEU. Does this provision really give the EU the competence to change its own competences? The traditional answer has always been in the negative, because the EU is not a sovereign state, and therefore it cannot have the power to grant itself competences which had not been conferred upon it beforehand by the Member States.[841] Yet once we abandon this classic sovereigntist preconception of the constitutional division of powers, it becomes clear that it is the very purpose of Article 352 TFEU to bridge the gap between the Union's objectives and its given powers through an expansion of these powers.[842]

Hence there are two plausible reasons to consider this provision as giving the EU some degree of legislative *Kompetenz-Kompetenz*: first, procedurally speaking, Article 352 TFEU provides, upon a proposal by the Commission, for the Council

[839] See Article 48(4) and (6) TEU. [840] Nettesheim, 'Kompetenzen' (n 800) 402.

[841] Robert Schütze, 'EU Competences: Existence and Exercise' in Anthony Arnull and Damian Chalmers (eds), *The Oxford Handbook of European Union Law* (Oxford University Press, 2015) 79.

[842] Andrea Giardina, 'The Rule of Law and Implied Powers in the European Communities' (1975) 1 *Italian Yearbook of International Law* 99, 102.

to obtain the consent of the European Parliament and subsequently to adopt appropriate measures unanimously. In other words, since neither approval by the Member States is required, nor any national authority can block such measures, this procedure represents an entirely Union-internal procedure. And secondly, substantively speaking, Article 352 TFEU enables the EU to extend its own competences (albeit only restrictively), which was also acknowledged by the Bundesverfassungsgericht when it expressly stated that this provision can lead to a *Kompetenz-Kompetenz* of the European Union.[843]

In this respect, it has also been remarked that it is a mistake to distinguish between a judicial and a legislative *Kompetenz-Kompetenz* of the EU,[844] since, ultimately, the CJEU is an institution of the Union, and has allowed the Union legislator almost complete freedom to interpret its own competences.[845] And nonetheless, as some important decisions show, the CJEU also accepts some limits to the scope of its competence sphere.[846] Article 352 TFEU should therefore be seen as a partial *Kompetenz-Kompetenz*,[847] which is partly within and partly outside the Treaty framework.[848] Thus, from the perspective of the Member States, measures adopted under Article 352 TFEU come very close to a small and informal Treaty amendment.[849]

Finally, to conclude, it has become clear that any amendments to the EU Treaties (i.e. the constitutional basis of the Union) can only be made based on EU law itself. And although the Member States continue to play a paramount role in this respect, they are now bound by the relevant rules on derogation enshrined in Union law. Therefore, there is no evidence for a superior position of the Member States on the chain of derogation vis-à-vis Union law.

iii. When monism turns into pluralism: a practical argument

In addition to the positive legal evidence against monism under the primacy of Member State law, there is also a very persuasive practical argument against it, namely the expediency and *effet utile* of European Union law.[850] If we assumed that the *Grundnorm* of the overall EU system was located within national law, this would turn the effectiveness of Union law upside down and seriously impair it. Such a state-centred reading would probably result in national courts disregarding any determination of matters affecting EU law, and the administration of justice would in

[843] BVerfGE 123, 267—*Lissabon* (n 582) paras 327–8.

[844] See the criticism by Schütze, 'EU Competences' (n 841) 80 fn 18. For Schütze, the main issue with this distinction is that one cannot grant the Union judicial *Kompetenz-Kompetenz* as the competence to declare and determine the limits of the EU's competences, and, at the same time, deny that the Union can determine the limits of its legislative competences. This is an obvious inconsistency.

[845] Ibid., 78.

[846] See e.g. Opinion 2/94 *Accession by the Community to the European Convention on Human Rights* [1996] ECR I-1759, paras 29–30; Opinion 2/13 *EU Accession to the ECHR* (n 782) paras 160–1.

[847] Schütze, 'EU Competences' (n 841) 80.

[848] A fact which has also been recognized by the Bundesverfassungsgericht; see BVerfGE 123, 267—*Lissabon* (n 582) para 328. See also for the UK the European Union Act (2011) part 1, section 8, which states that any ministerial decision on Article 352 TFEU in the Council requires prior authorization from Parliament.

[849] Schütze, 'EU Competences' (n 841) 80–1.

[850] Kaufmann (n 642) 541; and Kirchhof, 'Gewaltenbalance' (n 789) 967–8.

the long run devolve into the hands of private parties, because any party could at any given time claim that the final determination of legal questions by national courts is void for reasons of Union law.[851] The logical consequence of this view would be that Union law was only *apparently* a uniform legal order.

To begin with, this approach is—as monism under the primacy of national law in the context of general international law—out of line with reality from a practical aspect. If one believed that Union law only existed as delegated by Member State law, the result would be that there existed as many Union legal orders as they are Member States. Thus, the emergence of an, inter alia, French, Polish, Austrian, and Danish EU legal order would lead to the paradoxical outcome that the unity of the law, as promoted by monism, would be forfeited in favour of pluralism.[852] This fragmentation would clearly contradict EU legislation and the CJEU's long-standing jurisprudence; furthermore, in the light of the Member States' duty to cooperate in the project of European integration under Article 4(3) TEU, such a plethora of national basic norms would be utterly absurd.[853] If every single Member State really had the individual right to auto-interpret the Union Treaties,[854] and beyond that the right to disapply Union law at their discretion and with reference to constitutional law, the compulsory jurisdiction of the CJEU would become dispensable.[855] Yet it is a fact that the Member States enshrined in the Treaties highly elaborate provisions for centralized judicial review in order to escape this pragmatic nightmare.[856] On top of that, monism under the primacy of Member State law would justify the dreaded disintegration of EU law, as well as realize it in practice, given the lack of uniform validity and supremacy of Union law in this scenario.

State-centred monists might interject at this point that a Member State-based *Grundnorm* could nevertheless prove highly expedient. They might argue that this version of monism would not only be able to guarantee the unity of the law with the *topos* of real political power (i.e. national law), but also to liberate the Union legal order from the burden of seeking legitimacy by firmly anchoring its roots in the political entities of the Member States.[857] However, since political science has meanwhile acknowledged that the European Union is a political system in its own right, it is highly doubtful whether the legitimacy issue would simply disappear by locating the *Grundnorm* in national law.[858] Furthermore, the practical price to be paid for state-centred monism would be too high: this scenario would see the Member States abandoning the validity of Union law, which would then leave a mere torso of EU law, collapsing into national law. The remainder of Union law—if it is still worthy of

[851] Somek, 'Monism' (n 558) 357.

[852] Gerhard Baumgartner, 'Der Rang des Gemeinschaftsrechts im Stufenbau der Rechtsordnung' (2000) 8 *Journal für Rechtspolitik* 84, 77.

[853] Richmond (n 496) 396–7; Schmid (n 768) 429–31; Schroeder (n 486) 230–1.

[854] As suggested by Schilling, 'Autonomy' (n 635) 404 and 407–8.

[855] Schroeder (n 486) 231.

[856] Weiler and Haltern, 'Autonomy' (n 794) 433.

[857] Kaufmann (n 642) 527 and 530; Kirchhof, 'Die Gewaltenbalance' (n 789) 967; Schilling, 'Autonomy' (n 635) 399–400; Schroeder (n 486) 231.

[858] Weiler and Haltern, 'Autonomy' (n 794) 422.

this name—would then no longer require any political legitimacy. Metaphorically speaking, the operation might have been successful, but it left the patient dead.[859]

d. Conclusion: the shortcomings of monism under the primacy of Member State law

The foregoing sections have shown that conceiving of the relationship between Member State law and EU law in a monist fashion under the primacy of national law is not sufficiently convincing. To assume the existence of a national *Grundnorm* (or rather: a plethora of national *Grundnormen*) does not and cannot contribute to a better understanding of the EU legal order, let alone explain it in the light of contravening Union as well as Member State practice. It would therefore be extremely misleading to say that monism under the primacy of Member State law would give us the most useful and empirically accurate tool to describe the workings of EU law.[860]

It is evident that the practical ramifications of monism with national law superordinated to Union law would be devastating in terms of legal stability. This model would presuppose that the EU is principally defenceless against any national intervention. If a Member State were to give up its constitutional self-restraint and to repeal its ratification statute or the respective legal act giving domestic effect to Union law, substantive EU law as well as any ensuing infringement proceedings would have to be regarded as non-law or unlawful, because they would both be entirely incompatible with the national *Grundnorm*.[861] Hence the EU would only exist by the grace of the Member States, which would also entail that the Union could only barely guarantee the uniformity and effectiveness of its own law. This, in turn, would mean that the Member States would have retained full sovereignty, but this is a view which is not even held any more with regard to general international law,[862] where both scholars and practitioners either advocate a view that is altogether non-monist (dualism or pluralism) or monist under the primacy of international law[863]—but never monist under the primacy of national law.

This result also further corroborates the observation that regarding the disapplication of national law (if found to conflict with Union law) and the derogation of EU law itself, it is the European Union legal order that has the last say. With regard to the former situation, it is absolutely clear that any normative conflicts between national and EU law will be resolved on the basis of EU law itself, and if a Member State refuses to comply, sanctions on the basis of EU law itself can ensue.[864] With regard to the latter scenario, it is of course true that the power to amend the treaties rests with the Member States and their powers under general international law.[865] However,

[859] Schroeder (n 486) 232. [860] Richmond (n 496) 397; Schroeder (n 486) 232.

[861] Schmid (n 768) 430. [862] Ibid.

[863] Alfred Verdross and Bruno Simma, *Universelles Völkerrecht* (3rd edn; Duncker & Humblot, 1984) 23 ff.

[864] Somek, 'Monism' (n 558) 358; Somek, 'Inexplicable Law' (n 829) 630–3.

[865] Katja S. Ziegler, 'The Relationship between EU Law and International Law' in Dennis Patterson and Anna Södersten (eds), *A Companion to European Union Law and International Law* (Wiley & Blackwell, 2016) 43–4.

the reference in Article 48 TEU to the respective national ratification procedures does not mean that Treaty revisions are exclusively based on national constitutions; in fact, they are also dependent on Article 48 TEU and thereby Union law itself.[866]

Furthermore, this also means that there is no clearly identifiable chain of delegation between (allegedly) superordinated national law and subordinated EU law, and that the argument that EU law owes its validity and effectiveness entirely to the national mandate enshrined in the respective ratification statutes, is plainly wrong. The source of validity of positive Union law does not lie in national law, but in the EU Treaties, and by creating the EU and transferring powers to it, the Member States also gave up any claim to contain this very source of validity any longer. Thus, the Union today exists as an autonomous legal order which is valid independently of the Member States.[867]

Even if every single Member State repealed its national ratification statute, the EU would continue to exist (probably with an immensely decreased degree of domestic effectiveness and an overabundance of infringement proceedings, but it would continue to exist as a valid legal order). The EU and its institutions constitute more than just the sum of the cumulatively ceded and then reassembled competences of the Member States. The law of the European Union cannot be accurately perceived through the eyes of national law any more, not even by 'adding' all national legal orders,[868] as this would never equal the very entity that is the current EU legal order. Lastly, it also untrue that only a monist model under the primacy of national law would allow for the full use of the democratic legitimacy potentials of the Member States on behalf of the European Union. This argument does not take into consideration that these potentials can also be fulfilled by other models, not just state-centred monism, but also, for example, autonomous 'legitimacy-building' on the European level. This, however, is still work in progress, since the mere transfer of democratic legitimacy of the Member States to the EU institutions is not sufficient as long as autonomous European devices with a view to supplementing the state-based democratic legitimacy of the EU have not been realized.[869]

Therefore, in conclusion, a monist view of the relationship between the EU and the Member States under the primacy of the latter seems to be of little practical use to explain this very relationship. In addition to highly problematic theoretical issues such as the collapse of this version of monism into pluralism and the subsequent breakdown of the *effet utile* of Union law itself, it is simply not in accordance with the law as it is. In this vein, the last model to be explored at this point remains a monist conception of the relationship between European Union law and Member State law under the primacy of the former. Let us now investigate whether this model is capable of describing the relationship between national and EU law in a plausible way.

[866] Barents, *Autonomy* (n 588) 258.

[867] Ipsen, *Europäisches Gemeinschaftsrecht* (n 799) 58 and 62–3.

[868] Wendel (n 539) 23.

[869] Schmid (n 768) 431.

(5) *Monism under the primacy of European Union law*

a. Preliminary problems of the EU-centred monist model

The following sections will now discuss the relationship between EU and Member State from the viewpoint of monism under the primacy of European Union law, i.e. the model probably favoured by the proponents of the Vienna School of Jurisprudence. To this end, and since it is the overall purpose of this book to defend this version of monism, the structure of these sections will also differ from the foregoing sections: after a short introduction, two different approaches to monism under the primacy of EU law will be discussed. Subsequently, EU-centred monism will be defended against the most fervent attacks and be presented as the most plausible model to describe the relationship between Union and Member State law.

At the outset, it is again crucial to stress that if we consider European Union law as an autonomous legal order, then there is, *per definitionem*, no place for another independent source of law.[870] However, the main weakness of this approach, when considered empirically, is that the national legal orders could not be considered autonomous any more; in fact, they would be regarded as delegated and derived from the Union legal order. In other words, in this scenario EU law, by its own authority, would have unilaterally modified the nature and scope of national constitutions to the extent that the Member States cannot in any way prevent or control their competences any more.[871] Not only does this mean that the Member States have lost all of their legislative *Kompetenz-Kompetenz* to the European Union, but also that the *Grundnorm* has shifted to the EU legal order.[872] One could therefore say that a 'legal revolution' has taken place which replaced those national *Grundnormen* by one single European Union *Grundnorm*.[873] Thus, the Member States would have been transformed into pre-federated states in a pre-federated model,[874] which, as is most obvious, would not correspond to the reality of European integration.[875]

Perhaps we should therefore employ a model of monism, which could—by way of a more nuanced and elaborate analysis—explain how EU law became autonomous through emancipation and thereby established itself as the hierarchically superior body of law, including its own *Grundnorm*, without transforming the Member States into federal states. To this end, the subsequent section will examine two models of 'legal revolution': first, the EU's *a posteriori* emancipation from international law; and, secondly, the EU's a priori emancipation from Member State law on the basis of the so-called *Gesamtakttheorie*.

[870] See Kelsen, *Pure Theory* (n 24) 195; Barents, *Autonomy* (n 588) 174.
[871] Jean-Louis Seurin, 'Towards a European Constitution? Problems of Political Integration' [1994] *Public Law* 625, 625.
[872] Grussmann (n 138) 46. [873] Barents, *Autonomy* (n 588) 185.
[874] René Barents, 'The Precedence of EU Law from the Perspective of Constitutional Pluralism' (2009) 5 *European Constitutional Law Review* 421, 432.
[875] See also Case 33/67 *Kurrer* [1968] ECR 127, 135, referring to the Union as being 'composed of States, each of which retains its own national legal order'.

b. Two possible models of EU-centred monism

i. (R)Evolution: a posteriori emancipation from international law

One way to regard the EU legal order as having primacy in a unitary system is to assume that the Union Treaties have been gradually uncoupled from their international legal source of validity a posteriori;[876] in this sense, the international legal *Grundnorm* of EU law was subsequently replaced by another one.[877] To be more precise, this monist model—quite uncontroversially—holds that the EU legal order was not born as a constitutional order as it is today and that, at least at its inception, it plainly was a creature of international law.[878] Furthermore, one can also undeniably state that the Union has subsequently taken on an autonomous legal life of its own.

What is more controversial, nevertheless, is the question of whether—by moving away from the status of an international organization, in which the Member States were the sole 'Masters of the Treaties', towards the recognition of a new *pouvoir constituant*, giving rise to a genuinely autonomous legal order—a change in the *Grundnorm* has occurred. Kelsen himself clarifies that such a change is possible, most notably in the case of a revolution, but if and only if individuals behave in conformity with the new order and the previous government is hence removed successfully and efficaciously.[879] Given the EU's original international law status and the Treaties' initial character as ordinary international agreements, their transformation must have occurred later on, or a posteriori, through the constitutionalizing jurisprudence of the CJEU.[880] When asked to pinpoint such a possible revolution in the Union legal order, lawyers will instinctively mention the revolutionary cases *Van Gend en Loos* and *Costa v ENEL*. By introducing constitutional principles such as direct effect and supremacy, the Court constitutionalized the Treaties and transformed the EU Treaties into a 'Treaty-Constitution'.[881] Beyond that, because of their transferring of powers to the Union, the Member States have definitively and irreversibly set up a system whose very foundations cannot even be compromised by Treaty revision.[882] This approach entirely dismisses international law as the source of validity of Union law and the Member States as the 'Masters of the Treaties'. This is also in accordance with the CJEU's stance that the EU legal order does not form

[876] Dowrick (n 487) 184–5; Richmond (n 496) 393–4; Grussmann (n 138) 59–60. Cf. against this view, Schilling, 'Autonomy' (n 635) 403–9.

[877] Schroeder (n 486) 236.

[878] Aidan O'Neill, *Decisions of the European Court of Justice and their Constitutional Implications* (Butterworths, 1994) 8; Schilling, 'Autonomy' (n 635) 403; J.H.H. Weiler, 'The Transformation of Europe' (1991) 100 *Yale Law Journal* 2403, 2413.

[879] Kelsen, *General Theory* (n 26) 118; Kelsen, *Pure Theory* (n 24) 209.

[880] Koen Lenaerts, 'Constitutionalism and the Many Faces of Federalism' (1990) 38 *American Journal of Comparative Law* 205, 208–9.

[881] See Eric Stein, 'Toward Supremacy of Treaty-Constitution by Judicial Fiat: On the Margin of the *Costa* Case' (1965) 63 *Michigan Law Review* 491–518.

[882] Case 6/64 *Costa v ENEL* (n 485) 593; Opinion 1/91 *European Economic Area I* [1991] ECR I-6079, para 71.

part of general international law any more,[883] which strongly insinuates a newly and revolutionarily established EU *Grundnorm*.[884]

Some, however, argue that this process of constitutionalization was a gradual evolutionary, and not an abrupt revolutionary development, and that the CJEU was in fact authorized to decouple the Union legal order from general international law by way of Article 19 TEU.[885] This approach is nonetheless highly problematic, as it remains illusionary to think that the original intent or the will of the historical Treaty framers can be determined[886]—in particular given the fact that the *travaux préparatoires* of the original Treaties remain unpublished and largely inaccessible. It could therefore be argued that the Member States—as the original constituent powers—withdrew when the Treaties entered into force, and nowadays only act as revising powers within the course of Treaty amendments under Article 48 TEU. Thus, the historical will of the Member States can only be taken into consideration to the extent that there are any indications in this respect in the positive law.[887]

Another argument in favour of the evolutionary approach is that the constitutionalizing jurisprudence of the CJEU was inspired by the constitutional traditions of the Member States and their supreme or constitutional courts which also further develop national law through their case law.[888] Especially the Constitution of the UK is, in the words of A.V. Dicey, entirely judge-made and hence not the source, but the result of the courts' jurisprudence.[889] The constitutionalization of the EU could therefore be easily compared with the development of the British Constitution, which is characterized more by a creeping process of accumulating crucial and principal decisions by the courts than by the formal activities of the *pouvoir constituant* in a constitutional assembly.[890] This argument would then plausibly explain the change of the *Grundnorm* in evolutionary, rather than in revolutionary terms, and as the constitutional basis of the EU legal order.[891]

If we consider these issues in terms of the pure theory of law, it needs to be stressed, however, that the *Grundnorm* can only change by way of a legal revolution (which does not necessarily need to be a political revolution),[892] but not constitutional evolution. This means that the preconditions under which the legal acts of a given legal order are interpreted as valid have changed, because a new constitution came into existence by a means not recognized by the pre-existing constitution.[893] The

883 Case 6/64 *Costa v ENEL* (n 485) 593, wherein the CJEU, in contrast to Case 26/62 *Van Gend en Loos* (n 650) 12, suddenly changes its description of the EU as a 'new legal order of international law' to simply 'new legal order'; Opinion 1/91 *EEA I* (n 882) para 21.

884 Schroeder (n 486) 238.

885 Federico Mancini and David Keeling, 'Democracy and the European Court of Justice' (1994) 57 *Modern Law Review* 175, 186.

886 Schroeder (n 486) 238–9.

887 Robert Lecourt, *Le juge devant le marché commun* (Institut universitaire de hautes études internationales, 1970) 64; Schroeder (n 486) 239.

888 O'Neill (n 878) 8.

889 Albert Venn Dicey, *Introduction to the Study of the Law of the Constitution* (10th edn; Palgrave Macmillan, 1979) 196–7.

890 Stefan Oeter, 'Souveränität und Demokratie als Probleme in der "Verfassungsentwicklung" der Europäischen Union' (1995) 55 *Zeitschrift für ausländisches öffentliches Recht und Völkerrecht* 659, 689.

891 Schroeder (n 486) 240.

892 Ibid.

893 Kelsen, *General Theory* (n 26) 118; Kelsen, *Pure Theory* (n 24) 209–10.

decisive question thus is whether this change or replacement of the positive-legal constitution of the EU was lawful under the pre-existing constitution. In this vein, the constitutionalization of the Treaties through the case law of the CJEU indeed represents a legal revolution,[894] because the Treaties themselves do not contain any provision which could legally legitimize the replacement of the EU's international legal source of validity with a judicially made Treaty-constitution. Neither Article 19 TEU nor Article 48 TEU constitute a panacea in this respect unless one is willing to transgress the boundaries of the positive law and cross over into the realm of natural law.[895] Admittedly, the principles to observe the law and to protect the rule of law serve as gap-filling instruments to correct and complement the positive law, but it does not enable it to go beyond itself and to change its source of validity.[896]

Thus, in the eyes of the CJEU and majority of European scholars, the normative force of EU law is no longer derived from its international legal foundations. Its historically first constitution is the Rome Treaty[897] which, 'albeit concluded in the form of an international agreement, nonetheless constitutes the constitutional charter of a Community based on a rule of law …'.[898] This constitutional jurisprudence certainly represents a 'juridical-revolutionary' attack on the pre-existing *Grundnorm*, but leaves the question unanswered whether it indeed succeeded.[899] For Kelsen, a legal revolution and the change of the basic norm can only be legitimate if and only if a new constitution is established on the basis of this new *Grundnorm* by legislative act or custom, and if this new constitution is effective, because the norms created in conformity with it are by and large applied and obeyed.[900]

Since the constitution of the European Union in its current form was not created by a legislative act, it can only have been created by custom in the same way as the British constitution.[901] Furthermore, it is undisputable that this custom-based EU constitution is, by and large, effective, since the norms created in accordance with it—inter alia, the decisions of the CJEU, secondary EU law, and international agreements concluded by the Union—are by and large effective. This efficacy is ultimately safeguarded not only by the Union institutions themselves, but also by the national courts and authorities as well as individuals who comply with EU law.[902] The question remains, however, whether there is an *opinio iuris*, i.e. whether the acts, which constitute the custom, take place in the belief that they ought to take place.[903] What is more, we also need to ask whose *opinio iuris* is decisive in this respect. As has been correctly observed, the national courts largely accept the views reflected in the

[894] Grussmann (n 138) 59–60; Richmond (n 496) 393 and 399.

[895] O'Neill (n 878) 24–5 and Schilling, 'Autonomy' (n 635) 401.

[896] Schroeder (n 486) 240; di Fabio (n 610) 952.

[897] Schütze, 'On "Federal" Ground' (n 634) 1082.

[898] Opinion 1/91 *EEA I* (n 882) para 21; Case 294/83 *Les Verts v Parliament* [1986] ECR 1339, para 23.

[899] Schroeder (n 486) 241.

[900] Kelsen, *Pure Theory* (n 24) 210.

[901] Dicey (n 889) 39.

[902] Schroeder (n 486) 242; Neil Walker, 'The Philosophy of European Union Law' in Anthony Arnull and Damian Chalmers (eds), *The Oxford Handbook of European Union Law* (Oxford University Press, 2015) 23.

[903] Kelsen, *Pure Theory* (n 24) 225–6.

case law of the CJEU, but there are also several constitutional and supreme courts which balk at the claim that the EU legal order is supreme and autonomous. This finding would therefore speak against a custom-based constitution of the EU legal order.[904]

In terms of the pure theory of law, however, customary law is not created through a centralized procedure, but by the behaviour of individuals who are subject to the legal order in question. Thus, if an overwhelming majority of individuals participate in the creation of custom and thereby accept it as valid and binding law, this custom-based law becomes valid and binding on all individuals. As a result, the behaviour and *opinio iuris* of national courts and authorities is irrelevant for the creation of customary law, and their decisions may only be indicative, not constitutive, in ascertaining whether something is custom or not.[905]

If we acknowledge that individuals have now behaved for several decades in conformity with the Union constitution, and that even in the few cases in which individuals have tried to contest the basis of this constitution before national courts, they were subsequently ordered to comply with it, then no doubt remains that an according *opinio iuris* has successfully developed. In particular with regard to the practice of the Union institutions, first and foremost the jurisprudence of the CJEU, which has been accepted so far by the Member States, the assumption that the international law-based *Grundnorm* of Union law has been replaced by a genuine *Grundnorm* of EU law is not unreasonable at all.[906]

ii. Big bang: a priori emancipation from national law and the Gesamtakttheorie

In contrast to an a posteriori development of the EU's *Grundnorm* by way of judicial revolution, it has also been argued that the Union legal order already possessed its own *Grundnorm* right from the start, i.e. a priori. This theory is best explained by Hans Peter Ipsen's *Gesamtakttheorie* ('collective act theory'). Although this theory accepts the initial international legal character of the Union Treaties, it concurrently denies that this quasi-contractual basis necessarily entails a contractual-obligatory and thus a non-constitutional content of the created legal order.[907] In other words, the basis for the creation of this legal order may be one thing, but its content and nature are another one.[908] Hence there is no continuity between the founding treaty and the subsequent constitutional legal order, and one needs to distinguish sharply between genesis and validity.[909]

Ipsen emphasizes that his concept of *Gesamtakt* denotes the fusion of the individual will of states into one collective will, which subsequently enables the creation of legal norms beyond their own remits and the original consensus of the participating states. Accordingly, Ipsen describes the creation of the European Union as a 'collective act of State integrational powers' (*Gesamtakt staatlicher*

904 Schilling, 'Autonomy' (n 635) 397; Schmid (n 768) 433.

905 Kelsen, *Pure Theory* (n 24) 228–9, 232–6 and 255.

906 Schroeder (n 486) 242–3.

907 Ipsen, *Europäisches Gemeinschaftsrecht* (n 799) 59.

908 Albert Haenel, *Die vertragsmäßigen Elemente der deutschen Reichsverfassung* (Haessel, 1873) 38.

909 Peters, 'Rechtsordnungen und Konstitutionalisierung' (n 407) 36.

Integrationsgewalt) through which an autonomous legal order with defined competences and its own supranational public powers was established.[910] The innovative element of this thesis is that this transfer of powers indeed curtails the Member States' powers. These powers are not to be considered akin to virginity, as MacCormick puts it, which can be lost without anybody else gaining it.[911] Once these powers were transferred, the Member States lost control over them, and subsequently, these competences can only be exercised jointly with the other Member States and the EU itself.[912] In this regard, not the existing powers, in the proper meaning of the word, were transferred, but rather new powers were thereby created.[913]

Consequently, the *Gesamtakttheorie* implies that the constitution and the legal order of the EU are originary and therefore rooted neither in international law nor national law;[914] that Union law is superior to Member State law, which means that it cannot be derogated through a national *lex posterior*;[915] that, in contrast to international law, individual Member States cannot simply repeal the Treaties and the created legal order through individual decisions;[916] and that although the Union is not a federal state, it is more than an ordinary international organization or confederation, and possesses some of the Member States' sovereignty, which is thus shared between the states and the EU.[917] Some scholars argue that the *Gesamtakttheorie* has considerably influenced the case law of the CJEU.[918] And indeed, the Court seems to have appropriated this theory in *Costa v ENEL* when stating that 'in contrast with ordinary international treaties, the EEC Treaty *has created* its own legal system which, on the entry into force of the Treaty, became an integral part of the legal systems of the Member States and which their courts are bound to apply'.[919] It is interesting to note that the CJEU uses the present perfect tense here: it does not say that the EU Treaties were enacted as international agreements which subsequently changed into a constitution; rather, it considers the Treaties as autonomous and underived sources of law as of the very moment of their entry into force. As a result, their source of validity could have never been located in a norm of international law, but only in a particular EU *Grundnorm*.[920] Hence all of the founding Treaties in the shape of the Paris and Rome Treaties need to be seen as a uniform[921] and historically first constitution of the EU, whose provisions are to be complied with in accordance with the Union's own *Grundnorm*.[922] In this light, former President of the CJEU Hans Kutscher also regarded the Treaties as disconnected from international law, because they were

[910] Ipsen, *Europäisches Gemeinschaftsrecht* (n 799) 60–3.
[911] MacCormick, 'Beyond the Sovereign State' (n 486) 16.
[912] Karl-Heinz Klein, *Die Übertragung von Hoheitsrechten* (Duncker & Humblot, 1952) 27–8.
[913] Dana Burchardt, *Die Rangfrage im europäischen Normenverbund* (Mohr-Siebeck, 2015) 88.
[914] Ipsen, *Europäisches Gemeinschaftsrecht* (n 799) 63 and 195.
[915] Ibid., 59 and 279. [916] Ibid., 59. [917] Ibid., 190–1 and 229–30.
[918] Thomas Oppermann, *Europarecht* (2nd edn; C.H. Beck, 1999) paras 525–6; Gert Nicolaysen, *Europarecht I* (Nomos, 1991) 30; Badura (n 638) 72.
[919] Case 6/64 *Costa v ENEL* (n 485) 593 (emphasis added).
[920] Schroeder (n 486) 244.
[921] Joined Cases 27 and 39/59 *Campolongo* [1960] ECR 391, 405; Case 6/60 *Humblet* (n 585), 569; Case 221/88 *Busseni* [1990] ECR I-495, paras 13–14.
[922] Schroeder (n 486) 244.

ratified without reservations, and because national authorities were aware that national law could not be relied upon any more to escape obligations under Union law. Therefore, the Treaties established a common constitution for the Member States, and it is this specific character which makes it impossible to consider the Union a mere association of states under international law.[923]

Consequently, the *Gesamtakttheorie* has also been coined the 'big bang'[924] theory because it brought the European Union and its autonomous *Grundnorm* into existence from the quasi-gravitational singularity of the common will and the respective acts of the Member States. If one agrees with this approach, then a new *Grundnorm* was accepted concurrently with the entry into force of the EU Treaties. And this new *Grundnorm* of Union law states that the addressees of EU law ought to behave as the historically first EU constitution prescribes.[925] Hence, since the Union constitution was created by a legislative act, it should suffice that it is, by and large, effective—a fact which is beyond any doubt. The question remains, however, what this means for any possibly existing customary law within the EU legal order. This should, however, not be an issue within the context of European Union law. Although the development of customary Union law within the boundaries of the Treaties is possible, in particular to fill gaps in the positive law,[926] the CJEU is not only very reluctant to recognize custom as a source of law,[927] but has also clarified that customary law *contra legem* can never be accepted,[928] as this would be incompatible with the strict requirements of Treaty revision under Article 48 TEU.[929] Therefore, the entry into force of the codified Union constitution by way of the EU *Grundnorm* remains the only valid source of law within the Union legal order.[930]

In conclusion, the notion of the *Gesamtakt* attempts to develop a theory which explains the relationship between national and EU law in an eclectic fashion and thus on the basis of various other theories, thereby taking into consideration their numerous advantages: the creation of the EU itself on the basis of international agreements is being described by way of traditional international law; the Union's originary powers on the basis of federal integration theory through the respective constitutional provisions in national law; and the supremacy of EU law via the co-existence of two bodies of law which necessitates the resolution of normative

923 Hans Kutscher, 'Thesen zu den Methoden der Auslegung des Gemeinschaftsrechts, aus der Sicht eines Richters' in Gerichtshof der Europäischen Gemeinschaften (ed), *Begegnungen von Justiz und Hochschule am 27.–29.9.1976* (Gerichtshof der Europäischen Gemeinschaften, 1976) I-32.

924 Weiler, 'Transformation of Europe' (n 878) 2407; Schilling, 'Autonomy' (n 635) 391.

925 Schroeder (n 486) 246; Kelsen, *Pure Theory* (n 24) 8.

926 Case C-133/06 *Parliament v Council (Refugee Status)* [2008] ECR I-3189, Opinion of Advocate General Maduro, para 28.

927 Thijmen Koopmans, 'The Theory of Interpretation and the Court of Justice' in David O'Keeffe and Antonio Bavasso (eds), *Judicial Review in European Union Law: Essays in Honour of Lord Slynn of Hadley* (Kluwer, 2000) 56.

928 Case C-426/93 *Germany v Council (Business Registers)* [1995] ECR I-3723, para 21; Case C-133/06 *Parliament v Council (Refugee Status)* [2008] ECR I-3189, para 60.

929 Case 43/75 *Defrenne v Sabena* (n 832) para 58.

930 Schroeder (n 486) 247.

conflicts between them.[931] However, the decisive factor for monism is that the *Gesamtakttheorie* is capable of unifying national and EU law from a procedural perspective, most importantly on the basis of the preliminary ruling procedure and the direct applicability of regulations.[932] Thus, the relevant acts of ratification or constitutional provisions giving effect to Union law within domestic law are not the source of validity of the EU legal order; rather, it is valid and effective in itself. The consensus of the Member States is proof that they have generally accepted the case law of the CJEU in this respect,[933] and that there now is a *Grundnorm* of EU law which came about by a *Gesamtakt*.

iii. Interim conclusion

Both approaches—the revolutionary a posteriori emancipation of EU law from international law via judicial constitutionalization as well as its a priori emancipation from national law through a potential *Gesamtakt*—undoubtedly have their merits, and both appear to be very plausible from their individual and yet slightly different perspectives. However, ultimately, what remains crucial is that both approaches follow a monist way under the primacy of Union law: either the *Grundnorm* of the legal order of EU and Member States has gradually shifted there *qua* constitutionalizing jurisprudence, or it was immediately transplanted there via the *Gesamtakt* of the Member States. Either way, this *Grundnorm* constitutes the source of validity of the Union constitution in the shape of the Treaties, which, in turn, gives validity to secondary EU law. And even though there is no clear chain of delegation between Union and national law (a problem that will be discussed below), Member State law ranks inferior to EU law and must give way in the case of conflict. The interim conclusion, therefore, is that the difference between the two theories does not matter very much in the end, as both result in monism under the primacy of EU law. The subsequent sections will nonetheless now discuss arguments against this version of monism and also engage with counterarguments to them, trying to defend monism and to rebut those arguments against a potential change in the *Grundnorm* of European Union law.

c. Defending monism under the primacy of EU law: six arguments

The section at hand will now present six arguments against the thesis that there is a European Union *Grundnorm* and that EU law is thus superior to Member State law, or—succinctly put—that the EU law system can be best seen as a monist legal order under the primacy of Union law. Each argument will be discussed critically and then contrasted with plausible counterarguments in order to maintain this Union-centred monist view. These arguments, which are mostly based on Trevor

[931] Heribert Franz Köck, *Der Gesamtakt in der deutschen Integrationslehre* (Duncker & Humblot, 1978) 72–4.

[932] Ibid., 74 fn 107 and 108; Bleckmann, *Grundgesetz und Völkerrecht* (n 184) 304.

[933] Nicolaysen (n 918) 23–4; Waldemar Hummer, '"Etatisierung" der Union durch die neue Verfassung?' in Erhard Busek and Waldemar Hummer (eds), *Die Konstitutionalisierung der Verbandsgewalt in der (neuen) Europäischen Union* (Böhlau, 2006) 24–5.

C. Hartley's analysis of the relationship between international law and EU law,[934] are: first, that the form of the EU constitution in their shape of international treaties rather points against a change of the *Grundnorm*; second, that the procedure under which the EU Treaties were negotiated and concluded speaks against a monist view under the primacy of Union law; third, that the lack of physical enforcement mechanisms on part of the Union puts the Member States—not the EU—in control; fourth, that a change of the *Grundnorm* is only possible on the grounds of democratic legitimacy, and that the EU possesses little to none; fifth, that the overall *Kompetenz-Kompetenz* remains with the Member States; and last, that there is no real chain of delegation between Union and national law, thus making a hierarchy of norms between those two bodies of law inconceivable. At the beginning, however, two preliminary points need to be examined with respect to a potential change of the *Grundnorm*.

i. Two preliminary arguments

At the outset, Hartley correctly notes that the change of the *Grundnorm* is not an everyday occurrence. It rather is a cataclysmic event, resulting from changes in the basic political structure, and these very changes are of such magnitude that they fracture the foundations of the existing legal order.[935] As some courts in Pakistan, Uganda, and South Rhodesia (now Zimbabwe) have held regarding revolutions[936] and in accordance with Kelsen's thoughts on the change of the basic norm, such an event would usually involve the seizure of power by force and the removal of the hitherto legitimate government. If the revolution is successful, the old order will cease to exist and a new order begin to be efficacious, since the individuals whose behaviour the new order regulates behave, by and large, in conformity with this new order. Consequently, this new legal order will be considered a valid legal order under a new presupposed *Grundnorm*.[937] Another example of such a legal and political cataclysm includes the Glorious Revolution of 1688,[938] in which the English Parliament declared William and Mary, on the basis of the Bill of Rights, the new monarchs without the necessary assent of the old king, James II, who had fled the country.[939]

The paradoxical problem with this situation is that under the constitution, a statute was only valid if it was consented to by the monarch. William and Mary, however, were not King and Queen unless and until the Bill of Rights became valid law, and the Bill of Rights was not valid law unless and until the monarch had consented to it. James II did of course not consent to it, and therefore under the old

934 Trevor C. Hartley, 'International Law and the Law of the European Union—A Reassessment' (2001) 22 *British Yearbook of International Law* 1, 1–35.

935 Ibid., 6.

936 For Pakistan: *The State v Dosso* [1958] 2 Pakistan SCR 180; for Uganda: *Uganda v Commissioner of Prisons, ex parte Matovu* [1966] EA 514; for South Rhodesia/Zimbabwe: *Madzimbamuto v Lardner-Burke* [1969] AC 645 (PC), and *R v Ndhlovu* [1968] 4 SA 515.

937 Kelsen, *Pure Theory* (n 24) 208–11; Kelsen, *General Theory* (n 26) 437.

938 Hartley (n 934) 5.

939 See Frederic William Maitland, *The Constitutional History of England* (Cambridge University Press, 1908) 283–5.

Grundnorm, the Bill of Rights was invalid, William and Mary were not the rightful King and Queen, and all Acts of Parliament were null and void. These consequences can only be avoided by postulating a new *Grundnorm* which reflects the actual power relationships in England at that time: William and Mary ruled successfully and effectively, whilst James II never succeeded in regaining the throne. Thus, since a change of the *Grundnorm* appears to be an affront to the principle of legality and a denial of the rule of law, a possible change of the *Grundnorm* in the context of the EU legal order needs to be considered on very strict grounds.[940]

From this follows, as a second preliminary argument, that in most instances the new constitution—after a change of the *Grundnorm*—would have been invalid under the pre-existing legal order, i.e. under the old *Grundnorm*. This means that one can only maintain that the new constitution was valid by concurrently arguing that the *Grundnorm* has indeed changed.[941] In the case of the EU, one could therefore argue that since the founding Treaties are perfectly valid under international law,[942] there is no need to assert a change of the *Grundnorm* to explain why they are being applied. This certainly makes a change of the *Grundnorm* much harder to justify, but it cannot be ruled out on this ground alone, given that there are historical precedents for such a change.[943] The original Canadian Constitution, for instance, was a schedule to a British Act of Parliament, the Canada Act 1982,[944] and hence it derived its legal validity from British law and its respective *Grundnorm*. Yet it is nowadays generally accepted that if the issue ever arose, the Canadian courts would conclude that there has been a change of the *Grundnorm* and that the Canadian Constitution is now self-sustaining.[945]

In the light of these two preliminary arguments, let us now examine the already mentioned six arguments against a potential change of the *Grundnorm* in the context of EU law and the respective six counterarguments speaking in favour of such a change.

ii. The form of the EU constitution

The first argument concerns the form of the constitutional basis of the European Union. Whenever the Member States acted, they always intended to conclude agreements under international law, not a constitution.[946] After all, there is no European *demos* that could have acted as a *pouvoir constituant*.[947] This is true for the earliest treaties, as well as for all other subsequent treaties, and even for the failed constitutional treaty which, at least in name, used more state-like language. This is

[940] Hartley (n 934) 5–6. [941] Ibid., 6.

[942] Bill Davies, *Resisting the European Court of Justice* (Cambridge University Press, 2012) 49.

[943] Hartley (n 934) 6. [944] Canada Act 1982, c. 11, 29 March 1982.

[945] Hartley (n 934) 6. This view is also supported by, inter alia, Edward McWhinney, 'The Constitutional Patriation Project, 1980–82' (1984) 32 *American Journal of Comparative Law* 241, 243 and 248–63; Samuel V. LaSelva, *The Moral Foundations of Canadian Federalism* (McGill-Queen's University Press, 1996) 89–90.

[946] Schilling, 'Autonomy' (n 635) 393–4.

[947] Paul Kirchhof, 'Deutsches Verfassungsrecht und Europäisches Gemeinschaftsrecht' [1991] *Europarecht-Beiheft 1/1991*, 11, 12 ff.

further underscored by the fact that the EU Treaties open with a reference to the heads of state of the contracting parties, followed by a preamble. After that, they provide a list of plenipotentiaries and state that they, 'having exchanged their full powers, found in good and due form, have agreed as follows: … '.[948] At the end, the Treaties are then signed by the plenipotentiaries.[949] This is the language of traditional treaty-making,[950] not constitutional state-building, and therefore it is highly unlikely that a change of the *Grundnorm* in the relationship between the EU itself and the Member States has in fact occurred.[951]

This argument, however, remains unconvincing. It is of course true that the form of the EU constitution was concluded, in its original form, as international agreements. But neither the proponents of the gradual constitutionalization theory nor those of the *Gesamtakttheorie* deny this claim, which is, ultimately, compatible with both monist theories. Again, it should be emphasized that the basis for the creation of a legal order may be one thing, but its content and nature are another one.[952] The argument that the form of the EU constitution speaks against a possible change of the *Grundnorm* becomes even less convincing if compared with the early days and the further development of the United States Constitution. The framers of the American Constitution originally understood the future states of the United States to have the same legal status as foreign states, and the First Congress recognized that those states that had initially not ratified the constitution (i.e. North Carolina and Rhode Island) were to be considered foreign states.[953] It is especially the language used in Article VII of the constitution which hints at the original international legal nature of the United States: the *ratification* of a legal document by *states*, first through their representatives by name and subsequently their individual legislatures, 'the supreme authority in each State'.[954] Thus, it was the governments of the states which ratified the constitution, and it is this fact which put the United States of America at the outset, just as the EU, in between an international and national legal structure.[955]

Furthermore, it could also be argued that the concept of the *pouvoir constituant* is merely a political device developed within the course of the French Revolution. In pure constitutional law terms, i.e. *after* the entry into force of the constitution, however, this concept is irrelevant, because it denotes a pre-legal category.[956]

948 Treaty on European Union, Preamble, and Treaty on the Functioning of the European Union, Preamble.

949 Treaty on European Union, after Article 55 TEU; Treaty on the Functioning of the European Union, after Article 358 TFEU.

950 Particularly in the light of Articles 6–18 of the VCLT.

951 Hartley (n 934) 7–8.

952 Haenel (n 908) 38.

953 Act of 16 September 1789, 1 Stat 69 (North Carolina and Rhode Island goods imported into the United States considered to be goods imported from a foreign state, country, or kingdom). See Francisco Forrest Martin, *The Constitution as Treaty* (Cambridge University Press, 2007) 6.

954 James Madison, *The Federalist No 39* (McLean, 1788).

955 Schütze, *From Dual to Cooperative Federalism* (n 426) 23.

956 Kelsen, *Allgemeine Staatslehre* (n 302) 313–15; Gerd Roellecke, 'Verfassungsgebende Gewalt als Ideologie' (1992) 47 *Juristen-Zeitung* 929 ff; Josef Isensee, *Das Volk als Grund der Verfassung* (Westdeutscher Verlag, 1995) 43 ff and 68 ff.

Accordingly, it is not entirely far-fetched that international agreements are equally capable of founding constitutional orders. Examples include the so-called 'Treaty-Constitutions' (*Vertragsverfassungen*)[957] of the North German Confederation of 1866, the German Confederation of 1871,[958] and the German Reunification Treaty of 1990.[959] Another example against the argument by form is the Constitution of Bosnia and Herzegovina which was first concluded as a treaty and then adopted as a constitution. This fluidity between constitution and treaty was also confirmed by the Bosnian Constitutional Court when it held that Article 31 VCLT must still be applied when interpreting the constitution.[960]

Hence it can be concluded that the birth of legal orders may take various forms, from constitutional convention to international treaty. Each new creature inherits a genetic legal code that is altogether different from that of the parents, and the constitutive act may even extinguish the separate existence of the constituent units. But in any event, it will subordinate the constituent units to the new creation[961] lest its uniformity and effectivity be undermined. Thus, the form of a given legal document is not a convincing argument against its constitutional nature and a potential change of the basic norm.

iii. Procedural questions and the original intentions of the Member States

The second argument against a possible change of the *Grundnorm* and thus against a monist view under the primacy of EU law is of procedural nature. It holds that the procedure under which the EU Treaties were negotiated, signed, and ratified is absolutely standard for international agreements. This fact strongly suggests that it has always been the intention of the Member States—both at the time of the earliest Treaty and in the case of all subsequent Treaty amendments—to enter into regular agreements under international law, and not to establish a new *Grundnorm*. Therefore, some sceptics consider it very hard to believe that a legal instrument such as the EU Treaties could have resulted in the establishment of a new *Grundnorm* if this change was not the intention of those responsible for it.[962]

This argument certainly sounds very plausible *prima facie*, and it effectively contradicts the *Gesamtakttheorie*, which implicitly insinuates a particular intention on the part of the Member States to create something new *uno actu*. Yet if one really claims that the *Grundnorm* has been changed in the context of the EU legal order, then it could also be postulated that this change was not initiated by the Member States, but by the Court of Justice in its quasi-revolutionary jurisprudence a posteriori. And in fact, there are several arguments in favour of this view. To begin with, one should critically examine the significance of the so-called subjective-historical method of interpretation, first in international law and then in EU law. Principally,

957 Ipsen, *Europäisches Gemeinschaftsrecht* (n 799) 59; Lenaerts, 'Constitutionalism' (n 880) 207 ff.

958 Oeter, 'Souveränität und Demokratie' (n 890) 678 ff; Isensee, 'Vorrang des Europarechts' (n 613) 1262.

959 Treaty on the Establishment of German Unity, 31 August 1990, BGBl 1990 II, 889 ff.

960 Constitutional Court of Bosnia and Herzegovina, Partial Decision U-5/98 III, Judgment of 1 July 2000—*Izetbegović*; paras 19 ff.

961 Weiler and Haltern, 'Autonomy' (n 794) 419.

962 Hartley (n 934) 8.

this specific interpretative tool under which the will of the historical norm-creator is to be determined, is less favoured than objective methods of interpretation, thereby positioning Article 31 VCLT as the main source of interpretation[963] (i.e. the interpretation of the ordinary meaning of a text in its context and in the light of its object and purpose). The use of the *travaux préparatoires* of a treaty, basically reflecting the original intentions of the negotiating parties, conversely, only represents a supplementary means of interpretation under Article 32 VCLT. The reason for this is that while the text itself is an objective common denominator, externally ascertainable by any party and therefore a guarantor for an appreciable degree of legal certainty, historical intentions are subjective and elusive, as they tend to shade into the moody ground of motives.[964]

Sceptics will probably concede that this is of course correct in international law terms. They will, however, subsequently argue that conditions are entirely different under EU law, since the CJEU has not even once applied the relevant rules of interpretation of the Vienna Convention when interpreting the EU Treaties.[965] Therefore, it is not a given that the historical-subjective method of interpretation is per se irrelevant in EU law. This objection is also correct, but can easily be rebutted. In the same way as general international law, the CJEU also favours objective over subjective interpretation methods,[966] above all the teleological interpretation of EU law. After all, the decisive difference between a subjective-historical and a teleological approach is that the Court does not focus on the actual will of the Member States, but on what they should have reasonably agreed upon in the light of the overall object and purpose of the Treaties.[967] Thus, ultimately, it becomes evident that the CJEU is not interested in the original intention and will of the Member States, but will always prefer that method of interpretation which is more suitable to realize the goals of the Treaties, i.e. European integration as well as the most uniform and effective interpretation and application of EU law.

In this vein, one could also argue that if the Member States in fact had had the intention to conceal any hint of a change of the *Grundnorm*, then they have already had plenty of occasions, for instance when adopting a new Treaty, to 'set the record straight' and explicitly to deny the Court its powers and the law of the EU its supremacy and direct effect.[968] To be more concrete, if one follows through with

[963] Helmut Philipp Aust, Alejandro Rodiles, and Peter Staubach, 'Unity or Uniformity? Domestic Courts and Treaty Interpretation' (2014) 27 *Leiden Journal of International Law* 75, 80; International Law Commission Commentary, UN Conference on the Law of Treaties, Official Records: Documents of the Conference, A/CONF.39/11/Add 2, 40 para 11: '[T]he starting point of interpretation is the elucidation of the meaning of the text, not an investigation *ab initio* into the intention of the parties'.

[964] Robert Kolb, *The Law of Treaties: An Introduction* (Edward Elgar Publishing, 2016) 131–2.

[965] Kirsten Schmalenbach, 'Article 5' in Oliver Dörr and Kirsten Schmalenbach (eds), *Vienna Convention on the Law of Treaties: A Commentary* (Springer, 2012) para 9. See also Joined Cases T-27/03, T-46/03, T-58/03, T-79/03, T-80/03, T-97/03, and T-98/03 *SP SpA and Others v Commission* [2007] ECR II-1357, para 58.

[966] Matthias Pechstein and Carola Drechsler, 'Die Auslegung und Fortbildung des Primärrechts' in Karl Riesenhuber (ed), *Europäische Methodenlehre* (3rd edn; de Gruyter, 2015) 130 and 135–7.

[967] Winter (n 327) 433; Pierre Pescatore, 'International Law and Community Law—A Comparative Analysis' (1970) 7 *Common Market Law Review* 167, 172–4.

[968] Weiler and Haltern, 'Autonomy' (n 794) 432–3.

this thought, then the basic norm did not change when the Member States concluded the Treaties, but when jurists, in the aftermath of the CJEU's revolutionary decisions, started to change their thinking and began to make 'post-revolutionary' assertions to the effect that 'the law of the land *now* is the following', whereby the 'now' refers to some revolutionarily established source of the law. In other words, the *Grundnorm* may have changed when lawyers first deduced laws from some newly promulgated constitution (in this case the written EU constitution[969]). The existence of this new way of thinking is unquestionable in the light of European legal scholarship and practice. This, lastly, also relates to the second element in the change of the basic norm, i.e. the effectivity of the new legal order. Legal science and practice can only be socially useful activities, if they describe and practice in accordance with positive law that is by and large effective and being observed.[970] Again, a quick look at legal practice demonstrates that the law of the EU is, by and large, effective and being observed as a valid legal order. Hence the lack of original intention on the part of the Member States to change the *Grundnorm* is not a conclusive argument against such a change.

iv. Political power and physical enforcement mechanisms

The third argument against a potential change of the *Grundnorm* relates to more of a political and factual issue than a legal problem. If it is correct to assume that a change of the basic norm reflects a shift in political power, then there can be no doubt that actual power still lies with the Member States, and not the Union. There are no EU soldiers or police officers to counter physical resistance, and therefore—provocatively speaking—one can conclude that the EU only exists because the Member States permit it to exist. The Union is hence completely incapable of securing the physical enforcement of any of its decisions. This state of affairs suggests that no change of *Grundnorm* could have taken place.[971]

Proponents of this argument are right that there is no armed 'EU police' or 'army' operating within Union territory to enforce EU law vis-à-vis recalcitrant Member States. There are of course forces such as the European Gendarmerie Force or the EU Battle Groups whose members carry firearms, but their task is not to enforce Union law within the Union itself; all EU police and military missions are carried out in third countries, either under a mandate of the United Nations or upon consent and invitation by the respective country.[972] But these facts in themselves are insufficient to rebut a possible change of the basic norm. As already discussed above,[973] theoretically speaking, it is true that Kelsen mentions the infliction of an evil such as the deprivation of life, health, liberty, or economic values, on the responsible individual as

[969] J.W. Harris, 'When and Why Does the *Grundnorm* Change?' (1971) 29 *Cambridge Law Journal* 103, 117–18; Kelsen, *Pure Theory* (n 24) 221–4.

[970] Kelsen, *General Theory* (n 26) 437; Harris (n 969) 118–19.

[971] Hartley (n 934) 8; Schroeder (n 486) 215.

[972] See e.g. Alistair J.K. Shepherd, 'The European Security Continuum and the EU as an International Security Provider' (2015) 29 *Global Society* 156.

[973] See section 3B(3)b.iii above.

coercive acts to react to violations of the law or to influence human behaviour. This may also certainly require the application of physical force, but not in all cases.[974]

Inflicting an evil on a perpetrator (particularly a Member State) may, as Union law does, also include penalty payments[975] or the suspension of voting rights.[976] It is therefore undoubtedly true that EU law is capable of effectively sanctioning breaches of the law.[977] Again, physical enforcement constitutes only one way to enforce the law, and Union law simply uses other means to achieve this end. And lastly, it is crucial to emphasize that all conflicts between EU and Member State law are being resolved on the basis of Union law, not national law. Therefore, it appears rather implausible to deny a change of the *Grundnorm* on the argumentative basis of political power.

v. Democracy revisited

The fourth argument concerns democracy and claims that a change of the *Grundnorm* is thought to also reflect a shift in public opinion and the development of a genuine European democracy. In the European Union, there can be no doubt that people usually consider themselves citizens of their respective Member States first and Europeans only second, and that owing to increasing Euroscepticism, this status is not likely to change very soon. Citizens across Europe may certainly support the Union and its underlying idea, but only as a free association of states based on the continuing consent of its Member States, and not as something imposed on them in the shape of a new *Grundnorm*. They regard their home countries as independent, despite their membership of the Union, and this view is completely incompatible with a possible change of the *Grundnorm*.[978]

In terms of democracy and from a purely political position, this sceptical diagnosis is correct, yet it is concurrently amiss for the purposes of identifying a change of the basic norm. Ideally, and in a political sense, a democratic state (or an entity such as the European Union aspiring to democratic ideals)[979] should certainly never content itself with a purely formal *Grundnorm*, and instead aim for the highest possible democratic legitimacy. However, this is not the epistemological function of the basic norm. Kelsen sees the main functions of this hypothesis in terminating the infinite regress of the hierarchy of norms, in serving as the highest basis of validity,

[974] Kelsen, *Pure Theory* (n 24) 33–4.
[975] Article 260 TFEU.
[976] Article 7 TEU and Article 354 TFEU. It should be noted, however, that despite (or perhaps because of) their labelling as the 'nuclear option', proceedings under Article 7 TEU will most likely remain toothless and dead letter law. In December 2017, the European Commission initiated such proceedings for the first time, in this case to defend judicial independence in Poland. However, seeing that Article 7(2) TEU requires unanimity in the Council of the EU to determine the existence of a serious and persistent breach by a Member State of the values mentioned in Article 2 TEU, and that Hungary has already declared that it will not vote against Poland, the result of these proceedings remains uncertain. See European Commission, *Rule of Law: European Commission Acts to Defend Judicial Independence in Poland*, Press Release of 20 December 2017, http://europa.eu/rapid/press-release_IP-17-5367_en.htm, and Kim Lane Scheppe, 'Can Poland Be Sanctioned? Not Unless Hungary Is Sanctioned Too', *Verfassungsblog* (24 October 2016) http://verfassungsblog.de/can-poland-be-sanctioned-by-the-eu-not-unless-hungary-is-sanctioned-too/.
[977] Mayer, 'Reine Rechtslehre und Gemeinschaftsrecht' (n 480) 130.
[978] Hartley (n 934) 8.
[979] See e.g. Articles 2, 10–12, and 14 TEU.

and in unifying the legal order. The *Grundnorm* can thus be seen as the guarantor of a valid, meaningful, and reasonably structured legal order, but not *prima facie* as a guarantor of a fair and just system.[980] The respective form and substance of the law are independent from one another, and to claim that valid norms can only be created within a democratic system is simply wrong; democracy or autocracy are mere methods to create law and social order,[981] and from a purely legal aspect, a change of the *Grundnorm* does not require democratic legitimization.[982] As long as citizens across Europe accept that EU law is valid (in accordance with a presupposed and thus hypothesized *Grundnorm*), a change of the basic norm is conceivable and plausible. Particularly to avoid any misunderstandings in this context, it needs to be stressed that the *Grundnorm*, as an epistemological tool, cannot legitimize a legal order.[983] Therefore, it is otiose to argue that a change of the basic norm cannot occur owing to the lack of democratic legitimacy of the Union legal order. Such legitimacy would of course be desirable from a political viewpoint, but it is not necessary from a legal-epistemological position.

After all, the gap between the concept of the *Grundnorm* and democracy might not be unbridgeable, and it would be socially, politically, and legally ideal to bring about a change of the basic norm through democratic means (e.g., a referendum). But it is nonetheless correct that these two ideas—*Grundnorm* and democracy—engage with two different problems and two distinct areas: the pure theory of law studies the law in an objective and scientific sense and without engaging with the question of why the law functions as part of human society (which may be democratic or autocratic), whilst the concept of democracy exactly fills that very blank space, which the hypothetical *Grundnorm* highlights but omits to materialize in a substantive manner.[984]

vi. Again: legislative and judicial Kompetenz-Kompetenz

In addition to the democratic argument, i.e. that the European people never consented to a change of the *Grundnorm*, there is also a similar argument with respect to the national courts, especially the national supreme and constitutional courts. So far, there is not the slightest suggestion in any of their judgments that there has indeed been a change of the *Grundnorm*. Whenever they have to deal with the effects of Union law within domestic law, they start from the premise that EU norms are derived from international treaties. Consequently, their validity is rooted in international law, not an autonomous EU legal order, and their disagreement with this

[980] Kelsen, 'Die philosophischen Grundlagen' (n 611) 295. See also Stanley L. Paulson, 'Die unterschiedlichen Formulierungen der Grundnorm' in Aulis Aarnio and others (eds), *Rechtsnorm und Rechtswirklichkeit* (Duncker & Humblot, 1993) 61–2. But see also Chapter 5, section 3B arguing that a hypothetical *Grundnorm* is more conducive to democracy than the absolute values of natural law theory.

[981] Kelsen, *Allgemeine Staatslehre* (n 302) 368–9.

[982] Horst Dreier, *Rechtslehre, Staatssoziologie und Demokratietheorie bei Hans Kelsen* (Nomos, 1986) 193.

[983] Robert Walter, 'Entstehung und Entwicklung des Gedankens der Grundnorm' in Robert Walter (ed), *Schwerpunkte der Reinen Rechtslehre* (Manz, 1992) 47–59.

[984] Georg Kohler, 'Basiskonsens und Willensnation: Die Kontingenz des Unverfügbaren und das Modell der Schweiz' in Hans Vorländer (ed), *Demokratie und Transzendenz* (Transcript, 2013) 129.

notion of legal autonomy should therefore be understood to the effect that there has never been a change of the *Grundnorm*.[985]

It should be admitted that the sceptics are principally correct with respect to the EU's legislative *Kompetenz-Kompetenz*, which rests with the Union *in conjunction with* the Member States, not the EU alone—as already examined above.[986] Yet, from the viewpoint of monism, it is even more important to emphasize that the Member States merely remain in the collective plural the 'Masters of the Treaties'; individual Member States have lost their *Kompetenz-Kompetenz*.[987] Hence the Member States are unilaterally no longer competent to determine the limits of their own competences themselves.[988] On top of that, Article 48 TEU also bars the Member States from multilaterally amending the EU Treaties outside the official revision procedure by effectively subordinating the legal regime governing subsequently concluded agreements between Member States to the supremacy of European Union law.[989]

This perfectly segues into the issue of the CJEU's judicial *Kompetenz-Kompetenz*.[990] The Court's exclusive jurisdiction in both applying and interpreting Union law (including the division of powers) under Article 19 TEU as well as Articles 258, 259, 260, 263, 265, 267, and 344 TFEU is a fact, and even if a national court deems a Union legal act to be ultra vires, it has to refer this case to Luxembourg. It is thus undoubtedly the CJEU that has the final say in matters of Union law[991] and, to date , all of the national courts have accepted this fact (albeit some of them grudgingly). Therefore, the argument that the *Grundnorm* has not changed because the national courts have never consented to this very change is not convincing at all. In a contribution from 2003, Trevor C. Hartley correctly argues that a change in the *Grundnorm* at the expense of the Member States through the case law of the Court would turn the Union Treaties into a self-validating constitution and the Member States would be members whether they liked it or not, because there was no provision in the Treaties permitting a Member State to withdraw from the EU.[992] In the light of the introduction of Article 50 TEU and thus of this very right to withdraw from Union membership, one might argue that it is, ironically, this right to withdraw which might actually bolster the argument for a change in the *Grundnorm*. As the case of the UK's Brexit referendum of June 2016 demonstrates, it remains entirely a Member State's unilateral decision to leave the Union, but there is nevertheless a procedural obligation under EU law to comply with the procedure under

[985] Hartley (n 934) 9. [986] See section 3B(4)c.ii above.

[987] Hans Peter Ipsen, 'Europäische Verfassung—Nationale Verfassung' (1987) 22 *Europarecht* 195, 202.

[988] Armin von Bogdandy and Jürgen Bast, 'The European Union's Vertical Order of Competences: The Current Law and Proposals for its Reform' (2002) 39 *Common Market Law Review* 227, 237.

[989] Schütze, 'On "Federal" Ground' (n 634) 1082–3. [990] See section 3B(4)c.ii above.

[991] Weiler and Haltern, 'Autonomy' (n 794) 430 ff.

[992] Trevor C. Hartley, 'National Law, International Law and EU Law—How Do They Relate?' in Patrick Capps, Malcolm Evans, and Stratos Konstadinides (eds), *Asserting Jurisdiction* (Hart Publishing, 2003) 68.

Article 50 TEU.[993] This means, in conclusion, that even in the act of withdrawing from the EU, the Member States are bound by its legal order: Member States may leave if they wish to do so, and if they do, they need to adhere to the procedure set out in Article 50 TEU; but if, conversely, they decide to stay they have to accept the system which they never explicitly changed according to their wishes. Again, this finding does not speak against a possible change of the *Grundnorm*.

vii. A chain of delegation between EU and Member State law?

The last argument against a potential change of the *Grundnorm* in the relationship between EU and Member State law concerns the hierarchy of norms or, to be more precise, the question of whether and how there can be a chain of delegation between those two bodies of law. If we assume that the common *Grundnorm* of the EU-Member State system rests at the apex of Union law itself, this would also entail that EU norms would create national norms or that, alternatively, the validity of national law would depend on Union law. In addition to the fact that the CJEU itself has never even claimed that national law can only be valid if created in accordance with Union law, there seems to be no norm of positive EU law which would subsequently allow for the creation of Member State law.[994] Therefore, the assumption that such a chain of delegation under the primacy of Union law exists is highly debatable, indeed extremely grotesque.[995]

Again, non-monists are of course correct that there is no clear-cut chain of delegation, running down from the *Grundnorm* of EU law via the Treaties and secondary law, thereby validating national law. In the light of the *lex lata*, this would indeed be absurd. But things are not as easily ascertainable as they might appear at first glance. As has become clear in the discussion above on monism under the primacy of Member State law,[996] a view, which would base the validity of Union law exclusively on national law, is currently only tenable on purely historical, but not juridical grounds.[997] This raises the question of whether the opposite view could also be possible, i.e. whether Member State law is not historically, but juridically dependent on Union law. In this scenario, the validity of the supreme positive norms of national law (i.e. their respective constitutions) is derived from a norm of EU law by which national legal acts can be considered to be either lawful or unlawful from the point of view of the Union legal order.[998] This principle can be compared to the principle of effectiveness in international law which regulates the behaviour of states; and in the same ways as it must determine what a state is in international legal terms, it must also determine under what conditions their acts are to be regarded as acts of a state, i.e. as legal acts in the meaning of international law.[999]

[993] Christophe Hillion, 'Accession and Withdrawal in the Law of the European Union' in Anthony Arnull and Damian Chalmers (eds), *The Oxford Handbook of European Union Law* (Oxford University Press, 2015) 136.

[994] Kammerhofer, 'Kelsen—Which Kelsen?' (n 724) 241–2.

[995] Schilling, *Rang und Geltung* (n 616) 181; Kruis (n 490) 9; Wendel (n 539) 21–3.

[996] See section 3B(4)c above.

[997] Stefan Haack, *Verlust der Staatlichkeit* (Mohr-Siebeck, 2007) 179.

[998] Richmond (n 496) 413.

[999] Kelsen, *Pure Theory* (n 24) 337.

Equally, the legal order of the European Union regulates the behaviour of its Member States, and consequently, it must also determine under what conditions their acts are to be regarded as lawful acts in the meaning of EU law.[1000] In this light, the term 'lawful' of course only refers to the application or possible disapplication of national law if found in conflict with Union law along the lines of the principle of supremacy and the *Simmenthal* doctrine—and not its actual validity or invalidity. The reason for this is that the CJEU—in the same way as international law and international courts or tribunals—is incapable of invalidating national law in contravention with EU law. Thus, the positive norm, which 'connects' the chain of validity between Union and national law, is the principle under which national law remains applicable under EU law. And this principle is further bolstered by the positive law which, on the one hand, admits the Member States into the Union, contained either in the original Treaties or in the relevant Accession Treaties,[1001] and the positive law, on the other hand, which gives effect to Union law within domestic law.

Furthermore, if we assume that the basic norm of the EU has shifted towards Union law itself, then there is another principle of EU law to be considered, namely the rather elusive concept of the scope of application of Union law. Under this concept, the Member States are bound by Union law not only if they are merely implementing Union law (in the rather narrow[1002] wording of Article 51(1) of the Charter of Fundamental Rights), but also if the Member States are acting within the wider notion of the scope of application of EU law, as defined by the Court of Justice in *Åkerberg Fransson*.[1003] In this light, Member State law is entirely delegated by EU law if a Member State is fulfilling an obligation imposed by Union law or if a national measure aims at preventing infringements of secondary law.[1004] This, lastly, also means that a Member State may apply the standards of its own constitutionally guaranteed fundamental rights only if those standards are higher than those guaranteed by the Charter and if 'primacy, unity and effectiveness of [EU] law are not thereby compromised'.[1005] Thus, one might say that Member State legislation is in fact constrained and hence delegated by the 'constitution' of the European Union and its *Grundnorm*.

But the principle of the scope of application of EU law should not be understood as a boundless constraint upon national law, as this principle itself acts as a limit to Union law. Accordingly, it needs to be taken into consideration as a large *caveat* to the chain of delegation: not the entire domestic law of the Member States is delegated by EU law, but only that law which falls within the scope of application of

[1000] Richmond (n 496) 413 and fn 130. [1001] Ibid., 413.

[1002] Craig, *EU Administrative Law* (n 687) 462; Case 5/88 *Wachauf* [1989] ECR 2609, para 19.

[1003] Case C-617/10 *Åkerberg Fransson* (n 736).

[1004] Koen Lenaerts and José A. Gutiérrez-Fons, 'The Place of the Charter in the EU Constitutional Edifice' in Steve Peers and others (eds), *The EU Charter of Fundamental Rights: A Commentary* (Hart Publishing, 2014) 1567–8, para 55.26.

[1005] Case C-617/10 *Åkerberg Fransson* (n 736) para 29; Case C-399/11 *Melloni* (n 568) paras 55–64.

Union law. And besides this scope of application, national law remains delegated by general international law and the presupposed *Grundnorm* of international law.[1006]

C. Conclusion

The foregoing sections have all shown that explaining and assessing the relationship between European Union law and Member State law through the prism of pluralism, dualism, and monism under the primacy of Member State law fail to convince. They all share the same shortcomings, namely their inadequacy to consider the law as it is and to reconcile it with their theoretical preconceptions.

This chapter can of course not ascertain beyond any reasonable doubt whether the *Grundnorm* within the relationship between the Member States and the European Union has changed and shifted towards the EU legal order; but it is now also clear that the arguments against such a change are not convincing either. It therefore seems that a monist interpretation of the relationship between Union law and Member State with the primacy of the former (only to the extent, however, of its scope of application) allows for the best and most plausible explanation,[1007] and that neither pluralism nor dualism seem to be tenable theories in this respect.[1008] Some are more cautious and warn of premature conclusions, because the mutual interlocking of EU and Member State law cannot be seen as the former actually delegating the latter.[1009]

It is of course true that such delegation—from a historical viewpoint—seems implausible. However, we are here dealing with a situation that is analogous to that of international and national law: States and their legal orders remain unconstrained except for the relevant scope of application in which they find themselves normlogically delegated by international law (which restrains their jurisdictional competences vis-à-vis other international legal subjects) and EU law (which curtails their competences with respect to the powers of the EU). Lastly, this analogy and the existence of a moderate monist system between national and EU law becomes even more visible when taking a look at the principle of primacy of Union norms: such as international norms, they do not and cannot invalidate or annul conflicting national norms (*Geltungsvorrang*), but merely obligate the respective state in question to set them aside and disapply them (*Anwendungsvorrang*)—which has also been confirmed by the Court of Justice itself.[1010] The principle of supremacy is thus perfectly capable of explaining not only the fact that Union law itself determines its own binding character, but also its supreme status vis-à-vis national law, meaning that violations of obligations under the Treaties entail legal consequences. Therefore, the relationship between EU and national law appears to be best described by a

[1006] Rill, 'Internationales, supranationales und nationales Recht' (n 102) 693–4.

[1007] Griller, 'Stufenbau' (n 647) 284.

[1008] Rill, 'Internationales, supranationales und nationales Recht' (n 102) 697–9; Potacs, 'Verhältnis' (n 104) 120.

[1009] Öhlinger, 'Einheit' (n 139) 171.

[1010] Joined Cases C-10/97 to C-22/97 *IN.CO.GE'90* (n 552) para 21; Case C-409/06 *Winner Wetten* [2010] ECR I-8015, para 55.

moderate monism under the primacy of Union law which is limited by the scope of its application.

In conclusion, it should be emphasized again that Union and national law form part of the same unitary legal order via a common *Grundnorm*, located at the top of EU law, and—as in the context of public international law—one must accept this unless he or she is prepared to deny the legal nature of Union law. And again, a definition of the law that excludes EU law does not verify pluralism or dualism or monism under the primacy of national law.[1011]

[1011] Rill, 'Internationales, supranationales und nationales Recht' (n 102) 695.

5

The Moral Appeal of Legal Monism

1. Introduction: Beyond Epistemology and Description

The previous chapters of this book have explored the philosophical as well as the epistemological foundations of legal monism and the question of whether its claims can be tested in the light of the law as it is, respectively. In contrast to these issues, the focus of the present chapter will be on the question of what exactly follows from legal monism in a normative sense. In other words, one could ask what the benefit of monism under the primacy of international law or EU law is and why one should—in addition to epistemological reasons or empirical data—favour this approach over dualism, pluralism, and monism under the primacy of national law. A justification of monism merely resting on its epistemological explanatory and factual descriptive powers may be *necessary*, but not *sufficient* to convince the staunchest sceptics, especially not the dualists and pluralists among the readers. Therefore, it seems to be apposite to look beyond the mere epistemological and descriptive horizon of legal monism and to enquire as to what follows from a unitary view of the law in normative sense. Furthermore, this necessitates the question of whether monism is indeed capable of improving the law as it is, and if the answer is yes, in what way it can achieve this goal.

A. Ethical dimensions of legal monism

Both legal epistemology and legal doctrine are concerned with the *law as it is*, or the *lex lata*: the former with the method as to how valid law (as it is) can be cognized, and the latter as to how the law (as it is) can be described. Yet the central thesis of this chapter is that we cannot understand what monism really is or what it intends to do without connecting this project of legal unity to deep ethical convictions,[1] or the idea of the *lex ferenda: the law as it ought to be*. As an equally legitimate object of scholarly research, the idea of the *lex ferenda* serves as a label for something that has conceptual existence in contrast to the *lex lata*, and states that some rule *should* be part of the positive law.[2]

[1] George Rodrigo Bandeira Galindo, 'Revisiting Monism's Ethical Dimension' in James Crawford and Sarah Nouwen (eds), *Select Proceedings of the European Society of International Law: Volume 3* (Hart Publishing, 2012) 142.

[2] Hugh Thirlway, 'Reflections on Lex Ferenda' (2001) 32 *Netherlands Yearbook of International Law* 3, 4.

Of course, in order to maintain the scientific objectivity of the law, these two concepts—*lex lata* and *lex ferenda*—certainly need to be strictly distinguished from one another, as political or moral considerations cannot form part of the law if we wish to cognize it as valid in itself. But this does not mean that arguments *de lege ferenda* cannot be objects of legal analysis, all the more since legal decision-making will always have a moral and political impact. Thus perhaps lawyers, and in particular international lawyers, should be allowed to express their political ideologies and to be activists and revolutionaries for a better world, because in every single approach to the relationship between different bodies of law, ethical choices also need to be made.[3]

The subsequent normative defence of monism does of course not mean that dualism or pluralism have no ethical value at all. On the contrary, by emphasizing sovereignty, the dualist tradition is deeply committed to the idea that international law is a law of coordination,[4] while pluralism is to be very much commended in the social, economic, and political spheres.[5] Nonetheless, their respective ethical dimensions are essentially reluctant to accept change[6] and the definitive resolution of normative conflicts under clearly defined legal rules. In contrast to that, monism commends itself owing to its superb constitutionalist sensibilities[7] and the rule of law. By its curtailing effect on state sovereignty and its respect for the individual and human rights, it becomes a bulwark[8] against legal fragmentation and a 'promise that there is some system in all the madness',[9] as monism attempts to provide unity to a system and thereby to strengthen this system's nature as a *legal* system.[10]

Avoiding fragmentation and maintaining systemic unity, in turn, also avoids arbitrariness in the law. Furthermore, one should not underestimate the mutual influence between democracy and legal monism: on the one hand, legal clarity *qua* legal unity informs and strengthens democracy by providing for the rules of representation in the respective decision-making institutions;[11] and on the other hand, it is indisputable that democratic systems with their emphasis on internal peace and rationality (in contrast to ideology and irrationality prevailing in autocratic systems) also corroborate a specific attitude in foreign policy, namely pacifism.[12] Legal monism and a democratic outlook on the world therefore go hand in hand, and

[3] Galindo (n 1) 141–2.

[4] Murray Forsyth, 'The Tradition of International Law' in Terry Nardin and David R. Mapel (eds), *Traditions of International Ethics* (Cambridge University Press, 1992) 23.

[5] Nico Krisch, *Beyond Constitutionalism* (Oxford University Press, 2012) 78 ff.

[6] Galindo (n 1) 142.

[7] Alexander Somek, 'Monism: A Tale of the Undead' in Matej Avbelj and Jan Komárek (eds), *Constitutional Pluralism in the European Union and Beyond* (Hart Publishing, 2012) 344.

[8] Anne Peters, 'Rechtsordnungen und Konstitutionalisierung: Zur Neubestimmung der Verhältnisse' (2010) 65 *Zeitschrift für Öffentliches Recht* 3, 25–6 and 28–9.

[9] Jan Klabbers, 'Constitutionalism Lite' (2004) 1 *International Organizations Law Review* 31, 49.

[10] Ernst-Ulrich Petersmann, 'Multilevel Judicial Governance as Guardian of the Constitutional Unity of International Economic Law' (2008) 30 *Loyola of Los Angeles International and Comparative Law Review* 367, 367.

[11] Hans Kelsen, 'Foundations of Democracy' (1955) 66 *Ethics* 1, 8.

[12] Hans Kelsen, 'State-Form and World-Outlook' in Hans Kelsen and Ota Weinberger (eds), *Essays in Legal and Moral Philosophy* (Reidel, 1973) 101–11.

democracy, in the end, could then serve as a more plausible argument for the rule of law against non-monists than pure logic and epistemology. Lastly, given this pacifist objective, legal monism should also be seen under the aspect of cosmopolitanism and the morally desirable concept of a *civitas maxima*,[13] especially in the sense that monism could eventually help bring about a Kantian world society.[14]

The constructivist approach in international relations theory, for example, holds that 'anarchy is what States make of it'.[15] Consequently, it is absolutely possible for states to construct an international system socially that is not shaped by materialist forces such as power, interests, and geography alone, but also ideas, concepts, and norms, in particular an overarching international legal order and a monist view under the primacy of international law. Kantian cosmopolitanism hence is not only desirable, but also becomes feasible under an international law-centred monist approach.

In this light, this chapter will underscore that the great legacy of monism is not only its internal logic or its precise depiction of various developments in the relationship between international and domestic law. Beyond the ideas of unity and coherence, monism also provides a conception about how to change the world in a time of peril,[16] and to make it a better place.

B. A heretical reading of the pure theory of law?

This normative reading of legal monism as envisaged by the pure theory of law faces, however, a major problem, as this epistemologically informed monism never intended to be a theory of a world legal order which may develop over the course of time. Legal monism in this sense could only foster this process if one deliberately misinterprets this pure theory by way of methodological syncretism[17]—which is the very concept that the proponents of the pure theory of law intended to cast off in their works.[18] It is well known that Kelsen himself—whilst evidently believing that the adoption of a monist view under the primacy of international law would entail morally desirable consequences[19]—went to great lengths to avoid making the claim that monism *ought* to be adopted by legal science because of its moral superiority to other legal theories. Such a defence of monism would not have been, after all, 'scientific' in Kelsen's understanding of the term, and hence he is definitely not

[13] Lars Vinx, *Hans Kelsen's Pure Theory of Law: Legality and Legitimacy* (Oxford University Press, 2007) 176.

[14] Martin Wight, *International Theory: The Three Traditions* (Leicester University Press, 1991).

[15] See particularly Alexander Wendt, 'Anarchy Is What States Make of It' (1992) 46 *International Organization* 391, and Alexander Wendt, *Social Theory of International Politics* (Cambridge University Press, 1999).

[16] Galindo (n 1) 144.

[17] See e.g. Hans Kelsen, 'Was ist die Reine Rechtslehre?' in Hans R. Klecatsky, René Marcic, and Herbert Schambeck (eds), *Die Wiener rechtstheoretische Schule: Schriften von Hans Kelsen, Adolf Merkl, Alfred Verdross, Band 1* (Verlag Österreich, 2010) 509–10.

[18] Theo Öhlinger, 'Die Einheit des Rechts: Völkerrecht, Europarecht und staatliches Recht als einheitliches Rechtssystem?' in Stanley L. Paulson and Michael Stolleis (eds), *Hans Kelsen: Staatsrechtslehrer und Rechtstheoretiker des 20. Jahrhunderts* (Mohr-Siebeck, 2005) 167.

[19] Hans Kelsen, *Das Problem der Souveränität und die Theorie des Völkerrechts* (Mohr-Siebeck, 1920) 241–74.

'guilty' of trying to defend monism in normative terms under the false guise of a legal-theoretical argument.[20]

However, in this regard, legal monism is being confronted with a veritable dilemma: either one eliminates all moral components of monism and maintains it as a theory pure and devoid of interesting terms such as pacifism and world peace, but concurrently takes away its fascination and impetus for a better world; or one ends up associating it with normative (and thus 'impure') elements, such as a worldwide and peaceful legal order, but goes against the methodological purity of the very theory that represents the epistemological basis for legal monism.[21] But what if the key to this problem were to be the above sentence that legal monism in this sense *could* foster the process towards a peaceful and democratic world legal order? What if legal monism in its pure sense should be seen as something as Wittgenstein's ladder, i.e. as something that—once it has been understood by having been used and climbed up—needs to be thrown away?[22]

Perhaps an analogy with Kantian philosophy is appropriate at this point. According to Kant, all philosophy principally aims at answering the three questions of 'What can I know?' (i.e. epistemology), 'What should I do?' (i.e. ethics), and 'What may I hope?' (i.e. religion).[23] Traditionally, an orthodox reading of his *Critique of Pure Reason* is intended to provide an answer to the first question in the shape of Kant's transcendental philosophy and the concept of the synthetic a priori. Answers to the other two questions can consequently be found in the *Critique of Practical Reason*[24] and in *Religion within the Bounds of Bare Reason*,[25] respectively. Yet in contrast to this view, it has been argued that the first *Critique* is driven not only by theoretical, but also by practical (i.e. ethical) considerations, in particular if one takes into account the motto included in the second edition and the often-ignored second part, the Transcendental Doctrine of Method.[26] It is of course correct that the predominant part of the *Critique of Pure Reason* is indeed concerned with the epistemic faculties and their limits, but even here, Kant concedes that the ultimate purpose of philosophy is morality. In this light, he seeks to forever silence 'all objections to morality ... and this in Socratic fashion, namely by the clearest proof of the ignorance of the objectors'.[27]

A fully heterodox reading of the first *Critique*, however, regards it as focusing on all three questions (whereas the third question concerning religion is of no interest here), wherein '[a]ll the interests of my reason, speculative [i.e. theoretical] as well as practical' are combined.[28] Thereby theoretical philosophizing becomes of 'cosmopolitan

[20] Vinx (n 13) 182. [21] Öhlinger, 'Einheit des Rechts' (n 18) 172.

[22] Ludwig Wittgenstein, *Tractatus Logico-Philosophicus* (Kegan Paul, 1922) § 6.54. The analogy of the ladder is lent from Arthur Schopenhauer, *The World as Will and Representation, Vol II* (transl E.F.J. Payne; Dover, 1958) ch VII, 80.

[23] Immanuel Kant, *Kritik der reinen Vernunft* (Johann Friedrich Hartknoch, 1781/1787) B 832.

[24] Immanuel Kant, 'Kritik der praktischen Vernunft' in Immanuel Kant (ed), *Gesammelte Schriften* (Deutsche Akademie der Wissenschaften, 1913) AA 5:1.

[25] Immanuel Kant, 'Die Religion innerhalb der Grenzen der bloßen Vernunft' in Immanuel Kant (ed), *Gesammelte Schriften* (Deutsche Akademie der Wissenschaften, 1907) AA 6:1.

[26] Otfried Höffe, *Kants Kritik der praktischen Vernunft* (C.H. Beck, 2012) 39 and 41.

[27] Kant, *Kritik der reinen Vernunft* (n 23) B xxxi. [28] Ibid., B 832.

significance',[29] and both motives—morality and cosmopolitanism—become intertwined. By not only responding to the first, but also to the second question, the *Critique of Pure Reason* contains a certain kind of encyclopedia of philosophical sciences. But since morality plays the decisive role in all of these sciences, this mere heterodox reading pinnacles in a full-blown heretical reading, as it puts epistemology at the service of morality.[30] The result of this is the 'epistemic World Republic' because all epistemological principles of the first *Critique*—as a synthetic a priori—are universally valid and independent of history or culture, thereby establishing a global and peaceful commonwealth among all humans.[31]

Therefore, the objective of this chapter is to argue the following: in the same way that the primarily epistemology-oriented *Critique of Pure Reason* can be read heterodoxically or even heretically to the effect that it already contains ethical-practical consequences which only become fully visible in the chiefly morality-geared *Critique of Practical Reason*, the scientifically neutral *Pure Theory of Law* and all the other juridico-epistemological works of the Vienna School can also be read and interpreted in a heterodox manner. As will be shown, these works also offer the resources to come up with something more substantive than pure epistemology to defend monism, especially if read against the letter in the light of other works on ideological criticism, democracy, and pacifism as well as cosmopolitanism. Going beyond the 'jurist Kelsen' also means to acknowledge that his comprehensive work in political science is equally significant, although it remains largely unnoticed.[32] Kelsen's theory of law and state can be understood as a political theory of a pluralist democracy, and as a consequence of a pluralist-democratic society.[33] Hence the pure theory of law's strict exclusion of all extra-legal and potentially ideological elements should not hide the fact that its proponents, in the same way as Georges Scelle, were concerned about the endangered status of democracy during the inter-war years. Scelle's monism was an essentially juridico-political perspective on international law, and utterly inseparable from the core issues at stake within domestic political societies. Similarly, epistemological monism—despite its pure logical deduction—forms an integral part of a defence of democracy and the individual. It can consequently be interpreted as an attempt to curtail the sovereignty and the wide-ranging powers of the nation-State, to empower the individual, and to protect human dignity.[34] Accordingly, it

[29] Immanuel Kant, 'Logik: Ein Handbuch zu Vorlesungen' in Immanuel Kant (ed), *Gesammelte Schriften* (Deutsche Akademie der Wissenschaften, 1923) AA 9:25.

[30] Höffe, *Kants Kritik der praktischen Vernunft* (n 26) 37–8. See also Otfried Höffe, *Kants Kritik der Reinen Vernunft* (C.H. Beck, 2003) 292–7.

[31] Kant, *Kritik der reinen Vernunft* (n 23) B 879; Höffe, *Kants Kritik der praktischen Vernunft* (n 26) 52.

[32] Ota Weinberger, 'Vorwort' [1982] *Rechtstheorie (Beiheft 4)* 5, 6; Tamara Ehs, 'Vorwort' in Tamara Ehs (ed), *Hans Kelsen: Eine politikwissenschaftliche Einführung* (Facultas, 2009) 6.

[33] Robert Christian van Ooyen, *Der Staat der Moderne: Hans Kelsens Pluralismustheorie* (Duncker & Humblot, 2003) 70.

[34] Janne Nijman and André Nollkaemper, 'Introduction' in Janne Nijman and André Nollkaemper (eds), *New Perspectives on the Divide between National and International Law* (Oxford University Press, 2007) 9.

goes very much hand in hand with endeavours such as constitutionalization and democratization.[35]

As Kelsen himself says, a scientifically pure theory of law should not be seen as barring lawyers from engaging in sociological, psychological, or historical research. Quite the contrary, such extra-legal investigations are necessary to uphold a functioning legal system. However, at the same time, lawyers must be aware that by concurrently working as sociologists, psychologists, or historians, they pursue a way that differs from that of specific legal cognition, and that the results of these investigations must not form part of the conception of the law per se.[36] In that way, Kelsen's legal theory does not exclude cooperation with other academic disciplines; it only insists on the specific characteristics of the legal method.[37] Thus, it becomes possible to go beyond the law as a purely epistemological and logical category and to ask what normatively follows from the findings of the Vienna School of Jurisprudence—particularly legal monism—without automatically 'tainting' its methodological purity. Can legal monism thereby be shown as highly superior to both dualism and pluralism as a robust foundation for the rule of law and legal certainty, a democratic structure of the law, and a (Kantian) cosmopolitan outlook on the international legal order?

C. The threefold normative significance of monism

In Kelsen's general theory of the law, politics and law are clearly separated from each other to the extent that the validity of the law is dependent neither upon democratic legitimacy nor the existence of the rule of law or individual fundamental rights. According to the pure theory of law, these elements can certainly form part of the positive law, but only by way of the positive law itself,[38] and not through supra-positive or natural-legal norms.[39] In this context, the criticism is often raised that such a pure theory of law, devoid of any substance, regards totalitarian and democratic legal systems as equally valid. This criticism is, however, entirely amiss, as it not only deliberately misjudges the Vienna School's constant fight against authoritarian ideas and for democracy, but also the actual objective of the pure theory which is to extend, and not to constrict, the scope of criticism concerning existing social and normative orders.[40] Especially regarding international law, it has consequently been argued that the pure theory of law is very open to extra-legal elements, namely in three distinct areas,[41] which will also form the main sections of this chapter: ideological

[35] Peters, 'Rechtsordnungen und Konstitutionalisierung' (n 8) 25–6.

[36] Hans Kelsen, *Hauptprobleme der Staatsrechtslehre* (1st edn; Mohr-Siebeck, 1911) 42.

[37] Horst Meier, 'Lob des Rechtspositivismus' (2005) 673 *Merkur* 430, 431.

[38] Hans Kelsen, *Pure Theory of Law* (2nd edn; University of California Press, 1967) 138–45.

[39] Alfred Rub, *Hans Kelsens Völkerrechslehre: Versuch einer Würdigung* (Schulthess Polygraphischer Verlag, 1995) 82.

[40] See e.g. Adolf Julius Merkl, 'Die Wandlungen des Rechtsstaatsgedankens' in Hans R. Klecatsky, René Marcic, and Herbert Schambeck (eds), *Die Wiener rechtstheoretische Schule: Schriften von Hans Kelsen, Adolf Merkl, Alfred Verdross, Band 2* (Verlag Österreich, 2010) 1599–613; Hans Kelsen, *The Essence and Value of Democracy* (Rowman & Littlefield, 2013).

[41] Rub (n 39) 83.

criticism; democracy; and pacifism (as well as cosmopolitanism). Let us now engage with this threefold normative significance of monism in detail.

2. Ideological Criticism and Legal Monism

A. Introduction: ideology and ideological criticism

A comprehensive definition of the terms 'ideology' and 'ideological criticism' would definitely go beyond the scope of this section. Nonetheless, and especially because of the elusive and often misunderstood nature of these terms, a short introduction and brief clarification of their respective meanings seems to be in order. Generally, 'ideology' appears to denote a set of beliefs, ideas, or ideals held by individuals, groups, or entire societies. And since these beliefs are often socially motivated or form the basis of economic or political theories,[42] the word has acquired a pejorative connotation to the effect that ideology, like halitosis, is something that only the other person has. Therefore, nobody would claim that their own thinking was ideological.[43]

It is interesting to note that although the development of a pure theory of law takes centre stage in his writings, Kelsen's contributions to ideological criticism are not unrelated to his juridical work. On the contrary, they aim at giving the pure theory a scientific-theoretically substantiated basis.[44] If we take, for instance, Kelsen's example of the difference between a legal community and a gang of robbers, this objective becomes much clearer: seeing that both the law and a gang of robbers may command you to hand over your money lest an evil will be inflicted on you, they both seem to constitute valid coercive acts. The difference between them is, however, that the command by the legal order itself ('give me your tax money or you will be arrested') is ultimately validated by its traceability to a *Grundnorm*. Conversely, the 'validity' of the command by the gang of robbers ('give us your money or we will kill you') is founded in brute force and the factual element of retribution. Hence without the assumption of a *Grundnorm*, a purely normative question would be automatically transformed into a descriptive-empirical one, thereby possibly legitimizing violence.[45] Consequently, the connecting element between the law and ideology is the attempt to elaborate a 'consistent post-metaphysical legal theory',[46] which becomes most obvious in the addition of an ideology-critical chapter on 'Law and Science'[47] in the second edition of The *Pure Theory of Law*.

[42] See the definition in the *Oxford English Dictionary* (7th edn; Oxford University Press, 2012) 358.
[43] Terry Eagleton, *Ideology: An Introduction* (Verso, 1991) 2.
[44] Clemens Jabloner, 'Ideologiekritik bei Kelsen' in Robert Walter (ed), *Schwerpunkte der Reinen Rechtslehre* (Manz, 1992) 97.
[45] Kelsen, *Pure Theory* (n 38) 44–50. See also Hans Kelsen, *Vergeltung und Kausalität* (van Stockum, 1941).
[46] Horst Dreier, *Rechtslehre, Staatssoziologie und Demokratietheorie bei Hans Kelsen* (Nomos, 1986) 23.
[47] In ch 3 in Kelsen, *Pure Theory* (n 38) 70–107.

When dealing with the vagueness and ambiguousness of the term 'ideology',[48] Kelsen eventually distinguishes two concepts of ideology: on the one hand, if we understand 'ideology' as merely relating to mental or intellectual entities—in contrast to actually existing facts—then the law itself, as a mental content, is ideological. The reason for this is that the reality of facts or the physical world is best described by the principle of causality, whereas law is ordered on the basis of the concept of imputation, which works in ways that are similar to causality, but which is nevertheless entirely different in kind.[49] On the other hand, ideology can also be seen in a much narrower sense which directly turns it into a problem, namely if objectively unjustifiable value judgments become part of scientific argumentation. In doing so, the empirically given legal material often tends to be justified ethically, to be glorified, or to be concealed if it conflicts with moral values.[50] And this means that if we understand positive law as part of an objective reality, 'then a presentation of [it] must keep itself free from ideology ...'.[51]

Accordingly, *ideology* in the sense of the pure theory of law denotes, as false jurisprudence or false legal doctrine, the antonym to a pure and non-ideological science of law. Such jurisprudence breaches the scientific principle of objectivity and may be abused for political purposes, for example if it is conflated with naturalist theories and subsequently used to legitimize a disfigured view of the legal reality.[52] In other words, problematic 'ideology' therefore is a conflation of 'ideology' in the first meaning of the world (i.e. simply the mental world) with the physical reality. This is often done to explain and interpret the world by projecting social theories onto the natural world.[53]

Thus, for Kelsen, *ideological criticism* means to assess whether an interpretation of reality is in conformity with reality, and concurrently to uphold the dualism of *ideology* (through which social entities present themselves in the consciousness of those people who constitute these very entities) and *reality* (which is the reality of the actually existing relations between those individuals constituting these entities).[54] Metaphorically, Kelsen intends to expose and unmask the actual reality, or—as the proverb goes—'to call a spade a spade' without beating about the bush, even if everybody else calls the spade a shovel.[55] Regarding his specific ideology-critical method, it has been noted that ideologically charged statements usually utilize words

[48] Especially in Hans Kelsen, 'Allgemeine Rechtslehre im Lichte materialistischer Geschichtsauffassung' (1931) 66 *Archiv für Sozialwissenschaft und Sozialpolitik* 449–521.

[49] Kelsen, *Pure Theory* (n 38) 103–4.

[50] Kelsen, 'Allgemeine Rechtslehre im Lichte materialistischer Geschichtsauffassung' (n 48) 435–54.

[51] Kelsen, *Pure Theory* (n 38) 105.

[52] Otto Pfersmann, 'Kelsens Ideologiekritik' in Nikitas Aliprantis and Thomas Olechowski (eds), *Hans Kelsen: Die Aktualität eines großen Rechtswissenschafters und Soziologen des 20. Jahrhunderts* (Manz, 2014) 54.

[53] Ernst Topitsch, *Erkenntnis und Illusion* (Mohr-Siebeck, 1988) 63–77.

[54] Hans Kelsen, 'Zur Soziologie der Demokratie' in Hans R. Klecatsky, René Marcic, and Herbert Schambeck (eds), *Die Wiener rechtstheoretische Schule: Schriften von Hans Kelsen, Adolf Merkl, Alfred Verdross, Band 2* (Verlag Österreich, 2010) 1417.

[55] Friedrich Lachmayer, 'Ideologiekritik und Deutungskampf' [1982] *Rechtstheorie (Beiheft 4)* 63, 65–6.

that have been emotionally charged, and which tend to stimulate sentiments and feelings in order to influence the attitude and behaviour of individuals. And particularly those words, concepts, and terms, which possess a dual normative-descriptive function, play an enormously important role in sociology and politics, i.e. in areas where persuasion by way of linguistic means is key to achieving certain goals. At that, the value-laden and emotional components often predominate, whilst the descriptive components are much less pronounced and remain indistinct. In this context, one only needs to think of the use of words such as 'freedom', 'justice', or 'sovereignty' as perfect examples, whose positive emotional connotations (which may of course also be used in a neutral or negative manner) frequently support ideologies with very different objectives to generate approval and sympathy for these objectives. Therefore, it is the task of ideological criticism to unmask these disguised valuations and to showcase any value premises which are often only implicitly included in ideological statements. In doing so, this criticism can help restrict the manipulative effects of ideologies and prevent the brain-washing of individuals by an ideological system with whose convictions they would never agree if their value premises were openly declared in broad daylight.[56]

B. Critique of natural law as a way to legal monism

One object of Kelsen's ideological criticism is the idea of natural law, and it is there where we find the origin of his attack on ideological thinking in general. Yet his critical investigations are not only concerned with elucidating the implications of natural law, but also with legal positivism itself. The pure theory of law thus becomes a critique of any predominant legal theory, which may be abused to serve certain political interests, and a sociological as well as scientific-theoretical analysis of a pre-scientific worldview, in which natural law thinking is deeply rooted.[57]

(1) Taking on the giants

Until the nineteenth century and the rise of modern legal positivism, the legal sciences were principally coterminous with natural law doctrine. This did not mean that the study of positive law was completely excluded, but rather that positive law could only be assessed in close connection with natural law and thus with the concept of justice as *the* material basic norm of all law. Therefore, natural law assumes, as the name suggests, that law is natural, not artificial or posited. Rather, law consists of norms that can be deduced from God, reason, or the nature of human behaviour itself. In contrast to that, legal positivism is concerned with the separation of the

[56] Ernst Topitsch and Kurt Salamun, *Ideologie: Herrschaft des Vor-Urteils* (Langen-Müller, 1972) 106–7 and 110.

[57] Peter Römer, 'Die Reine Rechtslehre Hans Kelsens als Ideologie und Ideologiekritik' (1971) 12 *Politische Vierteljahresschrift* 579, 580–1; Ernst Topitsch, 'Hans Kelsen als Ideologiekritiker' in Salo Engel and Rudolf A. Métall (eds), *Law, State, and International Legal Order: Essays in Honour of Hans Kelsen* (University of Tennessee Press, 1964) 330.

terms 'just' and 'legal',[58] and with law as a human-made coercive normative order under the paradigm of ethical relativism: such positive law can have any arbitrary content and eludes the yardstick of a morally superior body of natural or divine law. Accordingly, any political concept or view can be 'poured' into positive law without it having to submit to a non-human power.[59]

The ultimate logical mistake of natural lawyers is therefore attempting to deduce legal norms concerning just behaviour from nature itself (i.e. the physical reality) and to apply the yardstick of justice to positive law. One could say that thereby normative statements are derived from descriptive statements, which breaches the dichotomy of 'is' and 'ought', or the dualism of reality and ideology.[60] One problem of this assumption is circular reasoning, because natural law already presupposes certain values to be inherent in nature, which it then concurrently tries to deduce from it.[61] The other and more challenging problem is that both legal orders—natural law and positive law—claim to be normative orders, and hence it is not the rule of causality, but the essentially different rule of the 'ought', i.e. normativity and imputation, that governs both orders. However, the 'ought' of natural law is absolute, because it reflects the immutable ideal of justice, whereas the 'ought' of positive law is merely relative and hypothetical, as its norms are only valid under the assumption of a *Grundnorm*.[62] Thus, legal positivism is tantamount to epistemic relativism in the same way as natural law amounts to metaphysical absolutism. For Kelsen, any attempt to disrupt the relative-hypothetical foundation of positive law and to justify it with an allegedly superior cause (i.e. by replacing the hypothetical *Grundnorm* with an absolute one for political reasons) consequently entails that any differences between positive and natural law are entirely neutralized. In this light, metaphysics interferes with experience, and the eternal validity and immutability of natural law and its ideals, first and foremost justice, can be abused as an ideological strategy to legitimize any social order.[63]

There is simply no answer to the question 'what is justice?', which would satisfy everyone in an equal manner. Whoever thinks that they are able to ascertain a universally valid or a supreme legal principle in a scientific-rational way falls victim to the illusion[64] that it would be possible to discover such principles in human rationality. In fact, however, these principles are constituted by irrational emotions. Any attempt to establish absolute values in general and to define 'justice' in particular proves to be an utterly empty formula through which any desired social order can be regarded as 'just'.[65] To demonstrate the parallel legal insignificance

[58] Hans Kelsen, 'Die philosophischen Grundlagen der Naturrechtslehre und des Rechtspositivismus' in Hans R. Klecatsky, René Marcic, and Herbert Schambeck (eds), *Die Wiener rechtstheoretische Schule: Schriften von Hans Kelsen, Adolf Merkl, Alfred Verdross, Band 1* (Verlag Österreich, 2010) 232.

[59] Kelsen, *Pure Theory* (n 38) 65; van Ooyen, *Staat der Moderne* (n 33) 50.

[60] Kazimierz Opałek, 'Kelsens Kritik der Naturrechtslehre' [1982] *Rechtstheorie (Beiheft 4)* 71, 73; Jabloner, 'Ideologiekritik' (n 44) 99.

[61] Hans Kelsen, 'Justice et droit naturel' in Hans Kelsen and others (eds), *Le droit naturel: Annales de philosophie politique, Vol III* (Paris: Presses universitaires de France, 1959) 74–102.

[62] Kelsen, 'Philosophische Grundlagen' (n 58) 234–5.

[63] Ibid., 237. Kelsen uses the term 'social order' interchangeably with 'legal order'.

[64] Topitsch, 'Ideologiekritiker' (n 57) 331.

[65] Hans Kelsen, *Was ist Gerechtigkeit?* (Deuticke, 1953) 18.

and ideological destructiveness of the ideal of justice, Kelsen takes on the giants of Western philosophy and its purportedly unshakable foundations, especially the philosopher who has moulded this concept more than anyone else: Plato. Above all, the central issue for Kelsen is that Plato's dualism of 'good versus evil'[66] does not provide an answer as to what actually constitutes justice. Plato's first explanation of 'justice' is that justice is retribution in the afterlife, where good behaviour is rewarded and evil deeds are punished.[67] But this is nothing more than a pseudo-answer, because it does not tell us anything about a particular moral standard of good and evil, which would underlie the principle of retribution. Plato simply defers this problem to his theory of forms[68] and identifies the form of the good as the core of justice.[69]

Not even in his extensive *Republic*, is Plato able to offer a clear-cut answer as to what is 'good'. In his view, 'good' is initially defined along the lines of the state constitution, which mirrors the hierarchically structured tripartite human soul, i.e. appetite, spirit, and reason, reflecting workers, warriors, and rulers. Ultimately, it is of course the rulers, the 'philosopher-kings',[70] who know and tell the people what is good, namely to act in conformity with nature, whilst anything against nature is evil.[71] Again, a potential solution to the problem of justice is merely postponed,[72] since Plato equates 'nature' with the individuals' duty to take up the role within society that has been assigned to them according to the content of their souls.[73] At the same time, this irrational mysticism is intricately linked to an emphatic claim to power, as the contemplation of good and evil is exclusively reserved for the philosopher-kings. Since everybody else is precluded from finding and knowing what is good, they are also banned from partaking in the governing of the state. Their only purpose is to serve by subjecting themselves to the rulers, and thus, Plato's mysticism becomes capable of justifying any antidemocratic policy; it becomes the ideology of every autocracy.[74]

Similarly, Aristotle does not escape Kelsen's ideological criticism either, as he simply refers to the 'absolute good' in the shape of a deity,[75] and thereby fails to answer the question as to what good really is.[76] Furthermore, Aristotle also fails

[66] Hans Kelsen, 'Die platonische Liebe' in Ernst Topitsch (ed), *Hans Kelsen: Aufsätze zur Ideologiekritik* (Luchterhand, 1964) 114; Hans Kelsen, 'Die platonische Gerechtigkeit' in Ernst Topitsch (ed), *Hans Kelsen: Aufsätze zur Ideologiekritik* (Luchterhand, 1964) 198–204.

[67] Kelsen, 'Platonische Gerechtigkeit' (n 66) 218–21.

[68] Ernst Topitsch, 'Einleitung' in Ernst Topitsch (ed), *Hans Kelsen: Aufsätze zur Ideologiekritik* (Luchterhand, 1964) 15.

[69] Kelsen, 'Platonische Liebe' (n 66) 165–7; Kelsen, 'Platonische Gerechtigkeit' (n 66) 216 and 221–2.

[70] Plato, *Republic* (ed John M. Cooper, Hackett, 1997) 443b–444d and 506b–520d.

[71] Kelsen, 'Platonische Gerechtigkeit' (n 66) 222–5; Kelsen, 'Platonische Liebe' (n 66) 162.

[72] Jabloner, 'Ideologiekritik' (n 44) 100–1.

[73] Plato, *Republic* (n 70) 414b–415d, i.e. gold for the rulers, silver for the warriors, and iron ore for the workers and peasants.

[74] Kelsen, 'Platonische Gerechtigkeit' (n 66) 209, 213–16, and 225–30. See also the similarities to Kelsen's position in Karl Popper, *The Open Society and its Enemies, Vol I* (5th edn; Routledge, 1966).

[75] Aristotle, *Metaphysics* (ed and transl J. Barnes, *The Complete Works of Aristotle, Vol 2* (Oxford University Press, 1984) 1072a.

[76] Hans Kelsen, 'Die hellenisch-makedonische Politik und die "Politik" des Aristoteles' in Ernst Topitsch (ed), *Hans Kelsen: Aufsätze zur Ideologiekritik* (Luchterhand, 1964) 293–7.

with his famous *mesótes* formula as *the* determinant of the moral good, namely the golden mean lying between the two extremes of excess and deficiency.[77] The logical problem of this formula is that it already presupposes the existence of certain vices as self-evident in a given social order, which it then tries to determine. This automatically leads to its practical problem: this formula is materially meaningless and hence applicable to any social order. And this ultimately means that in assuming the validity of the existing social order in question, this ethic justifies it. Its inherent tautology is that it amounts to saying that good is what the existing social order considers good, and it legitimizes and maintains the predominant ideologies of an existing social order. Accordingly, justice is simply the opposite of injustice, and injustice is what positive morality and the law consider to be unjust.[78] Thereby, Aristotelian ethics is being immunized against critical analysis and becomes scientifically worthless.[79]

Another example of the tautological application of the moral good or the principle of justice is the so-called golden rule,[80] which, again, presupposes already existing positive moral and legal rules regarding the infliction of pain and the prohibition thereof, respectively. Here, Kelsen concurs with Kant that the golden rule might eventually lead to the abolition of all law and morality, as a duly convicted prisoner could, on the basis of this rule, ask to be released, arguing that the judge would not want anyone else to send to prison, so he should not do so unto others. Or a person may have nothing at all against others telling her or him lies, as she or he thinks themselves clever enough to find out the truth in any event. But then the golden rule would, ultimately, permit lies, and that is certainly not its intention.[81] Kant's own attempt to formulate a universally valid moral rule, the categorical imperative,[82] has—due to its similarity—been thought to be identical or at least to be a very close cousin of the golden rule, hence calling into question whether it materially improves the golden rule's basic concept. However, although Kant adamantly insists that the categorical imperative is not another version of the golden rule,[83] it does not escape Kelsen's ideological criticism either. For Kelsen, Kant's rule only states that 'human conduct is good or just when it is determined by norms, of

[77] Aristotle, *Nicomachean Ethics* (ed and transl J. Barnes, *The Complete Works of Aristotle, Vol 2* (Oxford University Press, 1984) 1109a20–1109b26; e.g. the μεσότης (mesótes) between recklessness and cowardice being the virtue of courage.

[78] Kelsen, 'Hellenisch-makedonische Politik' (n 76) 302.

[79] Hans Kelsen, 'What Is Justice?' in Hans Kelsen and Ota Weinberger (eds), *Essays in Legal and Moral Philosophy* (Reidel, 1973) 20.

[80] Among the most famous variations of the golden rule, there are both positive ('Do unto others as you would have them do unto you') and negative formulations ('Do *not* do unto others as you would *not* have them do unto you').

[81] Kelsen, 'What Is Justice?' (n 79) 17–18; Immanuel Kant, 'Grundlegung zur Metaphysik der Sitten' in Immanuel Kant (ed), *Gesammelte Schriften* (Deutsche Akademie der Wissenschaften, 1911) AA 4:430.

[82] At this point, only the first version of the Categorical Imperative is relevant, namely: 'Act only according to that maxim whereby you can at the same time will that it should become a universal law without contradiction'. See Kant, 'Grundlegung zur Metaphysik der Sitten'(n 81) AA 4:421; and with slight variations at AA 4: 434 and 436.

[83] Ibid., AA 4:430.

which the agent can or should will that they be binding on all men. But what are these norms of which we can or should will that they be universally binding? That is the crucial question of justice; and to this question the categorical imperative—like its prototype, the golden rule—gives no answer'.[84] Thus, the categorical imperative can also serve as a justification for any given social order and any ideological concept, especially if justice is considered to be 'natural' because it is derived from human reason.[85]

In conclusion, it becomes obvious that natural law doctrine tries to deduce immutable values of justice from nature itself, but by doing so, it transposes the 'is-rules' of reality into 'ought-norms' of morality or law. Thereby natural law creates the illusion that there are objective, absolute, and eternal values inherent in physical reality.[86] Yet not only is this assumption entirely wrong, but it is also highly susceptible to abuse by political ideologies of any kind, most dangerously by autocracies. The reason for this is that if *the* defining criterion of positive law is its creation by human acts, and that consequently this law can only claim relative and thus voidable, but never absolute and permanent validity,[87] then the assumption that only *just* law can be valid law carries the inherent risk that necessarily imperfect human-made law will always be assessed against the standards of unascertainable and unobtainable ideals.[88] And such assessment can be used by autocratic governments both to undermine positive law and the rule of law, *or* to glorify it to the effect that it becomes impregnable to any change.[89]

The reader might wonder at this point how this foregoing critical discussion relates to legal monism. Rest assured that this was only the first step of the argument that is necessary to assess the relationship between natural and positive law in the subsequent section.

(2) *The positivity of natural law*

After this analysis, the differences between positive and natural law are evident: the former is valid only in relation to a hypothetical *Grundnorm*, and because it was posited in a certain manner (e.g., in conformity with the applicable rules on norm-creation); the latter is absolutely valid since it is derived from nature, a deity, or human reason. However, this comparison also shows that there is one significant overlap between those two conceptions of the law, which ultimately illustrates the inherent problem of the natural law doctrine. This problem is that every normative order—positive law as well as natural law—necessarily requires structuring from general to concrete norms by way of individualization. Nonetheless, at this very point where natural law needs to be implemented and applied to real facts, the

84 Kelsen, 'What Is Justice?' (n 79) 18.

85 Ibid., 18.

86 Ibid., 20–1.

87 Hans Kelsen, 'Science and Politics' (1951) 45 *American Political Science Review* 641, 653.

88 Dreier (n 46) 163.

89 Hans Kelsen, 'Metamorphoses of the Idea of Justice' in Paul Sayre (ed), *Interpretations of Modern Legal Philosophies: Essays in Honor of Roscoe Pound* (Oxford University Press, 1947) 390.

question arises whether natural law can even maintain its own existence beyond all positivity and completely independent from positive law. Thus, the question is whether natural law as such is even conceivable,[90] and whether positive and natural law are perhaps mutually exclusive.[91]

To answer these questions, Kelsen hypothetically presupposes the existence of a material content of natural law, which subsequently raises the question as to what form natural law has. As every other normative order, the natural law order can, at the outset, only be thought of in a general and abstract form, for example under the material *Grundnorm* of justice. But these general norms cannot possibly be the only manifestation of the law, since it needs to be applied to concrete cases in order to have a regulative function. Analogously, it becomes obvious that *every* normative order, including natural law, consists of at least two hierarchical steps, i.e. a general-abstract and an individual-concrete level on which abstract norms are being individualized, concretized, and applied.[92] And this is exactly where the theory of the hierarchy of norms comes into play once again. As Merkl states, a judicial decision does not constitute a simple logical deduction from general law, but is the result of a norm-creating act of will.[93] But if such an act of will is required to apply general norms to concrete cases, then the second (or hierarchically inferior step) of natural law is necessarily human-made. Consequently, applied natural law cannot be regarded as 'natural' *stricto sensu* any more; it must be 'artificial' or 'posited'. This means that natural law, on the level of individual norms, inevitably becomes positive, human-made law.[94]

If we take, for example, the natural law-based principle of *pacta sunt servanda*, then we can see that on the individualized level, first, additional positive rules on, say, the specificities of the obligations in question are required; and second, that the consequences of non-performance need to be further specified. Natural law itself is incapable of answering these questions, since its principal goal is the cognition of absolute truth and justice. Positive law, conversely, aims at settling disputes, and therefore its ideal is the creation and preservation of peace. And even though an individual judicial decision in an allegedly natural law-inspired legal order will certainly claim conformity with natural law itself, it is valid even if it does not conform to these claimed standards. Accordingly, positive law has replaced natural law not only in a formal, but also a substantial sense.[95] From the perspective of ideological criticism, this means that the legitimizing function of natural law also disappears, as the question of whether positive law is legitimate under natural law subsequently becomes meaningless. If only positive and human-made law is accepted as valid law,

[90] Kelsen, 'Philosophische Grundlagen' (n 58) 238; Hans Kelsen, 'Die Idee des Naturrechts' in Hans R. Klecatsky, René Marcic, and Herbert Schambeck (eds), *Die Wiener rechtstheoretische Schule: Schriften von Hans Kelsen, Adolf Merkl, Alfred Verdross, Band 1* (Verlag Österreich, 2010) 211.

[91] Opałek (n 60) 74; Jabloner, 'Ideologiekritik' (n 44) 101.

[92] Kelsen, 'Idee des Naturrechts' (n 90) 211–13.

[93] Adolf Julius Merkl, 'Das doppelte Rechtsantlitz' in Hans R. Klecatsky, René Marcic, and Herbert Schambeck (eds), *Die Wiener rechtstheoretische Schule: Schriften von Hans Kelsen, Adolf Merkl, Alfred Verdross, Band 1* (Verlag Österreich, 2010) 895–7.

[94] Kelsen, 'Idee des Naturrechts' (n 90) 213 and 216.

[95] Ibid., 217–19 and 226–7.

then the law can be cognized by everybody, can always be changed, and does not claim absolute validity. In contrast to that, natural law as a normative order, which can only be cognized by a selected few ('the good', 'the just', or 'the reasonable') will always tend towards concealing the existing power structures as ideology[96] and legitimizing autocratic governments.[97] In Kelsen's own words, the principal question at which natural law is aiming, is: 'what lies beyond positive law?'. 'And whoever looks for an answer to this question, will unfortunately neither find an absolute metaphysical truth nor absolute justice. Whoever lifts the veil and does not close their eyes, will have to face the look of the Gorgon's head of power'.[98]

The conclusion is that positive and natural law are mutually exclusive. From its absolutist viewpoint, natural law claims to be the only valid legal order,[99] but in particular for this very reason it has to face a dilemma which eventually undermines its conceptual core: if natural law refuses to be individualized by way of concretization in the context of an actual case, and insists on remaining an eternally valid general norm, it never really applies and hence ceases to have any regulative function. Or natural law finally gives in to individualization and application, but in doing so, becomes positive law. Either way, the concept of natural law is doomed and only leaves positive law in place as valid law.

(3) *The monist purification of positive law*

If we deliberately leave aside for a moment the foregoing finding that natural law necessarily becomes positive law or obsolete, then it becomes obvious that natural law is, in its very substance, profoundly dualist. This means that natural law inevitably distinguishes between itself as an ideal, natural, and immutable normative system and positive law as a real, human-made, and changeable legal order. Positive law itself, conversely, is inherently monist, because it only acknowledges the existence of human-made, changeable, and thus relative laws.[100] Nonetheless, the question remains whether this monist claim is actually true. To answer this question, Kelsen continues using the instrument of ideological criticism to discover and analyse any natural law residues in the positive law in order eventually to purify these elements from it. In fact, there are plenty of these residual elements in positive law in the shape of ideologically charged dualisms, and these elements must be somehow overcome before the law can be considered ideologically neutral. After all, the best way to do so is through an entirely monist conception of the positive law.

For Kelsen, ideologically charged dualisms in the positive law still play an enormous role in legal doctrine today. Especially the concept of 'authority' (*Gewalt*) and

[96] Dreier (n 46) 100 and 173–4; Jabloner, 'Ideologiekritik' (n 44) 101–2.

[97] Kelsen, 'Idee des Naturrechts' (n 90) 229.

[98] Hans Kelsen, 'Diskussionsbeitrag zu den Berichten "Der Begriff des Gesetzes in der Reichsverfassung"' (1927) 3 *Veröffentlichungen der Vereinigung der deutschen Staatsrechtslehrer* 53, 54–5.

[99] Opałek (n 60) 74.

[100] Hans Kelsen, 'Naturrecht und positives Recht' in Hans R. Klecatsky, René Marcic, and Herbert Schambeck (eds), *Die Wiener rechtstheoretische Schule: Schriften von Hans Kelsen, Adolf Merkl, Alfred Verdross, Band 1* (Verlag Österreich, 2010) 183–5.

its various manifestations, such as 'State authority' (*Staatsgewalt*), contribute to a dualizing effect on the law which may introduce new or perpetuate existing ideologies. These dualisms are well known and particularly effective in the shape of the distinction between public and private law; objective law and subjective rights; and lastly between national and international law.[101] In the context of this book, however, only the last dualism is of immediate relevance.

Kelsen's method in unmasking false dualisms is the ideology-critical 'monist method'. In the same way as positive law itself cannot be divided by false dichotomies on the basis of potential natural law residues in it (such as the above-mentioned public-private or the subjective-objective divide), national and international law are not to be separated along the same lines. In this light, the Vienna School's fight against naturalism and the reducibility of the normative material to empirical facts or metaphysical speculation is directed against the brute power of the state on the international level. Kelsen's ideological criticism attempts to reveal the power of the state, i.e. its sovereignty, as a remnant of natural law which enables this erroneous dualist thinking and the separation of national and international law in the first place. The roots of state sovereignty and unlimited state power can be traced back to, inter alia, Hobbes and his *Leviathan*, wherein he sets the stage for individual states to pursue their goals and interests relentlessly over legal obligations in a 'realist fashion',[102] as well as Hegel and his theological deification of the state.[103] Yet there were also legal positivists who proved influential in incorporating this natural law residue into positive law, such as Georg Jellinek. For him, the state represents a power that is original and cannot be derived from anything else, and it is this power to create law that designates a state as sovereign.[104]

For Kelsen, the ideological component of the concept of state sovereignty is its inherent impediment for the 'technical improvement of international law', that is, 'every effort toward further centralization of the international legal system'.[105] In this sense, the pure theory of law intends to expose the use of the concept of sovereignty as an allegedly legal concept lending to a purely political argument in order to uphold and maintain the absolute power of the state, which is grounded in natural law. And precisely by doing so, the pure theory facilitates developments in international law which, so far, have been stunted by mistaken notions, but does not ideologically justify or postulate them.[106]

Natural law *qua* state sovereignty tries to rationalize the triumph of 'might' over 'right', thereby regarding the state as a self-fettering and untamed Leviathan who could, for political reasons, always cast off those legal fetters if need be. Ideologically

[101] Jabloner, 'Ideologiekritik' (n 44) 103; Römer (n 57) 582.

[102] Thomas Hobbes, *Leviathan* (Andrew Crooke, 1651) ch XIII.

[103] Georg Wilhelm Friedrich Hegel, *Elements of the Philosophy of Right* (transl H.B. Nisbet; Cambridge University Press, 1991) §§ 258 and 270.

[104] Georg Jellinek, *Allgemeine Staatslehre* (3rd edn; Häring, 1914) 475, 481, and 489–91.

[105] Hans Kelsen, *Introduction to the Problems of Legal Theory: A Translation of the First Edition of the Reine Rechtslehre or Pure Theory of Law* (transl Bonnie Litschewski Paulson and Stanley L. Paulson; Clarendon Press, 1997) 124.

[106] Ibid.

speaking, this notion entails the possibility of self-liberation from the legal fetters on the grounds of 'higher' political interests of the state organism.[107] But this assumption again amounts to an undue naturalist interpretation of the state in the international legal order: either the state derives its power in a purely natural law interpretation from metaphysical entities such as God, or from its own natural and factual existence, which simply amounts to positive law interspersed with natural law residues.[108] However, since this conception ideologically conflates empirical facts with the normative material, the state—as a substantial and sovereign subject, as a quasi-living organism—needs to be reduced to its legal dimension.[109] Only then, by way of monistically integrating national law into the international legal fabric, can sovereignty be overcome as an idea that is profoundly detrimental to an ideology-free legal science.

In a second step, Kelsen confronts the ideological import of the question as to what body of law—national or international law—enjoys primacy in this monist construct. As was already discussed in detail before,[110] Kelsen advocates a scientifically objective 'choice hypothesis' according to which both versions of primacy are epistemology equal and possible. This means that the eventual choice for one of them is guided by ethical or political preferences, not scientific criteria: imperialism (under the primacy of national law) or pacifism (under the primacy of international law).[111] Alternatively, this element of Kelsen's international law theory is explicitly marked as political, not legal.[112]

Despite his cosmopolitan attitude, Kelsen had to make this concession for the sake of his own credibility and for the theoretical 'purity' of his legal theory.[113] However, and even though it is clear that both versions of primacy are indubitably ideologically charged, particularly Kelsen's student Josef L. Kunz argues that international law is especially susceptible to ideological distortions by international legal scholarships, mainly because of its highly political nature and the paucity of codified norms. Hence there are immense trends toward the nationalistic instrumentalization of international law, and that is why international law is 'often taught less what was "lawful among nations" ... and instead how the politics of one's own country could be justified in terms of international law. The motto of many international law jurists was not the legal question: Quid juris?, but the purely ethical or political maxim: Right or wrong—my country'.[114] Therefore, if one intends to take international law seriously, the choice must be made for the primacy of international law.

[107] Hans Kelsen, *Der soziologische und der juristische Staatsbegriff* (2nd edn; Mohr-Siebeck, 1928) 138; Dreier (n 46) 213.

[108] Kelsen, *Problem der Souveränität* (n 19) 56–9.

[109] Hans Kelsen, *Allgemeine Staatslehre* (Springer, 1925) 376.

[110] See Chapter 3, section 5A(3)c.

[111] Kelsen, *Pure Theory* (n 38) 345–6; Hans Kelsen, *Principles of International Law* (Rinehart, 1952) 446–7; Kelsen, *Problem der Souveränität* (n 19) 317.

[112] András Jakab, 'Kelsens Völkerrechtslehre zwischen Erkenntnistheorie und Politik' (2004) 64 *Zeitschrift für ausländisches öffentliches Recht und Völkerrecht* 1045, 1051.

[113] Jochen von Bernstorff, *The Public International Law Theory of Hans Kelsen* (Cambridge University Press, 2010) 106.

[114] Josef L. Kunz, *Völkerrechtswissenschaft und Reine Rechtslehre* (Deuticke, 1923) 70.

Regardless of his postulated purity of the law, even Kelsen emphasizes that the assumption of a primacy of national law would eventually result in a denial of international law and thereby in a legal absurdity.[115] But there is more to this argument than meets the eye, in particular from an ideology-critical standpoint. Certainly, from an entirely objective and 'pure' view, both versions of primacy are ideological: under the primacy of national law, sovereignty and the power of the state form the dominant ideology, whilst under the primacy of international law, pacifism and peaceful cooperation become ideological ideals. Nonetheless the strong argument in favour of pacifism (and thus monism under the primacy of international law) is that the former is a subjective ideology which, by proceeding from the observers' own *ego* (i.e. the state), only interprets the external world as the will and idea of the subject. Such an ideology is incapable of comprehending other subjects and results in utter solipsism.[116] The latter, conversely, focuses on law as an ideology, and thus becomes an objective ideology which presupposes the validity of the law by way of the hypothesized *Grundnorm*.[117] However, beyond that, the crucial ideological argument in favour of monism under the primacy of international law is that '[t]he idea of law, in spite of everything, seems still to be stronger than any other ideology of power'.[118]

Having said that, it needs to be acknowledged that the positive law is also an ideology of power, but it is the best functioning ideology,[119] because it is objective and therefore also in line with the objectivization programme of the pure theory of law. State sovereignty, conversely, is entirely rooted in the mysticism of natural law, and wrongfully poses as an objective, absolute, and eternal value. But in fact, if regarded as a defining characteristic of the state, the concept of sovereign states—in the same way as the idea of 'justice' or the 'good'—not only becomes a meaningless tautology,[120] but also a very potent factor in transgressing the is-ought dichotomy and thus in perpetuating power politics at the expense of the rule of law. Ultimately, one can therefore say that a monist view under the primacy of international law is both legally pure and ideologically neutral.[121]

C. Conclusion

It was Kelsen's intention to localize any remaining natural law-based dualisms in the positive law in order to purify it of all ideological residues. The main point is that the strict distinction between natural law and positive law eventually results in the

[115] Hans Kelsen, "Souveränität" in Karl Strupp (ed), *Wörterbuch des Völkerrechts und der Diplomatie* (de Gruyter, 1925) 555.

[116] Hans Kelsen, *General Theory of Law and State* (reissue edn; Transaction Publishers, 2007) 386–7.

[117] Kelsen, *Problem der Souveränität* (n 19) 316–17.

[118] Hans Kelsen, *Law and Peace in International Relations: The Oliver Wendell Holmes Lectures, 1940–1941* (Harvard University Press, 1942) 170.

[119] Jakab (n 112) 1051 fn 52.

[120] Michael Keating, 'Sovereignty and Plurinational Democracy: Problems in Political Science' in Neil Walker (ed), *Sovereignty in Transition* (Hart Publishing, 2003) 191–2.

[121] Heinz Peter Rill, 'Internationales, supranationales und nationales Recht—eine Einheit' in Clemens Jabloner and others (eds), *Gedenkschrift Robert Walter* (Manz, 2013) 683 fn 24.

collapse of natural law, which, in turn, necessarily entails a monist perspective of all law. And it is exactly this monist view of the positive law itself which enables a scientifically clear and objective as well as ideology-free description and analysis of the law. In other words, the ideological criticism of natural law and monism under the primacy of international law should be seen as a hermeneutic circle, and that they can only be understood with reference to each other: ideological criticism leads to and supports monism, but monism itself is also directed against any ideology and works as a remedy against ideology-based dualisms in the positive law. One cannot be thought without the other, and this is precisely where the normative value of monism in the context of ideological criticism is to be found.

3. Democracy and Legal Monism

A. Introduction: a peculiar encounter

The members of the Vienna School in general and Kelsen in particular are, first and foremost, known as legal scholars, not political scientists. The reader will therefore be puzzled how Kelsen's strict 'separation of . . . legal theory from politics'[122] and his epistemological legal positivism can be reconciled with his political thought on democracy. Indeed, his legal theory claims to be universally applicable and axiologically neutral,[123] and nothing can better prove its purity in terms of politics than the criticism that this theory was accused of being concurrently democratic, fascist, communist, capitalist, catholic, and atheist.[124]

Furthermore, this raises the question of why democracy should be favoured as a specific system of government, if the pure theory is equally applicable to democratic and autocratic systems, and the *Grundnorm* may confer substantively unlimited powers on an absolute monarch.[125] Nonetheless, these arguments do not prevent an analysis of this peculiar encounter of democracy theory and the pure theory of law, particularly with a view towards legal monism. On the contrary, as a sincere and convinced democrat,[126] Kelsen highlights the main purpose of his theory, which is to liberate the law from any metaphysical exaltation or empirical reduction. As his ideological criticism above has shown, he intends to expose the view of the law as a natural given as an ideological chimera,[127] and thus to claim that only a democratic constitution can legitimize the positive law. The reason for this is—in contrast to autocratic regimes—that democracy ensures that the substance of the law will be more than the mere expression of the subjective will of a single ruler, and that it

[122] Jerzy Wróblewski, 'Democracy and Procedural Values of Law-Making' [1982] *Rechtstheorie (Beiheft 4)* 275, 276.

[123] Kelsen, *General Theory* (n 116) 5; Kelsen, *Pure Theory* (n 38) 1.

[124] Hans Kelsen, 'The Function of the Pure Theory of Law' in Alison Reppy (ed), *Law: A Century of Progress, 1835-1935, Vol 2* (New York University Press, 1936) 239.

[125] Vinx (n 13) 101.

[126] Rudolf A. Métall, *Hans Kelsen: Leben und Werk* (Deuticke, 1969) 110.

[127] Dreier (n 46) 250.

subjects acts of legislation to the legitimizing conditions of legality.[128] Thereby, it becomes evident that absolute values such as 'justice' or 'sovereignty' cannot be included in a democratic system without being subordinate to an ideology rooted in the will, desire, and interests of an autocratic ruler.[129] The legitimacy of a legal norm is based on its legality, which entails that the state falls exclusively within the realm of the 'ought'. Neither does the law create the state nor the state the law, but, again, the state and its law are identical, and hence the ultimate criterion for legitimacy is legality;[130] a conclusion that also resolves the oft-discussed tension between democracy and the rule of law. Kelsen's value-relativism does not automatically imply indifference or a denial of values or democracy;[131] it merely means to stand unflinchingly for one's convictions, and to realize concurrently their relative validity.[132]

B. From democracy to monism: there and back again

In times when everybody talks about democracy, but means a different thing, it seems apposite to provide a definition first. Democracy, in its original meaning as 'rule of the people', is a political postulate as well as a legal yardstick, and in a constitutional legal meaning, it legitimizes the exercise of public power over the people by the people.[133] For Kelsen, democracy is a formal process, not a substantive value or content. The crucial element thus is that there are no prescribed values attached to democracy, but only that the people participate in the creation and application of the law.[134] This participation may be direct or indirect, and this makes democracy the most rational form of government and consequently the most tolerable.

(1) A defence of representative democracy

Nonetheless, Kelsen favours the indirect, or representative, form of democracy. Given the current rise of populism on the basis of 'popular sovereignty' and the call for more direct forms of democracy, which might work momentarily, but eventually destabilize democracy itself,[135] Kelsen's views are now all the more important and should be defended. This section will take up this task and offer reasons why representative democracy remains the superior form of democracy. Given the immense scope of Kelsen's writings on democracy, it must, however, necessarily remain superficial and will only analyse the relevant parts in connection with legal monism.

[128] Vinx (n 13) 102.

[129] Hans Kelsen, 'La méthode et la notion fondamentale de la théorie pure du droit' (1934) 41 *Revue de métaphysique et de morale* 183, 191.

[130] Kelsen, *Staatsbegriff* (n 107) 135.

[131] Sandrine Baume, *Hans Kelsen and the Case for Democracy* (ECPR Press, 2012) 5 and 9–10.

[132] Kelsen, 'Foundations' (n 11) 4.

[133] Oliver Lepsius, 'Kelsens Demokratietheorie' in Tamara Ehs (ed), *Hans Kelsen: Eine politikwissenschaftliche Einführung* (Facultas, 2009) 68–9.

[134] Kelsen, *Essence and Value* (n 40) 98; Kelsen, 'Foundations' (n 11) 66.

[135] As the 'Brexit' referendum has shown, see e.g. Erik Jones, 'Brexit's Lessons for Democracy' (2016) 58 *Survival* 41, 42.

In Kelsen's analysis, the central element of democracy is, first, individual freedom, and second, that this freedom is equal for all, and this principle constitutes—in reference to Jean-Jacques Rousseau's philosophy[136]—a presupposed axiom. Consequently, any state power needs to be justified vis-à-vis individual autonomy, because the exercise of this very power will result in conflicts between the subjective individual will and the objective social or legal order, inevitably leading to an 'agony of heteronomy'.[137] This raises the question of how this unbridgeable opposition between nature, demanding freedom, and the coercive nature of the social condition can be best reconciled. Kelsen replies that the socialization of the individual does not allow for complete autonomy, and since perfect identity between the subject and object of state power is impossible, the individual is being 'denaturized', thus transforming 'anarchical freedom into democratic freedom'.[138] Democracy is therefore the attempt to at least approximate this original state of natural individual freedom and to minimize government as best as possible.[139] Hence, although freedom in a social order presupposes the exercise of state power, individual submission to the law is merely submission to its own, and not to another's will; and this is the very essence of democracy, which distinguishes it from autocratic systems.[140]

Furthermore, it is evident that individual autonomy could only be fully guaranteed if all decisions in such a state were made unanimously. But since such a *modus operandi* would be highly impractical and counterproductive to the social order itself, the only sensible premise to decide is the principle of majority. Then, at least, as many individuals as possible will be free, and the number of individual wills in conflict with the general will of the social order can be minimized.[141] Accordingly, democracy is not leaderless or, as an autocracy, governed by only one leader, but in fact, by a plethora of leaders.[142] The individual will of these leaders will, however, remain ineffective, unless they congregate in groups, or political parties, in order to be able to resolve any clashes of interests within society.[143] For Kelsen, democracy therefore amounts to a division of labour and is based on a pluralist society. In contrast to his antipode, Carl Schmitt, for whom democracy is constituted by the homogenous identity between the state and its people as well as between the constitution and the people's will,[144] Kelsen emphasizes again societal pluralism and mocks the idea of a static and homogenous will of the people, because this idea is based on a pre-legal and deeply ideological concept which does not exist in an empirical sense.[145]

Lastly, Kelsen does not tire to stress that the majority also needs to consider the will of the minority in order not to become an autocracy where no balancing of interests is possible. Accordingly, and under the principle of value-relativism, neither the

[136] Jean-Jacques Rousseau, *Du contrat social* (Marc Michel Rey, 1762) book I, ch 6.
[137] Kelsen, *Essence and Value* (n 40) 27–8. [138] Ibid., 27–32.
[139] Kelsen, *Allgemeine Staatslehre* (n 109) 323; Kelsen, 'Foundations' (n 11) 26.
[140] Kelsen, 'Foundations' (n 11) 19; Dreier (n 46) 253–4.
[141] Kelsen, *Essence and Value* (n 40) 29–32; Kelsen, 'Foundations' (n 11) 25.
[142] Kelsen, *Allgemeine Staatslehre* (n 109) 323; Kelsen, *Essence and Value* (n 40) 88.
[143] Kelsen, *Essence and Value* (n 40) 40–1.
[144] Carl Schmitt, *Verfassungslehre* (Duncker & Humblot, 1928) 10 and 227.
[145] Kelsen, *Allgemeine Staatslehre* (n 109) 317 and 344; Lepsius (n 133) 84.

majority nor the minority can claim to have the absolute truth; they can only try to persuade, which for the majority means trying to persist, and for the minority trying to have their interests heard and considered. Compromise thus also constitutes an essential component of democracy.[146]

Let us now return, in the next step, to the above-mentioned crucial element of indirect or representative democracy, which this section intends to defend. In contrast to Rousseau who only accepts the direct voting of all citizens as truly democratic,[147] Kelsen realizes that, given the complexity of social conditions in a modern state, direct democracy is impossible, and that representative democracy in the form of parliamentarism constitutes the 'only realistic of government capable of putting the democratic ideal into practice ...'.[148] And even though parliamentarism thereby amounts to yet another reduction of individual autonomy, it is a necessary compromise between the claim to personal freedom and the division of labour which makes social progress possible in the first place.[149] In this light, the parliament becomes the meeting place of the representatives of the people through free elections, and where these representatives can resolve differences peacefully and without bloodshed, balancing the interests of the majority and the minority.[150] This said, it is, however, certainly equally true that direct democracy is also desirable, as it fosters immediate participation of the people in the law-making process and hence leads to a higher convergence of the objective and the subjective will within a social order. Kelsen freely accepts this argument and underscores the importance of referenda and petitions to face the argument of elitism in parliament and to keep democracy alive. Nonetheless, parliamentarism continues to constitute a 'fateful question' for democracy.[151]

The apparently paradoxical reason for the enduring importance of representative democracy is that this very representation is a mere fiction. At second glance, however, it becomes clear why this fiction is so crucial; namely, because this representation is based on the free mandate of the representatives in parliament, and not on an actual identity of wills between the representative and the voters.[152] Schmitt and modern populists attack this representative system by arguing that it ignores 'the homogenous will of the people' and 'popular sovereignty',[153] and that only direct democracy could reinvolve the disenfranchised people. The problem with this argument is that it starts from a wrong premise, i.e. that democracy and popular sovereignty are the same. In fact, popular sovereignty legitimizes the constitution as the *pouvoir constituant*, which then establishes democracy as a positive-legal principle. It follows that 'popular sovereignty' is a legally relevant category, but not a legal principle in itself, and that what accounts for the dignity of popular sovereignty is

[146] Kelsen, *Essence and Value* (n 40) 67–8; Baume (n 131) 13.
[147] Rousseau (n 136) book III, chapter 15 and book IV, ch 2.
[148] Kelsen, *Essence and Value* (n 40) 48–9. [149] Ibid., 49.
[150] Kelsen, *Allgemeine Staatslehre* (n 109) 361; Dreier (n 46) 256.
[151] Kelsen, *Essence and Value* (n 40) 48 and 57–8.
[152] Ibid., 49–50; Kelsen, *Allgemeine Staatslehre* (n 109) 301 ff.
[153] Carl Schmitt, *Politische Theologie* (10th edn; Duncker & Humblot, 2015) 67; Carl Schmitt, *Legalität und Legitimität* (Duncker & Humblot, 1932) 40–7.

the same thing, which bereaves it of its practical effect. For in the very moment in which a constitution becomes valid law, the *pouvoir constituant* has done its part and must retreat; it may certainly return at any time and act, but only by concurrently destroying the constitutional legal order[154] and thereby changing the *Grundnorm*.

Kelsen correctly complains that the dogma of popular sovereignty is used against parliamentarism, because the latter has been overburdened with promises which it is has never been able to fulfil. The concept of popular sovereignty precedes the normativity of the law, whilst parliamentarism requires this very normativity. Hence, if populists try to explain 'real democracy' based on the 'will of the people' (a term which cannot be explained in legal vocabulary either) and pit popular sovereignty against representative democracy, parliamentarism will always appear to be deficient.[155] But parliament is not identical with the people, nor are the representatives mere messengers; its task is to have its own will as an organ and as a representative of the people.[156]

In a last step, Kelsen also succeeds in neutralizing the ideological potential of the concept of popular sovereignty by disentangling it from indeterminate factual aspects and by 'legalizing' it through international law. If we recall that the state is identical with its legal order, then the people cannot be claim to be sovereign if they have conferred this power, by way of a constitution, to a parliament.[157] Consequently, neither the term 'people' nor 'sovereignty' remain part of the concept of popular sovereignty as a non-normative and ideology-susceptible residue, and the sovereignty of the state can only be explained by way of the primacy of international law in a unitary legal order.[158] In this manner, it becomes obvious how intricately related and mutually reinforcing democracy and legal monism are. Sceptics might still doubt that the law is a unitary body under the primacy of international law. Nevertheless, in the light of the arguments made above in favour of representative democracy, they must—if they continue to do so—then also face very strong normative arguments for monism *qua* democracy and answer the question of why they are against democracy. Democracy is and remains the only form of government in which it is possible to be subject to a social order *and* still to be free.[159]

(2) *Constitutional review as an essential instrument of democracy*

Democracy often finds itself in tension with the instrument of constitutional review,[160] especially when there is public rant about so-called 'unelected judges' in the light of unpopular decisions. In this vein and on the basis of Kelsen's writings, this

[154] Lepsius (n 133) 71–2.

[155] Kelsen, *Essence and Value* (n 40) 51; Kelsen, *Allgemeine Staatslehre* (n 109) 313–15; Kelsen, *Problem der Souveränität* (n 19) §§ 9, 10, 21, 39, 42, and 51; Lepsius (n 133) 72–3.

[156] Kelsen, 'Foundations' (n 11) 2, 14 and 20–1; Kelsen, *Allgemeine Staatslehre* (n 109) 312–14.

[157] Kelsen, *Allgemeine Staatslehre* (n 109) 115; Kelsen, *General Theory* (n 116) 181 ff.

[158] Lepsius (n 133) 73.

[159] Kelsen, *General Theory* (n 116) 285.

[160] See e.g. Jeremy Waldron, 'The Core of the Case against Judicial Review' (2006) 115 *Yale Law Journal* 1346; Samuel Freeman, 'Constitutional Democracy and the Legitimacy of Judicial Review' (1990/1991) 9 *Law and Philosophy* 327.

section intends to demonstrate that this tension cannot only be easily resolved, but also that constitutional review is essential to democracy. Furthermore, it will show that it is also pivotal in guaranteeing the unity of the law and thus conducive to legal monism. Democracy and judicial review are mutually supporting institutions, and both are required to legitimize a social order through objective legality.[161]

Kelsen is very eager to defend the concept of constitutional review against any criticism. Concerning the first criticism, namely that constitutional review is incompatible with parliamentary democracy, Kelsen replies that it would be politically naïve to leave the decision on the unconstitutionality of a statutory law and its eventual derogation to the same body that adopted this law in the first place, namely the legislature in the shape of parliament. This would merely result in the principle of constitutional legality being rendered ineffective, especially when it comes to individual citizens who might then be uncertain whether to comply with the act in question or not.[162] Furthermore, this criticism must be rejected when taking into account the hierarchy of norms under which the constitution is regarded as the supreme echelon of positive law.[163] The decisive point is that this very constitution determines both the process of legislation in parliament *and* the procedure of constitutional review, and that the demand for statutes to be in conformity with the constitution does not mean anything else than the demand for administration and jurisprudence to comply with statutory law. Alternatively, constitutional review does not stand above legislation, but it is also not foreign to the constitutional legal order. Therefore neither constitutional review itself nor the existence of 'unelected judges' can be undemocratic.[164]

On a different note, there is another argument against the alleged undemocratic nature of constitutional review, namely its power in moderating relations between the majority and minority in parliament. As a control mechanism overseeing the conformity of the law with the constitution, the constitutional court becomes an independent guardian of constitutional liberties[165] by effectively protecting the minority against a despotic majority. Constitutional amendments, for example, are tied to the requirement of a heightened majority, which ensures the participation of the minority lest the amendment in question be subsequently annulled. Furthermore, the interests of a vulnerable minority against majoritarian abuse may sometimes be even protected by the mere threat of making appeal to the constitutional court.[166] Under this viewpoint, constitutional review is far from being undemocratic.

The second line of criticism, forcefully voiced by Schmitt, relates to the allegation that the constitutional court, as an organ of the judicial branch, interferes with the

[161] Vinx (n 13) 145.

[162] Hans Kelsen, 'Wesen und Entwicklung der Staatsgerichtsbarkeit' in Hans R. Klecatsky, René Marcic, and Herbert Schambeck (eds), *Die Wiener rechtstheoretische Schule: Schriften von Hans Kelsen, Adolf Merkl, Alfred Verdross, Band 2* (Verlag Österreich, 2010) 1503–4; Vinx (n 13) 146.

[163] See Adolf Julius Merkl, *Die Lehre von der Rechtskraft entwickelt aus dem Rechtsbegriff* (Deuticke, 1923) 213 and 217; Kelsen, *Pure Theory* (n 38) 221–67.

[164] See also Alexander Hamilton, *The Federalist No 78* (McLean, 1788).

[165] Baume (n 131) 53.

[166] Kelsen, 'Wesen und Entwicklung' (n 162) 1526; Miguel Poiares Maduro, *We, the Court: The European Court of Justice and the European Economic Constitution* (Hart Publishing, 1998) 158–64.

separation of powers if it annuls a legal act, which has been adopted by the legislative branch. For Schmitt, calls for a 'guardian of the constitution' grow only louder in times of a constitutional crisis, and such a crisis is always necessarily of a political nature. Hence, for a constitutional court to adjudicate such matters would require it to act politically and thereby in violation of its judicial function. To avoid such an interference, the only neutral power in a state, the president, democratically elected by the people, should have the competence to mediate, regulate, and preserve the normal order in the case of an emergency.[167]

Kelsen replies by way of a twofold argument: first, Kelsen concedes that all legal decisions are partly discretionary and therefore political. Yet the critical addendum is that such a decision is a valid exercise of authority only if it fits within the hierarchy of norms and thus fully complies with all relevant superior legal norms.[168] Alternatively, one must understand that a constitutional judge, reviewing the constitutionality of a statute, does not apply a general law to a particular case; in fact, such a reviewing judge authoritatively interprets the legal norm in question, thereby voiding it (if unconstitutional), but not enacting it. One could hence argue that the constitutional judge is not making a political decision because he or she is not usurping the discretionary powers of the legislative. The judge is simply making an authoritative judgment of attribution on behalf of the individual whose primary powers of review have been internalized by the legal system.[169] The constitutional court does not legislate positively; it legislates negatively by repealing laws.[170]

Secondly, it is obvious that these exclusive and comprehensive powers of a president in terms of constitutional review, as envisaged by Schmitt, might easily result in an autocracy.[171] Therefore, Kelsen highlights the fact that especially the most important cases of constitutional review involve the legislative and the executive branches as disputing parties. This subsequently requires a *judicial* body, that stands apart from this conflict and which is not itself involved in the exercise of power divided up between the legislature and the executive, to resolve this conflict in an impartial and neutral fashion. Thus, democracy is not simply about the rule of the majority; it is essentially about the constitutional restraint of power, the peaceful search for compromise, and the acknowledged supremacy of a system of procedural rules and minority rights which gives voice and standing to all groups in a social order. A constitutional court, impartially guarding these procedures and rights, is therefore an indispensable element of a democratic state.[172]

167 Carl Schmitt, *Der Hüter der Verfassung* (Duncker & Humblot, 1931) 128–59.

168 Hans Kelsen, 'Wer soll der Hüter der Verfassung sein?' in Hans R. Klecatsky, René Marcic, and Herbert Schambeck (eds), *Die Wiener rechtstheoretische Schule: Schriften von Hans Kelsen, Adolf Merkl, Alfred Verdross, Band 2* (Verlag Österreich, 2010) 1539–53.

169 Kelsen, 'Wesen und Entwicklung' (n 162) 1505–6; Vinx (n 13) 150.

170 Kelsen, 'Hüter der Verfassung' (n 168) 1550 fn 10.

171 A consequence which Schmitt seems ready to accept; see Carl Schmitt, 'Die Diktatur des Reichspräsidenten nach Artikel 48 der Weimarer Verfassung' (1924), reproduced as an appendix to Carl Schmitt, *Die Diktatur* (Duncker & Humblot, 1922) 213–18. See also Kelsen, 'Hüter der Verfassung' (n 168) 1572 fn 13.

172 Kelsen, 'Wesen und Entwicklung' (n 162) 1526; Kelsen, 'Hüter der Verfassung' (n 168) 1551–3.

The last argument in favour of constitutional review finally concerns the unity of the law, and in this light, we need to consider the hierarchy of norms again. Merkl reinterprets the traditional doctrine of the constitutional separation of powers as an utter and complete subjection of the executive under the legislative branch, because the former applies concretely what the latter adopts abstractly. Consequently, the executive must be subordinated to the legislature, and their respective powers are no more than different layers within the hierarchy of norms,[173] which—as briefly mentioned above—entails that the powers of the legislature must be derived from the constitution itself. The task of the constitutional court is then to police the grounds of legal legitimacy and the conditions which make it possible for individuals to defer to the law. Moreover, this legal legitimacy is implicit in the thesis of the identity of law and state and the realization of democracy as a means of extending the idea of legal legitimacy to the legislative level. Hence, the role of the constitutional court is to protect the integrity of these two conditions of legal legitimacy,[174] which is, ultimately, nothing less than securing the unity of the legal order.

Eventually, the main argument for legal monism *qua* constitutional review is that as long as there is no guarantee that unconstitutional acts can be annulled, then the constitution also lacks a legally binding character and supremacy vis-à-vis statutory law, administrative acts, and even contracts between individuals. This, however, stands in stark contrast to the reality of constitutional law. Kelsen concedes that the complete absence of constitutional review does not render a constitutional order absolutely irrelevant, if there are other mechanisms to ensure the effectiveness of the constitution, e.g. the concept of ministerial responsibility as a punitive sanction.[175] However, the crucial argument is that it is the constitution alone that defines how law can be lawfully created and repealed as well as violations be sanctioned. It is of course true that there might be statutes in existence that have not been created in full accordance with the constitution, and it nonetheless allows for their existence until their formal abrogation.[176]

Therefore, the constitution needs to be read not as an unequivocal manual to law-creation, but as an alternation or 'alternative authorization',[177] which certainly allows for an allegedly unconstitutional statute to exist and to conflict with the constitution. But at the same time, the constitution also provides for a special procedure—i.e. constitutional review—through which such a statute can be repealed and the normative conflict be resolved.[178] This means that the unity of the legal order can only be guaranteed if the constitution is fully binding within this hierarchy of norms, and this is the case if a constitutional court has the power

[173] Adolf Julius Merkl, 'Prolegomena einer Theorie des rechtlichen Stufenbaus' in Hans R. Klecatsky, René Marcic, and Herbert Schambeck (eds), *Die Wiener rechtstheoretische Schule: Schriften von Hans Kelsen, Adolf Merkl, Alfred Verdross, Band 2* (Verlag Österreich, 2010) 1104–7.

[174] Vinx (n 13) 171.

[175] Or the so-called 'declaration of incompatibility' used in the United Kingdom, through which courts may declare legislation incompatible (but not invalid or unenforceable) with the European Convention on Human Rights; Human Rights Act 1998, ch 42 s 4.

[176] Kelsen, 'Wesen und Entwicklung' (n 162) 1524–5.

[177] See also Chapter 3, section 4C(4).

[178] Hans Kelsen, *General Theory of Norms* (reprint; Clarendon Press, 2011) 125.

to quash unconstitutional statutes and acts[179]—a conclusion that has also been acknowledged by the European Commission for Democracy through Law in one of its reports.[180]

When compared with a domestic law that is in contravention with international law, critics will certainly cite the absence of such a repeal procedure as proof against the legal nature of international law. Kelsen agrees that international law lacks the same effectiveness and enforceability as domestic law, but this does not speak against its legal nature. In the same way as a constitutional order without constitutional review may react to an unconstitutional statute through the instrument of ministerial responsibility, a state may respond to another state's domestic law in violation of its international obligations through sanctions. And again, it is international law, as the 'constitution' of this unitary legal order, that defines under which conditions domestic law is in accordance with it and violations can be sanctioned. Hence, Kelsen concludes that the same critics who oppose the instrument of constitutional review as an enforcer of constitutional law, also deny international law its legal character and resist the establishment of an international court with reviewing powers.[181] This leaves monism under the primacy of international law as the only morally acceptable choice.

(3) Monism and a democratic world outlook

We have now seen that only democratic systems subject their law to the legitimizing conditions of legality, and that this legality thereby becomes the yardstick to assess the legitimacy of all public acts within a social order.[182] Legality and democracy are therefore mutually reinforcing concepts, and in the same way as strict legality buttresses democracy, democracy expands the rule of law and legal monism beyond the scope of national law. In a social order where the president, according to Schmitt, is authorized to circumvent the legal order in the case of a constitutional crisis, the state and the law are separate from each other. This dualism results in the concept of sovereignty being defined and expressed outside of the legality of ordinary times, paving the way for autocracy. For Kelsen, however, as we have learnt, sovereignty in this political manifestation is a chimera, and nothing more than the identity of law and state. Sovereignty merely means that the state applies and implements the law constrained by the constitution, thereby realizing the ideal of democracy.[183] Following up on these conclusions, this section will argue that democracy on the national level constitutes a precondition for a monist view under the primacy of international law and world peace.

179 Kelsen, 'Wesen und Entwicklung' (n 162) 1525.

180 European Commission for Democracy through Law (Venice Commission), 'The Limits of Constitutional Review of the Ordinary Courts' Decisions in Constitutional Complaint Proceedings', CDL-JU(2005)068, 20 December 2005, 12.

181 Kelsen, 'Wesen und Entwicklung' (n 162) 1525–6.

182 Kelsen, *Staatsbegriff* (n 107) 135.

183 Baume (n 131) 49.

At the outset, Kelsen stresses that there is a close inner connection between politics and philosophy. The centre of both is dominated by a subject-object relation, which is decisive in shaping the intuition that the subject develops regarding its relation to the object. In the same way as a person has ideas about their relation to their neighbour, this person also has a particular view of life and a particular political attitude, which corresponds to it. This is certainly not a logical necessity, but as a matter of intellectual history, such a connection can indeed be made out as a congenial contingency.[184] An autocratic system is characterized by the will to dominate through absolute authority, the negation of freedom, inequality, the subjection to the will of a single ruler, aggression, and an enhanced consciousness of self, which goes hand in hand with a neglect of the others. A democratic system, conversely, strives for freedom, equality, the subjection to the law, and the experiencing of others: the *tat twam asi* of Indian philosophy,[185] according to which we all recognize ourselves in one another,[186] and should refrain from imposing our will on the other.[187] Democracy limits authority and absolute dominance through discussion and compromise between the majority and the minority, and thereby secures internal peace. The life-principle of every democracy therefore is freedom in all its facets, and in particular freedom of science, objectivity, self-criticism, and rationality. This freedom, however, is not possible in an autocracy, where no opposition can be tolerated. Even the freedom of science will be abolished, and its findings can be tolerated only as a serviceable tool of the ruling power as long as they affect its interests. Thus, objectivity is abandoned in favour of the irrational, and emotions and passions triumph over reason.[188]

For Kelsen, the rationalism of democracy shows itself especially clearly in its endeavour to set up its social order as a system of written rules, through which general norms determine individual judicial and administrative acts. This echoing of the hierarchy of norms demonstrates that democracy tends to shift the centre of gravity of governmental functions into legislation, and to constrain governmental power through law. Legality plays again a crucial role in legitimizing power, and emphasizes that legal certainty (i.e. the ability to justify and assess the exercise of public power rationally through its conformity to the law, accountability, and control mechanisms) mirrors an inclination to legal positivism over natural law. Autocracy, on the other hand, claims to be a realization of the problematic natural law residue of 'justice', thereby holding on to irrational and unfalsifiable mystic-religious ideologies.[189]

In the next step, Kelsen extrapolates this analysis of the relationship between character, philosophy, and domestic politics to the international sphere by considering

184 Kelsen, 'World-Outlook' (n 12) 95–8; Kelsen, 'Foundations' (n 11) 98 fn 71.

185 Meaning 'thou art that'; Chandogya Upanishad, 6.8.7. According to Métall (n 126) 3, awareness of this principle probably stems from Kelsen's early engagement with Schopenhauer (n 22) ch XLVII, 600.

186 Kelsen, 'World-Outlook' (n 12) 100–1.

187 Clemens Jabloner, 'Menschenbild und Friedenssicherung' in Robert Walter and Clemens Jabloner (eds), *Hans Kelsens Wege sozialphilosophischer Forschung* (Manz, 1997) 64.

188 Kelsen, 'World-Outlook' (n 12) 101–2. See also Karl Popper, *The Open Society and Its Enemies, Vol II* (5th edn; Routledge, 1971) 224.

189 Kelsen, 'World-Outlook' (n 12) 103–4.

the specific attitudes in foreign policy, thus transforming the plea for democracy into a strong argument for monism under the primacy of international law. Democracies definitely incline towards an ideal of pacifism; autocracies, conversely, towards imperialism. It is of course true that democracies also wage wars of conquest, but the important factor is that their readiness to do so is much weaker and the inner political inhibitions to be overcome much stronger than in an autocratic system. Foreign policy of democracies will therefore be justified by a rational and pacifist ideology based on international law and self-defence, and not on the heroic stance or greatness of the nation, as prevalent in autocracies.[190] This claim is strongly reminiscent of the 'democratic peace theory', as first described by Immanuel Kant and Thomas Paine,[191] holding that democracies do not go to war with each other, because the democratic system itself gives influence to those probably wounded or killed in wars.[192] More convincingly, one could also argue that it was the existence of non-violent dispute resolution mechanisms, inherent to democracies, which led to the emergence of a social norm that democracies *should* not fight each other due to their shared norms and values. This conviction would send a very credible signal to other democratic states of an aversion to the use of force and hence guarantee peaceful relations.[193]

Accordingly, the idea of a state's foreign policy gives us clear evidence of the differences of outlook on the nature of the state: in an autocracy, the heightened ego-feeling of the leader corroborates the ideology that the state is a supreme being and the realization of absolute values. The concept of sovereignty therefore brings about the absolutization and deification of the state, and international law only holds as far as the state acknowledges it, assuming it considers it law at all.[194] In diametrical contrast to that, democracy relativizes the state and regards it as something not above its subjects and the law, but as something made through them. Thereby the state is recognized as a legal entity, which disposes of the concept of sovereignty as an obstacle to a valid and binding international legal order above the state. Ultimately, only democracy has the capacity as well as the inclination to pass a scientifically objective judgment on the form of state appropriated to it,[195] thereby paving the way to respect for international law and subsequently to a monist view under its primacy.

Kelsen does certainly not provide any empirical evidence in his comprehensive philosophical thesis that there is a connection between individual character, form of government, and foreign policy. Furthermore, one could also criticize that he explains the differences between democracy and autocracy based on human mentality

[190] Kelsen, 'Foundations' (n 11) 32.

[191] Immanuel Kant, 'Zum Ewigen Frieden' in Immanuel Kant (ed), *Gesammelte Schriften* (Deutsche Akademie der Wissenschaften, 1923) AA 8:349–53; Thomas Paine, *Common Sense* (R. Bell, 1776) section III.

[192] Bruce Russett, *Grasping the Democratic Peace* (Princeton University Press, 1993) 30. This argument, however, fails to explain why democracies sometimes wage war against non-democratic States; see Michael Doyle, *Ways of War and Peace* (Norton, 1997) 272.

[193] Christopher F. Gelpi and Michael Griesdorf, 'Winners or Losers? Democracies in International Crisis, 1981–94' (2001) 95 *American Political Science Review* 633, 634; Russett (n 192) 59–62 and 73–4.

[194] Kelsen, 'World-Outlook' (n 12) 107–8.

[195] Ibid., 108–9.

and indeterminable 'peculiarities of the human mind'[196] by way of a psychologist reduction,[197] possibly influenced by Sigmund Freud's work.[198] Yet regardless of the persuasiveness of these arguments or their lack thereof, one must admit that, by pointing out the psychological substructure and epistemological ramifications of the respective autocratic and democratic attitudes, Kelsen successfully draws attention to those foundations, which are indispensable in stabilizing a democratic social order. A democracy, which intends to preserve its inherent principles of functioning and thriving, and to prevent the danger of self-destruction, requires certain social-psychological prerequisites in the behavioural repertoire of individuals,[199] such as political education.[200] Moreover, democracy presupposes the state as something human-made and thus as something relative, and what is true for the state is equally true for the law: democracy has an affinity with legal positivism, whereas autocracy prefers natural law.[201]

It may certainly remain doubtful whether a world of democratic states would automatically lead to a cosmopolitan and monist utopia under the primacy of international law, but Kelsen's arguments are convincing that such a state of the world would be highly conducive to it. In this vein, democracy does not only improve life on the domestic scale, but also entails more peaceful relations under the legitimacy of international law.

C. Conclusion

This section showed that Kelsen's understanding of democracy must not be read in a formalistic and narrow fashion.[202] On the contrary, the nexus between the pure theory of law and democracy theory demonstrates that it is exactly the relativist theory of the *Grundnorm* as well as the legitimizing function of the law and the battle against absolutist ideologies, such as natural law, which makes real democracy possible in the first place. Furthermore, only a strictly scientific and objective view on democracy enables the ideal of representative democracy and constitutional review, which in turn protects the minority against a potentially despotic majority through discussion, compromise, and judicial impartiality. What is more important in the context of this book, however, is to realize how beneficial democracy in this form is for a monist view of the law under the primacy of international law: representative democracy helps overcome the non-legal and highly harmful concept of 'popular sovereignty'; constitutional review sustains the hierarchy of norms and the unity of the law; and lastly, a democratic outlook on the world endorses peaceful international relations under the normative shield of international law.[203] Thus,

[196] Kelsen, 'Foundations' (n 11). [197] Dreier (n 46) 274.
[198] See e.g. Métall (n 126) 40–1; Jabloner, 'Menschenbild' (n 187) 65.
[199] Dreier (n 46) 277. [200] Kelsen, *Essence and Value* (n 40) 38 and 95.
[201] Dreier (n 46) 278. [202] Vinx (n 13) 171.
[203] As, one might argue, the United Kingdom Supreme Court has demonstrated in *R (on the application of Miller) v Secretary of State for Exiting the European Union* [2017] UKSC 5, by deciding that, first, Parliament has to be involved in notifying the withdrawal from the EU; and, second, that the withdrawal procedure itself is governed by EU law.

democracy and monism under the primacy of international law form two intricately related and mutually reinforcing concepts, which—from a moral standpoint—can only be seen as a force of good in this world.

4. Pacifism, Cosmopolitanism, and Legal Monism

A. Introduction: methodological purity and the *civitas maxima*

Although monism under the primacy of international law does not necessarily entail the development of a world state, its underlying ideas and close interdependencies with a critical stance towards ideology and a sympathetic outlook on democracy are highly beneficial to this very process. In this light, the last aspect of a potential moral consequence of this version of monism are the concepts of pacifism and cosmopolitanism. Kelsen was deeply convinced of pacifism[204] and essentially considered the law to be *the* social order for the promotion of peace.[205] The greatest hindrance to the development of such an international legal order remains, however, the dogma of sovereignty, because it mistakenly claims that the independence of states is necessarily incompatible with the existence of international legal norms that bind states even against their will. The crucial point is that in order to remove this hindrance, we do not have to commit to the view that the development of such a *civitas maxima* is morally desirable; on the contrary, value-free legal-scientific arguments alone suffice to argue that a binding global legal order is compatible with independent statehood. Thus, any objections to the realization of the *civitas maxima* and the unwillingness to accept the subjection of one's own state to international law are merely politically motivated.[206]

As already mentioned several times throughout this book, (the young) Kelsen as well as his students Verdross and Kunz advocate monism under the primacy of international law, as it corresponds to an objective and pacifist view, and goes beyond the *ego* of the state, recognizing ourselves in the other.[207] Whilst monism under the primacy of national law entails subjectivism and imperialism, international law-centred monism limits sovereignty and the waging of war through the instrument of law, thereby securing world peace. Let us now discuss and defend these morally desirable implications of monism under the primacy of international law, in particular with an innovative view on constructivism in international relations theory.

[204] Thomas Olechowski, 'Kelsen als Pazifist' in Nikitas Aliprantis and Thomas Olechowski (eds), *Hans Kelsen: Die Aktualität eines großen Rechtswissenschafters und Soziologen des 20. Jahrhunderts* (Manz, 2014) 119.

[205] Kelsen, *Law and Peace* (118) 1; Hans Kelsen, *Peace through Law* (University of North Carolina Press, 1944) 3.

[206] Vinx (n 13) 176; Kelsen, *Problem der Souveränität* (n 19) 52–5.

[207] Kelsen, 'World-Outlook' (n 12) 100–1.

B. Cosmopolitanism and law as the basis for peace

Although it seems astounding, the world has indeed seen a considerable decline in violence and increase in peace over the last centuries.[208] However, peace needs to be secured constantly and recent events throughout the world, which threaten to unravel the world order established after the Second World War, have to be taken seriously. It is evident that '[n]early everybody wants peace, ... but there is practically nobody thinking out the arrangements needed'.[209] Therefore, it is high time to make a strong plea for such arrangements in the shape of cosmopolitanism, understood as a belonging of all human beings to a single community, and pacifism, as a general criticism of war, to tackle and overcome these worrisome developments on the basis of monism under the primacy of international law.

(1) From Kantian to judicial cosmopolitanism

The term 'cosmopolitanism' in its meaning as 'citizen of the world' has a long history and can be traced back to Diogenes of Sinope and Stoicism in ancient times. For its modern revitalization, we are indebted to Kant who defends a truly universal politics based upon reason and optimism rather than sentiment and gloominess.[210] In his *Toward Perpetual Peace*, Kant calls for the establishment of a federal league of nations, which is indispensable for securing and promoting a genuine and perpetual peace. The establishment of such a league is a 'direct moral duty',[211] flowing from the principle that any action is right as long as it does not constrain the freedom of others. The problem is, however, that in an anarchical state of nature and in the absence of any institutionalized law, individuals will, in their dealings with one another, probably resort to force.[212] In the same way, each state will, in such a state of nature where it is not subject to any external lawful coercion, resort to violence and command individuals to sacrifice themselves in war. To avoid this use of individuals as mere means and thus a violation of the formula of humanity,[213] it becomes a duty to leave the international state of nature and to establish a league of nations, which would then act as a dispute settlement mechanism and peacekeeper.[214] Lastly, individuals should enjoy the 'cosmopolitan right' of hospitality, which means that they

208 See the comprehensive study by Steven Pinker, *The Better Angels of Our Nature* (Penguin, 2011).

209 H.G. Wells, *What Is Coming?* (Cassel, 1916) ch I.

210 Martha C. Nussbaum, 'Kant and Stoic Cosmopolitanism' (1997) 5 *Journal of Political Philosophy* 1, 3.

211 Kant, 'Zum Ewigen Frieden' (n 191) AA 8:354–7. See also Bryan Lueck, 'Appendix: On Cosmopolitanisms' in Lucian Stone (ed), *Iranian Identity and Cosmopolitanism* (Bloomsbury, 2014) 164.

212 Immanuel Kant, 'Die Metaphysik der Sitten' in Immanuel Kant (ed), *Gesammelte Schriften* (Deutsche Akademie der Wissenschaften, 1907) AA 6:230, 237, and 312.

213 Stating that you should '[a]ct in such a way that you treat humanity, whether in your own person or in the person of any other, never merely as a means to an end, but always at the same time as an end': see Kant, 'Grundlegung zur Metaphysik der Sitten' (n 81) AA 4:429.

214 Kant, 'Die Metaphysik der Sitten' (n 212) AA 6:350; Kant, 'Zum Ewigen Frieden' (n 191) AA 8:354–7.

have the right to visit other countries. Access can be refused, but not with hostility, if visitors behave peacefully, and not if it leads to their demise.[215]

In these considerations, Kant does not reject the idea of a world state as such.[216] He concedes, however, that since this ideal cannot and should not be reached completely, it should at least be approximated through a league of nations.[217] The reason for this is that, on the one hand, he believes that states would never be willing to renounce their sovereignty in order to establish a genuine world state; and on the other hand, he argues that human rights can only be effectively protected by individual states, and not by nations extending over vast regions.[218] Accordingly, Kantian cosmopolitanism is best seen as a complementary or subsidiary cosmopolitanism,[219] in which states continue to exist under a league of nations and individuals remain state citizens in addition to their cosmopolitan citizenship.

The younger Kelsen proved to be very susceptible to this idea of Kantian cosmopolitanism, which, in his view, would be able 'to eliminate the most terrible employment of force—namely, war—from inter-State relations' by means of a world state.[220] To this end, he first adopts Christian Wolff's notion of the *civitas maxima*, understood as the superior universal community of 'all nations and the whole human race',[221] which he regards as the personification of the international legal order, encompassing all state legal orders.[222] In this light, the ideal of the *civitas maxima* becomes the political core of the hypothesis of the primacy of international law.[223]

The profoundly ethical dimension of this argument is that the scourge of war can only be overcome by guaranteeing peace, and global and lasting peace can only be achieved through cosmopolitan monism. The primacy of international law is hence merely a consequence of a deep ethical conviction on the unity of law and humankind in a single state.[224] Soon, however, Kelsen agrees with Kant and drops the notion of the *civitas maxima* from his later works upon realizing the utopian character of this endeavour and that the establishment of such a world state must necessarily fail due to insurmountable practical difficulties.[225] What is even more problematic with this deduction of the primacy of international law from a moral premise is Kelsen's own violation of Hume's law and his transgression of the methodological boundary between scientific-legal purity and ethical value-laden subjectivity.[226]

215 Kant, 'Zum Ewigen Frieden' (n 191) AA 8:357–60.

216 Pauline Kleingeld, *Kant and Cosmopolitanism* (Oxford University Press, 2012) 52–3; Otfried Höffe, *'Königliche Völker'* (Suhrkamp, 2001) 226–7.

217 Kant, 'Die Metaphysik der Sitten' (n 212) AA 6:350.

218 Ibid.; Kant, 'Zum Ewigen Frieden' (n 191) AA 8:354.

219 Höffe, *'Königliche Völker'* (n 216) 200.

220 Kelsen, *Peace through Law* (n 205) 4–5.

221 Christian Wolff, *Ius Gentium methodo scientifica pertractatum* (Renger, 1749) § 2.

222 Kelsen, *Problem der Souveränität* (n 19) 249–57.

223 Hans Kelsen, 'Les rapports de système entre le droit interne et le droit international public' (1926-IV) 14 *Recueil des cours* 227, 325; Galindo (n 1) 145.

224 Galindo (n 1) 145.

225 Kelsen, *Peace through Law* (n 205) 5–6 and 10–11. See also Charles Leben, 'Hans Kelsen and the Advancement of International Law' (1998) 9 *European Journal of International Law* 287, 295; Olechowski (n 204) 124.

226 See the criticism by Danilo Zolo, 'Hans Kelsen: International Peace through International Law' (1998) 9 *European Journal of International Law* 306, 310.

Yet perhaps this moral ideal of a *civitas maxima*, promising global peace, can be saved through a different avenue, namely on the basis of law itself and through a purely epistemological approach. As already discussed in the introduction to this chapter, Kant's *Critique of Pure Reason* can be understood as establishing a cosmopolitan community through the ahistorical and acultural concept of the synthetic a priori, which founds, as the polity of human reason, an 'epistemic World Republic'.[227] In the same way, the pure theory of law represents a general theory of positive law itself,[228] independent from any historical or cultural preconditions and only reliant on epistemic human reasoning. In this light, the completion and perfection of the law in a cosmopolitan international legal order is nothing more than a radical anti-solipsism,[229] respecting and co-existing with the other in a peaceful way. Therefore, monism under the primacy of international law should not be deduced from moral presuppositions, but *vice versa*, it is the epistemological purity of the law which not only allows for this monism in the first place, but also for the moral ideal of peace through law. In his eponymous work *Peace through Law*, Kelsen intends to prove this claim.

(2) *Pacifism: peace through law*

It might be trivial to note that the law has always been an essential means in creating and securing peace.[230] It is, however, not trivial to emphasize that the utilization of international law to the same end represents a rather recent development of the twentieth century.[231] Thus, and even though Kelsen continues to adhere to the idea of a 'World Federal State' as a long-term objective, he pleads that, for the time being, the second best option is to pursue durable peace 'within the framework of international law—that is to say, by an organization which, in the degree of centralization, does not exceed that of the usual type of international communities'.[232] In Kelsen's view, law is—for a very simple reason—the only order capable of promoting peace through the peaceful living-together and non-violent settlement of conflicts: namely, through the assumption of a *Grundnorm*. The *Grundnorm* does not only require that coercive force be applied in accordance with the legal norms validated by it; it also determines that the application of coercive force on any other basis is impermissible.[233] In the face of frequent and serious violations of the prohibition of the use of force in international law, Kelsen's view of international law as a guarantor of peace was of course heavily criticized as mere 'wishful thinking'.[234]

[227] Kant, *Kritik der reinen Vernunft* (n 23) B 879; Höffe, *Kants Kritik der praktischen Vernunft* (n 26) 52.

[228] Kelsen, *Pure Theory of Law* (n 38) 1.

[229] Höffe, *'Königliche Völker'* (n 216) 263.

[230] Kelsen, *Pure Theory of Law* (n 38) 38. See also Grenville Clark and Louis B. Sohn, *World Peace through World Law* (Harvard University Press, 1958).

[231] Jabloner, 'Menschenbild' (n 187) 70.

[232] Kelsen, 'Les rapports' (n 223) 5 and 12.

[233] Kelsen, *Law and Peace* (118) 1; Kelsen, *Peace through Law* (n 205) 3. See also Vinx (n 13) 194–5.

[234] Hedley Bull, 'Hans Kelsen and International Law' in Richard Tur and William Twining (eds), *Essays on Kelsen* (Clarendon Press, 1986) 329.

Yet in addition to the fact that breaches of the law do not disprove the legal quality of international law,[235] this argument is, at this point, entirely amiss, as this section does not intend to prove the legal quality of international law—this has already been done in the previous parts of this book. This section rather intends to show that if one accepts monism under the primacy of international law, law can bring about durable peace as a moral ideal. Alternatively, the legal quality of international law must already be presupposed at this point. A sceptic may certainly reject this presupposition, but then he or she might not be interested in the moral implications of monism anyway.

The creation of a world state to secure peace remains utopian and could, if ever, only be realized as the outcome of a long historical process and only through numerous intermediate stages.[236] In the meantime, however, the international legal order is entrusted with this goal. Kelsen readily accepts that international law is a 'primitive legal order', currently lacking specialized institutions of compulsory jurisdiction and law-enforcement. Nevertheless the subjects of this legal order, i.e. primarily states, accept that the use of force is prohibited,[237] unless they react to prior breaches of the law on the part of others, for instance by way of self-defence or collective security measures.[238] Yet in addition to the active engagement of the United Nations Security Council in certain situations, the ascertainment of a breach of law largely falls to each individual state, and the subsequent enforcement usually takes place by way of self-help.[239] To support Kelsen's interpretation of international law, one could highlight the undeniable fact that states very rarely engage in the use of force without offering any justification provided for by international law. Therefore, states seem to accept that the use of force is only lawful if it takes the form of the application of a sanction against a prior breach of a norm of international law.[240]

This finding strongly speaks in favour of the moral superiority of monism under the primacy of international law, because only law derived from one common hypothesized and purely formal *Grundnorm* can guarantee the unlawfulness of the use of force by monopolizing it and thereby deter states or make it more difficult for them to engage in it. If we contrast that with the other theories discussed throughout this book—State-centred monism, dualism, and pluralism—one can easily see their shared defect: none of them could guarantee world peace (as imperfect as it may be at the moment) as monism under the primacy of international law. The reason for this is that all of them would allow states to develop their legal orders according to their own basic norm. And these respective basic norms could be substantive and

[235] See Chapter 3, sections 5A.2 and 5B.2.c. See also Kelsen, *Principles of International Law* (n 111) 422–3; Alexander Somek, 'Kelsen Lives' (2007) 18 *European Journal of International Law* 409, 435–6.

[236] Zolo (n 226) 317.

[237] See Article 2(4) of the UN Charter.

[238] See Articles 51 and 42, respectively, of the UN Charter.

[239] Kelsen, *Pure Theory of Law* (n 38) 323.

[240] Vinx (n 13) 195–6. For two examples of such a justification for obviously unlawful incidents (i.e. the war in Iraq 2003 and the annexation of Crimea 2014, respectively) see John Yoo, 'International Law and the War in Iraq' (2003) 97 *American Journal of International Law* 563–76; and Anatoly Kapustin, 'Crimea's Self-Determination in the Light of Contemporary International Law' (2015) 75 *Zeitschrift für ausländisches öffentliches Recht und Völkerrecht* 101–18.

value-laden, which would allow ideological concepts such as 'justice' or 'the good' to dominate the law again. In this respect, one can easily see how such a scenario could seriously endanger the concept of peace under one common and shared *Grundnorm* of international law.

Kelsen nonetheless takes the argument a step further. It is indisputable that the international legal system suffers from the absence of a court with compulsory jurisdiction.[241] Particularly owing to the failure of the League of Nations, he therefore suggests the creation of a 'Permanent League for the Maintenance of Peace'.[242] Yet in contrast to the League of Nations (and the current system, one might add), Kelsen does not place the centre of operations of this new League in a legislative or executive organ. Not only should the establishment of such bodies simply be the last step towards a centralized world organization; their inherent problem also is that their decisions are taken unanimously, binding no state against its will and thus undermining the effectiveness of the international legal order.[243]

Conversely, the centre of the Permanent League should be a court with compulsory jurisdiction. To begin with, a court can be relatively easily centralized early on in the process, and furthermore, courts usually decide on the basis of the majority principle, which would also solve the problem of decision-making within the organization. Without the existence of such a court, however, every state would retain its competence to self-help, to decide who is in breach of international law and to resort to war or reprisals against the alleged perpetrator.[244]

Lastly, echoing his debate with Schmitt[245] discussed above, Kelsen extrapolates his analysis of constitutional review to the international judiciary: he argues that no distinction can be made between legal and political disputes, since such a distinction would be entirely subjective in character and would only consist in the way the parties to the conflict justify their respective attitude.[246] Positive law can be applied to any conflict, and therefore the League becomes a legal community instead of a political one to which all partaking states have subjected themselves voluntarily.[247] Their political independence would hence not be endangered.

In conclusion, we see now that the notion of the *civitas maxima* requires an international court with the power of compulsory jurisdiction in all disputes among states, and that the appropriate means of achieving international peace does not lie in political methods, but in legal relations.[248] The moral component is, again, that

[241] Cf. Article 36(2) of the ICJ Statute, stating that States '*may* at any time declare that they recognize' the compulsory jurisdiction of the Court (emphasis added). Furthermore, even if States have recognized the jurisdiction of the ICJ by way of special agreement, they often withdraw from said agreement after having lost their case. See e.g. the United States after *LaGrand (Germany v United States of America)* [2001] ICJ Rep 466.

[242] Kelsen, *Peace through Law* (n 205) 14–15 and 56 ff.

[243] Ibid., 50.

[244] Ibid., 13–15 and 21; Kelsen, *Law and Peace* (118) 152–3.

[245] Olechowski (n 204) 125.

[246] Kelsen, *Peace through Law* (n 205) 24 and 28–30. See also Judith von Schmädel, 'Kelsen's Peace through Law and Its Rejection by his Contemporaries' (2011) 39 *Hitotsubashi Journal of Law and Politics* 71, 75.

[247] Kelsen, *Peace through Law* (n 205) 27 and 66.

[248] Vinx (n 13) 198; von Schmädel (n 246) 76.

only through this avenue, all law would unquestionably form a unitary order and international law would be supreme in any event, thereby excluding the use of force in the case of conflict and thus guaranteeing global peace. Until the eventual establishment of such a powerful court, however, the primacy of international law in its current form remains the best hope of securing peace.

(3) Monism and constructivism in international relations theory

Despite the existence of international law, however, anarchy—here understood as the absence of a centralized and effective world government—remains a considerable factor in international relations, and thus a significant threat to peace. How should we deal with this anarchical international society of states, where the 'law of the jungle' and brute force might easily take over and disregard the normative constraints of international law? Given these issues, this section will look into International Relations theory and determine what it says about international law and its potential power to secure peace. The moral implications of monism under the primacy of international law will accordingly be scrutinized from a political side, which will allow us to understand state behaviour not only through power relationships (as claimed by realism), but also through social interaction and the normativity of the law. The theory most suitable to do so is *constructivism*, which is interested in legal norms and their influence on the international system. This interest has proven to be the strongest bridging point between international lawyers and constructivists,[249] which emphasizes even more that this specific theory can be interpreted as having strong ties to a monist understanding of the law. Regardless of its cursory character, this section will nonetheless try to show some overlaps between constructivism and monism under primacy of international law as envisaged by the pure theory of law.

To begin with, it should be briefly explained why other theories should be disqualified as serious competitors to constructivism in this context. On the one hand, realism in all its diverse manifestations focuses on power and materialism. It is therefore intrinsically hostile to international law and tends to devalue the role of norms in the international system.[250] Accordingly, there is not much love lost between realists, seeing 'might as right' as well as deriving 'ought' from 'is', and legal positivists, seeking to separate the validity of the law from everyday politics and morality.[251] More cynically speaking, realism holds that states only help each other if there is 'something in it for them', but never because of a sense of legal obligation or

[249] Jutta Brunnée and Stephen J. Toope, 'Constructivism and International Law' in Jeffrey L. Dunoff and Mark A. Pollack (eds), *Interdisciplinary Perspectives on International Law and International Relations* (Cambridge University Press, 2013) 119.

[250] Ibid., 120; Ian Hurd, 'Constructivism' in Christian Reus-Smit and Duncan Snidal (eds), *The Oxford Handbook of International Relations* (Oxford University Press, 2008) 299.

[251] David Armstrong, Theo Farrell, and Hélène Lambert, *International Law and International Relations* (2nd edn; Cambridge University Press, 2012) 83; Jack Donnelly, 'The Ethics of Realism' in Christian Reus-Smit and Duncan Snidal (eds), *The Oxford Handbook of International Relations* (Oxford University Press, 2008) 153.

normative legitimacy.[252] On the other hand, liberalism with its focus on institutions may—at least *prima facie*—be suitable for the purposes of this section. However, it is also inexpedient since it not only challenges the separability thesis of law, morality, and facts defended throughout this book, but also pursues a prescriptive approach (in contrast to the merely descriptive approach of the pure theory of law).[253] Above all, neo-liberalism stresses that social action is to be achieved through value-laden institutions as well as non-binding soft law[254]—two assumptions which are evidently anathema to the core tenets of the pure theory of law.

In contrast to these two theories, constructivism takes a mid-way approach and argues that state interests are defined both in material *and* non-material terms, the latter being constitutive rules of a complex 'social system' with multiple layers of actors operating with mixed motivations through institutions.[255] Particularly the colourful example that '500 British nuclear weapons are less threatening to the United States than five North Korean nuclear weapons, because the British are friends ... and the North Koreans are not'[256] shows that the international system is somehow socially constructed, similar to the law as something posited and not natural. Alternatively, the focus of constructivism is on the material basis of international relations *and* its being supervened by ideas, culture, and norms. Thereby moderate constructivism offers a very promising line of engagement with positivism, focuses on norms as explanatory variables in world politics, and seeks to develop objective knowledge of the social world and the workings of international law.[257]

Radical constructivism, conversely, which puts more emphasis on hermeneutics and linguistics at the expense of material elements, can be discounted for the purposes of this section, as it explicitly rejects Kelsen's legal positivism.[258] Moderate constructivism, however, helps explain how international law can influence state behaviour; not through legal norms as direct causes of action, but rather how these norms constrain, enable, and constitute actors and thus help shape world politics.[259] In particular the concept of 'compliance pull' exerted by legitimate legal norms plays an important rule here, and this compliance with international law can be explained by law's clarity, communication of authority, consistency, and creation through a hierarchical structure. The source of the binding effect of law is, eventually, a general belief that it is indeed binding, and hence a social construct.[260]

[252] Wendt, *Social Theory* (n 15) 242.

[253] Armstrong and others (n 251) 92–3.

[254] Ibid., 98; Robert Keohane and Joseph Nye, *Power and Interdependence* (Longman, 1977) 20 and 137–9.

[255] Phillip A. Karber, '"Constructivism" as a Method in International Law' (2000) 94 *Proceedings of the Annual Meeting (American Society of International Law)* 189, 189; Brunnée and Toope (n 249) 121.

[256] Alexander Wendt, 'Constructing International Politics' (1995) 20 *International Security* 71, 73.

[257] Armstrong and others (n 251) 107–9.

[258] See e.g. Nicholas Onuf, 'Do Rules Say What They Do? From Ordinary Language to International Law' (1985) 26 *Harvard International Law Journal* 385, 395; Friedrich Kratochwil, *Rules, Norms, and Decisions* (Cambridge University Press, 1989) 186 and 200–1.

[259] Brunnée and Toope (n 249) 120 and 124.

[260] Thomas M. Franck, 'The Power of Legitimacy and the Legitimacy of Power: International Law in an Age of Power Disequilibrium' (2006) 100 *American Journal of International Law* 88, 91–3.

Although constructivists argue that international politics and international law are mutually constitutive, law remains distinctive and institutionally autonomous from politics due to its obligatory character. This obligatory effect is rooted in the deep constitutional structure of modern international society, which explains why states feel compelled to provide legal justifications for their actions: they all value long-term cooperation and predictability which is promoted by appearing to be law-abiding.[261] From the viewpoint of this book, one might add that this course of action is only possible if states accept monism under the primacy of international law, because otherwise national law could always prevail in the case of conflict and thereby disrupt such cooperation.

Certain similarities of moderate constructivism with the main features of the pure theory of law should have become obvious to the reader by now. Both share a philosophical lineage that can be traced back to Kant,[262] namely (i) that international politics and law are socially constructed or posited and not reducible to nature or materialist facts (i.e. the dichotomy of 'is' and 'ought'); (ii) hence a relativist epistemology where international politics is based on social relations supervening material facts, and international law on a hypothetical *Grundnorm* allowing for the validity of positive law; and finally (iii) a process-oriented ontology in which the object of cognition (i.e. social relations and positive law, respectively) is created through the method of cognition. Owing to these similarities, constructivism appears to be extremely suitable to explain the morally desirable ramifications of monism under the primacy of international law. However, at this point, one central issue remains unexplained, namely the claimed legitimacy of international law as *the* factor for state compliance. Is its legitimacy indeed the only reason for compliance or are there other arguments as well? And, if in the affirmative, what makes legitimacy superior to these other reasons?

In fact, constructivism answers the question as to why states comply with international law by recourse to the three cultures of anarchy as exemplified by Hobbes, Locke, and Kant, and three degrees of norm-internalization within them, namely (i) at the lowest level, to avoid sanctions or because of coercion; (ii) at an intermediate level, to realize self-interest; or (iii) at the highest level, because legal norms are accepted as legitimate and states *want* therefore to comply with them.[263] Anarchy continues to pose a distinctive and important problem of order for international politics and a threat to peace, and accordingly, constructivism suggests some new solutions in the form of these three cultures of anarchy, as adapted from the English School of International Relations.[264] The first culture is *Hobbesian anarchy* in which

[261] Christian Reus-Smit, 'The Politics of International Law' in Christian Reus-Smit (ed), *The Politics of International Law* (Cambridge, 2004) 42–3; Ian Johnstone, *The Power of Deliberation: International Law, Politics, and Organizations* (Oxford University Press, 2011) 33–4.

[262] See Karber (n 255) 189–90.

[263] Filipe dos Reis and Oliver Kessler, 'Constructivism and the Politics of International Law' in Anne Orford and Florian Hoffmann (ed), *The Oxford Handbook of the Theory of International Law* (Oxford University Press, 2016) 350–1.

[264] Wendt, *Social Theory* (n 15) 247 and 257. See also Wight (n 14) and Hedley Bull, *The Anarchical Society* (Macmillan, 1977).

the representation of the other by the self boils down to enmity. In this violent state of nature, foreign policy focuses on the destruction of the enemy, the significance of military capabilities, and—in the case of armed conflict—the absence of any limits to violence. Thus, the entire international system is taken over by the representation of the enemy, which generates patterns of state behaviour, namely the Hobbesian 'war of all against all' and a true self-help system. Knowledge-sharing in such a culture of anarchy starts at a very low level and boils down to the common denominator that 'there are other States, and they are enemies'.[265] Yet even though there are also three degrees of norm-internalization in a Hobbesian anarchy, none of them suffices to guarantee peace: coercion can be resisted or violently overcome, and self-interest might change in the face of threats. Even the legitimacy of norms becomes paradoxical in such a system, as the enmity amongst states itself is thereby being legitimized in the shape of an 'adversary symbiosis'.[266] It is evident that such a system of isolation and solipsism,[267] where no norms except for enmity itself are shared, is intrinsically inimical to the concept of international law and its peace-securing functions. From a moral viewpoint, it can therefore only be rejected.

The second culture is *Lockean anarchy*, reflecting, more or less, the Westphalian international system, where the 'kill or be killed' logic of Hobbes is replaced by the motto of 'live and let live'. Representations of the self and the other in this culture are less threatening, because states recognize each other's territory as their 'property'. Hence enmity becomes rivalry, but violence might still occur. The most important difference to the Hobbesian system is, however, the right to sovereignty and its transformation into a formal institution of international law which prohibits other states from trying to take away one another's life, liberty, and property. Despite the absence of centralized enforcement, international law becomes a key part of the deep structure of contemporary international politics,[268] as it constrains rivalry among states. Nonetheless, the Lockean system is not a complete 'rule of law system' (in the sense of Kelsen's 'primitive legal order'[269]), because violence may still be exercised—but only within the limits set out by international law.[270]

Accordingly, the principle of sovereignty becomes crucial as a restraining force in international relations, but of course under the significant *caveat* that is to be understood as a *legal*, and not a *political* concept. When we now look into the abovementioned three degrees of internalization, we will see that the existence of and respect for the international legal order in a Lockean culture makes an enormous difference: whereas coercion alone is ill-equipped to account for the long-term stability of the Westphalian system, self-interested states pursue legal norms because it helps them advance their interests. Yet a relatively peaceful and stable system is only

[265] Wendt, *Social Theory* (n 15) 259–68.

[266] Ibid., 268–75; Howard Stein, 'Adversary Symbiosis and Complementary Group Dissociation' (1982) 6 *International Journal of Intercultural Relations* 55, 55–83.

[267] C. Fred Alford, *Group Psychology and Political Theory* (Yale University Press, 1994) 87.

[268] Stephen Kocs, 'Explaining the Strategic Behaviour of States: International Law as System Structure' (1994) 38 *International Studies Quarterly* 535, 542–3.

[269] Kelsen, *Problem der Souveränität* (n 19) 267.

[270] Wendt, *Social Theory* (n 15) 279–81.

durable once 'self-interest' turns into genuine 'interest' to comply with the law not as a mere object, but because it is accepted as legitimate. This legitimacy stems from an expanded sense of the self that includes other members of the international system whose right to life, liberty, and property is therefore respected.[271] The Lockean culture of anarchy, having dominated the last three centuries, certainly represents a very welcome first step into the right direction of a peaceful world under the rule of law, but it remains deficient nevertheless: albeit within the boundaries of the law, states continue to see each other as rivals and violence might flare up in times of crisis.

Eventually, only a culture of *Kantian anarchy* will be able to succeed in securing perpetual peace.[272] Instead of enmity or rivalry, this political culture is based on friendship which means that all disputes are settled without violence through negotiation, arbitration, or courts, and security threats against one will be regarded as threats against all. The logic of Kantian anarchy is accordingly predominated by the view that real assurance of peace comes from shared knowledge of one another's peaceful intentions and collective security.[273] War is simply not considered a legitimate way of settling disputes any more. Again, coercion—as the lowest degree of norm-internalization—fails to explain such close cooperation, whilst self-interest would degrade friendship to a mere strategy and render it an empty concept. Only the highest degree of norm-internalization through which states accept the legitimacy of international law and identify themselves with each other leads to a situation in which one another's security is not just related to their own, but literally being their own. By extending the cognitive boundaries of the self to include the other, they both begin to form a single 'cognitive region' of solidarity.[274] International interests become part of the national interest, and friendship is a preference over an outcome, not just preference over a strategy. Lastly, one should, however, acknowledge that this Kantian culture remains a culture of anarchy. But the crucial factor is that anarchy and hierarchy should not be seen as dichotomical terms, but as a continuum. Otherwise, the international system would be *per definitionem* an anarchy until the successful formation of a world government. Rather, the Kantian system under the accepted legitimacy of international law constitutes a domesticated international system under a de facto rule of law and decentralized authority.[275]

The question remains how such cultures can be changed and reach a higher level of stability and peace. Change is of course not a historical necessity, but simply morally desirable, and especially the 'high death rate' of states within the Hobbesian anarchy creates incentives to create a Lockean culture.[276] Constructivism thus explains how anarchy can be transformed into something that is less anarchic, and where law helps advance a normative agenda in world politics and translate political disputes

[271] Ibid., 285–93.

[272] Andrew Hurrell, 'Kant and the Kantian Paradigm in International Relations' (1990) 16 *Review of International Studies* 183, 188.

[273] Wendt, *Social Theory* (n 15) 297–300. See e.g. Karl Deutsch and others, *Political Community and the North Atlantic Area* (Princeton University Press, 1957) 29.

[274] Emanuel Adler, 'Imagined (Security) Communities: Cognitive Regions in International Relations' (1997) 26 *Millenium* 249, 251–5; Deutsch and others (n 273) 129.

[275] Wendt, *Social Theory* (n 15) 301–8. [276] Ibid., 311.

into legal claims[277] in order to 'civilize nations'.[278] This explains particularly well the transformation of a Lockean system into a Kantian one wherein especially self-restraint is highly conducive to democratic peace. Only once states start to engage in mutual prosocial behaviour through which they can overcome the fear of each other, does perpetual peace become tangible. The traditional solution to this problem of trust is the imposition of external constraint by a third party, for example the protective behaviour of Great Powers or military technology. Yet what is even more effective than that is the creation of institutions and a normative framework, which guarantee the mutual respect for sovereignty, and the non-violent resolution of conflict—namely international law. Through repeated compliance with international norms, states begin to internalize it as an institution and external constraint suddenly becomes internal constraint or self-control.[279] In the terms of the pure theory of law, this norm-internalization or legal 'acculturation'[280] could be seen as the acceptance of the *Grundnorm* of international law by states, which would necessarily entail a monist view under the primacy of international law. Moreover, mutual trust can also be created by externalizing domestic policies, especially conflict-resolution and democracy, through changed foreign policy behaviour,[281] which would corroborate Kelsen's hypothesis that a democratic world outlook goes hand in hand with peaceful international relations. Lastly, trust can be secured through unilateral self-binding, for instance by subordinating one's foreign policy to a collective. The European Union represents an excellent example for this course of action.[282]

We now see that monism under the primacy of international law corresponds, more or less, to the Kantian culture of anarchy where legitimacy of state behaviour is rooted in and promoted by legality. This legitimacy through legality comes into play when the logics of the Hobbesian and Lockean cultures, respectively, fail to explain certain situations, such as the fact that Great Powers respect the norms of international law or at least try to justify their actions in legal terms in dubious cases. Thus, the legitimacy-based approach of the Kantian culture provides a much-needed opportunity to leave behind the confines of inter-State politics and finally to embrace normative aspirations of world politics.[283] In this light, constructivism is to be lauded as it can speak about legal reasoning and justification as well as legitimacy in a way other approaches in international relations cannot. But what is most important in the context of this book, is that constructivism is able to explain a monist approach under the primacy of international law from an international politics perspective. Law is certainly never perfect and it is of course not be the positive endpoint of normative development in international politics, but it can at least help as a gentle civilizer amongst states.[284] Under a dualist or pluralist view, such conflicts remain political and are not amenable to legal and thus entirely peaceful resolution.

[277] Hurd (n 250) 308; dos Reis and Kessler (n 263) 359–60.

[278] See Martti Koskenniemi, *The Gentle Civilizer of Nations* (Cambridge University Press, 2002).

[279] Wendt, *Social Theory* (n 15) 344 and 357–61.

[280] Ryan Goodman and Derek Jinks, 'How to Influence States: Socialization and International Human Rights Law' (2004) 54 *Duke Law Journal* 621, 643–5.

[281] David Lumsdaine, *Moral Vision in International Politics* (Princeton University Press, 1993) 288.

[282] Wendt, *Social Theory* (n 15) 361–2.

[283] dos Reis and Kessler (n 263) 353.

[284] Brunnée and Toope (n 249) 128–30 and 137–8.

C. Conclusion

This section demonstrated that there is a clear moral relevance to cosmopolitanism, namely its value in establishing and securing a possibly perpetual peace as envisaged by Kant. However, perhaps a world state is neither desirable nor feasible, and therefore international law constitutes the best fallback option we currently have at our disposal to found an 'epistemic *civitas maxima*' through legal means, as Kelsen suggests. The crucial point of this judicial cosmopolitanism is that only the respect for international law in settling disputes and its supremacy over conflicting domestic law—i.e. monism under the primacy of international law—can ensure civilized and de-politicized social interactions between states. By resorting to a third superordinated authority—namely the law—States can extend their self to the other, thus overcoming the egoism and solipsism of blind state sovereignty. A global legal order claiming a monopoly of force makes good moral sense, and it is explicable on the basis of a value internal to law, whilst the choice for anything else than monism under the primacy of international law can only be defended on the basis of values external to the ideal of legality. This conclusion entails that states have a moral duty to support the growth of such an order or to provide us with a substantive moral argument for their position why legal peace on the international level would be undesirable.[285] Lastly, as a constructivist view of international relations proves, it is indeed possible for states socially to construct an international system that is not shaped by materialist forces such as power, interests, and geography, but ideas, concepts, and norms, in particular an overarching international legal order and a monist view under the primacy of international law. This further underlines that states have a moral duty to bring about a better and peaceful word. Judicial cosmopolitanism hence is not only desirable, but also becomes feasible under an international law-centred monist approach.

5. Appraisal

In addition to the question of whether monism under the primacy of international law is epistemologically necessary or empirically falsifiable, we can now see that it is also morally highly desirable and superior to other approaches. Even though this version of monism is a result of the Vienna School's 'pure approach' to the law, it is not a purely formal concept. On the contrary, it is capable of bringing forth moral ideas, which further corroborate its epistemic and neutral stance towards the law. Monism as envisaged by the pure theory of law does not claim moral superiority; this moral superiority simply follows from its scientific and objective quality, especially when we apply its methods to ideological criticism, democracy theory, constitutional review, and cosmopolitanism as well as the desire for peace.

Having said that, it is of course obvious that international law should not fall into the realm of idealism, as this would be highly irresponsible in the face of the many

[285] Vinx (n 13) 201–2.

problems afflicting our world today. However, conversely, the mere act of describing and providing answers to a given world with no perspectives of change, is too reductionist to the role of lawyers as political participants. One should therefore not forget that it was critical sense which has, throughout history, helped forge concepts such as freedom and equality.[286] Moreover, the monist framework as explained and defended here, attempts to put the burden of moral proof on those who would disregard international law in favour of national law or due to political necessity. Such a course of action would hence force a state to bear the stigma of the denier of international law and the disturber of peace,[287] which should convince any remaining sceptics of monism's inherent ethical dimension and moral benefits. The central point remains that international lawyers should not succumb to the given reality of the positive law. The objective of the pure theory of law to be able to distinguish clearly between the 'legal' and the 'non-legal' is a necessary requirement to be in a position to talk about the law. But the heterodox twist to this is that methodological purity does not legitimize narrow-mindedness. Lawyers can and should be sociologists, historians, and philosophers as well, but they must be aware that in their capacities as lawyers, they have to apply different methods.[288] Thereby, lawyers will realize that the inspiration for building a better world can also be found outside the boundaries of the positive law. The concluding moral component of the monist message is that a different world is conceivable, and that this world is to be regarded as an open reality for different projects; and one of these projects should be the creation of a better world in the shape of democracy and a *civitas maxima* based on law.[289]

[286] Galindo (n 1) 152. [287] Vinx (n 13) 205–6.

[288] Hans Kelsen, 'Zur Soziologie des Rechts' (1912) 34 *Archiv für Sozialwissenschaft und Sozialpolitik* 601, 602.

[289] Galindo (n 1) 152–3.

PART III

CONCLUSION

6
Conclusion

1. The Principal Question Answered

At the end of this book, we can now return to its central question, which was raised first in the introduction, namely: is there only one 'law'? This question is particularly pressing in the context of normative conflicts between different bodies of law, since the choice for a specific theory will necessarily determine the resolution or non-resolution of such a conflict. Yet courts need to decide cases, and individuals need to know what the law is, lest they end up in a dilemma of contradicting legal rules. Theories such as dualism and pluralism fail to explain the relationship of different bodies of law and remain incapable of resolving such normative conflicts. At best, they ask 'what happens next?' and resort to extra-legal solutions, such as moral norms or political expedience. However, they never ask 'what happens next *legally*?'[1] in a coherent way, and therefore they are entirely inapt as *legal* theories to deal with normative conflicts. This question can only be answered if we also answer the main question of this book in the affirmative, i.e. that there is only one legal order in this world, and this is only possible under a *monist* view of the law. As this book has shown, monism is not a moribund or dead concept; it is, on the contrary, indispensable in cognizing and explaining the law as well as capable of demonstrating its moral superiority over competitor theories.

2. Findings of This Book

The *first* finding of this book is the epistemological necessity of legal monism. If we accept the dichotomy of 'is' and 'ought' as well as the separability and normativity theses of law, then there can only be a unitary body of law. This means that, first, prescriptive statements cannot be derived from descriptive statements; and that, secondly, the law is concurrently separate from morality as something posited and substance-relative, and separate from social and empirical facts as something normative and behaviour-regulating. By incorporating these key principles as its core tenets, the pure theory of law pursues to establish the law as an objective science,

[1] Alexander Somek, 'Monism: A Tale of the Undead' in Matej Avbelj and Jan Komárek (eds), *Constitutional Pluralism in the European Union and Beyond* (Hart Publishing, 2012) 354–5.

Legal Monism: Law, Philosophy, and Politics. Paul Gragl. © Paul Gragl 2018. Published 2018 by Oxford University Press.

and thus as an epistemic and universal theory of the law, accessible to everybody and ideologically neutral. It is Kelsen's use of the methodological toolbox of Kant and the neo-Kantians—the transcendental argument—which then makes the unity of cognition and hence the cognition of the law as one unitary body possible. Through the hypothesis of the *Grundnorm* as the logical terminus of Merkl's hierarchy of norms and its function of giving validity to the law, the method of cognizing the law as valid creates it as the object of legal science. Accordingly, the very concept of legal validity is conterminous with the existence of the law.

Alternatively, only law that has been created in accordance with a superior norm within the hierarchy of norms will withstand review and remain valid—otherwise it will cease to be law. Applied to the relationship between international and national law, this entails that these two bodies of law either find themselves in a hierarchical connection with one another in a unitary body of law, or that they are created by a third superimposed legal order. However, since there is no third legal order creating international and national law, it must necessarily be the case that they are part of the same monist legal order through the principle of effectiveness. Furthermore, by exposing the concept of sovereignty as a mere legal concept and equating the state with its own legal order, Kelsen succeeds in demystifying the last political arguments against monism and the legal nature of international law.

Lastly, if one accepts international law as genuine law and one intends to avoid the utterly absurd multiplication of the international legal order, Verdross and Kunz show that, within this unitary body of international and national law, it is necessarily the former, which has primacy and prevails in the case of conflict. Nonetheless, this primacy of international law remains 'modest' and does not entail the automatic invalidation of national law in contravention to it. A state is certainly obligated to bring its domestic law into conformity with national law, but if it fails to do so, sanctions under international law and short of the use of force can be used to bring the defaulting state back in line with its international obligations. Dualists and pluralists are certainly right that other bodies of law may prevail in the case of conflict, but only if they are willing to give up the concept of legal validity or to turn the concept of 'international law' into an oxymoron. In this case, however, we would not speak about law any more, and dualism and pluralism cease to be theories about the *law*.

The *second* finding of this book is that monism under the primacy of international law is not only epistemologically necessary, but also empirically falsifiable and better equipped to explain and describe the positive law than dualism or pluralism. This should convince the sceptics that the pure theory of law is not just quixotical philosophizing, but also of practical relevance in resolving normative conflicts. By applying the above definition of the law—i.e. that positive law is an effective and self-creating system of coercive norms that have been posited by human beings for the regulation of their behaviour—to the relationship between different bodies of law, we can see that the law can indeed be explained as a unitary body. In the context of international law, the fact that certain domestic constitutions or courts declare themselves non-monist is entirely irrelevant and without prejudice to monism under the primacy of international law. Even if they make the validity, supremacy, or applicability of international norms within municipal law dependent on national law, this unity is not jeopardized. The effectiveness of international law might certainly suffer in cases of non-compliance, but its formal unity remains as long as international law provides for the above-mentioned sanctions and has the last say on what is lawful and unlawful.

It is evident that both international and domestic law share the same source, namely the common *Grundnorm* at the apex of the international legal order; that international law itself determines its own binding character as well as its supreme status over national law; and that international and national law share the same substance and the same addressees, especially individuals. Thus again, if one accepts that international law is genuine law, monism under the primacy of international law appears to be the better theory to describe and explain the positive law. The same is also true for the relationship between the law of the EU and Member State law where neither pluralism nor dualism or monism under the primacy of national law are able to account for the law as it is.

The law of the EU is a hierarchically ordered legal system in which this law itself, under the Treaties, has the last say on its application, supremacy, and interpretation vis-à-vis national law. Resistance on the part of some national courts or governments against the supremacy (in application), direct effect, and potential legislative and judicial *Kompetenz-Kompetenz* of Union law is, as in the context of international law, equally irrelevant, because EU law itself provides for enforcement mechanisms to deal with non-compliance. Due to this formal unity, it can be argued that a change in the *Grundnorm* from national law to EU law has taken place, at least within the scope of application of Union law. These findings leave monism under the primacy of international law or EU law, respectively, as the only plausible description of the relationship between different bodies of law and as the only theory that can effectively resolve normative conflicts.

The *third and last* finding of this book is that monism under the primacy of international law is not only epistemologically necessary and empirically better equipped to explain and describe the positive law, but also morally superior to its competitor theories. This should eventually convince the staunchest sceptics who were—so far—not convinced by epistemological and practical arguments. By using the purely formal approach of the pure theory of law and by ultimately going beyond it, one can also see its normative 'side effects' or consequences, which do not compromise its scientific objectivity. On the contrary, only with this very objectivity, are lawyers able to localize any remaining natural legal residues in the positive law and to draw attention to the fact that natural law ultimately collapses into positive law and a monist perspective. Particularly once the ideological and pre-legal concept of 'State sovereignty' is overcome, monism under the primacy of international law remains as the only ideology-free choice to perceive the law.

This mutually reinforcing effect can also be observed in democracy theory. Only representative democracy, where parliamentarians are permitted to form their own political will (and can be held accountable in general elections) and are not reduced to mere envoys of the people, the equally pre-legal and ideologically harmful concept of 'popular sovereignty' can be replaced with a fully legal and constitutional concept of democracy under the legitimacy of the law. Furthermore, only a legal order that allows for constitutional review can effectively protect the minorities in such a democracy and concurrently sustain the hierarchy of norms and thus the unity of the law.

Lastly, it is evident that only a democratic outlook on the world is capable of endorsing peaceful international relations under an international legal order. Such peaceful relations on the international level are further strengthened by monism under the primacy of international law if we think of its cosmopolitan effect: following up on Kant's *Perpetual Peace*, the Vienna School's project understood that a world state remains too utopian an idea to be ever realized. Yet on the way there, the law—and especially international law—can take up the role of the 'civilizer of nations' by constraining the use of force and by turning political clashes into legal disputes before international courts and tribunals. The moral force of monism then becomes clearly visible once we think of international relations as socially constructed. This means, in other words, that states can always change the anarchic system of international politics and make it less anarchic, first and foremost by internalizing the normative force of international law and by establishing a Kantian culture under the legitimacy of the law. Such a culture, where states can trust each other that they act in conformity with the law and which generally corresponds to a monist view under the primacy of international law, is of course more peaceful and therefore morally more desirable than any other culture. Accordingly, this finding also leaves international law-centred monism as the most ethical theory in describing the relationship between different bodies of law.

3. Monism in Our Times

At the time of writing, this book has seen the emergence of turbulent times. With the United Kingdom's decision to withdraw from the European Union and the election of Donald Trump as President of the United States, the liberal and democratic order established after the Second World War in the West appears to be under attack by populism, illiberalism, autocratic politics, and a disdain for the rule of law. Tectonic shifts in international politics suddenly threaten the most important and hard-won accomplishments of the Age of the Enlightenment. Not only objective facts, but also objectivity itself is being questioned, which also adversely affects the law and its validity. However, if the law, its validity, and legal obligations become arbitrary and nothing more than well-intentioned and not binding guidelines, human society and living-together become arbitrary as well. As this book has shown, however, legal monism includes a healthy respect for all of these principles, and it is therefore all the more important to remember the benefits of a world governed by law and a binding international legal order. This book attempts to do its small part and hopes to restore some of this respect for international cooperation based on the rule of law.

Dualism and pluralism are not to be rejected as theories right away; in particular, pluralism in its political and social form is to be lauded and defended. Yet in their legal manifestations, they can contribute neither to global unity nor to the resolution of conflicts through legal means.[2] Only legal monism under the primacy of international law can do this, as it comes closest to the ideal of a world system of legal legitimacy, a monopoly of force, and a judicial law enforcement mechanism based on objective findings—in other words: a coherent and meaningful unitary legal order which can secure peace among states. It has been remarked that it would be highly ironic if a doctrine as formalistic and positivist as the pure theory of law could ultimately attain realization as the practised ideal of a common law of humankind. Nonetheless, at the same time, and given the Vienna School's inherent cosmopolitan intentions, it would also be deeply satisfactory.[3]

In a time of political and legal fragmentation, it is therefore crucial that the Kelsenian notion of systemic unity of international and domestic law is not given up. On the contrary, it is now required even more than ever. And even if such unity has not been achieved yet in an institutional manner, 'it needs to be upheld intellectually by lawyers in international legal practice'.[4] It is hoped that this book will serve as a tool for reflection for them and others—reflection on the factors for how a liberal, peaceful, and democratic world under the rule of law can be preserved.

[2] Lars Vinx, 'The Kelsen-Hart Debate: Hart's Critique of Kelsen's Legal Monism Reconsidered' in Jeremy Telman (ed), *Hans Kelsen in America—Selective Affinities and the Mysteries of Academic Influence* (Springer, 2016) 80–1.

[3] John H. Herz, 'The Pure Theory of Law Revisited: Hans Kelsen's Doctrine of International Law in the Nuclear Age' in Salo Engel and Rudolf A. Métall (eds), *Law, State, and International Legal Order* (University of Tennessee Press, 1964) 117.

[4] Jochen von Bernstorff, *The Public International Law Theory of Hans Kelsen* (Cambridge University Press, 2010) 266.

Bibliography

Note: The abbreviations 'WRS I' and 'WRS II' used in this bibliography stand for the two volumes by Hans R. Klecatsky, René Marcic, and Herbert Schambeck (eds), *Die Wiener rechtstheoretische Schule: Schriften von Hans Kelsen, Adolf Merkl, Alfred Verdross* (Verlag Österreich, 2010).

Aaron DM, 'Reconsidering Dualism: The Caribbean Court of Justice and the Growing Influence of Unincorporated Treaties in Domestic Law' (2007) 6 *Law and Practice of International Courts and Tribunals* 233.

Abashidze A, 'The Relationship between International and Municipal Law: Significance of Monism and Dualism Concepts' in M Novaković (ed), *Basic Concepts of Public International Law: Monism & Dualism* (University of Belgrade, 2013) 23–33.

Adler E, 'Imagined (Security) Communities: Cognitive Regions in International Relations' (1997) 26 *Millenium* 249.

Alchourrón CE and Bulygin E, *Normative Systems* (Springer, 1971).

——, 'The Expressive Conception of Norms' in SL Paulson and B Litschewski Paulson (eds), *Normativity and Norms: Critical Perspectives on Kelsenian Themes* (Oxford University Press, 2007) 383–410.

Alexy R, 'Hans Kelsens Begriff des relativen Apriori' in Robert Alexy and others (eds), *Neukantianismus und Rechtsphilosophie* (Nomos, 2002) 179–202.

Alford CF, *Group Psychology and Political Theory* (Yale University Press, 1994).

Alkema EA, 'Netherlands' in D Shelton (ed), *International Law and Domestic Legal Systems* (Oxford University Press, 2011) 407–28.

Allars M, 'International Law and Administrative Discretion' in BR Opeskin and DR Rothwell (eds), *International Law and Australian Federalism* (Melbourne University Press, 1997) 232–79.

Allison HE, *Kant's Transcendental Idealism* (revised edn; Yale University Press, 2004)

d'Almeida LD, *Allowing for Exceptions: A Theory of Defences and Defeasibility in Law* (Oxford University Press, 2015).

D'Amato A, 'Is International Law Really "Law"?' (1984/1985) 79 *Northwestern University Law Review* 1293.

Amerasinghe CF, *Local Remedies in International Law* (2nd edn; Cambridge University Press, 2004).

Amrhein-Hofmann C, *Monismus und Dualismus in den Völkerrechtslehren* (Duncker & Humblot, 2003).

Annacker C, *Der fehlerhafte Rechtsakt im Gemeinschafts- und Unionsrecht* (Springer, 1998).

Anzilotti D, *Corso di diritto internazionale* (2nd edn; Athenaeum, 1912).

——, *Corso di diritto internazionale privato* (Athenaeum, 1925).

——, *Corso di diritto internazionale, Vol I* (3rd edn; Athenaeum, 1928).

Arangio-Ruiz G, 'International Law and Interindividual Law' in J Nijman and A Nollkaemper (eds), *New Perspectives on the Divide between National and International Law* (Oxford University Press, 2007) 15–51.

Aristotle, *De Anima* (ed and transl J Barnes), *The Complete Works of Aristotle, Vol 1* (Oxford University Press, 1984).

——, *Metaphysics* (ed and transl J Barnes), *The Complete Works of Aristotle, Vol 2* (Oxford University Press, 1984).
——, *Nicomachean Ethics* (ed and transl J Barnes), *The Complete Works of Aristotle, Vol 2* (Oxford University Press, 1984).
——, *On Interpretation* (ed and transl J Barnes), *The Complete Works of Aristotle, Vol 1* (Oxford University Press, 1984).
——, *Politics* (ed and transl J Barnes), *The Complete Works of Aristotle, Vol 2* (Oxford University Press, 1984).
——, *Posterior Analytics* (ed and transl J Barnes), *The Complete Works of Aristotle, Vol 1* (Oxford University Press, 1984).
Armstrong D, Farrell T, and Lambert H, *International Law and International Relations* (2nd edn; Cambridge University Press, 2012).
Arnull A, *The European Union and its Court of Justice* (2nd edn, Oxford University Press 2006).
Aron R, *Guerre et paix entre les nations* (3rd edn; Calmann-Lévy, 1962).
Asimow M, 'Delegated Legislation: United States and United Kingdom' (1983) 3 *Oxford Journal of Legal Studies* 253.
D'Aspremont J, 'The Systemic Integration of International Law by Domestic Courts: Domestic Judges as Architects of the Consistency of the International Legal Order' in OK Fauchald and A Nollkaemper (eds), *The Practice of International and National Courts and the (De-) Fragmentation of International Law* (Hart Publishing, 2012) 141–65.
Aufricht H, 'On Relative Sovereignty' (1944) 30 *Cornell Law Quarterly* 137.
Aust A, 'United Kingdom' in D Sloss (ed), *The Role of Domestic Courts in Treaty Enforcement: A Comparative Study* (Cambridge University Press, 2009) 476–503.
Aust HP, Rodiles A, and Staubach P, 'Unity or Uniformity? Domestic Courts and Treaty Interpretation' (2014) 27 *Leiden Journal of International Law* 75.
Austin J, *The Province of Jurisprudence Determined* (reprint; Hackett Publishing, 1998).
Avbelj M, 'Supremacy or Primacy of EU Law—(Why) Does it Matter?' (2011) 17 *European Law Journal* 744.
Bacon F, *The New Organon* (John Bill, 1620).
Badura P, 'Supranationalität und Bundesstaatlichkeit durch Rangordnung des Rechts' in J Schwarze (ed), *Verfassungsrecht und Verfassungsgerichtsbarkeit im Zeichen Europas* (Nomos, 1998) 63–79.
Bailyn M, *A Survey of Thermodynamics* (American Institute of Physics, 1994).
Baker GP and Hacker PMS, *Frege: Logical Excavations* (Blackwell, 1984).
Baker RB, 'Customary International Law in the 21st Century: Old Challenges and New Debates' (2010) 21 *European Journal of International Law* 173.
Baquero Cruz J, 'The Legacy of the Maastricht-Urteil and the Pluralist Movement' (2008) 14 *European Law Journal* 389.
——, 'Legal Pluralism and Institutional Disobedience in the European Union' in M Avbelj and J Komárek (eds), *Constitutional Pluralism in the European Union and Beyond* (Hart Publishing, 2012) 249–68.
Barber NW, 'Legal Pluralism and the European Union' (2006) 12 *European Law Journal* 306.
Barents R, *The Autonomy of Community Law* (Kluwer, 2004).
——, 'The Precedence of EU Law from the Perspective of Constitutional Pluralism' (2009) 5 *European Constitutional Law Review* 421.
Bartolini G, 'A Universal Approach to International Law in Contemporary Constitutions: Does It Exist?' (2014) 4 *Cambridge Journal of International and Comparative Law* 1287.
Basdevant J, 'Règles générales du droit de la paix' (1936) 58 *Recueil des cours* 471.
Baume S, *Hans Kelsen and the Case for Democracy* (ECPR Press, 2012).

Baumgartner G, 'Der Rang des Gemeinschaftsrechts im Stufenbau der Rechtsordnung' (2000) 8 *Journal für Rechtspolitik* 84.
Behrend J, *Untersuchungen zur Stufenbaulehre Adolf Merkls und Hans Kelsens* (Duncker & Humblot, 1977).
Bentham J, *An Introduction to the Principles of Morals and Legislation* (reprint; Athlone Press, 1970).
Bentsi-Enchill K, 'The Colonial Heritage of Legal Pluralism' (1969) 1 *Zambia Law Journal* 1.
Berlin I, *The Hedgehog and the Fox* (2nd edn; Princeton University Press, 2013).
Berman PS, 'Global Legal Pluralism' (2006/2007) 80 *Southern California Law Review* 1155.
——, 'A Pluralist Approach to International Law' (2007) 32 *Yale Journal of International Law* 301.
——, 'Federalism and International Law through the Lens of Legal Pluralism' (2008) 73 *Missouri Law Review* 1149.
——, *Global Legal Pluralism: A Jurisprudence of Law Beyond Borders* (Cambridge University Press, 2013).
Bernstorff J von, *The Public International Law Theory of Hans Kelsen* (Cambridge University Press, 2010).
Besson S, 'European Legal Pluralism after *Kadi*' (2009) 5 *European Constitutional Law Review* 237.
Beutler B, 'State Liability for Breaches of Community Law by National Courts: Is the Requirement of a Manifest Infringement of the Applicable Law an Insurmountable Obstacle?' (2009) 46 *Common Market Law Review* 773.
Beyleveld D and Brownsword R, 'Normative Positivism: The Mirage of the Middle-Way' (1989) 9 *Oxford Journal of Legal Studies* 463.
Bieber R, Jacqué J-P, and Weiler JHH, 'Introduction' in R Bieber, J-P Jacqué, and JHH Weiler (eds), *An Ever Closer Union: A Critical Analysis of the Draft Treaty Establishing the European Union* (Office for Official Publications of the European Communities, 1985) 7–14.
——, 'Presupposing the Basic Norm' (2001) 14 *Ratio Juris* 143.
Bindreiter U, *Why* Grundnorm*? A Treatise on the Implications of Kelsen's Doctrine* (Kluwer Law, 2010).
Bingham T, 'International Law in National Courts' in J Crawford and M Young (eds), *The Function of Law in the International Community: An Anniversary Symposium* (Lauterpacht Centre for International Law, 2008) 1–10.
Bix BH, 'Rules and Normativity in Law' in M Araszkiewicz and others (eds), *Problems of Normativity, Rules, and Rules-Following* (Springer, 2015) 125–46.
Björgvinsson DT, *The Intersection of International and Domestic Law* (Edward Elgar Publishing, 2015).
Blackstone W, *Commentaries on the Laws of England* (Clarendon Press, 1765–1769).
Bleckmann A, 'Vorrang des Völkerrechts im Landesrechtsraum? Zum Urteil der belgischen Cour de cassation vom 27. Mai 1971' (1972) 32 *Zeitschrift für ausländisches öffentliches Recht und Völkerrecht* 516.
——, *Grundgesetz und Völkerrecht* (Duncker & Humblot, 1975).
——, 'Monismus mit Primat des Völkerrechts' [1984] *Rechtstheorie (Beiheft 5)* 337.
——, 'Self-Executing Treaty Provisions' in Rudolf Bernhardt (ed), *Encyclopedia of Public International Law, Vol VII* (North-Holland, 1984) 414–17.
——, *Allgemeine Staats- und Völkerrechtslehre: Vom Kompetenz- zum Kooperationsvölkerrecht* (Heymanns, 1995).
Bluntschli JC, *Das moderne Völkerrecht der civilisirten Staten* (CH Beck, 1878).

Bobbio N and Zolo D, 'Hans Kelsen, the Theory of Law, and the International Legal System: A Talk' (1998) 9 *European Journal of International Law* 355.

Bobek M, 'Of Feasibility and Silent Elephants: The Legitimacy of the Court of Justice through the Eyes of National Courts' in Maurice Adams and others (eds), *Judging Europe's Judges* (Hart Publishing, 2013) 197–234.

Bodin J, *De re publica libri sex* (Jacob Dupuys, 1576).

Bogdandy A von, 'Pluralism, Direct Effect, and the Ultimate Say: On the Relationship between International and Domestic Constitutional Law' (2008) 6 *International Journal of Constitutional Law* 397.

——and Bast J, 'The European Union's Vertical Order of Competences: The Current Law and Proposals for its Reform' (2002) 39 *Common Market Law Review* 227.

—— and Dellavelle S, 'Georg Wilhelm Friedrich Hegel (1770–1831)' in B Fassbender and A Peters (eds), *The Oxford Handbook of the History of International Law* (Oxford University Press, 2012) 1127–31.

Bolton JR, 'Is There Really "Law" in International Affairs?' (2000) 10 *Transnational Law and Contemporary Problems* 1.

Bonafé BI, 'International Law in Domestic and Supranational Settings' in J Kammerhofer and J d'Aspremont (eds), *International Legal Positivism in a Post-Modern World* (Cambridge University Press, 2014) 378–400.

Borchard E, 'The Relation between International Law and Municipal Law' (1940) 27 *Virginia Law Review* 137.

Borowski M, 'Die Lehre vom Stufenbau des Rechts nach Adolf Julius Merkl' in SL Paulson and M Stolleis (eds), *Hans Kelsen: Staatsrechtslehrer und Rechtstheoretiker des 20. Jahrhunderts* (Mohr-Siebeck, 2005) 122–59.

——, 'Legal Pluralism in the European Union' in AJ Menéndez and JE Fossum (eds), *Law and Democracy in Neil MacCormick's Legal and Political Theory* (Springer, 2011) 185–210.

——, 'Concretized Norm and Sanction *qua* Fact in the Vienna School's *Stufenbaulehre*' (2014) 27 *Ratio Juris* 79.

Bos M, 'The Hierarchy among the Recognized Manifestations ("Sources") of International Law' (1978) 25 *Netherlands International Law Review* 334.

——, 'Prolegomena to the Identification of Custom in International Law' in *Essays on International and Comparative Law* [no editor] (Springer, 1983) 1–13.

Bothe M, 'Article 46 Convention of 1969' in O Corten and P Klein (eds), *The Vienna Conventions on the Law of Treaties: A Commentary, Vol II* (Oxford University Press, 2011) 1090–9.

Brierly JL, 'The Basis of Obligation in International Law' in Hersch Lauterpacht and Humphrey Waldock (eds), *The Basis of Obligation in International Law and Other Papers by the Late James Leslie Brierly* (Clarendon, 1958) 1–67.

Brockhaus RR, 'Realism and Psychologism in 19th Century Logic' (1991) 51 *Philosophy and Phenomological Research* 493.

Brodherr A, *Alfred Verdross' Theorie des gemäßigten Monismus* (Utz, 2005).

Broude T and Shany Y, 'The International Law and Policy of Multi-Sourced Equivalent Norms' in T Broude and Y Shany (eds), *Multi-Sourced Equivalent Norms in International Law* (Hart Publishing, 2011) 1–15.

——, 'The Constitutional Function of Contemporary International Tribunals, Or Kelsen's Visions Vindicated' (2012) 4 *Goettingen Journal of International Law* 519.

Brunnée J, 'Consent' in R Wolfrum (ed), *Max Planck Encyclopedia of Public International Law* (2nd edn; Oxford University Press, 2013) 679–84.

—— and Toope SJ, 'Constructivism and International Law' in JL Dunoff and MA Pollack (eds), *Interdisciplinary Perspectives on International Law and International Relations* (Cambridge University Press, 2013) 119–45.
Buergenthal T, 'Self-Executing and Non-Self-Executing Treaties in National and International Law' (1992-IV) 235 *Recueil des cours* 303.
Bühler KG, *State Succession and Membership in International Organizations* (Kluwer, 2001).
Bull H, *The Anarchical Society* (Macmillan, 1977).
——, 'Hans Kelsen and International Law' in R Tur and W Twining (eds), *Essays on Kelsen* (Clarendon Press, 1986) 321–36.
Bulygin E, 'Das Problem der Geltung bei Kelsen' in SL Paulson and M Stolleis (eds), *Hans Kelsen: Staatsrechtslehrer und Rechtstheoretiker des 20. Jahrhunderts* (Mohr-Siebeck, 2005) 80–95.
Burchardt D, *Die Rangfrage im europäischen Normenverbund* (Mohr-Siebeck, 2015).
Burckhardt W, *Über die Unvollkommenheit des Völkerrechts* (Haupt, 1923).
Busch J and Ehs T, 'The EU as "Rechtsgemeinschaft": A Kelsenian Approach to European Legal Philosophy' (2008) 85 *Rivista internazionale di filosofia del diritto* 195.
Bydlinski F, *Juristische Methodenlehre und Rechtsbegriff* (2nd edn; Springer, 1991).
Çalı B, *The Authority of International Law* (Oxford University Press, 2015).
Carnap R, 'Überwindung der Metaphysik durch logische Analyse der Sprache' (1931/1932) 2 *Erkenntnis* 219.
Cassese A, *International Law in a Divided World* (Clarendon, 1994).
——, 'Towards a Moderate Monism: Could International Rules Eventually Acquire the Force to Invalidate Inconsistent National Laws?' in A Cassese (ed), *Realizing Utopia: The Future of International Law* (Oxford University Press, 2012) 187–99.
Chase J and Reynolds J, *Analytic versus Continental: Arguments on the Methods and Value of Philosophy* (Acumen, 2011).
Chemerinsky E, 'The Rehnquist Court and Justice: An Oxymoron?' (1999) 37 *Washington University Journal of Law and Policy* 1.
Chiasson P, '*Wiener* Realism' in LD d'Almeida, J Gardner, and L Green (eds), *Kelsen Revisited: New Essays on the Pure Theory of Law* (Hart Publishing, 2013) 131–62.
Christoffersen J and Madsen MR, 'The End of Virtue? Denmark and the Internationalisation of Human Rights' (2011) 80 *Nordic Journal of International Law* 257.
Cicero MT, *Pro Balbo* (revised edn; trans R Gardner, Loeb, 1989).
Claes M, 'The Primacy of EU Law in European and National Law' in A Arnull and D Chalmers (eds), *The Oxford Handbook of European Union Law* (Oxford University Press, 2015) 178–211.
Clapham A, 'The Role of the Individual in International Law' (2010) 21 *European Journal of International Law* 25.
Clark G and Sohn LB, *World Peace through World Law* (Harvard University Press, 1958).
Cohen H, *Ethik des reinen Willens* (2nd edn; Cassirer, 1907).
——, *Logik der Reinen Erkenntnis* (Cassirer, 1922).
Cohen JL, 'Sovereignty in the Context of Globalization: A Constitutional Pluralist Perspective' in S Besson and J Tasioulas (eds), *The Philosophy of International Law* (Oxford University Press, 2010) 261–80.
Coleman JL, 'Beyond the Separability Thesis: Moral Semantics and the Methodology of Jurisprudence' (2007) 27 *Oxford Journal of Legal Studies* 581.
Conforti B, *International Law and the Role of Domestic Legal Systems* (Martinus Nijhoff, 1993).
Conklin WE, *The Invisible Origins of Legal Positivism: A Re-Reading of a Tradition* (Kluwer Law, 2001).

Corwin ES, 'The Passing of Dual Federalism' (1950) 36 *Virginia Law Review* 1.

Coyle JF, 'Incorporative Statutes and the Borrowed Treaty Rule' (2009/2010) 50 *Virginia Journal of International Law* 655.

Craven M, 'The Problem of State Succession and the Identity of States under International Law' (1998) 9 *European Journal of International Law* 142.

Craig P, 'Once Upon a Time in the West: Direct Effect and the Federalization of EEC Law' (1992) 12 *Oxford Journal of Legal Studies* 453.

——, 'Constitutions, Constitutionalism, and the European Union' (2001) 7 *European Law Journal* 125.

——, *EU Administrative Law* (2nd edn; Oxford University Press, 2012).

—— and Gráinne de Búrca, *EU Law: Text, Cases, and Materials* (6th edn; Oxford University Press, 2015).

Crawford J, 'International Law and the Rule of Law' (2004) 24 *Adelaide Law Review* 3.

——, *The Creation of States in International Law* (2nd edn; Oxford University Press, 2006).

——, *Brownlie's Principles of Public International Law* (8th edn; Oxford University Press, 2012).

Crilly T, *The Big Questions: Mathematics* (Quercus, 2011).

Curd PK, 'Parmenidean Monism' (1991) 36 *Phronesis* 241.

Curtin D and Manucharyan T, 'Legal Acts and Hierarchy of Norms in EU Law' in A Arnull and D Chalmers (eds), *The Oxford Handbook of European Union Law* (Oxford University Press, 2015) 103–25.

Cutler AC, 'The "Grotian Tradition" in International Relations' (1991) 17 *Review of International Studies* 41.

d'Almeida LD, *Allowing for Exceptions: A Theory of Defences and Defeasibility in Law* (Oxford University Press, 2015).

D'Amato A, 'Is International Law Really "Law"?' (1984/1985) 79 *Northwestern University Law Review* 1293.

D'Aspremont J, 'The Systemic Integration of International Law by Domestic Courts: Domestic Judges as Architects of the Consistency of the International Legal Order' in OK Fauchald and A Nollkaemper (eds), *The Practice of International and National Courts and the (De-) Fragmentation of International Law* (Hart Publishing, 2012) 141–65.

Davies B, *Resisting the European Court of Justice* (Cambridge University Press, 2012).

Davies G, 'Constitutional Disagreement in Europe and the Search for Pluralism' in M Avbelj and J Komárek (eds), *Constitutional Pluralism in the European Union and Beyond* (Hart Publishing, 2012) 269–84.

de Bellescize D, 'L'article 169 du Traité de Rome et l'efficacité du contrôle communautaire sur les manquements des États membres' (1977) 13 *Revue trimestrielle de droit européen* 173.

de Búrca G, 'The European Court of Justice and the International Legal Order after *Kadi*' (2010) 51 *Harvard International Law Journal* 1.

——, 'The ECJ and the International Legal Order: A Re-Evaluation' in G de Búrca and JHH Weiler, *The Worlds of European Constitutionalism* (Cambridge University Press 2012) 105–49.

Decaux E, 'France' in D Shelton (ed), *International Law and Domestic Legal Systems* (Oxford University Press, 2011) 207–39.

Décencière-Ferrandière A, 'Considérations sur le droit international dans ses rapports avec le droit de l'État' (1933) 40 *Revue Générale de Droit International Public* 45.

Delacroix S, 'Hart's and Kelsen's Concepts of Normativity Contrasted' (2004) 17 *Ratio Juris* 501.

Delfs H, *Komplementäre Integration: Grundlegung und Konstitutionalisierung des Europarechts im Kontext* (Mohr-Siebeck, 2015).

Delmas-Marty M, *Towards a Truly Common Law: Europe as a Laboratory for Legal Pluralism* (Cambridge University Press, 2002).

——, *Les forces imaginantes du droit (II): Le pluralisme ordonné* (Seuil, 2006).

Descartes R, 'Meditations on First Philosophy' in J Cottingham, R Stoothoff, and D Murdoch (transl), *The Philosophical Writings of René Descartes, Vol II* (Cambridge University Press, 1984) 17–62.

Deutsch K and others, *Political Community and the North Atlantic Area* (Princeton University Press, 1957).

Dicey AV, *Introduction to the Study of the Law of the Constitution* (10th edn; Palgrave Macmillan, 1979).

Dickson J, 'Towards a Theory of European Union Legal Systems' in J Dickson and P Eleftheriadis (eds), *Philosophical Foundations of European Union Law* (Oxford University Press, 2012) 25–53.

—— and Eleftheriadis P, 'Introduction: The Puzzles of European Union Law' in J Dickson and P Eleftheriadis (eds), *Philosophical Foundations of European Union Law* (Oxford University Press, 2012) 1–22.

Diels H and Kranz W, *Die Fragmente der Vorsokratiker* (4th edn; Weidmannsche Buchhandlung, 1922).

Dougan M, 'The Convention's Draft Constitutional Treaty: Bringing Europe Closer to Its Lawyers?' (2003) 28 *European Law Review* 763.

——, 'When Worlds Collide! Competing Visions of the Relationship between Direct Effect and Supremacy' (2007) 44 *Common Market Law Review* 931.

Douglas-Scott S, *Law after Modernity* (Hart Publishing, 2013).

Dowrick FE, 'A Model of the European Communities' Legal System' (1983) 3 *Yearbook of European Law* 169.

Doyle M, *Ways of War and Peace* (Norton, 1997).

Dreier H, *Rechtslehre, Staatssoziologie und Demokratietheorie bei Hans Kelsen* (Nomos, 1986).

Duguit L, *Souveraineté et Liberté* (Alcan, 1922).

——, *Traité de droit constitutionnel, Vol I* (2nd edn; Boccard, 1921).

——, *Traité de droit constitutionnel, Vol II* (2nd edn; Boccard, 1923).

Dupuy P-M, 'International Law and Domestic (Municipal) Law' in R Wolfrum (ed), *Max Planck Encyclopedia of Public International Law* (2nd edn; Oxford University Press, 2013) 836–61.

Dworkin R, *Law's Empire* (Hart Publishing, 1986).

Eagleton T, *Ideology: An Introduction* (Verso, 1991).

Ebenstein W, 'The Pure Theory of Law: Demythologizing Legal Thought' (1971) 59 *California Law Review* 617.

Eckes C and Hollenberg S, 'Reconciling Different Legal Spheres in Theory and Practice: Pluralism and Constitutionalism in the Cases of *Al-Jedda, Ahmed,* and *Nada*' (2013) 20 *Maastricht Journal of European and Comparative Law* 220

Eeckhout P, 'Human Rights and the Autonomy of EU Law: Pluralism or Integration?' (2013) 66 *Current Legal Problems* 169.

Ehrlich, Grundlegung der Soziologie des Rechts (Duncker & Humblot, 1913).

——, *Fundamental Principles of the Sociology of Law* (Harvard University Press, 1936).

Ehs T, 'Vorwort' in T Ehs (ed), *Hans Kelsen: Eine politikwissenschaftliche Einführung* (Facultas, 2009) 5–14.

Eleftheriadis P, 'Begging the Constitutional Question' (1998) 36 *Journal of Common Market Studies* 255.

——, 'Pluralism and Integrity' (2010) 23 *Ratio Juris* 365.

Engliš K, 'Die Norm ist kein Urteil' (1964) 50 *Archiv für Rechts- und Sozialphilosophie* 305.

Ewald O, 'Die deutsche Philosophie im Jahre 1911' (1912) 17 *Kant-Studien* 382.

Fabbrini F, *Fundamental Rights in Europe: Challenges and Transformations in Comparative Perspective* (Oxford University Press, 2014).

di Fabio U, 'Richtlinienkonformität als ranghöchstes Auslegungsprinzip? Überlegungen zum Einfluss des indirekten Gemeinschaftsrechts auf die nationale Rechtsordnung' (1990) 43 *Neue Juristische Wochenschrift* 947.

Fackeldey HG, *Handlungsnormen: Typologie und Logik* (Peter Lang, 2005).

Feldman D, 'Monism, Dualism, and Constitutional Legitimacy' (1999) 20 *Australian Yearbook of International Law* 105.

Ferdinandusse WN, *Direct Application of International Criminal Law in National Courts* (TMC Asser Press, 2006).

Ferrari-Bravo L, 'International and Municipal Law: The Complementarity of Legal Systems' in R St. John MacDonald and DM Johnston (eds), *The Structure and Process of International Law: Essays in Legal Philosophy, Doctrine, and Theory* (Martinus Nijhoff, 1983) 715–44.

Fitzmaurice G, 'The General Principles of International Law' (1957-II) 92 *Recueil des Cours* 1.

——, 'Some Problems Regarding the Formal Sources of International Law' in FM van Asbeck and others (eds), *Symbolae Verzijl. Présentées au Prof. J.H.W. Verzijl à l'occasion de son LXX-ième anniversaire* (Martinus Nijhoff, 1958) 153–76.

——, *The Law and Procedure of the International Court of Justice, Vol II* (Grotius, 1986).

Forsyth M, 'The Tradition of International Law' in T Nardin and DR Mapel (eds), *Traditions of International Ethics* (Cambridge University Press, 1992) 23–41.

Franck TM, 'The Power of Legitimacy and the Legitimacy of Power: International Law in an Age of Power Disequilibrium' (2006) 100 *American Journal of International Law* 88.

Freeman S, 'Constitutional Democracy and the Legitimacy of Judicial Review' (1990/1991) 9 *Law and Philosophy* 327.

Frege G, *The Foundations of Arithmetic* (2nd edn; Blackwell, 1959).

——, *The Basic Laws of Arithmetic* (transl Montgomery Furth; University of California Press, 1964).

——, 'Logic' in H Hermes and others (eds), *Gottlob Frege: Posthumous Writings* (University of Chicago Press, 1979) 126–51.

——, 'Thoughts' in B McGuinness (ed), *Gottlob Frege: Collected Papers on Mathematics, Logic, and Philosophy* (Blackwell, 1984) 351–72.

Frenz W, *Europarecht* (2nd edn; Springer, 2015).

Frowein J, 'Die Europäisierung des Verfassungsrechts' in P Badura and H Dreier (eds), *Festschrift 50 Jahre Bundesverfassungsgericht – Band 1: Verfassungsgerichtsbarkeit – Verfassungsprozess* (Mohr-Siebeck, 2001) 209–22.

Funk B-C, 'Die Leistungsfähigkeit der Stufenbaulehre: Zur Wissenssoziologie eines reduzierten Positivismus' in S Griller and HP Rill (eds), *Rechtstheorie: Rechtsbegriff – Dynamik – Auslegung* (Springer, 2011) 195–208.

Gabriel G, 'Frege als Neukantianer' (1986) 77 *Kant-Studien* 84.

Gänswein O, *Der Grundsatz unionsrechtskonformer Auslegung nationalen Rechts* (Peter Lang, 2009).

Gaja G, 'Positivism and Dualism in Dionisio Anzilotti' (1992) 3 *European Journal of International Law* 123.

——, 'Dualism – A Review' in J Nijman and A Nollkaemper (eds), *New Perspectives on the Divide Between National and International Law* (Oxford University Press, 2007) 52–62.
Galindo GRB, 'Revisiting Monism's Ethical Dimension' in J Crawford and S Nouwen (eds), *Select Proceedings of the European Society of International Law, Vol 3* (Hart Publishing, 2012) 141–53.
García-Salmones Rovira M, *The Project of Positivism in International Law* (Oxford University Press, 2013).
Gardiner R, *Treaty Interpretation* (2nd edn; Oxford University Press, 2015).
Gehring T, 'Treaty-Making and Treaty Evolution' in D Bodansky, J Brunnée, and E Hey (eds), *The Oxford Handbook of International Environmental Law* (Oxford University Press, 2007) 467–97.
Gelpi CF and Griesdorf M, 'Winners or Losers? Democracies in International Crisis, 1981–94' (2001) 95 *American Political Science Review* 633.
Ghandhi S, 'Human Rights and the International Court of Justice: The *Ahmadou Sadio Diallo* Case' (2011) 11 *Human Rights Law Review* 527.
Giardina A, 'The Rule of Law and Implied Powers in the European Communities' (1975) 1 *Italian Yearbook of International Law* 99.
Giudice M, 'Hart and Kelsen on International Law' in Leslie Green and Brian Leiter (eds), *Oxford Studies in Philosophy of Law, Vol 2* (Oxford University Press, 2013) 148–74.
Glendinning S, *The Idea of Continental Philosophy* (Edinburgh University Press, 2006).
Gödel K, 'Über formal unentscheidbare Sätze der Principia Mathematica und verwandter Systeme I' (1931) 38 *Monatshefte für Mathematik und Physik* 173.
Goldsmith JL and Posner EA, *The Limits of International Law* (Oxford University Press, 2006).
Goodman R and Jinks D, 'How to Influence States: Socialization and International Human Rights Law' (2004) 54 *Duke Law Journal* 621.
Green M, 'Hans Kelsen and the Logic of Legal Systems' (2003) 54 *Alabama Law Review* 365.
Griffiths J, 'What is Legal Pluralism?' (1986) 24 *Journal of Legal Pluralism* 1.
Griller S, *Die Übertragung von Hoheitsrechten auf zwischenstaatliche Einrichtungen* (Springer, 1989).
——, 'Der Stufenbau der österreichischen Rechtsordnung nach dem EU-Beitritt' (2000) 8 *Journal für Rechtspolitik* 273.
——, 'Völkerrecht und Landesrecht – unter Berücksichtigung des Europarechts' in R Walter, C Jabloner, and K Zeleny (eds), *Hans Kelsen und das Völkerrecht* (Manz, 2004) 83–120.
Gross L, 'States as Organs of International Law and the Problem of Autointerpretation' in Leo Gross (ed), *Essays on International Law and Organization* (reprint; Springer, 1984) 367–97.
Grotius H, *De iure belli ac pacis* (Nicolas Buon, 1646).
Grussmann W-D, 'Grundnorm und Supranationalität – Rechtsstrukturelle Sichtweisen der Europäischen Integration' in Thomas von Danwitz, and others (eds), *Auf dem Wege zu einer Europäischen Staatlichkeit* (Boorberg, 1993) 47–64.
Guggenheim P, *Lehrbuch des Völkerrechts: Band 1* (Recht und Gesellschaft, 1948).
——, 'Les principes de droit international public' (1952-I) 80 *Recueil des cours* 1.
Haack S, *Verlust der Staatlichkeit* (Mohr-Siebeck, 2007).
Habermas J, *Faktizität und Geltung* (Suhrkamp, 1998).
Haenel A, *Die vertragsmäßigen Elemente der deutschen Reichsverfassung* (Haessel, 1873).
Haesaert JP, 'Book Review: Hans Kelsen, *Principles of International Law*' (1953) 2 *American Journal of Comparative Law* 576.
Hafner G and Novak G, 'State Succession in Respect of Treaties' in DB Hollis (ed), *The Oxford Guide to Treaties* (Oxford University Press, 2012) 396–427.

Halberstam D, 'Constitutional Heterarchy: The Centrality of Conflict in the European Union and the United States' in JL Dunoff and JP Trachtman (eds), *Ruling the World? Constitutionalism, International Law, and Global Governance* (Cambridge University Press, 2009) 326–55.

Haljan D, *International Law and the Separation of Powers* (TMC Asser, 2013).

Hamilton A, *The Federalist No 78* (McLean, 1788).

Hammer S, 'Kelsens Grundnormkonzeption als neukantianische Erkenntnistheorie des Rechts?' in SL Paulson and R Walter (eds), *Untersuchungen zur Reinen Rechtslehre* (Manz, 1986) 210–31.

——, 'A Neo-Kantian Theory of Legal Knowledge in Kelsen's Pure Theory of Law?' in SL Paulson and B Litschewski Paulson (eds), *Normativity and Norms: Critical Perspectives on Kelsenian Themes* (reprint; Clarendon Press, 2007) 177–94.

Handl-Petz E, 'Austria' in D Shelton (ed), *International Law and Domestic Legal Systems* (Oxford University Press, 2011) 55–97.

Hansson SO, *The Structure of Values and Norms* (Cambridge University Press, 2001).

Harris JW, 'When and Why Does the *Grundnorm* Change?' (1971) 29 *Cambridge Law Journal* 103.

Hart HLA, 'Positivism and the Separation of Law and Morals' (1957/1958) 71 *Harvard Law Review* 593.

——, 'Kelsen Visited' (1962/1963) 10 *UCLA Law Review* 709.

——, *Essays in Jurisprudence* and Philosophy (Clarendon Press, 1983).

——, *The Concept of Law* (2nd edn; Clarendon Press, 1994).

——, 'Kelsen's Doctrine of the Unity of Law' in SL Paulson and B Litschewski Paulson (eds.), *Normativity and Norms: Critical Perspectives on Kelsenian Themes* (reprint; Clarendon Press, 2007) 553–81.

——, 'Answers to Eight Questions' in LD d'Almeida, J Edwards, and A Dolcetti (eds), *Reading HLA Hart's* The Concept of Law (Hart Publishing, 2013) 279–98.

Hartley TC, 'International Law and the Law of the European Union – A Reassessment' (2001) 22 *British Yearbook of International Law* 1.

——, 'National Law, International Law and EU Law – How Do They Relate?' in P Capps, M Evans, and S Konstadinides (eds), *Asserting Jurisdiction* (Hart Publishing, 2003) 65–82.

Hees M van, *Legal Reductionism and Freedom* (Kluwer Law, 2000).

Hegel GWF, *Elements of the Philosophy of Right* (transl HB Nisbet; Cambridge University Press, 1991).

Heidemann C, *Die Norm als Tatsache: Zur Normentheorie Hans Kelsens* (Nomos, 1997).

——, 'Hans Kelsen and the Transcendental Method' (2004) 55 *Northern Ireland Legal Quarterly* 358.

Henkin L, *How Nations Behave* (Columbia University Press, 1979).

——, 'International Law: Politics, Values, and Functions' (1989-IV) 216 *Recueil des cours* 19.

Herz JH, 'The Pure Theory of Law Revisited: Hans Kelsen's Doctrine of International Law in the Nuclear Age' in S Engel and RA Métall (eds), *Law, State, and International Legal Order* (University of Tennessee Press, 1964) 107–18.

Hesselink MW, 'How Many Systems of Private Law Are There in Europe?' L Niglia (ed), *Pluralism and European Private Law* (Hart Publishing, 2013) 199–248.

Hicks SV, 'Hegel on Cosmopolitanism, International Relations, and the Challenges of Globalization' in Andrew Buchwalter (ed), *Hegel and Global Justice* (Springer, 2012) 21–47.

Higgins R, *Problems and Process – International Law and How We Use It* (Oxford University Press, 1994).

Hillion C, 'Accession and Withdrawal in the Law of the European Union' in A Arnull and D Chalmers (eds), *The Oxford Handbook of European Union Law* (Oxford University Press, 2015) 126–52.

Hobbes T, *Leviathan* (Andrew Crooke, 1651).

Höffe O, *'Königliche Völker'* (Suhrkamp, 2001).

——, *Kants Kritik der Reinen Vernunft* (CH Beck, 2003).

——, *Kants Kritik der praktischen Vernunft* (CH Beck, 2012).

Hofstadter DR, *Gödel, Escher, Bach: An Eternal Golden Braid* (reprint; Penguin, 2000).

Hold-Ferneck A von, 'Anerkennung und Selbstbindung. Ein Beitrag zur Lehre vom Wesen des Völkerrechts' (1929) 4 *Zeitschrift für Rechtsphilosophie* 161.

——, *Lehrbuch des Völkerrechts I* (Meiner, 1930).

Hoof GJH van, *Rethinking the Sources of International Law* (Kluwer Law, 1983).

Hume D, *A Treatise of Human Nature* (John Noone, 1738).

——, *An Enquiry Concerning Human Understanding* (A Millar, 1748).

Hummer W, '"Etatisierung" der Union durch die neue Verfassung?' in E Busek and W Hummer (eds), *Die Konstitutionalisierung der Verbandsgewalt in der (neuen) Europäischen Union* (Böhlau, 2006) 19–52.

Hurd I, 'Constructivism' in C Reus-Smit and D Snidal (eds), *The Oxford Handbook of International Relations* (Oxford University Press, 2008) 298–316.

Hurrell A, 'Kant and the Kantian Paradigm in International Relations' (1990) 16 *Review of International Studies* 183.

Husserl E, *Logical Investigations, Vol I* (transl JN Findlay; Routledge, 1970).

Ipsen HP, *Europäisches Gemeinschaftsrecht* (Mohr-Siebeck, 1972).

——, 'Europäische Verfassung – Nationale Verfassung' (1987) 22 *Europarecht* 195.

Isensee J, *Das Volk als Grund der Verfassung* (Westdeutscher Verlag, 1995).

——, 'Vorrang des Europarechts und deutsche Verfassungsvorbehalte – offener Dissens' in J Burmeister (ed), *Verfassungsstaatlichkeit: Festschrift für Klaus Stern zum 65. Geburtstag* (CH Beck, 1997) 1239–68.

Jabloner C, 'Ideologiekritik bei Kelsen' in R Walter (ed), *Schwerpunkte der Reinen Rechtslehre* (Manz, 1992) 97–106.

——, 'Menschenbild und Friedenssicherung' in R Walter and C Jabloner (eds), *Hans Kelsens Wege sozialphilosophischer Forschung* (Manz, 1997) 57–73.

——, 'Der Rechtsbegriff bei Hans Kelsen' in S Griller and HP Rill (eds), *Rechtstheorie: Rechtsbegriff – Dynamik – Auslegung* (Springer, 2011) 21–39.

Jack B, 'Article 260(2) TFEU: An Effective Judicial Procedure for the Enforcement of Judgments?' (2013) 19 *European Law Journal* 404.

Jackson JH, 'Status of Treaties in Domestic Legal Systems: A Policy Analysis' (1992) 86 *American Journal of International Law* 310.

Jakab A, 'Kelsens Völkerrechtslehre zwischen Erkenntnistheorie und Politik' (2004) 64 *Zeitschrift für ausländisches öffentliches Recht und Völkerrecht* 1045.

——, 'Problems of the *Stufenbaulehre*: Kelsen's Failure to Derive the Validity of a Norm from Another Norm' (2007) 20 *Canadian Journal of Law and Jurisprudence* 35.

Jaklic K, *Constitutional Pluralism in the EU* (Oxford University Press, 2014).

Jellinek G, *Die rechtliche Natur der Staatenverträge* (Hölder, 1880).

——, *Allgemeine Staatslehre* (3rd edn; Häring, 1914).

Jenks CW, 'The Conflict of Law- Making Treaties' (1953) 30 *British Yearbook of International Law* 401.

——, *The Common Law of Mankind* (Stevens & Sons, 1958).

Jennings R and Watts A (eds), *Oppenheim's International Law* (9th edn; Longman, 1992).

Jestaedt M, 'Der Europäische Verfassungsverbund' in C Calliess (ed), *Verfassungswandel im europäischen Staaten- und Verfassungsverbund* (Mohr-Siebeck, 2007) 93–128.
Jöckel W, *Hans Kelsens rechtstheoretische Methode* (Mohr-Siebeck, 1930).
Johnstone I, *The Power of Deliberation: International Law, Politics, and Organizations* (Oxford University Press, 2011).
Jones E, 'Brexit's Lessons for Democracy' (2016) 58 *Survival* 41.
Jones JW, 'The "Pure" Theory of International Law' (1935) 16 *British Yearbook of International Law* 5.
Jones ML, 'The Legal Nature of the European Community: A Jurisprudential Analysis Using H.L.A. Hart's Model of Law and a Legal System' (1984) 7 *Cornell International Law Journal* 1.
Jørgensen J, 'Imperatives and Logic' (1937/1938) 7 *Erkenntnis* 288.
Jørgensen S, 'Grundnorm und Paradox' [1984] *Rechtstheorie (Beiheft 5)* 179.
Jouannet E, 'Universalism and Imperialism: The True-False Paradox of International Law?' (2007) 18 *European Journal of International Law* 379.
Kadelbach S, *Allgemeines Verwaltungsrecht unter europäischem Einfluss* (Mohr-Siebeck, 1999).
Kaiser K, 'Treaties, Direct Applicability' in R Wolfrum (ed), *The Max Planck Encyclopedia of Public International Law* (2nd edn; Oxford University Press, 2013) 1108–13.
Kammerhofer J, 'Uncertainty in the Formal Sources of International Law: Customary International Law and Some of Its Problems' (2004) 15 *European Journal of International Law* 523.
——, 'Kelsen – Which Kelsen? A Reapplication of the Pure Theory to International Law' (2009) 22 *Leiden Journal of International Law* 225.
——, 'Hans Kelsen's Place in International Legal Theory' in A Orakhelashvili (ed), *Research Handbook on the Theory and History of International Law* (Edward Elgar Publishing, 2011) 143–67.
——, *Uncertainty in International Law: A Kelsenian Perspective* (Routledge, 2011).
——, 'Robert Walter, die Normkonflikte und der zweite Stufenbau des Rechts' in C Jabloner and others (eds), *Gedenkschrift Robert Walter* (Manz, 2013) 237–56.
——, 'Hans Kelsen in Today's International Legal Scholarship' in J Kammerhofer and J d'Aspremont (eds), *International Legal Positivism in a Post-Modern World* (Cambridge University Press, 2014) 81–113.
Kant I, *Kritik der reinen Vernunft* (Johann Friedrich Hartknoch, 1781/1787).
——, 'Die Religion innerhalb der Grenzen der bloßen Vernunft' in Immanuel Kant (ed), *Gesammelte Schriften* (Deutsche Akademie der Wissenschaften, 1907) AA 6:1–202.
——, 'Die Metaphysik der Sitten' in Immanuel Kant (ed), *Gesammelte Schriften* (Deutsche Akademie der Wissenschaften, 1907) AA 6:203–493.
——, 'Prolegomena zu einer jeden künftigen Metaphysik, die als Wissenschaft wird auftreten können' in Immanuel Kant (ed), *Gesammelte Schriften* (Deutsche Akademie der Wissenschaften, 1911) AA 4:253–383.
——, 'Grundlegung zur Metaphysik der Sitten' in Immanuel Kant (ed), *Gesammelte Schriften* (Deutsche Akademie der Wissenschaften, 1911) AA 4:384–463.
——, 'Kritik der praktischen Vernunft' in Immanuel Kant (ed), *Gesammelte Schriften* (Deutsche Akademie der Wissenschaften, 1913) AA 5:1–163.
——, 'Über den Gemeinspruch: Das mag in der Theorie richtig sein, taugt aber nicht für die Praxis' in Immanuel Kant (ed), *Gesammelte Schriften* (Deutsche Akademie der Wissenschaften, 1923) AA 8:273–315.
——, 'Zum Ewigen Frieden' in Immanuel Kant (ed), *Gesammelte Schriften* (Deutsche Akademie der Wissenschaften, 1923) AA 8:341–86.

——, 'Logik: Ein Handbuch zu Vorlesungen' in Immanuel Kant (ed), *Gesammelte Schriften* (Deutsche Akademie der Wissenschaften, 1923) AA 9:1–150.
Kapustin A, 'Crimea's Self-Determination in the Light of Contemporary International Law' (2015) 75 *Zeitschrift für ausländisches öffentliches Recht und Völkerrecht* 101.
Karber PA, ' "Constructivism" as a Method in International Law' (2000) 94 *Proceedings of the Annual Meeting (American Society of International Law)* 189.
Kaufmann M, 'Permanente Verfassungsgebung und verfassungsrechtliche Selbstbindung im europäischen Staatenverbund' (1997) 36 *Der Staat* 521.
Keating M, 'Sovereignty and Plurinational Democracy: Problems in Political Science' in N Walker (ed), *Sovereignty in Transition: Essays in European Law* (Hart Publishing, 2003) 191–208.
Keller H, *Rezeption des Völkerrechts* (Springer, 2003).
—— and Sweet AS, 'Assessing the Impact of the ECHR on National Legal Systems' in H Keller and AS Sweet (eds), *A Europe of Rights: The Impact of the ECHR on National Legal Systems* (Oxford University Press, 2008) 677–712.
Kelsen H, *Hauptprobleme der Staatsrechtslehre* (1st edn; Mohr-Siebeck, 1911).
——, 'Zur Soziologie des Rechts' (1912) 34 *Archiv für Sozialwissenschaft und Sozialpolitik* 601.
——, *Das Problem der Souveränität und die Theorie des Völkerrechts* (Mohr-Siebeck, 1920).
——, *Hauptprobleme der Staatsrechtslehre* (2nd edn; Mohr-Siebeck, 1923).
——, *Allgemeine Staatslehre* (Springer, 1925).
——, 'Souveränität' in K Strupp (ed), *Wörterbuch des Völkerrechts und der Diplomatie—Band 2* (de Gruyter, 1925) 554–61.
——, 'Les rapports de système entre le droit interne et le droit international public' (1926-IV) 14 *Recueil des cours* 227.
——, 'Diskussionsbeitrag zu den Berichten "Der Begriff des Gesetzes in der Reichsverfassung" ' (1927) 3 *Veröffentlichungen der Vereinigung der deutschen Staatsrechtslehrer* 53.
——, 'Die Bundesexekution' in Z Giacometti and D Schindler (eds), *Festgabe für Fritz Fleiner zum 60. Geburtstag* (Mohr-Siebeck, 1927) 127–87.
——, *Der soziologische und der juristische Staatsbegriff* (2nd edn; Mohr-Siebeck, 1928).
——, 'Souveränität' (1929) 40 *Die neue Rundschau* 433.
——, 'Allgemeine Rechtslehre im Lichte materialistischer Geschichtsauffassung' (1931) 66 *Archiv für Sozialwissenschaft und Sozialpolitik* 449.
——, 'Théorie générale du droit international public. Problèmes choisis' (1932-IV) 42 *Recueil des cours* 116.
——, 'La méthode et la notion fondamentale de la théorie pure du droit' (1934) 41 *Revue de métaphysique et de morale* 183.
——, 'Völkerrechtliche Verträge zu Lasten Dritter' (1934) 14 *Prager Juristische Zeitschrift* 419.
——, *The Legal Process and International Order* (Constable, 1935).
——, 'La transformation du droit international public en droit interne' (1936) 43 *Revue générale de droit international public* 5.
——, 'The Function of the Pure Theory of Law' in A Reppy (ed), *Law: A Century of Progress, 1835–1935, Vol 2* (New York University Press, 1936) 231–41.
——, 'Zur Lehre vom Primat des Völkerrechts' (1938) 12 *Internationale Zeitschrift für Theorie des Rechts* 211.
——, *Vergeltung und Kausalität* (van Stockum, 1941).
——, *Law and Peace in International Relations: The Oliver Wendell Holmes Lectures, 1940–1941* (Harvard University Press, 1942).
——, *Peace through Law* (University of North Carolina Press, 1944).
——, *Society and Nature: A Sociological Enquiry* (Kegan Paul, 1946).

——, 'Zur Grundlegung der Völkerrechtslehre. Eine Auseinandersetzung mit Heinrich Drost' (1946) 1 *Österreichische Zeitschrift für öffentliches Recht* 20

——, 'Metamorphoses of the Idea of Justice' in P Sayre (ed), *Interpretations of Modern Legal Philosophies: Essays in Honor of Roscoe Pound* (Oxford University Press, 1947) 390–418.

——, *The Law of the United Nations* (Praeger, 1951).

——, 'Science and Politics' (1951) 45 *American Political Science Review* 641.

——, *Principles of International Law* (Rinehart & Company, 1952).

——, 'Théorie du droit international public' (1953-III) 84 *Recueil des cours* 1.

——, *Was ist Gerechtigkeit?* (Deuticke, 1953).

——, 'Collective Security under International Law' (1954) 49 *Naval War College International Law Studies* 1.

——, 'Foundations of Democracy' (1955) 66 *Ethics* 1.

——, 'Die Einheit von Völkerrecht und staatlichem Recht' (1958) 19 *Zeitschrift für ausländisches öffentliches Recht und Völkerrecht* 234.

——, 'Justice et droit naturel' in H Kelsen and others (eds), *Le droit naturel: Annales de philosophie politique, Vol III* (Paris: Presses universitaires de France, 1959) 1–123.

——, 'On the Basic Norm' (1959) 47 *California Law Review* 107.

——, 'Adolf Merkl zu seinem siebzigsten Geburtstag' (1959/1960) 10 *Österreichische Zeitschrift für Öffentliches Recht* 313.

——, 'Eine "Realistische" und die Reine Rechtslehre. Bemerkungen zu Alf Ross: On Law and Justice' (1959/1960) 10 *Österreichische Zeitschrift für öffentliches Recht* 1.

——, 'Die hellenisch-makedonische Politik und die "Politik" des Aristoteles' in E Topitsch (ed), *Hans Kelsen: Aufsätze zur Ideologiekritik* (Luchterhand, 1964) 293–357.

——, 'Die platonische Liebe' in E Topitsch (ed), *Hans Kelsen: Aufsätze zur Ideologiekritik* (Luchterhand, 1964) 114–97.

——, 'Die platonische Gerechtigkeit' in E Topitsch (ed), *Hans Kelsen: Aufsätze zur Ideologiekritik* (Luchterhand, 1964) 198–231.

——, 'On the Pure Theory of Law' (1966) 1 *Israel Law Review* 1.

——, 'Recht, Rechtswissenschaft und Logik' (1966) 52 *Archiv für Rechts- und Sozialphilosophie* 545.

——, *Pure Theory of Law* (2nd edn; University of California Press, 1967).

——, 'Der Wandel des Souveränitätsbegriffs' in Hanns Kurz (ed), *Volkssouveränität und Staatssouveränität* (reprint; Wissenschaftliche Buchgesellschaft, 1970) 164–78.

——, 'Derogation' in H Kelsen and O Weinberger, *Essays in Legal and Moral Philosophy* (Reidel, 1973) 261–75.

——, 'Law and Logic' in H Kelsen and O Weinberger (eds), *Essays in Legal and Moral Philosophy* (Reidel, 1973) 228–53.

——, 'State-Form and World-Outlook' in H Kelsen and O Weinberger (eds), *Essays in Legal and Moral Philosophy* (Reidel, 1973) 95–113.

——, 'What Is Justice?' in Hans Kelsen and Ota Weinberger (eds), *Essays in Legal and Moral Philosophy* (Reidel, 1973) 1–26.

——, 'Rechtswissenschaft und Recht' in SL Paulson (ed), *Die Rolle des Neukantianismus in der Reinen Rechtslehre: Eine Debatte zwischen Sander und Kelsen* (Scientia, 1988) 279–411.

——, *Introduction to the Problems of Legal Theory: A Translation of the First Edition of the Reine Rechtslehre or Pure Theory of Law* (transl B Litschewski Paulson and SL Paulson; Clarendon Press, 1997).

——, 'Autobiographie' in M Jestaedt (ed), *Hans Kelsen im Selbstzeugnis* (Mohr-Siebeck, 2006) 31–94.

——, *General Theory of Law and State* (reissue edn; Transaction Publishers, 2007).
——, 'Natural Law Doctrine and Legal Positivism' (as an appendix) to Hans Kelsen, *General Theory of Law and State* (reissue edn; Transaction Publishers, 2007).
——, 'The Pure Theory of Law, "Labandism", and Neo-Kantianism: A Letter to Renato Treves' in SL Paulson and B Litschewski Paulson (eds), *Normativity and Norms: Critical Perspectives on Kelsenian Themes* (reprint; Clarendon Press, 2007) 169–75.
——, 'Die soziologische und die juristische Staatsidee' in M Jestaedt (ed), *Hans Kelsen: Werke, Band 3; Veröffentlichte Schriften 1911–1917* (Mohr-Siebeck, 2010) 201–34.
——, *The Essence and Value of Democracy* (Rowman & Littlefield, 2013).
——, 'Die Grundlagen der Naturrechtslehre' in WRS I 711–46.
——, 'Die Idee des Naturrechts' in WRS I 201–30.
——, 'Die philosophischen Grundlagen der Naturrechtslehre und des Rechtspositivismus' in WRS I 231–88.
——, 'Die Selbstbestimmung des Rechts' in WRS II 1181–88.
——, 'Naturrecht und positives Recht' in WRS I 177–200.
——, 'Recht und Logik' in WRS II 1201–24.
——, 'Über Staatsunrecht' in WRS I 785–866.
——, 'Was ist die Reine Rechtslehre?' in WRS I 499–514.
—— 'Wesen und Entwicklung der Staatsgerichtsbarkeit' in WRS II 1485–1532.
——, 'Zur Soziologie der Demokratie' in WRS II 1417–28.
——, 'Wer soll der Hüter der Verfassung sein?' in WRS II 1533–74.
——, *General Theory of Norms* (reprint; Clarendon Press, 2011).
Kenny A, 'Frege, Gottlob' in T Honderich (ed), *The Oxford Companion to Philosophy* (2nd edn; Oxford University Press, 2005) 316–20.
Keohane R and Nye J, *Power and Interdependence* (Longman, 1977).
Kinley D, 'Bendable Rules: The Development Implications of Human Rights Pluralism' in BZ Tamanaha, C Sage, and M Woolcock (eds), *Legal Pluralism and Development: Scholars and Practitioners in Dialogue* (Cambridge University Press, 2012) 50–65.
Kirchhof P, 'Deutsches Verfassungsrecht und Europäisches Gemeinschaftsrecht' [1991] *Europarecht-Beiheft 1/1991*, 11.
——, 'Die Gewaltenbalance zwischen staatlichen und europäischen Organen' (1998) 53 *Juristen-Zeitung* 965.
Kirchmair L, *Die Theorie des Rechtserzeugerkreises* (Duncker & Humblot, 2013).
——, 'The Theory of the Law Creators' Circle: Re-Conceptualizing the Monism-Dualism-Pluralism Debate' (2016) 17 *German Law Journal* 179.
——, 'Constitutionalism Lite' (2004) 1 *International Organizations Law Review* 31.
——, 'Setting the Scene' in J Klabbers, A Peters, and G Ulfstein (eds), *The Constitutionalization of International Law* (Oxford University Press, 2011) 1–44.
—— and Touko Piiparinen (eds), *Normative Pluralism and International Law: Exploring Global Governance* (Cambridge University Press, 2013).
——, 'Straddling the Fence: The EU and International Law' in A Arnull and D Chalmers (eds), *The Oxford Handbook of European Union Law* (Oxford University Press, 2015) 52–71.
Klamert M, *The Principle of Loyalty in EU Law* (Oxford University Press, 2014).
Klein K-H, *Die Übertragung von Hoheitsrechten* (Duncker & Humblot, 1952).
Kleingeld P, *Kant and Cosmopolitanism* (Oxford University Press, 2012).
Kleinlein T, 'Alfred Verdross as a Founding Father of International Constitutionalism' (2012) 4 *Goettingen Journal of International Law* 385.
Kletzer C, 'Kelsen's Development of the *Fehlerkalkül*-Theory' (2005) 18 *Ratio Juris* 46.

——, 'The Role and Reception of the Work of Hans Kelsen in the United Kingdom' in R Walter, C Jabloner, and K Zeleny (eds), *Hans Kelsen anderswo – Hans Kelsen abroad* (Manz, 2010) 133–66.
Köck HF, *Der Gesamtakt in der deutschen Integrationslehre* (Duncker & Humblot, 1978).
Kocs S, 'Explaining the Strategic Behaviour of States: International Law as System Structure' (1994) 38 *International Studies Quarterly* 535.
Koh HH, 'Why Do Nations Obey International Law?' (1996/1997) 106 *Yale Law Journal* 2599.
Kohler G, 'Basiskonsens und Willensnation: Die Kontingenz des Unverfügbaren und das Modell der Schweiz' in H Vorländer (ed), *Demokratie und Transzendenz* (Transcript, 2013) 121–41.
Kolb R, *The International Court of Justice* (Hart Publishing, 2013).
——, *The Law of Treaties: An Introduction* (Edward Elgar Publishing, 2016).
Koller P, 'Zur Theorie des rechtlichen Stufenbaus' in SL Paulson and M Stolleis (eds), *Hans Kelsen: Staatsrechtslehrer und Rechtstheoretiker des 20. Jahrhunderts* (Mohr-Siebeck, 2005) 106–21.
Komárek J, 'Institutional Dimension of Constitutional Pluralism' in M Avbelj and J Komárek (eds), *Constitutional Pluralism in the European Union and Beyond* (Hart Publishing, 2012) 231–48.
Koopmans T, 'The Theory of Interpretation and the Court of Justice' in D O'Keeffe and A Bavasso (eds), *Judicial Review in European Union Law: Essays in Honour of Lord Slynn of Hadley* (Kluwer, 2000) 45–58.
Koskenniemi M, *The Gentle Civilizer of Nations* (Cambridge University Press, 2002).
Kotzur M, 'Overcoming Dichotomies: A Functional Approach to the Constitutional Paradigm in Public International Law' (2012) 4 *Goettingen Journal of International Law* 585.
——, 'Über Monismus und Dualismus hinaus: Ansätze zu einer Neukonzeptualisierung des Völkerrechts mit einer konstitutionellen Matrix' in M Novaković (ed), *Basic Concepts of Public International Law: Monism & Dualism* (University of Belgrade, 2013) 157–73.
Krabbe H, *Die Lehre von der Rechtssouveränität* (Wolters, 1906).
——, *Die moderne Staatsidee* (2nd edn; Martinus Nijhoff, 1919).
——, 'L'idée moderne de l'état' (1926-III) 13 *Recueil des cours* 513.
Krasner SD, 'Realist Views of International Law' (2002) 96 *Proceedings of the Annual Meeting of the American Society of International Law* 265.
Kratochwil F, *Rules, Norms, and Decisions* (Cambridge University Press, 1989).
Krawietz W, 'Die Lehre vom Stufenbau des Rechts – eine säkularisierte politische Theologie?' [1984] *Rechtstheorie (Beiheft 5)* 255.
Krisch N, *Beyond Constitutionalism* (Oxford University Press, 2010).
Kruis T, *Der Anwendungsvorrang des EU-Rechts in Theorie und Praxis* (Mohr-Siebeck, 2013).
Kühne D, 'Die Grundnorm als inhaltlicher Geltungsgrund der Rechtsordnung' [1984] *Rechtstheorie (Beiheft 5)* 193.
Kumm M, 'Who Is the Final Arbiter of Constitutionality in Europe: Three Conceptions of the Relationship between the German Federal Constitutional Court and the European Court of Justice?' (1999) 36 *Common Market Law Review* 351.
——, 'The Legitimacy of International Law: A Constitutionalist Framework of Analysis' (2004) 15 *European Journal of International Law* 907.
——, 'The Jurisprudence of Constitutional Conflict: Constitutional Supremacy in Europe Before and After the Constitutional Treaty' (2005) 11 *European Law Journal* 262.
——, 'The Cosmopolitan Turn in Constitutionalism: On the Relationship between Constitutionalism in and beyond the State' in JL Dunoff and JP Trachtman (eds), *Ruling*

the World? Constitutionalism, International Law, and Global Governance (Cambridge University Press, 2009) 258–324.

——, 'The Moral Point of Constitutional Pluralism' in J Dickson and P Eleftheriadis (eds), *Philosophical Foundations of European Union Law* (Oxford University Press, 2012) 216–46.

Kunz JL, *Völkerrechtswissenschaft und Reine Rechtslehre* (Deuticke, 1923).

——, 'La primauté de droit des gens' (1925) 6 *Revue de droit international et de legislation comparée* 556.

——, 'On the Theoretical Basis of the Law of Nations' (1925) 10 *Transactions of the Grotius Society* 115.

——, 'Die Rechts- und Staatslehre Léon Duguits' (1926/1927) 1 *Revue internationale de la théorie du droit* 140.

——, 'The "Vienna School" and International Law' in JL Kunz (ed), *The Changing Law of Nations: Essays on International Law* (Ohio State University Press, 1934) 59–124.

——, 'The Meaning and the Range of the Norm *pacta sunt servanda*' (1945) 39 *American Journal of International Law* 180.

——, 'An Introduction to Latin-American Philosophy of Law' (1964) 15 *University of Toronto Law Journal* 259.

Kutscher H, 'Thesen zu den Methoden der Auslegung des Gemeinschaftsrechts, aus der Sicht eines Richters' in Gerichtshof der Europäischen Gemeinschaften (ed), *Begegnungen von Justiz und Hochschule am 27.–29.9.1976* (Gerichtshof der Europäischen Gemeinschaften, 1976) I-1–56.

Kwiecień R, 'The Primacy of European Union Law over National Law under the Constitutional Treaty' in P Dann and M Rynkowski (eds), *The Unity of the European Constitution* (Springer, 2010) 67–86.

Lacey N, *A Life of HLA Hart: The Nightmare and the Noble Dream* (Oxford University Press, 2004).

Lachmayer F, 'Ideologiekritik und Deutungskampf' [1982] *Rechtstheorie (Beiheft 4)* 63.

Lagrange E, 'L'efficacité dans l'ordre juridique interne des normes internationales concernant la situation des personnes privées' (2012) 356 *Recueil des cours* 239.

Lando M, 'Intimations of Unconstitutionality: The Supremacy of International Law and Judgment 238/2014 of the Italian Constitutional Court' (2015) 78 *Modern Law Review* 1028.

LaSelva SV, *The Moral Foundations of Canadian Federalism* (McGill-Queen's University Press, 1996).

Laski HJ, *A Grammar of Politics* (Allen & Unwin, 1938).

La Torre M, 'Legal Pluralism as Evolutionary Achievement of Community Law' (1999) 12 *Ratio Juris* 182.

Lauterpacht H, 'Some Observations on the Prohibition of *Non Liquet* and the Completeness of the Law' in FM van Asbeck and others (eds), *Symbolae Verzijl. Présentées au Prof. J.H.W. Verzijl à l'occasion de son LXX-ième anniversaire* (Martinus Nijhoff, 1958) 196–221.

——, 'General Rules of the Law of Peace' in Elihu Lauterpacht (ed), *International Law: Being the Collected Papers of Hersch Lauterpacht, Vol 1: General Works* (Cambridge University Press, 1975) 179–444.

——, 'The Nature of International Law and General Jurisprudence' in E Lauterpacht (ed), *International Law: Being the Collected Papers of Hersch Lauterpacht, Vol 2: The Law of Peace* (Cambridge University Press, 1975) 3–21.

——, *The Function of Law in the International Community* (reprint; Oxford University Press, 2011).

Leben C, 'Hans Kelsen and the Advancement of International Law' (1998) 9 *European Journal of International Law* 287.

——, *The Advancement of International Law* (Hart Publishing, 2010).
Lecourt R, *Le juge devant le marché commun* (Institut universitaire de hautes études internationales, 1970).
Lee TH and Sloss DL, 'International Law as an Interpretive Tool in the Supreme Court, 1861–1900' in DL Sloss, MD Ramsay, and WS Dodge (eds), *International Law in the U.S. Supreme Court: Continuity and Change* (Cambridge University Press, 2011) 124–63.
Lenaerts K, 'Constitutionalism and the Many Faces of Federalism' (1990) 38 *American Journal of Comparative Law* 205.
—— and Desomer M, 'Towards a Hierarchy of Legal Acts in the European Union? Simplification of Legal Instruments and Procedures' (2005) 11 *European Law Journal* 744.
—— and Gutiérez-Fons JA, 'The Constitutional Allocation of Powers and General Principles of EU Law' (2010) 47 *Common Market Law Review* 1629.
——and Gutiérrez-Fons JA, 'The Place of the Charter in the EU Constitutional Edifice' in S Peers and others (eds), *The EU Charter of Fundamental Rights: A Commentary* (Hart Publishing, 2014) 1559–94.
Lepsius O, 'Kelsens Demokratietheorie' in T Ehs (ed), *Hans Kelsen: Eine politikwissenschaftliche Einführung* (Facultas, 2009) 67–89.
Leser N, 'Die Reine Rechtslehre im Widerstreit der philosophischen Ideen' in *Die Reine Rechtslehre in wissenschaftlicher Diskussion* [no editor] (Manz, 1982) 97–104.
Letsas G, 'Harmonic Law: The Case against Pluralism' in J Dickson and P Eleftheriadis (eds), *Philosophical Foundations of European Union Law* (Oxford University Press, 2012) 77–108.
Lev A, 'The Transformation of International Law in the 19th Century' in A Orakhelashvili (ed), *Research Handbook on the Theory and History of International Law* (Edward Elgar Publishing, 2011) 111–42.
Linarelli J, 'Anglo-American Jurisprudence and Latin America' (1996/1997) 20 *Fordham International Law Journal* 50.
Linderfalk U, 'The Principle of Rational Decision-Making: As Applied to the Identification of Normative Conflicts in International Law' (2013) 73 *Zeitschrift für ausländisches öffentliches Recht und Völkerrecht* 591.
Lippold R, *Recht und Ordnung* (Manz, 2000).
Llewellyn KN, *Jurisprudence: Realism in Theory and Practice* (Chicago University Press, 1962).
Lohmar D, *Erfahrung und kategoriales Denken* (Springer, 1998).
Losano MG, 'Das Verhältnis von Geltung und Wirksamkeit in der Reinen Rechtslehre' in *Die Reine Rechtslehre in wissenschaftlicher Diskussion* [no editor] (Manz, 1982) 82–96.
——, 'Kelsen's Theory on International Law during His Exile in Geneva' (2015) 28 *Ratio Juris* 470.
Loughlin M, 'Constitutional Pluralism: An Oxymoron?' (2014) 3 *Global Constitutionalism* 9.
Lueck B, 'Appendix: On Cosmopolitanisms' in L Stone (ed), *Iranian Identity and Cosmopolitanism* (Bloomsbury, 2014) 159–76.
Luf G, 'On the Transcendental Import of Kelsen's Basic Norm' in SL Paulson and B Litschewski-Paulson (eds), *Normativity and Norms: Critical Perspectives on Kelsenian Themes* (Oxford University Press, 2007) 221–34.
MacCormick N, 'Beyond the Sovereign State' (1993) 56 *Modern Law Review* 1.
——, 'The *Maastricht*-Urteil: Sovereignty Now' (1995) 1 *European Law Journal* 259.
——, 'Risking Constitutional Collision in Europe?' (1998) 18 *Oxford Journal of Legal Studies* 517.
——, *Questioning Sovereignty* (Oxford University Press, 1999).

MacMillan GM, 'The European Union: Is It a Supranational State in the Making?' in A Heineman-Grüder (ed), *Federalism Doomed? European Federalism between Integration and Separation* (Berghahn, 2002) 63–82.
MacWhinney E, 'The Constitutional Patriation Project, 1980–82' (1984) 32 *American Journal of Comparative Law* 241.
Madison J, *The Federalist No 39* (McLean, 1788).
Maduro MP, *We, the Court: The European Court of Justice and the European Economic Constitution* (Hart Publishing, 1998).
——, 'Contrapunctual Law: Europe's Constitutional Pluralism in Action' in N Walker (ed), *Sovereignty in Transition: Essays in European Law* (Hart Publishing, 2006) 501–37.
——, 'Three Claims of Constitutional Pluralism' in M Avbelj and J Komárek (eds), *Constitutional Pluralism in the European Union and Beyond* (Hart Publishing, 2012) 67–84.
Maitland FW, *The Constitutional History of England* (Cambridge University Press, 1908).
Mancini F and Keeling D, 'Democracy and the European Court of Justice' (1994) 57 *Modern Law Review* 175.
Marek K, *Identity and Continuity of States in Public International Law* (Librairie Droz, 1968).
——, 'Paul Guggenheim, 1899–1977' (1987) 44 *Schweizerisches Jahrbuch für internationales Recht* 9.
Martin FF, *The Constitution as Treaty* (Cambridge University Press, 2007).
Matthews HE, 'Strawson on Transcendental Idealism' (1969) 19 *Philosophical Quarterly* 204.
Mayer FC and Wendel M, 'Multilevel Constitutionalism and Constitutional Pluralism' in M Avbelj and J Komárek (eds), *Constitutional Pluralism in the European Union and Beyond* (Hart Publishing, 2012) 127–52.
Mayer H, 'Die Theorie des rechtlichen Stufenbaus' in R Walter (ed), *Schwerpunkte der Reinen Rechtslehre* (Manz, 1992) 37–46.
——, 'Rechtstheorie und Rechtspraxis' in C Jabloner and F Stadler (eds), *Logischer Empirismus und Reine Rechtslehre: Beziehungen zwischen dem Wiener Kreis und der Hans Kelsen-Schule* (Springer, 2001) 319–31.
——, 'Reine Rechtslehre und Gemeinschaftsrecht' in R Walter, C Jabloner, and K Zeleny (eds), *Hans Kelsen und das Völkerrecht* (Manz, 2004) 121–38.
——, G Kucsko-Stadlmayer and K Stöger, *Grundriss des Österreichischen Bundesverfassungsrechts* (11th edn; Manz, 2015).
Meier H, 'Lob des Rechtspositivismus' (2005) 673 *Merkur* 430.
Menchaca VA, 'Die "Unreinheit" der Reinen Rechtslehre' [1984] *Rechtstheorie (Beiheft 5)* 131.
Meng W, *Das Recht der Internationalen Organisationen – eine Entwicklungsstufe des Völkerrechts* (Nomos, 1979).
Menon P, 'An Enquiry into the Sources of Modern International Law' (1986) 64 *Revue de droit international, de sciences diplomatiques et politiques* 181.
Merkl AJ, *Die Lehre von der Rechtskraft entwickelt aus dem Rechtsbegriff* (Deuticke, 1923).
——, *Allgemeines Verwaltungsrecht* (Springer, 1927).
——, 'Das doppelte Rechtsantlitz' in WRS I 893–912.
——, 'Gesetzesrecht und Richterrecht' in WRS II 1323–30.
—— 'Justizirrtum und Rechtswahrheit' in WRS I 159–70.
——, 'Prolegomena einer Theorie des rechtlichen Stufenbaus' in WRS II 1071–112.
——, 'Das Recht im Lichte seiner Anwendung' in WRS I 955–83.
——, 'Die Rechtseinheit des österreichischen Staates' in WRS I 913–54.
——, 'Die Unveränderlichkeit von Gesetzen – ein normlogisches Prinzip' in WRS I 883–92.
——, 'Die Wandlungen des Rechtsstaatsgedankens' in WRS II 1599–614.

——, 'Zum Problem der Rechtskraft in Justiz und Verwaltung' in WRS II 983–92.
Merry SE, 'Legal Pluralism' (1988) 22 *Law and Society Review* 869.
Métall RA, 'Skizzen zu einer Systematik der völkerrechtlichen Quellenlehre' (1931) 11 *Zeitschrift für Öffentliches Recht* 416.
——, *Hans Kelsen: Leben und Werk* (Deuticke, 1969).
Mettenheim C von, *Recht und Rationalität* (Mohr-Siebeck, 1984).
Meyer-Hesemann W, 'Zur rechtstheoretischen Rekonstruktion der Reinen Rechtslehre' [1984] *Rechtstheorie (Beiheft 5)* 63.
Mill JS, *A System of Logic, Vol I* (Parker, 1843).
Mohl R von, *Staatsrecht, Völkerrecht und Politik, Bd. 1* (Laupp, 1860).
Möllers C, 'Pouvoir constituant – Constitution – Constitutionalisation' in A von Bogdandy and J Bast (eds), *Principles of European Constitutional Law* (2nd edn; Hart Publishing, 2009) 169–204.
Moore JB (ed), *History and Digest of International Arbitrations to which the United States Has Been A Party, Vol 2* (Government Printing Office, 1898).
Moorhead T, *The Legal Order of the European Union* (Routledge, 2014).
Morgenstern F, 'Judicial Practice and the Supremacy of International Law' (1950) 27 *British Yearbook of International Law* 42.
Mowbray A, 'The Creativity of the European Court of Human Rights' (2005) 5 *Human Rights Law Review* 57.
Muñiz-Fraticelli VM, *The Structure of Pluralism* (Oxford University Press, 2014).
Munzer S, *Legal Validity* (Martinus Nijhoff, 1972).
Navarro PE and Rodríguez JL, *Deontic Logic and Legal Systems* (Cambridge University Press, 2014).
Needham CW, 'The Exclusive Power of Congress over Interstate Commerce' (1911) 11 *Columbia Law Review* 251.
Neff SC, 'United Kingdom' in D Shelton (ed), *International Law and Domestic Legal Systems* (Oxford University Press, 2011) 620–30.
Nettesheim M, 'EU-Recht und nationales Verfassungsrecht' [2002] *XX FIDE Report* 1.
——, 'Kompetenzen' in A von Bogdandy and J Bast (eds), *Europäisches Verfassungsrecht: Theoretische und dogmatische Grundzüge* (2nd edn; Springer, 2009) 389–440.
Neves M, 'Grenzen der Autonomie des Rechts in einer asymmetrischen Weltgesellschaft: Von Luhmann zu Kelsen' in H Brunkhorst and R Voigt (eds), *Rechts-Staat: Staat, internationale Gemeinschaft und Völkerrecht bei Hans Kelsen* (Nomos, 2008) 301–46.
Nicholas B, *An Introduction to Roman Law* (revised edn; Oxford University Press, 1975).
Nicolaïdis K, 'The New Constitution as European Demoi-cracy? (2004) 7 *Critical Review of International Social and Political Philosophy* 76.
——, 'European Demoicracy and Its Crisis' (2013) 51 *Journal of Common Market Studies* 351.
Nicolaysen G, *Europarecht I* (Nomos, 1991).
Nijman J and Nollkaemper A, 'Introduction' in J Nijman and A Nollkaemper (eds), *New Perspectives on the Divide between National and International Law* (Oxford University Press, 2007) 1–14.
——, 'Beyond the Divide' in J Nijman and A Nollkaemper (eds), *New Perspectives on the Divide between National and International Law* (Oxford University Press, 2007) 341–60.
Nollkaemper A, 'The Netherlands' in D Sloss (ed), *The Role of Domestic Courts in Treaty Enforcement: A Comparative Study* (Cambridge University Press, 2009) 326–69.

——, 'Rethinking the Supremacy of International Law' (2010) 65 *Zeitschrift für Öffentliches Recht* 65.
——, *National Courts and the International Rule of Law* (Oxford University Press, 2012).
——, 'Inside or Out: Two Types of International Legal Pluralism' in J Klabbers and T Piiparinen (eds), *Normative Pluralism and International Law: Exploring Global Governance* (Cambridge University Press, 2013) 94–139.
——, 'The Duality of Direct Effect in International Law' (2014) 25 *European Journal of International Law* 105.
——, 'The Effects of Treaties in Domestic Law' in CJ Tams, A Tzanakopoulos, and A Zimmermann (eds), *Research Handbook on the Law of Treaties* (Edward Elgar Publishing, 2014) 123–50.
Nolte G, 'From Dionisio Anzilotti to Roberto Ago: The Classical International Law of State Responsibility and the Traditional Primacy of a Bilateral Conception of Inter-State Relations' (2002) 13 *European Journal of International Law* 1083.
Noonan HW, *Frege: A Critical Introduction* (Polity Press, 2001).
Nussbaum MC, 'Kant and Stoic Cosmopolitanism' (1997) 5 *Journal of Political Philosophy* 1.
O'Brien-Thomond AH, 'Positivism and Monism in International Law' (1948) 8 *Franciscan Studies* 321.
O'Connell M, 'Peace and War' in B Fassbender and A Peters (eds), *The Oxford Handbook of the History of International Law* (Oxford University Press, 2012) 272–93.
Oeter S, 'Souveränität und Demokratie als Probleme in der "Verfassungsentwicklung" der Europäischen Union' (1995) 55 *Zeitschrift für ausländisches öffentliches Recht und Völkerrecht* 659.
Öhlinger T, 'Artikel 9, Absatz 1' in K Korinek and M Holoubek (eds), *Österreichisches Bundesverfassungsrecht – Textsammlung und Kommentar* (Springer, 2002).
——, 'Die Einheit des Rechts: Völkerrecht, Europarecht und staatliches Recht als einheitliches Rechtssystem?' in SL Paulson and M Stolleis (eds), *Hans Kelsen: Staatsrechtslehrer und Rechtstheoretiker des 20. Jahrhunderts* (Mohr-Siebeck, 2005) 160–73.
Olechowski T, 'Der Beitrag Hans Kelsens zur österreichischen Bundesverfassung' in R Walter and others (eds), *Hans Kelsen: Leben – Werk – Wirksamkeit* (Manz, 2009) 211–30.
——, 'Kelsen als Pazifist' in N Aliprantis and T Olechowski (eds), *Hans Kelsen: Die Aktualität eines großen Rechtswissenschafters und Soziologen des 20. Jahrhunderts* (Manz, 2014) 119–29.
O'Neill A, *Decisions of the European Court of Justice and their Constitutional Implications* (Butterworths, 1994).
Onuf N, 'Do Rules Say What They Do? From Ordinary Language to International Law' (1985) 26 *Harvard International Law Journal* 385.
Ooyen RC van, *Der Staat der Moderne: Hans Kelsens Pluralismustheorie* (Duncker & Humblot, 2003).
Opałek K, *Überlegungen zu Hans Kelsens "Allgemeiner Theorie der Normen"* (Manz, 1980).
——, 'Kelsens Kritik der Naturrechtslehre' [1982] *Rechtstheorie (Beiheft 4)* 71.
Opeskin B, 'Constitutional Modelling: The Domestic Effect of International Law in Commonwealth Countries: Part I' [2000] *Public Law* 607.
Ophüls CF, 'Vom Internationalen zum Übernationalen' (1952) 2 *Das Parlament* 1.
Oppermann T, *Europarecht* (2nd edn; CH Beck, 1999).
Orakhelashvili A, 'The Position of the Individual in International Law' (2000) 31 *California Western International Law Journal* 241.
——, *Peremptory Norms in International Law* (Oxford University Press, 2008).
Paine T, *Common Sense* (R. Bell, 1776).

Pallieri GB, 'Le dottrine di Hans Kelsen e il problema dei rapporti fra diritto interno e diritto internazionale' (1935) 27 *Rivista di diritto internazionale* 24.
Palombino FM, 'Compliance with International Judgments: Between Supremacy of International Law and National Fundamental Principles' (2015) 75 *Zeitschrift für ausländisches öffentliches Recht und Völkerrecht* 503.
Panhuys JFH van, 'The Netherlands Constitution and International Law' (1953) 47 *American Journal of International Law* 537.
Partsch KJ, *Die Anwendung des Völkerrechts im innerstaatlichen Recht* (CF Müller, 1964).
Paulson SL, 'Material and Formal Authorization in Kelsen's Pure Theory of Law' (1980) 39 *Cambridge Law Journal* 172.
——, 'Zum Problem der Normenkonflikte' (1980) 66 *Archiv für Rechts- und Sozialphilosophie* 487.
——, 'Stellt die "Allgemeine Theorie der Normen" einen Bruch in Kelsens Lehre dar?' in *Die Reine Rechtslehre in wissenschaftlicher Diskussion* [no editor] (Manz, 1982) 122–41.
——, 'On the Status of the *lex posterior* Derogating Rule' in R Tur and W Twining (eds), *Essays on Kelsen* (Clarendon Press, 1986) 229–47.
——, 'Methodological Dualism in Kelsen's *Das Problem der Souveränität*' in A Carrino (ed), *Kelsen e il problema della sovranità* (Edizione scientifiche italiane, 1990) 83–103.
——, 'Zur Stufenbaulehre Merkls in ihrer Bedeutung für die Allgemeine Rechtslehre' in R Walter (ed), *Adolf J. Merkl: Werk und Wirksamkeit* (Manz, 1990) 93–105.
——, 'The Neo-Kantian Dimension of Kelsen's Pure Theory of Law' (1992) 12 *Oxford Journal of Legal Studies* 311.
——, 'Die unterschiedlichen Formulierungen der "Grundnorm" in A Aarnio and others (eds), *Rechtsnorm und Rechtswirklichkeit* (Duncker & Humblot, 1993) 53–74.
——, 'On the Kelsen-Kant Problematic' in EG Valdés and others (eds), *Normative Systems in Legal and Moral Theory* (Duncker & Humblot, 1997) 197–213.
——, 'Four Phases in Hans Kelsen's Legal Theory? Reflections on a Periodization' (1998) 18 *Oxford Journal of Legal Studies* 153.
——, 'The Great Puzzle: Kelsen's Basic Norm' in LD d'Almeida, J Gardner, and L Green (eds), *Kelsen Revisited: New Essays on the Pure Theory of Law* (Hart Publishing, 2013) 43–62.
Paust JJ, 'Self-Executing Treaties' (1988) 82 *American Journal of International Law* 760.
Pauwelyn J, *Conflict of Norms in Public International Law* (Cambridge University Press, 2003).
Pawlik M, *Die Reine Rechtslehre und die Rechtstheorie H.L.A. Harts: Ein kritischer Vergleich* (Duncker & Humblot, 1993).
Pechstein M and Drechsler C, 'Die Auslegung und Fortbildung des Primärrechts' in K Riesenhuber (ed), *Europäische Methodenlehre* (3rd edn; de Gruyter, 2015) 125–45.
Peirce CS and Jastrow J, 'On Small Differences in Sensation' (1885) 3 *Memoirs of the National Academy of Sciences* 73.
Pelletier FJ, Elio R, and Hanson P, 'Is Logic All in Our Heads? From Naturalism to Psychologism' (2008) 88 *Studia Logica: An International Journal for Symbolic Logic* 3.
Pernice I, 'Multilevel Constitutionalism and the Treaty of Amsterdam: European Constitution-Making Revisited?' (1999) 36 *Common Market Law Review* 703.
——, 'Multilevel Constitutionalism in the European Union' (2002) 8 *European Law Review* 511.
——, 'Art. 25' in H Dreier (ed), *Grundgesetz-Kommentar: Band II* (2nd edn; Mohr-Siebeck, 2006).
——, 'Theorie und Praxis des Europäischen Verfassungsverbundes' in C Calliess (ed), *Verfassungswandel im europäischen Staaten- und Verfassungsverbund* (Mohr-Siebeck, 2006) 61–92.

Pernthaler P, 'Die neue Doppelverfassung Österreichs' in H Haller and others (eds), *Staat und Recht: Festschrift für Günter Winkler* (Springer, 1997) 773–96.
Pescatore P, 'International Law and Community Law – A Comparative Analysis' (1970) 7 *Common Market Law Review* 167.
——, 'The Doctrine of Direct Effect: An Infant Disease of Community Law' (1983) 8 *European Law Review* 155.
Petev V, 'Rechtsquellenlehre und Reine Rechtslehre' [1984] *Rechtstheorie (Beiheft 5)* 273.
Peters A, *Elemente einer Theorie der Verfassung Europas* (Duncker & Humblot, 2001).
——, 'The Globalization of State Constitutions' in J Nijman and A Nollkaemper (eds), *New Perspectives on the Divide Between National and International Law* (Oxford University Press, 2007) 251–308.
——, 'Supremacy Lost: International Law Meets Domestic Constitutional Law' (2009) 3 *Vienna Online Journal on International Constitutional Law* 170.
——, 'Rechtsordnungen und Konstitutionalisierung: Zur Neubestimmung der Verhältnisse' (2010) 65 *Zeitschrift für Öffentliches Recht* 1.
——, *Jenseits der Menschenrechte: Die Rechtsstellung des Individuums im Völkerrecht* (Mohr-Siebeck, 2014).
Petersen N, 'Customary Law without Custom? Rules, Principles, and the Role of State Practice in International Norm Creation' (2007) 23 *American University International Law Review* 275.
——, 'Determining the Domestic Effect of International Law through the Prism of Legitimacy' (2012) 72 *Zeitschrift für ausländisches öffentliches Recht und Völkerrecht* 223.
Petersmann E-U, 'Multilevel Trade Governance in the WTO Requires Multilevel Constitutionalism' in C Joerges and E-U Petersmann (eds), *Constitutionalism, Multilevel Trade Governance and Social Regulation* (Hart Publishing, 2006) 5–58.
——, 'Multilevel Judicial Governance as Guardian of the Constitutional Unity of International Economic Law' (2008) 30 *Loyola of Los Angeles International and Comparative Law Review* 367.
Pfeffer R, *Das Verhältnis von Völkerrecht und Landesrecht* (Mohr Siebeck, 2009).
Pfersmann O, 'Kelsens Ideologiekritik' in N Aliprantis and T Olechowski (eds), *Hans Kelsen: Die Aktualität eines großen Rechtswissenschafters und Soziologen des 20. Jahrhunderts* (Manz, 2014) 53–66.
Pinker S, *The Better Angels of Our Nature* (Penguin, 2011).
Pisillo-Mazzeschi R, 'Die reine Lehre Kelsens und die Realität des heutigen Völkerrechts' in A Carrino and G Winkler (eds), *Rechtserfahrung und Reine Rechtslehre* (Springer, 1995) 129–55.
Planck M, *Vorträge und Erinnerungen* (Hirzel, 1949).
Plato, *Phaedo* (ed John M. Cooper; Hackett, 1997).
——, *Republic* (ed John M. Cooper; Hackett, 1997).
Popper K, *The Open Society and its Enemies, Vol I* (5th edn; Routledge, 1966).
——, *The Open Society and its Enemies, Vol II* (5th edn; Routledge, 1971).
——, *Objective Knowledge: An Evolutionary Approach* (revised edn; Oxford University Press, 1979).
——, *Logik der Forschung* (8th edn; Mohr-Siebeck, 1984).
Pospisil L, *Anthropology of Law: A Comparative Theory* (Harper and Row, 1971).
Potacs M, 'Das Verhältnis zwischen der EU und ihren Mitgliedstaaten im Lichte traditioneller Modelle' (2010) 65 *Zeitschrift für Öffentliches Recht* 117.
——, 'Die Grundnormproblematik' in S Griller and HP Rill (eds), *Rechtstheorie: Rechtsbegriff–Dynamik–Auslegung* (Springer, 2011) 135–52.

Priest G, *In Contradiction: A Study of the Transconsistent* (2nd edn; Clarendon Press, 2006).
——, *One* (Oxford University Press, 2014).
Priester J-M, 'Die Grundnorm – Eine Chimäre' [1984] *Rechtstheorie (Beiheft 5)* 211.
Prost M, *The Concept of Unity in Public International Law* (Hart Publishing, 2012).
Puder M, 'Supremacy of the Law and Judicial Review in the European Union: Celebrating *Marbury v. Madison* with *Costa v. ENEL*' (2004) 36 *George Washington International Law Review* 567.
Pulkowski D, *The Law and Politics of International Regime Conflict* (Oxford University Press, 2014).
Putnam H, 'Why Reason Can't Be Naturalized' (1982) 52 *Synthese* 3.
Quine WVO, *Methods of Logic* (4th edn; Harvard University Press, 1982).
Radbruch G, 'Gesetzliches Unrecht und übergesetzliches Recht' (1946) 1 *Süddeutsche Juristen-Zeitung* 105.
Ranganathan S, 'Responding to Deliberately Created Treaty Conflicts' in CJ Tams, A Tzanakopoulos, and A Zimmermann (eds), *Research Handbook on the Law of Treaties* (Edward Elgar Publishing, 2014) 447–75.
Raz J, 'The Identity of Legal Systems' (1971) 59 *California Law Review* 795.
——, 'Kelsen's Theory of the Basic Norm' (1974) 19 *American Journal of Jurisprudence* 94.
——, *The Concept of a Legal System: An Introduction to the Theory of Legal System* (2nd edn; Oxford University Press, 1980).
——, 'The Purity of the Pure Theory' (1981) 35 *Revue internationale de philosophie* 441.
——, *Ethics in the Public Domain* (Oxford University Press, 1994).
——, 'Two Views of the Nature of the Theory of Law: A Partial Comparison' (1998) 4 *Legal Theory* 249.
——, *The Authority of Law* (2nd edn; Oxford University Press, 2009).
Reis F dos and Kessler O, 'Constructivism and the Politics of International Law' in A Orford and F Hoffmann (eds), *The Oxford Handbook of the Theory of International Law* (Oxford University Press, 2016) 344–64.
Rensmann T, 'Article 46' in O Dörr and K Schmalenbach (eds), *Vienna Convention on the Law of Treaties: A Commentary* (Springer, 2012) 775–804.
Reus-Smit C, 'The Politics of International Law' in C Reus-Smit (ed), *The Politics of International Law* (Cambridge, 2004) 14–44.
Reuter P, 'Le plan Schuman' (1952-II) 81 *Recueil des cours* 519.
Réveillard C, *Les premières tentatives de construction d'une Europe fédérale, des projets de la Résistance au Traité de la CED* (1940–1954) (Oeil, 2001).
Ricoeur P, *Oneself as Another* (transl Kathleen Blamey; University of Chicago Press, 1990).
Richmond C, 'Preserving the Identity Crisis: Autonomy, System and Sovereignty in European Law' (1997) 16 *Law and Philosophy* 377.
Riesenfeld S, 'The Doctrine of Self-Executing Treaties and *US v. Postal*: Win at Any Price?' (1980) 74 *American Journal of International Law* 892.
Rigaux F, 'Hans Kelsen on International Law' (1998) 9 *European Journal of International Law* 325.
Rill HP, 'Internationales, supranationales und nationales Recht – eine Einheit' in C Jabloner and others (eds), *Gedenkschrift Robert Walter* (Manz, 2013) 679–700.
Rintelen F-J von, 'Philosophical Idealism in Germany: The Way from Kant to Hegel and the Present' (1977) 38 *Philosophy and Phenomological Research* 1.
Roellecke G, 'Verfassungsgebende Gewalt als Ideologie' (1992) 47 *Juristen-Zeitung* 929.
Roermund B van, 'Norm-Claims, Validity, and Self-Reference' in LD d'Almeida, J Gardner, and L Green (eds), *Kelsen Revisited: New Essays on the Pure Theory of Law* (Hart Publishing, 2013) 11–42.

Römer P, 'Die Reine Rechtslehre Hans Kelsens als Ideologie und Ideologiekritik' (1971) 12 *Politische Vierteljahresschrift* 579.
Rotter M, 'Die Reine Rechtslehre im Völkerrecht – eine eklektizistische Spurensuche in Theorie und Praxis' in R Walter, C Jabloner, and K Zeleny (eds), *Hans Kelsen und das Völkerrecht* (Manz, 2004) 51–81.
Rousseau J-J, *Du contrat social* (Marc Michel Rey, 1762).
Rozakis C, *The Concept of Jus Cogens in the Law of Treaties* (North-Holland, 1976).
Rub A, *Hans Kelsens Völkerrechslehre: Versuch einer Würdigung* (Schulthess Polygraphischer Verlag, 1995).
Rudolf W, *Völkerrecht und deutsches Recht* (Mohr Siebeck, 1967).
——, 'Incorporation of Customary International Law into Municipal Law' in GI Tunkin and R Wolfrum (eds), *International Law and Municipal Law* (Duncker & Humblot, 1988) 24–40.
Ruffert M, 'The European Debt Crisis and European Union Law' (2011) 48 *Common Market Law Review* 1777.
Russell B, 'On Denoting' (1905) 14 *Mind* 479.
Russell YI and Gobet F, 'What Is Counterintuitive? Religious Cognition and Natural Expectation' (2013) 4 *Review of Philosophy and Psychology* 715.
Russett B, *Grasping the Democratic Peace* (Princeton University Press, 1993).
Sauer H, 'Vorrang ohne Hierarchie' (2013) 44 *Rechtstheorie* 503.
Scelle G, *Précis de droit des gens: Principes et systématique, Vol 1: Introduction, le milieu intersocial* (Sirey, 1932).
——, 'Règles générales du droit de la paix' (1933-IV) 46 *Recueil des cours* 331.
Schabas W, 'Reservations to the Convention on the Rights of the Child' (1996) 18 *Human Rights Quarterly* 472.
Schaus A, 'Article 27 Convention of 1969' in O Corten and P Klein (eds), *The Vienna Conventions on the Law of Treaties: A Commentary, Vol I* (Oxford University Press, 2011) 688–701.
Schermers HG, 'The Role of the Member States in Filling Lacunae in EC-Law' in R Bieber and G Ress (eds), *Die Dynamik des Europäischen Gemeinschaftsrechts* (Nomos, 1987) 311–17.
Schiffer W, *Die Lehre vom Primat des Völkerrechts in der neueren Literatur* (Deuticke, 1937).
Schilling T, *Rang und Geltung von Normen in gestuften Rechtsordnungen* (Nomos, 1994).
——, 'The Autonomy of the Community Legal Order: An Analysis of Possible Foundations' (1996) 37 *Harvard International Law Journal* 389.
——, 'Zum Verhältnis von Gemeinschafts- und nationalem Recht' (1998) 39 *Zeitschrift für Rechtsvergleichung, Internationales Privatrecht und Europarecht* 149.
——, 'Das Verhältnis zwischen Völkerrecht, Gemeinschaftsrecht und staatlichem Recht' in S Griller and HP Rill (eds), *Rechtstheorie: Rechtsbegriff – Dynamik – Auslegung* (Springer, 2011) 153–94.
Schlick M, 'Meaning and Verification' (1936) 45 *The Philosophical Review* 339.
Schmädel J von, 'Kelsen's Peace through Law and Its Rejection by his Contemporaries' (2011) 39 *Hitotsubashi Journal of Law and Politics* 71.
Schmalenbach K, 'Article 5' in O Dörr and K Schmalenbach (eds), *Vienna Convention on the Law of Treaties: A Commentary* (Springer, 2012) 89–99.
——, 'Article 26' in O Dörr and K Schmalenbach (eds), *Vienna Convention on the Law of Treaties: A Commentary* (Springer, 2012) 427–51.
——, 'Article 27' in O Dörr and K Schmalenbach (eds), *Vienna Convention on the Law of Treaties: A Commentary* (Springer, 2012) 453–73.
——, 'Article 53' in O Dörr and K Schmalenbach (eds), *Vienna Convention on the Law of Treaties: A Commentary* (Springer, 2012) 897–942.

Schmid CU, 'From Pont d'Avignon to Ponte Vecchio: The Resolution of Constitutional Conflicts between the European Union and the Member States through Principles of Public International Law' (1998) *18 Yearbook of European Law* 415.
Schmitt C, 'Die Diktatur des Reichspräsidenten nach Artikel 48 der Weimarer Verfassung' (1924), reproduced as an appendix to Schmitt C, *Die Diktatur* (Duncker & Humblot, 1922).
——, *Verfassungslehre* (Duncker & Humblot, 1928).
——, *Der Hüter der Verfassung* (Duncker & Humblot, 1931).
——, *Legalität und Legitimität* (Duncker & Humblot, 1932).
——, *Politische Theologie* (10th edn; Duncker & Humblot, 2015).
Scholz R, 'Europäische Union und deutscher Bundesstaat' (1993) 12 *Neue Zeitschrift für Verwaltungsrecht* 817.
Schopenhauer A, *The World as Will and Representation, Vol II* (transl EFJ Payne; Dover, 1958).
Schroeder W, *Das Gemeinschaftsrechtssystem* (Mohr-Siebeck, 2002).
Schütze R, *From Dual to Cooperative Federalism: The Changing Structure of European Law* (Oxford University Press, 2009).
——, 'On "Federal" Ground: The European Union as an (Inter)National Phenomenon' (2009) 46 *Common Market Law Review* 1069.
——, *An Introduction to European Law* (2nd edn; Cambridge University Press, 2012).
——, *European Constitutional Law* (Cambridge University Press, 2012).
——, 'EU Competences: Existence and Exercise' in A Arnull and D Chalmers (eds), *The Oxford Handbook of European Union Law* (Oxford University Press, 2015) 75–102.
Schwarzenberger G, 'The Forms of Sovereignty' (1957) 10 *Current Legal Problems* 264.
Schweitzer M, '*Ius cogens* im Völkerrecht' (1971) 15 *Archiv des Völkerrechts* 197.
Seidl-Hohenveldern I, 'Transformation or Adoption of International Law into Municipal Law' (1963) 12 *International and Comparative Law Quarterly* 88.
Seurin J-L, 'Towards a European Constitution? Problems of Political Integration' [1994] *Public Law* 625.
Shany Y, 'Toward a General Margin of Appreciation Doctrine in International Law?' (2006) 15 *European Journal of International Law* 908.
Shelton D, 'Introduction' in D Shelton (ed), *International Law and Domestic Legal Systems* (Oxford University Press, 2011) 1–22.
Shepherd AJK, 'The European Security Continuum and the EU as an International Security Provider' (2015) 29 *Global Society* 156.
Simma B, 'Self-Contained Regimes' (1985) 16 *Netherlands Yearbook of International Law* 111.
——, 'The Contribution of Alfred Verdross to the Theory of International Law' (1995) 6 *European Journal of International Law* 33.
——and Tams CJ, 'Reacting against Treaty Breaches' in DB Hollis (ed), *The Oxford Guide to Treaties* (Oxford University Press, 2012) 576–604.
——, 'Human Rights Before the International Court of Justice: Community Interests Coming to Life?' in CJ Tams and J Sloan (eds), *The Development of International Law by the International Court of Justice* (Oxford University Press, 2013) 301–25.
Simpson AWB, *Reflections on* The Concept of Law (Oxford University Press, 2011).
Sinagra A and Bargiacchi P, *Lezioni di diritto internazionale pubblico* (Giuffrè, 2009).
Sloss D, 'United States' in David Sloss (ed), *The Role of Domestic Courts in Treaty Enforcement: A Comparative Study* (Cambridge University Press, 2009) 504–54.
——, 'Domestic Application of Treaties' in DB Hollis (ed), *The Oxford Guide to Treaties* (Oxford University Press, 2012) 367–95.

——, 'Treaty Enforcement in Domestic Courts: A Comparative Analysis' in D Sloss (ed), *The Role of Domestic Courts in Treaty Enforcement: A Comparative Study* (Cambridge University Press, 2014) 1–60.

Sluga H, *Gottlob Frege* (Routledge, 1980).

Slyz G, 'International Law in National Courts' (1995/1996) 28 *New York University Journal of International Law and Politics* 65.

Solomon RC, *From Rationalism to Existentialism: The Existentialists and Their Nineteenth-Century Backgrounds* (Rowman & Littlefield, 2001).

Somek A, 'Inexplicable Law: Legality's Adventure in Europe' (2006) 15 *Transnational Law and Contemporary Problems* 627.

——, 'Kelsen Lives' (2007) 18 *European Journal of International Law* 409.

——, *Individualism: An Essay on the Authority of the European Union* (Oxford University Press, 2008).

——, 'The Spirit of Legal Positivism' (2011) 12 *German Law Journal* 729.

——, 'Monism: A Tale of the Undead' in M Avbelj and J Komárek (eds), *Constitutional Pluralism in the European Union and Beyond* (Hart Publishing, 2012) 343–80.

——, *The Cosmopolitan Constitution* (Oxford University Press, 2014).

Somló F, *Juristische Grundlehre* (2nd edn; Meiner, 1927).

Sørensen M, 'Die Verpflichtungen eines Staates im Bereich seiner nationalen Rechtsordnung aufgrund eines Staatsvertrages' in Rechts- und staatswissenschaftliche Fakultät an der Universität Wien (ed), *Menschenrechte im Staatsrecht und im Völkerrecht* (CF Müller, 1967) 15–33.

Spagnolo B, *The Continuity of Legal Systems in Theory and Practice* (Hart Publishing, 2015).

Spiermann O, 'Højesterets anvendelse af folkeret i det 20 århundrede' [2001] *Juristen* 1.

Starke JG, 'Monism and Dualism in the Theory of International Law' (1936) 17 *British Yearbook of International Law* 66.

——, 'The Primacy of International Law' in S Engel and RA Métall (eds), *Law, State, and International Legal Order* (University of Tennessee Press, 1964) 307–16.

Starr WC, *Kelsen and Hart on International Law* (University of Wisconsin, 1977).

Steiger H, 'The Relationship of German National Law with Public International Law and with European Community Law' in AJA Vandamme and J-H Reestman (eds), *Ambiguity in the Rule of Law* (Europa Law Publishing, 2001) 63–84.

Stein E, 'Toward Supremacy of Treaty-Constitution by Judicial Fiat: On the Margin of the *Costa* Case' (1965) 63 *Michigan Law Review* 491.

Stein H, 'Adversary Symbiosis and Complementary Group Dissociation' (1982) 6 *International Journal of Intercultural Relations* 55.

Stoitzner B, 'Die Lehre vom Stufenbau der Rechtsordnung' in SL Paulson and R Walter (eds), *Untersuchungen zur Reinen Rechtslehre* (Manz, 1986) 51–90.

Stone J, 'Mystery and Mystique in the Basic Norm' (1963) 26 *Modern Law Review* 34.

Stotz R and Škvařilová-Pelzl P, 'Europarechtliche Gesetzeskontrolle' in W Kluth and G Krings (eds), *Gesetzgebung: Rechtsetzung durch Parlamente und Verwaltungen sowie ihre gerichtliche Kontrolle* (CF Müller, 2014) 957–1032.

Strawson P, *Bounds of Sense: Essay on Kant's* Critique of Pure Reason (Routledge, 1966).

Stuart JM, *The Acceptance of Community Law in the English Legal Order* (Zentrum für Europäisches Wirtschaftsrecht, 1991).

Suárez F, *De legibus, Vol II* (Johannes Keerberg, 1612).

Suy E, 'Article 53 Convention of 1969' in O Corten and P Klein (eds), *The Vienna Conventions on the Law of Treaties: A Commentary, Vol II* (Oxford University Press, 2011) 1224–33.

Swaine ET, 'Reserving' (2006) 31 *Yale Journal of International Law* 307.

Tamanaha BZ, 'The Folly of the "Social Scientific" Concept of Legal Pluralism' (1993) 20 *Journal of Law and Society* 192.
——, 'Understanding Legal Pluralism: Past to Present, Local to Global' (2008) 30 *Sydney Law* Review 375.
Tarski A, 'The Concept of Truth in Formalized Languages' in J Corcoran (ed), *Logic, Semantics, Metamathematics: Papers from 1923 to 1938* (2nd edn; Hackett, 1983) 152–278.
Tasioulas J, 'The Legitimacy of International Law' in S Besson and J Tasioulas (eds), *The Philosophy of International Law* (Oxford University Press, 2010) 97–117.
Telman J, 'A Path Not Taken: Hans Kelsen's Pure Theory of Law in the Land of the Legal Realists' in R Walter, C Jabloner, and K Zeleny (eds), *Hans Kelsen anderswo – Hans Kelsen Abroad* (Manz, 2010) 353–76.
——, 'A Monist Supremacy Clause and a Dualistic Supreme Court: The Status of Treaty Law as U.S. Law' in M Novaković (ed), *Basic Concepts of Public International Law: Monism and Dualism* (University of Belgrade, 2013) 571–90.
Téson F, 'The Relations between International Law and Municipal Law: The Monism/Dualism Controversy' in Michael Bothe and Raul E. Vinuesa (eds), *International Law and Municipal Law* (Duncker & Humblot, 1982) 107–16.
Tessar H, *Der Stufenbau nach der rechtlichen Autorität und seine Bedeutung für die juristische Interpretation* (Verlag Österreich, 2010).
Thaler M, 'Rechtsphilosophie und das Verhältnis zwischen Gemeinschaftsrecht und nationalem Recht' (2000) 8 *Journal für Rechtspolitik* 75.
Theodossiou MA, 'An Analysis of the Recent Response of the Community to Non-Compliance with Court of Justice Judgments: Article 228(2) EC' (2003) 27 *European Law Review* 25.
Thienel R, 'Geltung und Wirksamkeit' in SL Paulson and R Walter (eds), *Untersuchungen zur Reinen Rechtslehre* (Manz, 1986) 20–50.
——, 'Derogation: Eine Untersuchung auf Grundlage der Reinen Rechtslehre' in R Walter (ed), *Untersuchungen zur Reinen Rechtslehre II* (Manz, 1988) 11–43.
——, *Kritischer Rationalismus und Jurisprudenz* (Manz, 1991).
Thirlway H, *International Customary Law and Codification* (Sijthoff, 1972).
——, 'Reflections on *Lex Ferenda*' (2001) 32 *Netherlands Yearbook of International Law* 3.
——, *The Sources of International Law* (Oxford University Press, 2014).
Thürer D, 'Internationales "Rule of Law"—innerstaatliche Demokratie' (1995) 5 *Schweizerische Zeitschrift für internationales und europäisches Recht* 454.
Topitsch E, 'Hans Kelsen als Ideologiekritiker' in S Engel and RA Métall (eds), *Law, State, and International Legal Order: Essays in Honour of Hans Kelsen* (University of Tennessee Press, 1964) 329–38.
——, *Erkenntnis und Illusion* (Mohr-Siebeck, 1988).
—— and Salamun K, *Ideologie: Herrschaft des Vor-Urteils* (Langen-Müller, 1972).
Torres Pérez A, 'The Challenges for Constitutional Courts as Guardians of Fundamental Rights in the European Union' in P Popelier, A Mazmanyan, and W Vandenbruwaene (eds), *The Role of Constitutional Courts in Multilevel Governance* (Intersentia, 2013) 49–75.
Tridimas T, *The General Principles of EU Law* (2nd edn; Oxford University Press, 2007).
——, 'The ECJ and the National Courts: Dialogue, Cooperation, and Instability' in A Arnull and D Chalmers (eds), *The Oxford Handbook of European Union Law* (Oxford University Press, 2015) 403–430.
Triepel H, *Völkerrecht und Landesrecht* (C.L. Hirschfeld, 1899).
——, 'Les rapports entre le droit interne et le droit international' (1923-I) 1 *Recueil des Cours* 77.

Trindade AC, *The Construction of a Humanized International Law* (Brill, 2015).
Türk AH, *Judicial Review in EU Law* (Edward Elgar Publishing, 2009).
Tunkin G, 'Remarks on the Juridical Nature of Customary Norms of International Law' (1961) 49 *California Law Review* 419.
——, 'Is General International Law Customary Law Only?' (1993) 4 *European Journal of International Law* 534.
Tuori K, *European Constitutionalism* (Cambridge University Press, 2015).
Turley J, 'Dualistic Values in the Age of International Legisprudence' (1992/1993) 44 *Hastings Law Journal* 158.
Tzanakopoulos A, 'Domestic Courts in International Law: The International Judicial Function of National Courts' (2011) 43 *Loyola of Los Angeles International and Comparative Law Review* 133.
——, 'Judicial Dialogue as a Means of Interpretation' in HP Aust and G Nolte (eds), *The Interpretation of International Law by Domestic Courts* (Oxford University Press, 2016) 72–95.
Ulfstein G, 'The International Judiciary' in J Klabbers, A Peters, and G Ulfstein (eds), *The Constitutionalization of International Law* (Oxford University Press, 2011) 126–52.
——, 'The Relationship between Constitutionalism and Pluralism' (2012) 4 *Goettingen Journal of International Law* 575.
Vandamme T, 'EU Directives and Multilevel Governance – Can Lessons Be Drawn from Cooperative Federalism?' (2014) 21 *Maastricht Journal of European and Comparative Law* 341.
Vattel E de, *Le droit des gens, ou principes de la loi naturelle*, 2 vols (Apud Liberos Tutior, 1758).
Vayssière B, *Vers une Europe fédérale? Les espoirs et les actions fédéralistes au sortir de la Seconde Guerre mondiale* (Peter Lang, 2006).
Vázquez CM, 'Treaties as Law of the Land: The Supremacy Clause and the Judicial Enforcement of Treaties' (2008/2009) 122 *Harvard Law Review* 599.
Verdross A, 'Völkerrecht und staatliches Recht' in Hans Robert Engelmann (ed), *Die völkerrechtswidrige Kriegshandlung und der Strafanspruch der Staaten* (Engelmann, 1920) 34–44.
——, 'Grundlagen und Grundlegungen des Völkerrechts – ein Beitrag zu den Hypothesen des Völkerrechtspositivismus' (1921) 29 *Niemeyers Zeitschrift für internationales Recht* 65
——, *Die Einheit des rechtlichen Weltbildes auf Grundlage der Völkerrechtsverfassung* (Mohr, 1923).
——, *Die Verfassung der Völkerrechtsgemeinschaft* (Springer, 1926).
——, 'Le fondement du droit international' (1927-I) 16 *Recueil des cours* 247.
——, 'Die Rechtstheorie Hans Kelsens' (1930) 59 *Juristische Blätter* 421.
——, 'Vierhundert Jahre Völkerrechtswissenschaft' (1933) 63 *Stimmen der Zeit* 36.
——, 'Droit international public et droit interne' (1954) 32 *Revue de Droit International, de Sciences Diplomatiques et Politiques* 219.
——, *Völkerrecht* (5th edn; Springer, 1964).
—— and Bruno Simma, *Universelles Völkerrecht* (3rd edn; Duncker & Humblot, 1984).
——, 'Zum Problem der völkerrechtlichen Grundnorm' in WRS II 1811–18.
Villiger ME, *Commentary on the 1969 Vienna Convention on the Law of Treaties* (Martinus Nijhoff, 2009).
Vinx L, *Hans Kelsen's Pure Theory of Law: Legality and Legitimacy* (Oxford University Press, 2007) 102.

——, 'The Kelsen-Hart Debate: Hart's Critique of Kelsen's Legal Monism Reconsidered' in J Telman (ed), *Hans Kelsen in America—Selective Affinities and the Mysteries of Academic Influence* (Springer, 2016) 59–84.
Voegelin E, 'Die Einheit des Rechtes und das soziale Sinngebilde Staat' (1930/1931) 5 *Zeitschrift für Theorie des Rechts* 58.
Vollmeyer J, *Der Staat als Rechtsordnung: Hans Kelsens Identitätsthese und ihre Bedeutung für den europäischen Konstitutionalisierungsprozess* (Nomos, 2011).
Vranes E, '*Lex Superior, Lex Specialis, Lex Posterior* – Zur Rechtsnatur der "Konfliktlösungsregeln"' (2005) 65 *Zeitschrift für ausländisches öffentliches Recht und Völkerrecht* 391.
——, 'The Definition of "Norm Conflict" in International Law and Legal Theory' (2006) 17 *European Journal of International Law* 395.
Wagner H, 'Monismus und Dualismus: eine methodenkritische Betrachtung zum Theorienstreit' (1964) 89 *Archiv des öffentlichen Rechts* 212.
Waldron J, '"Transcendental Nonsense" and System in the Law' (2000) 100 *Columbia Law Review* 16.
——, 'The Core of the Case against Judicial Review' (2006) 115 *Yale Law Journal* 1346.
——, 'Who Needs Rules of Recognition?' in MD Adler and KE Himma (eds), *The Rule of Recognition and the U.S. Constitution* (Oxford University Press, 2009) 327–49.
Walker K and Mitchell AD, 'A Stronger Role for Customary International Law in Domestic Law?' in H Charlesworth and others (eds), *The Fluid State: International Law and National Legal Systems* (Federation Press, 2005) 110–35.
Walker N, 'The Idea of Constitutional Pluralism' (2002) 65 *Modern Law Review* 317.
——, 'Late Sovereignty in the European Union' in N Walker (ed), *Sovereignty in Transition: Essays in European Law* (Hart Publishing, 2003) 3–32.
——, 'Beyond Boundary Disputes and Basic Grids: Mapping the Global Disorder of Normative Orders' (2008) 6 *International Journal of Constitutional Law* 373.
——, 'Constitutionalism and Pluralism in Global Context' in M Avbelj and J Komárek (eds), *Constitutional Pluralism in the European Union and Beyond* (Hart Publishing, 2012) 17–38.
——, 'The Philosophy of European Union Law' in A Arnull and D Chalmers (eds), *The Oxford Handbook of European Union Law* (Oxford University Press, 2015) 3–27.
Walter R, 'Können Verordnungen Gesetzen derogieren?' (1961) 16 *Österreichische Juristen-Zeitung* 2.
——, *Der Aufbau der Rechtsordnung* (2nd edn; Manz, 1974).
——, 'Die Lehre vom Stufenbau der Rechtsordnung' (1980) 13 *Archivum Iuridicum Cracoviense* 5.
——, 'Reine Rechtslehre und Gesetzgebungstechnik' in H Kindermann (ed), *Studien zu einer Theorie der Gesetzgebung 1982* (Springer, 1982) 144–51.
——, 'Entstehung und Entwicklung des Gedankens der Grundnorm' in R Walter (ed), *Schwerpunkte der Reinen Rechtslehre* (Manz, 1992) 47–59.
——, 'Die Grundnorm im System der Reinen Rechtslehre' in A Aarnio and others (eds), *Rechtsnorm und Rechtswirklichkeit* (Duncker & Humblot, 1993) 85–100.
——, 'Die Rechtslehren von Kelsen und Verdross unter besonderer Berücksichtigung des Völkerrechts' in R Walter, C Jabloner, and K Zeleny (eds), *Hans Kelsen und das Völkerrecht* (Manz, 2004) 37–49.
Walz G, *Völkerrecht und staatliches Recht* (Kohlhammer, 1933).
Ward I, 'Dualism and the Limits of European Integration' (1995) 17 *Liverpool Law Review* 29, 36.

Waters MA, 'Creeping Monism: The Judicial Trend Toward Interpretive Incorporation of Human Rights Treaties' (2007) 107 *Columbia Law Review* 628.
Watts SA, 'The International Rule of Law' (1993) 36 *German Yearbook of International Law* 15.
Weiler JHH, 'The Transformation of Europe' (1991) 100 *Yale Law Journal* 2403.
——, 'Prologue: Global and Pluralist Constitutionalism—Some Doubts' in G de Búrca and JHH Weiler (eds), *The Worlds of European Constitutionalism* (Cambridge University Press, 2012) 8–18.
—— and Haltern UR, 'The Autonomy of the Community Legal Order—Through the Looking Glass' (1996) 37 *Harvard International Law Journal* 411.
Weinberger O, 'Kelsens These von der Unanwendbarkeit logischer Regeln auf Normen' in *Die Reine Rechtslehre in wissenschaftlicher Diskussion* [no editor] (Manz, 1982) 108–21.
——, 'Vorwort' [1982] *Rechtstheorie (Beiheft 4)* 5.
——, *Rechtslogik* (Duncker & Humblot, 1989).
——, 'The Expressive Conception of Norms: An Impasse for the Logic of Norms' in SL Paulson and B Litschewski Paulson (eds), *Normativity and Norms: Critical Perspectives on Kelsenian Themes* (reprint; Clarendon Press, 2007) 411–32.
Weinert F, 'Einstein and Kant' (2005) 80 *Philosophy* 585.
Wells HG, *What Is Coming?* (Cassel, 1916).
Wendel M, *Permeabilität im Europäischen Verfassungsrecht* (Mohr-Siebeck, 2011).
Wendt A, 'Anarchy Is What States Make of It' (1992) 46 *International Organization* 391.
——, 'Constructing International Politics' (1995) 20 *International Security* 71.
——, *Social Theory of International Politics* (Cambridge University Press, 1999).
Wenzel M, *Juristische Grundprobleme* (Dümmler, 1920).
——, 'Der Begriff des Gesetzes in der Reichsverfassung' (1927) 4 *Veröffentlichungen der Vereinigung der Deutschen Staatsrechtslehrer* 136.
Wessel RA, 'Reconsidering the Relationship between International and EU Law: Towards a Content-Based Approach?' in E Cannizzaro, P Palchetti and RA Wessel (eds), *International Law as Law of the European Union* (Brill, 2012) 7–33.
Westfall R, *The Construction of Modern Science* (Cambridge University Press, 1977).
Weyland I, 'Idealism and Realism in Kelsen's Treatment of Norm Conflicts' in R Tur and W Twining (eds), *Essays on Kelsen* (Clarendon Press, 1986) 249–69.
——, 'The Application of Kelsen's Theory of the Legal System to European Community Law: The Supremacy Puzzle Resolved' (2002) 21 *Law and Philosophy* 1.
Wiederin E, 'Was ist und welche Konsequenzen hat ein Normenkonflikt?' (1990) 21 *Rechtstheorie* 311.
——, 'Die Stufenbaulehre Adolf Julius Merkls' in S Griller and HP Rill (eds), *Rechtstheorie: Rechtsbegriff – Dynamik – Auslegung* (Springer, 2011) 81–134.
Wight M, *International Theory: The Three Traditions* (Leicester University Press, 1991).
Wildhaber L and Breitenmoser S, 'The Relationship between Customary International Law and Municipal Law in Western European Countries' (1988) 48 *Zeitschrift für ausländisches öffentliches Recht und Völkerrecht* 163.
Wilson A, 'Joseph Raz on Kelsen's Basic Norm' (1982) 27 *American Journal of Jurisprudence* 46.
Winkler G, *Der Bescheid* (Manz, 1956).
Winter JA, 'Direct Applicability and Direct Effect: Two Distinct and Different Concepts in Community Law' (1972) 9 *Common Market Law Review* 425.
Witte B de, 'European Union Law: How Autonomous Is Its Legal Order?' (2010) 65 *Zeitschrift für Öffentliches Recht* 141.

——, 'Direct Effect, Primacy, and the Nature of the Legal Order' in P Craig and G de Búrca (eds), *The Evolution of EU Law* (2nd edn; Oxford University Press, 2011) 323–62.
Wittgenstein L, *Tractatus Logico-Philosophicus* (Kegan Paul, 1922).
Wolff C, *Ius Gentium methodo scientifica pertractatum* (Renger, 1749).
Wright GH von, *Norm and Action. A Logical Enquiry* (Routledge, 1963).
——, *Norm und Handlung* (Scriptor, 1979).
Wróblewski J, 'Kelsen, the Is-Ought Dichotomy, and Naturalistic Fallacy' (1981) 35 *Revue internationale de philosophie* 508.
——, 'Democracy and Procedural Values of Law-Making' [1982] *Rechtstheorie (Beiheft 4)* 275.
Yoo J, 'International Law and the War in Iraq' (2003) 97 *American Journal of International Law* 563.
Young EA, 'Dual Federalism, Concurrent Jurisdiction, and the Foreign Affairs Exception' (2000/2001) 69 *George Washington Law Review* 139.
Zbíral R, 'A Legal Revolution of Negligible Episode? Court of Justice Decision Proclaimed *Ultra Vires*' (2012) 49 *Common Market Law Review* 1475.
Zemánek J, 'An "Entirely-Specific" Situation or a Routine Limitation of the National Autonomy? *Slovak Pensions XVII* of the Czech Constitutional Court' in Rainer Arnold (ed), *Limitations of National Sovereignty through European Integration* (Springer, 2016) 125–40.
Ziegler KS, 'The Relationship between EU Law and International Law' in D Patterson and A Södersten (eds), *A Companion to European Union Law and International Law* (Wiley & Blackwell, 2016) 42–61.
Ziller J, 'Hierarchy of Norms, Hierarchy of Sources, and General Principles in European Union Law' in U Becker and others (eds), *Verfassung und Verwaltung in Europa: Festschrift für Jürgen Schwarze zum 70. Geburtstag* (Nomos, 2014) 334–52.
Zirk-Sadowski M, 'Legal Epistemology and Transformation of Legal Cultures' in M Van Hoecke (ed), *Epistemology and Methodology of Comparative Law* (Hart Publishing, 2004) 21–34.
Zolo D, 'Hans Kelsen: International Peace through International Law' (1998) 9 *European Journal of International Law* 306.

Index